Lecture Notes in Computer Science

Lecture Notes in Artificial Intelligence 16833

Founding Editor

Jörg Siekmann

Series Editors

Randy Goebel, *University of Alberta, Edmonton, Canada*
Wolfgang Wahlster, *DFKI, Berlin, Germany*
Zhi-Hua Zhou, *Nanjing University, Nanjing, China*

The series Lecture Notes in Artificial Intelligence (LNAI) was established in 1988 as a topical subseries of LNCS devoted to artificial intelligence.

The series publishes state-of-the-art research results at a high level. As with the LNCS mother series, the mission of the series is to serve the international R & D community by providing an invaluable service, mainly focused on the publication of conference and workshop proceedings and postproceedings.

Paweł Sobociński · Francesco Bellucci ·
Amirouche Moktefi · Dave Beisecker ·
Atsushi Shimojima · Erica de Vries ·
Reetu Bhattacharjee
Editors

Diagrammatic Representation and Inference

15th International Conference, Diagrams 2026 Tallinn, Estonia, August 25–28, 2026 Proceedings

Springer

Editors
Paweł Sobociński
Tallinn University of Technology
Tallinn, Estonia

Francesco Bellucci
Tallinn University of Technology
Tallinn, Estonia

Amirouche Moktefi
Tallinn University of Technology
Tallinn, Estonia

Dave Beisecker
University of Nevada
Las Vegas, NV, USA

Atsushi Shimojima
Doshisha University
Kyoto, Japan

Erica de Vries
Université Grenoble Alpes
Grenoble, France

Reetu Bhattacharjee
Universität Münster
Münster, Germany

ISSN 0302-9743 ISSN 1611-3349 (electronic)
Lecture Notes in Artificial Intelligence
ISBN 978-3-032-34177-8 ISBN 978-3-032-34178-5 (eBook)
https://doi.org/10.1007/978-3-032-34178-5

LNCS Sublibrary: SL7 – Artificial Intelligence

This Springer imprint is published by the registered company Springer Nature Switzerland AG
The registered company address is: Gewerbestrasse 11, 6330 Cham, Switzerland

Preface

The 15th International Conference on the Theory and Application of Diagrams (DIAGRAMS 2026) was held at Tallinn University of Technology, Tallinn, Estonia, from the 25th to the 28th of August. The conference continued the Diagrams tradition of bringing together researchers from a wide range of disciplines concerned with diagrammatic representation, visual reasoning, and the role of diagrams in cognition, communication, education, science, technology, and philosophy. The event provided an interdisciplinary forum in which established scholars and emerging researchers could exchange ideas, present new results, and explore future directions for diagrammatic research.

DIAGRAMS 2026 invited submissions in the categories of long papers, short papers, posters, and non-archival abstracts. All submissions underwent a rigorous peer-review process. Each contribution was evaluated by at least three reviewers using a single-blind review procedure in which reviewers were aware of the authors' identities, while authors did not know the identities of the reviewers. Authors were given the opportunity to respond to reviewers' comments during a rebuttal phase, after which the Program Committee carefully considered both reviews and author responses before reaching final decisions. We are grateful to all members of the Program Committee and the additional reviewers for their thoughtful evaluations, constructive feedback, and commitment to maintaining the high standards of the conference.

A total of 57 submissions were received forDIAGRAMS 2026. Submissions were distributed across the conference tracks as follows: 26 submissions to the Main Track, 21 submissions to the Philosophy Track, and 10 submissions to the Psychology and Education Track. Of these, 14 were accepted as long papers, 20 as short papers, 3 as abstracts, and 9 as posters. Together, the accepted contributions reflect the diversity and vitality of contemporary research on diagrams, spanning theoretical, empirical, historical, computational, and applied perspectives.

In addition to the main technical program,DIAGRAMS 2026 featured a Graduate Symposium, providing doctoral researchers with an opportunity to present their work and receive feedback from experienced scholars, plus a tutorial and a workshop on specific topics. These events fostered discussion, collaboration, and the exchange of ideas beyond the regular paper sessions.

The conference was further enriched by keynote lectures delivered by Jessica Carter (Aarhus University, Denmark), Peter Cheng (University of Sussex, UK), and Fabio Zanasi (University College London, UK). Their presentations highlighted important developments in the study of diagrams and visual reasoning and stimulated discussion across disciplinary boundaries. We are deeply grateful for their participation and for the insights they shared with the conference community.

Many individuals contributed to the success ofDIAGRAMS 2026. We would like to thank Gianluca Caterina for coordinating the workshop and the tutorials programs, and Nathan Haydon for organizing the Graduate Symposium. Pawel Sobocinski served as General Chair. Kristi Ainen and Amirouche Moktefi worked as Local Co-Chairs.

Francesco Bellucci served as Senior Program Chair and coordinated the scientific review process. Atsushi Shimojima, Dave Beisecker, and Erica de Vries led the Main Track, Philosophy Track, and Psychology and Education Track, respectively. Special thanks are due to Reetu Bhattacharjee for her work as Proceedings and Publicity Chair and for overseeing the preparation of this volume and the dissemination of conference information. We also thank Richard Burns for his generous help with the website of the conference. Many thanks also to Kristi Ainen for her help throughout the organization process to ensure the smooth running of the event.

Acknowledgements also go to Tallinn University of Technology, which hosted and supported the event, especially the Department of Software Science, the Ragnar Nurkse Department of Innovation and Governance, and the Estonian Maritime Academy. We are also grateful to the City of Tallinn for its generous support with local transportation during the conference.

Finally, we would like to express our sincere appreciation to the members of the Diagrams Steering Committee for their continued guidance and support. Most importantly, we thank all authors, presenters, reviewers, session chairs, and participants whose enthusiasm and contributions madeDIAGRAMS 2026 a stimulating and rewarding event.

August 2026

Paweł Sobocinski
Francesco Bellucci
Amirouche Moktefi
Dave Beisecker
Atsushi Shimojima
Erica de Vries
Reetu Bhattacharjee

Organization

General Chair

Pawel Sobocinski	Tallinn University of Technology, Estonia

Local Co-Chairs

Kristi Ainen	Tallinn University of Technology, Estonia
Amirouche Moktefi	Tallinn University of Technology, Estonia

Senior Program Chair

Francesco Bellucci	University of Bologna, Italy

Philosophy Track Chair

Dave Beisecker	University of Nevada, Las Vegas, USA

Main Track Chair

Atsushi Shimojima	Doshisha University, Japan

Psychology and Education Track Chair

Erica de Vries	Université Grenoble Alpes, France

Proceedings and Publicity Chair

Reetu Bhattacharjee	Universität Münster, Germany

Graduate Symposium Chair

Nathan Haydon	University of Waterloo, Canada

Tutorial and Workshop Chair

Gianluca Caterina	Endicott College, USA

Program Committee

Andrew Aberdien	Florida Institute of Technology, USA
Shaaron Ainsworth	University of Nottingham, UK
Mohanad Alqadah	Umm Al-Qura University, Saudi Arabia
Dave Barker-Plummer	Stanford University, USA
Dave Beisecker	University of Nevada, Las Vegas, USA
Francesco Bellucci	University of Bologna, Italy
Mireille Betrancourt	University of Geneva, Switzerland
Reetu Bhattacharjee	Universität Münster, Germany
Viktor Blasjo	Utrecht University, Netherlands
Ben Blumson	National University of Singapore, Singapore
Jean-Michel Boucheix	LEAD-CNRS, University of Burgundy, France
José-Martín Castro-Manzano	Universidad Popular Autónoma del Estado de Puebla, Mexico
Gianluca Caterina	Endicott College, USA
Mihir Chakraborty	Jadavpur University, India
Peter Chapman	Edinburgh Napier University, UK
Peter Cheng	University of Sussex, UK
Daniele Chiffi	Polytechnic University of Milan, Italy
James Corter	Columbia University, USA
Gennaro Costagliola	Università di Salerno, Italy
Lorenz Demey	KU Leuven, Belgium
Ian Dove	University of Nevada, USA
Jacques Fleuriot	The University of Edinburgh, UK
Amy Fox	University of California, San Diego, USA
Mari Fukuda	Kyoto University, Japan
Amar Hadzihasanovic	Tallinn University of Technology, Estonia
Reinhard von Hanxleden	Christian-Albrecht University of Kiel, Germany
Nathan Haydon	University of Waterloo, Canada
Mateja Jamnik	University of Cambridge, UK

Yasuhiro Katagiri	National Institute of Advanced Industrial Science and Technology, Japan
Brendan Larvor	University of Hertfordshire, UK
Javier Legris	University of Buenos Aires, Argentina
Jens Lemanski	University of Münster, Germany
Emmanuel Manalo	Kyoto University, Japan
Kim Marriott	Monash University, Australia
Ingolf Max	Leipzig University, Germany
Mark Minas	Universität der Bundeswehr München, Germany
Amirouche Moktefi	Tallinn University of Technology, Estonia
Arnold Oostra	University of Tolima, Colombia
Mario Piazza	Scuola Normale Superiore in Pisa, Italy
Ahti-Veikko Pietarinen	Hong Kong Baptist University, China
Uta Priss	Ostfalia University, Germany
Daniel Raggi	University of Cambridge, UK
Peter Rodgers	University of Kent, UK
Frank Thomas Sautter	Universidade Federal de Santa Maria, Brazil
Fabien Schang	HSE University, Russia
Dirk Schlimm	McGill University, Canada
Johanna Schoenherr	University of Osnabrück, Germany
Andrew Schumann	University of Information Technology and Management in Rzeszow, Poland
Stephanie Schwartz	Millersville University, USA
Marco Segala	University of L'Aquila, Italy
Atsushi Shimojima	Doshisha University, Japan
Hans Smessaert	KU Leuven, Belgium
Pawel Sobocinski	Tallinn University of Technology, Estonia
Michael Stoelzner	University of South Carolina, USA
Takeshi Sugio	Doshisha University, Japan
Silvia De Toffoli	Princeton University, USA
Yuri Uesaka	University of Tokyo, Japan
Jean Van Bendegem	Vrije Universiteit Brussel, Belgium
Ioannis Vandoulakis	Hellenic Open University, Greece
Ivan Varzinczak	University of Artois and CNRS, France
Petrucio Viana	Federal Fluminense University, Brazil
Erica de Vries	Université Grenoble Alpes, France
Julia Xing	Tarleton State University, USA

Contents

Logical Diagrams

Logical Diagrams

On Carroll Diagrams for Numerical Syllogistic

J.-Martín Castro-Manzano[1,2(✉)]

[1] UPAEP University, Puebla, Pue 72430, Mexico
[2] Consejo de Ciencia y Tecnología del Estado de Puebla, Puebla, Pue 72430, Mexico
josemartin.castro@upaep.mx

Abstract. In this contribution we combine Carroll's triliteral diagrams with Murphree's numerical syllogistic in order to obtain a system of logic diagrams *à la* Carroll for numerical syllogistic, and then we provide some evidence to the effect that the resulting system is sound and complete.

Keywords: Logic diagram · Syllogistic · Numerical syllogistic

1 Introduction

In this contribution we combine Carroll's triliteral diagrams ($\mathcal{CARR}$) —which are used to represent syllogistic ($\mathcal{SYLL}$)— with Murphree's numerical syllogistic ($\mathcal{SYLL}^{\nu}$) in order to obtain a system of logic diagrams *à la* Carroll for numerical syllogistic ($\mathcal{CARR}^{\nu}$). The intuition behind this combination can be explained by way of the next diagram:

$$\begin{array}{ccc} \mathcal{SYLL} & \xrightarrow{\text{extends to}} & \mathcal{SYLL}^{\nu} \\ \text{modeled by} \downarrow & & \downarrow \text{modeled by} \\ \mathcal{CARR} & \xrightarrow{\text{extends to}} & \mathcal{CARR}^{\nu} \end{array}$$

After doing that, we provide some evidence to the effect that the resulting combination is sound and complete. In order to achieve these goals, we first give some preliminaries, and then we offer our proposal.

2 Preliminaries

Traditional Aristotelian deductive logic, also known as *syllogistic* ($\mathcal{SYLL}$), is a term logic that deals with inference using categorical statements. A *categorical statement* is a statement of the form "*Quantity* S *Quality* P" where *Quantity* $\in$ {*All*, *Some*}, *Quality* $\in$ {*is* (*are*), *is* (*are*) *not*}, and S and P are term-schemas. The combination of these elements produces the four traditional categorical statements: the universal affirmative *All* S *are* P (S*a*P), the universal negative *All* S *are not* P (S*e*P), the particular affirmative *Some* S *are* P (S*i*P), and the particular negative *Some* S *are not* P (S*o*P). A sequence of exactly three

P. Sobociński et al. (Eds.): Diagrams 2026, LNAI 16833, pp. 3–10, 2027.
https://doi.org/10.1007/978-3-032-34178-5_1

categorical statements arranged in such a way that the first two statements are premises and the last statement is the conclusion is known as a *mood.* A categorical syllogism, then, is a mood with exactly three terms, one of which occurs in both premises but not in the conclusion. This special term, usually denoted by the term-schema M, works as a link between the remaining or extreme terms that connect each other in the conclusion and is known as the middle term. Thus, we can say, more precisely, that a *categorical syllogism* is a mood with exactly three terms, one of which is a middle term, and the rest are extreme terms. And then, given the position of the middle term, we get the four *figures* of a categorical syllogism. These remarks allow us to say that the *form* of a categorical syllogism is the conjunction of its mood and its figure. The traditional valid syllogisms forms are grouped into four figures. In what follows, however, for reasons of brevity, we focus only on the first figure, namely the *Barbara*, *Celarent*, *Darii*, and *Ferio* syllogisms.

Carroll's system of logic diagrams ($\mathcal{CARR}$) [1] has a vocabulary that includes the following basic elements: the *triliteral diagram*, the *biliteral diagram*, and the *counters* (Fig. 1). Each quarter in a diagram is called a *cell* and is labeled by positive (resp. negative) term-schemas S (resp. S′), P (P′), and M (M′). The semantics is straightforward: cells represent the terms in a categorical statement while the counters indicate whether such cells are full or empty. Black counters indicate a cell is non-empty, gray counters indicate a cell is empty. Given this language, $\mathcal{CARR}$ provides Algorithm 1, with which we can develop diagrammatic proofs of the syllogisms of $\mathcal{SYLL}$ (Fig. 2).

Algorithm 1: $\mathcal{CARR}$

Input: A triliteral diagram
Output: A corresponding biliteral diagram
initialize an empty biliteral diagram;
foreach *quarter q in the triliteral diagram* **do**
  let q_1 and q_2 be the two cells of q;
  let $b(q)$ be the corresponding quarter in the biliteral diagram;
  `// Case 1: black information survives directly`
  if q_1 *or* q_2 *contains at least one black counter* **then**
    place one black counter in $b(q)$;
    continue
  end
  `// Case 2: grey information requires paired cells`
  if q_1 *and* q_2 *both contain grey counters* **then**
    place one grey counter in $b(q)$;
  end
  `// Case 3: empty or single-grey quarters do nothing`
end

Numerical syllogistic ($\mathcal{SYLL}^{\nu}$) deals with numerical quantifiers. For instance, the statement *More than 430,000 Argentinians are Spanish speakers* differs clearly from *Some Argentinians are Spanish speakers*: if the first statement is true, the second is also true, but not necessarily the other way around. Therefore, precise numerical quantities cannot be treated as mere instances of the particular quantity (*i.e. Some*) without careful consideration. To address this, Murphree [2] extended $\mathcal{SYLL}$ to handle numerical quantifiers, thus producing $\mathcal{SYLL}^{\nu}$. In this system, a *numerical statement* is of the form "*Quantity* n S *Quality* P", where *Quantity* $\in$ {*All except*, *At most*, *At least*}, $\mathtt{n} \in \mathbb{Z}^+$, *Quality* $\in$

{*is* (*are*), *is* (*are*) *not*}, and S and P are term-schemas. The combination of these elements produces the following numerical statements: the universal affirmative *All except n* S *are* P (nS*a*P), the universal negative *At most n* S *are* P (nS*e*P), the particular affirmative *At least n* S *are* P (nS*i*P), and the particular negative *At least n* S *are not* P (nS*o*P). The decision algorithm for this system is presented in Algorithm 2, and to illustrate these concepts, consider the examples shown in Tables 1 and 2.

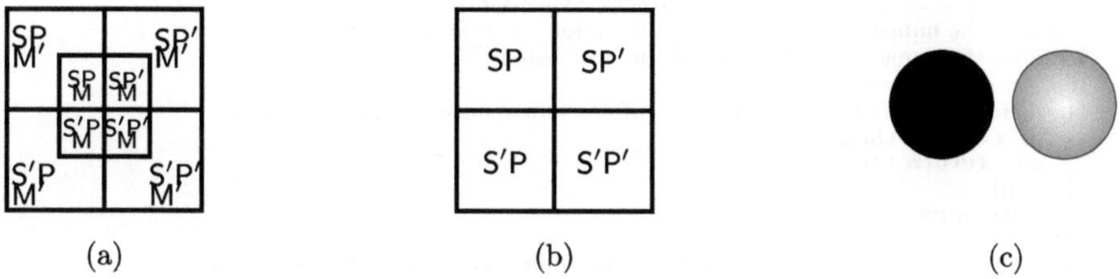

Fig. 1. *CARR*'s language: (a) triliteral diagram, (b) biliteral diagram, (c) counters.

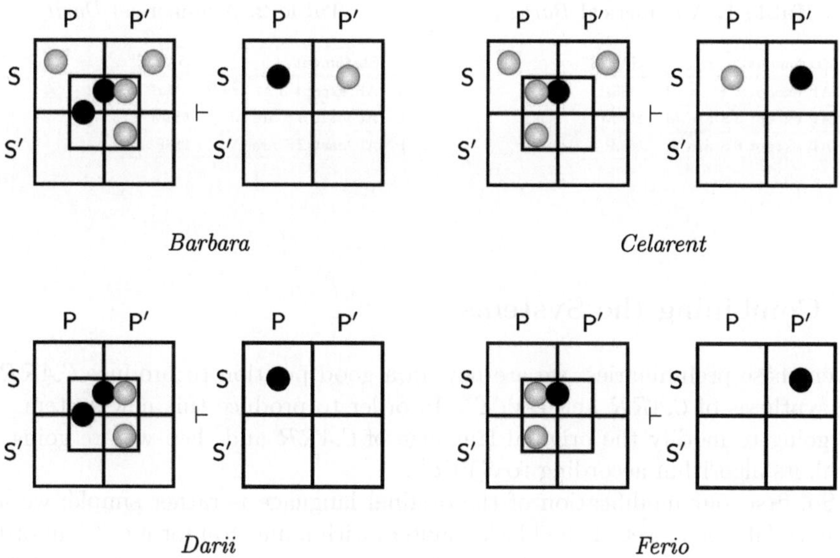

Fig. 2. First figure syllogisms.

Algorithm 2: $\mathcal{SYLL}^{\nu}$

```
Input: A numerical syllogism with premises P1, P2 and conclusion C
Output: VALID or INVALID
// Step 0: Identify roles
Identify the terms S, P, M;
Let P_maj be the premise containing M and P;
Let P_min be the premise containing S and M;
// Step 1: validity in SYLL
if the categorical syllogism is not valid in SYLL then
    return INVALID
end
// Step 2: numerical constraint (Murphree's expansion)
Let n be the numerical parameter of the major universal premise P_maj;
Let k be the numerical parameter of the conclusion C;
if P_min is universal then
    Let m be the numerical parameter of the minor universal premise P_min;
    if k = n + m then
        return VALID
    end
    return INVALID
else
    Let r be the numerical parameter of the minor particular premise P_min;
    if k = max(0, r − n) then
        return VALID
    end
    return INVALID
end
```

Table 1. A numerical *Barbara*

	Statement	$\mathcal{SYLL}^{\nu}$
1.	All except 5 M are P.	5M*a*P
2.	All except 3 S are M.	3S*a*M
⊢	All except 8 S are P.	8S*a*P

Table 2. A numerical *Darii*

	Statement	$\mathcal{SYLL}^{\nu}$
1.	All except 3 M are P.	3M*a*P
2.	At least 5 S are M.	5S*i*M
⊢	At least 2 S are P.	2S*i*P

3 Combining the Systems

Given these preliminaries, we are now in a good position to produce $\mathcal{CARR}^{\nu}$, the synthesis of $\mathcal{CARR}$ and $\mathcal{SYLL}^{\nu}$. In order to produce this new system, we are going to modify the original language of $\mathcal{CARR}$ and then we are going to tweak its algorithm according to $\mathcal{SYLL}^{\nu}$.

So, first, our modification of the original language is rather simple: we are going to label a subset of the black counters with a numeral for $\mathtt{n} \in \mathbb{Z}^+$ in order to accommodate the numerical quantifiers —we could also use, when suitable, $\mathtt{n}$ black counters to work with, but using single, numerically labeled counters is way simpler. And now, given this modification, we can provide a modified algorithm for $\mathcal{CARR}^{\nu}$. In order to do so, we need to introduce some definitions. So, first, let us fix arbitrary terms S, P, M; let us consider an arbitrary, solved, triliteral diagram D, and let q range over the 8 quarters (that will define regions) determined by a triliteral diagram.

Definition 1 (Adjacency). *For each biliteral region $X \cap Y$ (with $X \in \{\mathsf{S}, \mathsf{S}'\}$ and $Y \in \{\mathsf{P}, \mathsf{P}'\}$), define the* adjacency pair *collapsing to it by*

$$\mathrm{Adj}(X \cap Y) \ := \ \{X \cap Y \cap \mathsf{M}, \ X \cap Y \cap \mathsf{M}'\}.$$

Let $\mathrm{blk}(q) \in \mathbb{N}$ *be the sum of the numeric labels on the black counters in region q (and 0 if none). For a set of regions Q, write* $\mathrm{blk}(Q) := \sum_{q \in Q} \mathrm{blk}(q)$.

Definition 2 (Major/minor numeric parameters). *Let the* major *premise be the one involving* (M, P) *and the* minor *premise the one involving* (S, M). *Then:*
(Major universal parameter). *If the major is of form* $\mathtt{n}\mathsf{MaP}$, *set* $E_M := \mathsf{M} \cap \mathsf{P}'$. *If the major is of form* $\mathtt{n}\mathsf{MeP}$, *set* $E_M := \mathsf{M} \cap \mathsf{P}$. *Define*

$$\mathtt{n} \ := \ \mathrm{blk}(\{\mathsf{S} \cap E_M, \ \mathsf{S}' \cap E_M\}).$$

(Minor universal parameter). *If the minor is of form* $\mathtt{m}\mathsf{SaM}$, *set* $E_S := \mathsf{S} \cap \mathsf{M}'$. *If the minor is of form* $\mathtt{m}\mathsf{SeM}$, *set* $E_S := \mathsf{S} \cap \mathsf{M}$. *Define*

$$\mathtt{m} \ := \ \mathrm{blk}(\{E_S \cap \mathsf{P}, \ E_S \cap \mathsf{P}'\}).$$

(Minor particular parameter). *If the minor is of form* $\mathtt{r}\mathsf{SiM}$, *define*

$$\mathtt{r} \ := \ \mathrm{blk}(\{\mathsf{S} \cap \mathsf{M} \cap \mathsf{P}, \ \mathsf{S} \cap \mathsf{M} \cap \mathsf{P}'\}).$$

If the minor is of form $\mathtt{r}\mathsf{SoM}$, *define*

$$\mathtt{r} \ := \ \mathrm{blk}(\{\mathsf{S} \cap \mathsf{M}' \cap \mathsf{P}, \ \mathsf{S} \cap \mathsf{M}' \cap \mathsf{P}'\}).$$

Definition 3 (Numerical collapse τ). *Given a solved triliteral diagram D for terms* $\mathsf{S}, \mathsf{P}, \mathsf{M}$, *define $\tau(D)$ as follows:*
(Categorical). *Collapse D to a biliteral diagram in $\mathcal{CARR}$.*
(Numerical). *Compute the major parameter* $\mathtt{n}$ *as in Definition 2. Determine whether the minor is universal or particular by $\mathcal{CARR}$, then compute the corresponding parameter* $\mathtt{m}$ *or* $\mathtt{r}$ *as in Definition 2. Finally, set*

$$\mathtt{k} := \begin{cases} \mathtt{n} + \mathtt{m}, & \textit{if the minor is universal,} \\ \max(0, \, \mathtt{r} - \mathtt{n}), & \textit{if the minor is particular.} \end{cases}$$

And give the numerical conclusion $\mathtt{k}\mathsf{S}x\mathsf{P}$ *for* $x \in \{a, e, i, o\}$.

Consequently, given these conceptual conditions, the algorithm for $\mathcal{CARR}^{\nu}$ would look like Algorithm 3, and to show how this works, let us reconsider the examples of Tables 1 and 2 in Fig. 3.

Algorithm 3: $\mathcal{CARR}^{\nu}$

Input: A solved triliteral $\mathcal{CARR}^{\nu}$ diagram D for terms S, P, M
Output: The numerical conclusion k$\mathsf{S}x\mathsf{P}$ and its biliteral diagram
// Step 1: Categorical collapse
Collapse D to a biliteral diagram using Algorithm 1;
Let $x \in \{a, e, i, o\}$ be the categorical statement read from the collapsed biliteral conclusion;
// Step 2: Read the major universal parameter n (Def. 2)
if *the major premise is* nMaP **then**
  $E_M \leftarrow (\mathsf{M} \cap \mathsf{P}')$; // exception for MaP
else if *the major premise is* nMeP **then**
  $E_M \leftarrow (\mathsf{M} \cap \mathsf{P})$; // bound for MeP
else
  return *Error: major must be universal*;
end
$\mathtt{n} \leftarrow \text{blk}(\mathsf{S} \cap E_M) + \text{blk}(\mathsf{S}' \cap E_M)$;
// Step 3: Read the minor parameter (m if universal, r if particular) (Def. 2)
if *the minor premise is universal* **then**
  if *the minor is* mSaM **then**
    $E_S \leftarrow (\mathsf{S} \cap \mathsf{M}')$; // exception for SaM
  else if *the minor is* mSeM **then**
    $E_S \leftarrow (\mathsf{S} \cap \mathsf{M})$; // bound for SeM
  end
  $\mathtt{m} \leftarrow \text{blk}(E_S \cap \mathsf{P}) + \text{blk}(E_S \cap \mathsf{P}')$;
  $\mathtt{k} \leftarrow \mathtt{n} + \mathtt{m}$
else
  if *the minor is* rSiM **then**
    $\mathtt{r} \leftarrow \text{blk}(\text{Adj}(\mathsf{S} \cap \mathsf{M})) = \{\mathsf{S} \cap \mathsf{M} \cap \mathsf{P},\ \mathsf{S} \cap \mathsf{M} \cap \mathsf{P}'\}$
  else if *the minor is* rSoM **then**
    $\mathtt{r} \leftarrow \text{blk}(\text{Adj}(\mathsf{S} \cap \mathsf{M}')) = \{\mathsf{S} \cap \mathsf{M}' \cap \mathsf{P},\ \mathsf{S} \cap \mathsf{M}' \cap \mathsf{P}'\}$
  end
  $\mathtt{k} \leftarrow \max(0, \mathtt{r} - \mathtt{n})$
end
// Step 4: Give the numerical conclusion
return k$\mathsf{S}x\mathsf{P}$ *and the collapsed biliteral diagram*;

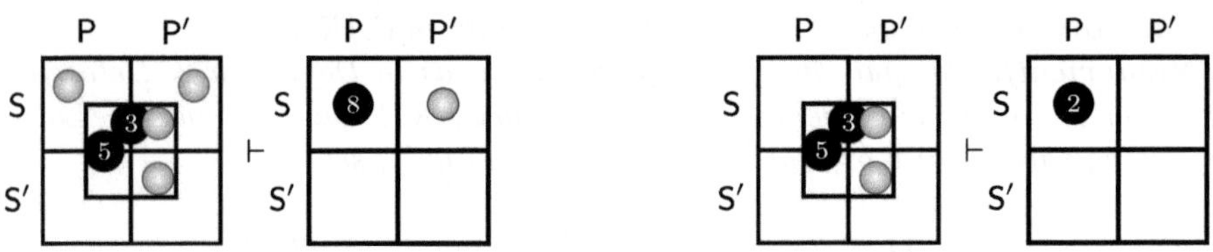

Barbara *Darii*

Fig. 3. Numerical *Barbara* and *Darii* syllogisms

And now, we would like to show some formal results, but first we require a reduction assumption:

Lemma 1 (Aristotle reduction). *Every valid mood of (numerical) syllogistic can be reduced, by a finite sequence of truth-preserving transformations, to one of the four first-figure moods:* Barbara, Celarent, Darii, *or* Ferio.

Theorem 1 (Soundness). *If a numerical syllogism is valid in $\mathcal{SYLL}^\nu$, then its diagrammatic instance is valid in $\mathcal{CARR}^\nu$ (the numerical label computed by τ is correct).*

Proof We proceed by cases. (Case 1) Numerical *Barbara*. Assume premises $\mathtt{n}\mathsf{M}a\mathsf{P}$ and $\mathtt{m}\mathsf{S}a\mathsf{M}$. In the triliteral diagram, $\mathtt{n}$ is placed in the major region $\mathsf{M} \cap \mathsf{P}'$ and $\mathtt{m}$ in the minor region $\mathsf{S} \cap \mathsf{M}'$. Under $\mathcal{CARR}$ collapse, the categorical conclusion is $\mathsf{S}a\mathsf{P}$. Numerically, $\mathsf{S}a\mathsf{P}$ must be either *i*) S outside M (accounted by $\mathtt{m}$) or *ii*) S inside M but outside P (accounted by $\mathtt{n}$). Hence the bound for $\mathsf{S}a\mathsf{P}$ is $\mathtt{n}+\mathtt{m}$, which is exactly $\mathtt{k}$ computed by τ.

(Case 2) Numerical *Celarent.* Assume premises $\mathtt{n}\mathsf{M}e\mathsf{P}$ and $\mathtt{m}\mathsf{S}a\mathsf{M}$. Now the major region is $\mathsf{M} \cap \mathsf{P}$, while the minor region is $\mathsf{S} \cap \mathsf{M}'$. $\mathcal{CARR}$ collapse yields $\mathsf{S}e\mathsf{P}$. Any $\mathsf{S} \cap \mathsf{P}$ items must either lie *i*) outside M (bounded by $\mathtt{m}$) or *ii*) inside M (bounded by $\mathtt{n}$). Thus at most $\mathtt{n}+\mathtt{m}$ S are P, i.e. the conclusion is $\mathtt{k} = \mathtt{n}+\mathtt{m}$, which is computed by τ.

(Case 3) Numerical *Darii.* Assume premises $\mathtt{n}\mathsf{M}a\mathsf{P}$ and $\mathtt{r}\mathsf{S}i\mathsf{M}$. The minor states that at least $\mathtt{r}$ items lie in $\mathsf{S}\cap\mathsf{M}$, i.e. in the union of the two adjacent cells $\mathsf{S} \cap \mathsf{M} \cap \mathsf{P}$ and $\mathsf{S} \cap \mathsf{M} \cap \mathsf{P}'$; thus $\mathtt{r}$ is read as in Definition 2. The major allows at most $\mathtt{n}$ items of M to fall in the exceptional region $\mathsf{M} \cap \mathsf{P}'$. In the worst case, up to $\mathtt{n}$ of the $\mathtt{r}$ items for $\mathsf{S}\cap\mathsf{M}$ lie in $\mathsf{S}\cap\mathsf{M}\cap\mathsf{P}'$, leaving at least $\max(0, \mathtt{r}-\mathtt{n})$ items in $\mathsf{S}\cap\mathsf{M}\cap\mathsf{P} \subseteq \mathsf{S}\cap\mathsf{P}$. Therefore the conclusion $\mathtt{k}\mathsf{S}i\mathsf{P}$ holds with $\mathtt{k} = \max(0, \mathtt{r}-\mathtt{n})$, which is computed by τ.

(Case 4) Numerical *Ferio.* Assume premises $\mathtt{n}\mathsf{M}e\mathsf{P}$ and $\mathtt{r}\mathsf{S}i\mathsf{M}$. Here at most $\mathtt{n}$ items of M lie in P (major $\mathsf{M}\cap\mathsf{P}$). Among the $\mathtt{r}$ items in $\mathsf{S}\cap\mathtt{M}$ (at least), at most $\mathtt{n}$ can be in $\mathsf{S} \cap \mathsf{M} \cap \mathsf{P}$, so at least $\max(0, \mathtt{r}-\mathtt{n})$ must be in $\mathsf{S} \cap \mathsf{M} \cap \mathsf{P}' \subseteq \mathsf{S} \cap \mathsf{P}'$. Thus the conclusion is $\mathtt{k}\mathsf{S}o\mathsf{P}$ with $\mathtt{k} = \max(0, \mathtt{r}-\mathtt{n})$, which is computed by τ.

So, since the four first figure moods are sound in $\mathcal{CARR}^\nu$, and every valid mood reduces to one of them by Aristotle's Lemma, it follows that every $\mathcal{SYLL}^\nu$ valid syllogism is $\mathcal{CARR}^\nu$ valid with the correct numerical conclusion. □

Theorem 2 (Completeness). *If a syllogistic inference is derivable in $\mathcal{CARR}^\nu$, then the corresponding syllogism is valid in $\mathcal{SYLL}^\nu$.*

Proof Let D be a solved triliteral $\mathcal{CARR}^\nu$ diagram for terms $\mathsf{S}, \mathsf{P}, \mathsf{M}$. Let the collapsed biliteral diagram determine $\mathsf{S}x\mathsf{P}$ (as in $\mathcal{CARR}$). We then show that the k produced by $\tau(D)$ is for a valid syllogism in $\mathcal{SYLL}^\nu$.

For the categorical case, if D is solved by $\mathcal{CARR}$ for a valid mood in $\mathcal{SYLL}$, then the inference is valid in $\mathcal{SYLL}^\nu$, for $\mathcal{SYLL} \subseteq \mathcal{SYLL}^\nu$.

For the numerical case, we have two sub-cases. (Case 1) The minor is universal. Then D encodes a universal major with parameter $\mathtt{n}$ and a universal minor with parameter $\mathtt{m}$, read as in Definition 2. In any interpretation compatible with D, an exception to the conclusion's universal statement must be either an exception contributed by the major exceptional M region (bounded by $\mathtt{n}$) or an exception contributed by the minor exceptional S region (bounded by $\mathtt{m}$). Therefore the conclusion bound is at most $\mathtt{n}+\mathtt{m}$. This is exactly the case of $\mathcal{SYLL}^\nu$ when we have two universal premises.

(Case 2) The minor is particular. Then D encodes a universal major with parameter $\mathtt{n}$ and a particular minor with lower bound $\mathtt{r}$, where $\mathtt{r}$ is read from the adjacent collapse-pair witnessing the minor (Definition 2). In any interpretation compatible with D, at most $\mathtt{n}$ of those $\mathtt{r}$ items can lie in the major region (either $\mathsf{M} \cap \mathsf{P}'$ for $\mathsf{M}a\mathsf{P}$ or $\mathsf{M} \cap \mathsf{P}$ for $\mathsf{M}e\mathsf{P}$). Hence at least $\max(0, \mathtt{r} - \mathtt{n})$ items must lie in the complementary region, which is exactly the conclusion region for $\mathsf{S}i\mathsf{P}$ (*Darii*) or $\mathsf{S}o\mathsf{P}$ (*Ferio*). This is exactly the case of $\mathcal{SYLL}^{\nu}$ when we have exactly one particular premise.

Thus, in all cases, $\tau(D)$ yields a conclusion whose number satisfies $\mathcal{SYLL}^{\nu}$ conditions. □

4 Conclusions

In this contribution we have combined Carroll's triliteral diagrams with Murphree's numerical syllogistic in order to obtain a system of logic diagrams *à la* Carroll for numerical syllogistic; and then we provided some evidence to the effect that the resulting system is sound and complete. The novelty of these results is twofold: on the one hand, Carroll diagrams provide a diagrammatic system for categorical syllogistic that lacks numerical expressivity, insofar as counters encode only emptiness and non-emptiness and do not support numerical inference [1,3]; on the other, the existing work on diagrammatic reasoning does not address numerical syllogistic as a deductive base [4,5]. The present proposal fills this gap by introducing a logic diagram system that is sound and complete with respect to numerical syllogistic. This shows that Carroll diagrams can be extended to model numerical syllogistic; and that Murphree's numerical syllogistic is not restricted to Murphree's own diagrams.

References

1. Carroll, L.: Symbolic Logic. Macmillan, London (1896)
2. Murphree, W.A.: Numerical Term Logic. Notre Dame Journal of Formal Logic **39**(3), 346–362 (1998). https://doi.org/10.1305/ndjfl/1039182251
3. Moktefi, A.: Lewis carroll's logic. In: Gabbay, D.M., Woods, J. (eds.) Handbook of the History of Logic, vol. 4, pp. 457–505. North-Holland, Amsterdam (2008). https://doi.org/10.1016/S1874-5857(08)80013-1
4. Shin, S.-J.: The Logical Status of Diagrams. Cambridge University Press, Cambridge (1994)
5. Howse, J., Molina, F., Taylor, J., Kent, S., Gil, J.Y.: Spider diagrams: a diagrammatic reasoning system. J. Vis. Lang. Comput. **12**(3), 299–324 (2001). https://doi.org/10.1006/jvlc.2000.0210

On Paraconsistent Diagrams

J.-Martín Castro-Manzano(✉)

UPAEP University, Consejo de Ciencia y Tecnología del Estado de Puebla, 72430
Puebla, Pue, Mexico
josemartin.castro@upaep.mx

Abstract. Given a graphical reading of $\mathcal{VENN}$ diagrams, we could say that they do not deal with truth or falsehood, but with emptiness or non-emptiness. On this reading, we think $\mathcal{VENN}$ allows us to define some sort of paraconsistent logic in the sense that there are diagram semantics whose induced consequence relation is paraconsistent.

Keywords: Venn diagrams · Paraconsistency · Semantics

1 Introduction

Given a graphical reading of $\mathcal{VENN}$ diagrams, we could say that they do not deal with truth or falsehood, but with emptiness or non-emptiness. This would be so because a region —a basic object of $\mathcal{VENN}$— is either empty or non-empty, but it is not true or false (propositions come with a truth-value, but regions are not propositions). On this reading, we think $\mathcal{VENN}$ allows us to define some sort of paraconsistent logic. Thus, our main argument is, right off the bat, as follows:

1. Paraconsistency is a property of a consequence relation that forbids explosion.
2. Semantics can be induced by diagrams.
3. There are diagrams that forbid explosion.

   ∴ There are diagram semantics whose induced consequence relation is paraconsistent.

Premise 1 holds by definition: a logic is paraconsistent if and only if explosion fails in it (i.e. $\{\phi, \neg\phi\} \not\vdash \psi$ for any ϕ, ψ). Since this definition is not dogmatically tied to truth-values, possible-worlds semantics, and the like, paraconsistency is not committed to any pre-established semantics. Premise 2 should also be granted, for it is undisputed that semantics can be induced by way of diagrams [1]. Premise 3, however, requires some explanation, but that is pretty much the rest of this contribution. So, our main goal is to show that a particular interpretation of $\mathcal{VENN}$ diagrams induces a consequence relation that is paraconsistent. In order to reach this objective, we first introduce $\mu\mathcal{VENN}$ —a particular interpretation of $\mathcal{VENN}$ diagrams—, and then we explore some of its properties. At the end, we close with a brief discussion.

P. Sobociński et al. (Eds.): Diagrams 2026, LNAI 16833, pp. 11–16, 2027.
https://doi.org/10.1007/978-3-032-34178-5_2

2 $\mu\mathcal{VENN}$

Consider an intuitive, direct physical interpretation of $\mathcal{VENN}$ diagrams in which *joining* two diagrams d_1 and d_2, say $d_1 \sqcup d_2$, produces a new diagram d_3 that keeps all visible features. The idea is that *join* represents *accumulation of information*, as in the following exhaustive examples:

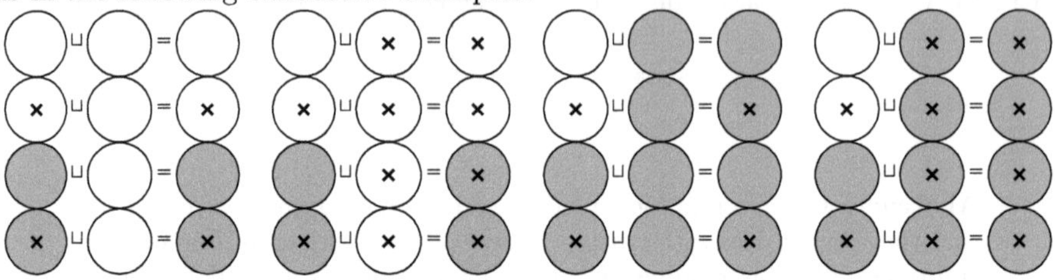

Similarly, consider that *meeting* two diagrams d_1 and d_2, say $d_1 \sqcap d_2$, produces a new diagram d_3 that shows what remains visible in both diagrams, so that *meet* represents *shared information*, as in the following exhaustive examples:

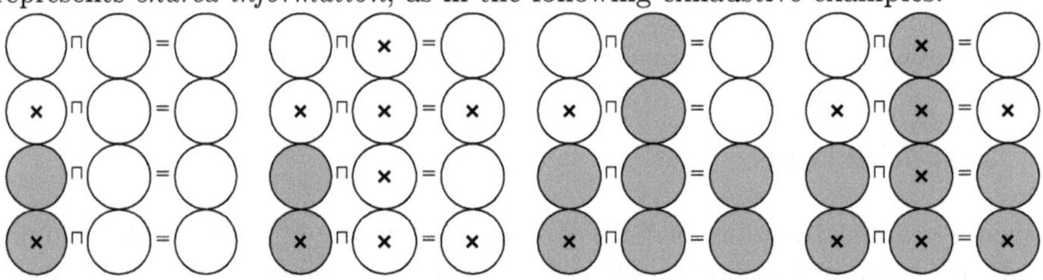

And finally, consider that *countering* a diagram d_1 is obtained by reversing the features that are present and absent in it, so that *counter*, say $\overline{d_1}$, represents *information opposition*, as in the following exhaustive examples:

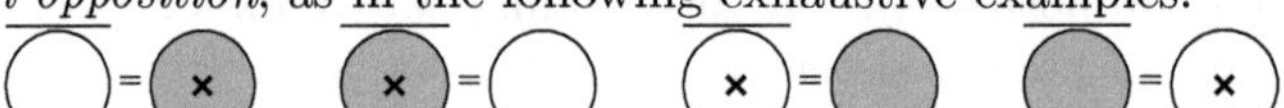

Now consider $\mu\mathcal{VENN}$, or micro $\mathcal{VENN}$, as a proxy for $\mathcal{VENN}$ designed to capture these basic features of $\mathcal{VENN}$'s treatment of regions. So, say a diagram d in $\mu\mathcal{VENN}$ is a basic region of $\mathcal{VENN}$ or a composition of diagrams. Basic regions are of four sorts: □, ⊠, ■, or ❖. As usual, □ stands for a neither empty nor non-empty region; ⊠ stands for a non-empty region; ■ represents an empty region; and finally, ❖ represents a region that is both empty and non-empty. With these remarks and the previous examples, we can define the following operations on diagrams: join ($\sqcup$), meet ($\sqcap$), and counter ($\overline{\cdot}$) (Table 1).

Under this interpretation, our claim is that $\mu\mathcal{VENN}$ induces a paraconsistent consequence relation. In order to make this more precise, we first introduce a structural notion of content inclusion between diagrams, and then we use it to motivate a valuation-based semantics.

So, let D be the set of $\mu\mathcal{VENN}$ diagrams and let $\sqcup, \sqcap$ be the operators of join and meet. We define a partial order $\leq$ on D by

$$d_1 \leq d_2 \quad \text{iff} \quad d_1 \sqcap d_2 = d_1 \qquad (\text{equivalently, } d_1 \sqcup d_2 = d_2).$$

Table 1. Operators of $\mu\mathcal{VENN}$: (a) Join, (b) Meet, and (c) Counter.

⊔	□	⊠	■	❖
□	□	⊠	■	❖
⊠	⊠	⊠	❖	❖
■	■	❖	■	❖
❖	❖	❖	❖	❖

(a)

⊓	□	⊠	■	❖
□	□	□	□	□
⊠	□	⊠	□	⊠
■	□	□	■	■
❖	□	⊠	■	❖

(b)

d	$\overline{d}$
□	❖
⊠	■
■	⊠
❖	□

(c)

Intuitively, $d_1 \leq d_2$ means that every graphical feature present in d_1 is also present in d_2. In general, for any finite set of diagrams $\Delta = \{d_1, \dots, d_n\} \subseteq D$, we write

$$\bigsqcup \Delta := d_1 \sqcup \cdots \sqcup d_n$$

for their informational aggregation. In this way, this order represents *content inclusion*, that is, an order of diagrams in terms of their informational value, and this order induces a Hasse diagram where □ ≤ ⊠, ■ ≤ ❖ (Fig. 1).

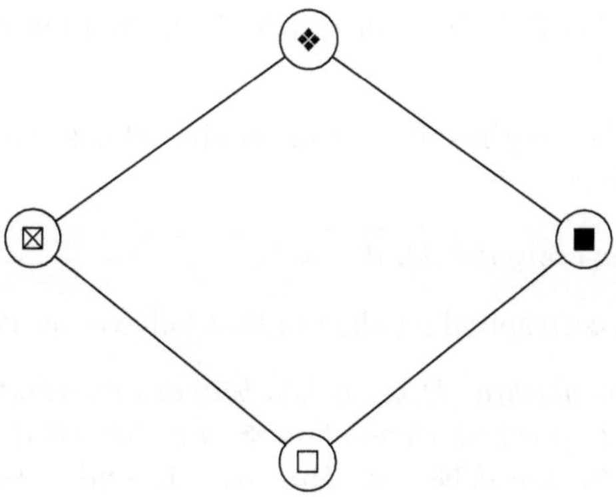

Fig. 1. An induced partial order

Now, to define semantic consequence, let us introduce a notion of valuation and a set of designated diagram-values motivated by the previous considerations. Let $\mathcal{L}$ be a language whose connectives are interpreted by $\sqcup$, $\sqcap$, and $\bar{\cdot}$. We then say a *valuation* is a homomorphism $v : \mathcal{L} \rightarrow D$ such that

$$v(A \sqcup B) = v(A) \sqcup v(B), \quad v(A \sqcap B) = v(A) \sqcap v(B), \quad v(\overline{A}) = \overline{v(A)}.$$

And we take the set of *designated* values to be $\mathsf{Des} = \{$⊠, ■, ❖$\}$, that is, all diagrammatic states containing some visible marks. The value □ is thus excluded from this set since it represents the absence of any information. Hence, we can say that a valuation v *satisfies* a formula A, written $v \models A$, iff $v(A) \in \mathsf{Des}$. Then, we define semantic consequence for any set of formulas Γ and any formula A as usual by

$$\Gamma \models_{\mu\mathcal{VENN}} A \quad \text{iff} \quad \text{for every valuation } v, \text{ if } v \models \Gamma \text{ then } v \models A.$$

Thus, $\models_{\mu\mathcal{VENN}}$ captures preservation of diagrammatic information: whenever the premises are assigned acceptable diagram-states, so is the conclusion —this notion of consequence is induced by the underlying diagrammatic structure encoded by $\leq$, although it is not identical with content inclusion.

And now, given these conceptual conditions, we are in a good position to establish the paraconsistency of $\mu\mathcal{VENN}$:

Proposition 1. *$\mu\mathcal{VENN}$ is paraconsistent.*

Proof. Let A and B be atomic formulas. Define a valuation v by $v(A) = \boxtimes$ and $v(B) = \square$. Then $v(\overline{A}) = \overline{v(A)} = \blacksquare$ by the counter. Since $\boxtimes, \blacksquare \in \mathsf{Des}$, we have $v \models A$ and $v \models \overline{A}$; however, $v(B) = \square \notin \mathsf{Des}$, so $v \not\models B$. Hence, there is a valuation that satisfies both A and $\overline{A}$ but does not satisfy B. Therefore, $A, \overline{A} \not\models_{\mu\mathcal{VENN}} B$ and explosion fails, thus making $\mu\mathcal{VENN}$ paraconsistent.

Consequently, in $\mu\mathcal{VENN}$:

Corollary 1. Ex falso *fails (i.e. inconsistent information does not entail any conclusions).*

But this is not the only result we can obtain. Almost trivially, we get involutivity of the counter:

Proposition 2. *For every $d \in D$, $\overline{\overline{d}} = d$.*

We also obtain a corresponding algebra that behaves as a distributive lattice:

Proposition 3. *The algebra $\langle D, \sqcup, \sqcap \rangle$ is a bounded distributive lattice. Its least element is $\square$ and its greatest element is ❖, i.e. for all $d \in D$, $d \sqcup \square = d$, $d \sqcap \square = \square$, $d \sqcup$❖$=$❖, and $d \sqcap$❖$= d$. Moreover, $\sqcup$ and $\sqcap$ satisfy commutative, associative, idempotent, and distributive properties.*

And finally, if we set an implication defined by content inclusion as

$$A \to B := \begin{cases} B & \text{if } v(A) \leq v(B), \\ \square & \text{otherwise.} \end{cases}$$

then we have a restricted *Modus Ponens* for designated values:

Proposition 4. *If $v(A) \leq v(B)$, then for every valuation v, if $v \models A$ and $v \models A \to B$, then $v \models B$. Consequently, if $A \leq B$, then $A,\ A \to B \models_{\mu\mathcal{VENN}} B$.*

Proof. Assume that $v(A) \leq v(B)$. By definition of $\to$, this implies that $v(A \to B) = v(B)$. Suppose $v \models A$ and $v \models A \to B$. Then $v(A) \in \mathsf{Des}$ and $v(A \to B) = v(B) \in \mathsf{Des}$. Hence $v \models B$. And since this holds for every valuation v, it follows that $A,\ A \to B \models_{\mu\mathcal{VENN}} B$.

These results, we think, support the claim that a particular interpretation of $\mathcal{VENN}$ diagrams induces a consequence relation that is paraconsistent, but what strikes us as interesting is that this type of paraconsistency is not stipulated at the level of inference rules, but rather induced by the physical status of diagrams, since diagrams are physical states of affairs [2].

At this point, however, someone may notice the similarity between this proposal and FDE semantics, which also employ four values that distinguish between "true," "false," "both," and "neither" [3]. In FDE, these values are typically interpreted as epistemic or semantic statuses of propositions. By contrast, in $\mu\mathcal{VENN}$ the four values represent physically instantiated diagrammatic situations. So, in FDE the operators are defined in terms of truth and falsity conditions, and paraconsistency is introduced at the semantic level; whereas in $\mu\mathcal{VENN}$ the operators are grounded in material manipulations of diagrams, so that paraconsistency emerges, so to speak, from representational practices.

There is another difference regarding negation (resp. counter). In FDE, negation fixes the values "both" and "neither," exchanging only "true" and "false.'n' In $\mu\mathcal{VENN}$, by contrast, the counter is given by complementation, exchanging both empty/non-empty and blank/both, reflecting a physical inversion of graphical features. Consequently, $\mu\mathcal{VENN}$ also validates involution (and hence De Morgan theorems) but in a different way.

Last, another important remark should be made. Although $\sqcap$ behaves algebraically as a lattice meet, it does not validate adjunction in the usual inferential sense. Thus, $\sqcap$ should not be interpreted as a standard conjunctive connective at the inferential level. In this sense, $\mu\mathcal{VENN}$ exhibits a non-adjunctive form of paraconsistency.

3 Conclusions

In this contribution we have tried to show that a particular interpretation of $\mathcal{VENN}$ diagrams induces a consequence relation that is paraconsistent. And while there is substantial literature on diagrammatic reasoning and on paraconsistent logics (notably FDE), we are not aware of an explicit development of paraconsistency arising from a physical reading of diagrams. At this point, however, some interesting objections may emerge. We answer just three.

Objection 1. The imposition. The paraconsistency of $\mu\mathcal{VENN}$ is not really discovered in the diagrams themselves; it is rather introduced by stipulating how values and operations are to be interpreted. *Answer:* In $\mu\mathcal{VENN}$ the semantic clauses are directly grounded in material constraints on diagrammatic manipulation. These clauses do not arbitrarily assign meanings to symbols, they codify how physical diagrams behave under standard, intuitive, visual transformations. So, the resulting semantics is constrained by practice rather than free imposition. In this sense, $\mu\mathcal{VENN}$ does not add paraconsistency to $\mathcal{VENN}$ diagrams: it rather makes explicit some logical consequences of their physical manipulations.

Objection 2. The nonnecessity. Standard FDE semantics are well-studied, elegant, and satisfy familiar inferential principles, so why bother with a more idiosyncratic system? *Answer:* The aim of $\mu\mathcal{VENN}$ is not to improve upon FDE or even compete. Our agenda is to show that paraconsistent behaviour can arise from diagrammatic practices in $\mathcal{VENN}$. So, in other words, we could say that with this proposal, a philosophical point is being made, rather than a novel contribution at the mathematical logic level.

Objection 3. The misrepresentation. Since $\mu\mathcal{VENN}$ differs from ordinary set-theoretic interpretations of $\mathcal{VENN}$ diagrams, it misrepresents the standard semantics of $\mathcal{VENN}$. *Answer:* This objection is based upon a misunderstanding: $\mu\mathcal{VENN}$ is not intended as a reconstruction of typical $\mathcal{VENN}$ semantics, its purpose is not to claim that standard $\mathcal{VENN}$ diagrams are already paraconsistent, but to show that once diagrammatic practices are idealized in this minimal way, paraconsistent structures naturally emerge.

References

1. Shin, S.-J.: The Logical Status of Diagrams. Cambridge University Press, Cambridge (1995)
2. Barwise, J., Etchemendy, J.: Visual Information and Valid Reasoning. In: Allwein, G., Barwise, J. (eds.) Logical Reasoning with Diagrams, pp. 3–25. Oxford University Press, New York (1996)
3. Omori, H., Wansing, H.: 40 years of first-degree entailment: an introductory overview. Stud. Logica. **105**, 1021–1049 (2017)

Reference by Occurrence in Quantification

Francesco Bellucci(✉)

University of Bologna, Bologna, Italy
francesco.bellucci4@unibo.it

Abstract. This paper investigates occurrence-referentiality at the quantificational level and argues that it clarifies distinctive features of Peirce's Beta Existential Graphs. Extending the distinction between type-referential and occurrence-referential systems to quantification, it contrasts standard first-order logic with identity (FOL=) with Beta Graphs. In FOL=, co-reference depends on reuse of the same variable type ("*x*"), while different types ("*x*" and "*y*") allow distinct reference; reference is thus determined at the level of type. In Peirce's Beta graphs, by contrast, reference depends on symbol occurrences: existential quantification is represented by Lines of Identity (LIs), where continuity expresses co-reference and disconnection distinctness. The system is therefore occurrence-referential at the quantificational level. Two consequences follow. First, Beta graphs display an equivalential observational advantage: logically equivalent FOL= formulas collapse into a single graph type and are directly observable as equivalent. Second, Existential Graphs achieve the expressive power of FOL= while using only one representational device—the LI—to express both variables and identity.

Keywords: Existential Graphs · Lines of Identity · Peirce · Quantification · Reference by Occurrence

1 Introduction

In previous work (Bellucci and Burton 2020; Bellucci 2024) we have introduced and discussed the notion of "reference by occurrence" or "occurrence-referentiality" with special regard to Euler-like diagrammatic systems. Extending a suggestion by John Etchemendy to Keith Stenning (Stenning 2000, p. 134), we called a system of representation in which the sameness of object represented (e.g. a class) is represented by the sameness of the symbol type "type-referential": in a type-referential system, each occurrence of a symbol type refers to one and the same object. I call a system in which the sameness of object represented is represented by the sameness of the symbol occurrences "occurrence-referential": in an occurrence-referential system, each occurrence of a symbol type refers to a distinct object. The system of unitary Euler diagrams is occurrence-referential: there is one symbol type, the circle; each occurrence of the symbol, i.e. each occurrence of the circle, represents a distinct class; two distinct occurrences of the symbol represent distinct classes. By contrast, the system of non-unitary Euler diagrams (see for example Howse, Molina, Taylor 2000) is type-referential: there is

P. Sobociński et al. (Eds.): Diagrams 2026, LNAI 16833, pp. 17–24, 2027.
https://doi.org/10.1007/978-3-032-34178-5_3

one single type, the circle, and yet what counts in the determination of the sameness or distinctness of the classes represented is not the symbol occurrence, but the sameness of labeled circles, each labeled circle being a distinct sub-type of the circle type. In unitary Euler diagrams, labeling is useful, but not necessary. By contrast, in non-unitary Euler diagrams, labeling is necessary, for otherwise we could not know how to determine the identity of the circles.

In previous works (Bellucci and Burton 2020; Bellucci 2024) we mentioned that the type- vs. occurrence-referentiality divide may apply at distinct representational levels in a system, for example at the predicate level (as in Euler diagrams, where circles represent classes), at the sentential level (as in standard language for sentential logic, in which the sentential variables P, Q, R etc. represent sentences), or at the quantificational level. In this paper, I focus on the type- vs. occurrence-referentiality at the quantificational level. The purpose of the paper is to show that just as occurrence-referentiality at the predicate level explains certain inferential properties of Euler diagrams (Bellucci 2024), so occurrence-referentiality at the quantificational level explains certain inferential properties of Peirce's system of Existential Graphs.

2 Quantification and Variables

In any notation for first-order logic (FOL) two properties are to be represented: the co-reference of the variables bound to certain quantifiers and the logical scope of the quantifiers that bind the variables. The linguistic condition of the sameness and the distinctness of reference of the variables is the sameness and distinctness of the variables themselves. Consider formulas (1a) and (1b). In (1a) there are two distinct variable types ("x" and "y"), while (1b) has two occurrences of one and the same variable type. The identity in type in (1b) is just as essential to the meaning of the sentence as is the distinctness in type in (1a). In (1b) I can uniformly substitute "x" with any other symbol type ("$y = y$," "$z = z$," etc.) without change in the meaning of the sentence; while in (1a) I cannot substitute "x" with "y" without a change in the meaning ("$y > y$" has not the same meaning as "$x > y$"). Now consider sentences (2a) and (2b). In (2a) the use of one and the same variable "x" requires that something is F and that the same thing is H, i.e. requires that the same thing is both F and H. In (2b) the use of distinct variables "x" and "y" requires that something is F and that something is H, but the two somethings may be different.

(1a) $x > y$
(1b) $x = x$
(2a) $(Fx \,\&\, Hx)$
(2b) $(\exists x)\,(Fx)\,\&\,(\exists y)\,(Hy)$
(2c) $(\exists x)\,(Fx)\,\&\,(\exists x)\,(Hx)$
(3) $(\exists x)(\exists y)(Lxy)$

In the standard language for FOL, sameness and distinctness of the variables are relative to the variable *type*. It is the sameness in type in (2a) that allows the two occurrences of "x" to be interpreted as referring to the same individual. It is the distinctness in type in (2b) that allows the two single occurrences of "x" and "y" to be interpreted as referring to possibly distinct individuals. This is what I mean by saying that the linguistic condition of the sameness and the distinctness of reference of the variables is the sameness and distinctness of the variables themselves. When such condition concerns the variable type, I call the language "type-referential". In a language that is type-referential at the quantificational level, each occurrence of a symbol type refers to one and the same object in the domain of quantification, and distinct symbol types refer, or may refer, to distinct objects in the domain of quantification.[1]

Of course, (2b) could also be written as (2c), as the two are in fact equivalent in FOL. This may seem to violate my definition of a type-referential language, because in (2c) there is one variable type (the "x") but the individuals referred to may be two. This impression disappears as soon as we consider FOL sentences in prenex form: in order to move all quantifiers to the left, variables are to be "standardized apart", i.e. each quantifier must have a distinct variable type. If this caveat is added, i.e. if a standardized version of FOL is considered, it will be seen that such a language is type-referential in the defined sense. In what follows, my comparison of the logical graphs with FOL is always meant to be to a "standardized" (or prenex) version of the usual language for FOL.

Languages for FOL that are not type-referential exist. One of these is Peirce's Existential Graphs (Peirce 2019–2025; Roberts 1973; Bellucci and Pietarinen 2024). In the Beta part of this system, corresponding roughly to FOL with identity (FOL=), predicates are represented by "spots", that is, by letters having a definite number of "hooks" or argument places. To each of the hooks of a spot a "Line of Identity" (LI) is attached to represent that an existential quantification has taken place with respect to that hook. For example, the graph in Fig. 1 contains the dyadic spot "L" ("_ loves _"), which has two hooks, one on the left and one on the right. To each of its hooks, a LI is attached. This corresponds to existentially quantifying in both positions. Thus the graph in Fig. 1 says precisely the same thing as the formula in (3), or "Something loves something". While in (3) the (possible) distinctness of the individuals referred to is represented by the distinctness of the variable types "x" and "y", in Fig. 1 the (possible) distinctness of the individuals referred to is represented by the distinctness of the variable occurrences. In Beta graphs, there is only one variable type, the LI. What counts in determining reference is the occurrences of the variable: each detached portion of a LI is a distinct occurrence of the LI. In Beta graphs, the linguistic condition of the sameness and the distinctness of reference of the variables is the sameness and distinctness of variable occurrence. In a language that is occurrence-referential at the quantificational level, each occurrence of a symbol type refers to a possibly distinct individual in the domain of quantification.

[1] The "refer" vs "may refer" distinction depends on whether the interpretation of the variables is exclusive ("refer") or inclusive ("may refer"). Since this distinction applies to both type- and occurrence-referential languages, I can abstract from it in what follows. FOL is usually interpreted inclusively. See Rogers and Wehmeier 2012.

Fig. 1. A Beta graph

3 Free Rides

In previous works (Bellucci and Burton 2020; Bellucci 2024) we argued that the possibility of having "free rides" (Shimojima 1996a; Shimojima 1996b), or, more generally, "observational advantages" (Stapleton, Jamnik, Shimojima 2017; Stapleton, Shimojima, Jamnik 2018) in Euler diagrams depends on their method of reference, i.e. depends on their being an occurrence-referential system of representation. The basic argument was like this: non-unitary Euler diagrams do not manifest free rides in the same way as unitary Euler diagrams; since non-unitary Euler diagrams are type-referential while unitary Euler diagrams are occurrence-referential (in the defined sense), and since this difference is the only difference in the convention underlying the systems, free rides must be due to the occurrence-referential nature of Euler diagrams. Now a parallel argument may be constructed about Existential Graphs and Lines of Identity.

A free ride is "where a reasoner attains a semantically significant fact *s* in a diagram site, while the instructions of the operations the reasoner has followed do not entail the realization of *s*" (Shimojima 1996b, p. 32). Roughly, the contrast is between *inferring* a "semantically significant fact" from a given representation of information and *observing* that fact without inferring it. When one is able to *observe* a "semantically significant fact" from a given representation of information without inferring it, one is exploiting a free ride of that system of representation, and more generally, that system of representation is observationally more advantageous than systems in which that "semantically significant fact" has to be inferred.

However, the definition says nothing about what the "semantically significant fact" may be taken to be. In Euler diagrams, the "semantically significant fact" that is obtained for free may be the conclusion of a syllogism, which is a logical consequence of the premises. For example, in constructing the syllogism for Celarent (Fig. 2), once the premises "All B are A" and No A is C" are constructed, the conclusion "No B is C" is also *ipso facto* constructed, or constructed "for free". The conclusion can be observed rather than inferred; it's a free ride. The system of Euler diagrams is observationally more advantageous with respect to other systems or languages, e.g. standard set theory language, in which that conclusion has to be inferred by application of rules of inference.

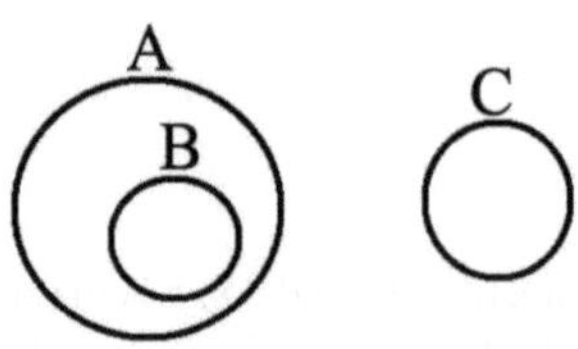

Fig. 2. Free rides in Euler diagrams

With Existential Graphs, the "semantically significant fact" is of a different type. Consider (4a) and (4b). They are logically equivalent in FOL=. In Existential Graphs, there is no way of expressing (4a) without thereby expressing (4b); only one single Beta graph, like that in Fig. 3, corresponds to (4a) and (4b), as well as to infinitely many FOL= sentences that may be constructed along these lines, i.e. by introducing new variables and identity statements, as in (4c), (4d), etc. The reason for this is that Beta graphs are occurrence-referential: one single symbol type, the LI, occurs in as many detached portions as there are distinct or potentially distinct individuals a certain formula is about. Once the graph for (4a) is constructed, the graphs for (4b), (4c), (4d) etc. are also *ipso facto* constructed, or constructed for free. Here there is an important distinction between Existential Graphs and Euler diagrams. I call a free ride "consequential" if the "semantically significant fact" that is observed (rather than inferred) is a logical consequence of a given representation of information. I call a free ride "equivalential" if the "semantically significant fact" that is observed (rather than inferred) is logically equivalent to a given representation of information. Euler diagrams allow free rides of the "consequential" kind: by constructing the diagram of the premises of a syllogism, you get the diagram of the conclusion, i.e. of a logical consequence, for free. Existential graphs allow free rides of the "equivalential" kind: by constructing the graph of a certain FOL= sentence, you get the graph of other sentences that are logically equivalent to the former, for free. The matter may also be put in terms of observational advantages. Existential Graphs are observationally more advantageous with respect to FOL=, because in FOL= you have to prove that, e.g. (4a) and (4b) are equivalent, and the proof of this equivalence involves at least some basic inferential transformation, while in Existential graphs the equivalence is directly observed, not inferred; namely, it is observed that the graph corresponding to (4a) and the graph corresponding to (4b) are the same graph type.

(4a) $(\exists x)\ (Lxx)$
(4b) $(\exists x)\ (\exists y)\ (Lxy\ \&\ x = y)$
(4c) $(\exists x)\ (\exists y)\ (\exists z)\ (Lxy\ \&\ x = y\ \&\ y = z)$
(4d) $(\exists x)\ (\exists y)\ (\exists z)\ (\exists u)\ (Lxy\ \&\ x = y\ \&\ y = z\ \&\ z = u)$
(4e) …

Fig. 3. Free rides in Existential Graphs

4 Expressivity

First-order logic without identity (FOL) is less expressive than first-order logic with identity (FOL=); for example, finite numerical quantification (quantifiers of the form "there are at least n objects such that") is expressible in FOL= but not in FOL (Wehmeier 2017). It is standardly claimed that Existential Graphs, and especially its Beta department, are as expressive as FOL=. In the first place, this is not strictly true due to the fact that the "hooks" of the "spots" of Beta graphs are unordered (for the space upon which the graphs are scribed is unordered), so there is no way to distinguish e.g. "*Lxy*" from "*Lyx*". As a result, Beta graphs are expressively equivalent to a fragment of FOL=, i.e. the fragment with monadic and symmetric binary predicates. If the full expressive power of FOL= has to be maintained, then some convention of interpretation has to be added to the system of conventions; in his very first papers on the logical graphs (Peirce 2019–2025, vol. 1, pp. 211–261; vol. 1 pp. 292–303) Peirce suggests that the hooks of a spot should have a definite order of interpretation beginning at a designated hook and continuing clockwise. He thought that this problem of expressivity could be fixed one way or another (cf. Bellucci and Pietarinen 2016; Bellucci and Pietarinen 2021).

But here I want to focus on another side of the graphs' expressive power. In any notation for FOL=, two things are to be represented: (i) variables and (ii) identity (plus of course quantifiers and quantification priorities, which is a distinct matter and cannot be addressed here; but see Bellucci and Pietarinen 2016; Bellucci and Pietarinen 2021). When it is said that Existential Graphs are expressively equivalent to FOL=, part of what is meant is that besides representing the variables, Existential Graphs can express identity, and thus, for example, finite numerical quantification. In the standard, type-referential notation for FOL=, the variables are represented by letters ("x", "y", "z" etc.) while the relation of identity is represented by the symbol "="; the identity of the individuals denoted by two distinct variables, say "x" and "y", is represented by connecting two occurrences of those variables by an occurrence of the symbol "=", as in (5).

(5) $(\exists x)\,(\exists y)\,(x = y)$

Now in what manner do Existential Graphs represent the relation of identity? More generally, in what manner can an occurrence-referential language for quantification represent the relation of identity? In an occurrence-referential language, it is the occurrence of the variable that determines identity and sameness of reference. Two distinct occurrences of the variable represent two possible distinct individuals (Fig. 4a). In order to say that those individuals are the same individual, one has simply to join the two distinct occurrences and turn them into a single occurrence of the variable (Fig. 4b). The only way to assert the identity of the individuals denoted by distinct occurrences of the variable is to join them, i.e. turn them into one single occurrence. Any other means of expressing identity would leave the two occurrences distinct, which in an occurrence-referential language means that the two individuals referred to are or may be distinct.

Let us then go back to expressive power. Everything that the standard notation for FOL= does with two distinct notational devices (the variables and the symbol of identity), Existential Graphs do by means of one single notational device (the variable, i.e. the LI). This can happen, of course, because of occurrence-referentiality. To use the famous

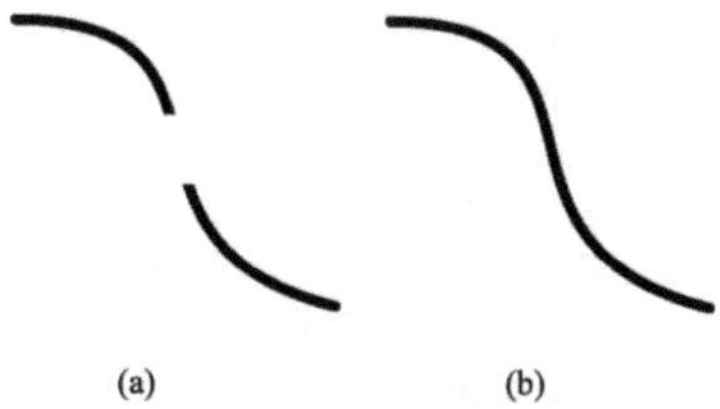

Fig. 4. Identity in an occurrence-referential language

Wittgensteinian distinction between "saying" and "showing", one might say that a type-referential language *says* by means of an *ad hoc* sign of identity that distinct variable types have the same reference, while in an occurrence-referential language the possibility of making identity statements is "embodied" in the language itself; the language itself *shows* identity and distinctness without saying it.

Existential Graphs do everything that the standard notation for FOL= does with one single notational device instead of two. They have distinct vocabularies (FOL= has the variables and the identity symbol, Existential Graphs have only the variable) but the same expressive power. Let us now consider a comparison between Existential Graphs and FOL *without* identity. FOL has the variables "x", "y" etc. (which are used type-referentially), Existential Graphs have the LI (which is used occurrence-referentially). In this sense, Existential Graphs and FOL have the same vocabulary. But Existential Graphs can express more than FOL without identity, i.e. it can express identity, and accordingly finite numerical quantification. So, while they have the same vocabulary of FOL, Existential Graphs have a greater expressive power. The result is that Existential Graphs have the expressive power of FOL= with the vocabulary of FOL.

References

Bellucci, F.: Reference by occurrence. In: Lemanski, J., et al. (eds.) Diagrammatic Representation and Inference, pp. 182–189. Springer (2024)

Bellucci, F., Pietarinen, A.-V.: From Mitchell to Carus. Fourteen years of logical graphs in the making. Trans. Charles S. Peirce Soc. **52**, 539–575 (2016)

Bellucci, F., Pietarinen, A.-V.: An analysis of existential graphs. Part 2: Beta. Synthese. **199**, 7705–7726 (2021)

Bellucci, F., Pietarinen, A.-V.: Existential graphs. History and interpretation. In: De Waal, C. (ed.) The Oxford Handbook of Charles S. Peirce, pp. 240–260. Oxford University Press, Oxford (2024)

Bellucci, F., Burton, J.: Observational advantages and occurrence-referentiality. In: Pietarinen, A.-V., et al. (eds.) Diagrammatic Representation and Inference, pp. 202–215. Springer (2020)

Howse, J., Molina, F., Taylor, J.: On the completeness and expressiveness of spider diagram systems. In: Anderson, M., et al. (eds.) Theory and Application of Diagrams, pp. 26–41. Springer, Dordrecht (2000)

Peirce, C.S.: Logic of the Future. Peirce's Writings on Existential Graphs. In: 3 vols Ed. by A.-V. Pietarinen. Berlin: De Gruyter (2019–2025)

Roberts, D.R.: The Existential Graphs of Charles S. Mouton, Peirce. The Hague (1973)

Rogers, B., Wehmeier, K.F.: Tractarian first-order logic: identity and the N-operator. Rev. Symbolic Logic. **5**, 538–573 (2012)

Shimojima, A.: On the efficacy of representation. Ph.D. thesis, Indiana University (1996a)
Shimojima, A.: Operational constraint in diagrammatic reasoning. In: Allwein, G., Barwise, J. (eds.) Logical Reasoning with Diagrams, pp. 27–48. Oxford University Press, Oxford (1996b)
Stapleton, G., Jamnik, M., Shimojima, A.: What makes an effective representation of information: a formal account of observational advantages. J. Log. Lang. Inf. **26**, 143–177 (2017)
Stapleton, G., Shimojima, A., Jamnik, M.: The observational advantages of Euler diagrams with existential import. In: Chapman, P., et al. (eds.) Diagrammatic Representation and Inference, 313–329. Springer, Cham (2018)
Stenning, K.: Distinctions with differences: comparing criteria for distinguishing diagrammatic from sentential systems. In: Anderson, M., et al. (eds.) Diagrammatic Representation and Inference, 132–148. Springer, Heidelberg (2000)
Wehmeier, K.F.: Identity and quantification. Philos. Stud. **174**, 759–770 (2017)

Syllogistic Diagrams and Existential Commitment: A Historical Study

Karol Wapniarski[1,2(✉)] and Mariusz Urbański[2]

[1] Faculty of Philosophy, University of Cambridge, Cambridge CB3 9DA, UK
[2] Faculty of Psychology and Cognitive Science, Adam Mickiewicz University Poznań, 60-568 Poznan, Poland
krw41@cam.ac.uk, mariusz.urbanski@amu.edu.pl

Abstract. We look into how logical diagrams used throughout the history of logic might have influenced the debate on the use of empty terms in logic. To this end, we survey Byzantine diagrams for syllogistic figures, Arabic linear diagrams of Al-Barakāt, European linear diagrams of Leibniz and Lambert, Euler circles, Venn, and Venn-Peirce diagrams. The diagrams are analysed with respect to their ability or inability to account for and represent (non-)empty terms. Additionally, we sketch parallels between the evolution of the diagrams and the historical perspectives on empty terms, arguing that an influence, albeit not necessarily conscious, might have been at work. Attention is also drawn to how Venn and post-Venn diagrams explicitly addressed the issue of representing non-emptiness – this is in order to show the influence that the development of modern formal logic has exerted on visually representing syllogistic.

Keywords: existential import · logic diagrams · syllogistic diagrams · history of logic · syllogisms

1 Introduction

The study of logical diagrams and their role throughout the history of logic is an ongoing trend, getting more and more scholarly attention over recent years. A subthread in this research area has been the study of the connection between visual thinking and recognizing existence in logic. A recent paper by Lemanski [20] proposes a detailed examination of nineteenth century circular diagrams and argues for viewing the evolution of Euler and Venn diagrams (and circular diagrams in general) as crucial in the process of recognizing existence in the nineteenth century logic.

By contrast to this example, we will not provide a detailed study of one group of diagrams, connecting them to the issue of existential import. Instead, we will offer a wide historical overview of how syllogistic diagrams evolved, connecting their ongoing evolution to the parallel evolution of how empty terms in syllogistic logic were viewed and how logicians dealt with the problem of existential import.

P. Sobociński et al. (Eds.): Diagrams 2026, LNAI 16833, pp. 25–40, 2027.
https://doi.org/10.1007/978-3-032-34178-5_4

What we aim to show is, in particular, that indeed, a parallel development of syllogistic diagrams and considerations on empty terms may be discerned. The main thesis is as follows: In times where the scholars were not openly addressing the issue of empty terms in logic, the type of diagrams used could not properly represent existence or non-existence of logical terms' denotata; in times where the scholars were addressing the issue with more and more detail, the diagrammatic representations used were more and more apt to represent individual existence and hence to mark the non-emptiness of terms. We should stress that we do not wish to address individual authors' opinions on existential import – these may be found elsewhere; nor are we concerned with the question(s) of the intellectual influence of one author upon another. Our investigation focuses solely on the interplay between logical diagrams and logical theory (on the example of recognising the importance of marking non-emptiness), analysing subsequent individual instances of this interplay and showing its gradual evolution. We therefore limit ourselves to cover only facts directly relevant to our main thesis. Apart from analysing this historical case, we treat it as a case study which illustrates that a use of a particular kind of diagrammatic representation may have a significant influence on philosophical views on logic and its development.

To these ends, we draw attention to several most significant kinds of diagrams that were used to visually render syllogistic reasoning throughout the history of logic. We begin by briefly sketching, in Sect. 2, the history of how empty terms were considered by logicians. Section 3 is devoted to Byzantine diagrams for syllogistic figures: We show that as existential import in syllogistic was not considered by Aristotle, these diagrams could not represent the emptiness (or non-emptiness) of terms. In Sect. 4, we take a look at Arabic diagrams and specifically Al-Barakāt's linear diagrams, showing that with existential import being reflected upon by Arabic logicians, the diagrams used could also account for the emptiness of terms, and hence represent existence. In Sect. 5, we show two kinds of linear diagrams developed by Leibniz, connecting them to his analysis of the problem of empty terms present in his *Difficultates quaedam logicae* – we show how two modes of treating empty terms recognised by him in this paper get reflected in the diagrams he devised. Next, in Sect. 6, we survey diagrams of Lambert, Euler, Venn, and Peirce, showing how singular terms and individual existence gradually get more and more articulated as these diagrams develop, culminating in Peirce's "existential" diagrams, where the representation of existence is the primary building-block of visual representations. Lastly, we draw attention to how the development of modern logic influenced these diagrams and, subsequently, the understanding of empty terms in syllogistic. The paper ends with more general speculations about the epistemological significance of visual representations in logic.

2 Existential Commitments Throughout the History of Logic

For reasons of space, we give just a brief description of how the considerations concerning existential commitments proceeded throughout the history of logic,

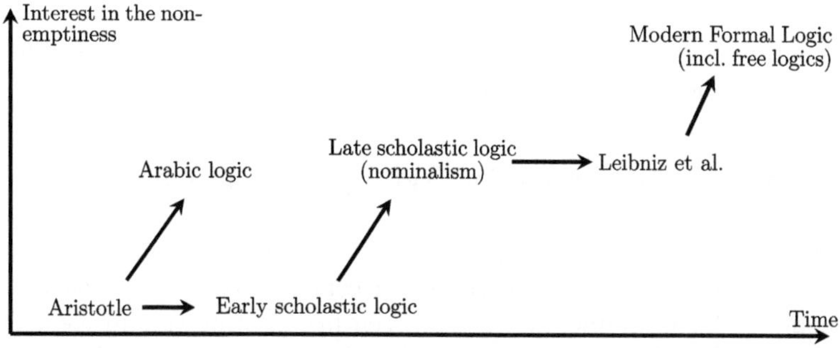

Fig. 1. Interest in the non-emptiness of terms throughout the history of logic

marking the most important periods. An interested reader may consult the abundant literature on this subject [9,11,30,33][1]. As pertains to the goal of this paper, we are interested in distinguishing points in history when the existence of subjects of terms in syllogistic was debated avidly and, by contrast, periods in which it was significantly less relevant for scholars.

Although much has been said about Aristotle making the assumption of the non-emptiness of all syllogistic terms (most importantly [21]), the consensus in recent studies is that this issue is not present in sections of *Prior Analytics* devoted to assertoric syllogistic (see [22, p. 82] and [30]). Consequently, the problem of existential import has not been addressed by Aristotle, nor by subsequent Greek scholars. The first one we know to talk about existential import explicitly is Al-Farabi [16, p. 39] – after him, the issue was debated in considerable detail by Avicenna, Averroes, and also later figures of Arabic logic [2,11]. In the West, existential import was not considered until late scholasticism, having been briefly raised by the main expounders of nominalism (Ockham, Buridan) [9], and then neglected in the mainstream until Leibniz, who considers it in detail [18, p. 115-121]. The problem of existential import and empty terms was then getting more and more attention as the "new logic", built upon the notion of set, started to emerge. The emergence of this new logic, itself not allowing for the emptiness of terms, brought with it commentaries on Aristotelian logic containing the untrue statement that this "ancient" logic was restricted to the use of non-empty terms as well. The history of the issue may be thus depicted as presented in Fig. 1 (note that we are interested in the "intensity" of the scholarly discussions taking place and not in the precise solutions being discussed).

In what follows, we shall see that the periods in which the diagrams used by logicians allowed for marking empty terms usually overlap with the periods in

[1] The most important issue with existential import was the validity of subalternations (inferences from universal affirmative to particular affirmative and from universal negative to particular negative) and p-conversion (inference from universal affirmative to particular affirmative with the terms converted). Such inferences are problematic as they necessitate adoption of an additional existential premise stating existence of the universal statement's subject.

which the issue of empty terms was addressed – and conversely for periods in which diagrams were *not* able to account for the emptiness of terms. The thesis that this is not merely a coincidence is the main thesis of this paper.

3 Byzantine Diagrams for Syllogistic Figures

Byzantine diagrams for syllogistic figures, known from a manuscript tradition (consult [8]) which originated in the sixth century AD, have been developed into a concrete form around the eleventh century [1] and were in use as late as Renaissance Italy [25]. Nevertheless, their origins are traced back to antiquity and modern scholarship argues that the underlying mechanism of the Byzantine diagrams was used already by Aristotle, and was only given a more articulate form by later scholars [23,31]. With some oversimplification, we may claim that the diagrams are an integral part of the so-called "Greek" tradition of encoding syllogistic moods – as opposed to the "Latin" tradition, which originated in the Latin West[2] – and were used mainly for mnemonic purposes, as devices that help to classify and remember different moods.

The study of these diagrams received a considerable amount of scholarly attention recently [5,19,28,31,32]. As a result, we have several modern reconstructions of their working mechanism [25,28]. For reasons of space, we will not comprehensively describe this mechanism, but only give an overview of it and pinpoint features most significant to purposes of this work.

There are three types of Byzantine diagrams, representing three syllogistic figures as defined by Aristotle[3]: A moon-like diagram for Figure 1, a triangle diagram for Figure 2, and an inverted-triangle diagram for Figure 3. With the type of diagram representing syllogistic *figure* and terms located on vertices, a specific syllogistic *mood* can be represented by specifying the relationship between the terms (i.e. which kind of categorical sentence holds between them). This is done by annotating sides between any two given terms. Below are examples of the three types of Byzantine diagrams with annotated terms (P, M, S).
The most pronounced feature of these diagrams, and the most important, from our point of view, is the fact that they are primarily used to distinguish between figures. As such, they are constructed so as to reflect the structural aspect of figures and not of individual moods within the figures, whose representation is visually the same apart from different annotations of sides. This characteristic is true not only for individual figures, but also for relationships between them. Most importantly, the shapes are so matched that the Figure 1 (moon-like) diagram

[2] In the Latin West, a different mnemonic system has been developed throughout the Middle Ages, consisting of Latin hexameter verses encoding subsequent syllogistic moods and their proofs (see e.g. relevant section in [1]). Explaining the precise functioning of this mnemonic is well beyond the scope of this paper, but one important point regarding it will be made later (see footnote 7).

[3] Each syllogistic figure gathering syllogistic moods of a specific subject-predicate arrangement across premises. We will not go into detail about this, as basic knowledge of syllogistic is assumed. A reader in need may consult [26].

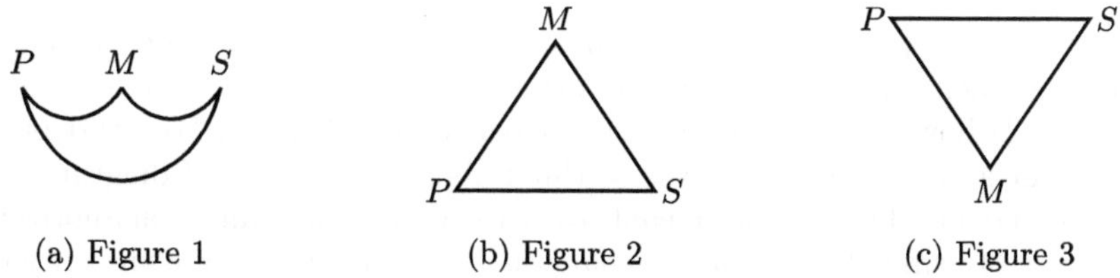

Fig. 2. Byzantine diagrams for syllogistic figures

can be overwritten on Figure 2 or 3 (triangle) diagrams to express the reducibility of the latter ones to the former, in accordance with the usual account of Aristotle[4]. An example of how such a diagrammatic proof may look is presented below – a Figure 2 mood (triangle) is shown to be expressible by the means of a Figure 1 mood (moon-like shape):

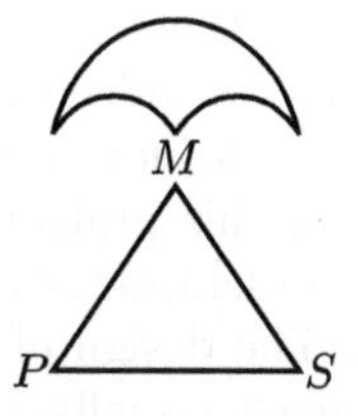

Fig. 3. A moon-like diagram representing Figure 1 overwritten on a triangle diagram representing Figure 2

The Byzantine diagrams were therefore constructed so that they could accurately express relations between figures: Precisely those relations deemed important by the tradition of thought they originated in. As a side effect of this, they are not capable of expressing variations within individual moods, nor the structure of them. Most importantly, they are not capable of expressing either extension or intension of individual terms that construct the moods and, consequently, *they do not allow for expressing whether a term is empty or not.* This lack, we argue, stems from the fact that empty terms were not considered by logicians on a theoretical level. What we claim is that since logicians were not aware of the non-emptiness problem, the type of diagrams they designed was not constructed (or perhaps even could not have been constructed) to account for this problem[5].

[4] I.e. with the Aristotelian claim that Figure 2 and 3 moods are reducible, i.e. can be expressed by, Figure 1 moods.

[5] It is true that syllogistic figures can be represented using other types of diagrams as well, e.g. Venn diagrams. What is important for our argument is, however, that representing the figure is an inherent feature of the Byzantine diagrams – there is no simple Byzantine diagram that would *not* by the sole virtue of being a Byzantine diagram represent a given figure. We thank an anonymous reviewer for raising this point.

A somewhat epistemological significance[6] of this claim may be made more convincing when one considers 1) the primarily mnemonic function of the diagrams [1], 2) how prevalent they were in teaching syllogistic. For students, to think about a syllogistic mood was to think about it in terms of diagrams; and to reduce one mood to another meant overwriting one diagram upon another. In the process of using the diagrams, what was important was again the structure of figures and not of individual moods – in practice, the term letters, as well as the sentence letters, were often overlooked or even not written at all by some scholars (see [1, p. 54] and [25, p. 35]), which again suggests their secondary importance.

The primarily mnemonic and pedagogic use of diagrams multiplied the epistemological effect – the diagrams were structuring how people thought about syllogistic, which properties of syllogisms they were likely to spot, and which they were not[7]. The fact that the diagrams could not express the non-emptiness of terms consequently reinforced the tendency to overlook the non-emptiness issue on a theoretical level as well.

A careful reader may spot that there is at least some level of circularity involved here. What we argue for is indeed a circular movement: The diagrams are constructed so that they do not allow for expressing non-emptiness *because* scholars were not aware of this problem; but then *since* the diagrams were not allowing for expressing non-emptiness, the issue remained obscure and was not noticed by the scholars. The design of the diagrams, not allowing the non-emptiness issue to manifest itself visually, paired with their ubiquitous use further prohibited this issue from being spotted.

Indeed, as we shall see from other examples in this paper, it is not implausible to state that if, by a pure chance, diagrams constructed with a purpose of expressing figure-relations were *also* accidentally able to express the non-emptiness of terms, allowing for visually marking if a term is empty or not, the issue would get spotted by logicians and discussed. But since it was not the case, the non-emptiness of terms remained obscure for Greek logicians and was vividly discussed only in the Arabic world. Such a scenario, in which a type of diagram

[6] By epistemological here we mean that the habitual use of diagrams to think about syllogistic moods is also significantly structuring how one think about these moods and more importantly *what* can one think about them.

[7] Here let us note that the same effect can be said to occur with the "Latin tradition" mnemonic system (see footnote 2). What it has in common with the Greek one (diagrams) is that they both did not allow for representing empty terms, nor did they provide any theoretical tools for understanding how admitting empty terms influences validity of some of the moods.

Considering that, our argument about the epistemological significance of using a particular type of mnemonic can be stretched out to the Latin mnemonic as well – in both traditions, the major system of representation in use did not allow for marking whether a term was empty or not, and in this way, the issue of empty terms has not been prone to appear as an issue to logicians for a long time. The mnemonic devices – Greek diagrams and Latin verses – have in this way prompted the neglect of empty terms in the early and mid Middle Ages.

induces (or forces) one to consider the emptiness of terms, is not implausible, as we will see in the next Section.

4 Al-Barakāt's Linear Diagrams: an Epistemic Contraction

We have so far seen that the Byzantine diagrams for syllogistic figures could not accommodate for marking whether a term is empty or not, which coincides with the previous observation that empty terms were not considered by Aristotle, nor by the early Greek scholars. Now, we shall consider Arabic diagrams, showing that with Arabic scholars debating the issue of non-emptiness of terms, the diagrams in use were sensitive to that issue. The example hereby described will also assure us of the epistemological significance of using a specific kind of diagrams.

Unfortunately, not many studies on Arabic diagrams for syllogistic logic exist. We will therefore constrain ourselves to but a one, although very illustrative, type of diagrams developed and used by an Arabic logician and follower of Avicenna, Al-Barakāt [15]. The diagrams of Al-Barakāt were developed in his major work, *Kitāb al-Mut̀abar* [3], in the mid twelfth century. In this work, he devises a method for diagrammatically determining whether a specific pair of premises yields a conclusion and, if so, for determining what this conclusion is. This is done through sketching a pair of lines, each line corresponding to one term, for a given categorical sentence. In Fig. 4a and Fig. 4b, there are example diagrams for a universal affirmative and particular affirmative sentences.

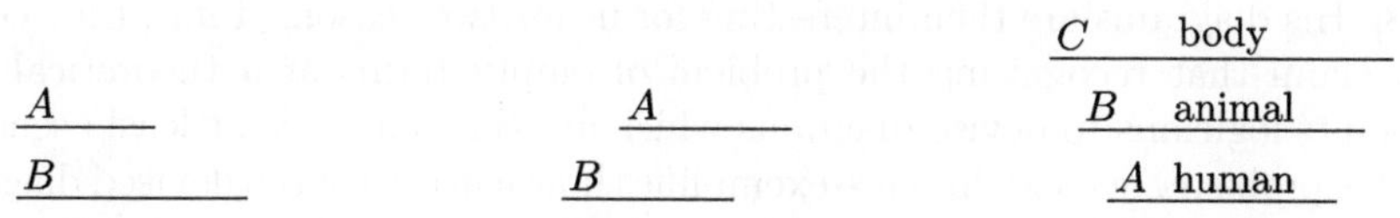

(a) All A's are B's (b) Some A's are B's (c) Barbara

Fig. 4. Examples of Al-Barakāt's diagrams

In order to show a whole syllogistic mood, such diagrams are then compounded accordingly, resulting in a diagram consisting of three lines: One for major term, one for middle term, and one for minor term. As an example for the syllogistic mood Barbara, Al-Barakāt gives the diagram portrayed in Fig. 4c. This consists of three simpler diagrams for sentences: That every B is C and every A is B (every animal has a body, every human is an animal), yielding the conclusion that every A is C (every human has a body). A three-line diagram therefore includes three two-line diagrams.

One may immediately recognise that although the end goal of Al-Barakāt's diagrams is similar to that of the Byzantine diagrams, namely checking the validity of syllogistic moods, the way this is done in both systems is entirely different. Whereas Byzantine diagrams are primarily concerned with structural aspects of syllogistic figures, the diagrams of Al-Barakāt are primarily about the semantics of individual sentences. The simplest way of seeing that is to consider that Al-Barakāt's diagrams represent individual sentences first, and the representations of moods are built upon them. It is also important to see that the individual lines represent what we may in today's language call an extension of a term.

The second startling and imposing feature of Al-Barakāt's diagrams pertains directly to the issue of non-emptiness. As we have mentioned, Arabic logicians were aware of empty terms at least since Al-Farabi, and admitting empty terms was discussed e.g. by Avicenna of whom Al-Barakāt was a follower. Arabic logicians were also considering structures of individual types of subject-predicate sentences in much more detail (see e.g. [10]). Al-Barakāt was therefore perfectly aware of the problem of non-emptiness, as well as sensitive to the internal structure of categoricals (as evidenced by his diagrams). Indeed, even before devising his diagrams, he discussed the non-emptiness of terms and allowed for the terms to be interpreted as empty.

The relevant feature of the diagrammatic system he devised is, however, that his linear diagrams have no way of representing empty terms[8]. Whereas the Byzantine diagrams were "concealing" the problem, having no way of representing *whether* a term is empty or not, Al-Barakāt's diagrams prove to be aware of the possibility of marking a term as empty or not, but they only allow to represent one type of terms, namely the non-empty ones.

This leads us to an interesting observation that Al-Barakāt, having recognised this feature of his diagrams, decided to change his views on a theoretical level and restricted his logic to structures that operate on non-empty terms only [15, p. 8]. His diagrams are then interesting for us for two reasons: First, they certify our claim that recognising the problem of empty terms at a theoretical level prompts logicians to devise diagrams which are (in some way, at least) sensitive to this problem. Second, his case exemplifies how features of the devised diagrams can influence logicians' thinking about logic. In the case of Byzantine diagrams, this influence was tacit and spread over generations, consisting in the diagrams

[8] If this is not obvious from how the diagrams look like, one may consult [15, p. 375-376]. Although according to Hodges the case is that "There is one obvious reason for Al-Barakāt to turn his back on empty terms", which is that "his diagrams have no way to represent empty sets" [15, p. 376], it may be argued that nothing prevents one from substituting e.g. "unicorn" for "human", with the validity of the diagram (Fig. 4c) unchanged. To this we respond that one may also follow a modern interpretation of pre-Venn diagrams which states that if a term exists, an object is drawn to represent it; if it does not exist, it is simply not represented at all (see e.g. [7]) – i.e., drawing something presupposes its existence. Considering Al-Barakāt's decision of restricting his theory to non-empty terms only following the adoption of his diagrams, it seems to us that both of these lines of argument stem from imposing a post-Venn perspective on pre-Venn diagrams: It is true that for Al-Barakāt, drawing something presupposes its existence, but it seems not to be true that not drawing something represents its non-existence: empty terms are simply not considered by him at all. We thank reviewers for raising these important issues.

inhibiting the awareness of the problem of non-empty terms. In the case of Al-Barakāt, it was open and constrained to the life of one scholar, and therefore manifested itself clearly.

We can be therefore sure that in this example, the expressive powers of diagrams influenced theoretical decision about the admission of empty terms. We also note that this influence elicited a contraction, and not an expansion, of a logical system, causing Al-Barakāt to restrict empty terms. As will become evident in subsequent sections, the interplay of diagrams and theory can manifest itself in different ways, e.g. with a richer theory eliciting richer system of diagrams.

5 Linear Diagrams of Leibniz and His *Difficultates Quaedam Logicae*

The manuscript of Leibniz in which he presents his views on existential import and empty terms in a most detailed way are his *Difficultates quaedam logicae* [*Some logical difficulties*] [18, p. 115-121]. In this paper, he discusses two interpretations of syllogistic terms, an intensional and an extensional interpretation. An extensional interpretation takes term denotata to be objects in the external world, and the syllogistic inferences to describe relations between those objects; an intensional interpretation takes term denotata to be concepts, viz. mental objects, and syllogistic inferences to describe relations between those concepts. Thus, an example sentence "Every human is an animal" is, on the first interpretation, saying that the set of humans is contained in the set of animals, and, on the second interpretation, that the concept of being a human contains the concept of being an animal (cf. [12, p. 29-30]). What Leibniz argues for regarding the problem of empty terms is that, shall both categorical sentences involved in subalternation or p-conversion (see footnote 2) be interpreted according to the same interpretation, the problem does not occur[9]. Below are example universal affirmative categoricals drawn for both interpretations using Leibniz's linear diagrams[10]:
On the first diagram (Fig. 5a), the solid lines indicate extension of terms, and the dashed lines tell us where the range of S ends. On the second diagram (Fig. 5b), the solid lines indicate intensions of terms, whereas the dashed line indicates the *possible* intension of terms (in this case, of P), and the vertical lines mark the limit of the range for both terms. The first diagram thus states that the set S is

[9] There is no space to elaborate on this idea here, a curious reader may consult *Difficultates* himself. What is important for our argument is that Leibniz, having considered two interpretations of categoricals for his treatment of existential import, has also developed two types of diagrams that reflect these interpretations – this, again, might not have been a causal relation, but is nevertheless representative of the interplay between diagrams and theory we investigate in the present work.

[10] Although *Difficultates* themselves contain no diagrams, they were written at a time when Leibniz made extensive use of linear diagrams. For more information regarding Leibniz's linear diagrams, including works where they appear, consult [12, p. 27-31].

(a) Every S is P (extensional) (b) Every S is P (intensional)

Fig. 5. Leibniz's linear diagrams for universal categorical sentences

contained within the set P; the second says that the concept of S contains the concept of P (for clarifications see [18, p. xxxviii-xlii] and [4]).

What is important in this case is not precisely how the diagrams work, but the fact that Leibniz did devise two different diagrammatic systems for two interpretations of terms he considered – these interpretations being closely connected to his treatment of empty terms. We can see a clear parallel between the developed systems of diagrammatic representations and Leibniz's theoretical investigations: Having considered intensional and extensional interpretations theoretically, he devised his diagrams accordingly; and, since his stance on empty terms is that the problem does not occur if both categorical sentences are interpreted in the same way (i.e. either intensionally or extensionally), his diagrams' expressive powers aptly represent his theoretical considerations.

The case is therefore different from the case of Al-Barakāt. In the latter, the design of diagrams elicited restriction of logical theory; here, the logical theory influences creation of diagrams, honing their expressive powers. This not only certifies our main claim that theoretical considerations of empty terms and expressive powers of logical diagrams coincide, but adds to this claim an important detail: When empty terms are considered, the diagrams are not only capable of expressing the non-emptiness of terms, but their design can also reflect what a particular scholar thought about this problem.

The diagrams of Leibniz are thus capable of visually representing an intensionally or extensionally non-empty term, but they are not yet able to represent a single denotatum within that term, i.e. an existence of a singular term. This feature, closely connected to the development of modern formal logic and the algebra of Boole, has become crucial in the next period, in which syllogistic logic was viewed more and more through the lenses of the newly emerging systems.

6 Recognizing Existence Through Singular Terms: Lambert, Euler, Venn, and Peirce

Leibniz was thus one step further compared to Al-Barakāt – the latter restricts his logic to non-empty terms only because of his diagrams, the former expands his system of diagrams to account for his theoretical stance on empty terms. In both cases, however, the diagrams are not able to represent what we might call an empty set. I.e., their default is representing sets that are non-empty (only extensional in Al-Barakāt, extensional or intensional in Leibniz).

During the period from Leibniz to the nineteenth century, scholars were apparently prompted more and more to consider representations whose "default mode" of visualising terms allows for them to be either empty or non-empty. The set itself, if interpreted as empty by default, could then be marked non-empty using a special diagrammatic feature, usually boiling down to marking an existence of a singular term within a set. This change of approach to diagrams can be traced back to Lambert, and a tendency to stress singular terms more and more can be observed with subsequent diagrammatic systems considered – Euler diagrams, Venn diagrams, and some features of diagrammatic systems devised later by Peirce.

As we shall argue, this evolution stems from (1) empty terms being given more attention, (2) modern formal logic, considering only non-empty terms but based on a notion of a set that technically *can* be empty, being developed. This confirms the last piece of our history: That with empty terms being given considerable attention in the modern times, the devised diagrams were getting more and more sensitive to marking non-emptiness. The case in the following Sections will also form our last example of how diagrams and theory are interconnected: This time, theoretical advancements in a new theory (formal logic, emerging) influence how diagrams originally devised for old theory (syllogistic) are reconsidered, which in turn influences how the old logic itself is interpreted.

As numerous studies on the representation of non-empty sets with Euler and Venn diagrams exist (e.g. [20,24,27]), we will limit ourselves to remarks necessary for making the main point of this paper. We will also not deal with contemporary interpretations of Euler and Venn diagrams, but rather take into consideration the historical texts of analysed authors.

6.1 Lambert's Linear Diagrams

The first step towards recognising individual existence may be illustrated by looking at the linear diagrams of Lambert. The principal idea of these diagrams is roughly equivalent to that of Al-Barakāt or Leibniz – to represent the extension (or intension) of a set using a line and then combine lines to draw representations of sentences and inferences. What is new in Lambert is that he has a method for indicating non-emptiness: And that is by having a term letter in place of a line. Examples of A and I categorical sentences are shown in the Figure 6 below.

(a) All A's are B's (b) Some A's are B's

Fig. 6. Lambert's diagrams for categorical statements

About this term letter he writes that: "when we retain only a letter without a line for the concept A, this indicates that we know only of some, *and perhaps only of one* individual A that it is B" ([17, p. 113-114]; our emphasis)[11]. That

[11] All translations are due to the first author of this paper unless otherwise indicated.

is, the primary purpose is to indicate that *some* individuals fall under a term, i.e. that the represented sentence is a particular and not a universal categorical; the secondary purpose is to represent that only *one* such individual exists, i.e. to mark a singular term. This secondary feature will become the standard usage of such new diagrammatic properties later, in Euler and Venn.

6.2 Euler's, Venn's, and Peirce's Circular Diagrams

This quality of diagrams, witnessed in Lambert, became more explicit with Euler and Venn. This did not happen automatically, but was adopted gradually. As we shall see, Euler did not himself introduce additional way of marking singular terms yet; this was considered by Venn, and was strongly advocated by Peirce. What is different from Lambert in these examples is, however, that the primary function of these diagrammatic innovations was not to represent particular categoricals and only secondarily mark existence of singular terms, but that their sole purpose was to mark non-emptiness, i.e. explicitly indicate the existence of a term[12].

The diagrams of Euler were devised by him in four letters, from CII to CV, of his *Letters to a German Princess* [13, p. 95-126]. Euler does not introduce an explicit way of marking non-emptiness yet[13]. However, such explicit marking of non-emptiness – or emptiness – of terms became even more important with Venn's system of logical diagrams developed in his *Symbolic Logic* [29, p. 100-125], the purpose of which was to "provide a visual mapping of Boole's new algebraic logic" [12, p. 35]. As depicting an empty term became important – and as Venn himself considered the issue of existence of terms in considerable detail (in the chapter following the chapter on diagrams) – the diagrams themselves had a built-in method of depicting emptiness, and that was by shading the relevant area. The visualisations of categoricals sketched using the shading method are depicted in Fig. 7a and 7b.

For a long time, it was thought that what Venn did not yet do was to introduce a symbol similar to Euler's asterisk for explicitly marking non-emptiness. Further, it was thought that this was done by Peirce, who was even more devoted to advancing modern algebraic and mathematical logic, and who aimed to optimise Venn diagrams' expressive powers to account for this new logic (see e.g. [14]). This narrative has been shown untrue and it has been recognised that Venn himself did introduce several methods of representing existential which, however,

[12] We are not claiming that in the discussed types of diagrams, terms were viewed as empty by default and had to be marked to be recognised as non-empty: What we do claim is that there was a raising need for *explicitly* marking the non-emptiness of terms. I.e., at certain point non-emptiness of terms became so important an issue that diagrams could no longer be silent about it and it had to be marked *explicitly*.

[13] Although this is debated, with claims that Euler diagrams either have or do not have to do with existence. Englebretsen, for example, states that Euler did introduce a special asterisk symbol "$*$" for indicating that a cell is non-empty [12, p. 33]. This interpretation aligns with our claim as it shows that explicitly marking non-emptiness has started already with Euler.

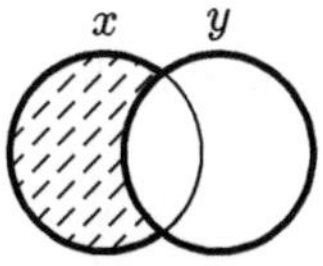

(a) Venn diagram for "All x is y", shading indicating emptiness

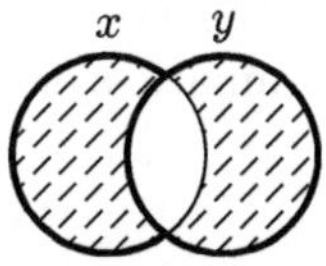

(b) Venn diagram for "All x is all y", shading indicating emptiness

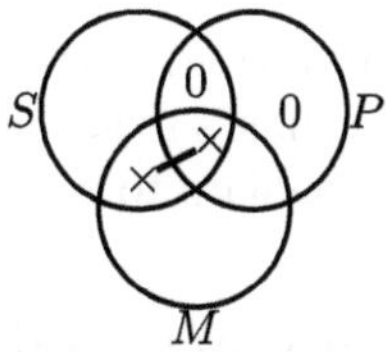

(c) Peirce's Diagram for Festino

Fig. 7. Examples of circular diagrams with emptiness and non-emptiness explicitly marked

he deemed unsatisfactory [24]. Whatever the case may be, Peirce's refinement of Venn diagrams consisted of using an x for marking non-emptiness of a term, viz. existence of a singular term within a specified domain – which then became a standard to use in Venn diagrams. More importantly, he proposed several other refinements concerning emptiness of terms, which together resulted in a new type of diagram, Venn-Peirce diagram: There, empty terms were marked by 0's, and non-emptiness by x's – to mark that either of the two areas is non-empty, two x's were supposed to be drawn [6], connected by a line as shown in Fig. 7c.

The development of these diagrams is in direct parallel with the development of the new logic and discussions around empty terms connected to it. The striking feature of schemes such as Euler, Venn, and Venn-Peirce diagrams is that the distinction between predicate and subject, fundamental for Aristotelian division of moods into figures is, as Venn himself notes, "entirely robbed of its significance" [29, p. 6]. We can see that what was the intrinsic feature of Byzantine diagrams – the division into figures – became inexpressible in modern representations; what was on the other hand inexpressible in Byzantine diagrams – the non-emptiness of terms – has become one of the crucial features of these modern representations.

These advancements in diagrammatic tools, as we argue, over time influenced how syllogistic itself was understood (with a prevalent use of them an epistemological effect, as in the case of Byzantine diagrams, might also be argued for). It has been argued in the literature that the ability of Venn diagrams to account for empty terms helped to explicate this issue and prompted researchers to become aware of it in the realm of syllogistic [33]. What we argue for here is a more nuanced view: Venn diagrams, being devised with Boolean algebra in mind, have been constructed so as to account for the empty terms; they have been then applied to render categoricals and also used to interpret syllogistic logic; this use of Venn diagrams for syllogistic logic has imposed a Boolean algebra framework on it, prompting researchers to consider the emptiness of terms in syllogistic as well. As the prevalent assumption amongst modern logicians was to consider all terms to be non-empty, this view was transposed to syllogistic (notably by Łukasiewicz [21]) and remained the standard view for a long time. Thus in the first step, similar to our Leibniz example, a diagrammatic system has been devised with a particular theory in mind; in the second step, similarly to Al-Barakāt's example, a diagrammatic system has influenced a theory, again causing scholars to restrict it.

7 Summary and Conclusions

We have surveyed some prominent examples of diagrammatic reasoning, evaluating them for their ability or inability to express the non-emptiness of terms. As the survey prompted us to spot a significant interplay between the design of diagrams and the logical theory in use, we have also commented on how theory can influence "diagrammatic practice", and vice versa. The survey has confirmed our assumption that during the periods in which empty terms were avidly debated, the diagrams were apt to express them; in periods in which the scholars were silent on the issue, analogously, the diagrams were silent as well. Lest one say that this is an obvious statement, we proposed a nuanced approach that better explains the observed phenomena: That not only logical theory influences the design of diagrams, but also the design of diagrams secondarily affects the logical theory.

In this regard, we have shown that diagrams' expressive powers have the propensity to influence not only conscious decisions on what logical theory to adopt (Al-Barakāt), but also the somewhat unconscious perception of logic, structuring what can be and what cannot be thought of about logical inferences in a given period (Byzantine diagrams, circular diagrams).

We should perhaps stress that the goal of this paper was not to provide a detailed analysis of any given type of diagrams, but rather to offer a wide perspective on a case study that may be illustrative when it comes to understanding how different visual representations of the same structures can stimulate (or restrict) evolution of philosophical views. It was also to propose that by looking at the history of diagrams, we might better understand historical shifts in attention regarding empty terms. We are sure that there is much more work to do, and every Section could be expanded in ways that this preliminary study could not accommodate.

References

1. Agiotis, N.: Remarks on the Greek tradition of syllogistic diagrams on Prior Analytics I 4–6 (sixth-fifteenth century). In: Hegel, P., Krewet, M. (eds.) Wissen und Buchgestalt, pp. 41–85. Harrassowitz Verlag, Wiesbaden (2022)
2. Bäck, A.T.: Avicenna on existence. J. Hist. Philos. **25**(3) (1987)
3. al-Barakāt Hibat Allāh ibn ʻAlī ibn Malkā al Baghdādī, A.: al-Kitāb al-muʻtabar fī al-ḥikmah. Idārat Jamʻīyat Dā'irat al-Maʻārif al-ʻUthmānīyah, Ḥaydarābād al-Dakkan, 1 edn. (1938)
4. Bellucci, F., Moktefi, A., Pietarinen, A.: Diagrammatic autarchy: linear diagrams in the 17th and 18th centuries. In: Burton, J., Choudhury, L. (eds.) First International Workshop on Diagrams, Diagrams, Logic and Cognition. CEUR Workshop Proceedings, vol. 1132, pp. 31–35 (2013). http://ceur-ws.org/Vol-1132/paper4.pdf

5. Bhattacharjee, R.: Direct reduction of syllogisms with Byzantine diagrams. Hist. Philos. Logic **46**(2), 236–257 (2025). https://doi.org/10.1080/01445340.2024.2336411
6. Bhattacharjee, R., Moktefi, A.: Revisiting Peirce's rules of transformation for Euler-Venn diagrams. In: Basu, A., Stapleton, G., Linker, S., Legg, C., Manalo, E., Viana, P. (eds.) Diagrammatic Representation and Inference. Diagrams 2021. LNCS, vol. 12909. Springer, Cham (2021). https://doi.org/10.1007/978-3-030-86062-2_14
7. Bhattacharjee, R., Moktefi, A., Pietarinen, A.V.: The Representation of Negative Terms with Euler Diagrams. In: Béziau, J.Y., Desclés, J.P., Moktefi, A., Pascu, A.C. (eds.) Logic in Question. Studies in Universal Logic, Birkhäuser, Cham (2022). https://doi.org/10.1007/978-3-030-94452-0_3
8. Cacouros, M.: Les schémas dans les manuscrits grecs de contenu logique. Gazette du livre médiéval **39**(1), 21–33 (2001)
9. Church, A.: The History of The Question of Existential Import of Categorical Propositions. In: Logic, Methodology and Philosophy of Science: Proceedings of The 1964 International Congress, North-Holland Publishing Company, Amsterdam (1964)
10. Daşdemir, Y.: Propositions with negative predicates in Arabic logic. Hist. Philos. Logic, 1–19 (2024). https://doi.org/10.1080/01445340.2024.2410107
11. Dasdemir, Y.: The Problem of Existential Import in Metathetic Propositions: Qutb al-Din al-Tahtani contra Fakhr al-Din al-Razi. Nazariyat 5(2) (2019)
12. Englebretsen, G.: Some Historical Figures. In: Figuring It Out: Logic Diagrams, pp. 8–57. De Gruyter, Berlin, Boston (2020)
13. Euler, L.: Lettres a une princesse d'Allemagne sur divers sujets de physique & de philosophie, Tome Second. De l'Imprimerie de l'Academie impériale des sciences, Saint Petersbourg (1768)
14. Hammer, E., Shin, S.J.: Euler's Visual Logic. Hist. Philos. Logic **19**(1), 1–29 (1998). https://doi.org/10.1080/01445349808837293
15. Hodges, W.: A Correctness Proof for al-Barakāt's Logical Diagrams. Rev. Symbol. Logic **16**(2), 369–384 (2023). https://doi.org/10.1017/S1755020321000332
16. Hodges, W., Chatti, S.: Al-Farabi: Syllogism: An Abridgment of Aristotle's Prior Analytics. Bloomsbury Academic, London (2020)
17. Lambert, J.H.: Neues Organon oder Gedanken über die Erforschung und Bezeichnung des Wahren und dessen Unterscheidung vom Irrthum und Schein, vol. 1, Wendler, Leipzig (1764)
18. Leibniz, G.W.: Logical Papers. Clarendon Press, Oxford,: translated and edited by G. H. R, Parkinson (1966)
19. Lemanski, J., Bhattacharjee, R.: On the expressivity of Byzantine diagrams in logic. In: Lemanski, J., Johansen, M.W., Manalo, E., Viana, P., Bhattacharjee, R., Burns, R. (eds.) Diagrammatic Representation and Inference. Diagrams 2024. LNCS, vol. 14981. Springer, Cham (2024). https://doi.org/10.1007/978-3-031-71291-3_35
20. Lemanski, J.: Individuals, existence, and existential commitment in visual reasoning. Open Philosophy **7**(1), 20240042 (2024). https://doi.org/10.1515/opphil-2024-0042
21. Łukasiewicz, J.: Aristotle's Syllogistic. Clarendon Press, Oxford (1951)
22. Malink, M.: Aristotle's Modal Syllogistic. Harvard UP, Cambridge, MA (2013)
23. McConaughey, Z.: Logical diagrams in the pons asinorum. Philos. Antiq. **25**, 57–88 (2025). forthcoming

24. Moktefi, A., Pietarinen, A.V.: On the diagrammatic representation of existential statements with venn diagrams. J. Logic, Lang. Inf. **24**(4), 361–374 (2015), http://www.jstor.org/stable/43919286
25. Panizza, L.: Learning the syllogisms: Byzantine visual aids in Renaissance Italy-Ermolao Barbaro (1454–93) and others. In: Blackwell, C., Kusukawa, S. (eds.) Philosophy in the Sixteenth and Seventeenth Centuries, pp. 22–47. Routledge, London (2017)
26. Smith, R.: Aristotle's Logic. In: Zalta, E.N., Nodelman, U. (eds.) The Stanford Encyclopedia of Philosophy, Metaphysics Research Lab, Stanford University (2022) winter 2022 edn
27. Stapleton, G., Shimojima, A., Jamnik, M.: The Observational Advantages of Euler Diagrams with Existential Import. In: Chapman, P., Stapleton, G., Moktefi, A., Perez-Kriz, S., Bellucci, F. (eds.) Diagrammatic Representation and Inference. Diagrams 2018. Lecture Notes in Computer Science, vol. 10871. Springer, Cham (2018). https://doi.org/10.1007/978-3-319-91376-6_29
28. Triantafyllou, V.: Aristotle's syllogistic as a form of geometry. History Philosophy Log. Anal. **27**(1), 30–78 (2023). https://doi.org/10.30965/26664275-bja10066
29. Venn, J.: Symbolic Logic. Macmillan & Co, London (1881)
30. Wapniarski, K., Urbański, M.: Exploring Aristotelian syllogistic in first-order logic: an overview of the history and reality of ontological commitments. In: Kayvos, A., Gregoriades, V. (eds.) Proceedings of the 14th Panhellenic Logic Symposium. Aristotle University of Thessaloniki, July 2024. http://panhellenic-logic-symposium.org/14/papers/PLS14_Wapniarski_Urbanski.pdf
31. Wesoly, M.: Analysis peri ta schemata: restoring Aristotle's lost diagrams of the syllogistic figures. Peitho **3**(1), 83–114 (2012)
32. Wesoly, M.: The elements of aristotle's analytics: three terms through one mediating diagrammed into three syllogistic figures. In: Borbone, G., Brzechczyn, K. (eds.) From Scientific Philosophy to Myth: An Unquiet Philosophical Journey. Volume 2: Studies Offered to Francesco Coniglione, Poznań Studies in the Philosophy of the Sciences and the Humanities, vol. 126, pp. 22–35. Brill, Leiden (2026). https://doi.org/10.1163/9789004756502
33. Wu, J.S.: The Problem of Existential Import. From George Boole to P. F. Strawson. Notre Dame J. Formal Logic **10**(4) (1969)

Diagrammatic Inference for Ancient Logic: Formalising Aristotle's Topics via Graph Transformations

José David García Cruz(✉)

Universidad del Valle de Puebla, Dirección de Educación y Desarrollo Estudiantil, Puebla, Mexico
jose.garcia@uvp.edu.mx

Abstract. We argue that Aristotle's *Topics*—a two-thousand-year-old dialectical manual—instantiates a fully computable system of diagrammatic inference. The core observation is that each of the text's rules is naturally expressed as a commutative diagram condition on an ontological graph: given that certain labelled paths exist, a further edge must hold or be blocked. This diagrammatic character has been systematically overlooked by prior formalisations, which treat the Topics either as rhetorical heuristic or as propositional inference scheme.

We introduce $\mathcal{L}_{\mathrm{Dial}}$, a formal graph language whose seven primitive relation types capture Aristotle's predicable vocabulary (genus, accident, proper, definition, contrary, privation, intermediate). Over this language we define thirty graph-transformation rules that encode the dialectic of contraries and privatives across all four predicable categories. We prove that these rules instantiate three canonical diagrammatic patterns—direct composition, parallel propagation, and compound conditions—and show that the privation operator $\mathcal{P}$ exhibits the structural behaviour of a partial endofunctor on the category of dialectical graphs, a claim we develop and partially verify in Sect. 8.3.

The framework is validated by ARISTOTELES.JS, a zero-backend, single-file browser application built on Cytoscape.js that performs fixed-point graph completion in real time. Users input assertions in plain English; the engine derives and visualises all reachable consequences, distinguishing asserted from inferred edges with colour-coded dashed overlays. Experiments with classical examples (sight/blindness, health/disease, justice/injustice) confirm that the engine recovers every inference Aristotle explicitly draws, and discovers several that he leaves implicit. The complete source code and interactive demo are available at: https://github.com/0010x0101x0000x0110/topic-diagrams.

Keywords: Diagrammatic Reasoning · Graph Transformation · Aristotle · Dialectical Logic · Existential Graphs · Knowledge Graphs · History of Logic · Automated Deduction

P. Sobociński et al. (Eds.): Diagrams 2026, LNAI 16833, pp. 41–54, 2027.
https://doi.org/10.1007/978-3-032-34178-5_5

1 Introduction

When Aristotle writes that "if vigour is an attribute of health, then weakness is an attribute of disease" [1], he is not constructing a syllogism. He is observing that a square commutes: the contrary-relation edges cross the attribute-relation edges in a consistent pattern. This paper demonstrates that Aristotle is, in effect, reasoning in a graph-based diagrammatic calculus two millennia before such calculi were formalised.

The *Topics* [1,21] comprises approximately three hundred topoi—rules for attacking or defending predications of genus, accident, proper, or definition. Despite the structural richness of these rules, they have received far less formal attention than the syllogistic. The few existing formalisations either focus on medieval rhetorical reinterpretations [5,12] or absorb the Topics into classical first-order logic [21], losing the relational geometry that gives the rules their inferential force.

We propose a different framing. The Topics' rules are not linear inference chains but *diagram conditions*: they assert that whenever a certain pattern of labelled edges is present in an ontological graph, one may complete the pattern by adding (or blocking) a further edge. This is exactly the semantics of graph transformation systems [7,18], and it aligns the Topics with the tradition of diagrammatic reasoning initiated by Peirce's Existential Graphs [16,17] and axiomatised by Shin [19], Barwise & Etchemendy [4], and Hammer [10].

Contributions.

1. We define $\mathcal{L}_{\text{Dial}}$, a formal dialectical language over seven primitive relation types, and characterise its ontological validity conditions (Sect. 3).
2. We encode thirty Aristotelian rules as graph-transformation rules over $\mathcal{L}_{\text{Dial}}$ graphs (Sects. 4–5).
3. We identify three canonical diagrammatic patterns underlying the rule system and present a partial categorical analysis of the privation operator as a structure-preserving map on dialectical graphs (Sect. 8).
4. We validate the framework with ARISTOTELES.JS, a real-time inference engine with natural-language input (Sect. 7).

2 Background and Related Work

2.1 Diagrammatic Reasoning as a Proof Paradigm

The programme of diagrammatic reasoning, launched by Peirce's Existential Graphs [16,17] and systematised by Shin [19] and Hammer [10], studies inference systems whose well-formed representations are spatial or relational structures rather than linear strings. Shin's proof that Venn-II diagrams constitute a sound and complete formal system for monadic predicate logic [19] established that visual representation can carry full logical force. Barwise and Etchemendy [4] further argued that heterogeneous reasoning—mixing diagrammatic and linguistic representations—is irreducibly natural to human cognition.

The philosophical significance of this programme extends beyond proof theory. If the Topics can be reconstructed as a diagrammatic calculus, its rules are not merely useful heuristics or rhetorical moves but *necessary* consequences of relational structure: any domain satisfying the premiss pattern must satisfy the conclusion. This reframes the Topics—typically read as a handbook of dialectical strategy—as a *computable inference system* whose rules are derivable from the topology of the ontological graph rather than stipulated by convention. The epistemological implication is substantive: it places Aristotelian dialectic within the same formal tradition as Peirce's graphs, Shin's logical diagrams, and modern graph transformation systems, and opens the possibility of machine-assisted reasoning over ancient philosophical corpora.

The commutative diagram conditions that constitute $\mathcal{L}_{\text{Dial}}$ rules are squarely within this tradition: each rule asserts that a certain diagram commutes, i.e. that traversing two paths in an ontological graph between the same endpoints yields the same relational result. This is a formally precise, topological claim [20].

Existing diagrammatic provers—Speedith [24] and GraPEL [23]—implement diagram-specific inference for Euler/Venn systems; our contribution extends the diagrammatic proof paradigm to an entirely different representational regime: labelled relational graphs.

2.2 Formal Accounts of the Topics

Slomkowski's monograph [21] is the most systematic modern formalisation, identifying the predicable framework as the backbone of dialectical inference. Krabbe [13] traces a direct lineage from the topoi to formal dialogue games, arguing that each topos licenses a move type in a regulated exchange. Neither account, however, supplies a computational model of the rules, nor does either recognise their essentially diagrammatic character.

2.3 Computational Argumentation

Abstract Argumentation Frameworks [6] and structured systems such as ASPIC+ [15] and Carneades [9] model dialectical exchange as graphs of attacking and supporting arguments. These systems capture the procedural dimension of debate but treat arguments as atomic nodes, abstracting away the contentual relational structure that the Topics explicitly theorises. Our work complements this programme by formalising the intra-argument relational level.

2.4 Graph Transformation and Ontology

Graph Transformation Systems (GTS) [7] provide the algebraic machinery for our encoding. The double-pushout (DPO) formalism of Ehrig et al. underpins our `addInf()` mechanism, while the conditional DPO extension accounts for rules with existential side conditions. Description logics and OWL [3] model predication via the $\sqsubseteq$ relation but have no account of contrarity, privation, or intermediacy—precisely the relations that give the Topics its distinct logical character.

3 The Dialectical Language $\mathcal{L}_{\text{Dial}}$

3.1 Syntax

Definition 1. (Dialectical Language). $\mathcal{L}_{\text{Dial}} = \langle \text{Var}, \text{Rel} \rangle$, *where* Var $= \{X, Y, Z, W, U, V, \ldots\}$ *is a countably infinite set of ontological variables and* $\text{Rel} = \{a, g, c, p, i, d, f, \bar{a}, \bar{g}, \bar{f}\}$ *is the set of relation symbols.*

Relation symbols partition into three classes:

Class	Symbols	Notation
Positive directed	a, g, f	$X \xrightarrow{a} Y$, $X \xrightarrow{g} Y$, $X \rightleftharpoons^{f} Y$
Positive symmetric	c, p, i, d	$X \leftrightarrow^{c} Y$, $X \leftrightarrow^{p} Y$, $X \leftrightarrow^{i} Y$, $X \rightleftharpoons^{d} Y$
Negative	$\bar{a}$, $\bar{g}$, $\bar{f}$	$X \xrightarrow{\bar{a}} Y$, $X \xrightarrow{\bar{g}} Y$, $X \rightleftharpoons^{\bar{f}} Y$

A *dialectical graph* is a directed multigraph $G = (V, E)$ with $V \subseteq \text{Var}$; each $e \in E$ carries a label in Rel. Symmetric relations are stored as directed arcs but matched bidirectionally during inference.

3.2 Derived Relations and Ontological Commitments

Two predicable types reduce to primitive combinations:

$$X \rightleftharpoons^{d} Y \iff X \xrightarrow{g} Y \wedge Y \xrightarrow{g} X \qquad \text{(mutual genus)}$$
$$X \rightleftharpoons^{f} Y \iff X \xrightarrow{a} Y \wedge Y \xrightarrow{a} X \qquad \text{(mutual accident)}$$

This follows from Aristotle's remark that definition is the "giving of the essence" and proper is the "universally accompanying attribute" (*Top.* 102a18, 102b6).

Notation for d and f. Both definition (d) and proper (f) use the semi-arrow notation $\rightleftharpoons$ to visually distinguish them from the full double-arrow $\leftrightarrow$ used for contrary (c) and privation (p). The distinction is semantic: c and p are *primitive* symmetric relations, whereas d and f are *derived* symmetric relations, each decomposing into two directed edges. The semi-arrow encodes this derived, biconditional character at a glance.

3.3 Inference Rules and Commutative Diagrams

A graph-transformation rule $\rho = (L_\rho, R_\rho)$ consists of a left-hand pattern L_ρ (matching condition) and a right-hand edge R_ρ (conclusion). A dialectical graph G is *valid with respect to* ρ if every match of L_ρ into G extends to a match of R_ρ.

Let $\mathcal{R}$ denote the full set of thirty rules. The *dialectical closure* $\overline{G}$ is the least fixed point of the operator

$$T_{\mathcal{R}}(G) = G \cup \{\, e \mid \exists \rho \in \mathcal{R},\ \exists \text{ match morphism } m : L_\rho \to G,\ e = m(R_\rho) \,\},$$

where $m(R_\rho)$ is the image of the conclusion edge under the match morphism m. We use $\mathcal{R}$ consistently for the rule set, reserving R_ρ (or R when ρ is clear) for the right-hand side of an individual rule.

Equivalently, each rule ρ can be drawn as a commutative diagram: nodes are variables, solid arcs are premisses, and the dashed blue arc is the conclusion. Commutativity of a face asserts the validity of the corresponding inference—connecting $\mathcal{L}_{\text{Dial}}$ to the diagrammatic proof tradition of Peirce and Shin [16,19].

4 Rules for Contraries

We present fifteen rules governing contrary opposites, grouped by predicable type. Each rule is grounded in a passage of the *Topics* and illustrated with its commutative diagram. Relation labels appear as superscripts on arrows; the redundant prefix notation used in earlier drafts has been harmonised to the superscript convention throughout.

4.1 Group A — Contrary Accidents (*Top.* II.8)

R1/R2 (Contraposition). Contraposition of directed attributes over contradictory conjugates:

$$X \xrightarrow{a} Y,\quad X \xrightarrow{\bar{a}} \bar{Y},\quad \bar{Y} \xrightarrow{\bar{a}} \bar{X} \ \therefore\ \bar{Y} \xrightarrow{a} \bar{X} \qquad \text{(R1)}$$

and its converse (R2). These encode Aristotle's observation at *Top.* 113b15 that contrapositives of attribute assertions hold across negated terms.

R3 (SD^{+-}, Direct Sequence). The central rule of Group A, grounded at *Top.* 113b28–30:

$$X \leftrightarrow^{c} Y,\quad Z \xrightarrow{a} X,\quad Z \leftrightarrow^{c} W \ \therefore\ W \xrightarrow{a} Y \qquad \text{(R3)}$$

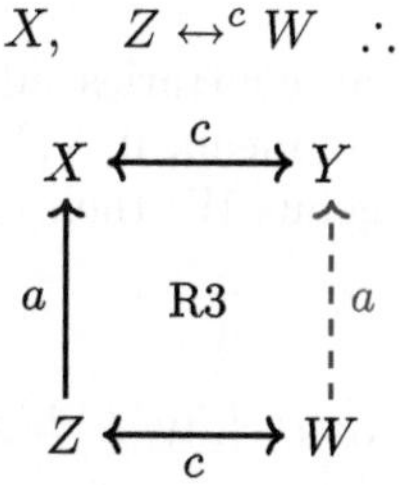

Reading. If Z has attribute X, and Z, W are contraries just as X, Y are, then W must have attribute Y. The diagram commutes: the inferred arc (dashed) closes a structure-preserving square across the contrary relation. Aristotle's philosophical insight at *Top.* 113b28–30 is that attribute-opposition *tracks* subject-opposition: a property belonging to one extreme forces the contrary property onto the contrary extreme. This is not merely a useful heuristic—it is a necessary consequence of the relational geometry of the ontological graph. R4 (SC^{+-}, converse) yields $Y \xrightarrow{a} W$; R5 (SI^{+-}, indirect) yields $W \xrightarrow{\bar{a}} Y$.

4.2 Group B — Contrary Genera, Destructive (*Top.* IV.3)

R6/R7/R8. Three rules governing genus membership of contraries. R7 (GI^{-}) is structurally R3 with $a \mapsto g$, illustrating the systematic parallelism between accidental and generic predication:

$$X \leftrightarrow^{c} Y, \quad Z \leftrightarrow^{c} W, \quad Z \xrightarrow{g} X \ \therefore\ W \xrightarrow{g} Y \quad \text{(R7)}$$

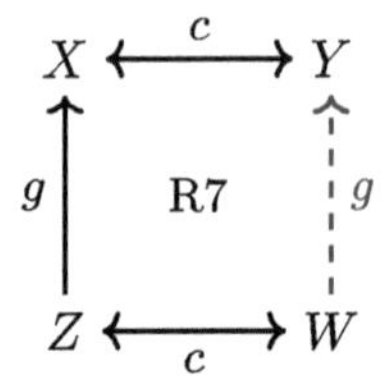

R6 adds $Y \xrightarrow{g} Z$ when $\nexists c(Z)$ (genus with no contrary); R8 propagates the negated-genus relation $\bar{g}$ in the same conditions.

R9 (HG^{-}, Generic Heritage). The inheritance rule: contrary species of contrary genera are themselves contrary:

$$X \leftrightarrow^{c} Y, \quad Z \xrightarrow{g} X, \quad W \xrightarrow{g} Y \ \therefore\ Z \leftrightarrow^{c} W \quad \text{(R9)}$$

This is Pattern I (Sect. 8.1): the inferred edge closes a commutative square whose boundary consists of two g-edges and two c-edges. The philosophical basis, at *Top.* 123b29, is that genus-membership is co-variant with opposition: if two species belong to contrary genera, those species are themselves contrary. This makes the genus hierarchy sensitive to the opposition structure of its nodes—a non-trivial topological claim about Aristotelian ontology that is directly expressible as a commutative square condition. See Listing 1 for the JavaScript implementation.

R10/R11/R12. These rules treat contraries admitting an intermediate. R12 encodes Aristotle's doctrine of the mean: if X, Y are extreme contraries under genus Z, and Z has a contrary genus W, then any species U of W not in Z is contrary to both X and Y:

$$X \leftrightarrow^{c} Y,\ X \xrightarrow{g} Z,\ Y \xrightarrow{g} Z,\ Z \leftrightarrow^{c} W,\ U \xrightarrow{g} W,\ U \xrightarrow{\bar{g}} Z \ \therefore\ U \leftrightarrow^{c} X,\ U \leftrightarrow^{c} Y \quad \text{(R12)}$$

4.3 Group C — Contrary Genera, Constructive (*Top* IV.3)

R13–R15 are the constructive duals of R6, R7, R11: they establish rather than block genus membership. R13 is the exact mirror of R6:

$$X \leftrightarrow^{c} Y, \quad Y \xrightarrow{g} Z, \quad \nexists c(Z) \ \therefore\ X \xrightarrow{g} Z \quad \text{(R13)}$$

4.4 Groups D–E — Propria and Definition

R16–R17 apply contrarity to proper predication (f), structurally identical to R3/R4 with $a \mapsto f$. R18 (CD$^+$) states that contrary terms have contrary definitions. R19 (CD$^-$) is the guard rule: it blocks the circular definition $X \rightleftharpoons^d Z$ whenever $X \leftrightarrow^c Y$ and $Y \leftrightarrow^c Z$ hold simultaneously (*Top.* 147b16–20). In the engine, R19 fires a structured warning rather than adding an edge—a negative diagrammatic conclusion.

5 Rules for Privatives

Privation (*stéresis*) is the asymmetric counterpart of contrarity: blindness is the absence of sight in a subject naturally apt to have it, not merely its opposite. The privative rules mirror the contrary rules structurally but encode the ontological asymmetry: possession may ground inferences that privation cannot.

5.1 Group F — Privation as Inferential Weakening

R20 (SDP^{+-}) is the only accident rule that transfers from contraries to privatives. The converse sequence (R4) and indirect sequence (R5) both fail for privation (*Top.* 114a9–13):

$$X \leftrightarrow^p Y, \quad Z \leftrightarrow^p W, \quad Z \xrightarrow{a} X \ \therefore\ W \xrightarrow{a} Y \quad \text{(R20)}$$

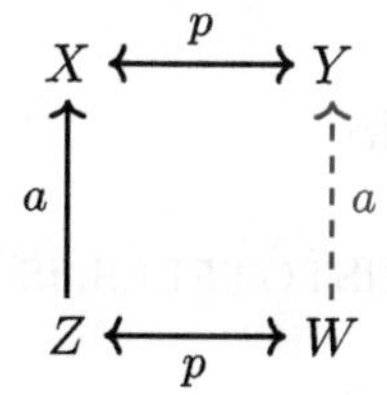

5.2 Group G — Privation Inverts the Genus Hierarchy

The privation genus rules are the most striking departure from contrarity: they do not merely share but *invert* the genus structure.

R21 (CGP$^-$, Genus Cancellation).

$$X \leftrightarrow^p Y, \quad X \xrightarrow{g} Z \ \therefore\ Y \xrightarrow{\bar{g}} Z \quad \text{(R21)}$$

Privation is never in the same ultimate genus as its possession (*Top.* 124a35–39): if sight belongs to perception, blindness is *not* a perception. R21 produces a positive $\bar{g}$-edge (not merely the absence of a g-edge), which then serves as a premiss for R23. The philosophical depth here is considerable: Aristotle is claiming that the ontological categories are not merely distinguished but *repelled*— privation actively excludes genus membership in a way that contrarity does not. Contraries may share a genus (health and disease are both states of the body); privation cannot (blindness is no kind of sight). This categorical polarity is the most distinctive structural feature of the privation relation and the primary motivation for the endofunctor analysis of Sect. 8.3.

R22/R23. R22 (PPO$^-$): shared privation prohibits the genus relation between possessions. R23 (IGP$^+$) is the constructive converse of R21:

$$X \leftrightarrow^p Y, \quad Y \xrightarrow{\bar{g}} Z \ \therefore\ X \xrightarrow{g} Z \quad \text{(R23)}$$

The trio R21–R23 defines a strict ontological polarity: the genus-graph splits cleanly into a possession side and a privation side, with no mixed genus memberships possible.

5.3 Groups H–I — Privation Propria and Definition

R24–R25 parallel R16–R17 with $c \mapsto p$. R26–R27 establish definitional substitution: accidental predication is invariant under interchange of definitionally equivalent terms. R28 (DIP$^+$) is the deepest rule of Group I:

$$X \leftrightarrow^p Y, \quad Z \leftrightarrow^p W, \quad X \rightleftharpoons^d Z \ \therefore\ Y \rightleftharpoons^d W \quad \text{(R28)}$$

Defining the possession automatically defines the privation (*Top.* 147a15: "in defining knowledge, a man in a sense defines ignorance as well"). R29/R30 propagate privation through definitional chains while preserving the one-way dependency: possession may be defined without reference to privation, but not vice versa (Table 1).

6 Complete Rule Table

7 Implementation: ARISTOTELES.JS

7.1 Architecture

ARISTOTELES.JS is a zero-backend single-file web application (HTML, CSS, and Vanilla JavaScript) with Cytoscape.js [8] as its only external dependency. The portability constraint is deliberate: the file runs with a double-click on any browser, with no server required. Three layers interact as follows.

Graph Layer. A Cytoscape.js instance maintains $G \in \mathcal{L}_{\text{Dial}}$. Nodes store canonical identifiers and human-readable labels; edges carry their relation type, display colour, and an `inferred` boolean flag.

Inference Layer. Thirty rule functions implement the match-and-apply semantics of DPO graph-transformation rules. `addInf()` enforces idempotency and logs each new edge with its deriving rule identifier.

Presentation Layer. A dark-themed interface with a live statistics bar, per-node hover tooltips, and a scrollable log. Inferred edges render as dashed cyan arcs; asserted edges appear in relation-type colours.

Table 1. The thirty Aristotelian graph-transformation rules. Bars over a relation symbol denote its negation; $\nexists c(Z)$ means no c-edge is incident on Z.

ID	Name	Premisses	Conclusion	Locus
Group A—Contrary Accidents (Top. *II.8, 113b15–114a5*)				
R1	Contra^{+}	$X \xrightarrow{a} Y$, $X \xrightarrow{\bar{a}} \bar{Y}$, $\bar{Y} \xrightarrow{\bar{a}} \bar{X}$	$\bar{Y} \xrightarrow{a} \bar{X}$	113b15
R2	Contra^{-}	$\bar{X} \xrightarrow{a} \bar{Y}$, $\bar{X} \xrightarrow{\bar{a}} Y$, $\bar{Y} \xrightarrow{\bar{a}} X$	$\bar{Y} \xrightarrow{\bar{a}} \bar{X}$	113b15
R3	SD^{+-}	$X \leftrightarrow^{c} Y$, $Z \xrightarrow{a} X$, $Z \leftrightarrow^{c} W$	$W \xrightarrow{a} Y$	113b28
R4	SC^{+-}	same as R3	$Y \xrightarrow{a} W$	113b35
R5	SI^{+-}	$X \leftrightarrow^{c} Y$, $Z \xrightarrow{\bar{a}} X$, $Z \leftrightarrow^{c} W$	$W \xrightarrow{\bar{a}} Y$	114a3
Group B—Contrary Genera, Destructive (Top. *IV.3, 123b2–123b29*)				
R6	CG^{-}	$X \leftrightarrow^{c} Y$, $X \xrightarrow{g} Z$, $\nexists c(Z)$	$Y \xrightarrow{g} Z$	123b2
R7	GI^{-}	$X \leftrightarrow^{c} Y$, $Z \leftrightarrow^{c} W$, $Z \xrightarrow{g} X$	$W \xrightarrow{g} Y$	123b4
R8	GC^{-}	$X \leftrightarrow^{c} Y$, $X \xrightarrow{\bar{g}} Z$, $\nexists c(Z)$	$Y \xrightarrow{\bar{g}} Z$	123b8
R9	HG^{-}	$X \leftrightarrow^{c} Y$, $Z \xrightarrow{g} X$, $W \xrightarrow{g} Y$	$Z \leftrightarrow^{c} W$	123b29
R10	SimIn^{-}	$X \leftrightarrow^{i} Y$, $Z \xrightarrow{g} X$, $W \xrightarrow{g} Y$	$Z \leftrightarrow^{i} W$	123b12
R11	IC^{-}	$X \leftrightarrow^{c} Y$, $X{,}Y \xrightarrow{g} Z$, $\nexists c(Z)$, $W \leftrightarrow^{c} X{,}Y$	$W \xrightarrow{g} Z$	123b23
R12	JM^{-}	(see Sect. 4)	$U \leftrightarrow^{c} X{,}Y$	123b27
Group C—Contrary Genera, Constructive (Top. *IV.3, 124a4–124a9*)				
R13	GC^{+}	$X \leftrightarrow^{c} Y$, $Y \xrightarrow{g} Z$, $\nexists c(Z)$	$X \xrightarrow{g} Z$	124a4
R14	GI^{+}	$X \leftrightarrow^{c} Y$, $Z \leftrightarrow^{c} W$, $W \xrightarrow{g} Y$	$Z \xrightarrow{g} X$	124a7
R15	IC^{+}	$X \leftrightarrow^{c} Y$, $W \xrightarrow{g} Z$, $W \leftrightarrow^{c} X{,}Y$, $\nexists c(Z)$	$X{,}Y \xrightarrow{g} Z$	124a6
Group D—Contrary Propria (Top. *V.6, 135b8–135b14*)				
R16	CP^{-}	$X \leftrightarrow^{c} Y$, $Z \leftrightarrow^{c} W$, $X \rightleftharpoons^{\bar{f}} Z$	$Y \rightleftharpoons^{\bar{f}} W$	135b8
R17	CP^{+}	same, with f	$Y \rightleftharpoons^{f} W$	135b12
Group E—Contrary Definition (Top. *VI.9, 147a32–147b20*)				
R18	CD^{+}	$X \leftrightarrow^{c} Y$, $Z \leftrightarrow^{c} W$, $X \rightleftharpoons^{d} Z$	$Y \rightleftharpoons^{d} W$	147a32
R19	CD^{-}	$X \leftrightarrow^{c} Y$, $Y \leftrightarrow^{c} Z$	$\neg(X \rightleftharpoons^{d} Z)$	147b16
Group F—Privation Accidents (Top. *II.8, 114a9–13*)				
R20	SDP^{+-}	$X \leftrightarrow^{p} Y$, $Z \leftrightarrow^{p} W$, $Z \xrightarrow{a} X$	$W \xrightarrow{a} Y$	114a9
Group G—Privation Genera (Top. *IV.4, 124a35–124b5*)				
R21	CGP^{-}	$X \leftrightarrow^{p} Y$, $X \xrightarrow{g} Z$	$Y \xrightarrow{\bar{g}} Z$	124a35
R22	PPO^{-}	$X \leftrightarrow^{p} Y$, $Z \leftrightarrow^{p} Y$	$Z \xrightarrow{\bar{g}} X$	124a39
R23	IGP^{+}	$X \leftrightarrow^{p} Y$, $Y \xrightarrow{\bar{g}} Z$	$X \xrightarrow{g} Z$	124b3
Group H—Privation Propria (Top. *V.6, 135b27–136a4*)				
R24	PP^{-}	$X \leftrightarrow^{p} Y$, $Z \leftrightarrow^{p} W$, $X \rightleftharpoons^{\bar{f}} Z$	$Y \rightleftharpoons^{\bar{f}} W$	135b27
R25	PP^{+}	same, with f	$Y \rightleftharpoons^{f} W$	135b33
Group I—Privation Definition (Top. *VI.9, 147a12–148a9*)				
R26	IPI	$X \xrightarrow{a} Y$, $X \rightleftharpoons^{d} Z$	$Z \xrightarrow{a} Y$	147a12
R27	IPD	$X \xrightarrow{a} Y$, $Y \rightleftharpoons^{d} Z$	$X \xrightarrow{a} Z$	147a12
R28	DIP^{+}	$X \leftrightarrow^{p} Y$, $Z \leftrightarrow^{p} W$, $X \rightleftharpoons^{d} Z$	$Y \rightleftharpoons^{d} W$	147a15
R29	PD^{+}	$X \leftrightarrow^{p} Y$, $Y \rightleftharpoons^{d} Z$	$X \leftrightarrow^{p} Z$	147b5
R30	DP^{+}	$X \rightleftharpoons^{d} Y$, $Z \leftrightarrow^{p} Y$	$Z \leftrightarrow^{p} X$	148a2

7.2 Natural Language Input and Graph Completion

The engine accepts natural-English assertions (e.g., *"Sight is privation of Blindness"*, *"Health is contrary to Disease"*) that are parsed into $\mathcal{L}_{\text{Dial}}$ edges. Pressing PROVE triggers `runAllRules()`, which iterates all thirty rules until fixed point ($\overline{G}$). Because newly derived edges can re-enable other rules (notably: R21 produces $\bar{g}$-edges that enable R23), a multi-pass loop is required.

7.3 Representative Implementation: R9

```
function rule_R9() {
  let n = 0;
  // For each contrary edge c: X <-> Y
  cy.edges('[rel="c"]').forEach(eXY => {
    const X = eXY.source().id(), Y = eXY.target().id();
    // Find Z: g -> X
    getSources(X, 'g').forEach(Z => {
      // Find W: g -> Y
      getSources(Y, 'g').forEach(W => {
        if (Z !== W && addInf(Z, W, 'c', 'R9')) n++;
      });
    });
  });
  return n; // count of new inferences
}
```

Listing 1. Rule R9 (HG^-, Generic Heritage). `getSources(id,rel)` returns all nodes Z with a directed `rel`-edge to `id`.

Rules with existential side conditions (R6, R8, R11, R13, R15) call `hasNoContrary(id)`. Rules with negative conclusions (R19, R21) produce either a structured warning (R19) or an explicit $\bar{g}$-edge (R21)—a positive assertion about genus exclusion that can serve as a premiss for R23.

7.4 Validation Example: Sight, Blindness, Perception

From the asserted basis {p:sight $\leftrightarrow^p$ blindness, g:sight $\xrightarrow{g}$ perception, a: perceive $\xrightarrow{a}$ sight, p:perceive $\leftrightarrow^p$ noperceive}, the engine derives:

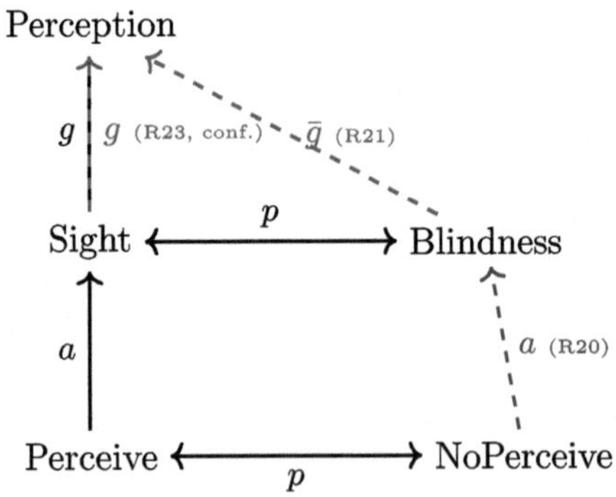

R20 infers noperceive $\xrightarrow{a}$ blindness; R21 infers blindness $\xrightarrow{\bar{g}}$ perception; R23 confirms sight $\xrightarrow{g}$ perception idempotently. Every inference is one Aristotle himself draws (or explicitly endorses) in Book IV.

8 Structural Analysis

8.1 Three Canonical Diagrammatic Patterns

Inspecting the thirty rules reveals that all of them instantiate one of three diagrammatic patterns. This is not accidental: it reflects the combinatorial structure of the predicable system.

Pattern I—Direct Composition. The inferred edge closes a commutative *triangle* or *square*.
Triangular Case. Given paths $X \xrightarrow{r_1} Y$ and $Y \xrightarrow{r_2} Z$, one infers $X \xrightarrow{r_3} Z$, where r_3 is determined by the composition table of $\mathcal{L}_{\text{Dial}}$ relations.
Square Case. Given nodes X, Y, Z, W with edges $X \xrightarrow{r_1} Y$, $Z \xrightarrow{r_1} W$, and $Z \xrightarrow{r_2} X$, one infers $W \xrightarrow{r_2} Y$, closing a commutative square in which both horizontal edges carry r_1 and both vertical edges carry r_2. Rules R3, R7 are instances of the square case; R9 is an instance in which the horizontal edges are c-edges and the vertical edges are g-edges, yielding a square that closes by inferring the second c-edge. Rules R6, R13, R21, R23 are triangular instances.

Pattern II—Parallel Propagation. A relation r between two nodes propagates to their "opposite" partners under a symmetric opposite relation $\odot$:

$$\odot{:}X \odot Y, \quad \odot{:}Z \odot W, \quad r{:}X \sim Z \ \therefore\ r{:}Y \sim W \qquad (\Pi_2)$$

for various $\odot \in \{c, p\}$ and $r \in \{a, g, f, d\}$. Rules R7, R14, R17, R18, R24, R25, R28 are Pattern II instances. This pattern captures the key philosophical claim: whatever structure holds among possessions holds, with appropriate sign, among their opposites.

Pattern III—Compound Conditions. Rules R10, R11, R12, R22, R15 require three or more matched subgraphs plus existential side conditions. These are computationally the most expensive (nested iteration over three edge sets) and logically the richest—they encode Aristotle's subtler claims about genera admitting intermediates and the doctrine of the mean (Fig. 1).

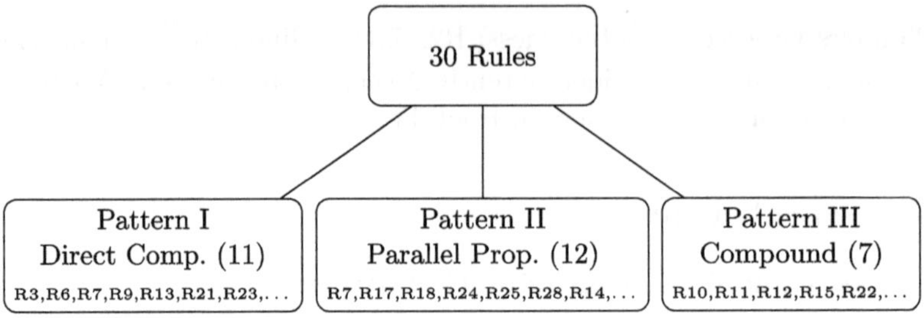

Fig. 1. Partition of the thirty $\mathcal{L}_{\text{Dial}}$ rules by diagrammatic pattern. Pattern II is the most philosophically significant: it encodes the parallelism of opposite pairs across all predicable types.

8.2 The Privation Asymmetry: A Meta-Theorem

Theorem 1. (Privation as Inferential Restriction). *The set of privative accident rules* $\{\text{R20}\}$ *is a strict subset of the contrary accident rules* $\{\text{R3}, \text{R4}, \text{R5}\}$. *Specifically, rules R4 and R5 have no privative counterparts.*

Proof. (Proof sketch). R4 transfers to the converse direction; R5 transfers negated attributes. Both require that the opposite relation be symmetric under complementation—a property of contrarity (each extreme implies the other's opposite) but not of privation, where the implication runs only from possession to privation, not vice versa (*Top.* 114a9).

Conversely, privation is stronger in the genus domain: contraries may share a genus (R6), but R21 categorically prohibits this for privation. The genus-graph thus splits into two disconnected components—possession and privation—a partition with no counterpart in the contrary rules.

8.3 Stéresis as a Structure-Preserving Map

The structural parallel between Groups B/C (contrary genera) and Group G (privation genera), and between Groups D/E and H/I, points to a deeper algebraic characterisation.

Definition 2. (Privatisation Map). *Let* **Dial** *be the category whose objects are dialectical graphs and whose morphisms are graph homomorphisms preserving relation labels. Define the privatisation map* $\mathcal{P}$: **Dial** $\rightharpoonup$ **Dial** *by:*

- $\mathcal{P}(X) = X^{\text{priv}}$ *(a fresh privation node for each possession node* X*);*
- $\mathcal{P}(r) = r^{\text{priv}}$*, where c-edges map to p-edges and g-edges map to* $\bar{g}$*-edges (genus inversion);*
- $\mathcal{P}$ *is undefined (partial) on paths whose commutativity would require R4 or R5, which fail for privation.*

Proposition 1. *Rules R20, R24, R25, R28, R29, R30 are precisely the images of R3, R16, R17, R18, R29, R30 under $\mathcal{P}$, modulo the genus inversion performed by R21–R23.*

This establishes that stéresis is a structure-preserving map that inverts the ontological domain: it preserves the accident, proper, and definition predication structures while reversing the genus hierarchy. Whether $\mathcal{P}$ constitutes a genuine partial endofunctor in the categorical sense—satisfying functoriality and the relevant coherence conditions—remains to be verified. Specifically, it needs to be shown that **Dial** satisfies all the axioms of a category, that $\mathcal{P}$ preserves composition of morphisms on its domain of definition, and that the possession/privation pairing can be made into an adjoint pair in the sense of Lawvere [14]. These verifications, which require the categorical framework developed in Awodey [2] and Spivak [22], are left to future work.

9 Conclusion

We have demonstrated that Aristotle's *Topics* constitutes a well-defined, computable system of diagrammatic inference. Three results support this claim.

1. **Formal completeness.** The thirty graph-transformation rules of $\mathcal{L}_{\text{Dial}}$ cover all four predicable types for both contraries and privatives, and exhibit an exhaustive partition into three canonical diagrammatic patterns (direct composition, parallel propagation, compound conditions).
2. **Architectural insight.** The privation operator $\mathcal{P}$ is not merely an analogy of contrarity: it is a structure-preserving partial map that inverts the genus hierarchy while preserving positive predication—a claim with precise categorical content that we have formalised at the level of rules and proposed as a functorial conjecture.
3. **Practical validation.** Aristoteles.js recovers every inference Aristotle explicitly draws in the passages underlying the thirty rules, and fires warnings for the two negative rules (circular definition, genus contradiction) that Aristotle flags as dialectical faults.

Future work falls into four directions: (a) *Fixed-point guarantee*: replace the manual re-invocation with an automatic least-fixed-point loop and prove termination for finite input graphs; (b) *Completeness*: extend coverage from $\approx 10\%$ to the remaining ≈ 270 topoi of the *Topics*; (c) *Categorical formalisation*: verify that $\mathcal{P}$ is a partial endofunctor and, if so, that it is a left adjoint to a possession functor, connecting $\mathcal{L}_{\text{Dial}}$ to Lawvere's programme of logical operations as adjoints [14]; (d) *Ontology integration*: map $\mathcal{L}_{\text{Dial}}$ to OWL/RDF [3] to enable the engine to reason over existing historical and philosophical knowledge graphs [11,22].

The broader implication is methodological: diagrammatic reasoning systems are not a modern invention. The *Topics*—read through the lens of graph transformation and commutative diagram conditions—anticipates, with remarkable precision, the inferential architecture of Peirce's Existential Graphs [16,17], Shin's logical diagrams [19], and modern GTS [7,18].

References

1. Aristotle: Topics. In: Barnes, J. (ed.) The Complete Works of Aristotle: The Revised Oxford Translation, vol. 1. Princeton University Press, Princeton, NJ (1984), translated by W. A. Pickard-Cambridge
2. Awodey, S.: Category Theory, 2nd edn. Oxford University Press, Oxford (2010)
3. Baader, F., Calvanese, D., McGuinness, D., Nardi, D., Patel-Schneider, P. (eds.): The Description Logics Handbook. Cambridge University Press, Cambridge (2003)
4. Barwise, J., Etchemendy, J.: Visual information and valid reasoning. In: Allwein, G., Barwise, J. (eds.) Logical Reasoning with Diagrams, pp. 3–25. Oxford University Press, New York (1996)
5. Bird, O.: The formalizing of the topics in mediaeval logic. Notre Dame J. Formal Logic **1**(4), 138–149 (1960)
6. Dung, P.M.: On the acceptability of arguments and its fundamental role in nonmonotonic reasoning, logic programming, and n-person games. Artif. Intell. **77**(2), 321–357 (1995)
7. Ehrig, H., Ehrig, K., Prange, U., Taentzer, G.: Fundamentals of Algebraic Graph Transformation. Springer, Berlin (2006)
8. Franz, M., Lopes, C.T., Huck, G., Dong, Y., Sumer, O., Bader, G.D.: Cytoscape.js: a graph theory library for visualisation and analysis. Bioinformatics **32**(2), 309–311 (2016)
9. Gordon, T.F., Prakken, H., Walton, D.: The Carneades model of argument and burden of proof. Artif. Intell. **171**(10–15), 875–896 (2007)
10. Hammer, E.: Logic and Visual Information. CSLI Publications, Stanford (1995)
11. Hogan, A., et al.: Knowledge graphs. ACM Comput. Surv. **54**(4), 71:1–71:37 (2021)
12. Huseman, R.C.: Aristotle's system of topics. Southern J. Commun. **30**(3), 243–252 (1965)
13. Krabbe, E.C.W.: Topical roots of formal dialectic. Argumentation **27**(1), 71–87 (2013)
14. Lawvere, F.W.: Adjointness in foundations. Dialectica **23**(3–4), 281–296 (1969)
15. Modgil, S., Prakken, H.: The ASPIC+ framework for structured argumentation: a tutorial. Argument Comput. **5**(1), 31–62 (2014)
16. Peirce, C.S.: Collected Papers, Vols. 4–5. Harvard University Press, Cambridge, MA (1933), Existential Graphs: CP 4.347–584
17. Roberts, D.D.: The Existential Graphs of Charles S. Peirce. Mouton, The Hague (1973)
18. Rozenberg, G. (ed.): Handbook of Graph Grammars and Computing by Graph Transformation, vol. 1. World Scientific, Singapore (1997)
19. Shin, S.J.: The Logical Status of Diagrams. Cambridge University Press, Cambridge (1994)
20. Shin, S.J., Lemon, O., Mumma, J.: Diagrams. In: Zalta, E.N., Nodelman, U. (eds.) *The Stanford Encyclopedia of Philosophy*. Metaphysics Research Lab, Stanford University (2024). https://plato.stanford.edu/entries/diagrams/
21. Slomkowski, P.: Aristotle's Topics, Philosophia Antiqua, vol. 74. Brill, Leiden (1997)
22. Spivak, D.I.: Category Theory for the Sciences. MIT Press, Cambridge (2014)
23. Stapleton, G., Howse, J., Taylor, J.: A decidable constraint language for graph-based notations. J. Vis. Lang. Comput. **22**(3), 203–222 (2011)
24. Urbas, M., Jamnik, M.: Speedith: A reasoner for spider diagrams. In: Dwyer, T., Purchase, H., Delaney, A. (eds.) Diagrammatic Representation and Inference. LNCS, vol. 7352, pp. 261–263. Springer, Berlin (2012)

The Multifaceted Sorites Diagram

Christina Kittsteiner(✉)

FernUniversität in Hagen, Hagen, Germany
christina.kittsteiner@studium.fernuni-hagen.de

Abstract. The nowadays relatively unknown Sorites diagram visualizes Sorites syllogisms, i.e., chains of multiple interconnected syllogisms which form large arguments, proofs or chains of evidences. Since these chains of syllogisms are not limited in size or the number of syllogisms they contain, Sorites syllogisms can become very complex and confusing. The Sorites diagram depicts them in a comprehensible way and enables a clear reading that supports the understanding of the matter. Despite its long history and frequent use by various logicians all over the world in the 18th and 19th century, the Sorites diagram fell into oblivion at the beginning of the 20th century and has not yet made its comeback into the field of diagrammatic logic. Because of this, it is very underrepresented in research. This paper aims to shed some light on the forgotten diagram by presenting the Sorites diagram and its many different styles that include lines, trees and circles. Because of its flexibility and comprehensibility, many current fields of science including, among others, diagrammatic logic and argumentation theory, can benefit from the features the Sorites diagram offers.

Keywords: Sorites Diagram · Logic Diagram · Visual Representation

1 The Sorites Syllogism at the Core of the Diagram

Today the Sorites diagram is a relatively unknown type of diagram, but that was not always the case. In fact it has a long history starting in ancient times with already Cicero [9, p.376] and Seneca laying the foundation for the diagram by employing the concept of interconnected 'heaped' syllogisms that were called something else back then, but are known today under the designation of 'Sorites syllogisms'. Seneca's Sorites syllogism in the epistle no. 85 from the *Epistulae Morales Ad Lucilium* was heavily used by various logic authors in their textbooks to explain how Sorites syllogisms work (for an example concerning Schopenhauer, see [11]).

The Sorites chains together multiple syllogisms, whereby the individual conclusions are preliminary suppressed to have only one overall conclusion at the end of the chain. Since there is no limit to that, potentially very large chains of syllogisms can be generated. They can be used for different purposes: from connecting multiple arguments in a debate to extensive scientific chains of evidence

P. Sobociński et al. (Eds.): Diagrams 2026, LNAI 16833, pp. 55–62, 2027.
https://doi.org/10.1007/978-3-032-34178-5_6

during the conduction of experiments or the process of rather theoretic research such as mathematical proofs (see below, Sect. 2.2). But on the downside, this also can quickly become confusing, which means the Sorites syllogisms can endanger the gain of knowledge, which they actually are supposed to promote.

To get a more clear picture of how a Sorites syllogism looks like, the following example may be considered:

Bucephalus is a horse;
A horse is a quadruped;
A quadruped is an animal;
An animal is a substance;
Therefore, Bucephalus is a substance. [9, p.367]

Since 'Bucephalus' is the first subject in the Sorites syllogism, it automatically becomes the subject in the conclusion. After this, the following predicate 'horse' is the subject of the next syllogism and the predicate 'quadruped' becomes the subject of the next syllogism, etc. When looking at the middle terms (horse, quadruped, animal) and their occurrence, which is first at the predicate's position and then at the subject's position, it is noticeable that the structure corresponds to the fourth syllogistic figure. That serves the purpose of clarifying the overall conclusion between the first subject, 'Bucephalus', and the last predicate 'is a substance' which can be observed with just one glance at the syllogism. When the Sorites gets disassembled into its individual syllogisms the first two premises change places and every individual syllogism becomes a *Modus Barbara* of the first syllogistic figure. Since there are three middle terms in the example Sorites syllogism, three individual syllogisms can be disassembled as follows:

A horse is a quadruped,	A quadruped is an animal,	An animal is a substance,
Bucephalus is a horse;	Bucephalus is a quadruped;	Bucephalus is an animal.
Therefore, Bucephalus is a quadruped.	Therefore, Bucephalus is an animal.	Therefore, Bucephalus is a substance.

For the ease of handling (and a nicer reading), each term of a syllogism can be designated with a short label, e.g., 'Bucephalus' may just be described as A; 'horse' as B, 'quadruped' as C, 'animal' as D and 'substance' as E which gives a much cleaner overview of the three disassembled syllogisms:

$$\begin{array}{lll} B \text{ is } C & C \text{ is } D & D \text{ is } E \\ A \text{ is } B & A \text{ is } C & A \text{ is } D \\ A \text{ is } C & A \text{ is } D & A \text{ is } E \end{array}$$

Nevertheless, this is far from an intuitive reading and very time-consuming if this process must be executed every time one wants to take a closer look at a

Sorites syllogism. At this point, the Sorites diagram comes into play. The diagram enables both the depiction of transitions between the individual syllogisms, as well as a clean and comprehensible overview. Visualizing precisely such Sorites syllogisms, the Sorites diagram has been used in multiple different forms of representation throughout the centuries.

Putting the Sorites syllogisms in a proper diagram, as the Sorites diagram is, clearly provides advantages regarding the handling of the syllogisms compared to the tedious manual way which was shown here.

In the following some of the most common types of Sorites diagrams will be introduced to show the variety of forms and styles it may take.

2 A Rich Bouquet of Visualizations

Unlike most other diagrams that follow a strict style, the Sorites diagram comes in many different types and looks. The most frequently used and best known representatives of the Sorites diagram will be introduced in the following. These comprise the line-shaped diagrams as well as the tree-shaped diagrams and finally the circle-shaped Sorites diagrams.

2.1 Line-Shaped Sorites Diagram

The first Sorites diagrams that fall into the category of the line-shaped diagrams are the so-called 'Byzantine' diagrams. They are called 'Byzantine' because they became known through Byzantine scholars who brought this kind of diagram to Europe after Constantinople had fallen. Some researchers assume that the Byzantine diagram is originally much older and was even used in ancient times. Typically Byzantine diagrams are composed of arcs that show the relation between entities like the following example given in Fig. 1, that dates back to the 16th century [4,15]. Because of that, they can more likely be denoted as 'curved-line-shaped' or 'bow-shaped' diagrams.

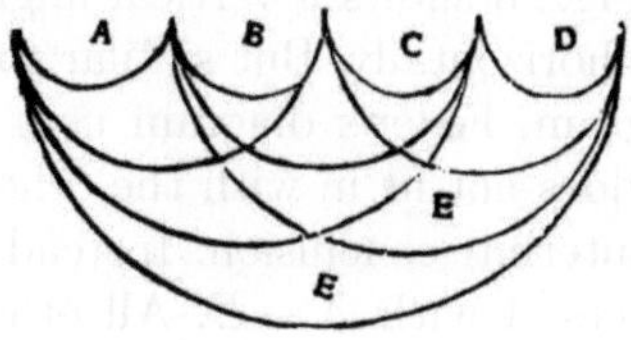

Fig. 1. A Sorites depicted by a Byzantine diagram from 1545 [3, p.68].

As Fig. 1 shows, the Byzantine Sorites diagram uses several arcs to connect the different entities with each other. In the case of the Byzantine Sorites diagram, the entities are mostly terms which are not labeled individually with letters here, but are symbolized by the five points at the top of the diagram. The letters A, B, C, D and E show the several judgments of the Sorites whereby the last entity E can be seen twice in the diagram. On the one hand E stands for the conclusion between the second and fifth point, on the other hand E stands for the conclusion between the first and last point and therefore for the overall conclusion of the diagram.

A rather big similarity to the shape of the Byzantine diagram can be found in Hamilton's variant of a line-shaped Sorites diagram from 1860 in Fig. 2a. Both his diagram and the Byzantine diagram of Fig. 1 combine lines and arcs, but differently to the Byzantine diagram, Hamilton labels the terms in Fig. 2a with letters – not the judgments. Further, he depicts what the judgements from Fig. 1 were (A, B, C and D) with colons and lines that become wider in their curves. These lines actually look like very pointed isosceles triangles. Hamilton explains that a "comma, denotes *some*; the colon: *all*; the line [...] denotes the affirmative copula [...]; the thick end of the line denotes the subject, the thin end the predicate, of Extension." [10, pp.277f.]. E is again the conclusion.

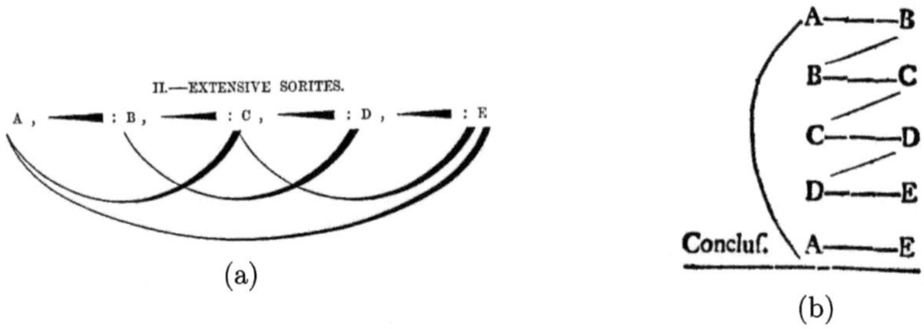

Fig. 2. Different variants of the line-shaped Sorites diagram. (a) Hamilton's Sorites diagram [10, p.397]. (b) Feder's Sorites diagram from 1791.

One of the earliest line-shaped Sorites diagrams that differ from the Byzantine style was used by Feder in 1791 in his work *Logik und Metaphysik* [7, pp.56f.]. His diagram, depicted in Fig. 2b shows a vertical alignment, unlike Hamilton's diagram which was placed horizontally. But similar to both the Byzantine diagram and Hamilton's diagram, Feder's diagram uses an arc on the left of his Sorites diagram. This arc does not fit in with the other two arcs which connect the first entity with the (interim) conclusion. Instead of connecting A directly with E, Feder's arc connects A with $A - E$. All other possibilities to show a connection from A to E would maybe have looked rather peculiar, so Feder just indicated the connection from A to E and made it clear with the last line that shows the conclusion $A - E$ eventually. To highlight the conclusion line, Feder also disconnects it visually by not inserting an EE line. The diagonal lines BB, CC and DD show the position of the middle term according to the fourth syllogistic figure and their transfer of a term into the next judgment. This illustrates the chain-like transitivity of the Sorites syllogism very well (see also Sect. 1). The horizontal lines AB, BC, CD and DE depict the judgments while the letters A, B, C, D and E stand for terms.

2.2 Tree-Shaped Sorites Diagram

Another variant of the Sorites diagram is the tree-shaped form, for which four examples are depicted in Fig. 3. At the first glance they look very similar because the branches immediately give the impression of a tree form and indeed all four diagrams have the structure of a so called 'Seneca tree (S-tree)' which ramifies on every level into two subunits [14, pp.69ff.]. However, these diagrams differ significantly regarding their individual reading direction and the way information is depicted so that they really have little in common.

While Lambert's tree diagram in Fig. 3a and Fries' diagram in Fig. 3b show their judgments on the leaves and the justification (i.e., the premises) by the branches, Read's diagram in Fig. 3c and Beisecker's diagram in Fig. 3d place the terms on the leaves instead. Further, Fig. 3c depicts the judgments with its branches whereas Beisecker's diagram in Fig. 3d shows a tree that uses the branches to depict inclusive disjunction [5, p.3]. Thus, Beisecker's diagram, inspired by Carroll and Wilson, also goes beyond syllogistics since, among other things, disjunctions are not used in syllogistics.

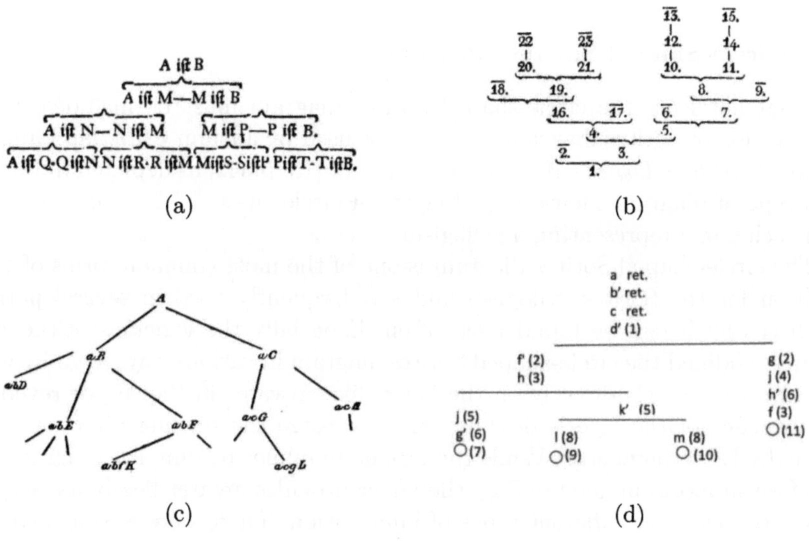

Fig. 3. Different variants of the tree-shaped Sorites diagram. (a) Lambert's Sorites diagram from 1764 [12, p.191]. (b) Fries' Sorites diagram from 1811 [8, p.267]. (c) Read's Sorites diagram from 1878 [17, p.246]. (d) Beisecker's Sorites diagram from 2024 [5, p.11].

In addition to that, Fig. 3a also shows some horizontal lines which stand for the middle terms, e.g., $M - M$, $N - N$ and $P - P$. This makes the syllogisms in the diagram to appear in a triangle-like structure. The diagram in Fig. 3b is on the contrary not showing any syllogisms, but numbers that stand for axioms and propositions in informal mathematical proofs. The horizontal lines on the numbers are used as a symbol to indicate termination at the respective part of the diagram. Comparing the numbers 2, 6, 17 which are terminated in the first and third level of the tree's branching structure with their original text passages it is revealed that these are axioms. The rest of the terminations are placed at the upper end of the diagram (13, 15, 22 and 23) and once all branches have terminated, the entire proof is complete indicating that the argument has been proven. While Fries thus terminates a branch at an axiom or at the end of the proof, the terminating branches in Fig. 3d are contradictions and therefore exactly the opposite of Fries'. The only thing, which the terminations of Fries and Beisecker have in common is the use of a symbol to depict the termination in form of a line above the numbers at Fries and a circle at Beisecker.

Finally, a last striking point is Fig. 3c's apparent lack of visual complexity compared to the other three tree-shaped diagrams. Read chose this structure for his diagram because of his intention to show some classification including "Classes" (the capital letters), "attributes" (the small letters), an "Order" ('A'), "Tribes" ('B' and 'C'), "Genera" ('D', 'E', 'F', 'G' and 'H'), and "Species" ('K', 'L') [17, p.247]. This does not only show that the visual appearance of tree-shaped Sorites diagrams has a broad spectrum, but also that there exists a variety of use cases one can apply these diagrams on.

2.3 Circle-Shaped Sorites Diagram

Last but not least the circle-shaped Sorites diagram must be included in the presentation of Sorites diagrams. It was first used by Johann Christian Lange in the work *Nucleus Logicae Weisianae* from 1712 [13, p.342] as depicted in Fig. 4a. This type of diagram shows several layers of circles nested within one another, with each circle representing a syllogism.

The circle-shaped Sorites diagram is one of the most common forms of visualization for the Sorites syllogism and was frequently used in several periods which is why it can be found most often. Especially the logicians of the 19th century modified the circle-shaped Sorites diagram in various ways, e.g., by writing expressive labels directly on the layers like Atwater in Fig. 4b, or reversing the sequence of the layer's designations to change the reading direction as in Fig. 4c by De Reiffenberg.[1] While the former simplifies reading the diagram and therefore supports understanding, the latter provides greater flexibility when it comes to presenting different types of information. There were also made some attempts by Schuyler regarding the depiction of a negative Sorites diagram like it can be seen in Fig. 4d.

The advantage of the circle-shaped Sorites diagram is certainly the ability to make such alterations easily, but also to have all information of the Sorites syllogism concentrated in a structure that is grouped around a center and therefore enables the observer to grasp the entire structure with just a glance.

[1] Due to the limited scope of this paper, no further details regarding the reading direction and the Aristotelian and Goclenian variants can be provided here. Further information on this topic can be found at [11].

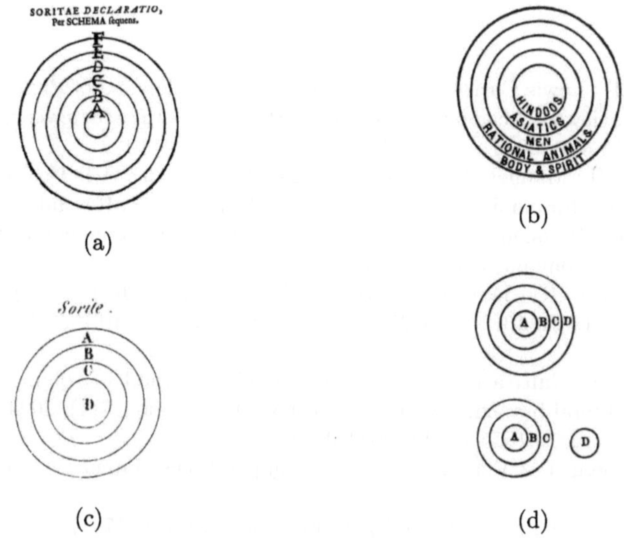

Fig. 4. Different variants of the circle-shaped Sorites diagram. (a) Lange's Sorites diagram from 1712. (b) Atwater's Sorites diagram from 1867 [2, p.154]. (c) De Reiffenberg's Sorites diagram from 1833 [6, p.421]. (d) Schuyler's Sorites diagram from 1869 [18, pp.87ff.].

3 Conclusion

The Sorites diagram has a long history with some very popular logicians using it. At the end of the 19th century, it fell into oblivion, not due to its lack of usefulness, but rather the prevailing zeitgeist which was generally skeptical of (logical) diagrams and rejected them.[2]

All of the diagrams presented in this paper are merely representative for the Sorites diagram and surely there are much more to discover. What they all have in common is that they can be favored to the normal textual representation of long chains of syllogisms where it is easy to lose track of things. Because of this, the Sorites diagram deserves to be lifted out of its current unrenownedness to ultimately enable further research on it. This should not only cover its different visual representations, but also its functioning principle and potential use for various diagrammatic, argumentative and other information-related questions.

Acknowledgement. I would like to thank Jens Lemanski for his valuable input and support, and Amirouche Moktefi for motivating the topic.

[2] John Venn and Lewis Carroll are deliberately not mentioned in this paper because their diagrams do not primarily show (Sorites) syllogisms but rather inferences withing the framework of Boolean algebra [16] [1, 3.b.]. They thus lie outside the scope of classical syllogistic and have been excluded for methodological reasons. A detailed discussion of this issue would go beyond the scope of this paper and constitutes a separate project.

References

1. Abeles, F.F.: Lewis Carroll: Logic. In: Internet Encyclopedia of Philosophy (IEP). A Peer-Reviewed Academic Resource. https://iep.utm.edu/lewis-carroll-logic/. Accessed 14 May 2026
2. Atwater, L.H.: Manuel of Elementary Logic. J.B. Lippincott & Co. (1867)
3. Bagolini, H., Burana J.F.: Aristotelis Priora Analytica seu Resolutiora a Io. Francisco Burana Veronensi in Latinum Sermonem versa, et Commentariis doctissimis illustrata. Hieronymus Scotus, Venice (1545)
4. Bhattacharjee, R.: Direct reduction of syllogisms with Byzantine diagrams. Hist. Philos. Logic **46**(2), 236–257 (2025). https://doi.org/10.1080/01445340.2024.2336411
5. Beisecker, D.: Cultivating trees: Lewis Carroll's method of solving (and creating) multi-literal branching sorites problems. Open Philos. **7**(1), 20240044 (2024). https://doi.org/10.1515/opphil-2024-0044
6. De Reiffenberg, F.A.F.T.: Principes de Logique. Louis Hauman et Com, Brussels (1833)
7. Feder, J.G.H.: Logik und Metaphysik. Fleischer, Leipzig (1791)
8. Fries, J.F.: System der Logik. Ein Handbuch für Lehrer und zum Selbstgebrauch. Mohr und Zimmer, Heidelberg (1811)
9. Hamilton, W.: Lectures on Metaphysics and Logic. In: Four Volumes, vol. III. William Blackwood and Sons, Edinburgh and London (1860)
10. Hamilton, W.: Lectures on Metaphysics and Logic. In: Four Volumes, vol. IV. William Blackwood and Sons, Edinburgh and London (1860)
11. Kittsteiner, C.: Schopenhauer's sorites diagram. In: Lemanski, J., Johansen, M.W., Manalo, E., Viana, P., Bhattacharjee, R., Burns, R. (eds) Diagrammatic Representation and Inference. Diagrams 2024. Lecture Notes in Computer Science, vol. 14981, pp. 145–152. Springer, Cham (2024). https://doi.org/10.1007/978-3-031-71291-3_12
12. Lambert, J.H.: Neues Organon [...]. Johann Wendler, Leipzig (1764)
13. Lange, J.C.: Nucleus Logicae Weisianae. Editus antehac Actore Christiano Weisio. Henning Müller, Gissae-Hassorum (1712)
14. Lemanski, J.: Seneca's and Porphyry's trees in modern interpretation. In: Lemanski, J., Max, I. (eds.) Historia Logicae and its Modern Interpretation, pp. 61–87. College Publications, London (2023)
15. Lemanski, J., Bhattacharjee, R.: On the expressivity of Byzantine diagrams in logic. In: Lemanski, J., Johansen, M.W., Manalo, E., Viana, P., Bhattacharjee, R., Burns, R. (eds) Diagrammatic Representation and Inference. Diagrams 2024. Lecture Notes in Computer Science, vol 14981, pp. 429–445. Springer, Cham (2024). https://doi.org/10.1007/978-3-031-71291-3_35
16. Moktefi, A., Lemanski, J.: On the Origin of Venn Diagrams. Axiomathes **32**(Suppl 3), 887–900 (2022). https://doi.org/10.1007/s10516-022-09642-2
17. Read, C.: On the Theory of Logic. An Essay. C. Kegan Paul & Co., London (1878)
18. Schuyler, A.: The Principles of Logic. Hinkle & Co., Cincinnati, Wilson (1869)

Modal Euler Diagrams: Diagrammatic Reasoning Patterns for Modal Logic

Yuri Sato(✉) and Hazuki Kawamitsu

Ochanomizu University, Tokyo, Japan
sato.yuri@ocha.ac.jp

Abstract. Traditional Euler diagrams are commonly regarded as representing only a fragment of monadic predicate logic, and much work in diagrammatic logic has therefore sought to extend their expressive scope. This paper proposes *modal Euler diagrams*, an extension of Euler-style diagrams designed to represent modal notions of necessity and possibility. The proposed notation augments standard Euler diagram components with additional graphical conventions, including thick-lined ellipses for necessity and dashed ellipses for possibility. The framework also distinguishes between predicate-level (*de re*) and sentence-level (*de dicto*) modality by placing modal notation either on predicates within the diagram or on the diagram as a whole. As an initial investigation, we examine modal syllogisms containing modal operators expressing necessity or possibility. Through representative examples, we illustrate how modal reasoning can be represented diagrammatically using modal Euler diagrams. The examples demonstrate how modal distinctions can be incorporated into Euler-style reasoning while preserving its overall diagrammatic structure. The paper is intended as an exploratory step toward diagrammatic representations of modal reasoning.

Keywords: Diagrammatic reasoning · Euler diagrams · Modal reasoning · Modal syllogisms

1 Introduction

Euler diagrams were originally introduced as a graphical device for representing Aristotelian syllogistic reasoning (for a historical overview, see [1]). In modern diagrammatic logic, the expressive power of such diagrams has been extensively investigated. In particular, Shin's seminal work [5] showed that Venn diagrams, a variant of Euler diagrams equipped with additional conventions, can capture the expressive power of monadic predicate logic. Subsequent developments, such as spider diagrams [2] and concept diagrams [6], have further extended diagrammatic representations toward richer fragments of predicate logic. Against this background, the present paper proposes *modal Euler diagrams*, a graphical notation designed to represent modal notions of necessity and possibility within Euler-style diagrams. Building on graphical devices used in diagrammatic reasoning research, we introduce thick-lined ellipses to represent necessity and dashed

P. Sobociński et al. (Eds.): Diagrams 2026, LNAI 16833, pp. 63–67, 2027.
https://doi.org/10.1007/978-3-032-34178-5_7

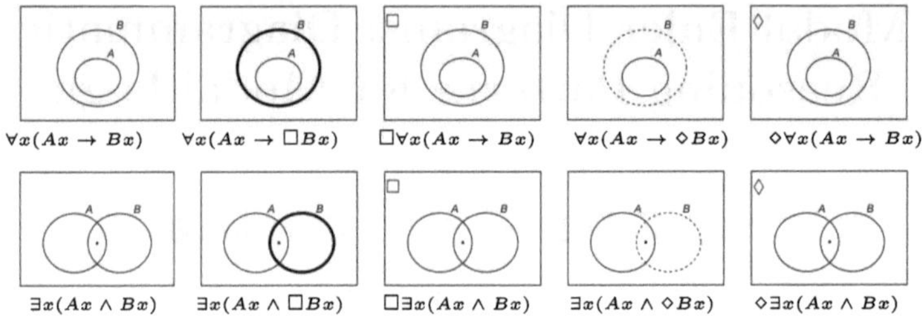

Fig. 1. Representative configurations of modal Euler diagrams

ellipses to represent possibility. In addition, we distinguish between predicate-level (*de re*) and sentence-level (*de dicto*) modality by attaching modal notation either to predicates within the diagram or to the diagram as a whole.

Graphical approaches to modal reasoning are not entirely new. Peirce's existential graphs, particularly gamma graphs, provide a diagrammatic system for modal propositional logic [3]. However, Peircean graphs differ substantially from Euler-style diagrams, since closed curves in Peirce's system do not represent sets or predicates. Hybrid approaches combining Peircean and Euler-style mechanisms have also been explored [7], although the present work focuses on extending Euler-style set representations. The present work instead investigates how modal distinctions can be incorporated into set-theoretic diagrammatic representations.

The aim of this paper is exploratory rather than fully axiomatic. Instead of developing a complete proof system, we demonstrate how modal reasoning patterns can be represented and supported using modal Euler diagrams. As an initial domain of investigation, we focus on *modal syllogisms*, understood here as valid syllogistic inference patterns containing modal operators expressing necessity or possibility. Aristotle's modal syllogistic has been widely studied in modern logic [4], and such patterns can be naturally formalized in quantified modal logic. The remainder of the paper is organized as follows. Section 2 introduces the basic syntactic components of modal Euler diagrams. Sections 3 and 4 illustrate representative forms of diagrammatic reasoning involving necessity and possibility. Finally, Sect. 5 discusses limitations of the current framework and directions for future work.

2 Modal Euler Diagrams

Modal Euler diagrams extend the graphical vocabulary of Euler-style diagrams with modal distinctions. As in standard Euler and Venn diagrams, a rectangle represents a world, an ellipse represents a set or unary predicate, a point represents an individual, and shading represents emptiness. To represent modality, modal Euler diagrams introduce two additional graphical conventions. First, in the case of *de re* modality, modal status is encoded directly in the graphical properties of ellipses: thick-lined ellipses represent necessity, while dashed

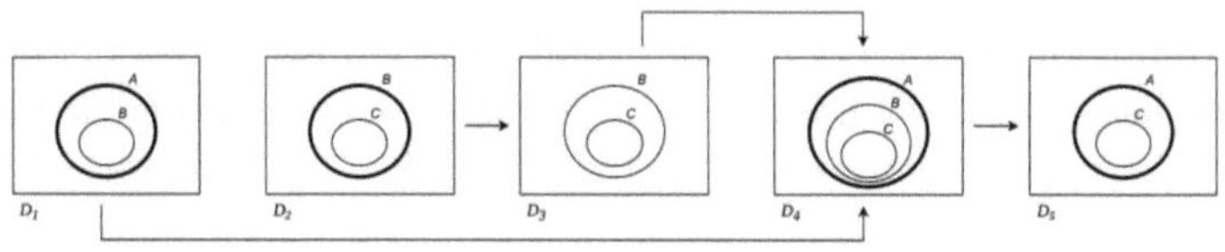

Fig. 2. Derivation of D_5 for $\forall x(Cx \to \Box Ax)$ from the premise diagrams D_1 for $\forall x(Bx \to \Box Ax)$ and D_2 for $\forall x(Cx \to \Box Bx)$.

ellipses represent possibility. Second, in the case of *de dicto* modality, where the modal operator applies to the entire proposition, the diagram is annotated with a modal label ($\Box$ or $\Diamond$) placed at the corner of the world rectangle. Figure 1 illustrates representative configurations of modal Euler diagrams. The second and fourth columns correspond to *de re* modality, in which the modal operator modifies the predicate, whereas the third and fifth columns correspond to *de dicto* modality, in which the modal operator applies to the entire statement.

3 Reasoning with Necessity

We illustrate modal reasoning using modal Euler diagrams through representative examples involving necessity under a *de re* interpretation. The reasoning process combines standard diagrammatic operations such as diagram unification with modal transformations. In particular, when two premise diagrams contain the same predicate with different modal status, direct unification is not always possible. To address this, we introduce a graphical operation called *line weakening*, which converts a thick-lined ellipse representing necessity into a normal solid ellipse. This operation corresponds to the modal principle expressed by axiom T ($\Box P \vdash P$).

Figure 2 illustrates a representative reasoning process. The diagram D_1 represents the premise $\forall x(Bx \to \Box Ax)$, while D_2 represents $\forall x(Cx \to \Box Bx)$. In D_2, the ellipse corresponding to B is drawn with a thick boundary, whereas the corresponding ellipse in D_1 is a normal solid ellipse. Because the modal markings differ, the two diagrams cannot be directly unified. To enable unification, line weakening is applied to the thick-lined ellipse in D_2, producing D_3. The diagrams can then be unified by identifying the ellipses corresponding to the predicate B, producing D_4. Finally, extracting the relation between C and A yields D_5, representing the conclusion $\forall x(Cx \to \Box Ax)$.

4 Reasoning with Possibility

Modal Euler diagrams can also represent reasoning involving possibility under a *de re* interpretation. Figure 3 illustrates a representative reasoning process involving possibility. The first premise diagram represents $\exists x(Ax \wedge Bx)$, while the second represents $\forall x(Bx \to Cx)$. The two diagrams are first unified by identifying the ellipses labeled B. Extracting the relation between C and A yields a diagram representing $\exists x(Cx \wedge Ax)$. Finally, the ellipse corresponding to A is transformed into a dashed ellipse, yielding a diagram representing $\exists x(Cx \wedge \Diamond Ax)$.

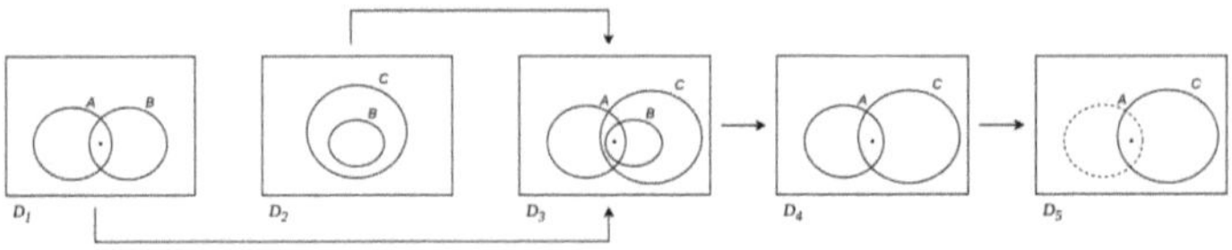

Fig. 3. Derivation of D_5 for $\exists x(Cx \wedge \Diamond Ax)$ from the premise diagrams D_1 for $\exists x(Ax \wedge Bx)$ and D_2 for $\forall x(Bx \rightarrow Cx)$.

5 Discussion and Future Work

The present paper introduced modal Euler diagrams as an extension of Euler-style diagrammatic representations for expressing modal distinctions involving necessity and possibility. The examples discussed in the previous sections focused mainly on *de re* modality, where modal operators are associated with predicates through graphical properties such as thick or dashed ellipses. The framework also supports *de dicto* modality by attaching modal labels to the world rectangle, although detailed reasoning examples involving *de dicto* interpretations were omitted in this paper. The proposed framework remains exploratory rather than fully axiomatic. Future work includes a more systematic classification of diagrammatic operations and their relation to proof-theoretic principles in modal logic. In particular, extending the framework toward interactive hybrid systems combining diagrams and logical formulas may provide useful support for human reasoning involving modal concepts. Beyond modal syllogisms, modal Euler diagrams may also be applicable to broader forms of conceptual and ontological representation involving modal constraints.

Acknowledgments. This study was supported by Grant-in-Aid for JSPS KAKENHI Grant Number JP24K15676 and JP24K00004 to the first author.

References

1. Baron, M.E.: A note on the historical development of logic diagrams: Leibniz, Euler and Venn. Math. Gaz. **53**(384), 113–125 (1969). https://doi.org/10.2307/3614533
2. Howse, J., Stapleton, G., Taylor, J.: Spider diagrams. LMS J. Comput. Math. **8**, 145–194 (2005). https://doi.org/10.1112/S1461157000000942
3. Ma, M., Pietarinen, A.V.: Gamma graph calculi for modal logics. Synthese **195**(8), 3621–3650 (2018). https://doi.org/10.1007/s11229-017-1390-3
4. Malink, M.: Aristotle's Modal Syllogistic. Harvard Univ Press (2013)
5. Shin, S.J.: The Logical Status of Diagrams. Cambridge Univ Press (1994)

6. Stapleton, G., Compton, M., Howse, J.: Visualizing OWL 2 using diagrams. In: Proceedings of VL/HCC 2017, pp. 245–253. IEEE (2017). https://doi.org/10.1109/VLHCC.2017.8103474
7. Tosaka, Y., Sato, Y.: Introducing modality De Re/De Dicto into Euler diagrams: implication to ontology visualization. In: Proceedings of VINCI 2025, pp. 1–5. ACM (2025). https://doi.org/10.1145/3769534.3769553

From Peirce to Zellweger: Evolution of the Notation for Propositional Connectives

Arnold Oostra(✉)

Universidad del Tolima, Ibagué, Colombia
noostra@ut.edu.co

Abstract. In this paper, we examine the notations developed by Peirce, Zellweger, and other authors for the sixteen binary connectives of classical propositional logic and highlight the most relevant features of each. These notations reveal interesting symmetries within the system of classical binary connectives. The analysis of these sign systems might allow us to identify properties useful for logical notation.

Keywords: Binary propositional connectives · Charles S. Peirce · Shea Zellweger

1 Introduction

In propositional logic, a binary connective is a particle that combines two variables or propositions. From a mathematical point of view, it is a function that assigns a proposition to an ordered pair of propositions. In the classical case, since a proposition only has two possibilities: being true (T) or false (F), a binary connective is simply a function from $\{V, F\} \times \{V, F\}$ to $\{V, F\}$and, therefore, is completely determined by its four-line truth table. Since there are n^m functions from a set with m elements to one with n elements, there are $2^4 = 16$ binary connectives in classical propositional logic. Four of them depend functionally on only one of the two variables, and two others are constant. In a sense, then, there are only ten truly binary connectives. However, for the sake of completeness, the system of classical binary connectives has sixteen members.

Unlike basic arithmetic, the notation for propositional connectives is far from standardized. Only a few of the sixteen connectives are considered usual in logic and have an associated symbol. Beyond tradition, it is difficult to justify the choice of signs, except perhaps the arrow for material implication ($p \to q$ means "if p then q" and, somehow, the antecedent p leads to the consequent q) or the wedge for conjunction ($p \wedge q$ means "p and q" and, in lattice theory, corresponds to the greatest lower bound, which represents the heap of lower bounds of p and q). This opens the search for a notation for the binary propositional connectives, with a sign for any of the sixteen connectives and with some method behind its construction.

P. Sobociński et al. (Eds.): Diagrams 2026, LNAI 16833, pp. 68–76, 2027.
https://doi.org/10.1007/978-3-032-34178-5_8

Throughout the 20th century, various logicians proposed different notations with the aforementioned characteristics, and many more properties. Each of them used the notation to forward a particular idea or solve a specific problem. Apparently, the first of these notations was devised by Charles S. Peirce in 1903 [12], and another widely developed notation is the Logic Alphabet conceived by Shea Zellweger [3]. In Sect. 2 of this article, we discuss Peirce's notation and point out some symmetries of the system of classical binary connectives that these symbols reveal. In Sect. 3 we review some similar notations subsequently proposed by other authors and finally, in Sect. 4 we analyse Zellweger's Logic Alphabet.

2 Peirce's Notation

In *A Proposed Logical Notation*, written around 1901 but only published recently [12, vol.1], C. S. Peirce introduced a notation for all sixteen binary connectives. He used it amply in *The Simplest Branch of Mathematics*, written in 1903 [11, vol.3], where he studied the complete connectives and searched for tautologies with a predetermined form. This notation was studied by Clark [2], Zellweger [14], and Oostra [7,9].

Peirce's notation starts from the form ×, whose four quadrants are labeled with the combinations of two truth values as follows: the upper quadrant is TT, the lower one is FF, the left one is TF, and the right one is FT. See the center of Fig. 1. The next step is to *close the false quadrants*, that is: the quadrants whose combination is F in the connective are closed with a segment that joins the corresponding endpoints of the form ×. The right side of Fig. 1 shows the sign for the material implication, which assigns F only to the combination TF. Incidentally, this idea of enclosing the false quadrants is consistent with the drawing of existential graphs, where a closed curve denies the graph it contains.

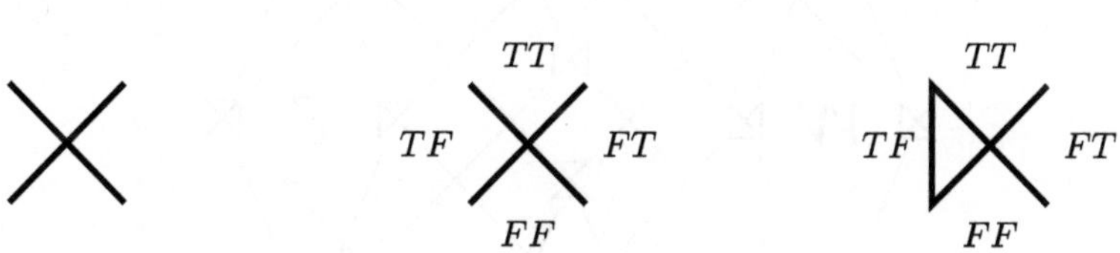

Fig. 1. Three stages in the definition of Peirce's notation.

Table 1 shows the signs of the sixteen connectives. In this system, conjunction is ⊠, disjunction is X̲, implication is ⋉, and equivalence is ⋈. This table shows an interesting left-right antisymmetry of complementary connectives.

With Peirce's notation, it is straightforward to define a natural partial order in the set of connectives: one sign precedes another if the second is obtained from the first by opening one or more closed quadrants. Figure 2 shows the resulting ordered set. In fact, this is a lattice, moreover, a Boolean algebra, specifically

Table 1. Peirce's notation

TT	F	F	F	F	T	T	T	T	F	F	F	F	T	T	T	T
TF	F	F	F	T	F	T	F	F	T	T	F	T	F	T	T	T
FT	F	F	T	F	F	F	T	F	T	F	T	T	T	F	T	T
FF	F	T	F	F	F	F	F	T	F	T	T	T	T	T	F	T
	⊠	[illegible]	[illegible]	[illegible]	[illegible]	[illegible]	[illegible]	⋈	⧖	[illegible]	[illegible]	[illegible]	[illegible]	[illegible]	[illegible]	✕
	⊕	⅄	<	>	∨	◿	◺	∞	8	◹	◸	ꝸ	∝	ꝏ	♉	✕

the free Boolean algebra with two generators. From a geometric point of view, this lattice represents the 4-dimensional cube and its wealth of symmetries is reflected in the system of propositional connectives. For instance, in this diagram the opposite vertices of the 4-cube have complementary connectives. Although Peirce apparently did not consider this order between the connectives, he did draw a similar figure which shows some of the symmetries of this structure. Also, he classified the connectives in the four groups $\mathcal{N}$ = {✕, [illegible], [illegible], ⋈}, $\mathcal{W}$ = {[illegible], [illegible], [illegible], [illegible]}, $\mathcal{E}$ = {[illegible], [illegible], [illegible], [illegible]}, and $\mathcal{S}$ = {⧖, [illegible], [illegible], [illegible]}, according to the upper and lower quadrants.

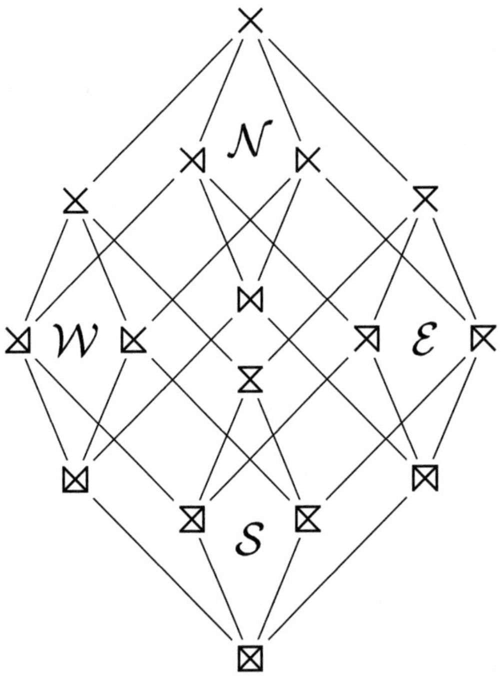

Fig. 2. Lattice of classical binary connectives with Peirce's notation.

In his manuscript Peirce simultaneously introduced a cursive version of his notation, shown in the bottom row of Table 1, which greatly improves the ease of handwriting. Surprisingly, in at least two cases, these signs are similar to those designed by Peirce elsewhere: the cursive form $\propto$ of implication somehow resembles the sign $\prec$ used since 1870, while the sign for the complete connective ⅄ is called by Peirce *ampheck* (from αμφήκης, cutting both ways) [8].

Peirce used his notation in the search for tautologies in the following forms:

1. $x \; \mathrm{O} \; x$
2. $x \Diamond (x \; \mathrm{O} \; x)$
3. $(x \Diamond x) \; \mathrm{O} \; (x \heartsuit x)$
4. $(x \Diamond y) \; \mathrm{O} \; (x \heartsuit y)$
5. $(x \spadesuit y) \heartsuit [(y \clubsuit z) \Diamond (x \; \mathrm{O} \; z)]$

Here O, $\Diamond$, $\heartsuit$, $\spadesuit$, and $\clubsuit$ are variable connectives and in each form the values are looked for such that the expression is true for any propositions x, y, and z. Peirce arranged his solutions for forms 4 and 5 into 16×16 tables with striking symmetries [2]. Figure 3 shows a similar table for form 3, for example: if $\Diamond$ is taken from the group $\mathcal{N}$ in Fig. 2 and $\heartsuit$ from the group $\mathcal{W}$, then $(x \Diamond x)$ ⊠ $(x \heartsuit x)$ is a tautology for any proposition x. The symmetry lies in the fact that any reflection or rotation of the table perfectly matches the same transformation performed by all the signs in each position.

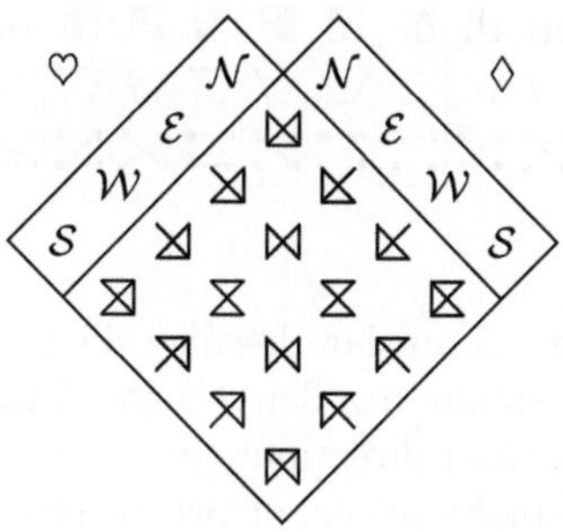

Fig. 3. Table of tautologies of the form $(x \Diamond x) \; \mathrm{O} \; (x \heartsuit x)$.

In summary, in Peirce's notation, the sign of each connective is its truth table, by means of a simple convention. The sign reveals properties of the connective, for instance, the connective is commutative if and only if its sign is right-left symmetrical. Furthermore, the system of signs reveals hidden symmetries of the entire system of classical propositional connectives. In addition to its basic form, Peirce's notation includes a cursive script useful for facilitating handwriting.

3 Other Peirce-Like Notations

There are several notations very similar to Peirce's, which were introduced throughout the 20th century, some of which are discussed below.

Warren S. McCulloch proposed a notation that begins with exactly the same form X as Peirce, labeled with the combinations of two truth values in the same way. But he decided to *draw a dot in the true quadrants*, see the first row of Table 2. This notation later became known as *Randolph diagrams*, because it was published and further developed by John F. Randolph [13]. Each sign is the table of its connective by a simple convention, and it has exactly the same symmetries as Peirce's symbolism. However, McCulloch's symbols are not topologically connected, which complicates their handwriting a little. In particular, the dots can be confused with each other or with other symbols.

Table 2. A spectrum of Peirce-like notations

T T	*F*	*F*	*F*	*F*	*T*	*T*	*T*	*T*	*F*	*F*	*F*	*F*	*T*	*T*	*T*	*T*
T F	*F*	*F*	*F*	*T*	*F*	*T*	*F*	*F*	*T*	*T*	*F*	*T*	*F*	*T*	*T*	*T*
F T	*F*	*F*	*T*	*F*	*F*	*F*	*T*	*F*	*T*	*F*	*T*	*T*	*T*	*F*	*T*	*T*
F F	*F*	*T*	*F*	*F*	*F*	*F*	*F*	*T*	*F*	*T*	*T*	*T*	*T*	*T*	*F*	*T*

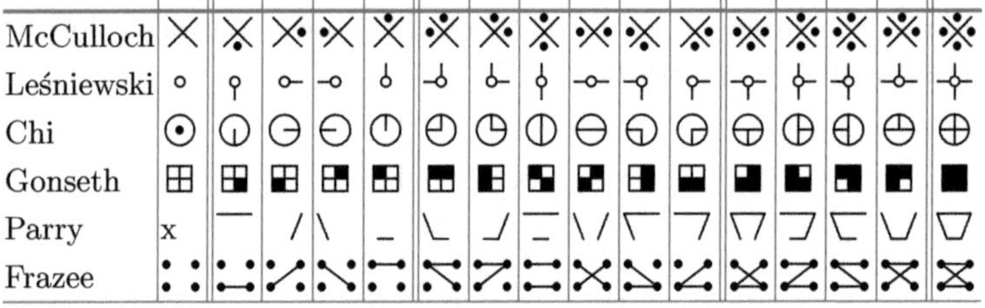

In many of his writings, Stanisław Leśniewski used a notation for classical propositional connectives similar to Peirce's [6]. This notation begins with a small circle with lines in the four directions (up, down, left, and right), directions that are labeled with the combinations of two truth values just as in the earlier notations. See the second line of Table 2. This symbolism shares all the features of Peirce's notation, including the fact that all its signs are connected. The notation introduced by Richard S. Y. Chi [1] is exactly the same, only the circle surrounds the lines, see the third row of Table 2.

Ferdinand Gonseth [5] introduced a notation for propositional connectives based on a square divided into other four smaller squares, like the panes of a window. The four smaller squares are labeled with the combinations of truth values, and the next step is to *fill in the true panes*, see the fourth row of Table 2. This symbolism shares all the characteristics of Peirce's notation except for a 45-degree rotation to the left. All the signs are topologically connected, but they are certainly not easy to draw quickly by hand.

There are also some notations with less symmetry. William T. Parry begins with a trapezoid with its top longer than the base [10]. The four sides are labeled with the truth value combinations as follows: the top side is FF, the bottom side is TT, the left side is TF, and the right side is FT. The next step is to *remove the false sides* arriving at the notation shown on the fifth row of Table 2. The author points out some similarities to the usual notations and some abbreviations. While each sign is the truth table of its connective by means of a simple code, this notation has fewer symmetries than Peirce's symbolism. For instance, the symbols can not be rotated 90 degrees. Some of Frazee's signs are disconnected and could easily be mistaken for unrelated lines when handwritten.

Finally, Jerome Frazee [4] does not begin with the combinations of truth values but with four dots in a rectangular pattern. The upper dots are labeled T and the bottom dots F, the left pair represents the truth values of the first proposition and the right pair that of the second proposition. The next step is to *join the dots that form the true combinations*, see the bottom row of Table 2. Once more, each sign is the truth table of its connective by means of a simple agreement. This notation has less symmetries than Peirce's signs, for instance, many of the signs can not be rotated 90 degrees. Some of Frazee's signs are not topologically connected, which complicates their handwriting somewhat.

Many notations for the propositional connectives introduced after Peirce's share its characteristics to a greater or lesser degree. Most share the same symmetries, or at least partially. On the other hand, most of these notations seem more difficult to write by hand, especially more so than the cursive notation proposed by Peirce.

4 Shea Zellweger's Logic Alphabet

In the 1960s, S. Zellweger proposed a notation for the binary connectives and called it *Logic Alphabet* [3]. For decades, he developed applications of this notation to logic and education [14,15], and build numerous physical models that exhibit the symmetries of the classical connective system.

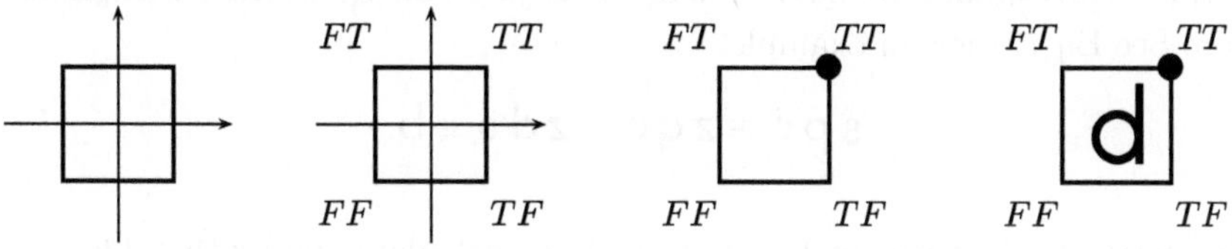

Fig. 4. Four stages in the definition of Zellweger's Logic Alphabet.

The Logic Alphabet begins with a square with one vertex in each quadrant of the Cartesian plane, see Fig. 4. By taking T as a positive value and F as a negative one, the four vertices are naturally labeled with the combinations of two truth values. The next step is to *mark the true vertices* with a heavy dot, see Table 3. Up to this point, the result is a notation similar to those mentioned earlier in this paper, sharing all the features of Peirce's signs except for a (right) 45-degree rotation. For instance, with this notation, a connective is commutative if and only if the sign is symmetric about the ascending diagonal.

Zellweger's further step is to choose, in each case, a letter with *stems in the marked corners*. Except for three cases, which are easily resolved, the English alphabet has lowercase letters for all connectives. The bottom row of Table 3 shows the final signs that make up Zellweger's Logic Alphabet.

Table 3. The Logic Alphabet

TT	F	F	F	F	T	T	T	T	F	F	F	F	T	T	T	T
TF	F	F	F	T	F	T	F	F	T	T	F	T	F	T	T	T
FT	F	F	T	F	F	F	T	F	T	F	T	T	T	F	T	T
FF	F	T	F	F	F	F	F	T	F	T	T	T	T	T	F	T
	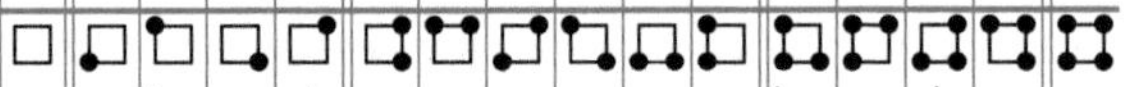															
	o	p	b	q	d	c	u	s	z	n	ɔ	h	μ	ɗ	ɥ	x

In the Logic Alphabet, a left-to-right flip of the sign amounts to negating the first component, while a top-to-bottom flip of the sign corresponds to negating the second component, see for instance Eq. (1) where we naturally use capital letters for propositional variables. In turn, negation of a connective amounts to taking the complement of the sign, in the sense that all existing stems disappear and the empty corners are replaced by new stems.

$$A\,\mathsf{b}\,B \equiv \overline{A}\,\mathsf{d}\,B \qquad\qquad A\,\mathsf{q}\,B \equiv A\,\mathsf{d}\,\overline{B} \tag{1}$$

These moves greatly simplify the algebraic calculation of the ternary operation in which the middle connective is applied to the two adjacent connectives, reducing the middle connective to one which is easy to calculate, such as conjunction d, which corresponds to intersection, or disjunction ɥ, which corresponds to union. See Eq. (2) for an example.

$$\mathsf{s}\,\mathsf{p}\,\mathsf{c} \equiv \mathsf{z}\,\mathsf{q}\,\mathsf{c} \equiv \mathsf{z}\,\mathsf{d}\,ɔ \equiv \mathsf{b}. \tag{2}$$

This operation, in turn, makes it possible to calculate the truth table of any formula, representing the letters also with connectives. For a formula with two letters, the propositional variables are expressed by connectives c and u, see an example in Eq. (3). Zellweger outlines the necessary steps to extend this method to formulas with more than two letters [14]. This procedure is already found in Randolph's paper [13] with McCulloch's notation.

$$(\mathsf{c}\,\mu\,\mathsf{u})\,\mu\,\mathsf{c} \equiv (ɔ\,ɥ\,\mathsf{u})\,\mu\,\mathsf{c} \equiv \mu\,\mu\,\mathsf{c} \equiv \mathsf{q}\,ɥ\,\mathsf{c} \equiv \mathsf{c}. \tag{3}$$

Over several decades, Zellweger developed a large number of hand-held models showing the symmetries of the classical binary propositional connectives revealed by the Logic Alphabet. There are one-dimensional, two-dimensional and three-dimensional models, as well as diagrams corresponding to four-dimensional objects. Some of these models are on display in a museum in Los Angeles.

Like Zellweger's preliminary square notation, the Logic Alphabet shares all the characteristics of Peirce's notation. The sign for each connective is its truth table by a simple convention. This notation also reveals the properties of each connective and the symmetries of the classical connective system. The symbols are topologically connected and are clearly easy to write, since almost all of them are familiar characters. On the other hand, a novel feature of the Logic Alphabet is that the signs have *names*, so any formula can be read directly aloud. All these features make the Logic Alphabet a truly interesting notation.

Disclosure of Interests. The author has no competing interests to declare that are relevant to the content of this article.

References

1. Chi, R.S.Y.: Buddhist Formal Logic. Motilal Banarsidass, Delhi (1969)
2. Clark, G.: New light on Peirce's iconic notation for the sixteen binary connectives. In: Houser, N., Roberts, D.D., Van Evra, J. (eds.) Studies in the Logic of Charles Sanders Peirce, pp. 304–333. Indiana University Press, Bloomington and Indianapolis (1997)
3. Clark, G., Zellweger, S.: Let the mirrors do the thinking. Mount Union Magazine **93**, 2–5 (1993)
4. Frazee, J.: A new symbolic representation of the basic truth-functions of the propositional calculus. Hist. Philos. Logic **9**, 87–91 (1987)
5. Gonseth, F.: Qu'est-ce que la logique? Hermann, Paris (1937)
6. Leśniewski, S.: Grundzüge eines neuen Systems der Grundlagen der Mathematik. Fundam. Math. **14**(1), 1–81 (1929)
7. Oostra, A.: La notación diagramática de C. S. Peirce para los conectivos proposicionales binarios. Revista de la Academia Colombiana de Ciencias **28**(106), 57–70 (2004)
8. Oostra, A.: Peirce y la completitud proposicional. Cuadernos de Sistemática Peirceana **7**, 157–180 (2015)
9. Oostra, A.: Shea Zellweger (1925–2022): creador del alfabeto lógico. In: Perry, P. (ed.) Encuentro de Geometría y sus Aplicaciones, vol. 26, pp. 3–7. Universidad Pedagógica Nacional, Bogotá (2024)
10. Parry, W.T.: A new symbolism for the propositional calculus. J. Symbolic Logic **19**(3), 161–168 (1954)
11. Peirce, C.S.: The New Elements of Mathematics, vol. 4. Mouton, The Hague (1976)
12. Peirce, C.S.: Logic of the future. In: Pietarinen, A.V. (ed.) Logic of the Future, Peirceana, vol. 1–3. De Gruyter, Berlin/Boston (2020–2024)
13. Randolph, J.F.: Cross-examining propositional calculus and set operations. Am. Math. Mon. **72**(2), 117–127 (1965)

14. Zellweger, S.: Untapped potential in Peirce's iconic notation for the sixteen binary connectives. In: Houser, N., Roberts, D.D., Van Evra, J. (eds.) Studies in the Logic of Charles Sanders Peirce, pp. 334–386. Indiana University Press, Bloomington and Indianapolis (1997)
15. Zellweger, S.: Mathelogical semiotics: a lesson in constructing a shape-value notation for elementary logic. In: Anderson, M., Sáenz-Ludlow, A., Zellweger, S., Cifarelli, V.V. (eds.) Educational Perspectives on Mathematics as Semiosis: From Thinking to Interpreting to Knowing, pp. 285–356. Legas, Toronto (2003)

Representational Normalization and Non-injective Translation in Peirce's Alpha Existential Graphs

Takashi Sasaki(✉)

Doshisha University, Kyoto, Japan
7sasaki@gmail.com

Abstract. Peirce's Existential Graphs (EGs) provide a diagrammatic system for classical propositional logic, representing negation by a cut and conjunction by juxtaposition. It is well known that the alpha system is expressively complete for propositional logic. This paper focuses on a different and less discussed property of the standard translation from formulas to EGs.

We argue that this translation is non-injective: distinct formulas that are logically equivalent can be mapped to the same graph. Consequently, certain equivalence transformations that must be demonstrated through derivations in symbolic systems are absorbed into the representation of EGs.

We refer to this phenomenon as representational normalization. In symbolic logic, logically equivalent formulas remain syntactically distinct expressions whose equivalence must be derived. In EGs, however, several equivalent formulas correspond to a single diagrammatic structure.

This perspective suggests that EGs function not merely as alternative notations for propositional formulas but as diagrammatic representations of equivalence classes of formulas. The analysis helps clarify phenomena such as transparency of equivalence and multiple readings that have been discussed in the literature on diagrammatic reasoning. This observation provides a structural explanation for why certain logical relations become visually immediate in EGs.

Keywords: Existential Graphs · Diagrammatic Reasoning · Peirce

1 Introduction

Peirce's existential graphs (EGs) constitute a diagrammatic system for classical propositional logic. The alpha system employs only two primitive graphical devices: the cut, representing negation, and juxtaposition, representing conjunction. Despite this minimal set of primitives, the system is expressively equivalent to standard propositional logic.

Previous studies on diagrammatic reasoning have suggested that diagrams may reveal logical relations in ways that are less transparent in symbolic systems. Norman (1999) argues that EGs are often more perspicuous than symbolic representations and introduces notions such as transparency of equivalence (TEQ), according to which logical equivalence can sometimes be recognized directly without explicit derivation. While

P. Sobociński et al. (Eds.): Diagrams 2026, LNAI 16833, pp. 77–84, 2027.
https://doi.org/10.1007/978-3-032-34178-5_9

related phenomena have been noted in previous studies, the structural basis of these observations has not been clearly articulated.

The present paper investigates a structural property of the translation from propositional formulas to alpha EGs. We show that this translation is non-injective: distinct but logically equivalent formulas may correspond to the same graph (Bellucci and Pietarinen 2016, 2021). We refer to this phenomenon as representational normalization, whereby several equivalent formulas collapse into a single diagrammatic representation in EGs. This property helps explain why certain logical relations become directly visible in diagrams and clarifies the relation between diagrammatic reasoning and multiple readings.

2 Alpha EGs and Translation

Peirce's existential graphs (EGs) are a diagrammatic system for propositional logic employing two primitive graphical devices: the cut and juxtaposition.

In the alpha system, the sheet of assertion represents the context of truth. The blank sheet itself is also regarded by Peirce as a graph representing truth. The proposition written directly on the sheet is thereby asserted as true. The cut, drawn as a closed curve, represents negation. A graph enclosed by a cut is interpreted as the negation of the proposition represented within that region. The juxtaposition of graphs within the same region represents conjunction. Consequently, the juxtaposition of two graphs, A and B, within the same region signifies the conjunction $A \wedge B$.

Other propositional connectives can be defined in terms of these primitives. For example, disjunction can be expressed using negation and conjunction via De Morgan's equivalence:

$$A \vee B \equiv \neg(\neg A \wedge \neg B)$$

Similarly, the conditional can be expressed as

$$A \rightarrow B \equiv \neg(A \wedge \neg B)$$

Utilizing these equivalences, formulas containing disjunction or conditional can be translated into EGs using only cuts and juxtaposition.

More formally, let F be the set of propositional formulas and G the set of alpha EGs (considered up to graphical isomorphism). A translation function

$$T : F \rightarrow G$$

can be defined recursively as follows:

$T(p)$ for an atomic proposition p is the occurrence of p placed on the sheet of assertion.

$T(\neg\varphi)$ is obtained by enclosing $T(\varphi)$ within a cut.

$T(\varphi \wedge \psi)$ is obtained by placing $T(\varphi)$ and $T(\psi)$ in the same region.

Other connectives are translated by first rewriting the formula using the equivalences above and then applying these rules.

This translation establishes a systematic correspondence between symbolic propositional formulas and EGs. However, as will be shown in the subsequent section, the mapping exhibits a salient structural property: it is not injective. It is noteworthy that distinct formulas may correspond to the same diagrammatic structure when translated into EGs. This property plays a crucial role in explaining certain features of diagrammatic reasoning with EGs.

3 Non-injective Translation and Representational Normalization

In the present paper, we consider translations from standard propositional languages containing connectives such as disjunction and conditional into existential graphs. Formulas involving these connectives are first rewritten in terms of negation and conjunction before translation. The phenomenon of representational normalization discussed here therefore concerns the relation between such symbolic languages and existential graphs, rather than properties internal to a minimal language containing only negation and conjunction.

A key structural feature of alpha EGs becomes visible when we examine the translation from propositional formulas to diagrams. Let F be the set of well-formed formulas of propositional logic and G the set of alpha EGs (considered up to graphical isomorphism). As mentioned in the previous section, a standard translation function, T: $F \rightarrow G$, can be defined recursively as follows: Atomic formulas are translated into atomic graph elements placed in the sheet of assertion. Negation is represented by enclosing the translated graph within a cut. Conjunction is represented by juxtaposition within the same region. Other connectives are defined in terms of these primitives. For instance, $(A \vee B)$ and $(A \rightarrow B)$ are translated as $\neg(\neg A \wedge \neg B)$ and $\neg(A \wedge \neg B)$, respectively.

Utilizing these definitions, it is possible to translate every propositional formula into an alpha graph. A salient property of this translation is that it is not injective: there exist formulas $\varphi \neq \psi$ such that $T(\varphi) = T(\psi)$ (up to graphical isomorphism).

This can be illustrated by simple examples. Consider the formulas $A \vee B$ and $\neg (\neg A \wedge \neg B)$. These expressions are syntactically distinct but logically equivalent. When translated into EGs, both yield the same graphical structure consisting of a double cut containing two separated occurrences of A and B. Similarly, the formulas $A \rightarrow B$ and $\neg (A \wedge \neg B)$ also translate into identical graph configurations. In both cases, distinct formulas collapse into a single diagrammatic representation. A similar phenomenon also occurs within languages containing only negation and conjunction. For example, the formulas $(A \wedge B)$ and $(B \wedge A)$ are syntactically distinct but correspond to the same graphical configuration in existential graphs, since juxtaposition is not order-sensitive. Likewise, $((A \wedge B) \wedge C)$ and $(A \wedge (B \wedge C))$ correspond to the same juxtaposition of graphs. These cases suggest that existential graphs collapse certain distinctions involving ordering and bracketing as well as definitional equivalences.

This phenomenon can be attributed to the minimal set of primitives present in the alpha system. Because EGs use only negation and conjunction as primitive operations, other connectives are defined through these operations prior to translation. Consequently, formulas that differ only by definitional equivalences are mapped to the same graphical structure.

This phenomenon is referred to as representational normalization. In symbolic propositional logic, logically equivalent formulas typically remain distinct syntactic expressions. The establishment of their equivalence must be achieved through derivations employing inference rules or equivalence transformations. In EGs, by contrast, certain classes of equivalent formulas are normalized into a unified diagrammatic representation during the process of translation.

Consequently, some logical relations that require explicit derivations in symbolic systems become directly observable in the diagrammatic representation. For example, once the formulas $(A \vee B)$ and $\neg(\neg A \wedge \neg B)$ are translated, their equivalence becomes immediately apparent due to their correspondence to the same graph. In this sense, the equivalence relations between formulas are partly absorbed into the representational structure of the diagrammatic system.

This property offers a structural explanation for phenomena that have been discussed in the literature on diagrammatic reasoning. In particular, Norman (1999) introduces the notion of transparency of equivalence (TEQ), according to which two representations are transparently equivalent when their logical equivalence can be recognized without applying inference rules. The representational normalization described here explains why such transparency frequently occurs in EGs: when multiple formulas are mapped to a common graph, their equivalence becomes visually immediate. This observation is closely related to Peirce's notion of "replica", according to which distinct inscriptions may instantiate the same graph type (Fig. 1).

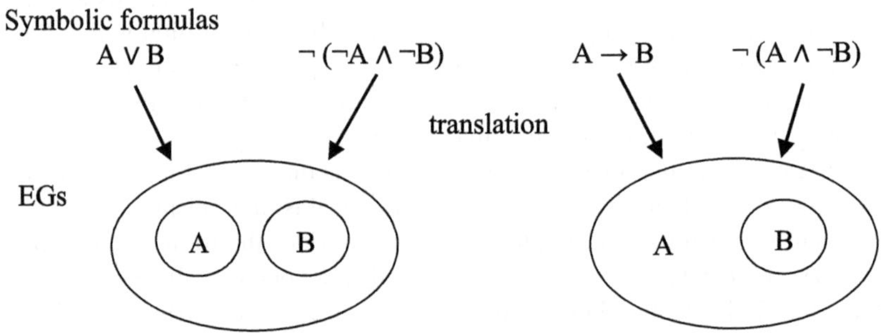

Fig. 1. Two distinct propositional formulas translated into the same alpha EGs.

Multiple Readings and Diagrammatic Semantics

The non-injective translation described in the previous section has a significant representational consequence. As distinct but logically equivalent formulas may correspond to the same diagram, existential graphs implicitly perform a form of normalization at the level of representation. We refer to this phenomenon as representational normalization.

This representational normalization also sheds light on Shin's well-known notion of multiple readings in EGs. Shin (2002) observes that a single diagram may correspond to multiple formulaic interpretations when translated into symbolic propositional logic. In other words, a diagram does not necessarily correspond to a unique formula but it can support multiple logically equivalent readings.

For example, consider the alpha graph consisting of a cut that contains two inner cuts around A and B. This diagram can be interpreted symbolically in at least two ways: $A \vee B$ and $\neg(\neg A \wedge \neg B)$

Shin interprets such cases as evidence that EGs function as an iconic logical system, in which diagrams represent logical relations through structural features rather than through syntactic composition alone. The interpretation of a diagram is therefore not confined to a single formulaic translation. Instead, diagrams can facilitate multiple readings that correspond to distinct but logically equivalent symbolic expressions.

The analysis developed in this paper provides a complementary perspective on this phenomenon. As shown in Sect. 3, the translation from formulas to EGs is not injective. Distinct formulas may correspond to the same graph under translation. This property implies that the mapping between formulas and diagrams is many-to-one. Consequently, when a diagram is translated back into symbolic notation, several formulas may serve as legitimate interpretations of the same graphical structure.

From this perspective, multiple readings are not merely a feature of interpretation but a structural consequence of representational normalization. Because EGs normalize certain equivalence transformations at the representational level, formulas that differ only by definitional equivalences are capable of being collapsed into a single diagram. When such a diagram is interpreted symbolically, the inverse mapping naturally yields multiple formulaic readings.

This observation suggests a slightly different way of understanding the semantics of EGs. Rather than perceiving diagrams as representations of individual formulas, it may be more appropriate to regard them as representations of equivalence classes of formulas under logical equivalence. In symbolic systems, equivalence relations between formulas are expressed through derivations. In EGs, by contrast, some of these relations are already reflected in the representational structure of the diagram.

This perspective clarifies why multiple readings arise naturally in diagrammatic reasoning. If a diagram represents an equivalence class of formulas, then different symbolic formulas belonging to that class can legitimately serve as valid readings of the same diagram. The phenomenon of multiple readings therefore reflects the fact that diagrammatic representations capture logical structure at a level that abstracts away from particular symbolic expressions.

In this sense, the phenomenon of multiple readings can be regarded as the interpretive counterpart of representational normalization. Representational normalization describes the process by which multiple formulas collapse into a single diagram during translation. Multiple readings, in turn, describe how that diagram can subsequently be interpreted through multiple equivalent symbolic expressions.

When considered as a whole, these observations reinforce the idea that EGs function as a diagrammatic representation of logical structure rather than merely as an alternative notation for symbolic formulas.

4 Implications for Diagrammatic Reasoning

The analysis developed in the preceding sections has implications for the broader study of diagrammatic reasoning. In particular, the notion of representational normalization offers a way of explaining why diagrammatic systems such as EGs can sometimes support efficient reasoning.

Research on diagrammatic reasoning has frequently emphasized that diagrams can reveal logical relations that remain implicit in symbolic representations. This observation has been discussed under various notions, including perspicuousness (Norman 1999), iconicity (Shin 2002), and free rides in diagrammatic reasoning. However, the mechanisms underlying these advantages are not always clearly specified.

The present analysis suggests that one important factor lies in the representational structure of the system. Because the translation from propositional formulas to EGs is not injective, certain equivalence transformations between formulas are absorbed into the diagrammatic representation itself. In symbolic logic, it is imperative to recognize that formulas that are logically equivalent remain syntactically distinct expressions. The demonstration of their equivalence must be substantiated through explicit derivations. In EGs, by contrast, some of these distinctions disappear at the representational level. Equivalent formulas may correspond to the same diagram, thereby allowing the logical relations between them to become visually apparent.

This structural feature helps explain Norman's notion of transparency of equivalence (TEQ). When equivalent formulas are mapped to the same diagrammatic configuration, their equivalence can be recognized directly without the application of transformation rules. In this sense, EGs do not merely display logical information but also encode certain logical equivalences within the geometry of the representation.

This observation also clarifies the role of Shin's notion of multiple readings. Because diagrams correspond to equivalence classes of formulas, the mapping from diagrams back to symbolic expressions naturally produces multiple formulaic interpretations. The phenomenon of multiple readings, therefore, stands in close relation to the representational normalization, a topic that is examined in this paper.

From a broader perspective, these observations suggest that diagrammatic reasoning systems may differ from symbolic systems not only in visual appearance but also in how logical structure is represented. In symbolic logic, logical relations are primarily established through the manipulation of syntactic expressions according to formal rules. In diagrammatic systems, some of these relations can be reflected directly in the structure of the representation. As a result, reasoning steps that require explicit derivations in symbolic systems may correspond to simple perceptual recognitions in diagrammatic systems.

This perspective is consistent with a predominant idea found in research on external representations: complex reasoning tasks can sometimes be simplified when a component of the logical structure is integrated into the representation itself. Diagrams can function as external cognitive artifacts that support reasoning by making relevant relations perceptually accessible.

This interpretation is also consistent with Peirce's own conception of diagrammatic reasoning. Peirce repeatedly emphasized that diagrams function not merely as visual aids but as representations of relational structure. According to Peirce, the objective of a diagram is to exhibit the structure of the relations involved, thereby enabling reasoning by observing the transformations of the diagram itself. In this sense, diagrams allow the reasoner to "experiment" upon representations whose structural features correspond to logical relations (Peirce, CP 4.530–4.552). This perspective is also related to Peirce's concern with "superfluous signs" in logical notation.

From this perspective, the phenomenon of representational normalization described in this paper can be understood as a consequence of the structural character of EGs. Diagrams, as representations of logical relations, utilize spatial and topological configurations rather than linear syntactic expressions. Consequently, certain equivalence transformations between formulas are inherently reflected in the graphical structure itself. Distinct symbolic expressions that differ only by definitional equivalences therefore collapse into the same diagrammatic configuration.

The analysis presented here does not imply that diagrammatic systems are universally superior to symbolic ones. Symbolic representations sometimes offer advantages in precision, compositionality, and formal analysis. However, the representational properties of systems such as EGs show that diagrammatic representations can offer distinctive benefits in certain reasoning contexts.

More generally, the present discussion indicates that comparisons between symbolic and diagrammatic reasoning should pay close attention to the representational properties of each system. Such disparities in efficiency may not only stem from visual characteristics but also from underlying structural properties, such as the normalization of equivalent expressions within the representational framework.

5 Conclusion

This paper has examined a structural feature of EGs that helps explain their role in diagrammatic reasoning. We showed that the translation from propositional formulas into alpha EGs is non-injective. This implies that distinct but logically equivalent formulas may correspond to the same diagrammatic representation. Consequently, EGs implicitly perform a form of representational normalization, in which certain equivalence transformations between formulas are absorbed into the representational structure of the diagram.

The concept of representational normalization thus provides a structural explanation for phenomena that have previously been described in terms of transparency or iconicity in diagrammatic reasoning. In particular, it helps clarify Norman's notion of transparency of equivalence, since equivalence relations between formulas can become directly discernible when those formulas are mapped to the same diagram. It also complements Shin's account of multiple readings, showing that the possibility of multiple symbolic interpretations emerges naturally when diagrams represent equivalence classes of formulas.

These considerations suggest the following further points regarding EGs. Although the alpha system formally employs only graphical counterparts of negation and conjunction, diagrams corresponding to disjunction or conditional can be represented as stable structural patterns within the graphical language itself. In pedagogical contexts or practical reasoning, these patterns can be treated as recognizable diagrammatic forms corresponding to familiar connectives, even without introducing additional primitive symbols.

In a broader sense, the analysis suggests that diagrammatic reasoning systems may encode logical structure in a manner that differs fundamentally from symbolic systems. In symbolic logic, equivalence relations between formulas must typically be established through explicit transformations. In EGs, some of these relations are already reflected in the geometry of the diagram itself.

A more systematic comparison between symbolic and diagrammatic reasoning may be facilitated by an understanding such representational properties. Subsequent research may further investigate how these structural features affect proof construction, cognitive accessibility, and the efficiency of reasoning in diagrammatic systems.

References

Charles Sanders Peirce: Collected Papers (CP), vol. 4 (1960)

Bellucci, F., Pietarinen, A.-V.: Existential graphs as an instrument of logical analysis: part 1. Alpha. Rev. Symbolic Logic. **9**(2), 209–237 (2016)

Bellucci, F., Pietarinen, A.-V.: An analysis of existential graphs–part 2: Beta. Synthese. **199**, 7705–7726 (2021)

Shin, S.-J.: The Iconic Logic of Peirce's Graphs. The MIT Press (2002)

Shin, S.-J.: Peirce's alpha graphs and propositional language. Semiotica. **186**(1/4), 333–346 (2011)

Jesse.: Norman, Diagrammatic Reasoning and Propositional Logic. University College London (1999)

Sasaki, T.: Multiple readings of existential graphs. In: Diagrammatic Representation and Inference, vol. 10871, pp. 598–604. Springer, LNAI (2018)

Sasaki, T.: Typical cases showing the efficiency of existential graphs. In: Diagrammatic Representation and Inference, Springer, LNAI, vol. 12169, pp. 494–497 (2020)

Logic Diagrams for Non-monotonic Relationships

Andrew Schumann(✉)

University of Information Technology and Management in Rzeszow, Sucharskiego 2, 35-225 Rzeszow, Poland

andrew.schumann@gmail.com

Abstract. This paper proposes a geometric framework for representing non-monotonic relationships using simplicial complexes. We introduce the notion of a logeme, defined as a fragment of a logical system represented by a simplicial complex derived from a partially ordered structure of semantic relations. Unlike graphs, which encode only pairwise relations, simplicial complexes allow the representation of higher-order dependencies and hierarchical interactions among propositions. This makes them suitable for modeling complex logical fragments that arise in natural language reasoning, knowledge representation, and defeasible inference systems.

Keywords: Simplicial complex · Non-monotonic Reasoning · Collapse

1 Introduction

In this article, we study logic diagrams in the context of synthetic judgments, with particular attention to an even more complex subtype: non-monotonic judgments, i.e., judgments whose semantic structure involves loops or feedback relations. Unlike analytic judgments, which rely on stable relations of conceptual containment, and unlike ordinary synthetic judgments, which can at least be grounded in empirical correlations between sets, non-monotonic judgments do not admit stable denotations in the same way. Their semantic structure may involve circular or self-referential dependencies, where the status of one statement depends on another that, directly or indirectly, depends on the first.

Because of these circular dependencies, such judgments cannot be adequately represented by classical order models, including Hasse diagrams. These models presuppose well-defined sets and stable inclusion or intersection relations. Non-monotonic reasoning, by contrast, requires representational frameworks capable of capturing cyclic dependencies among propositions.

2 Simplicial Complexes as Logic Diagrams

Let us recall that an *abstract simplicial complex* K on a vertex set V is a collection of finite subsets of V satisfying: (i) $\emptyset \in K$ (empty simplex), (ii) if $\sigma \in K$

P. Sobociński et al. (Eds.): Diagrams 2026, LNAI 16833, pp. 85–92, 2027.
https://doi.org/10.1007/978-3-032-34178-5_10

and $\tau \subseteq \sigma$, then $\tau \in K$ (downward closure of simplices). Elements $\sigma \in K$ with their dimensions $\dim(\sigma) := |\sigma| = k + 1$ are called *k-simplices*. The *geometric realization* $|K|$ is the topological space obtained by embedding each k-simplex as a geometric k-simplex in $\mathbb{R}^{|V|}$ and gluing along shared faces.

The simplicial complex allows us to represent any partially ordered set (poset) in a unique way within a topological space. Recall that a poset $(P, \leq)$ consists of a set P equipped with a reflexive, antisymmetric, and transitive relation $\leq$. A *chain* in P is a subset $C \subseteq P$ in which any two elements are comparable:

$$\forall x, y \in C, \quad x \leq y \text{ or } y \leq x.$$

The *order complex* $\Delta(P)$ of a poset P is the abstract simplicial complex defined by

$$\Delta(P) = \{C \subseteq P : C \text{ is a finite chain in } P\},$$

where vertices are elements of P and k-simplices are chains of length $k+1$ (i.e., $x_0 < x_1 < \cdots < x_k$). Hence, simplices of $\Delta(P)$ are identified with the chains in P.

3 Logic Diagrams for Logical Fragments (Logemes)

Let L be a deductive system (e.g., classical propositional logic) with (i) a countable set Form of formulas, (ii) a derivability relation $\vdash_L$ satisfying reflexivity, monotonicity, and transitivity. Define the *Lindenbaum-Tarski poset* $(\mathcal{P}_L, \leq)$ for any fragment $\Gamma \subseteq \mathsf{Form}$, where:

- $\mathcal{P}_L = \Gamma/{\equiv_L}$ is the set of equivalence classes under logical equivalence

$$[\varphi] = \{\psi \colon \varphi \vdash_L \psi \text{ and } \psi \vdash_L \varphi\},$$

- $[\varphi] \leq [\psi]$ iff $\varphi \vdash_L \psi$.

A *logeme* is an abstract simplicial complex that encodes a Lindenbaum-Tarski poset $\mathcal{P}_L = \Gamma/{\equiv_L}$ for the finite logical fragment Γ.[1] Formally, for a finite set of propositions $\Gamma = \{\varphi_1, \ldots, \varphi_n\} \subseteq \mathsf{Form}$, the logeme $\mathcal{L}(\Gamma)$ is defined as follows:

$$\mathcal{L}(\Gamma) := \Delta(\mathcal{P}_L) = \{\sigma \subseteq \mathcal{P}_L \colon \sigma \text{ is a chain under } \leq\}.$$

This is the *order complex* of the poset $\mathcal{P}_L$. Hence, geometrically, $\mathcal{L}(\Gamma)$ is built by gluing together standard geometric shapes according to a single rule: A set of points forms a simplex iff the corresponding logical elements are mutually comparable (form a chain under $\leq$). Here is how each dimension translates:

- *Vertices*: Every element of $\mathcal{P}_L$ becomes a point in space.
- *Edges*: Draw a line between a and b only if $a \leq b$ or $b \leq a$. If a and b are logically independent or incompatible, no edge exists.

[1] For the first time, the logeme was introduced in [5] and formally defined in [6,8].

- *Triangles*: Whenever you have three elements $a \leq b \leq c$, you don't just draw three edges; you *fill in the interior* to make a solid triangle. This happens automatically because transitivity guarantees all three pairwise edges exist.
- *Tetrahedrons & Higher*: Any chain of 4 elements yields a solid tetrahedron; chains of 5 yield 4-simplices, etc. The complex is the union of all such filled shapes, glued along shared faces.

Let us note that incomparable elements never share a simplex. If $a \parallel b$ (neither entails the other), they belong to disjoint parts of the complex or meet only at lower-dimensional faces that don't contain both.

Theorem 1. *Let* $L = \langle \mathsf{Form}, \vdash \rangle$ *be a propositional logic. If L is non-trivial (i.e.,* $[\top] \neq [\bot]$ *in the quotient* $\mathbf{A}_L := \mathsf{Form}/\equiv_L$*), then the Lindenbaum–Tarski algebra* $\mathbf{A}_{\mathcal{L}}$ *forms a non-degenerate logical matrix that verifies L. Moreover, L is strongly complete with respect to this single algebraic model.*

Thus, lattices, and more generally posets, serve as natural algebraic models for logical systems. Their ordered structure provides a semantic framework in which formulas can be interpreted as elements, and logical consequence corresponds to the preservation of order or designated values under valuations. The key reason for using such structures is that they support fundamental meta-logical properties. On the one hand, the existence of a non-trivial poset or lattice model guarantees that the logic is consistent, since not all formulas collapse to a single value. On the other hand, appropriately chosen classes of lattices make it possible to establish completeness, meaning that every semantically valid inference is also derivable within the logic.

If $\mathcal{L}(\Gamma)$ includes $[\top]$ or $[\bot]$, then $\mathcal{L}(\Gamma)$ is contractible to a point and its topology is trivial.

Proposition 1 (Cone Structure from Top Element). If $\mathcal{P}_L$ contains a greatest element $[\top]$, then $\Delta(\mathcal{P}_L)$ is a simplicial cone with apex $[\top]$. Consequently, its geometric realization $|\Delta(\mathcal{P}_L)|$ is contractible to the point $[\top]$.

In the same way we can prove a contractibility to $[\bot]$ if Γ contains $\bot$.

From the given proposition, one may infer that every lattice, including important special cases such as Boolean algebras, Heyting algebras, and MV-algebras, has a trivial homotopical structure in the sense that it can be contracted to a single point.

Theorem 2. *Each lattice (Boolean algebra, Heyting algebra, MV-algebra, etc.) presented as a logeme is contractible.*

Intuitively, this means that, despite their internal algebraic richness, these structures do not exhibit nontrivial "holes" or higher-dimensional features when viewed through a topological or order-theoretic lens. As a consequence, any logical system whose semantics is based on such lattices inherits this contractibility property at the level of its semantic models. In particular, well-known consistent systems, such as classical propositional logic (modeled by Boolean algebras), intuitionistic logic (modeled by Heyting algebras), and various many-valued logics (modeled by MV-algebras), can be regarded, in an appropriate abstract sense, as contractible to a point. This observation shows a certain structural simplicity underlying these logics: although they may differ significantly in expressive power and inferential behavior, their standard algebraic semantics share a common feature of homotopical triviality. In other words, from this perspective, these logical systems do not carry intrinsic higher-order topological complexity, but instead reduce, in a canonical way, to a single, degenerate point.

Theorem 3 (Topological Invariance of Logical Structure). Let T_1 and T_2 be finite theories in deductive systems L_1 and L_2. The geometric realizations of their order complexes are homeomorphic, $|\Delta(\mathcal{P}_{L_1})| \cong_{\text{homeo}} |\Delta(\mathcal{P}_{L_2})|$, if and only if T_1 and T_2 possess equivalent logic diagrams.

4 Logic Diagrams and (Non-)Monotonic Inference

Traditional deductive logics are *monotonic*, and this property can be understood as a form of *informational stability*: once a conclusion has been derived, it remains valid no matter how much additional information is added.

Formally, let L be a formal language and let $\vdash$ be a consequence relation on L. The relation $\vdash$ is monotonic if for all sets of premises $S, S' \subseteq L$,

$$S \subseteq S' \implies \{A \in L : S \vdash A\} \subseteq \{A \in L : S' \vdash A\}. \tag{1}$$

Equivalently, if $S \vdash A$ and $S \subseteq S'$, then $S' \vdash A$.

Non-monotonic reasoning violates it. This kind of reasoning was first introduced in the 1980s, see [2–4]. A consequence relation $\vdash_{\text{nm}}$ is *non-monotonic* if there exist $S \subseteq S'$ and a formula A such that

$$S \vdash_{\text{nm}} A \quad \text{but} \quad S' \nvdash_{\text{nm}} A. \tag{2}$$

Here, the addition of new information may force us to withdraw earlier conclusions. The key intuition is that conclusions are no longer final – they are *defeasible*, i.e., provisional and subject to revision in the light of further evidence [1]. This reflects realistic reasoning in contexts where information is incomplete, uncertain, or evolving.

This shift has a decisive structural consequence: it breaks the algebraic backbone of traditional logic. In monotonic (Tarskian) systems, the consequence relation behaves like a closure operator: it is extensive, idempotent, and monotone. This guarantees that logical equivalence,

$$\varphi \equiv \psi \iff (\varphi \vdash \psi \text{ and } \psi \vdash \varphi),$$

is a *congruence* on the algebra of formulas, i.e., it is preserved under all logical operations. As a result, one can pass to equivalence classes of formulas and construct the Lindenbaum–Tarski algebra, which provides a canonical algebraic semantics (e.g., Boolean algebras, Heyting algebras, MV-algebras). Non-monotonicity disrupts exactly this mechanism. Since the consequence relation is no longer monotone, it fails to define a closure operator, and interderivability ceases to behave well under substitution and composition. Two formulas that are interchangeable in one context may cease to be so when additional premises are introduced. Consequently, logical equivalence is no longer stable and does not form a congruence. Without a congruence, the passage to equivalence classes is ill-defined, and the Lindenbaum–Tarski construction is not possible.

For this reason, non-monotonic logics resist the standard algebraic treatment based on fixed truth values and operations. Their semantics must instead make the *dynamics of information* explicit. We aim to develop a rigorous mathematics for non-monotonic reasoning. These are forms of inference for which lattice-based semantics no longer suffice, because defeasible reasoning naturally generates *topological holes* in the underlying structure. Unlike monotonic systems, where the consequence relation induces a complete, transitive order suitable for lattice representation, non-monotonic inference violates the closure and congruence properties required for algebraic semantics. When exceptions, specificity conflicts, or defeated defaults arise, the poset of propositions ceases to form a coherent lattice; instead, it develops voids that explicitly encode logical tension.

To illustrate, consider the classic defeasible pattern: we initially accept the default rule "birds fly," encoded as a directed entailment Bird $\rightsquigarrow$ Flies. Upon discovering a penguin, we add the specific exception "penguins do not fly," yielding Penguin $\rightsquigarrow$ ¬Flies alongside Penguin $\rightsquigarrow$ Bird. The resulting configuration contains three vertices – Bird, Flies, and ¬Flies – with pairwise defeasible links that cannot be simultaneously realized in a single higher-dimensional simplex. The expected 2-simplex (filled triangle) that would represent the transitive closure Bird $\leq$ Flies $\leq$ ¬Flies is *absent* due to logical conflict. Topologically, this absence creates a *hole*: a 1-cycle formed by the three edges that is not the boundary of any 2-face, corresponding to a non-trivial element in the first reduced homology group $\tilde{H}_1$. Consequently, the implication "if A is a bird, then A flies" can no longer be maintained as a global entailment; it becomes locally valid but globally defeated.

Let $\Delta(\mathcal{P}_L)$ be a simplicial complex modeling a fragment $\Phi \subseteq \mathsf{Form}$ of a logical system L and $\Delta(\mathcal{P}'_L)$ be a simplicial complex modeling a subfragment $\Phi' \subseteq \Phi$. The guiding idea is that logical structure can be encoded geometrically so that inference corresponds to movement within a combinatorial-topological object rather than manipulation of purely symbolic expressions. For more detail about this idea see [7].

We assume that $\Delta(\mathcal{P}_L)$ is a complex, where:

- Vertices represent semantic interpretations $[\varphi]$ (or equivalence classes) of formulas $\varphi \in \Phi$.
- n-simplices encode nested deductions

$$(\psi_n \vdash_L \psi_{n-1}) \wedge \cdots \wedge (\psi_1 \vdash_L \psi_0),$$

  that is, totally ordered chains.
- A simplicial collapse $\Delta(\mathcal{P}_L) \searrow \Delta(\mathcal{P}'_L)$ represents a logical simplification: the logeme $\mathcal{L}(\Phi)$ is reduced to a subsystem $\mathcal{L}(\Phi')$ while preserving essential derivability relations.

Let us recall the definition of simplicial collapse $\Delta(\mathcal{P}_L) \searrow \Delta(\mathcal{P}'_L)$. A simplex $\tau \in K$ is a *free face* if it is a proper face of exactly one simplex $\sigma \in K$ with $\dim(\sigma) = \dim(\tau) + 1$. An *elementary collapse* removes the pair (σ, τ): $K \searrow K \setminus \{\sigma, \tau\}$.

Two complexes K and L are *simple-homotopy equivalent* if K can be transformed into L by a finite sequence of elementary collapses and their inverses (elementary expansions).

Let $\Gamma \subseteq \Phi$. We write $\Gamma \vdash_L \phi$ in $\mathcal{L}(\Phi)$ whenever there exists a loop-free (acyclic) path in $\mathcal{L}(\Phi)$ from the vertices corresponding to the premises Γ to the vertex corresponding to ϕ, where each edge or higher-dimensional simplex represents a valid inference step. In this interpretation, logical consequence becomes a path-existence property, and proof theory acquires a geometric realization.

A consequence relation is said to be

- *Monotonic* if $\Gamma \vdash_L \phi$ in $\mathcal{L}(\Phi') \implies \Gamma \cup \{\psi\} \vdash_L \phi$ in $\mathcal{L}(\Phi)$ for every added premise ψ, such that $[\psi] \in \mathcal{L}(\Phi)$, but $[\psi] \notin \mathcal{L}(\Phi')$ and $\mathcal{L}(\Phi') \subset \mathcal{L}(\Phi)$, i.e., enlarging the premise set never destroys existing paths.
- *Non-monotonic* if the addition of information may invalidate a prior conclusion: $\Gamma \vdash_L \phi$ in $\mathcal{L}(\Phi')$ but $\Gamma \cup \{\psi\} \nvdash_L \phi$ in $\mathcal{L}(\Phi)$, where $\mathcal{L}(\Phi') \subset \mathcal{L}(\Phi)$.

Proposition 2 (Monotonic Inference under Collapse, see [7]). If $\mathcal{L}(\Phi) \searrow \mathcal{L}(\Phi')$, then inference in $\mathcal{L}(\Phi)$ is monotonic in the sense that

$$\Gamma \vdash_L \phi \text{ in } \mathcal{L}(\Phi') \quad \Longrightarrow \quad \Gamma \cup \{\psi\} \vdash_L \phi \text{ in } \mathcal{L}(\Phi) \quad \text{for every } \psi.$$

such that $[\psi] \in \mathcal{L}(\Phi)$, but $[\psi] \notin \mathcal{L}(\Phi')$

Corollary 1 (Criterion for Non-Monotonicity). If $\Gamma \vdash_L \phi$ in $\mathcal{L}(\Phi')$ but $\Gamma \cup \{\psi\} \nvdash_L \phi$ in $\mathcal{L}(\Phi)$, then $\mathcal{L}(\Phi)$ cannot simplicially collapse to $\mathcal{L}(\Phi')$. Geometrically, the added information introduces a non-trivial cycle (hole) or obstruction that disrupts the original acyclic derivation path.

Corollary 2 (Boolean Algebras). Let B be a Boolean algebra and $K(B)$ its geometric realization via the order complex. Then inference in $K(B)$ is monotonic. Boolean lattices contain no topological obstructions that would invalidate existing inclusion chains when new elements are added; additional vertices only extend the lattice upward or downward without destroying previous relations.

According to these statements, *loops and higher-dimensional holes* become visual and topological indicators of non-monotonic behavior:

- A contractible region corresponds to stable, monotonic inference.
- A non-contractible cycle (hole) signals that additional information may override or invalidate previous conclusions.
- Missing faces represent higher-order inconsistencies or blocked derivations.

Let us consider an example of non-monotonic reasoning. Assume that we start with the chain Eagle $\vdash_S$ Bird $\vdash_S$ Flies. In the simplicial representation, these three terms form a 2-simplex (a filled triangle), expressing the transitive relation that an eagle is a bird and that birds fly. This simplex is contractible, i.e., it can collapse to a vertex (point). Now, let us introduce an additional vertex Penguin. Empirically, penguins are birds, but they do not fly. To represent this information, we add the relations Penguin $\vdash_S$ Bird and Penguin $\vdash_S$ not-Flies. Consequently, the vertex not-Flies must also be included in the complex. This addition creates a conflict with the previously assumed rule that birds fly. As a result, the complex contains the loop or hole that cannot be presented as a poset

$$\text{Bird} \longrightarrow \text{Flies} \longrightarrow \text{not-Flies} \longrightarrow \text{Bird},$$

which reflects the fact that within the fragment under consideration, birds are associated both with flying (as in the case of eagles) and with not flying (as in the case of penguins); see Fig. 1. It cannot collapse to a point.

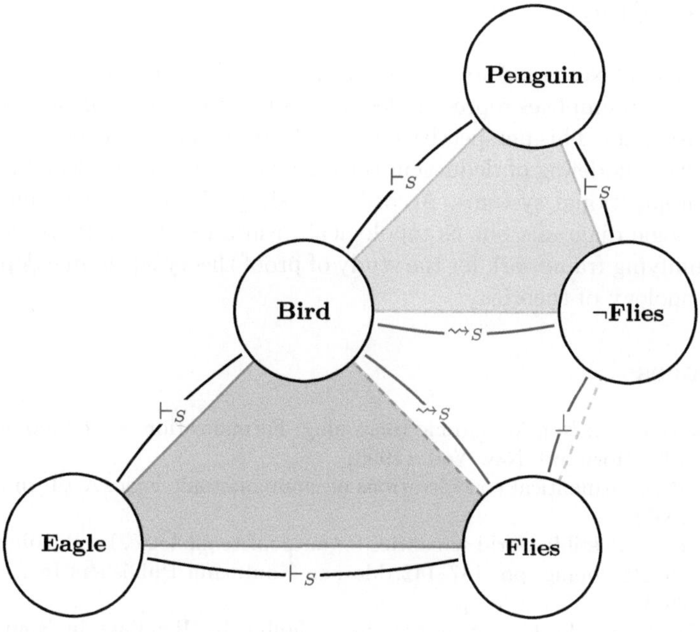

Fig. 1. Simplicial complex containing a loop: Bird $\longleftrightarrow$ Flies $\longleftrightarrow$ not-Flies.

Thus, the key feature of the structure is the *absence of a 2-simplex* on the vertices {Bird, Flies, ¬Flies}. Although there are edges connecting these vertices, the triangle is not filled. Topologically, this creates a *hole* (a non-trivial 1-cycle). This hole has a precise logical meaning: from Bird, one can defeasibly infer Flies, but also, via subclasses, ¬Flies is possible; hence no uniform conclusion can be drawn at the level of Bird alone. Thus, the inference Bird $\vdash$ Flies is *not stable under extension of information.* It is blocked by the presence of exceptions. The ambiguity induced by the hole is resolved not globally, but *locally*, by passing to coherent sub-simplices. The simplex {Eagle, Bird, Flies} represents a consistent context in which the default rule applies. Here, Eagle $\vdash$ Flies. The simplex {Penguin, Bird, $\neg$Flies} represents an exceptional context in which the default is overridden. Here, Penguin $\vdash \neg$Flies. Each triangle is internally consistent, but they cannot be merged into a single global simplex without contradiction.

This structure directly exhibits non-monotonic reasoning: Bird $\vdash_{\mathrm{nm}}$ Flies, but {Bird, Penguin} $\nvdash_{\mathrm{nm}}$ Flies. The addition of the premise Penguin invalidates the earlier conclusion. Thus, inference is *defeasible* and *context-dependent.* This example shows that non-monotonicity can be understood geometrically as the *failure of simplicial closure.* The presence of holes prevents the formation of global models and forces reasoning to proceed via compatible local contexts. In this sense, defeasibility is not an external feature of reasoning, but an intrinsic topological property of the underlying knowledge structure.

5 Conclusion

Simplicial complexes translate logical consistency into the language of algebraic topology, where simplices represent deductions and topological invariants encode global constraints. This perspective enables the detection of inconsistency cycles, the geometric modeling of deduction through collapse, and the scalable analysis of large propositional systems. Accordingly, simplicial complexes function not merely as logic diagrams but as topological invariants of logical structure, providing a unifying framework for the study of proof theory, epistemic dependency, and the topology of theories.

References

1. Łukaszewicz, W.: Non-Monotonic Reasoning: Formalization of Commonsense Reasoning. Ellis Horwood, New York (1990)
2. Moore, R.C.: Semantical considerations on nonmonotonic logic. Artif. Intell. **25**(1), 75–94 (1985)
3. Moore, R.C.: Possible-world semantics for autoepistemic logic. In: Readings in Nonmonotonic Reasoning, pp. 137–142. Morgan Kaufmann Publishers Inc., San Francisco (1987)
4. Riter, R., Criscuolo, G.: On interacting defaults. In: Readings in Nonmonotonic Reasoning, pp. 94–100. Morgan Kaufmann Publishers Inc., San Francisco (1987)
5. Schumann, A.: Archaeology of Logic. Taylor & Francis Group, London (2023)
6. Schumann, A.: Mozi's square of opposition and logemes as new logical approach. In: Lemanski, J., Johansen, M.W., Manalo, E., Viana, P., Bhattacharjee, R., Burns, R. (eds.) DIAGRAMS 2024, LNCS, vol. 14981, pp. 251–266. Springer, Cham (2024). https://doi.org/10.1007/978-3-031-71291-3_20
7. Schumann, A.: Logemes instead of logics. Synthese **207**(98) (2026)
8. Schumann, A., Gabbay, D., Król, J.: Logemes as a new approach to metalogic. Logic J. IGPL **34**(3) (2026)

Categorial Grammar and Existential Graphs

Nathan Haydon(✉)

University of Waterloo, Waterloo, ON, Canada
nhaydon@uwaterloo.ca

Abstract. Charles Peirce studied residuation and the linear negation laws in his early algebraic studies in the logic of relations. We demonstrate here that the Existential Graphs offer a concise, topological presentation of the residuation equivalences in terms of cyclic permutations inside the 'scroll.' We develop this direction by comparing to more recent geometric presentations of the laws of categorial grammar by Abrusci and Casadio, as well as a comparison to Cockett et al.'s circuit diagrams.

Keywords: Existential Graphs · Categorial Grammar · Residuation · Cyclic Linear Logic

1 Introduction

The *Neo-Peircean Calculus of Relations* provides a modern categorical presentation of the logic of relations found in Pierce's 'Note B' [7,19]. Following Peirce's original presentation, the calculus employs relational composition (;) and its De Morgan dual, which Peirce calls relative sum (†), along with linear distributivity and the corresponding linear negation laws.

A key feature of the Neo-Peircean Calculus is the presence of residuation, for which we list the well known residuation equivalences in Eq. 1.

$$R \leq T \dagger \breve{\bar{S}} \quad \text{iff} \quad R ; S \leq T \quad \text{iff} \quad S \leq \breve{\bar{R}} \dagger T \tag{1}$$

Note that relational composition appears on the left of the inclusion, with the dual relative sum appearing on the right. Also note that the combined complement-converse relation $(\breve{\bar{-}})$, which we will suggestively refer to as the *linear negation* or $(-)^{\perp}$, features prominently.[1] In fact, given the importance of linear distributivity, linear negation, and residuation to the multiplicative fragment of linear logic, the calculus has much in common with *classical linear logic* [10].

Peirce went on to give a concise rule for generating the residuation equivalences above (and more):

[1] Residuation takes the form of a division-like operation for relational composition. We can rewrite the residuals in Eq. 1 as the (perhaps) more well known $T \dagger S^{\perp} = T \,/\, S$ and $R^{\perp} \dagger T = R \setminus T$. We can also write $R \dagger S = (S^{\perp} \,;\, R^{\perp})^{\perp}$ (though the equivalent De Morgan dual with complement, $\overline{(\bar{R} \,;\, \bar{S})}$, is perhaps again more common).

P. Sobociński et al. (Eds.): Diagrams 2026, LNAI 16833, pp. 93–101, 2027.
https://doi.org/10.1007/978-3-032-34178-5_11

> "Hence the rule is that having a formula of the form $[R; S \leq T]$, the three letters may be cyclically advanced one place in the order of writing, those which are carried from one side of the copula to the other being both negatived and converted." [CP 3.341]

The rule above is an instance of the more well-known rule in sequent calculus presentations of linear logic that a term can be moved to the other side of the sequent so long as it is linearly negated.

While more emphasis has been placed in linear logic on the commutative case, the rule above specifically preserves cyclic order. These cyclic rules have a history throughout the development of linear logic—see [11,15,21]—and most notably arise in the discussion of non-commutative linear logic.

The cyclic rule suggests the need for a corresponding cyclic representation of the sequents, and yet the author knows of only a few—see, for example, Yetter's original presentation in [21, p. 52] and Blute and Scott's [6, p. 1424]—that have fully embraced cyclicity in an iconic way.

And yet residuation in the *Neo-Peircean Calculus* also takes on a topological flavor. Every inequation in the calculus can be rewritten in the form of Peirce's 'scroll' (see specifically Lemma 6.6 in [7]), allowing a shorthand route for representing cyclic equivalences in the Existential Graphs.

Perhaps the most notable application of the logic of residuation is Lambek's categorial grammar [14–16]. Following Abrusci, the laws for categorial grammar and the logic of residuation can be expressed in non-commutative multiplicative (cyclic) linear logic [1–3] Abrusci and Casadio have recently given certain geometric depictions to these laws [4,5] and it is these geometric representations that we use as comparison to Peirce's Existential Graphs. As the residuation equivalences are captured by one and the same graph (with simple topological deformations), we demonstrate here that the laws of categorial grammar are likewise easily presented in the Existential Graphs.

In Sect. 2 we give a background on the *Neo-Peircean Calculus* and using the 'scroll' to represent residuation. Section 3 demonstrates some simple laws from categorial grammar depicted in the graphs. Throughout, we mean this presentation to be a demonstration of the diagrammatic advantages of Peirce's Existential Graphs applied to the laws of categorial grammar.

Peirce recognized the composition of 'scrolls' in varying examples. We pave the way for future connections to proof nets and circuit diagrams in this setting by demonstrating 'scroll'-composition as (planar) polycategorical composition [8,10], giving depiction to Peirce's term *fusion*.

2 Residuation in Existential Graphs

We give a brief overview of the syntax of the Neo-Peircean Calculus and Peirce's Existential Graphs. A binary relation, xRy, is represented as a 'box' with an ingoing and outgoing wire for the domain and codomain (the forward 'notch' signally the left-to-right reading). Relational composition—defined verbosely as a relation from x to y, such that $\exists z(xRz \wedge zSy)$—is here absorbed by simply connecting an outgoing wire with an ingoing wire of another relation. Relative sum, as De Morgan dual, changes the quantifier and connective so that $R \dagger S$ is a relation from x to y, such that $\forall z(xRz \vee zSy)$. The converse relation has a 'notch' cut-out on the opposite corner, now to be read yRx[2]. We can now combine the features for the residual: S/R is a relation from x to y, such that $\forall z(yRz \Rightarrow xSz)$[3]. Finally, relational inclusion ($\leq$) is given by a 'scroll' with the antecedent on the once-enclosed section, and the consequent in the doubly enclosed section (Fig. 1).[4]

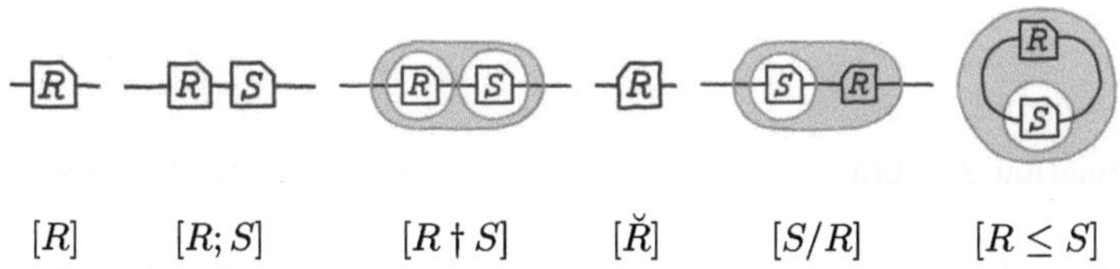

Fig. 1. Summary of relational operations in the NPR calculus

Returning to the residuation equivalences in Eq. 1, we give a sample derivation of left-most 'iff' in Fig. 2. The left column (a) uses the more well-known notation from relation algebra. The middle column (b) shows the same derivation in the Neo-Peircean Calculus. The right column (c) shows a graph of the inclusion $[R\,; S \leq T]$ and how one can show the equivalence more directly via a topological rearrangement inside the 'scroll.' In this setting, one imagines grabbing the 'S' and moving it around and down—like moving 'S' from the back of an '8-ball' around to the front—so that it induces a converse operation.[5] Similar derivations can be given for the other directions of the inclusion in Eq. 1.[6]

Another direction can be given by symmetry where a term in the †-context can be moved around and up to the antecedent side of the inclusion. Following Moortgat, we call this dual operation *coresiduation.* These operations feature prominently in what is called *bilinear logic* [10,15]. Figure 3 offers a shorthand notation for representing residuation and coresiduation via rotations inside the

2 One could rotate the wires around as in , but we find the notch removes the burden of extra bent wires.

3 We note that adding a 'scroll' around the $\breve{R}$ makes explicit the definition of residuation in terms of the †-context, i.e. $S \dagger \bar{\breve{R}}$ = .

4 A lengthier introduction in relation to Peirce's work can be found in [13].

5 The equivalence follows directly from topologically bending the wires in the original presentation in [12]. Here, we again use the 'notch' notation to omit the bending of wires.

6 Peirce's awareness of cyclicity in another instance seems to lead him as far back as 1882 towards presenting a two-dimensional graphical syntax. This suggests cyclicity perhaps played a role in the development of the later Existential Graphs. See discussion in [20, p. 18–19].

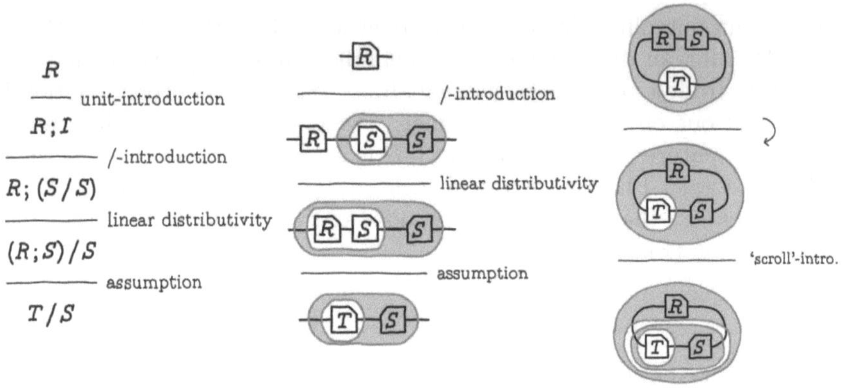

(a) Relation Algebra (b) NPR Calculus (c) Peirce's 'Scroll'

Fig. 2. Three depictions of the residuation equivalence: If $R;S \leq T$ then $R \leq T \dagger \bar{\breve{S}}$

'scroll'.[7] These moves make clear the overall preservation of the cyclic order.[8] Each introduction rule can correspondingly be undone, an act which we will simply refer to as *un*-residuation.

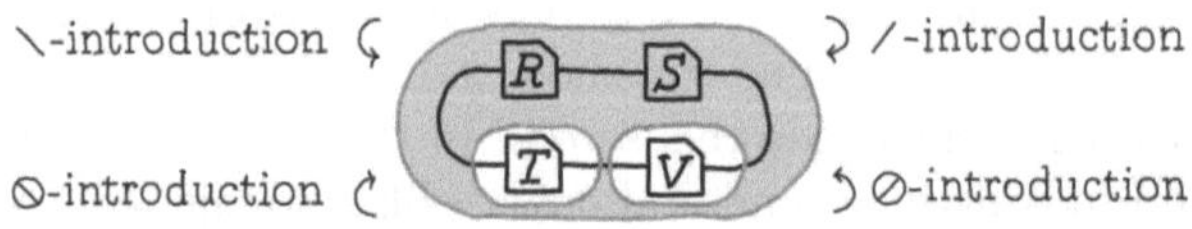

Fig. 3. Bilinear operations inside the 'scroll' for the inclusion: $R;S \leq T \dagger V$

Categorial grammar is the logic of residuation. In the next two sections we demonstrate the graphical advantages of the Existential Graphs applied to the basic laws of categorial grammar. The logic of residuation allows a large number of equivalent expressions. In Sect. 3 we show how the Existential Graphs and the bilinear operations in the 'scroll' allow a straightforward depiction of these equivalences.

3 Laws of Categorial Grammar in Existential Graphs

Following Abrsuci's work in [1,3] the derivable sequents and equivalencies in categorial grammar can be captured in the non-commutative multiplicative (cyclic) fragment of linear logic.

---

[7] This is also the setting for the *logic of generalized relations* given by Cockett et al. in [9] and in [8, Section 4].

[8] In the Neo-Peircean Calculus in [7] this is partly presented in Lemma 6.6.

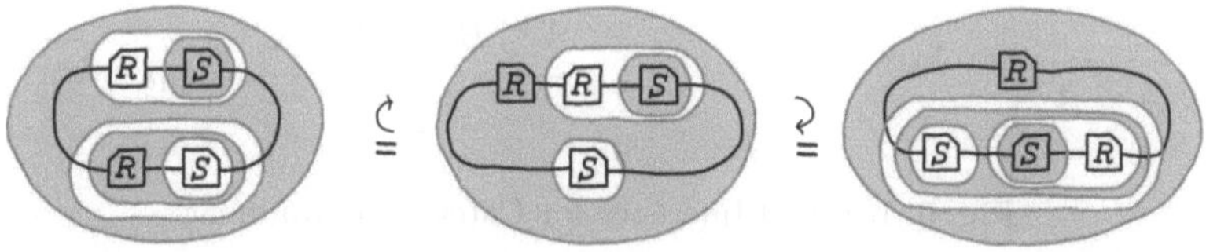

$R\backslash S \leq R\backslash S$ $\qquad$ $R;(R\backslash S) \leq S$ $\qquad$ $R \leq (S\backslash(R\backslash S))$

(a) Tautology ($id_{R\backslash S}$) (b) Application Law (c) Type-Raising Law

Fig. 4. Laws of categorial grammar following from residuation equivalences on $id_{R\backslash S}$

Given the graphical depiction in Existential Graphs in the last section, we turn to show these equivalences here. As an example, we show how a simple tautology with the residual (i.e. $R\backslash S \leq R\backslash S$, which we write suggestively as $id_{R\backslash S}$) yields a corresponding modus ponens rule for its elimination (an Application Law) and a further residuation introduction (a Type-Raising Law). These are shown in Fig. 4. We show another example of the Expansion Law in Fig. 5.

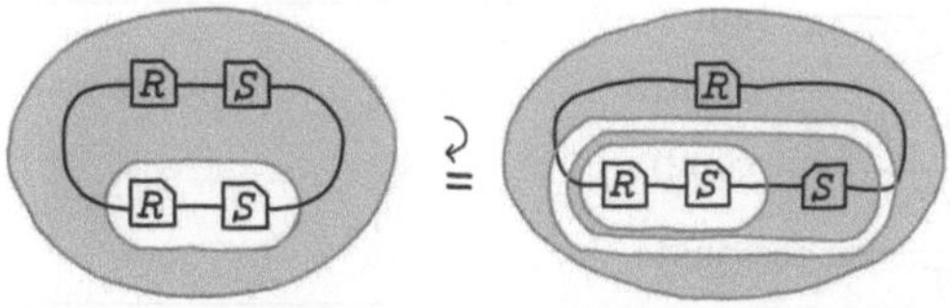

$R;S \leq R;S$ $\qquad$ $R \leq (R;S)\,/\,S$

(a) Tautology $id_{R\,;\,S}$ (b) Expansion Law

Fig. 5. Law of categorial grammar following from a residuation equivalence on $id_{R\,;\,S}$

Abrusci and Casadio arrive at these results by giving the various equivalences that come from translating a correct proof net [4,5]. Given a well-formed proof net, adding residuation-introduction or making explicit the De Morgan dual in the output does not change the meaning of the proof net. We go one step farther here, and show that these equivalences can be captured diagrammatically by the various rotations inside the 'scroll.'

4 Composition of 'Scrolls'

We turn now to the inference rules, for which we only add reflexivity and transitivity of the inclusion (see Fig. 6).

$$\dfrac{}{A \leq A}\ \text{tautology} \qquad\qquad \dfrac{A \leq B \qquad B \leq C}{A \leq C}\ \text{composition}$$

Fig. 6. Rules of Inference for Categorial Grammar

Certain derived rules become important. Following Lambek [15], we give as an example the derivation of a Monotonicity Law in Fig. 7. As a comparison we give the Peircean version in the right column using the 'scroll' notation.[9] As argued in Sect. 3 above, the residuation equivalences are nicely captured by rotations inside the 'scroll'. Transitivity of inclusion in this setting amounts to what we will call 'scroll'-composition. It corresponds to the cut-rule in the sense of proof theory.

$$\dfrac{\dfrac{R \leq S \qquad \dfrac{\dfrac{}{S;T \leq S;T}\ \text{taut.}}{S \leq (S;T)/T}\ \text{/-intro.}}{R \leq (S;T)/T}\ \text{comp.}}{R;T \leq S;T}\ \text{un-residuate}$$

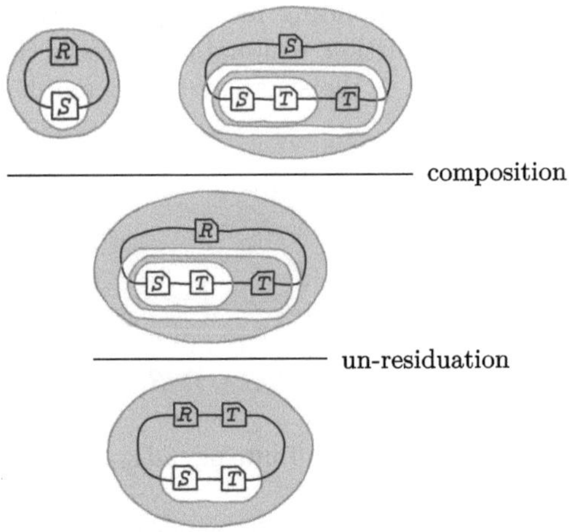

Fig. 7. Derivation of a Monotonicity Law

We find a number of examples where Peirce emphasizes 'scroll'-composition. Some of the examples in his early algebraic work in 'Note B' [19, see p. 195–198] focus specifically on the various compositions of residuals with relative sum. Of interest to us (and the cyclic case discussed above), is that the 'scroll' can be given a corresponding two-dimensional treatment. One such example is when Peirce derives the transitivity of residuation in [18, p. 305–307].

[9] The upper right graph starts with the expansion from Fig. 5 instead of the tautology $id_{S\,;\,T}$.

In a number of locations Peirce refers to 'scroll'-composition as *fusion*. We give an example of fusion in the composition of dyadic relations in Fig. 8 (the example is taken from [17, p. 281]). Note how Peirce intentionally squares the end of each 'scroll' to emphasize the fusing process.

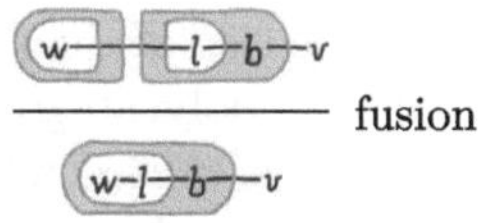

Fig. 8. Fusion of dyadic 'scrolls'

Peirce acknowledges that the inference in Fig. 8 follows from a simple application of linear distributivity. Peirce nonetheless develops the operation further—referring to it as a "derived rule" in [17, p. 240]—and goes on to extend it to more complicated 'scrolls'. Here is Peirce describing the operation in [17, p. 344]:

> Under even enclosures any two pairs of ovals, each consisting of one oval in another, but not usually the sole contents of that other, may be fused, by breaking all the ovals and uniting the two inner into one and the two outer into one [...]

Stated this way, where the 'scrolls' have corresponding elements in their antecedent parts, fusion tends to consist in two applications of linear distributivity—once for each of the two sides to be fused—and then a 'scroll' elimination over the middle term.

Perhaps the most notable example of fusion occurs in [17, p. 346] and is reproduced in Fig. 9. Here fusion brings together two 'scrolls' in a manner that preserves their antecedent parts. Of further interest here, is that fusion is followed by a linear negation where the middle term is eliminated. This is the 'cut' operation from proof theory [8].

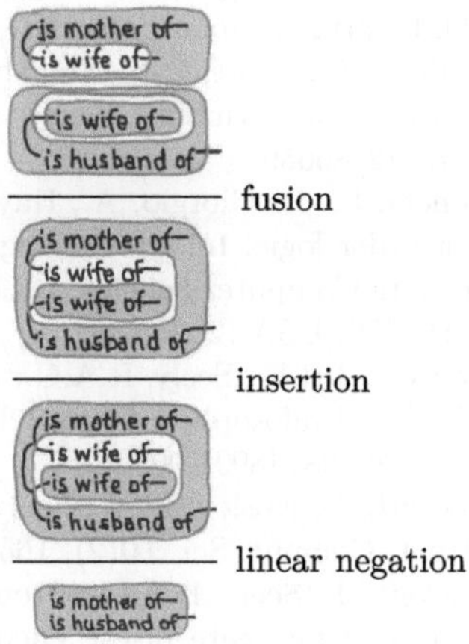

Fig. 9. Composition of 'scrolls'

Returning to categorial grammar, the 'scroll'-composition sought in the derivation of monotonicity in the upper right of Fig. 7 can be performed via the same moves demonstrated in Fig. 9. Both cases follow from the same strategy: use linear distributivity followed by linear negation to perform composition of 'scrolls' (or 'cut' in the sense of proof theory). We conclude that Peirce understood this setting.

Peirce understood residuation and the various residuation equivalences, and he understood 'scroll' composition. Combining these approaches leads to a diagrammatic alternative to presenting the laws of categorial grammar. One can scribe tautological inclusions using 'scrolls', performing cyclic permutations corresponding to the residuation (and co-residuation) equivalences, and perform analogous 'cuts' in the sense of proof theory via 'scroll'-composition. Such scrolls—see Fig. 3—employ a list of relationally composed terms in the antecedent and a list of dually composed terms in the consequent. This is the setting of (planar) polycategorical composition given by Cockett and Seely [8,10] for the *logic of generalized relations*, suggesting future connections between the Existential Graphs and proof theory.

References

1. Abrusci, V.M.: Non-commutative intuitionistic linear logic. Math. Log. Q. **36**(4), 297–318 (1990). https://doi.org/10.1002/malq.19900360405
2. Abrusci, V.M.: Phase semantics and sequent calculus for pure noncommutative classical linear propositional logic. J. Symbolic Logic **56**(4), 1403–1451 (1991). https://doi.org/10.2307/2275485
3. Abrusci, V.M.: On residuation. In: Casadio, C., Coecke, B., Moortgat, M., Scott, P. (eds.) Categories and Types in Logic, Language, and Physics. LNCS, vol. 8222, pp. 14–27. Springer, Heidelberg (2014). https://doi.org/10.1007/978-3-642-54789-8_2
4. Abrusci, V.M., Casadio, C.: A geometrical representation of the basic laws of categorial grammar. Studia Logica Int. J. Symbolic Logic **105**(3), 479–520 (2017). http://www.jstor.org/stable/45103018
5. Abrusci, V.M., Casadio, C.: Lambek's syntactic calculus and noncommutative variants of linear logic: laws and proof-nets. In: Joachim Lambek: The Interplay of Mathematics, Logic, and Linguistics. OCL, vol. 20, pp. 1–37. Springer, Cham (2021). https://doi.org/10.1007/978-3-030-66545-6_1
6. Blute, R.F., Scott, P.J.: The shuffle hopf algebra and noncommutative full completeness. J. Symbolic Logic **63**(4), 1413–1436 (1998). http://www.jstor.org/stable/2586659
7. Bonchi, F., Di Giorgio, A., Haydon, N., Sobocinski, P.: Diagrammatic algebra of first order logic. In: Proceedings of the 39th Annual ACM/IEEE Symposium on Logic in Computer Science, LICS '24. Association for Computing Machinery, New York, NY, USA (2024). https://doi.org/10.1145/3661814.3662078
8. Cockett, J.R.B., Seely, R.A.G.: Proof theory of the cut rule. In: Categories for the Working Philosopher. Oxford University Press (2017). https://doi.org/10.1093/oso/9780198748991.003.0010
9. Cockett, J., Koslowski, J., Seely, R.A.: Introduction to linear bicategories. Math. Struct. Comput. Sci. **10**(2), 165–203 (2000)
10. Cockett, J., Seely, R.A.G.: Proof theory for full intuitionistic linear logic, bilinear logic, and mix categories. Theory Appl. Categories **3**(5), 85–131 (1997). http://www.tac.mta.ca/tac//volumes/1997/n5/n5.pdf
11. Gianantonio, P.: Structures for multiplicative cyclic linear logic: deepness vs cyclicity. In: Marcinkowski, J., Tarlecki, A. (eds.) CSL 2004. LNCS, vol. 3210, pp. 130–144. Springer, Heidelberg (2004). https://doi.org/10.1007/978-3-540-30124-0_13
12. Haydon, N., Pietarinen, A.-V.: Residuation in existential graphs. In: Basu, A., Stapleton, G., Linker, S., Legg, C., Manalo, E., Viana, P. (eds.) Diagrams 2021. LNCS (LNAI), vol. 12909, pp. 229–237. Springer, Cham (2021). https://doi.org/10.1007/978-3-030-86062-2_21
13. Haydon, N., Sobociński, P.: Compositional diagrammatic first-order logic. In: Pietarinen, A.-V., Chapman, P., Bosveld-de Smet, L., Giardino, V., Corter, J., Linker, S. (eds.) Diagrams 2020. LNCS (LNAI), vol. 12169, pp. 402–418. Springer, Cham (2020). https://doi.org/10.1007/978-3-030-54249-8_32

14. Lambek, J.: The mathematics of sentence structure. Am. Math. Mon. **65**(3), 154–170 (1958)
15. Lambek, J.: From categorial grammar to bilinear logic. In: Heister, P.S., Došen, K. (eds.) Substructural Logics, chap. 8, pp. 207–238. Oxford University Press (1991)
16. Moortgat, M.: Symmetries in natural language syntax and semantics: the Lambek-Grishin calculus. In: Leivant, D., de Queiroz, R. (eds.) WoLLIC 2007. LNCS, vol. 4576, pp. 264–284. Springer, Heidelberg (2007). https://doi.org/10.1007/978-3-540-73445-1_19
17. Peirce, C.S.: The Logic of the Future: History and Applications, vol. 1. De Gruyter, Berlin, Boston (2020). https://doi.org/10.1515/9783110651409
18. Peirce, C.S.: The Logic of the Future: The 1903 Lowell Lectures, vol. 2/2. De Gruyter (2021). https://doi.org/10.1515/9783110740462
19. Peirce, C.S.: Studies in logic. By Members of the Johns Hopkins University. Little, Brown, and Company (1883)
20. Roberts, D.D.: The Existential Graphs of Charles S. Peirce, De Gruyter Mouton (1973)
21. Yetter, D.N.: Quantales and (noncommutative) linear logic. J. Symbolic Logic **55**(1), 41–64 (1990). https://doi.org/10.2307/2274953

A Magic Aristotelian Cube

J.-Martín Castro-Manzano[1,2(✉)]

[1] UPAEP University, Puebla Pue 72430, Mexico
josemartin.castro@upaep.mx
[2] Consejo de Ciencia y Tecnología del Estado de Puebla, Puebla Pue 72430, Mexico

Abstract. In this contribution we offer an embedding of the Aristotelian square into a $3 \times 3 \times 3$ Rubik's cube in order to obtain a magic Aristotelian cube. This embedding allows us to reinterpret the Aristotelian square not as a single diagram, but as a family of mechanically generated realizations, so that logical geometry becomes logical mechanics, so to speak.

Keywords: Rubik's Cube · Aristotelian square · Logical geometry

1 Introduction

We like logical geometry and we fancy mechanical puzzles. In particular, we enjoy logical structures, such as the Aristotelian square, and we take our time toying with Rubiks' cubes. Naturally, we ask ourselves: how could we enjoy our time even more? To answer this question, in this contribution we offer an embedding of the Aristotelian square into a $3 \times 3 \times 3$ Rubik's cube in order to obtain what we call a magic Aristotelian cube. This embedding allows us to reinterpret the Aristotelian square not as a single diagram but as a family of mechanically generated realizations, so that logical geometry becomes logical mechanics, so to speak: this is something that, to the best of our knowledge, has not been done before.

2 Preliminaries

The *Aristotelian square* is a traditional diagrammatic device used to represent logical relations among four categorical statements: the universal affirmative (A: *All S are P*), the universal negative (E: *No S are P*), the particular affirmative (I: *Some S are P*), and the particular negative (O: *Some S are not P*). These four statements are located at the corners of a square in such a way that certain logical relations are made visually explicit. The relations encoded in the square are the following: A and O, as well as E and I, stand in *contradiction* (they cannot both be true and cannot both be false); A and E are *contraries* (they cannot both be true, but may both be false); I and O are *subcontraries* (they cannot both be false, but may both be true); and finally, A stands in *subalternation* to I,

P. Sobociński et al. (Eds.): Diagrams 2026, LNAI 16833, pp. 102–105, 2027.
https://doi.org/10.1007/978-3-032-34178-5_12

and E to O, meaning that truth flows downward from universal to particular, while falsity flows upward. The square thus provides a geometric representation of basic inferential constraints among categorical statements [1]. Typically, we represent this device as in Fig. 1a.

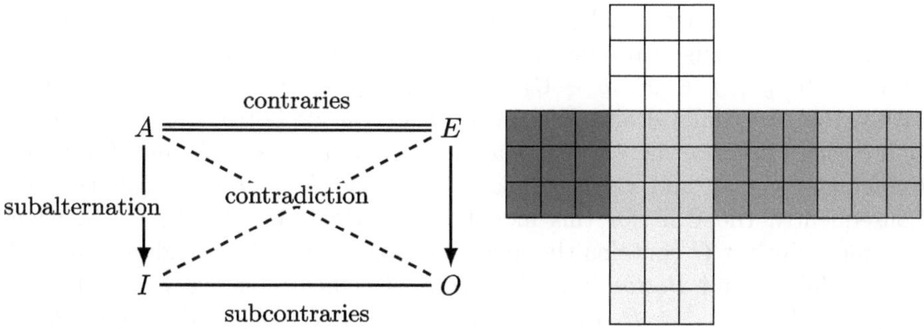

(a) The Aristotelian square. (b) $3 \times 3 \times 3$ cube schema.

Fig. 1. Structures.

The *Rubik's Cube* —originally named the Magic Cube— was invented in 1974 by the Hungarian architect and professor Ernő Rubik [2]. It has been listed among the most influential inventions of the twentieth century and is widely regarded as the world's best-selling toy [3] —although its underlying concept resonates with older traditions, such as the Chinese *Luoshu* (Luo Book) and the *Jiugong* (nine-palace) diagrams, which encode numerical and spatial symmetries that later inspired rearrangement puzzles during the Yuan Dynasty [5]. The standard $3 \times 3 \times 3$ Rubik's Cube has six faces, each subdivided into nine facelets, yielding a total of 54 visible facelets (Fig. 1b).

A *constraint satisfaction problem* (CSP) is a triple $\langle V, D, C \rangle$ where V is a finite set of variables, D is a finite domain of values, and C is a set of constraints restricting the admissible joint assignments of values to variables. Once we define a CSP, its solution is a total assignment satisfying all constraints in C [4]. Typical examples include Sudoku (each cell must contain a number from 1 to 9, with no repetitions in rows, columns, or grids), the Eight Queens Puzzle (place eight queens on a chessboard so that no two queens threaten each other), and map coloring (assign colors to regions on a planar map such that adjacent regions do not share the same color).

3 A Magic Aristotelian Cube

Now let us model a magic Aristotelian cube using a CSP on a $3 \times 3 \times 3$ cube with six faces $\mathcal{F} = \{U, D, L, R, F, B\}$ (for up, down, left, right, front, and back). Each face is a 3×3 grid of facelets (or positions) $\mathcal{P}_3 = \{(i, j) \mid i, j \in \{0, 1, 2\}\}$, from which we distinguish the corners ($\mathcal{C}$), edges ($\mathcal{E}$), and the center ($\mathcal{K}$) as follows: $\mathcal{C} = \{(0,0),(0,2),(2,0),(2,2)\}, \mathcal{E} = \{(0,1),(1,0),(1,2),(2,1)\}, \mathcal{K} = \{(1,1)\}$. Then we define the domains: for the corners, we use the set of categorical statements $D_4 = \{A,E,I,O\}$; for the edges, we use the set of glyphs $D_R = \{\downarrow, \Leftrightarrow, \leftrightarrow\}$; and for the center, we let a fixed marker $\times$ so that its domain is $\{\times\}$. So, for every face $f \in \mathcal{F}$: for each corner position $p \in \mathcal{C}$, we introduce a corner-variable $c_{f,p} \in D_4$; and for each edge position $p \in \mathcal{E}$, we introduce an edge-variable $r_{f,p} \in D_R$. Consequently, the full variable set is: $V = \{c_{f,p} \mid f \in \mathcal{F},\ p \in \mathcal{C}\} \cup \{r_{f,p} \mid f \in \mathcal{F},\ p \in \mathcal{E}\} \cup \{\times\}$. Intuitively, top edge links A and E are *contraries* via $\Leftrightarrow$; bottom edge links I and O are *subcontraries* via $\leftrightarrow$; diagonal links A and O, and E and I are *contradictories* via $\times$; and vertical links $A \downarrow I$, and $E \downarrow O$ are *subalternations.* Consequently, the CSP for this model is the triple $\langle V,\ (D_4, D_R),\ C\rangle$, where the constraint set C contains the following (for the intuitive reading *Top*, *Left*, *Right*, *Middle*, and *Bottom*): (C_1) Corner placement: for every face $f \in \mathcal{F}$, $c_{f,\mathrm{TL}_f} = A$, $c_{f,\mathrm{TR}_f} = E$, $c_{f,\mathrm{BL}_f} = I$, $c_{f,\mathrm{BR}_f} = O$. (C_2) Edge glyph placement: for every face $f \in \mathcal{F}$, $r_{f,\mathrm{TM}_f} = \Leftrightarrow$, $r_{f,\mathrm{BM}_f} = \leftrightarrow$, $r_{f,\mathrm{MM}_f} = \times$, $r_{f,\mathrm{ML}_f} = \downarrow$, $r_{f,\mathrm{MR}_f} = \downarrow$. And finally, ($C_3$) semantic constraints: for every face f: $r_{f,\mathrm{TM}_f} = \Leftrightarrow$ iff $\{c_{f,\mathrm{TL}_f}, c_{f,\mathrm{TR}_f}\} = \{A,E\}, r_{f,\mathrm{BM}_f} = \leftrightarrow$ iff $\{c_{f,\mathrm{BL}_f}, c_{f,\mathrm{BR}_f}\} = \{I,O\}, r_{f,\mathrm{MM}_f} = \times$ iff $\{\{c_{f,\mathrm{TL}_f}, c_{f,\mathrm{BR}_f}\}, \{c_{f,\mathrm{TR}_f}, c_{f,\mathrm{BL}_f}\}\} = \{\{A,O\},\{E,I\}\}, r_{f,\mathrm{ML}_f} = \downarrow$ iff $(c_{f,\mathrm{TL}_f}, c_{f,\mathrm{BL}_f}) = (A,I)$, $r_{f,\mathrm{MR}_f} = \downarrow$ iff $(c_{f,\mathrm{TR}_f}, c_{f,\mathrm{BR}_f}) = (E,O)$. We can summarize this embedding in Fig. 2.

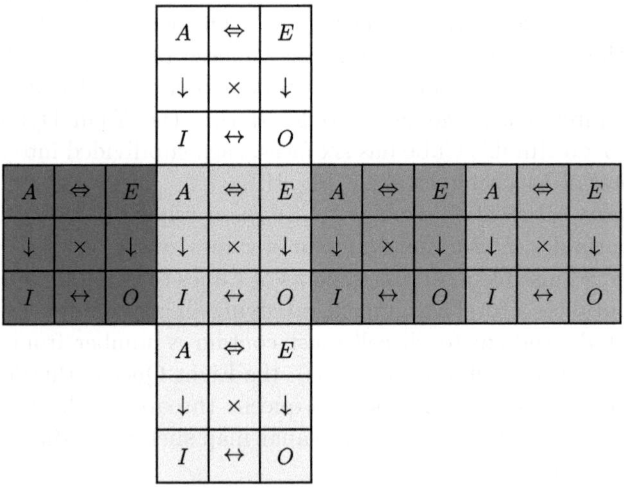

Fig. 2. $3 \times 3 \times 3$ Aristotelian cube.

Given this embedding, it is not difficult to prove that the action of the cube move group generates a large family of face patterns —at most 5,308,416— when projected onto a single colorless face. And if we add its colorful nature —or its texture, as in the Rubik's sensory cube— the action of the cube move group generates an even larger family of face patterns —at most 8,916,100,448— when projected onto a single face. This means that the cube supports a vast multiplicity of square configurations (Fig. 3), although only some of these correspond to the exact Aristotelian square; many others can be called pseudo-Aristotelian or non-Aristotelian in the sense that they may fail to validate one or more of the traditional Aristotelian constraints or they may succeed in validating relations that should canonically fail (they may be *disparatae*, to use medieval logic parlance).

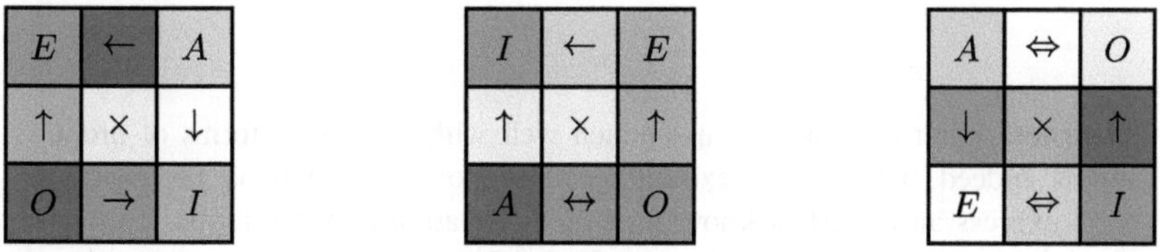

Fig. 3. Examples of squares.

4 Conclusion

All of this may be interesting because the traditional squares (of opposition) are static objects. Typically, a single diagram represents a fixed pattern of logical relations; by contrast, embedding the square into a Rubik's cube transforms logical geometry into what we could call *logical mechanics*. The idea is moving from a static plane to a dynamic space of logical diagrams under the cube transformations, which could provide a relatively novel interpretation of classical and non-classical logical structures —one in which logical pluralism is understood spatially. Of course, it is clear that we have more ~~playing~~ work to do, but in the meantime, let us mention three lines of research: *i)* embedding different logical structures (squares, hexagons, octagons, etc.) into different mechanical puzzles ($2 \times 2 \times 2$, $4 \times 4 \times 4$, $5 \times 5 \times 5$, etc.); *ii)* checking how bitstring semantics might work in these embeddings; and *iii)* testing different algorithms to solve these magic/logical cubes.

References

1. Béziau, J.-Y., Jacquette, D. (eds.): Around and Beyond the Square of Opposition. Springer, Basel (2012)
2. Rubik, E.: Cubed: The Puzzle of Us All. Weidenfeld & Nicolson, London (2020)
3. Hall, R.: Rubik's: 50 Years of the World's Most Famous Cube. White Lion Publishing, London (2024)
4. Dechter, R.: Constraint Processing. Morgan Kaufmann, San Francisco (2003)
5. Zeng, D.-X., Li, M., Wang, J.J., et al.: Overview of rubik's cube and reflections on its application in mechanism. Chin. J. Mech. Eng. **31**(1), Article 77 (2018). https://doi.org/10.1186/s10033-018-0269-7

Alternative Dotted Circle Diagrams

Reetu Bhattacharjee[1] and Amirouche Moktefi[2(✉)]

[1] Philosophisches Seminar, University of Münster, Münster, Germany
reetu.bhattacharjee@uni-muenster.de
[2] Ragnar Nurkse Department of Innovation and Governance, Tallinn University of Technology, Tallinn, Estonia
amirouche.moktefi@taltech.ee

Abstract. Euler diagrams do not match well with syllogistic forms of propositions. Indeed, while circles exhibit specific topological relations, propositions often express an imperfect knowledge of the relation between terms. To overcome this difficulty, early logicians often used dotted lines to express uncertainty. This technique was first employed in line diagrams. We argue that the transfer of the technique from line to circle diagrams could have led to another family of diagrams, if logicians had dotted spaces rather than lines. We develop these alternatives diagrams and discuss some of their features.

Keywords: Euler diagrams · Dotted lines · Ueberweg diagrams · Syllogistic

1 Introduction: Dotted Lines

In Euler diagrams, logical relations between the terms of a proposition are represented by topological relations between circles. However, there is no isomorphic correspondence between these relations of circles and traditional syllogistic propositions. Consider the proposition: 'All S is P'. Using Euler diagrams, this proposition is generally depicted with a circle S, which stands for the term S, drawn strictly inside a circle P, which stands for the term P, as shown in (Fig. 1)[1]. One readily observes the existence of an area of P which is outside S. Thus, one might infer that 'Some P is not-S'. This would be incorrect because S and P actually could coincide without violating the initial proposition 'All S is P'. Indeed, two relations between S and P are permitted: S might coincide or be strictly inside P. Hence, two distinct Euler diagrams are required to convey our imperfect knowledge of the relation between S and P. Logicians have long known this issue and used various techniques to lessen the inconvenience. Eventually, John Venn (1880) introduced his

[1] Since we are primarily interested in the employment of diagrammatic techniques rather than the historical development of the diagrams, we did not strictly reproduce the diagrams of the logicians we cite as they appear in their writings. At places, we introduced minor amendments to ease comparison and convey the ideas at work. For instance, we did not strictly follow the labeling practices of each logician and, rather, uniformly used letters S, P and M to stand for the terms depicted in the diagrams. The logicians that we cite used the techniques that we discuss but our paper should not be primarily read as a historical account of their diagrams.

P. Sobociński et al. (Eds.): Diagrams 2026, LNAI 16833, pp. 106–110, 2027.
https://doi.org/10.1007/978-3-032-34178-5_13

celebrated diagrams which, albeit not free from other shortcomings, tackle adequately this difficulty. Prior to him, the dominant technique to convey uncertainty employed dotted lines.

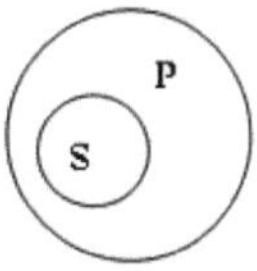

Fig. 1. Euler diagram

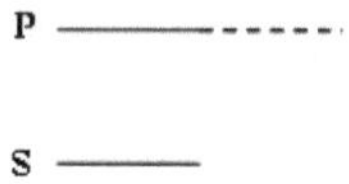

Fig. 2. Line diagram

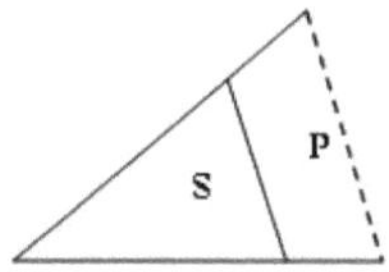

Fig. 3. Maass diagram

It seems that dotted lines were first employed in line diagrams. Such schemes resemble Euler's circles in that terms are represented with geometrical objects (here lines instead of areas), then logical relations between terms are conveyed by topological relations between these geometrical objects. Although known to his predecessors, line diagrams are often associated with Johann H. Lambert (1764) [2]. To represent 'All S is P', we draw two line-segments S and P, as shown in (Fig. 2). The continuous parts are known to exist, and the dotted part is uncertain. If one fills in the dotted part, the segment S appears strictly under the segment P. But if one strikes out that dotted part, the two segments coincide. Hence, this dotting technique conveys the two possible relations between S and P with a single line diagram.

Before their common usage on circle diagrams, dotted techniques are also found in the curious triangular diagrams of Johann Maass (1793) who combined Euler's and Lambert's ideas [5] (see [1, 3, pp. 316–317]). For 'All S is P', Maass proposes the diagram shown in (Fig. 3). It depicts a triangular area S within a triangular area P, as well as a small segment S subordinated to a larger segment P. Note that the dotted segment P is a border of the area P. If the dotted segment is filled in or stroked out, one gets different relations of S and P, as the proposition permits. Maass might be said to have opened the way to the employment of the dotting technique in circle diagrams by subsequent authors.

2 Dotted Circle Diagrams

Dotted circle diagrams appear in Arthur Schopenhauer's writings around 1820 [4, p. 12, 6, p. 117]. However, their use is commonly associated with Friedrich Ueberweg [8] (see [7]). The idea is simply to use dotted lines to indicate uncertain borders in an Euler diagram. There are various ways to apply this technique. For instance, for 'All S is P', one might simply use the diagram shown in (Fig. 4.a). If the dotted border is filled in, we obtain an area S strictly within an area P. However, if the dotted border is stroked out, we get coincident areas S and P. Thus, the diagram conveniently depicts the two possible relations of S and P permitted by the proposition. Note that, in line diagrams, the dots, applied to the entire portion of the extension whose status was undetermined, and not merely to the borders that delimit it. This differs from dotted circle diagrams discussed above, in which dots applied only to uncertain boundaries. Hence, the dotting technique is applied differently. If the convention of line diagrams were to be transferred consistently to spatial diagrams, the diagram would be represented by dotted areas (within dotted borders) rather than dotted borders alone. For instance, for 'All S is P', we dot the area of P which is outside S to indicate our uncertain knowledge regarding its existence. We obtain the diagram shown in (Fig. 4. b).

(a) Dotting borders (b) Dotting areas

Fig. 4. Dotted diagrams for 'All S is P'

The two methods of application, dotting borders and dotting areas, can be equally used to represent propositions. Yet, surprisingly, the logicians of the past seem to have only used the former method. Hence, we consider here how the latter can be used to represent categorical propositions. 'All S is P' was shown earlier in (Fig. 4) and 'No S is P' raises no uncertainty since the relation between S and P is adequately depicted by disjoint circles. In (Fig. 5), 'Some S is P' and 'Some S is not P' are represented with the dotting-borders and dotting-areas methods. In each case, the diagrams represent the possible relations between S and P. For instance, for 'Some S is P', S and P may coincide, may partially overlap, S may be strictly within P, or P may be strictly within S. Hence, the dotted technique, in both methods, allows the diagrams to accommodate the uncertainty of the relations between the terms in these propositions.

Propositions	Dotting borders	Dotting areas
Some S is P	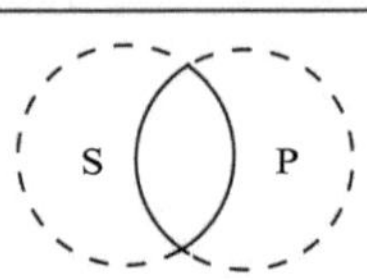	
Some S is not P	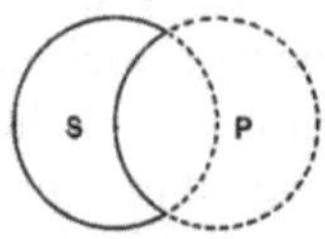	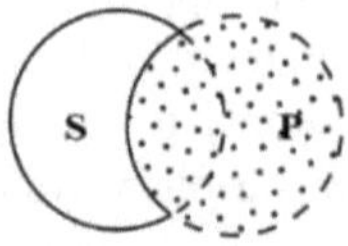

Fig. 5. Dotted diagrams for 'Some S is P' and 'Some S is not P'

Naturally, these methods can be used to represent syllogisms. For illustration, we present two examples of syllogisms, shown in (Fig. 6). Note that, in each case, the first premise would depict M with no dots. Then, the second premise renders the extension of M uncertain. Thus, M's border or area is dotted to convey this uncertainty.

The two methods produce analogous diagrams and one can easily transit from one to the other. One might argue that it is often easier to determine which regions (rather than which borders) should be dotted. Thus, the dotted-area method provides a more direct way of expressing uncertainty in circle diagrams. Note also that drawing border-dotted diagrams requires a special understanding of the logic of boundaries while dotted-area diagrams can be drawn with the common logic of the class relations. As such, dotted-area diagrams seem more intuitive and closer to the traditional practices of Euler diagrams. They may even be said to provide a bridge between Euler diagrams and dotted-border diagrams. Dotted-area diagrams also suggest Venn's subsequent practice of marking compartments to indicate their state. Hence, one might also view area-dotted diagrams as a conceptual bridge between Euler and Venn diagrams.

Syllogism	Dotting borders	Dotting areas
All M is P All S is M All S is P		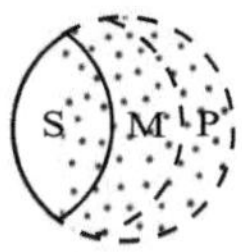
No M is P All S is M No S is P	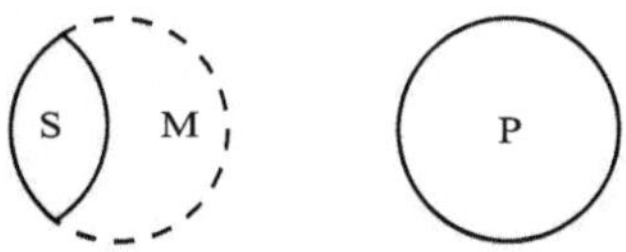	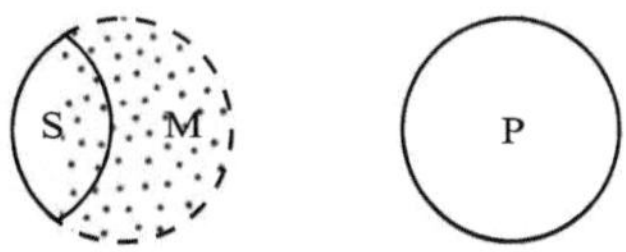

Fig. 6. Representation of syllogisms with dotted diagrams

3 Conclusion

The dotting technique is used to express uncertainty in circle diagrams. Two methods can be applied: dotting borders and dotting areas. The former has long been used by logicians while the latter is introduced in this paper. It is puzzling that dotted-borders diagrams alone have found their way to the practice of logicians. One might postulate the influence of Maass who, as we saw, employed a dotted segment as the border of an area. Albeit inherent to the design of his diagrams, this feature was unnecessary to the circle diagrams of his followers. Attitudes towards extensions, areas of diagrams as well as the occasional use of dots to express individuals might have also played a role in this 'historical accident' [4]. It remains that the dotted-area method to represent uncertainty remained uncharted and it was the aim of this paper to explore it.

References

1. Bernhard, P.: The remarkable diagrams of Johann Maass. In: Löffladt, G. (ed.) Mathematik - Logik - Philosophie, pp. 83–92. Harri Deutsch, Frankfurt (2012)

2. Lambert, J.H.: Neues Organon. Johann Wendler, Leipzig (1764)
3. Lemanski, J.: World and Logic. College Publications, London (2021)
4. Lemanski, J.: Individuals, existence, and existential commitment in visual reasoning. Open Philos. **7**(1), 20240042 (2024)
5. Maass, J.G.E.: Grundriss der Logik. Michaelis und Compagnie, Halle (1793)
6. Moktefi, A.: Schopenhauer's Eulerian diagrams. In: Lemanski, J. (ed.) Mathematics, Logic and Language in Schopenhauer, pp.111–127. Birkhäuser (2020)
7. Moktefi, A., Bhattacharjee, R., Lemanski, J.: Representing uncertainty with expanded Ueberweg diagrams. In: Lemanski, J., et al. (eds.) Diagrammatic Representation and Inference, pp. 207–214. Springer, Cham (2024)
8. Ueberweg, F.: System of Logic and History of Logical Doctrines. Green, and Co. London (1871)

Three Types of Scaffolding

Amirouche Moktefi(✉)

Ragnar Nurkse Department of Innovation and Governance, Tallinn University of Technology, Tallinn, Estonia
amirouche.moktefi@taltech.ee

Abstract. The scaffolding metaphor is widely used in scientific literature. Shvarts and Bakker (2019) pointed out a variety of interpretations that might cause confusion. They identified three usages of scaffolding in construction, where the scaffold may support a worker, be a prop that supports a structure or frame an entire structure. We provide a graphical representation of these three types. Then, we show that they are found in diagrams literature, with examples involving Venn diagrams. We argue that all readings can be maintained but, when used, one should carefully indicate which interpretation is at work.

Keywords: Scaffolding metaphor · Venn diagrams · Notation

1 The Metaphor

The scaffolding metaphor is frequently employed in the scientific literature that pertains to diagrams, notably on representations in education and cognition [5, 6]. Since metaphors transfer a concept from a context to another, one would justifiably expect a variety of interpretations. Roy D. Pea noted that "the concept of scaffolding has become so broad in its meanings [...] that it has become unclear in its significance" [10 , p. 423]. Part of the confusion springs from the polysemy of the term in the context where the metaphor originates, i.e. construction. Recently, Anna Shvarts and Arthur Bakker provided an insightful history of the metaphor and pointed out some of its ambiguities rooted in the construction context. In particular, they identified three "images that people may have as they think of scaffolding" in construction [12, pp. 17–18]. In (Fig. 1), we provide illustrations that convey these three forms of scaffolding. Here, the term 'scaffold' refers to the support structure while the term 'scaffolding' refers to the process of constructing, adjusting and removing, if at all, the scaffold.

In the first form of scaffolding, shown in (Fig. 1.a), a worker stands on a temporary supportive platform to build or reach a higher structure. We hereafter refer to this type of scaffold as a 'platform'. In the second form (Fig. 1.b), the scaffold directly supports the structure itself (although a worker might stand on the structure). We refer to this form of scaffold as a 'prop'. Finally, in the third form, the scaffold forms the skeleton of the structure or the building that is constructed (and a worker might stand inside the structure. We refer to this form as a 'frame'. For our ease, we introduce a graphical notation (inspired by the illustrations above) of these three forms of scaffolding in construction,

P. Sobociński et al. (Eds.): Diagrams 2026, LNAI 16833, pp. 111–114, 2027.
https://doi.org/10.1007/978-3-032-34178-5_14

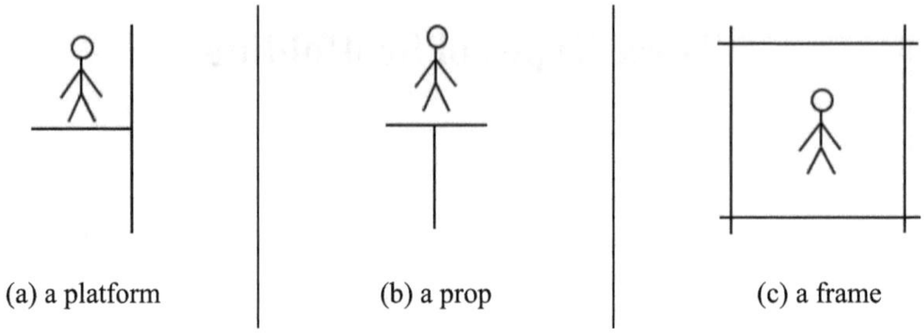

Fig. 1. Shvarts and Bakker's three types of scaffoldings in construction

as shown in (Fig. 2). Here, A and B refer to the scaffold and the structure that is the object of the scaffolding, respectively. In the following, we show that these three forms are found in the metaphors used in the literature that pertains to diagrams, with explicit reference to Venn diagrams.

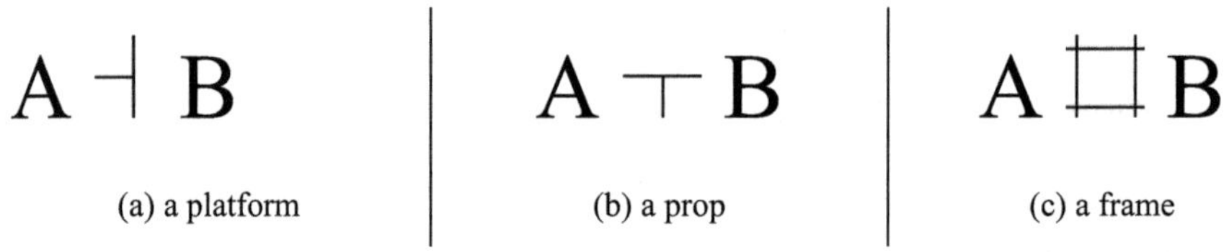

Fig. 2. A notation for the three types of scaffolding

2 Three Scaffoldings

The first type of scaffolding, i.e. the platform, is widely used in educational psychology [1, 13]. The idea is that the learner is temporarily supported to achieve a task which s/he would not be able to achieve unaided. Her/his position resembles that of the worker standing on a platform to achieve her/his task. It is important to keep in mind here that, although the scaffold itself might seem inert, scaffolding is interactive as the teacher continuously adjusts the scaffold to the progress of the learner. The scaffold is commonly removed when the student has acquired the skills needed to achieve the task unaided. An example of platform scaffolding is found in [9], where the task consists in reading a 2-term proposition on a 3-term Venn diagram. For instance, one might be offered the 3-term diagram shown in (Fig. 3, on the right) and be asked to formulate the relation between *x* and *y*. The beginner who is unable to achieve this task is invited to transfer information, following strict rules (see [3]), from the 3-term diagram to a 2-term diagram, as shown in (Fig. 3, on the left), where reading the proposition 'No *x* is not-*y*' is easier.

The second type of scaffolding, i.e. the prop, is found in studies on the cognitive role of representations. Andy Clark spoke of scaffoldings as "augmentations which allow us to achieve some goal which would otherwise be beyond us" [4, p. 163]. In construction, the prop supports a structure which, otherwise, would collapse. Similarly, notations

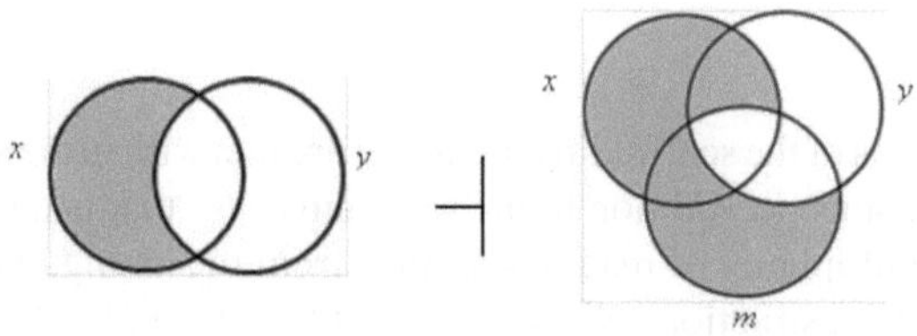

Fig. 3. Platform type of scaffolding

are external resources that help us achieve cognitive tasks which, otherwise, would be difficult, if possible at all. In this view, diagrams scaffold the ideas they represent. Thus, a Venn diagram is regarded as a scaffold that supports the propositions it represents, as shown in (Fig. 4). Clark refers to Venn diagrams in his discussion of inner rehearsal, which is the view that external resources can be internalized to assist the mind in its tasks without external aid. For instance, "experience with drawing and using Venn diagrams allows us to train a neural network which subsequently allows us to manipulate *imagined* Venn diagrams in our heads" [4 , p. 168].

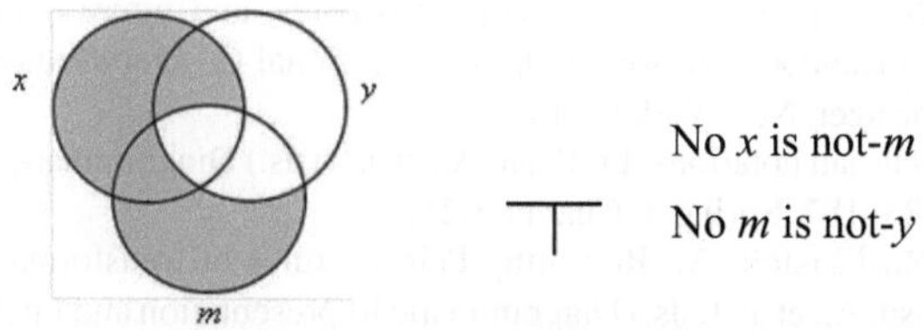

Fig. 4. Prop type of scaffolding

The third type of scaffolding, i.e. the frame, refers in construction to a contrivance which acts as a skeleton for an entire structure. Thus, a scaffold can be metaphorically understood as a framework in which other concepts are built. For instance, Venn's primary diagram, which exhibits the combinations of the terms, acts as a scaffold for the diagram that expresses propositions when syntactic marks are added, as shown in (Fig. 5). Ludwig Wittgenstein famously used the metaphor in this sense, or so it seems, when he spoke of the logical scaffolding and the scaffolding of the world [8]. In this respect, Gregory Landini precisely wrote that "Venn's propositional diagrams nicely illustrate Wittgenstein's ideas" [7 , p. 123] (see also [2]).

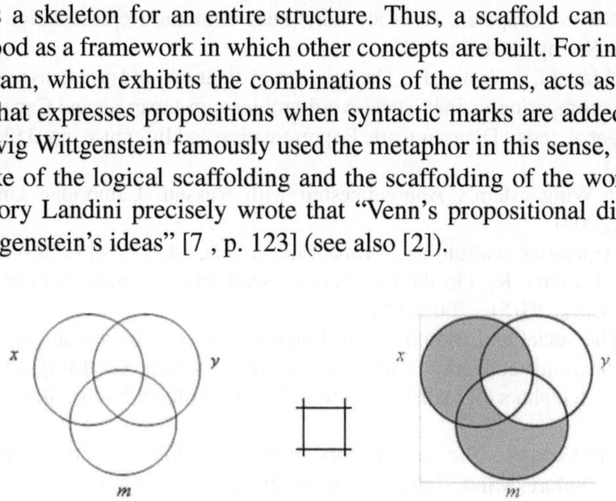

Fig. 5. Frame type of scaffolding

3 Conclusion

Diverse interpretations of the scaffolding metaphor are met with in the scientific literature that pertains to diagrams. In addition to the suggestiveness that is inherent to the usage of metaphors, the multiplicity of readings springs from the ambiguity of the term in its source context (here construction). We showed that Shvarts and Bakker's three types of construction scaffoldings are found in diagrams literature and outline different features of scaffolding.

This polysemy increases the risk of misinterpretation and over-interpretation. As Dirk Schlimm rightly pointed out, "because an object has a large number of features that can be relevant for its use in metaphors, it is important to pay careful attention to how the metaphors are actually used in each specific instance" [11 , p. 309]. As such, rather than promoting a specific interpretation that is believed to convey a better conception of the role of diagrams, we champion a refined usage of the metaphor where the interpretation is carefully explained and aligns with the specific function of the diagrams at work.

References

1. Belland, B.R.: Scaffolding: definition, current debates, and future directions. In: Spector, J.M., et al. (eds.) Handbook of Research on Educational Communications and Technology, pp. 505–518. Springer, New York (2014)
2. Bellucci, F.: Tractarian notations. In: Basu, A., et al. (eds.) Diagrammatic Representation and Inference, pp. 183–187. Springer, Cham (2021)
3. Bhattacharjee, R., Moktefi, A.: Revisiting Peirce's rules of transformation for Euler-Venn diagrams. In: Basu, A., et al. (eds.) Diagrammatic Representation and Inference, pp. 166–182. Springer, Cham (2021)
4. Clark, A.: Magic words: how language augments human computation. In: Carruthers, P., Boucher, J. (eds.) Language and Thought: Interdisciplinary Themes, pp. 162–183. Cambridge University Press, Cambridge (1998)
5. Fox, A.R., Hollan, J.: Read it this way: scaffolding comprehension for unconventional statistical graphs. In: Chapman, P., et al. (eds.) Diagrammatic Representation and Inference, pp. 441–457. Springer, Cham (2018)
6. Fukuda, M., Manalo, E., Ayabe, H.: The presence of diagrams and problems requiring diagram construction: comparing mathematical word problems in Japanese and Canadian textbooks. In: Basu, A., et al. (eds.) Diagrammatic Representation and Inference, pp. 353–357. Springer, Cham (2021)
7. Landini, G.: Wittgenstein's Apprenticeship with Russell. Cambridge University Press, Cambridge (2007)
8. Milkov, N.: Tractarian scaffoldings. Prima. Philosophia. **14**, 399–414 (2001)
9. Moktefi, A., Rumma, K.: On the metaphor of scaffolding in mathematical education and cognition. Theoria. **91**(5), e70028 (2025)
10. Pea, R.D.: The social and technological dimensions of scaffolding and related theoretical concepts for learning, education, and human activity. J. Learn. Sci. **13**(3), 423–451 (2004)
11. Schlimm, D.: Metaphors for mathematics from Pasch to Hilbert. Philos. Math. **24**(3), 308–329 (2016)
12. Shvarts, A., Bakker, A.: The early history of the scaffolding metaphor: Bernstein, Luria, Vygotsky, and before. Mind, Culture, Activity. **26**(1), 4–23 (2019)
13. Wood, D., Bruner, J.S., Ross, G.: The role of tutoring in problem solving. J. Child Psychol. Psychiatry. **17**, 89–100 (1976)

Mathematical Diagrams

Leibniz, Line Diagrams, and Euclidean Proportions

Jens Lemanski[1,2](✉)

[1] University of Münster, Zentrum für Wissenschaftstheorie, Domplatz 23, 48143 Münster, Germany
jenslemanski@uni-muenster.de
[2] University of Hagen, KSW, Universitätsstr, 23 58097 Hagen, Germany

Abstract. This paper examines Leibniz's line diagrams in fragments on logic from his posthumous works, thereby supplementing the widespread, primarily symbolic-algebraic interpretation of his logical program. Using key texts (including *De formae logicae comprobatione*, *Elementa de continente et contento*, plus/plus-minus calculi), the diagrammatic ideas are reconstructed: from (non-)parallelism of various lines to a reduction to a single 'basic' or 'proportion line', in which concepts are visualized as segments and relations as containment or intersection. Leibniz further developed the fundamental idea of a proportion line by incorporating curly brackets and semicircles, akin to those employed in so-called 'tape diagrams'. Nevertheless, the presence of divergent modern editions and the absence of consistent representation principles complicate the interpretation of these diagrams. It is systematically argued that Leibniz's line diagrams are strongly linked to Euclidean ratios and proportions (*Elements*, Book V and VI, Clavius commentary) as well as to Aristotelian principles (dictum de omni, transitivity, inesse). In conclusion, a mixed picture emerges: the diagrams are important for Leibniz's project of a calculus of logic; however, according to current findings, they present hardly any diagrammatic proof heuristics. Editorial work, detailed interpretations, and historical comparisons (Euclid, Clavius, Weigel, and others) remain central desiderata in current research.

Keywords: Linear diagrams · History of logic · Weigel School · History of mathematics · Euclid · Clavius · Ratios · Proportions · Logometrum · Tape diagrams · Euler Diagrams

1 Introduction

Leibniz is usually presented by historians as a precursor to the calculi of logic developed by Boole, Peirce, Frege, and subsequent scholars. In the 20th century, Leibniz's writings were often interpreted using modern symbolic logic. Only in recent years have there been increasing references to the fact that Leibniz used not only algebraic notation but also diagrams in his writings on logic (Bellucci et al. 2013, Oliveri 2025, Castro-Manzano 2017). Although it has been established that both algebraic and diagrammatic logic have a history that predates those developed by Leibniz, he is the first in European history before Lambert whose writings contain a large number of line diagrams.

P. Sobociński et al. (Eds.): Diagrams 2026, LNAI 16833, pp. 117–132, 2027.
https://doi.org/10.1007/978-3-032-34178-5_15

Line diagrams in logic have also been the subject of intense debate in recent years in computer science, mathematics, psychology, philosophy and others (Murata 2008, Rodgers et al. 2015, Wallinger et al. 2023, Moktefi 2024). However, both an overview and a detailed interpretation that deal historically only with Leibniz's line diagrams are lacking in research. In this regard, the present paper endeavors to make a preliminary contribution to addressing this lacuna. The focus of this paper is therefore on line diagrams in Leibniz's works on logic. There are several reasons why this paper is only a prelude to more intensive research: Firstly, Leibniz's manuscripts are still far from being completely edited, which is why it is not yet clear whether all of Leibniz's line diagrams are even known. Second, the paper cannot evaluate the symbolic interpretations to determine the extent to which they correspond with the line diagrams. Thirdly, it is not possible to discuss all diagrams, especially since we will see that individual diagrams and diagrammatic elements often deserve more detailed interpretations.

The following section provides an overview of Leibniz's known writings on line diagrams and analyses their basic diagrammatic principles. The central question addressed here concerns the functionality of line diagrams: How does Leibniz use line diagrams in his various writings? I will argue that Leibniz uses different forms of representation for line diagrams (Sects. 2.1–2.2), but that these can all be reduced to a basic idea and then expanded (Sects. 2.3–2.4). This basic idea seems to be based on the Euclidean theory of ratios and proportions, as found in Books V and VI of the *Elements* (Sect. 3).

2 The Leibniz Line Diagrams

This section first presents how Leibniz came into contact with logic diagrams and what his main writings on line diagrams are (2.1). Then, some basic line diagrams are presented (2.2), showing that these can be reduced to a basic idea that is also known from so-called 'tape diagrams' (2.3). This idea forms the basis for the calculus writings (2.4).

2.1 Leibniz's Study of (Line) Diagrams in Logic

Leibniz became acquainted with logic diagrams at Erhard Weigel's school. In 1663, Leibniz pursued his studies under Weigel's tutelage in Jena. Weigel had already dealt extensively with the use of diagrams and symbols in logic in his early magnum opus *Analysis Aristotelica ex Euclide restituta* from 1658. His diagrams bear a strong resemblance to those diagrams known today as 'Euler diagrams'. Weigel and his students usually called these diagrams 'Logometrum' or 'Schlussmaß' (inference/ logical measure). In 1663, Weigel's student Sturm published a lengthy treatise with Logometrum diagrams that went beyond their use in syllogistics, on the instructions of his teacher. In his dissertation of 1666, Leibniz dealt with this work by Sturm. However, according to current knowledge, Leibniz did not begin to draw the first logic diagrams himself, which correspond to the functioning of the logometrum, prior to the 1670s. Further information on Weigel and his school can be found in (Lemanski 2017, 2021 2025).

As explained in the writings just mentioned, Leibniz himself never published a logic diagram during his lifetime and tended to leave critical comments on visualizations in his publications. For this reason, Leibniz was often regarded as a critic of diagrams, especially in logic and mathematics, until the 19th century. The writings evaluated here therefore refer only to fragments of his literary estate. Apart from a few copies of these manuscripts becoming known over time, most line diagrams were not published until around 1900. For details, see Peckhaus 1997.

For this paper, series VI, vol. 4 of the Academy Edition was reviewed in its entirety (Leibniz 1999 = **A** VI 4), as well as Couturat's volume on logic (Leibniz 1903 = **C**), with comparisons to the editions of Erdmann, Gerhardt, Schmidt, Lenzen and the manuscripts. In addition to numerous other types of diagrams, these editions contain both line diagrams on logic and several line diagrams depicting natural philosophy, mechanics, and other subjects (e.g., A VI 4, p. 379). It should be noted that Leibniz sometimes also explains line diagrams in logic with the help of kinematics, mechanics, etc. (see below, Sect. 2.4). Conversely, line diagrams in mathematical or mechanical writings, for example, are sometimes analyzed with the help of logic. These cases will not be examined in the following.

A linear or line diagram for logic is understood here as a diagram consisting of lines that is found in a treatise on logic and primarily represents a logical issue. Of Leibniz's line diagrams for logic, the following writings in Table 1 are particularly noteworthy.

Table 1. Overview of the main writings on linear diagrams

Year	Title	Reference
1686	*Generales inquisitiones de analysi notionum et veritatum.*	A VI 4, N. 165, 739–788
1686/87	*Specimen calculi coincidentium et inexistentium*	A VI 4, N. 177, 830–845
1687	*Non inelegans specimen demonstrandi in abstractis*	A VI 4, N. 178, 845–885
1690	*De formae logicae comprobatione per linearum ductus*	C 292–321
1690	*Elementa de continente et contento*	C 321–324
1693	*Schedae de novis formis syllogisticis*	C 206–210
1697	*Essais de schèmes linéaires des syllogismes*	C 247–249

I will not proceed chronologically in the following, as I consider it questionable that there was a continuous development of line diagrams in Leibniz's work toward increasingly sophisticated diagrams. According to the prevailing opinion, the earliest document in Table 1, *i.e., Generales inquisitiones,* is Leibniz's most advanced calculus (Lenzen, p. 3; Malink). Perhaps the most complex line diagrams are found in *Non inelegans specimen demonstrandi in abstractis* and in *Specimen calculi coincidentium et inexistentium.* The first fragment is also known as *Plus-minus-calculus* or calculus XIX, the second as *Plus-calculus* or calculus XX. The most basic line diagrams, on the other hand, are found a few years later, around 1690. Nevertheless, this diagrammatic development should not be seen as a history of decline. As announced in the introduction, I will argue that behind all line diagrams (Sect. 2.2) there is a basic idea that can be most clearly seen in *Elementa de continente et contento* in 1690 and in *Essais de schèmes linéaires* in 1697 (Sect. 2.3). Leibniz expands on this basic idea in his calculus writings (Sect. 2.4) and connects it with Euclidean thought (Sect. 3).

2.2 Circle and Line Diagrams

Weigel had already pointed out in early writings that the form of the logometrum was irrelevant, meaning that lines, circles, letters, etc. could be used as long as the spatial relations of proximity and distance between two diagram objects could be clearly visualized as they correspond to the logical principles of identity and diversity (Lemanski 2017, 23). Leibniz also demonstrates that one and the same verbal-communicated inference can be expressed using both circles and lines. We find an example of this in his elementary work *De formae logicae comprobatione*. The elementary status of this work is evident from the introduction, in which Leibniz reflects that he has already thought about the use of line diagrams on several occasions:

> I have considered the verification of logical form by means of the drawing of lines. Let as many straight lines be drawn, one beneath another [una sub alia], as there are concepts; let propositions be expressed through the relations of the straight lines, insofar as straight lines contain straight lines [dum rectae rectas continent]. In this, caution is required, so that nothing more is expressed than the force of the form permits; and thus care must be taken both that a particular proposition is not represented as if it were universal, and that a proposition which is not always, or not by virtue of its form, convertible is not presented as convertible. It is also convenient [Commode etiam] that the major term always precede, since it is in the major proposition which we are accustomed to place first in syllogisms; the middle term should be placed in the middle position, and the minor in the lowest. Therefore, we shall explain separately the method of exhibiting propositions. [Itaque docebimus separatim modum exhibendi propositiones.] For the designation of the conclusion, however, no special caution is required, except that we not make the proposition more universal than it is. (C 292)

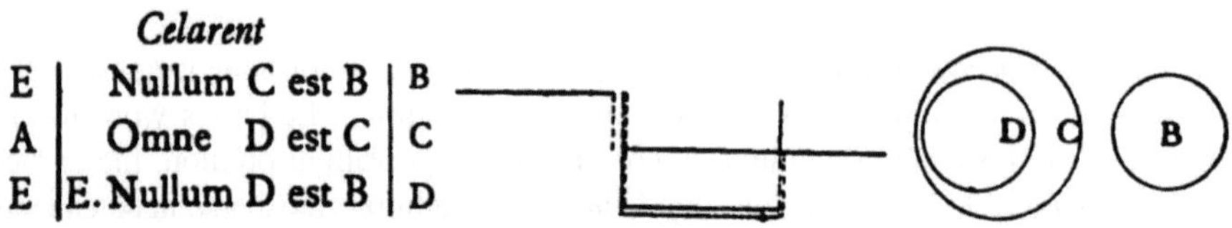

Fig. 1. Leibniz's linear and circle diagrams for Celarent (C, 294)

In Fig. 1, the modus C*ela*r*e*nt (No *C* is *B*, all *D* is *C*, thus no *D* is *B*) is represented verbally and then diagrammatically with both lines and circles. It is striking that the line diagrams in Fig. 1 are not labeled with letters on the corresponding lines, but rather that these are placed on the left from top to bottom (descending in Fig. 1: *B*, *C*, *D*). The upper horizontal line running to the far left represents concept *B*; the middle and longest horizontal line extending to the right end represents concept *C*. The double straight horizontal line running partially 'parallel' to *C* represents *D*. The vertical lines indicate the relationship between the lines. For example, the line starting at the right end of *B* shows that it is not parallel to *C* at any point. Since the left end of *C* is at the same height as that of *D*, as indicated by the middle vertical line, *B* is not parallel to *C* at any point. It follows that *B* is also not parallel to *D* at any point.

Although lines *D*, *C*, and *B* are geometrically parallel in Fig. 1, I will use the term 'parallel' in a narrower, diagrammatic sense in what follows. In this sense, two lines count as parallel only if their visible segments at least partially stand in a corresponding facing relation, such that their parallelism can be recognized without adding a guide line or mentally extending the lines. Accordingly, *C* and *D* are parallel in this restricted diagrammatic sense, whereas *B* is not parallel to either *C* or *D*.

It seems that line diagrams follow diagrammatically the 'una sub alia' principle, as mentioned in the quote above. Later authors such as Lambert usually called this 'subordination' and from of a modern perspective '(non-)parallelism of lines' may be a fitting term. One asks whether two lines are completely or partially parallel (or subordinated), or completely or partially non-parallel. In the first two cases, the two completely or partially parallel lines represent universal and particular affirmative judgments (A: *All S are P*; I: *Some S are P*). In the second case, the two completely or partially non-parallel lines represent the universal and particular negative judgments (E: *No S are P*; O: *Some S are not P*). The circle diagram, on the other hand, seem to follow the relation of (non-)containment, as is also typical of the so-called 'Euler diagrams' later on.

Both relations, parallelism and containment, can be generalized in Weigel's Logometrum terminology: if two circles contain each other at least partially or if two lines run parallel at least partially, this expresses spatial proximity and thus logical identity (A, I). If they do not, this expresses spatial distance and thus logical diversity (E, O).

The two diagrammatic relations mentioned above, parallelism and containment, not only give rise to analogous diagrams, as Fig. 1 shows, but can also be translated into one another (Moktefi 2024). Leibniz therefore sometimes mixes the concepts of the two diagrammatic relations (see Sect. 2.3 f.) and speaks of one line 'being contained' within another. We will see later that there are extensions of line diagrams that suggest this way of speaking, since the distinction between line and circle diagrams is not always unambiguous.

Leibniz did not develop uniform designations for the individual diagrammatic elements of his line diagrams, and in some cases did not designate them at all. For the sake of simplicity, we will refer to the horizontal lines as 'concept lines' and the vertical lines as 'guidelines' or 'comparison lines' (see Rodgers et al. 2015, sect. 2.3). The double line (as seen in Fig. 1) is a diagrammatic element that Leibniz uses in different ways, sometimes for distribution (C 312), sometimes as that which cannot be eliminated, i.e., as a kind of a 'minimum line' (C 384). For most diagrams in *De formae logicae comprobatione* the double line denotes the conclusion, as *D* and *B* in Fig. 1. In this case, one could speak of a 'conclusion line'. Leibniz sometimes refers to this line simply as "linea tractu continua" (Leibniz 1960, 375).

> Dotted lines connect adjacent lines and signify propositions formed from the middle term and one of the extremes. But a line drawn with a continuous stroke [linea tractu continua] signifies the conclusion. In the minor term [*D*], a double small line [duplex lineola], if it occupies the whole term, indicates a universal proposition; if not, a particular one. (C 294, Sch 375)

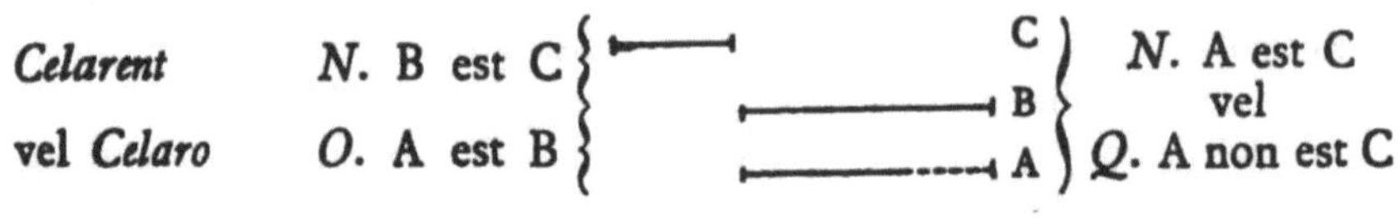

Fig. 2. Leibniz's solid and dotted line segments for Celarent or Celaro (C, 299)

As we can already see from the different functions of the double lines, Leibniz varied the line diagrams several times and changed the functions of the diagrammatic elements. In Fig. 2, for example, we see the modus Celarent again, but here the comparison lines are missing. All concept lines are also written as closed line segments here. As in Fig. 1, they continue to indicate the concepts, but are distinguished in two ways. The solid line segment is limited, the dotted one unlimited. The limited line segment corresponds approximately to the minimum line and indicates what cannot be taken away. The unlimited line segment thus indicates something that may or may not be. In this respect, the length of *A* in Fig. 2 is indeterminate, which is why either Celarent (thus no *A* is *C*) or Celaro (thus some *A* is not *C*) can follow from the premises (no *B* is *C*, all *A* is *B*).

The length of *A* is therefore not clearly defined; rather, the limited line segment only indicates that there is a minimum value for *A* that is parallel to *B* (and not to *C*). If we imagine removing the unlimited line segment from *A*, this results in the universally negative conclusion. If we imagine removing the unlimited line segment from *A*, this results in the partially negative conclusion.

2.3 The Basic Idea of Line Diagrams

In *Elementa de continente et contento*, Leibniz first uses diagrams based on Fig. 1 (C 321–323) and then introduces two axioms (C 323 f.) that deviate from previous conventions in several respects. The first axiom, connected to Fig. 3, concerns the containment relation 'inesse'.

> Whatever is in something that is itself in another is itself in that other [Quicquid inest inexistenti id ipsum inest]; for example, if *AB* is in *AC* and *AC* is in *AD*, then *AB* will be in *AD*. (C 323)

Three things are noteworthy in this quote, together with Fig. 3. First, we see here that Leibniz's formulation of the axiom resembles Aristotle's *dictum de omni* insofar as they both define a transitivity relation in logic. Second, we see here that Leibniz uses the containment relation (as with circles) and not the parallelism relation (as with lines).

In fact, we already encountered this in the first quotation from Sect. 2.1 ("dum rectae rectas continent"). Thirdly, it is noteworthy that we see a large closed line segment, i.e. *AD*, but it 'contains' different smaller closed line segments such as *AB*, *AC*, *BC*, ...

Since we have four collinear points on the line *AD*, Fig. 3 thus represents a total of six closed line segments that are distributed in such a way that some are 'contained' in another, while others are not. In this axiom, Leibniz only considers the intersecting or overlapping closed line segments, not the common end points that two closed line segments may have. *AB* and *AC*, for example, are intersecting because they have the common closed line segment *AB*. *AB* is therefore contained in *AC*. *AB* and *BD* do not intersect and do not contain each other, even though they both share endpoint *B*. If two line segments were explicitly superimposed, such *AB* and *AC*, they would be 'parallel' at *AB*, but not parallel at *BC*. Of the fifteen possible pairs of different closed line segments in Fig. 3, ten are intersecting line segments and five do not intersect at all. Of the ten pairs, there is exactly one relation, namely *AC* and *BD*, where each of the two lines has a segment of the other (*BC*) and no segment of the other (*AB* for *AC* and *CD* for *BD*).

Fig. 3. Leibniz's proportion line as the basic idea of line diagrams (C, 323)

By assigning a concept to each closed line segment between two points, all syllogistic inferences can be represented by the fifteen possible pairs. For example, the following mode Barbara could be read: 'All *AC* is *AD*, all *AB* is *AC*, thus all *AB* is *AD*'. If we substitute *B* for *CD*, *D* for *AB*, and *C* for *AC*, we could also read Fig. 1 from Fig. 3. In this way, the axiom with Fig. 3 seems to express the basic idea of all line diagrams (at least for positive judgments).

Looking again at the first quote from Sect. 2.2, it should now be apparent that Leibniz already had Fig. 3 in mind there. He writes that he only shows the lines separately ("separatim") in diagrams such as Fig. 1 for the sake of convenience ("commode"). Since diagrams such as Fig. 3 can be used to represent all syllogistic judgments, it shows the basic idea behind all line diagrams, and diagrams such as Fig. 1 or 2 are merely explications for more convenient reading.

Nevertheless, there is something peculiar about *Elementa de continente et contento*, which is illustrated with Axiom 2. This expresses verbally the relation of non-containment or exclusion, as required, for example, for the modus Celarent and for negative judgments. However, Leibniz does not represent this in Fig. 3, but modifies this diagram by not drawing the line segment *CD*, leaving a gap between *C* and *D* that is almost the length of an entire line segment. Instead, he adds another line segment, *DE*, to the right of this gap. I think that this diagram, which I will simply call Fig. 3*, is easy to imagine and does not need to be represented here. Axiom 2 reads:

> Whatever is in something that is excluded is itself excluded. [Quicquid inest excluso, id ipsum exclusum est.] For example, if *AB* is in AC and *AC* is outside [extra] *DE*, then *AB* too will be outside *DE*. (C 323)

What is surprising is not that the axiom is reminiscent of the dictum de nullo, but rather a peculiarity of this diagram. The point intersection, which played no role at all in Leibniz's axiom 1, Fig. 3, and most modern approaches (e.g., Rodgers et al. 2015, Wallinger et al. 2023) is now avoided in Fig. 3* by introducing the gap. Moktefi 2024 gives some arguments for using gaps in line diagrams, but Leibniz says nothing about this and some of his line diagrams seem not to introduce a gap. The diagrammatic question of which line diagrams in Leibniz's work still contain this gap cannot be answered here due to space constraints. The editions differ greatly in some respects, as the handwritten manuscripts are also highly debatable with regard to this question. However, we will see shortly that Leibniz clearly emphasizes this gap in some manuscripts, especially when he works with only one basic line.

My argument so far has been that Leibniz outlines a basic idea of line diagrams in Fig. 3. This basic idea shows that he can dispense with the comparison lines by circumscribing all conceptual lines in a large closed line segment with several collinear points (including several smaller closed line segments). These points then denote subsections or segments. I will call this entire line a 'basic', 'reference' or 'proportion line', whereby the last term is already connected to Euclidean diagrams (see Sect. 3).

Leibniz probably intended this proportion line to serve as a kind of orientation in his explicit line diagrams such as Figs. 1 and 2. Even if, for example, there is a gap between *B* and *C* (or *D*) in Fig. 1, this must have a relation or reference, otherwise we would have two diagrams instead of one. The basic or proportion line is explicitly shown, for example, in *Essais de schèmes linéaires*. Fig. 4a comes from Couturat's edition and is the oldest source of these diagrams. Here, the proportion line can be seen centrally in all four diagrams. The limited concept line and the comparison line are each combined with a curly bracket with horizontal and vertical diagrammatic elements. At the same time, the curly bracket indicates the segments or partial distances on the proportion line. The unlimited concept line continues to be indicated by a dotted line that extends the horizontal elements of the bracket. This type of line diagram including a basic line which serves as an orientation to other diagrammatic elements such as curly brackets is usually called today a 'single tape diagram' (Murata 2008, 380, 385).

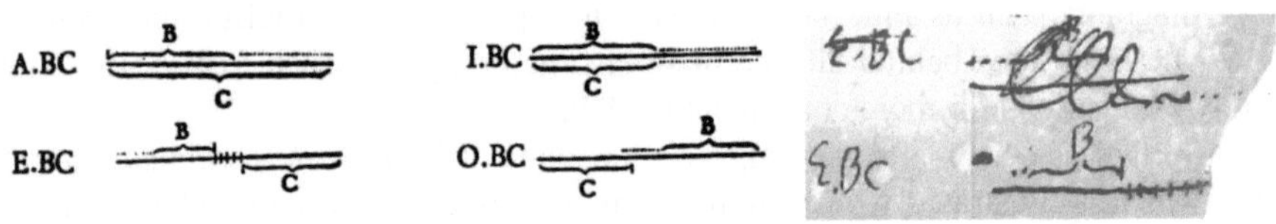

(a) (b)

Fig. 4 Leibniz's single tape diagrams of *Essais de schèmes linéaires* in (a) the Couturat edition (C, 249) and (b) the current status of the manuscript LH IV 7B, p. 19r.

Here in Fig. 4a, we see that Leibniz indicates the gap in the E-judgments, similar to Fig. 3*, with small vertical lines marked on the basic or proportion line between *B* and *C*. These small vertical lines on the proportion line serve as the gap here. In Fig. 4b, we see the corresponding manuscript showing only the E-judgement. We can see that Leibniz drew it twice: crossed out at the top maybe because he forgot the gap, and at the bottom with the gap indicated by the small vertical lines (similar to Fig. 4a). Unfortunately, we can also see in Fig. 4b that the edge of the manuscript is damaged, so that the bracket *C* after the gap is no longer there. Whether the manuscript was already damaged in 1903 and the E-judgement in Fig. 4a is an interpretation of Couturat is no longer traceable.

2.4 Extension of the Basic Idea

The four diagrams in Fig. 4a are already an extension of the basic idea shown in Fig. 3 thanks to the new diagrammatic elements such as curly brackets, but they still represent traditional syllogistics. In this section, however, we see a stronger diagrammatic and logical extension. In some of his calculus writings, Leibniz uses the single tape diagrams of Fig. 4a and extends the curly brackets to semicircles. An example of these semicircular line or tape diagrams can be found below in Fig. 5. This extension can be found primarily in *Non inelegans specimen demonstrandi in abstractis* and in *Specimen calculi coincidentium et inexistentium*, i.e., the plus and plus-minus calculi.

A paper by Schmidt illustrates well (Schmidt 1971, 271 f.) that, on the one hand, the semicircles can be replaced by curly brackets as in Fig. 4a and, on the other hand, diagrams can also be created for inferences for which Leibniz himself did not draw any diagrams. The problem is that all the editions reviewed differ greatly from one another, particularly with regard to the number and presentation of the respective diagrams in the plus calculus. Since these manuscripts are particularly difficult to decipher due to multiple revisions of Leibniz, the interpretation of Leibniz's diagrams always begins with the choice of the edition or with the question of what exactly the reader sees in the manuscripts. For this subsection, I am consulting the Academy edition as my primary source (A VI 4).

Let us first look at the rough structure of *Non inelegans specimen demonstrandi in abstracti*. In this calculus, Leibniz proceeds by first defining coincidence or identity (Def. 1), then diversity or difference (Def. 2), and introducing substitution in the latter. After introducing transitivity (Theorem 3), containment (Def. 3 and 5), and constitution (Def. 4), Leibniz defines disparate concepts (Def. 6). These are the first main topics, which are also represented diagrammatically.

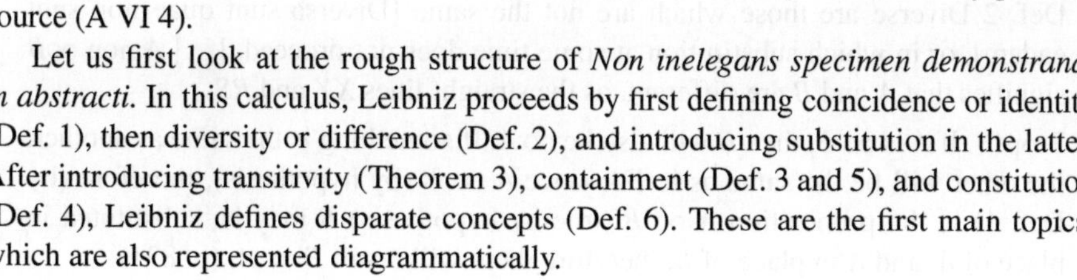

Fig. 5 Diagrams in *Non inelegans specimen demonstrandi in abstractis* (A VI 4, 831 f.)

Let us begin in Fig. 5a with the identity or coincidence of *A* (*XY*) and *B* (*YX*). The calculus is introduced with the following words.

> Def. 1. The same, or coincident [Eadem seu coincidentia], are those of which either can everywhere be substituted for the other while preserving truth [salva vertitate]. For example, triangle and trilateral; for in all propositions demonstrated by Euclid concerning the triangle, trilateral may be substituted, and conversely, with the truth preserved. $A \infty B$ signifies that A and B are the same [esse eadem]; as we shall say of the straight line XY and the straight line YX: $YX \infty XY$, that is, that the shortest path of a moving point from X to Y and from Y to X coincides [seu coincidere viam brevissimam mobilis]. (p. 831)

The last sentence shows, as we already noted in Sect. 2.1, that Leibniz also applies the diagrams in part to situations outside of logic, for example, to kinematics. Leibniz himself does not comment explicitly what the diagrams show or how they work. Fig. 5a is a kind of hybrid diagram between the mostly one-dimensional line diagrams and the mostly two-dimensional circle diagrams. (Int1) If, for example, we imagine removing the line XY in Fig. 5a, we are left with an oval that would be designated both as A and as B. Precisely this type of logical circle diagram can be found repeatedly in later generations, but independently of Leibniz, in order to represent identity. (Int2) However, if we imagine the semicircles A and B as brackets (as in Fig. 4) and then translate them as a conceptual line with a corresponding comparison line, we have reconstructed the typical line diagram as in Fig. 1. In my opinion, both interpretations, (Int1) and (Int2), are equally justifiable and may not necessarily be mutually exclusive.

However, (Int1) is further supported by Fig. 5b. Leibniz gives an example here that is intended to illustrate the definition of diversity or difference (Def. 2).

> Def. 2 Diverse are those which are not the same [Diversa sunt quae non sunt eadem], or in which substitution at some time does not proceed. [...] A non ∞B signifies that A and B are different, as the straight lines XY and RS.
>
> Prop. 1. If A is ∞ B, then B will also be ∞ A. If something is the same as another, the other will be the same as it. For since $A \infty B$ (by hypothesis), therefore (by Def. 1) in the proposition $A \infty B$ (true by hypothesis) B may be substituted in place of A, and A in place of B; therefore there will result $B \infty A$. (p. 831)

Fig. 5b corresponds exactly to Fig. 3 in terms of the line of proportion, except that the letters are different. The first sentence of the quotation, which still belongs to Def. 2, shows exactly the division of the line segments that we also discussed as a special feature in Fig. 3. Here we have a line segment YS that RS and XY have in common. However, the sub-segment RY and SX each belong to one of the two segments, but not to the other. In this respect, we can use the relations mentioned here to express particular judgments, as in the O-diagram in Fig. 4, for example.

In Fig. 5b, two interpretations are again possible: (Int3) A could correspond to the line segment RS and B to the segment YX. This would correspond exactly to the particular judgment "non" in the first sentence of the quotation. (Int4) Looking at the last two sentences of the quotation, A and B could also refer to the large semicircle marked L there. A and B are then identical and interchangeable, as shown in (Int1) for Fig. 5a. Here, too, both interpretations are possible. Leibniz may have been playing with the ambiguity of some diagrams.

Fig. 5c resembles the modus Celarent shown in Figs. 1 and 2 if one reads the diagram as "No *A* are *C*, all *B* are *A*, therefore no *B* are *C*." However, we see a difference here, because according to Fig. 5a (Int1) and Fig. 5b (Int4), *A* and *B* are identical in Fig. 5c. Leibniz therefore writes the following about Fig. 5c:

> If *A* ∞ *B* and *B* non ∞ *C*, then "*A* non ∞ *C*". If, of two things which are the same as each other [eadem inter se], one is different from a third [unum sit diversum a tertio], then the other will also be different from that same third. For if, in the proposition *B* non ∞ *C* (true by hypothesis), *A* is substituted in place of *B*, there will result (by definition, because *A* ∞ *B*) the true proposition *A* non ∞ *C*. (p. 832)

Notably, this Fig. 5c is only included in the Academy edition. Together with another diagram, it differs from the other twelve diagrams in that only the semicircles are labeled with letters, not the lines. In the Academy edition, it is also the only diagram that, like Fig. 3* (and also Fig. 4a), places a gap between the two lines, thus interrupting the proportion line. All other diagrams in the Academy Edition have an unbroken proportion line. This is also the case in Gerhardt's edition, although Fig. 5c is missing there. The Schmidt edition (Leibniz 1960) also lacks this and several other diagrams, but instead presents several diagrams with a broken proportion line. In manuscript LH IV 7B, 2 p. 60r, Fig. 5c is difficult to recognize because Leibniz made numerous corrections.

What is clear is that, unlike in Fig. 3*, Leibniz always designates the two segments separated by the broken proportion line with the same end and starting points in his plus calculus. This suggests that Leibniz did not have a uniform representation of line diagrams in mind, even though they all illustrate a common basic idea. The difference between Figs. 3, 3*, and the diagrams in the Academy edition is evident in the question of whether a common point also represents a common section of the concept line or not. Leibniz does not always seem to follow the same rules of representation in this regard. Whether similar discrepancies exist among other authors who use line diagrams would have to be investigated separately.

It is also remarkable that Leibniz draws Fig. 5c and the gap it contains before introducing disparate concepts in Def. 6. These are concepts that are completely separate from each other and have no overlapping line segments. While diversity (Fig. 5b) enables particular judgments, disparata (Fig. 5c) can be used to represent universal negative judgments. The universal affirmative judgments that are still missing have already been implicitly drawn according to (Int3) of Fig. 5b: According to this, for example, the semicircle *A* would be contained in *L*.

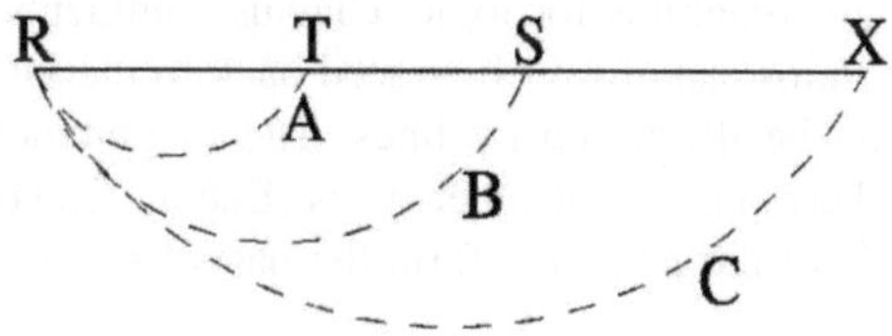

Fig. 6 Diagrams taken from A VI 4, 838.

In Fig. 6, for example, we see a diagram that allows for two interpretations (Int1) and (Int2), depending on whether one focuses more on the semicircles or more on the proportion line. In both interpretations, the diagram corresponds to the familiar diagrams for modus Barbara, whereby Leibniz sets the medius (*B* or *RS*) in such a way that premises 1 and 2 of modus Barbara would be reversed. He writes:

> If *A* is in *B* [Si *A* est in *B*] and *B* is in *C*, then *A* is in *C*. What is contained in the contained is contained in the containing. [Contentum contenti est contentum contientis.] [...] *RT* is in *RS* and *RS* is in *RX*, so *RT* is in *RX*. *A*= quadrilateral, *B*= parallelogram, *C*= rectangle. (p. 838)

While the first part of the quotation focuses on the semicircles, the second part focuses on the line. However, the terminology always refers to the relation of being contained, as can be seen not only in the containment relation, but above all in the second sentence of the quotation, which, again, reformulates Aristotle's transitivity axiom dictum de omni using the inesse vocabulary.

3 Euclidean Ratios and Proportions

As we have seen in the previous subsections, there are numerous points of contact between Leibniz and Aristotelian logic, even though Leibniz breaks with the prevailing scholastic interpretation of Aristotle in many places. Furthermore, Leibniz explicitly refers to Euclid as we have already seen in Def. 1 (Sect. 2.4), for example. The diagrams in the fragments discussed in Sects 2.2 and 2.3 also bear a clear resemblance to those found in books V and VI of the early modern editions of Euclid's *Elements* (and still today). Furthermore, the interpretation of Euclid with Aristotle is a clear hallmark of the Weigel school, which reached its first peak in 1658 with Weigel's *Analysis Aristotelica ex Euclide restituta* (transl. Aristotelian Analysis Restored from Euclid) and was continued by many of Weigel's numerous students. The name 'Logometrum' itself refers to the Euclidean doctrine of the measurement (μέτρον) of ratios (λόγος) and proportions (ἀναλογία) as defined in Book V of the *Elements*.

In the following, I can only provide an initial comparison of Leibniz's line and tape diagrams with Euclid's theory of ratios and proportions. A more in-depth investigation would require more detailed studies, which should also take into account Leibniz's relationship to Aristotle. In my comparison, I refer primarily to the Clavius edition of the *Elements* from 1607, which Leibniz is known to have studied intensively (Risi, p. 11).

In my view, we find the same basic idea in Euclid's *Elements* that we saw in Sect. 2.3 in Leibniz's line and tape diagrams for logic. Clavius comments on this basic idea in detail on many pages: ratios can always be traced back to the same type of magnitude (magnitudo), which can be illustrated by lines. The magnitudes represented can be geometric, arithmetic, harmonic, or of other types (Euclid, Clavius 1574, 392ff.). The straight lines in Book V of the *Elements* form the basis for the straight-line figures in Book VI.

The basic idea can be clearly seen in Definition VII of the *Elements*, which Clavius first mentions in the following quote and then describes with his own example, illustrated in Fig. 7a.

The same [sc. magnitudes] that have the same ratio shall be called proportional. [*Eandem* autem habentes rationem magnitudines, Proportionales vocentur.]

For example, if the magnitudes *A*, *B*, *C*, and *D* have the same ratio of *A* to *B* as *C* to *D*, then these magnitudes are called proportional. Similarly, if the same ratio exists between *E* and *F* as between *F* and *G*, then the magnitudes *E*, *F*, and *G* are called proportional. However, there are proportional magnitudes that are continuous, among which there is continuous proportionality; for example, the magnitudes *E*, *F*, *G*. Other proportional magnitudes are not continuous, but discrete; such are the magnitudes *A*, *B*, *C*, *D*. For in these there is an interruption of the proportions; in those, however, there is none whatsoever.

In Fig. 7a, *A* and *E* are the lines that correspond to what we have referred to above as the basic or proportion line. *B*, *C*, and *D* are closed line segments of *A*, just as *F* and *G* are segments of *E*. This would become clear if the comparison lines between *A*, *B*, *C*, and *D* were drawn in. *A*, for example, shows the points 0, 4, 8, 12, with only the number "12" being explicitly mentioned. However, line *B* is also a section of *A* (namely 0 to 4), as are *C* and *D*, whereby their points are only oriented towards *A*, but are not drawn in by corresponding points in *A*. In contrast to Leibniz, however, the horizontal lines in Euclid are not conceptual lines, but 'lines of magnitude' or, as in the example Fig. 7a of Clavius, 'number lines'. Based on modern terminology, Fig. 7a is a 'multiple tape diagram with number lines' (Murata 2008, 381).

The fact that early modern commentators on Euclid had such a basic line in mind can be clearly seen in the Byzantine diagram in Fig. 7b, where the basic line between points 2, 6, 18, and 54 is only implied. Leibniz was likely familiar with such diagrams, at least from his teacher Weigel, who discussed these diagrams in several places. However, combining the diagrammatic idea of a basic line, such as *A* or *E* in Fig. 7a, with the arcs as given in Fig. 7b leads to types of representation that correspond to the diagrams of the plus-minus calculus from Sect. 2.4. Some Clavius editions of the *Elements* also contain closed line segments that are continued elliptically by dots. However, I was unable to verify that Leibniz was familiar with these editions.

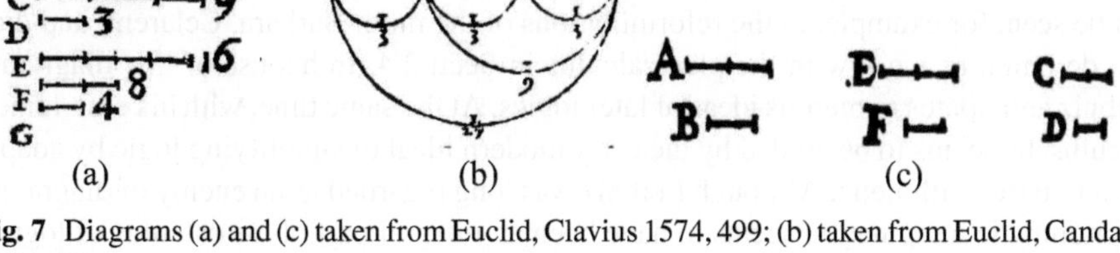

(a) (b) (c)

Fig. 7 Diagrams (a) and (c) taken from Euclid, Clavius 1574, 499; (b) taken from Euclid, Candalla 1566, 42

The fact that Leibniz's fragments also has similarities with Euclid's doctrine of ratio and proportion can also be seen by comparing Euclid's Def. VII given above with Leibniz's Def. 1 in Sect. 2.4. Both start from identity (eadem) and build transitivity relations on this basis. In Leibniz, we have already looked at these transitivity relations using the newly formulated dictum de omni axioms. In Fig. 3, for example, Leibniz presented the inference "if *AB* is in *AC* and *AC* is in *AD*, then *AB* will be in *AD*." In Euclid, we find something similar in Book V, Prop. 11, to which Clavius adds Fig. 7c.

> Those ratios that are one and the same to any one ratio, are also the same among themselves. [Quae eidem sunt eadem rationes, & inter se sunt eadem.] If the ratios *A* to *B* and *C* to *D* are each the same as the ratio *E* to *F*, then I say that the ratios *A* to *B* and *C* to *D* are also the same among themselves. (Euclid, Clavius 1574, 499)

Several more comparisons can be drawn between Leibniz and Euclid, but I can only hint at them here: Leibniz's inesse relation is reminiscent of the part-whole relation in *Elem.* V, Def. I and prop. XV, IXX. Substitution and coincidence in Leibniz resemble alternation and inversion in *Elem.* V, Def. XII and Prop. XVI. Detraction and remainder in Leibniz are reminiscent of *Elem.* V, Def. XV, Prop. XVIIff. and *Elem.* VI, Prop. III. However, these and many other possible comparisons must be examined in detail elsewhere.

4 Conclusion

This paper presented and analyzed some of Leibniz's line diagrams. These can be found in all of Leibniz's key fragments, which were regarded as precursors to modern logic calculi in the 20th century. These fragments are normally interpreted technically by using modern symbolic notations, and diagrams are often ignored. It is astonishing that, despite certain expressions of deference, Leibniz's program of a calculus of logic was considered a failure in the 18th century (Lemanski 2021). It was not until the late 19th century that this image began to change, culminating in the early 20th century in an almost unrestrained veneration of Leibniz in the field of logic. This was partly motivated by purely political considerations (Li/Rudolph 2013). It was not until the late 20th century that the first critical voices emerged, presenting a mixed picture of Leibniz and his influence (Peckhaus 1997). Based on the facts examined so far, I can agree with this mixed picture of modern research in the following.

It remains undisputed that Leibniz attempted to go beyond syllogistics using numerous creative means, without however completely losing a connection to Aristotle. This can be seen, for example, in the reformulations of the modi Barbara, Celarent, and dictum de omni, as we saw in the plus calculus in Sect. 2.4. In his use of line diagrams, Leibniz anticipates numerous ideas of later logics. At the same time, with his plus-minus calculus, he seems to be guided by the early modern ideal of simplifying logic by adapting it to basic arithmetic. Although Leibniz was long regarded as an enemy of diagrams, diagrammatic imagination seems to have been an integral part of his calculus of logic.

The problem, of course, is that we are not dealing with finalized texts. This expresses Leibniz's general dissatisfaction with his approaches and means that even a historically oriented interpretation always appears provisional from a systematic point of view. As we have seen in the course of this paper, there are also numerous open questions regarding the diagrams in the manuscripts and the interpretation of them in the published editions. There are even numerous external factors, such as damaged manuscripts, which make interpretation difficult. The extent to which Leibniz used diagrams for diagrammatic reasoning remains open to debate. Most linear diagrams discussed here are 'only' models that help to understand the text. So far, I have found not much evidence that Leibniz developed an algorithmic or at least heuristic method to prove the validity of inferences or extract new information from given premises using line diagrams, for example. Maybe this is the reason why modern technical interpretations rely solely on the symbolic elements. However, Leibniz's symbolic logic do not always proceed in a calculative manner also, but in some places merely represent abbreviated modes of speech.

As mentioned, however, these are only preliminary assessments based on an analysis of the diagrams in Leibniz's fragments. In my view, there are still numerous desiderata for future research. First, a complete diagrammatic analysis should be carried out to verify whether the impressions described above hold true. Secondly, the comparison between Leibniz and Euclid should be intensified, as should that with Aristotle. Thirdly, the evaluated material reveals a strong connection to Weigel and his school: Leibniz uses terminology that is very similar to Weigel's, which clearly distinguishes itself from other schools and thinkers of the time and combines Euclidean and Aristotelian approaches. Since Leibniz changed the representational characteristics of the logometrum in some ways, a more precise historical and systematic examination should be conducted to determine the extent to which Leibniz agrees with Ploucquet, Lambert, Euler, and their schools. I have been able to formulate some clues to these open questions in this paper. However, it is left to future research efforts to falsify the impressions and hypotheses formulated here or to show to what extent they stand up to scrutiny.

Acknowledgements. I would like to thank the Leibniz Research Centre in Münster for their support as well as Ingolf Max and Volker Peckhaus for helpful comments. This paper was supported by the funding of the Fritz Thyssen Foundation (project: History of Logic Diagrams in Kantianism) and the ViCom-project Gestures and Diagrams in Visual-Spatial Communication funded by the Deutsche Forschungsgemeinschaft (DFG, German Research Foundation) — (RE 2929/3-1).

References

Bellucci, F., Moktefi, A., Pietarinen, A.-V.: Diagrammatic autarchy. Linear diagrams in the 17th and 18th centuries. In: Ceur-ws 1132, pp. 23–30 (2013)

Castro-Manzano, J.M.: Re(dis)covering Leibniz's diagrammatic logic. Tópicos, Rev. Filosofía. **52**, 89–116 (2017)

Euclid, Candalla, F.F.: Elementa geometrica. Royer, Paris (1566)

Euclid, Clavius, C.: Euclidis elementorum libri XV. Accolt, Romae (1574)

Leibniz, G. W.: Sämtliche Schriften und Briefe. Ed. by Berlin-Brandenburgischen Akademie der Wissenschaften. Series VI, Vol. 4: Philosophische Schriften 1677–1690. Berlin, Akademie (1999)

Leibniz, G.W.: Opuscules et fragments inédits de Leibniz. Extraits des manuscrits de la Bibliothèque royale de Hanovre par Louis Couturat, Paris (1903)

Leibniz, G.W.: In: Schmidt, F. (ed.) Fragmente zur Logik. Akademie, Berlin (1960)

Leibniz, G. W.: Schriften zur Syllogistik. Ed. by W. Lenzen. Hamburg: Meiner (2019)

Lemanski, J.: Erhard Weigels Erfindung des Schlussmaßes. In: Herbst, K.-D. (ed.) Erhard Weigel (1625–1699) und seine Lehrer, pp. 29–55. Leipzig: Akadem. Verlagsanstalt (2025)

Lemanski, J.: Logic diagrams in the Weigel and Weise circles. Hist. Philos. Logic. **39**(1), 3–28 (2017)

Lemanski, J.: World and Logic. College Publications, London (2021)

Lenzen, W.: Leibniz's Logic. In: Gabbay, D.M., Woods, J. (eds.) The Rise of Modern Logic: Vol. 3: From Leibniz to Frege, pp. 1–85. Elsevier, Amsterdam et al. (2004)

Malink, M., Vasudevan, A.: The logic of Leibniz's Generales Inquisitiones de analysi notionum et veritatum. Rev. Symbolic Logic. **9**(4), 686–751 (2016)

Moktefi, A.: How linear are Englebretsen's line diagrams? In: New Directions in Term Logic, pp. 357–384. College Publications, London (2024)

Murata, A.: Mathematics teaching and learning as a mediating process: the case of tape diagrams. Math. Think. Learn. **10**(4), 374–406 (2008)

Oliveri, L.: Meditating and inquiring with imagination: Leibniz, Lambert, and Kant on the cognitive value of diagrams. Hist. Philos. Logic. **46**(1), 68–86 (2025)

Peckhaus, V.: Mathesis universalis und allgemeine Wissenschaft. Leibniz und die Wiederentdeckung der formalen Logik im 19. Jahrhundert. Akademie, Berlin (1997)

de Risi, V.: Leibniz on the Parallel Postulate and the Foundations of Geometry: the Unpublished Manuscripts. Springer, Cham (2016)

Rodgers, P., Stapleton, G., Chapman, P.: Visualizing sets with linear diagrams. ACM Trans. Comput. Hum. Interact. **22**(6), 27:1–27:39 (2015)

Schmidt, F.: Ganzes und Teil bei Leibniz. Archiv für Geschichte der Philosophie. **53**(3), 267–278 (1971)

Wallinger, M., Dobler, A., Nöllenburg, M.: LinSets.zip: compressing linear set diagrams. IEEE TVCG. **29**(6), 2875–2887 (2023)

Li, W.: In: Rudolph, H. (ed.) Leibniz in der Zeit des Nationalsozialismus. Steiner, Stuttgart (2013)

Graph-Based Proofs Can be Enlightening

Márcia R. Cerioli[1], Wagner Sanz[2], and Petrucio Viana[3(✉)]

[1] Programa de Engenharia de Sistemas e Computação-COPPE e Instituto de Matemática, UFRJ, Rio de Janeiro, RJ, Brazil
marcia@cos.ufrj.br

[2] Faculdade de Filosofia, UFG, Goiânia, GO, Brazil
wagnersanz@gmail.com

[3] Instituto de Matemática e Estatística, UFF, Niterói, RJ, Brazil
petrucio_viana@id.uff.br

Abstract. We provide diagrammatic proofs based on multigraphs (with two distinguished nodes and arcs labeled with relation algebra terms)—simply called *graphs*—to solve problems in binary relation arithmetic. First, we show that a graph-based proof helps us better understanding the fundamental *Dedekind-rule*, revealing a hidden diagrammatic aspect of it. Secondly, we apply the diagrammatic version of the Dedekind-rule to present a complete solution to a question raised by G. Birkhoff at the Jónsson Symposium. Thirdly, we present a graph-based proof that the dual composition of two functional relations is also a functional relation. In each case, we show that the use of graphs simplifies the search for a solution. Part of our work involves presenting proofs based on graphs and, when possible, transforming these proofs into standard proofs of binary relation arithmetic. We believe that, due to the informal way in which we present our graphical calculus and its application, this work can contribute to a greater recognition and dissemination of diagrammatic proofs in general and of this interesting system in particular.

Keywords: Graph calculus · Diagrammatic proofs · Relation algebra · Equational proofs

1 Introduction

We apply diagrammatic proofs based on multigraphs (with two distinguished nodes and arcs labeled with terms from relational algebra)—simply called *graphs*—to solve problems in binary relation arithmetic. We do this by presenting three examples: a proof and analysis of the Dedekind-rule of G. Schmidt and T. Ströhlein [9]; a complete solution to a question raised by G. Birkhoff at the Jónsson Symposium [3]; a graph-based proof that the dual composition of two functional relations is also a functional relation, a claim that L. Chin and A. Tarski considered false [2].

P. Sobociński et al. (Eds.): Diagrams 2026, LNAI 16833, pp. 133–149, 2027.
https://doi.org/10.1007/978-3-032-34178-5_16

Dedekind-Rule. The Dedekind-rule [9], p. 86, is the inclusion:

$$R \sqcap (S \circ T) \sqsubseteq [S \sqcap (R \circ T^{\smile})] \circ [T \sqcap (S^{\smile} \circ R)], \tag{1}$$

which is true for all binary relations R, S, T. Schmidt and Ströhlein's [9] proof for this inclusion is based on the equivalence they call Schröder-rule. To apply Schröder-rule, Schmidt and Ströhlein made essential use of the properties of complementation. In Sect. 4, we present a graph-based proof of (1) that does not use negation. Furthermore, by analyzing this proof, we are able to better understanding the meaning of (1).

Birkhoff-Question. According to S. Comer [3], p. 186, the following question was raised by G. Birkhoff at the Jónsson Symposium [4]:

> The implication
>
> $$R \circ S = \mathsf{I} \text{ and } S \circ R = \mathsf{I} \Rightarrow R = S^{\smile} \tag{2}$$
>
> holds in every relation algebra?

Comer [3] presents an affirmative answer to Birkhoff's question, providing a proof based on polygroupoids. This is a good illustration of how polygroupoids can be used in verifying properties of relation algebras. However, we believe that a complete answer to Birkhoff-question must necessarily be the presentation of an equational proof based exclusively on the axioms of relational algebra. In Sect. 5 we present a complete positive answer, providing a graph-based proof of (2) and translating it into a proof that does not use polygroupoids and is based solely on the axioms of relational algebra.

Chin-Tarski-Question. Functional relations are binary relations satisfying the unicity part of the condition for a relation to be a function, i.e., each element of the domain may have at most one image through the relation. The property of "being functional", for an arbitrary binary relation R, is expressed by the following formulas:

$$\forall x, y, z[(zRx \wedge zRy) \rightarrow x = y] \Leftrightarrow \forall x, y[\exists z(zRx \wedge zRy) \rightarrow x = y] \Leftrightarrow$$
$$\forall x, y[\exists z(xR^{\smile}z \wedge zRy) \rightarrow x\mathsf{I}y] \Leftrightarrow \forall x, y(xR^{\smile} \circ Ry \rightarrow x\mathsf{I}y) \Leftrightarrow R^{\smile} \circ R \sqsubseteq \mathsf{I}.$$

In [2], p.277, L. Chin and A. Tarski claimed that it is not difficult to verify that the set of functional relations is not closed under the operations of union, complementation, dual composition, and reversal. Here, dual composition is an operation introduced by Peirce [8], based on the idea that intersection and union are dual operations, as $R \sqcup S$ can be defined as $(R^{-} \sqcap S^{-})^{-}$. So, he defined a dual operation to composition by:

$$R \triangle S = (R^{-} \circ S^{-})^{-}, \tag{3}$$

for all relations R, S. Therefore, to prove that the dual composition of two relations is a functional relation, it suffices to prove that

$$R^{\smile} \circ R \sqsubseteq \mathsf{I} \text{ and } S^{\smile} \circ S \sqsubseteq \mathsf{I} \Rightarrow (R^{-} \circ S^{-})^{-\smile} \circ (R^{-} \circ S^{-})^{-} \sqsubseteq \mathsf{I}. \tag{4}$$

Although what Chin and Tarski affirmed was true for union, complementation, and reversion, it can be proven that the dual composition of two functional relations is, in fact, a functional relation. An arithmetic proof based on binary relations of (4),using only the axioms of relation algebra, was first presented by Monk [6], but remained unpublished until Maddux extended it to the arithmetic of weakly associative relation algebras [5]. In Sect. 7, we present a graph-based proof of (4) that can be translated into an arithmetic proof based on binary relations which uses only the axioms of relational algebra.

Warning. There are numerous automated proof assistants, theorem provers, and AI chats to help humans prove or disprove mathematical claims such as those we study here. However, our work follows a perpendicular direction: to help humans produce—without the aid of machines—detailed, explanatory, precise, and mechanical proofs of mathematical results. This article can be seen as a continuation of [1], where a more detailed presentation of the labels, graphs, and rules can be found.

2 Binary Relations and Inclusion

Let U be a non-empty set. As usual, a *binary* **relation** on U is a subset of $U \times U$. We denote the set of all binary relations on U by $2^{U\times U}$.

Let $a, b \in U$ and $R \in 2^{U\times U}$. To simplify, we write aRb instead of $(a, b) \in R$. Accordingly, we write $\neg aRb$ instead of $(a, b) \notin R$.

Now, let us consider a useful way to interpret both R and aRb. First, R may be seen as a *condition* that a and b must satisfy when given in this order. Whence, aRb means a followed by b satisfies condition R.

This *conditional view* can be represented by a labeled *graph* having two distinguished nodes:

$$- \xrightarrow{R} +$$

Here, $-$ is the *input node*, $+$ is the *output node*, and the *arc* labeled R which connects $-$ to $+$ means that any object a assigned to $-$ must satisfy the constraint expressed by R to be related to any object b assigned to $+$. As we illustrate in this work, the conditional view has some profound consequences for the diagrammatic representation of relations through graphs.

The Dedekind-rule (1) deals with inclusion between binary relations. Let $R, S \in 2^{U\times U}$:

$$R \sqsubseteq S \Leftrightarrow \forall a \forall b (aRb \rightarrow aSb) \tag{5}$$

Here, $\forall$ means *for everyone* and $\rightarrow$ means *if, then*. Therefore, $\sqsubseteq$ means that every ordered pair that happens to be in R already belongs to S.

Regarding inclusions, the conditional view of relational semantics provides us with three inference rules that allow us to solve the three problems proposed in Sect. 1.

First, we can consider that, for every $R, S \in 2^{U\times U}$, the fact that $R \sqsubseteq S$ means that every constraint expressed by R is already expressed by S and, at the same time, it may be that S expresses fewer constraints than R. This is because every ordered pair that belongs to R also belongs to S, and it is possible that S has ordered pairs that do not belong to R. This gives rise to the following inference rule:

We can infer that $R \sqsubseteq S$ by performing a sequence of transformations on $- \xrightarrow{R} +$ in such a way that constraints not present in R are not added during the transformation process until we arrive at $- \xrightarrow{S} +$.

Secondly, since a graph expresses constraints on the relationship between input and output nodes, when we delete a part of a graph without deleting the input or output nodes—assuming that what remains is still a graph—we obtain a graph that imposes fewer, or rather, no more constraints than the original graph. This gives rise to the following inference rule:

From a graph G we can infer the graph obtained from G by deleting a part of G—if what remains is still a graph.

Third, if we duplicate a part of a graph without introducing any new constraints we obtain a graph that express the same restrictions as the original graph. This gives rise to the following inference rule:

Starting from a graph G, we can infer the graph obtained from G by duplicating a part of G in such a way that no constraint that is not already present in G is generated.

We see these inference rules in action in Sects. 4, 5, and 7.

3 Composition, Reversion, and Intersection

In addition to inclusion, Dedekind-rule (1) deals with the usual operations of composition, reversion, and intersection from and into binary relations. For all $R, S \in 2^{U\times U}$ and $a, b \in U$:

$$aR \circ Sb \Leftrightarrow \exists c(aRc \wedge cSb) \tag{6}$$

$$aR^{\smile}b \Leftrightarrow bRa \tag{7}$$

$$aR \sqcap Sb \Leftrightarrow aRb \wedge aSb \tag{8}$$

Here, $\exists$ means *there is at least one* and $\wedge$ means *and*. Hence, by definition, $\circ$, and $\sqcap$, are, respectively, the operations of composition, and intersection. Besides, also by definition, $^{\smile}$ is the operation of reversion.

What is important here—and what forms the basis of all our applications—is that, according to the conditional view adopted in Sect. 2, the left-hand sides of (6), (7), and (8) can be directly represented by labeled graphs with distinguished nodes, while, by introducing appropriate new diagrammatic procedures, the right-hand sides can also be represented in this way.

Graphs and Rule Associated with Composition. The left hand side of (6) can be represented by the graph

$$- \xrightarrow{R \circ S} + \tag{9}$$

By adopting the dot $\bullet$ as a diagrammatic representation of an intermediate node, the right hand side of (6) can be represented by the graph

$$- \xrightarrow{R} \bullet \xrightarrow{S} + \tag{10}$$

Indeed, by the semantics of $\bullet$, the graph (10) means that any pair of objects a and b assigned to $-$ and $+$, respectively, must satisfy the restriction that there exists an intermediate object c, represented by $\bullet$, such that a is related to c according to R and c is related to b according to S.

The equivalence between (9) and (10) can be adapted into a diagrammatic inference rule to prove properties of relations whose definitions contains occurrences of the composition operator:

From a graph G of the form

$$H, x \xrightarrow{R \circ S} y \ ,$$

having nodes x and y that have an arc from x to y labeled $R \circ S$, and a new node $\bullet$ *that does not occur in G, we can infer the graph*

$$H, x \xrightarrow{R} \bullet \xrightarrow{S} y \ , \quad \text{(with an arc } x \xrightarrow{R \circ S} y \text{ curving above)} \tag{11}$$

obtained from G by adding two arcs $x \xrightarrow{R} \bullet$ and $\bullet \xrightarrow{S} y$.

This inference rule works in both directions. As a consequence of the erasing rule, in the rule for composition, we can choose not to keep the arc $x \xrightarrow{R \circ S} y$.

Graphs and Rule Associated with Reversion. The left hand side of (7) can be represented by the graph:

$$- \xrightarrow{R^{\smile}} + \tag{12}$$

On the other hand, the right hand side of (7) can be represented by the graph:

$$- \xleftarrow{R} + \tag{13}$$

Indeed, according to the arc orientation, (13) means that any object a assigned to $-$ must satisfy the condition expressed by R to be related to any object b

assigned to $+$, but in the opposite direction from that of a to b. That is, we must have bRa, which is the same as $aR^{\smile}b$.

The equivalence between the graphs (12) and (13) can be adapted into a diagrammatic inference rule to prove properties of the relations whose definitions contain occurrences of the reversion operator:

From any graph G of the form

$$H, x \xrightarrow{R^{\smile}} y\ ,$$

having an arc from x to y labeled $R^{\smile}$, we can infer the graph

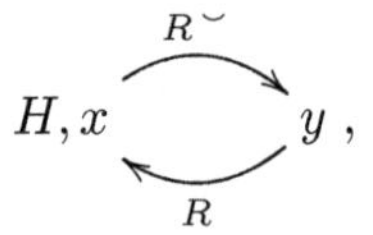

(14)

obtained from G by adding a new arc from y to x labeled R.

This inference rule works in both directions. As a consequence of the erasing rule, in the rule for reversion, we can choose not to keep the arc $x \xrightarrow{R^{\smile}} y$.

Graphs and Rule Associated with the Intersection. The left hand side of (8) can be directly represented by the graph

$$- \xrightarrow{R \sqcap S} + \qquad (15)$$

The right hand side of (8) can be represented by the graph

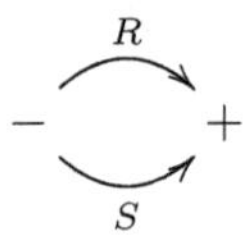

(16)

In fact, according to graph semantics, graphs express constraints on the relationship between input and output nodes. More specifically, a labeled arc connecting two nodes expresses that the objects associated with its ends must satisfy the constraints imposed by the relation represented by its label. Therefore, as in (16) we have a pair of parallel arcs connecting $-$ to $+$, given two objects a and b assigned to $-$ and $+$, respectively, for them to be related according to (16), we must have that a is related to b by R and also that a is related to b by S, that is, we must have $aR \sqcap Sb$.

The equivalence between (15) and (16) can be adapted into a diagrammatic inference rule to prove properties of relations whose definitions contains occurrences of the intersection operator:

From a graph G of the form

$$H, x \xrightarrow{R \sqcap S} y \ ,$$

having nodes x and y that have an arc from x to y labeled $R \sqcap S$, we can infer the graph

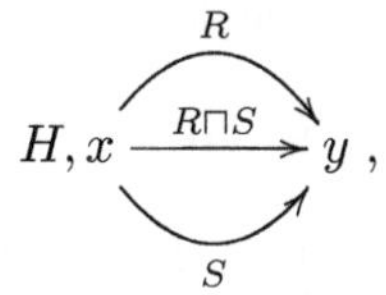

(17)

obtained from G by adding two parallel arcs from x to y, one labeled R and the other labeled S.

This inference rule works in both directions. As a consequence of the erasing rule, in the rule for intersection, we can choose not to keep the arc $x \xrightarrow{R \sqcap S} y$.

4 Dedekind-Rule

To obtain a graph-based proof of (1) that does not use complement, we transform $- \xrightarrow{R \sqcap (S \circ T)} +$ into $- \xrightarrow{[S \sqcap (R \circ T^{\smile})] \circ [T \sqcap (S^{\smile} \circ T)]} +$, applying three general demonstration strategies. First, we eliminate or introduce Boolean and Peircean operators according to their main occurrence in a term labelling some arc of the graph (Steps 1–3, 6–11). Second, we duplicate restrictions, in the form of labeled paths of length two in the graph (Steps 4 and 5). Third, we delete part of the graph which does not interest for the problem solution (Step 11).

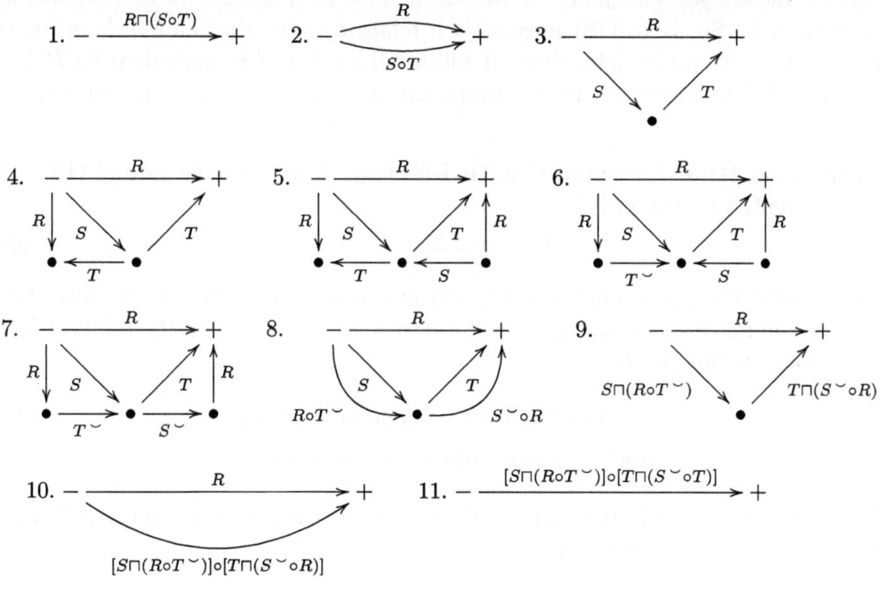

There are two aspects of the Dedekind-rule that our proof reveals. First, the transition from Step 10 to Step 11 can be replaced by the transition from Step 10 to

$$11'.\ - \xrightarrow{R\sqcap\{[S\sqcap(R\circ T^{\smile})]\circ[T\sqcap(S^{\smile}\circ T)]\}} +$$

Now, all the proof steps are reversible! So, as a matter of fact, this "new proof" shows, for all $R, S, T \in 2^{U\times U}$, the equality

$$R \sqcap (S \circ T) = R \sqcap \{[S \sqcap (R \circ T^{\smile})] \circ [T \sqcap (S^{\smile} \circ R)]\}.$$

Second, it seems there is no way to translate this graph-based proof into a binary relation arithmetic proof. This may be due to the essential role that the duplication of labeled paths of length two plays in the proof and to its seemingly intrinsic diagrammatic aspect, that is, non-arithmetical. In fact, we have a proof that the rule that allows us to duplicate labeled paths of length two in any given graph is equivalent to the truth of the Dedekind-rule. Therefore, we can say that our proof reveals a hidden diagrammatic aspect in Dedekind-rule!

4.1 Equality, Identity, and Hypothesis

In addition to composition and reversion, the Birkhoff-question (2) deals with equality and identity. Let $R, S \in 2^{U\times U}$ and $a, b \in U$:

$$R = S \Leftrightarrow \forall a \forall b (aRb \leftrightarrow aSb) \tag{18}$$

$$a\mathsf{I}b \Leftrightarrow a = b \tag{19}$$

Here, $\forall$ means *for everyone*, $\leftrightarrow$ means *if, and only if*, and $=$ in (19) means *equality in* U. So, $=$ in (18) means both relations have the same ordered pairs as elements. From the definitions, it follows that $R = S$ is equivalent to $R \sqsubseteq S$ and $S \sqsubseteq R$. Therefore, we do not adopt any inference rule for $=$ in relations.

Graph and Rule Associated with Identity. The left hand side of (19) can be represented by the graph

$$- \xrightarrow{\mathsf{I}} + \tag{20}$$

We express the right-hand side of (19) in our system indirectly by introducing two inference rules that translate the meaning of the identity relation into operations on the graphs:

Every object is identical to itself. (21)

Any two equal objects are identifiable. (22)

Based on (21) and (22), it is natural that we allow the *execution* of the following two *actions* in any graph. First:

From any graph G with node x, we can infer the graph

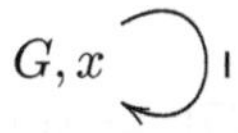

(23)

that is, the graph obtained from G by adding a loop from x to x labeled I.

This rule of inference works in both directions. Second:

From any graph G that has the form

$$G, x \xrightarrow{\mathsf{I}} y \tag{24}$$

that is, a graph that has an arc from node x to node y labeled with I, *we can infer the graph that results from G by* (1) *collapsing the nodes x and y;* (2) *replacing all the arcs that arrive or leave y with the respective arcs which arrive or leave x, but preserving input and output nodes.*

With the due care, this rule of inference works in both directions

Rule Associated with Hypothesis. Note that, according to the fact that an equality represents two inclusions, Birkhoff-question (2) may be reduced to two *sequents*:

$$\mathsf{I} \sqsubseteq S \circ R \text{ and } R \circ S \sqsubseteq \mathsf{I} \Rightarrow R \sqsubseteq S^{\smile} \tag{25}$$

$$\mathsf{I} \sqsubseteq R \circ S \text{ and } S \circ R \sqsubseteq \mathsf{I} \Rightarrow S^{\smile} \sqsubseteq R. \tag{26}$$

A natural way to prove a sequent as (25) is to assume the *antecedent* inclusions $\mathsf{I} \sqsubseteq S \circ R$ and $R \circ S \sqsubseteq \mathsf{I}$ and use them to prove the *consequent* inclusion $R \sqsubseteq S^{\smile}$. It is natural to consider that, assuming the *antecedent* inclusion $\mathsf{I} \sqsubseteq S \circ R$, we can add an arc labeled $S \circ R$ whenever we encounter an arc labeled I.

This fundamental idea can be adapted into a general rule of diagrammatic inference that allows us to transform a graph through inclusion taken as a hypothesis:

From any inclusion $R \sqsubseteq S$ and any graph of the form

$$G, x \xrightarrow{R} y\ ,$$

having an arc labeled R, we can infer the graph

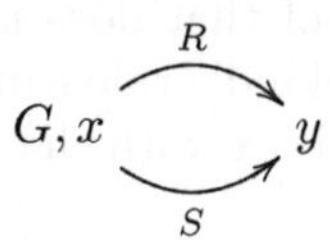

(27)

obtained from G by adding a new arc labeled S parallel to the old arc labeled R.

As a consequence of the erasing rule, in the rule for hypotheses, we can choose not to keep the arc $x \xrightarrow{R} y$.

5 Birkhoff-Question

To obtain a graph-based proof of (25), we transform the graph $- \xrightarrow{R} +$ into $- \xrightarrow{S^{\smile}} +$ applying the hypothesis $\mathsf{I} \sqsubseteq S \circ R$ and $R \circ S \sqsubseteq \mathsf{I}$ during the process of transformation. The proof consists of the following steps: 1. The graph of R; 2. Introduction of I; 3. Applying the hypothesis $\mathsf{I} \sqsubseteq S \circ R$; 4. Elimination of $\circ$; 5. Applying the hypothesis $R \circ S \sqsubseteq \mathsf{I}$; 6. Collapsing equal nodes; 7. Erasing irrelevant parts of the graph; 8. Introducing $^{\smile}$ to obtain $S^{\smile}$.

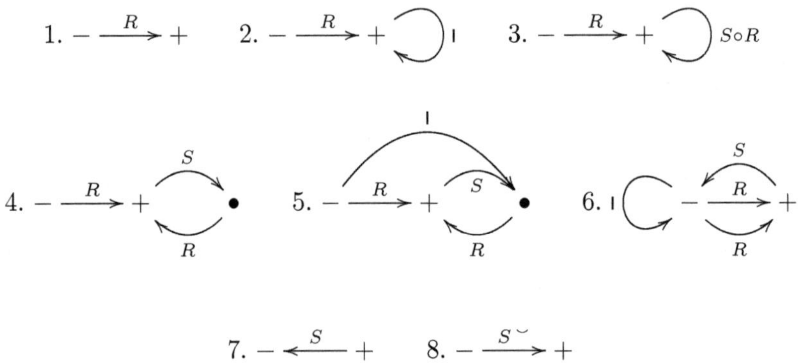

An interesting aspect of our graph-based proof is how close it is to an arithmetic proof based on binary relations, and at the same time, how far it is from it. Indeed, to obtain a relation algebraic proof of (25), the graph-based proof gives us the following start:

$$\begin{aligned} R &= R \circ \mathsf{I} && \text{Steps 1 and 2} \\ &= R \circ (S \circ R) && \text{Step 3} \\ &= (R \circ S) \circ R && \text{Step 4} \\ &= [(R \circ S) \sqcap \mathsf{I}] \circ R && \text{Step 5} \end{aligned}$$

Now, it seems there is no way to transform the transition from Step 5 to Step 6 into an arithmetic step since there is no obvious way to simulate the identification of $-$ and $\bullet$ performed in that transition. Furthermore, the arc labeled I, from $-$ to $\bullet$, represented in Step 5, extends beyond the arc labeled R, from $\bullet$ to $+$. But, in the last arithmetic step above, R is beyond the scope of the occurrence of I. What we need is a new proof that does not have this "flaw," and this is where our understanding of Dedekind's rule can be useful. By replacing Steps 3 through 7 of the demonstration above with the following steps, we obtain a new diagrammatic solution to Birkhoff-problem.

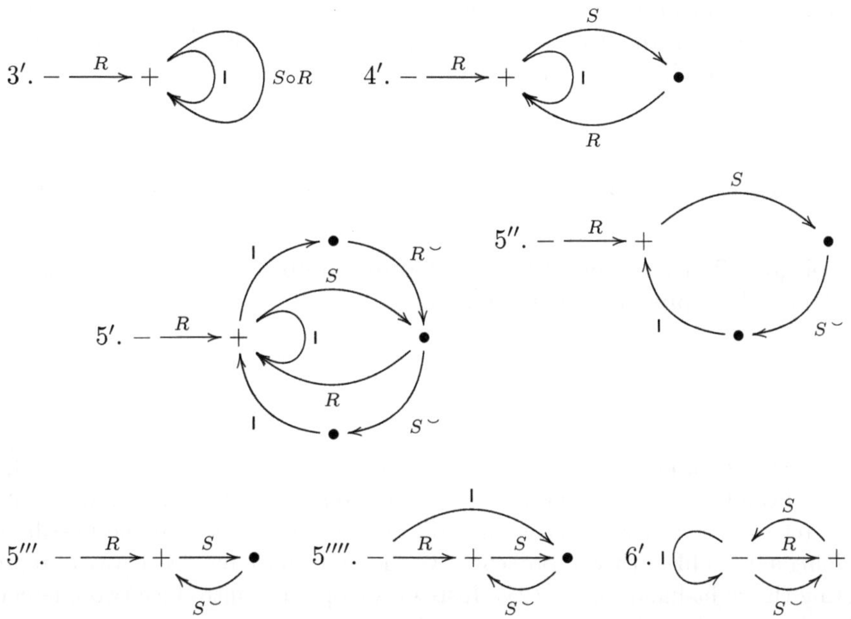

This new proof differs essentially from the previous one, because we use the strategy of duplicated paths of length two (Step 5). This becomes more evident when we notice that in Step 4 we have the triangle on the left on which we apply the diagrammatic reading of the Dedekind-rule, obtaining the structure on the right in Step 5:

Since this corresponds to one application of the Dedekind-rule, by doing so, we are able to translate the proof almost directly into an arithmetic proofs based on binary relations:

$$R = R \circ \mathsf{I} = R \circ [\mathsf{I} \sqcap (S \circ R)] \sqsubseteq R \circ \{[S \sqcap (\mathsf{I} \circ R^{\smile})] \circ [R \sqcap (S^{\smile} \circ \mathsf{I})]\} \sqsubseteq$$
$$R \circ [S \circ (S^{\smile} \circ \mathsf{I})] = R \circ (S \circ S^{\smile}) = (R \circ S) \circ S^{\smile} = \mathsf{I} \circ S^{\smile} = S^{\smile}.$$

Following completely analogous lines, we can present a graph-based proof of (26) that is directly translatable into an arithmetic proof based on binary relations. Due to space limitations, we leave this pleasant task to the reader.

6 Complementation

In addition to inclusion, composition, reversion, and identity, Chin-Tarski-question (4) deals with the usual operation of complementation from and to binary relations. For all $R \in 2^{U \times U}$ and $a, b \in U$:

$$aR^{-}b \Leftrightarrow \neg aRb \tag{28}$$

Here, $\neg$ means *not*. Hence, by definition, $^{-}$ is the operation of composition.

Graph and Rules Associated with Complementation. The left hand side of (28) can be represented by the graph

$$- \xrightarrow{R^{-}} + \tag{29}$$

A relevant philosophical and practical problem that, as far as we know, has not yet been fully solved, is how to graphically represent the negation of a statement (cf. [7] for a positive view and [10] for a negative view on the possibility of doing so). Unlike other approaches, we choose to have no direct way of representing the right-hand side of (28). Instead, we opted to introduce two inference rules that translate the meaning of classical negation.

To say that R^{-} is the complement of R is to say two things:

$$R \, \text{and} \, R^{-} \, \text{are} \, \textit{exhaustive}, \text{that is}, \mathsf{E} = R \sqcup R^{-}, \tag{30}$$

$$R \, \text{and} \, R^{-} \, \text{are} \, \textit{incompatible}, \text{that is}, R \sqcap R^{-} = \mathsf{E}^{-}. \tag{31}$$

Recall that E represents the universal relation. Therefore, E^{-} should be interpreted as the empty relation. Based on (30) and (31), it is natural that we allow the following two *actions* to be executed in any graph. First:

From any graph G with nodes x and y and any relation R, we can infer the graph

$$G, x \xrightarrow{R} y \;\Big|\; G, x \xrightarrow{R^{-}} y \tag{32}$$

that is the disjunction of two copies of G, one with a new arc from x to y labeled R the other with a new arc from x to y labeled R^{-}.

Second:

Any (*inconsistent disjunct* of a) graph of the form

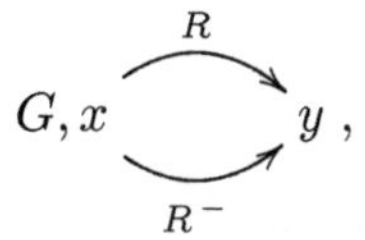

(33)

—that is, containing two nodes x and y that bear two parallel arcs, one labeled R and the other labeled R^-—can be deleted.

Indeed, according to graph semantics, (33) means that any pair of objects assigned to x and y, respectively, is related by both R and R^-, a contradiction according to (31).

7 Chin-Tarski-Question

To obtain a graph-based proof of (4) we transform $-\xrightarrow{(R^-\circ S^-)^{-\smile}\circ(R^-\circ S^-)^-}+$ into $-\xrightarrow{\mathsf{I}}+$, eliminating or introducing Peircean operators (Steps 2, 3, 7, 12, 18, 23), applying rule (32) (Steps 4, 5, 6, 9, 14, 17, 20), applying rule (33) (Steps 8, 11, 13, 16, 19, 22, 24) applying rule (27) (Steps 10, 15, 21), and deleting a part of the graph which does not interest for the problem solution (Step 25).

1. $-\xrightarrow{(R^-\circ S^-)^{-\smile}\circ(R^-\circ S^-)^-}+$ 2. $-\xrightarrow{(R^-\circ S^-)^{-\smile}}\bullet\xrightarrow{(R^-\circ S^-)^-}+$

3. $-\xleftarrow{(R^-\circ S^-)^-}\bullet\xrightarrow{(R^-\circ S^-)^-}+$

4.
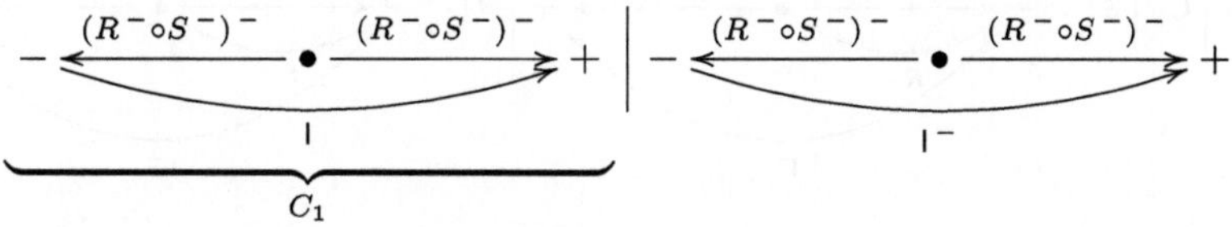

5.
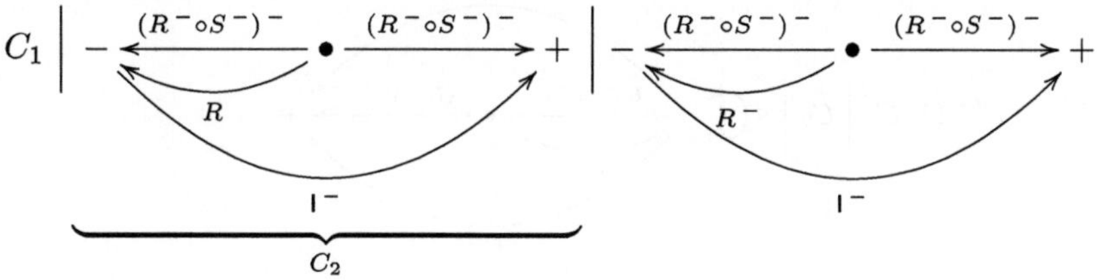

6. 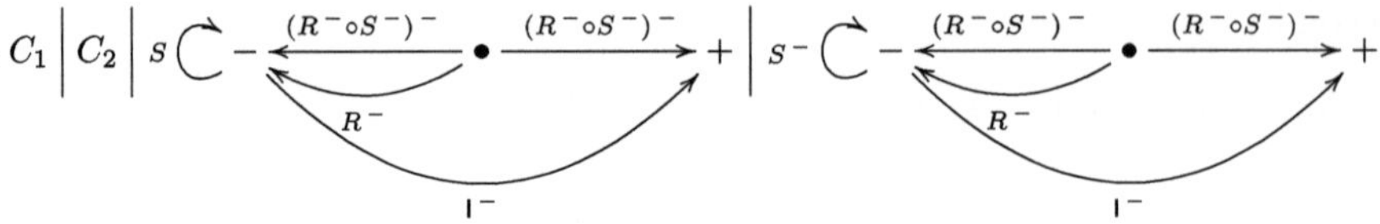
$C_1 \mid C_2 \mid s$
$(R^- \circ S^-)^-$
$(R^- \circ S^-)^-$
R^-
I^-
s^-
$(R^- \circ S^-)^-$
$(R^- \circ S^-)^-$
R^-
I^-

7. 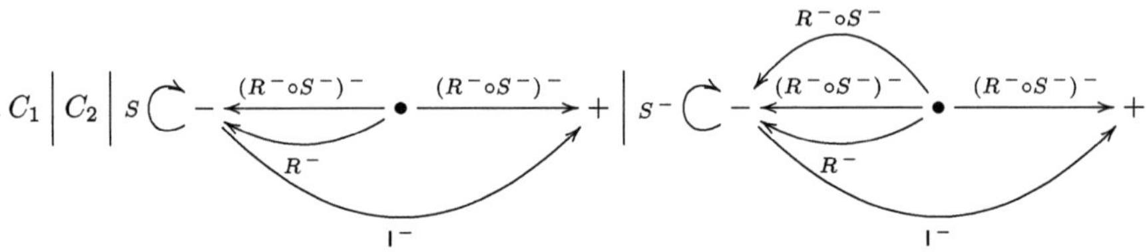
$C_1 \mid C_2 \mid s$
$(R^- \circ S^-)^-$
$(R^- \circ S^-)^-$
R^-
I^-
s^-
$R^- \circ S^-$
$(R^- \circ S^-)^-$
$(R^- \circ S^-)^-$
R^-
I^-

8. 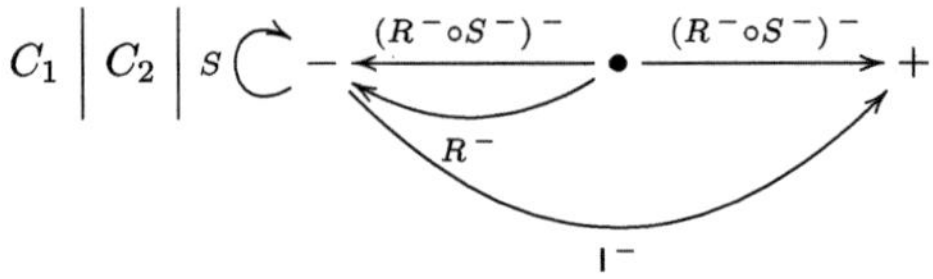
$C_1 \mid C_2 \mid s$
$(R^- \circ S^-)^-$
$(R^- \circ S^-)^-$
R^-
I^-

9. 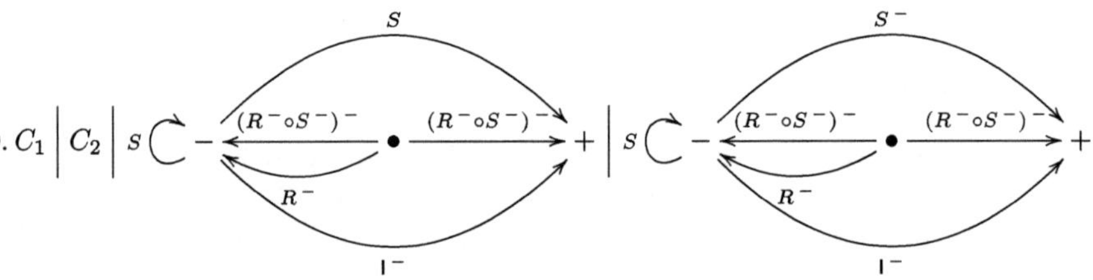
$C_1 \mid C_2 \mid s$
S
$(R^- \circ S^-)^-$
$(R^- \circ S^-)^-$
R^-
I^-
s
S^-
$(R^- \circ S^-)^-$
$(R^- \circ S^-)^-$
R^-
I^-

10. 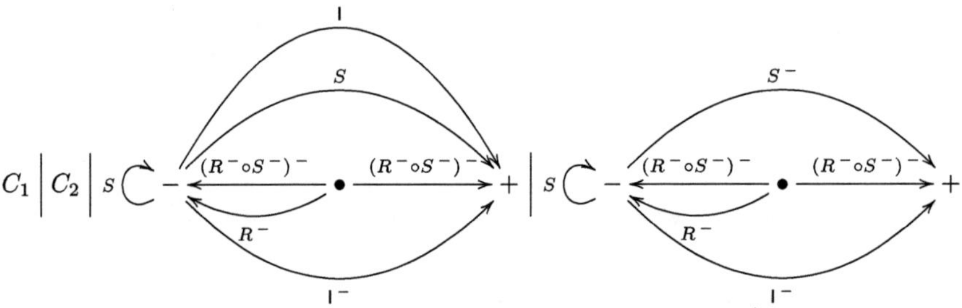
$C_1 \mid C_2 \mid s$
I
S
$(R^- \circ S^-)^-$
$(R^- \circ S^-)^-$
R^-
I^-
s
S^-
$(R^- \circ S^-)^-$
$(R^- \circ S^-)^-$
R^-
I^-

11. 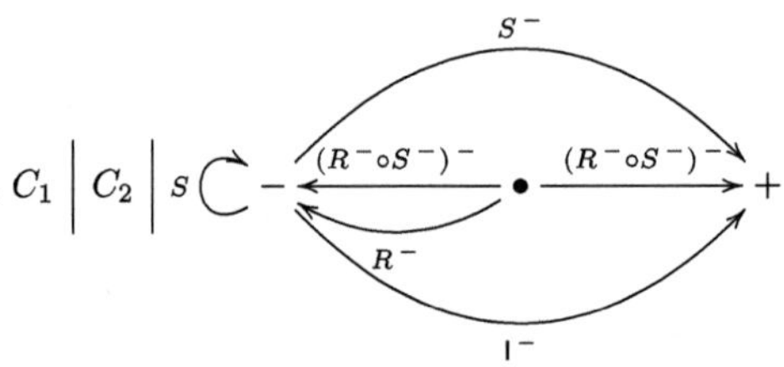
$C_1 \mid C_2 \mid s$
S^-
$(R^- \circ S^-)^-$
$(R^- \circ S^-)^-$
R^-
I^-

12. 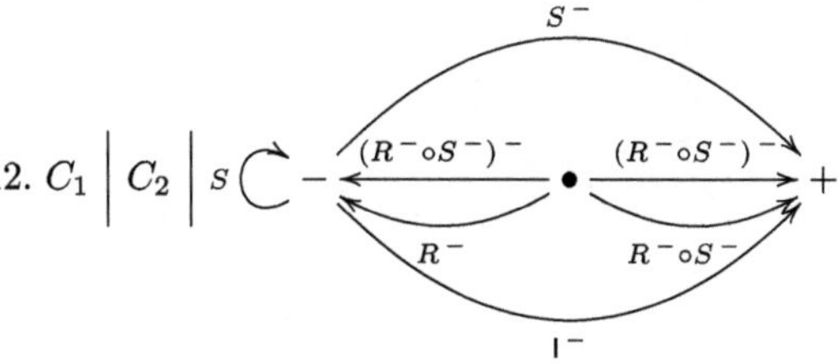

13. 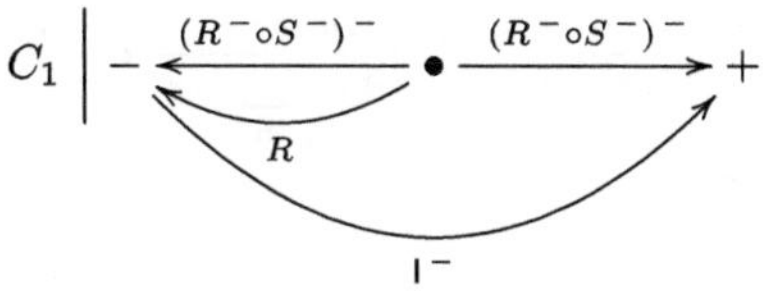

14. 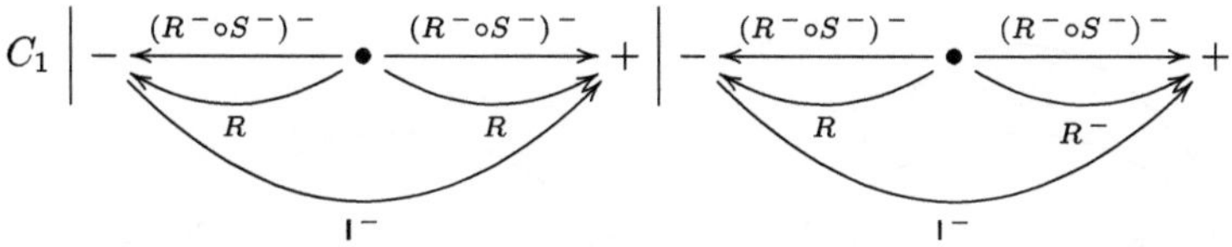

15. 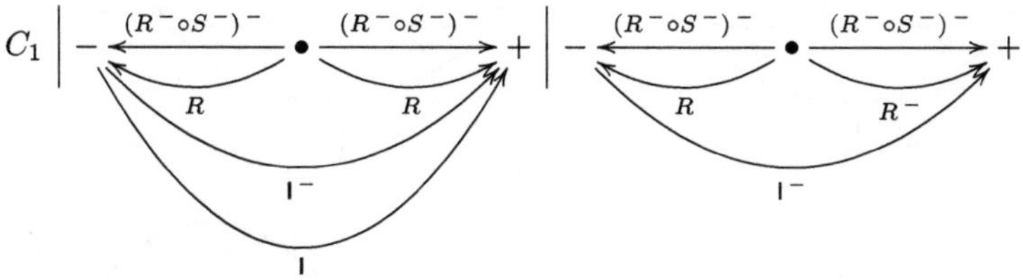

16. 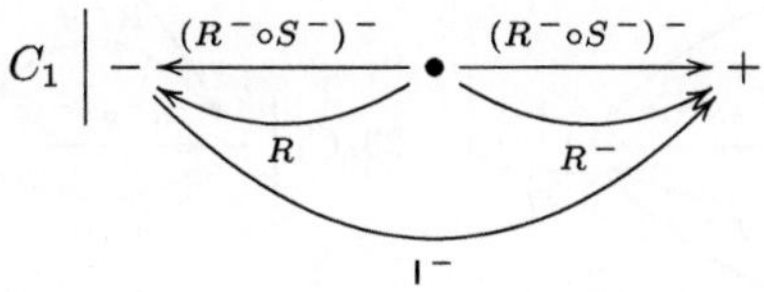

17. 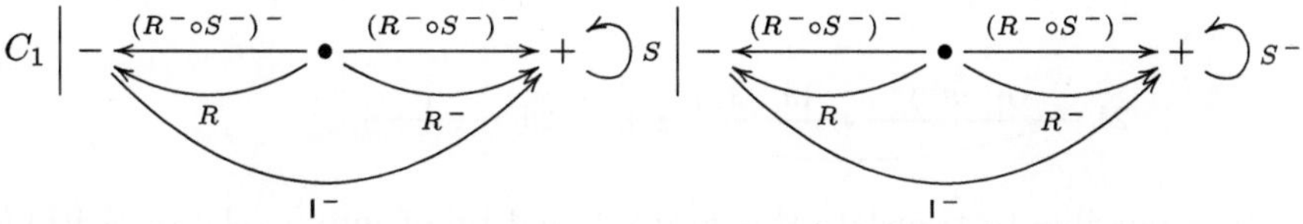

18. 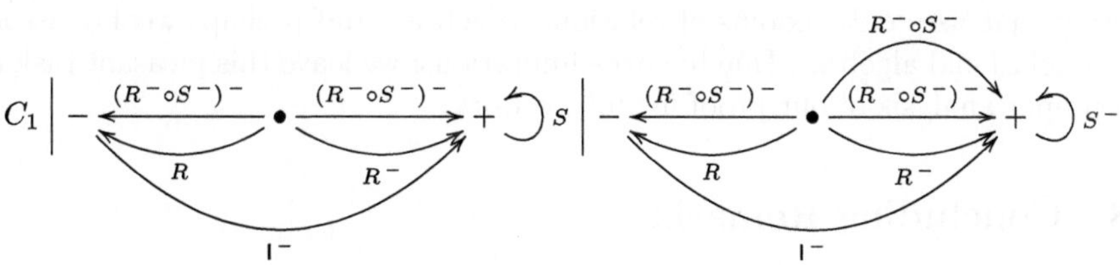

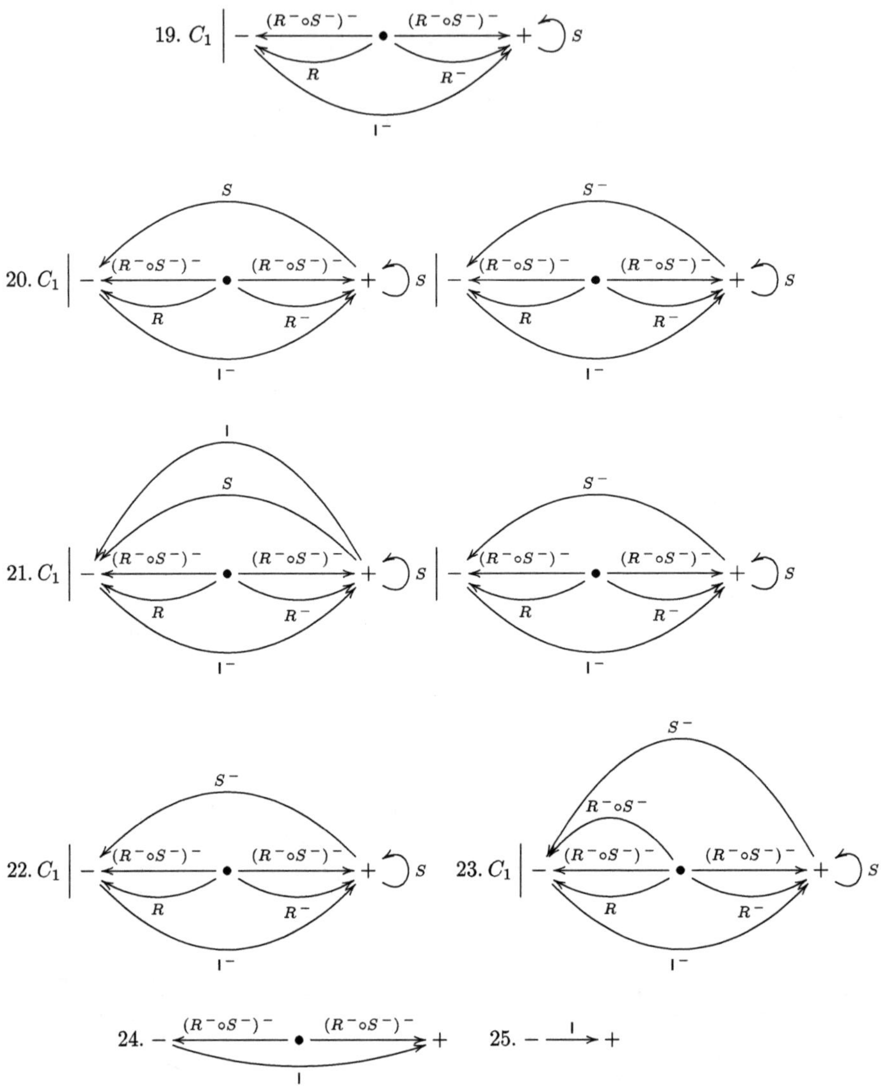

It is possible to translate this graph based proof into a relation arithmetic proof that uses only axioms of relational algebra—and perhaps weakly associative relational algebras. Due to space limitations, we leave this pleasant task and a proper analysis of our proof for future work.

8 Concluding Remarks

Whether diagrams in ancient geometry have an inferential role is a disputable question; however, they are certainly involved in reasoning. Here, it has been shown that graphs labeled with relation algebra terms can be used diagrammatically in a powerful inferential role, revealing certain aspects that are not expressible in arithmetical terms, such as the one hidden in Dedekind-rule. We believe that at least two features of our system make it attractive from the point of view of producing relatively simple and visually informative proofs:

- its language forces the user fragmenting the information into more or less disjoint parts whose formal treatment can be carried out without interference from the other parts (cf. the proof in Sect. 7);
- its inference mechanism acts strictly on the only diagram under scrutiny, forcing the user to operate step-wisely in the search for patterns that can lead to the next proof step (cf. the proofs in Sects. 4, 5, and 7).

A deeper understanding of these aspects in the form of proof strategies can help us simplify the solution to the heuristic problem of finding proofs.

References

1. Cerioli, M.R., Suguitani, L., Viana, P.: Presenting Basic Graph Logic. In: Basu, A., Stapleton, G., Linker, S., Legg, C., Manalo, E., Viana, P. (eds.) Diagrammatic Representation and Inference, Diagrams 2021, LNCS, vol. 12909, pp. 132–148. Springer, Heidelberg (2021)
2. Chin, L.H., Tarski, A.: Distributive and modular laws in the arithmetic of relation algebras. Univ. Calif. Publ. Math. **1**, 341–384 (1951)
3. Comer, S.D.: A new foundation for the theory of relations. Notre Dame J. Form. Log. **24**, 181–187 (1983)
4. Gold, M.: Symposium in honor of Bjarni Jónsson: announcement. Algebra Universalis **18**, 1–3 (1984)
5. Maddux, R.: A sequent calculus for relation algebras. Ann. Pure Appl. Logic **25**, 73–101 (1983)
6. Monk, J.D.: Studies in Cylindric Algebra. PhD Thesis. UC Berkley, Berkeley (1961)
7. Oversteegen, E., Schilperoord, J.: Can pictures say no or not? Negation and denial in the visual mode. J. Pragmat. **67**, 89–106 (2014)
8. Peirce, C.S.: Note B: the logic of relatives. In: Peirce, C.S. (ed.) Studies in logic by members of the Johns Hopkins University, pp. 187–203. John Benjamins Publishing Company, Amsterdam (1883)
9. Schmidt, G., Ströhlein, T.: Relation algebras: concepts of points and representability. Discrete Math. **54**, 83–92 (1985)
10. Worth, S.H.G.: Pictures can't say ain't. In: Gross, L. (ed.) Studying Visual Communication, pp. 162–184. University of Pennsylvania Press, Philadelphia (2016)

Inferring Relations from Relations

Stef Frijters(✉) and Atahan Erbas

Center for Logic and Philosophy of Science, KU Leuven, Leuven, Belgium
{stef.frijters,atahan.erbas}@kuleuven.be

Abstract. Aristotelian diagrams, such as the square of opposition, graphically depict logical relations holding between formulas. In previous work it has been noted that new logical relations can be inferred, and thus drawn in the diagram, based on information about other relations. However, this work rests on a number of assumptions about the formulas and diagrams. The most important of these assumptions are that in the diagram there is a contradictory formula for every formula, there are no equivalent formulas, there are only contingent formulas, and only four relations are depicted. In this paper we dispense with these assumptions and systematically work out what relations can be inferred from what other relations. This leads to a number of new discoveries, which in turn form the inspiration for a new and more general diagrammatic logic system for Aristotelian diagrams.

Keywords: Aristotelian Diagrams · Logical Relations · Logical Geometry · Square of Opposition · Logic Diagrams

1 Introduction

Aristotelian diagrams have been used to visualise logical relations since at least the second century BCE [1], and continue to be used in areas as diverse as philosophy, linguistics, law, computer science, and psychology [3]. It has been known for quite some time that the represented logical relations must always occur in certain patterns (see e.g. [4,12,14,15]). For example, if two formulas φ and ψ are contradictory (i.e. they cannot be true together and cannot be false together), and ψ' is in subalternation with ψ (i.e. ψ' implies ψ, but not vice versa), then φ and ψ' are contrary to each other (i.e. they cannot be true together, but they can be false together). Recently, [5] emphasized that this means that Aristotelian diagrams cannot only be seen as representing the logical relations, but also as inferential devices that allow us to derive new logical relations, or new diagrams. This led to the development of an *Aristotelian Diagrammatic Logic System* (**ADLS**), following the tradition of diagrammatic logic systems for all kinds of diagrams [8,11,13].

ADLS was developed to be suited for the most common types of Aristotelian diagrams. For example, Fig. 1.a depicts a square of opposition, the oldest and most well-known kind of Aristotelian diagram. This diagram depicts four Aristotelian relations holding between (in this case) formulas of propositional logic.

P. Sobociński et al. (Eds.): Diagrams 2026, LNAI 16833, pp. 150–166, 2027.
https://doi.org/10.1007/978-3-032-34178-5_17

An extension of this type of diagram is found in Fig. 1.d. Both these diagrams conform to a number of rules: there are no equivalent formulas present in the diagram, there are only contingent formulas present, and for every formula there is exactly one contradictory formula present. Most diagrams in the literature adhere to these three rules, and there are some theoretical considerations motivating these constraints [4,14]. Only diagrams conforming to these rules are covered by **ADLS**.

However, Aristotelian diagrams come in many shapes and sizes. Figure 1.c (taken from [2]) is an example of such a diagram. It breaks the rule that only contingent formulas are allowed to be present, and the rule that exactly one contradictory formula is present. The diagram in Fig. 1.b breaks the other rule: equivalent expressions occur in the diagram, and the equivalence relation is represented. This is a diagram often used to visualize the relations holding between different notions of 'right' in the Hohfeldian framework (see e.g. [9]). It contains equivalent notions denoted by a double-headed arrow (e.g. claim and duty), and also multiple contradictory notions: since 'Duty' and 'Privilege' are contradictory, and 'Duty' and 'Claim' are equivalent, it follows that 'Claim' and 'Privilege' are also contradictory.

This kind of inference is the central topic of this paper. Even without the mentioned rules for Aristotelian diagrams it is often still possible to derive many relations and new diagrams. We will systematically investigate what logical relations follow from what other logical relations, and then use that information to develop two new diagrammatic logic systems for Aristotelian diagrams: **ADLS**$^-$ and **ADLSC**. **ADLS**$^-$ makes no assumptions about the diagrams in play, while **ADLSC** only assumes that the formulas in the diagram are contingent.

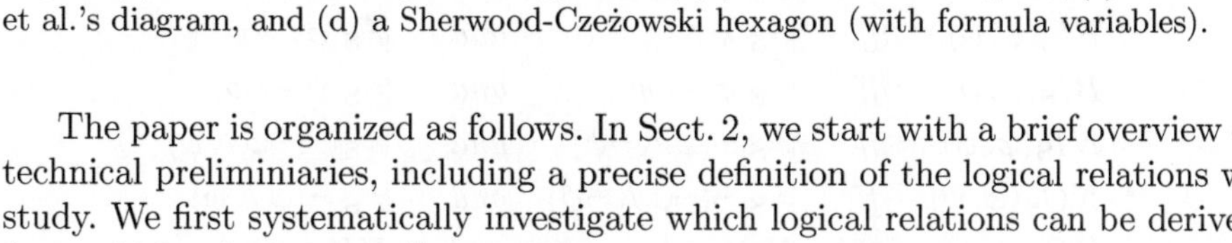

Fig. 1. (a) the traditional square of opposition, (b) the Hohfeldian square, (c) de Klerck et al.'s diagram, and (d) a Sherwood-Czeżowski hexagon (with formula variables).

The paper is organized as follows. In Sect. 2, we start with a brief overview of technical preliminiaries, including a precise definition of the logical relations we study. We first systematically investigate which logical relations can be derived from which other ones in Sect. 3. Then we use these result to construct two diagrammatic logic systems for Aristotelian diagrams in Sect. 4. The first of these, **ADLS**$^-$, is the most general, whereas the second system, **ADLSC** assumes that all the formulas in the diagram are consistent. In Sect. 4.1 we introduce the diagrammatic vocabulary of these systems, and in Sect. 4.2 the semantics. Then we present an axiomatization of **ADLS**$^-$ in Sect. 4.3, and an axiomatizaton of **ADLSC** in Sect. 4.4. We comment on the completeness of these systems in Sect. 4.5, before concluding in Sect. 5

2 Preliminaries

Let us start with some formal preliminaries. Definition 1 formally defines the logical relations that are central in this paper.[1] The traditional square of opposition depicts four of these relations: contradiction (CD), contrariety (C), subcontrariety (SC), and subalternation (SA). However, [14] argued that this set of relations should be extended to also include right implication (RI), bi-implication (BI), and unconnectedness (UC), and (to preserve symmetry) that SA should be replaced with left-implication (LI). They show that these seven relations form a partition of formula pairs: every ordered pair of contingent formulas is in exactly one of these relations.[2] In what follows, we refer to these seven relations as the 'Aristotelian relations'.

However, if we also include non-contingent formulas in our considerations, then the seven relations are no longer mutually exclusive. For example, for any contingent formula φ it is the case that a contradictory formula ($\perp$) is in both the LI and the C relation with φ (see e.g. Fig. 1.c). So when we consider non-contingent formulas as well, we will instead look at two different sets of relations. The 'opposition relations' (OR) are CD, C, SC and NO, and the 'implication relations' (IR) are BI, LI, RI and NI [14]. Both these sets of relations are partitions: every ordered pair of formulas are in exactly one opposition relation and one implication relation. For example, in classical proposition logic $LI(p, p \vee q)$ and $NO(p, p \vee q)$.

Definition 1. *Let* **S** *be a logical system based on a language* $\mathcal{L}_\mathbf{S}$*, which is assumed to have Boolean operators and a model-theoretic semantics* $\models_\mathbf{S}$*. The formulas* $\varphi, \psi \in \mathcal{L}_\mathbf{S}$ *are*

$$\begin{array}{llll}
CD_\mathbf{S}(\varphi,\psi) & \textit{iff} & \models_\mathbf{S} \neg(\varphi\wedge\psi) & \textit{and} & \models_\mathbf{S} \varphi\vee\psi \\
C_\mathbf{S}(\varphi,\psi) & \textit{iff} & \models_\mathbf{S} \neg(\varphi\wedge\psi) & \textit{and} & \not\models_\mathbf{S} \varphi\vee\psi \\
SC_\mathbf{S}(\varphi,\psi) & \textit{iff} & \not\models_\mathbf{S} \neg(\varphi\wedge\psi) & \textit{and} & \models_\mathbf{S} \varphi\vee\psi \\
SA_\mathbf{S}(\varphi,\psi) & \textit{iff} & \models_\mathbf{S} \varphi\to\psi & \textit{and} & \not\models_\mathbf{S} \psi\to\varphi \\
LI_\mathbf{S}(\varphi,\psi) & \textit{iff} & \models_\mathbf{S} \varphi\to\psi & \textit{and} & \not\models_\mathbf{S} \psi\to\varphi \\
RI_\mathbf{S}(\varphi,\psi) & \textit{iff} & \models_\mathbf{S} \psi\to\varphi & \textit{and} & \not\models_\mathbf{S} \varphi\to\psi \\
BI_\mathbf{S}(\varphi,\psi) & \textit{iff} & \models_\mathbf{S} \varphi\to\psi & \textit{and} & \models_\mathbf{S} \psi\to\varphi \\
NI_\mathbf{S}(\varphi,\psi) & \textit{iff} & \not\models_\mathbf{S} \neg(\varphi\wedge\neg\psi) & \textit{and} & \not\models_\mathbf{S} \neg(\neg\varphi\wedge\psi) \\
NO_\mathbf{S}(\varphi,\psi) & \textit{iff} & \not\models_\mathbf{S} \neg(\neg\varphi\wedge\neg\psi) & \textit{and} & \not\models_\mathbf{S} \neg(\varphi\wedge\psi) \\
UC_\mathbf{S}(\varphi,\psi) & \textit{iff} & NO(\varphi,\psi) & \textit{and} & NI(\varphi,\psi)
\end{array}$$

[1] We omit the subscript **S** when talking about the relation in general, without reference to a specific logic, or when the logic is clear from the context.

[2] The fact that these are a partition is not a new discovery by Demey and Smessaert, see for example [7].

In this paper we will only depict the seven Aristotelian relations in diagrams. To do so, we use the following convention. As usual, CD is represented by a solid line, C by a dashed line, and SC by a dotted line. Furthermore, since for any φ and ψ, $LI(\varphi, \psi)$ iff $RI(\psi, \varphi)$ (iff $SA(\varphi, \psi)$) we will use the single-headed arrow from φ to ψ to depict $LI(\varphi, \psi)$ and $RI(\psi, \varphi)$ (and $SA(\varphi, \psi)$). UC is usually not explicitly depicted. However, not drawing any connection between two formulas can mean that the two formulas are in the UC relation, or that the relation between the two formulas has not yet been derived (see e.g. Fig. 1.b). So, inspired by the convention from [14], we will represent UC by a grey line. If necessary, we could also represent NI by, for example, a grey double-headed arrow and NO by, for example, a grey dashed line, but we rarely encounter a depiction of such relations in Aristotelian diagrams ([14] is an exception to this rule).

3 Inferring Relations

In this section, we ask the central question of this paper: if we know that some formulas are in some relations, then what other relations can we derive? We start with Theorem 1, which specifically answers the question: if we know that φ and ψ are in a specific relation, and φ and χ are in a certain relation, then what do we know about the relation between ψ and χ? Here we do not have any assumptions about φ, ψ or χ: any one of them can be a tautology or a contradiction, and any two of them can be equivalent to each other. In Theorem 2 we answer the same question, but with our attention constricted to only contingent formulas.

Theorem 1. *For any φ, ψ, χ, the inferences in Fig. 2 hold. In case the background logic* **S** *cannot be trivial, CD is excluded from all results marked with † and BI is excluded from all results marked with ‡. In addition, for all entries marked by a '∗', not every combination of OR and IR is possible:*
2b If $BI(\psi, \chi)$, then not $CD(\psi, \chi)$.
2d If $BI(\psi, \chi)$, then $NO(\psi, \chi)$.
3c If $CD(\psi, \chi)$ or $SC(\psi, \chi)$, then $NI(\psi, \chi)$.
3e If $BI(\psi, \chi)$ or $LI(\psi, \chi)$, then $NO(\psi, \chi)$.
4b If $BI(\psi, \chi)$, then $NO(\psi, \chi)$.
4d If $CD(\psi, \chi)$ or $C(\psi, \chi)$, then $NI(\psi, \chi)$.
5c If $BI(\psi, \chi)$ or $RI(\psi, \chi)$, then $NO(\psi, \chi)$.
7g If $BI(\psi, \chi)$, $LI(\psi, \chi)$ or $RI(\psi, \chi)$, then $NO(\psi, \chi)$.

Proof. Proofs are easy in function of set theory, possibly using Venn diagrams. For example for 2c: the intersection of all models making φ true and making ψ true is empty because $C(\varphi, \psi)$. Because of $SC(\varphi, \chi)$, the intersection between the models making φ and χ true is not empty, but there are no models that make ψ true and not φ or χ. So all models that make ψ true make χ true, and there is at least one model that makes χ true. So $LI(\psi, \chi)$. All the information can also be depicted in a Venn (or Venn-Peirce) diagram, which makes it even easier to read off the relation between ψ and χ. See the Venn Diagrams in Fig. 3 for two examples (for more on Venn-Peirce diagrams, see [6,13]).

1. If $CD(\varphi, \psi)$, and (a) $CD(\varphi, \chi)$, then $BI(\psi, \chi)$ and any $OR\dagger$ (b) $C(\varphi, \chi)$, then $RI(\psi, \chi)$ and any OR (c) $SC(\varphi, \chi)$, then $LI(\psi, \chi)$ and any OR (d) $LI(\varphi, \chi)$, then $SC(\psi, \chi)$ and any IR (e) $RI(\varphi, \chi)$, then $C(\psi, \chi)$ and any IR (f) $BI(\varphi, \chi)$, then $CD(\psi, \chi)$ and any $IR\ddagger$ (g) $UC(\varphi, \chi)$, then $UC(\psi, \chi)$	2. If $C(\varphi, \psi)$, and (a) $CD(\varphi, \chi)$, then $LI(\psi, \chi)$ and any OR (b) $C(\varphi, \chi)$, then any OR and any IR^* (c) $SC(\varphi, \chi)$, then $LI(\psi, \chi)$ and any OR (d) $LI(\varphi, \chi)$, then any OR and any IR^* (e) $RI(\varphi, \chi)$, then $C(\psi, \chi)$ and any IR (f) $BI(\varphi, \chi)$, then $C(\psi, \chi)$ and any $IR\ddagger$ (g) $UC(\varphi, \chi)$, then $(C(\psi, \chi)$ or $NO(\psi, \chi))$ and $(LI(\psi, \chi)$ or $NI(\psi, \chi))$
3. If $SC(\varphi, \psi)$, and (a) $CD(\varphi, \chi)$, then $RI(\psi, \chi)$ and any OR (b) $C(\varphi, \chi)$, then $RI(\psi, \chi)$ and any OR (c) $SC(\varphi, \chi)$, then any OR and any IR^* (d) $LI(\varphi, \chi)$, then $SC(\psi, \chi)$ and any IR (e) $RI(\varphi, \chi)$, then any OR and any IR^* (f) $BI(\varphi, \chi)$, then $SC(\psi, \chi)$ and any IR (g) $UC(\varphi, \chi)$, then $(SC(\psi, \chi)$ or $NO(\psi, \chi))$ and $(RI(\psi, \chi)$ or $NI(\psi, \chi))$	4. If $LI(\varphi, \psi)$, and (a) $CD(\varphi, \chi)$, then $SC(\psi, \chi)$ and any IR (b) $C(\varphi, \chi)$, then any OR and any IR^* (c) $SC(\varphi, \chi)$, then $SC(\psi, \chi)$ and any IR (d) $LI(\varphi, \chi)$, then any OR and any IR^* (e) $RI(\varphi, \chi)$, then $RI(\psi, \chi)$ and any OR (f) $BI(\varphi, \chi)$, then $RI(\psi, \chi)$ and any OR (g) $UC(\varphi, \chi)$, then $(SC(\psi, \chi)$ or $NO(\psi, \chi))$ and $(RI(\psi, \chi)$ or $NI(\psi, \chi))$
5. If $RI(\varphi, \psi)$, and (a) $CD(\varphi, \chi)$, then $C(\psi, \chi)$ and any IR (b) $C(\varphi, \chi)$, then $C(\psi, \chi)$ and any IR (c) $SC(\varphi, \chi)$, then any OR and any IR^* (d) $LI(\varphi, \chi)$, then $LI(\psi, \chi)$ and any OR (e) $RI(\varphi, \chi)$, then any OR and any IR (f) $BI(\varphi, \chi)$, then $LI(\psi, \chi)$ and any OR (g) $UC(\varphi, \chi)$, then $(C(\psi, \chi)$ or $NO(\psi, \chi))$ and $(LI(\psi, \chi)$ or $NI(\psi, \chi))$	6. If $BI(\varphi, \psi)$, and (a) $CD(\varphi, \chi)$, then $CD(\psi, \chi)$ and any $IR\ddagger$ (b) $C(\varphi, \chi)$, then $C(\psi, \chi)$ and any IR (c) $SC(\varphi, \chi)$, then $SC(\psi, \chi)$ and any IR (d) $LI(\varphi, \chi)$, then $LI(\psi, \chi)$ and any OR (e) $RI(\varphi, \chi)$, then $RI(\psi, \chi)$ and any OR (f) $BI(\varphi, \chi)$, then $BI(\psi, \chi)$ and any $OR\dagger$ (g) $UC(\varphi, \chi)$, then $NO(\psi, \chi)$ and $NI(\psi, \chi)$
7. If $UC(\varphi, \psi)$, and (a) $CD(\varphi, \chi)$, then $NO(\psi, \chi)$ and $NI(\psi, \chi)$ (b) $C(\varphi, \chi)$, then $(C(\psi, \chi)$ or $NO(\psi, \chi))$ and $(RI(\psi, \chi)$ or $NI(\psi, \chi))$ (c) $SC(\varphi, \chi)$, then $(SC(\psi, \chi)$ or $NO(\psi, \chi))$ and $(LI(\psi, \chi)$ or $NI(\psi, \chi))$ (d) $LI(\varphi, \chi)$, then $(SC(\psi, \chi)$ or $NO(\psi, \chi))$ and $(LI(\psi, \chi)$ or $NI(\psi, \chi))$ (e) $RI(\varphi, \chi)$, then $(C(\psi, \chi)$ or $NO(\psi, \chi))$ and $(RI(\psi, \chi)$ or $NI(\psi, \chi))$ (f) $BI(\varphi, \chi)$, then $NI(\psi, \chi)$ and $NO(\psi, \chi)$ (g) $UC(\varphi, \chi)$, then any OR and any IR^*	

Fig. 2. Relations inferrable from two premisses

Theorem 2. *For any* contingent φ, ψ *and* χ, *the inferences in Fig. 4 hold.*

The results in Theorem 2 are already known in the literature, but in other contexts. For example, Table 2 in [10] comes to essentially the same results when investigating the 'joins' between 'basic entailment relations'. However, we are unaware of such a systematic approach in the context of Aristotelian diagrams. The results that have CD in the premisses have been known for quite some time

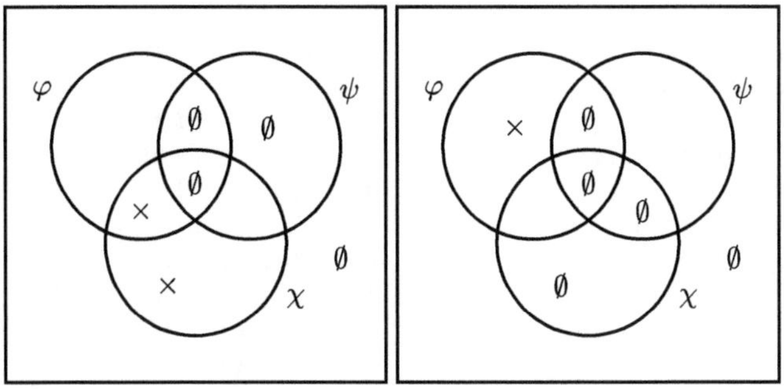

Fig. 3. Venn diagrams for cases 2.c and 2.e

(e.g. [5,14]), but for example cases 2c, 2e, 3b, or 4c of either theorem are quite surprising. It turns out that more relations can be inferred than was previously known, even when assuming very little about the diagrams in question.

In Theorems 1 and 2 we were only concerned with inferences with two premisses. There are also relations derivable when we have three inputs. For example, from $C(\varphi', \psi')$, $RI(\varphi', \varphi)$, and $RI(\psi', \psi)$ it follows that $C(\varphi, \psi)$. However, this already indirectly follows from Theorem 1. From $C(\varphi', \psi')$ and $RI(\varphi', \varphi)$ it follows by 2(e) that $C(\varphi, \psi')$. From this and $RI(\psi', \psi)$ it follows by another application of 2(e) that $C(\varphi, \psi)$. Now, does this hold for every derivation with more than two premisses? At this point we do not know. We will return to this question in Sect. 4.5, after we have set up a logic of Aristotelian diagrams.

There is however another question that we must first answer. So far we have looked at relations between arbitrary formulas. However, what follows if we know that one of the formulas is a tautology ($\top$) or a contradiction ($\bot$)? We list all of the possibilities in Fig. 5.[3]

4 Some Aristotelian Diagrammatic Logic Systems

In Sect. 3 we looked at the logical relations isolated from the diagrams in which they occur. We now return to these diagrams and present two Diagrammatic Logic Systems for Aristotelian diagrams. These new systems differ from the **ADLS** presented in [5]. Firstly, they include a representation of all seven Aristotelian relations. Secondly, they no longer make the three assumptions discussed before. They allow for diagrams with equivalent formulas, have no restriction on the contradiction relations, and one of the systems also allows diagrams containing non-contingent formulas.

[3] These results are easily checked. It suffices to simply apply the definitions of the relations.

1. If $CD(\varphi, \psi)$, and (a) $CD(\varphi, \chi)$, then $BI(\psi, \chi)$ (b) $C(\varphi, \chi)$, then $RI(\psi, \chi)$ (c) $SC(\varphi, \chi)$, then $LI(\psi, \chi)$ (d) $LI(\varphi, \chi)$, then $SC(\psi, \chi)$ (e) $RI(\varphi, \chi)$, then $C(\psi, \chi)$ (f) $BI(\varphi, \chi)$, then $CD(\psi, \chi)$ (g) $UC(\varphi, \chi)$, then $UC(\psi, \chi)$	2. If $C(\varphi, \psi)$, and (a) $CD(\varphi, \chi)$, then $LI(\psi, \chi)$ (b) $C(\varphi, \chi)$, then $C(\psi, \chi)$, $LI(\psi, \chi)$, $RI(\psi, \chi)$, $BI(\psi, \chi)$, or $UC(\psi, \chi)$ (c) $SC(\varphi, \chi)$, then $LI(\psi, \chi)$ (d) $LI(\varphi, \chi)$, then $CD(\psi, \chi)$, $C(\psi, \chi)$, $SC(\psi, \chi)$, $LI(\psi, \chi)$, or $UC(\psi, \chi)$ (e) $RI(\varphi, \chi)$, then $C(\psi, \chi)$ (f) $BI(\varphi, \chi)$, then $C(\psi, \chi)$ (g) $UC(\varphi, \chi)$, $C(\psi, \chi)$, $LI(\psi, \chi)$ or $UC(\psi, \chi)$
3. If $SC(\varphi, \psi)$, and (a) $CD(\varphi, \chi)$, then $RI(\psi, \chi)$ (b) $C(\varphi, \chi)$, then $RI(\psi, \chi)$ (c) $SC(\varphi, \chi)$, then $SC(\psi, \chi)$, $LI(\psi, \chi)$, $RI(\psi, \chi)$, $BI(\psi, \chi)$ or $UC(\psi, \chi)$ (d) $LI(\varphi, \chi)$, then $SC(\psi, \chi)$ (e) $RI(\varphi, \chi)$, then $CD(\psi, \chi)$, $C(\psi, \chi)$, $SC(\psi, \chi)$, $RI(\psi, \chi)$, or $UC(\psi, \chi)$ (f) $BI(\varphi, \chi)$, then $SC(\psi, \chi)$ (g) $UC(\varphi, \chi)$, then $SC(\psi, \chi)$, $RI(\psi, \chi)$, or $UC(\psi, \chi)$	4. If $LI(\varphi, \psi)$, and (a) $CD(\varphi, \chi)$, then $SC(\psi, \chi)$ (b) $C(\varphi, \chi)$, then $CD(\psi, \chi)$, $C(\psi, \chi)$, $SC(\psi, \chi)$, $RI(\psi, \chi)$, or $UC(\psi, \chi)$ (c) $SC(\varphi, \chi)$, then $SC(\psi, \chi)$ (d) $LI(\varphi, \chi)$, then $SC(\psi, \chi)$, $LI(\psi, \chi)$, $RI(\psi, \chi)$, $BI(\psi, \chi)$ or $UC(\psi, \chi)$ (e) $RI(\varphi, \chi)$, then $RI(\psi, \chi)$ (f) $BI(\varphi, \chi)$, then $RI(\psi, \chi)$ (g) $UC(\varphi, \chi)$, then $SC(\psi, \chi)$, $RI(\psi, \chi)$, or $UC(\psi, \chi)$
5. If $RI(\varphi, \psi)$, and (a) $CD(\varphi, \chi)$, then $C(\psi, \chi)$ (b) $C(\varphi, \chi)$, then $C(\psi, \chi)$ (c) $SC(\varphi, \chi)$, then $CD(\psi, \chi)$, $C(\psi, \chi)$, $SC(\psi, \chi)$, $LI(\psi, \chi)$ or $UC(\psi, \chi)$ (d) $LI(\varphi, \chi)$, then $LI(\psi, \chi)$ (e) $RI(\varphi, \chi)$, then $C(\psi, \chi)$, $LI(\psi, \chi)$, $RI(\psi, \chi)$c, $BI(\psi, \chi)$, or $UC(\psi, \chi)$ (f) $BI(\varphi, \chi)$, then $LI(\psi, \chi)$ (g) $UC(\varphi, \chi)$, then $C(\psi, \chi)$, $LI(\psi, \chi)$, or $UC(\psi, \chi)$	6. If $BI(\varphi, \psi)$, and (a) $CD(\varphi, \chi)$, then $CD(\psi, \chi)$ (b) $C(\varphi, \chi)$, then $C(\psi, \chi)$ (c) $SC(\varphi, \chi)$, then $SC(\psi, \chi)$ (d) $LI(\varphi, \chi)$, then $LI(\psi, \chi)$ (e) $RI(\varphi, \chi)$, then $RI(\psi, \chi)$ (f) $BI(\varphi, \chi)$, then $BI(\psi, \chi)$ (g) $UC(\varphi, \chi)$, then $UC(\psi, \chi)$
7. If $UC(\varphi, \psi)$, and (a) $CD(\varphi, \chi)$, then $UC(\psi, \chi)$ (b) $C(\varphi, \chi)$, then $C(\psi, \chi)$, $RI(\psi, \chi)$, or $UC(\psi, \chi)$ (c) $SC(\varphi, \chi)$, then $SC(\psi, \chi)$, $LI(\psi, \chi)$, or $UC(\psi, \chi)$ (d) $LI(\varphi, \chi)$, then $SC(\psi, \chi)$, $LI(\psi, \chi)$, or $UC(\psi, \chi)$ (e) $RI(\varphi, \chi)$, then $C(\psi, \chi)$, $RI(\psi, \chi)$, or $UC(\psi, \chi)$ (f) $BI(\varphi, \chi)$, then $UC(\psi, \chi)$ (g) $UC(\varphi, \chi)$, then any relation between ψ and χ is possible	

Fig. 4. Relations inferrable from two premisses, when only contingent formulas are involved

1. $CD(\varphi, \top)$ iff $\varphi \equiv \bot$.
2. There is no φ such that $C(\varphi, \top)$.
3. For any $\varphi \not\equiv \bot$: $SC(\varphi, \top)$.
4. For any $\varphi \not\equiv \top$: $LI(\varphi, \top)$.
5. There is no φ such that $RI(\varphi, \top)$.
6. $BI(\varphi, \top)$ iff $\varphi \equiv \top$.
7. There is no φ such that $UC(\varphi, \top)$.

1. $CD(\varphi, \bot)$ iff $\varphi \equiv \top$.
2. For any $\varphi \not\equiv \top$, $C(\varphi, \bot)$.
3. There is no φ such that $SC(\varphi, \bot)$.
4. There is no φ such that $LI(\varphi, \bot)$.
5. For any $\varphi \not\equiv \bot$: $RI(\varphi, \bot)$.
6. $BI(\varphi, \bot)$ iff $\varphi \equiv \bot$.
7. There is no φ such that $UC(\varphi, \bot)$.

Fig. 5. Relations of non-contingent formulas

4.1 Vocabulary and Syntax

In this section, we give the definition of the diagrammatic vocabulary (Definition 2) and the syntax (Definition 3) of both **ADLS**$^-$ and **ADLSC**. These are identical for both systems. They are a straightforward generalisation of the definitions from [5]. We have simply added double-headed arrows (representing BI-relations) and grey lines (representing UC-relations).[4]

Definition 2. (Vocabulary). *The vocabulary consists of (1) a set of formula-constants $\mathcal{C}$, (2) solid, dotted, dashed and grey lines, and (3) single and double-headed arrows.*

We use the formula-variables $\alpha, \beta, \gamma, \ldots$ as meta-variables ranging over $\mathcal{C}$, i.e. to refer to the formula-constants in the vocabulary.

Definition 3. (Syntax). *A well-formed Aristotelian diagram, WFAD, is defined as follows:*

1. *Every non-zero, but finite number of formula-constants written on a page is a WFAD.*
2. *If D is a WFAD containing the formula-constants α and β, then the diagram obtained by connecting α and β with a line (solid, dotted, dashed or grey) or an arrow (single or double-headed) is also a WFAD.*
3. *Only diagrams obtained in this way are WFADs.*

Definition 3 means that we make abstraction of any further visual elements of Aristotelian diagrams. For example, in most Aristotelian diagrams in the literature, contradiction is visualised not only by a solid line, but also by central symmetry [3]. Such visual elements are not relevant for our purposes in this paper, so we do not include them in Definition 3. This means that all of the diagrams in Figs. 1 and 6 are WFADs.

4.2 Semantics

In this section we present the semantics for our logical systems. Definition 4 defines models on which WFADs are interpreted, Definition 5 provides the

[4] When we refer to arrows without specifying whether they are single or double-headed, we mean single-headed arrows.

semantic clauses, and Definition 6 gives the semantic consequence relation. These definitions are mostly identical to those in [5].[5] The first important difference concerns Definition 4. In [5] there are three conditions on the models corresponding to the three rules discussed before (only contingent formulas, no equivalent formulas and exactly one contradictory formula) leading to a strong logical system named **ADLS**. Having none of these conditions gives the weakest system that we are concerned with. We will call it **ADLS**$^-$. Adding any combination of conditions gives us stronger variants. In this paper we will only be concerned with one strengthening: excluding non-contingent fomulas. We will call the resulting logic **ADLSC**.

Definition 4 (Models). *A* model *is a triple* $\langle \mathcal{F}, \mathbf{S}, I \rangle$ *such that* **S** *is a logical system that has a language* $\mathcal{L}_\mathbf{S}$*, Boolean operators and a model-theoretic semantics* $\models_\mathbf{S}$*,* $\mathcal{F} \subseteq \mathcal{L}_\mathbf{S}$*, and* $I : \mathcal{C} \to \mathcal{L}_\mathbf{S}$ *is a bijection.*

Definition 4 gives the most general definition of models, suitable for **ADLS**$^-$. The models of **ADLSC** are defined in exactly the same way, except that the following condition is added: there is no $\varphi \in \mathcal{F}$ such that $\models_\mathbf{S} \varphi$ or $\models_\mathbf{S} \neg\varphi$.

Definition 5 (Semantic Clauses). *Let* $M = \langle \mathcal{F}, \mathbf{S}, I \rangle$ *be a model, then* M *satisfies an Aristotelian diagram* D *iff all of the following conditions are met:*

1. *For every* α *occurring in* D*,* $I(\alpha) \in \mathcal{F}$*.*
2. *For every* α *and* β *occurring in* D *such that* α *and* β *are:*
   - *(a) connected by a solid line,* $CD_\mathbf{S}(I(\alpha), I(\beta))$*.*
   - *(b) connected by a dashed line,* $C_\mathbf{S}(I(\alpha), I(\beta))$*.*
   - *(c) connected by a dotted line,* $SC_\mathbf{S}(I(\alpha), I(\beta))$*.*
   - *(d) connected by a grey line,* $UC_\mathbf{S}(I(\alpha), I(\beta))$*.*
   - *(e) connected by an arrow from* α *to* β*,* $SA_\mathbf{S}(I(\alpha), I(\beta))$*.*
   - *(f) connected by a double-headed arrow,* $BI_\mathbf{S}(I(\alpha), I(\beta))$*.*

Definition 6 (Semantic Consequence). D *is a semantic consequence of* D'*, written as* $D' \models D$*, iff every model that satisfies* D' *also satisfies* D*.*

4.3 Axiomatization

In this section, we describe an axiomatization of **ADLS**$^-$. As in [5], we provide transformation rules, (Definition 8), axioms (Definition 7), structural rules (Definition 9), and a consequence relation (Definition 10).

Definition 7 (Axioms). *For every* α*,* β *and* γ *in a WFAD:*

1. *There is no solid or grey line between* α *and* α*, and no single-headed arrow from* α *to* α*. In addition, there is at most one line and one (single or double-headed) arrow between* α *and* β*.*

[5] As in [5], the *underlying logic* **S** should not be confused with the ADLS's.

2. *If there is a dashed line between α and β, and a grey line between α and γ, then between β and γ there is no solid line, dotted line or double-headed arrow, and there is no arrow from γ to β.*[6]
3. *If there is a dotted line between α and β, and a grey line between α and γ, then between β and γ there is no solid line, dashed line or double-headed arrow, and there is no arrow from β to γ.*
4. *If there is an arrow from α to β, and a grey line between α and γ, then between β and γ there is no solid line, dashed line or double-headed arrow, and there is no arrow from β to γ.*
5. *If there is an arrow from β to α, and a grey line between α and γ, then between β and γ there is no solid line, dotted line or double-headed arrow, and there is no arrow from γ to β.*
6. *If there is a dotted line from α to α, then there is no β such that there is a dashed or grey line between α and β, or an arrow from α to β.*
7. *If there is a dashed line from α to α, then there is no β such that there is a dotted or grey line between α and β, or an arrow from β to α.*
8. *If there is a dashed line between α and β, a dashed line between α and γ, and a double-headed arrow between β and γ, then there is no solid or dashed line between β and γ.*
9. *If there is a dashed line between α and β, an arrow from α to γ, and a double-headed arrow between β and γ, then there is no solid, dotted or dashed line between β and γ.*
10. *If there is a dotted line between α and β, a dotted line between α and γ, and a solid or dotted line between β and γ, then there are no (single or double-headed) arrows between β and γ.*
11. *If there is a dotted line between α and β, an arrow from γ to α, and a double-headed arrow between β and γ, then there is no solid, dashed or dotted line between β and γ.*
12. *If there is an arrow from α to β, a dashed line between α and γ, and a double-headed arrow between β and γ, then there is no solid, dashed or dotted line between β and γ.*
13. *If there is an arrow from α to β, an arrow from α to γ, and a solid line between β and γ, then there are no (single or double-headed) arrows between β and γ.*
14. *If there is an arrow from β to γ, a dotted line between α and γ, and a (single or double-headed) arrow between β and γ, then there is no solid, dashed or dotted line between β and γ.*
15. *If there is a grey line between β and γ, a grey line between α and γ, and a (single or double-headed) arrow between β and γ, then there is no solid, dashed or dotted line between β and γ.*
16. *There is at most one solid, dashed, or dotted line between α and β.*
17. *There is at most one double-headed or single-headed arrow (in any direction) between α and β.*

[6] When we talk about 'an arrow from A to B', we always mean a single-headed arrow.

Definition 8 (Transformation rules). *Apply the transformation rules only if the consequent hasn't been fulfilled. For every α, β and γ in a WFAD:*

1. *From any α, draw a double-headed arrow to itself.*
2. *If there is a solid line between α and β and*
   (a) *a solid line between α and γ, then draw a double-headed arrow between β and γ.*
   (b) *a dashed line between α and γ, then draw an arrow from γ to β.*
   (c) *a dotted line between α and γ, then draw an arrow from β to γ.*
   (d) *an arrow from α to γ, then draw a dotted line between β and γ.*
   (e) *an arrow from γ to α, then draw a dashed line between β and γ.*
   (f) *a double-headed arrow between α and γ, then draw a solid line between β and γ.*
   (g) *a grey line between α and γ, then draw a grey line between β and γ.*
3. *If there is a dashed line between α and β and*
   (a) *a dotted line between α and γ, then draw an arrow from β to γ.*
   (b) *an arrow from γ to α, then draw a dashed line between β and γ.*
   (c) *a double-headed arrow between γ and α, then draw a dashed line between β and γ.*
4. *If there is a dotted line between α and β and*
   (a) *an arrow from α to γ, then draw a dotted line between β and γ.*
   (b) *a double-headed arrow between α and γ, then draw a dotted line between β and γ.*
5. *If there is an arrow from α to β and*
   (a) *an arrow from γ to α, then draw an arrow from γ to β.*
   (b) *a double-headed arrow between α and γ, then draw an arrow from γ to β.*
6. *If there is an arrow from β to α and a double-headed arrow between α and γ, then draw an arrow from β to γ.*
7. *If there is a grey line between α and β and a double-headed arrow between α and γ, then draw a grey line between β and γ.*
8. *If there is a dotted line from α to α and a dashed line from β to β, then draw a solid line between α and β.*
9. *If there is a dotted line from α to α and a solid line between α and β, then draw a dashed line between β and β.*
10. *If there is a dashed line from α to α and a solid line between α and β, then there draw a solid line between α and β.*
11. *If there is dotted line from α to α, and*
    (a) *if there is a dotted line between α and β or an arrow from β to α, then draw a dotted line between α and γ.*
    (b) *if there is a dashed line between α and β or an arrow from α to β, then draw an arrow from α to γ.*
12. *If there is dashed line from α to α, and*
    (a) *if there is a dashed line between α and β or an arrow from α to β, then draw a dashed line between α and γ.*
    (b) *if there is a dotted line between α and β or an arrow from β to α, then draw an arrow from γ to α.*

Definition 9 (Structural Rules).
EFSQ If any of the axioms does not hold, then draw any new WFAD.
WEAK Remove any dashed line, dotted line, or arrow.

Definition 10 (Consequence Relation). *A Diagram D follows from a diagram D', written as $D' \vdash D$, iff D can be obtained by applying a finite number of transformation and/or structural rules to D'.*

Note that Definitions 7 and 8 are mostly just translations to the diagrammatic vocabulary of the results in Theorem 1 and Fig. 5. Rules 1 to 7 of Definition 8 are just a translation to the diagrammatic vocabulary of those results in Fig. 2 where a relation can be derived, whereas rules 8 to 12 are a translation of the results in Fig. 5 where a single relation can be derived. Similarly, axioms 2 to 5 of Definition 7 are a translation of those results in the figure where some relations are excluded. Axioms 6 and 7 follow from the observations around $\top$ and $\bot$ in Fig. 5 starting with 'there is no... ', and axioms 8 to 17 represent the information about the starred cases in Theorem 1. The definitions of the structural rules and the consequence relation are the same as those in [5]. Given this, the proof of soundness, Theorem 3, is quite straightforward.

Theorem 3 (Soundness of ADLS⁻). *If $D \vdash D'$, then $D \models D'$.*

Proof To prove soundness, it suffices to prove that each axiom and rule is valid. It would take up too much space (and it would be too tedious) to write this proof out for every rule and axiom. However, we give a few examples.

For axiom 2 and EFSQ, suppose there is a dashed line between α and β, a grey line between α and γ, and (for example) a dashed line between β and γ in a diagram D. It follows by the semantic clause that for every model $M = \langle \mathcal{F}, \mathbf{S}, I \rangle$ satisfying D, $C_{\mathbf{S}}(I(\alpha), I(\beta))$, $UC_{\mathbf{S}}(I(\alpha), I(\gamma))$, and $C_{\mathbf{S}}(I(\beta), I(\gamma))$. By case 2(g) of Fig. 2, this is not possible. Hence, there is no model satisfying D. Thus, for any WFAD D', $D \models D'$.

For transformation rule 3(a), suppose that there is dashed line between α and β, and a dotted line between α and γ in a diagram D. By the semantic clause, for every model $M = \langle \mathcal{F}, \mathbf{S}, I \rangle$ satisfying D, $C_{\mathbf{S}}(I(\alpha), I(\beta))$ and $SC_{\mathbf{S}}(I(\alpha), I(\gamma))$. By case 2(c) of Fig. 2, $LI_{\mathbf{S}}(I(\beta), I(\gamma))$. Hence, every model satisfying D also satisfies the diagram D' which is obtained from D by drawing an arrow from β to γ (if such an arrow was not yet present).

If we make the comparison with the transformation rules and axioms of [5], then we see a number of changes. Firstly, none of the axioms of **ADLS** are present in Definition 7. This is because these are no longer valid. Only axiom 1 in Definition 7 is a weakened version of axiom 1 of **ADLS**. In contrast, the transformation rules of **ADLS** are all present in a different form in Definition 8, or they are derivable. The transformation rules –I, →I and Tr. in Definition 5 of [5] are the same as transformation rules 2(e), 2(c) and 5(a) in Definition 8.

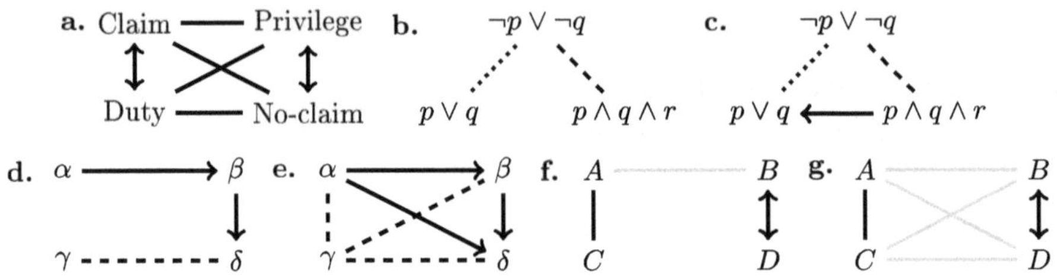

Fig. 6. The finished Hohfeldian square (a) and some other WFADs.

The rule •I in Definition 5 of [5] is derivable by applying rules 2(b), 2(d) and WEAK.

When working with Aristotelian diagrams to derive new diagrams (and new logical relations), we will most of the time only be interested in adding new lines or arrows. This is exclusively done by using the transformation rules (which are introduction rules, while WEAK is an elimination rule). The fact that all transformation rules of **ADLS** are also valid in **ADLS**$^-$ thus means that the additional assumptions (no equivalent formulas, only contingent formulas, exactly one contradictory formula) are not necessary for the majority of derivations made with Aristotelian diagrams. So for most practical applications, where we are only interested in adding lines or arrows to consistent diagrams, **ADLS**$^-$ is at least as suitable as **ADLS**. Furthermore, **ADLS**$^-$ can be used for a broader range of diagrams: those containing equivalences, non-contingent formulas, etc.

Let us conclude this section with some examples of diagrammatic reasoning using **ADLS**$^-$. The diagram in Fig. 6.a is derivable from the diagram in Fig. 1 by two applications of transformation rule 2(f). The diagram in Fig. 6.c can be derived from that in Fig. 6.b by an application of transformation rule 3(a). The diagram in Fig. 6.e follows from that in Fig. 6.d by transformation rules 5(a) and two applications of 3(b). Finally, the diagram in Fig. 6.g follows from that in Fig. 6.f by applications of the rules 2(g) and 7.

4.4 Axiomatization of ADLSC

We now move to the axiomatization of **ADLSC**. For **ADLSC** we will use the same definition of the consequence relation as we had for **ADLS**$^-$. Since **ADLSC** is a strengthening of **ADLS**$^-$, all of the axioms, transformation rules and structural rules of **ADLS**$^-$ also hold for **ADLSC**. This might seem strange, since e.g. axioms 6 and 7 are only relevant if there is a tautology or contradiction in the diagram. Strictly speaking, these axioms are valid, but redundant in **ADLSC**. The same goes for transformation rules 8 to 12.

One might expect new transformation rules as well as new axioms for **ADLSC**. However, a careful comparison between Figs. 2 and 4 shows that no additional transformation rules are needed, only new axioms. Definition 11 adds these new axioms and gets rid of redundant axioms.

Definition 11 (Axioms of ADLSC). *For every α, β and γ in a WFAD:*

1. *There is no solid, dotted, dashed or grey line between α and α, and no arrow from α to α.*
2. *For any α and β there is at most one line or arrow between them.*
3. *If there is a dashed lined between α and β, and a grey line between α and γ, then between β and γ there is no solid line, dotted line or double-headed arrow, and there is no arrow from γ to β.*
4. *If there is a dotted lined between α and β, and a grey line between α and γ, then between β and γ there is no solid line, dashed line or double-headed arrow, and there is no arrow from β to γ.*
5. *If there is an arrow from α to β, and a grey line between α and γ, then between β and γ there is no solid line, dashed line or double-headed arrow, and there is no arrow from β to γ.*
6. *If there is an arrow from β to α, and a grey line between α and γ, then between β and γ there is no solid line, dotted line or double-headed arrow, and there is no arrow from γ to β.*
7. *If there is a dashed lined between α and β, and a dashed line between α and γ, then there is no solid line between β and γ.*
8. *If there is a dashed lined between α and β, and an arrow from α to γ, then there is no double-headed arrow between β and γ, and no arrow from γ to β.*
9. *If there is a dotted lined between α and β, and a dotted line between α and γ, then there is no solid or dashed line between β and γ.*
10. *If there is a dotted lined between α and β, and an arrow from γ to α, then there is no double-headed arrow between β and γ, and no arrow from β to γ.*
11. *If there is an arrow from α to β, and an arrow from α to γ, then there is no solid or dashed line between β and γ.*
12. *If there is an arrow from β to α, and an arrow from γ to α, then there is no solid or dotted line between β and γ.*

Definition 12 (Semantic Consequence in ADLSC). *D is a semantic consequence of D' in* **ADLSC**, *written as $D' \models_C D$, iff for every model $M = \langle \mathcal{F}, \mathbf{S}, I \rangle$ such that $\mathcal{F}$ contains only contingent formulas, it holds that if M satisfies D', then M satisfies D.*

Definition 13 (Consequence Relation in ADLSC). *A Diagram D follows from a diagram D', written as $D' \vdash_C D$, iff D can be obtained by applying a finite number of transformation and/or structural rules to D'.*

Theorem 4 (Soundness of ADLSC). *If $D \vdash_C D'$, then $D \models_C D'$.*

Proof The proof is a straightforward variation on the proof for Theorem 3.

4.5 Completeness

We are not sure whether the logics presented in this paper are complete. As mentioned in Sect. 3, we are not sure whether there are possible derivations with three premisses that are not already covered by the cases discussed here. It might very well be that additional axioms or rules are needed for a complete axiomatization, or that for a complete axiomatization of **ADLS**$^-$ we need to expand the vocabulary in order to represent the NO and NI relations. However, we have some hope that a complete axiomatization is possible, since we prove the completeness of **ADLS** in a forthcoming paper.

5 Conclusion

In this paper we have looked in detail at the logical relations represented in Aristotelian diagrams. We have systematically investigated which relations can be derived from which other relations when no, or very few, assumptions about the formulas are made. Then we have used this information to construct two diagrammatic logic systems for Aristotelian diagrams. These systems are weaker than the already existing system **ADLS**, but therefore they are also more widely applicable.

Our main takeaway from this exercise is that a lot more is derivable in these circumstances than we would have thought at first. We can derive new relations, even when no contradiction-relations are in play, or when we are not sure whether the formulas that are involved are contingent. In addition, all of the introduction rules of **ADLS** are still valid in the new systems **ADLS**$^-$ and **ADLSC**. We claimed that in most practical cases we will only be interested in adding lines or arrows to a diagram. So for these cases, we do not really lose anything significant when switching from **ADLS** to **ADLS**$^-$ or **ADLSC**.

It should, however, be mentioned that the number of axioms and rules in **ADLS**$^-$ and **ADLSC** is much larger than those used in **ADLS**. It might be that further research, e.g. a completeness proof, shows that there is some redundancy in these axioms and rules. However, we doubt that this reduction would be significant. In practice, this large number of axioms and rules would make working with either of the newer systems more cumbersome than working with **ADLS**. This might explain why most diagrams encountered in the literature conform to the assumptions of **ADLS**. In turn, this gives an abductive argument for our inferential perspective on Aristotelian diagrams: most Aristotelian diagrams encountered in the literature conform to the rules needed to make inferring relations with the diagrams simple, and a good explanation for this fact is that Aristotelian diagrams were actually used to derive relations.

This paper opens the way to further work. Obviously, completeness of the systems developed here is still an open question. However, a further development of the systems is also a promising route. We could, for example, incorporate the idea of a "collapse" (when two equivalent formulas turn into one) into the diagrammatic logic system.

Another open problem was mentioned in the conclusion of [5]: can we develop a system that allows us to derive a diagram from two (or more) other diagrams? The systems in this paper are a good first step in that direction. If we combine two diagrams, we might end up with formulas that are equivalent to each other. This would have contradicted the axioms of **ADLS**, but it is no problem with

ADLS$^-$ or **ADLSC**. A possible way to (semantically) derive a diagram from two others is given by Definition 14.

Definition 14 (Semantic Consequence). *D is a semantic consequence of D' and D'', written as $D', D'' \models D$, iff for every model $M' = \langle \mathcal{F}', \mathbf{S}, I' \rangle$ that satisfies D' and every model $M'' = \langle \mathcal{F}'', \mathbf{S}, I'' \rangle$ it is the case that the model $M = \langle \mathcal{F}' \cup \mathcal{F}'', \mathbf{S}, I = \{\langle \alpha, \varphi \rangle \mid I'(\alpha) = \varphi$ or $I''(\alpha) = \varphi\}\rangle$ also satisfies D.*

However, more research in this direction is still necessary. In order to make this definition work, it seems like the background logic of the two diagrams needs to be the same, and that the diagrams need to agree on the interpretation of shared formula-constants.

Acknowledgments. The authors would like to thank Lorenz Demey and Hans Smessaert for valuable comments on earlier versions of this paper. This research was funded by the European Union (ERC, STARTDIALOG, 101040049). Views and opinions expressed are however those of the author(s) only and do not necessarily reflect those of the European Union or the European Research Council Executive Agency. Neither the European Union nor the granting authority can be held responsible for them.

References

1. Correia, M.: Boethius on the square of opposition. In: Around and Beyond the Square of Opposition, pp, pp. 41–52 (2012)
2. De Klerck, A., Vignero, L., Demey, L.: Morphisms between aristotelian diagrams: a. de klerck et al. Logica Universalis **18**(1), 49–83 (2024)
3. Demey, L., Smessaert, H.: A database of aristotelian diagrams: empirical foundations for logical geometry. In: International Conference on Theory and Application of Diagrams, pp. 123–131. Springer (2022)
4. Frijters, S., Demey, L.: The modal logic of Aristotelian diagrams. Axioms **12**(5), 471 (2023)
5. Frijters, S., Erbas, A.: Aristotelian diagrams as logic diagrams. In: International Conference on Theory and Application of Diagrams, pp. 275–283. Springer (2024)
6. Howse, J., Stapleton, G., Taylor, J.: Spider diagrams. LMS J. Comput. Math. **8**, 145–194 (2005)
7. Humberstone, L.: Logical relations. Philos. Perspect. **27**, 175–230 (2013)
8. Lemanski, J., Jansen, L.: A cl system for propositions and classes. In: Erkenntnis, pp. 1–28 (2025)
9. Li, X., Markovich, R.: A dynamic logic of the right to know. J. Appl. Logics **12**, 221–250 (2025)
10. MacCartney, B., Manning, C.D.: Natural logic and natural language inference. In: Computing Meaning, vol. 4, pp. 129–147. Springer (2014)
11. Moktefi, A., Shin, S.J.: A history of logic diagrams. In: Handbook of the History of Logic, vol. 11, pp. 611–682. Elsevier (2012)
12. Schang, F.: Logic in opposition. Studia Humana **2**, 31–45 (2013)
13. Shin, S.J.: The Logical Status of Diagrams. Cambridge University Press (1994)
14. Smessaert, H., Demey, L.: Logical geometries and information in the square of oppositions. J. Logic Lang. Inform. **23**, 527–565 (2014)
15. Smessaert, H., Shimojima, A., Demey, L.: Free rides in logical space diagrams versus Aristotelian diagrams. In: Diagrams 2020, pp. 419–435. Springer (2020)

Knowledge-How and Knowledge-That in the Construction and Use of Diagrams in Mathematics

Mary Elworth(✉)

Scuola Universitaria Superiore IUSS Pavia, Pavia, Italy
maryelworth.philmath@gmail.com

Abstract. Knowledge-how and knowledge-that underpin important competences that mathematicians operationalize in the production of mathematical knowledge. Briefly stated, knowledge-that is *propositional*, i.e., knowing that something is the case. Knowledge-how is *procedural*, i.e., knowing how to do an action. We consider these two kinds of knowledge, and their interplay, in the context of mathematical diagrams. My focus is a case study involving certain diagrams that are used in contemporary mathematical practice. The diagrams depict a construction procedure by which one mathematical object is obtained from another. I aim to show that constructing the objects exploits *knowledge-how*, while the knowledge of which relations are preserved in the objects resulting from this construction is an instance of *knowledge-that*. The fine-grained analysis of this case lays significant groundwork for understanding how these two kinds of knowledge complement each other in the context of diagrammatic practices in mathematics.

Keywords: Epistemology of diagrams · Mathematical practice · Knowledge-how · Knowledge-that · Constructions

1 Introduction

Over 80 years ago, Ryle [13] delivered his seminal analysis of the distinction between knowledge-how and knowledge-that which charted the course for how these kinds of knowledge have since been regarded. Following Ryle, the dominant view entertained by philosophers has been that knowledge-how and knowledge-that are fundamentally distinct, although some have expressed their dissent for this claim. Notably, Stanley and Williamson [14] make their case, through a syntactical and semantical analysis of sentences, that knowledge-how is a variant of knowledge-that. With regard to this ongoing debate, Cath [2] suggests that greater progress can be made concerning knowledge-how if we shift our focus away from the dichotomy of views about whether the distinction is tenable, and instead consider alternative accounts of what knowledge-how might be.

This paper lays significant groundwork for understanding how knowledge-how and knowledge-that complement each other in the context of mathematics

P. Sobociński et al. (Eds.): Diagrams 2026, LNAI 16833, pp. 167–174, 2027.
https://doi.org/10.1007/978-3-032-34178-5_18

by examining specific diagrammatic practices arising in a contemporary mathematical theory. A succinct description of these two kinds of knowledge is given in Tanswell [16]:

> Knowledge-that is propositional knowledge: knowledge that some fact is true. Knowledge-how is practical knowledge: knowledge of how to do some action or activity. ([16], p. 51)

What Tanswell refers to as "practical knowledge," we could, in some instances, think of as "procedural knowledge" in case the actions or activities involved serve as a means to accomplish a particular outcome. This characterization of knowledge-how and knowledge-that offers a fruitful starting point for revealing how these kinds of knowledge work together in beneficial ways in mathematics.

The motivation behind considering these kinds of knowledge in light of certain uses of diagrams in mathematics is to better understand how this practice contributes to the development of new mathematical theories. To this end, I am interested in a more fine-grained approach to understanding knowledge-how and knowledge-that than accounts that have tried to tackle this issue in more general terms. The point of view which I maintain is that knowledge-how and knowledge-that underpin important competences that mathematicians as finite agents operationalize in their daily work. One way that these competences appear in practice is through the use of diagrams. Significantly, diagrams play diverse epistemic roles in mathematics: for instance, they facilitate mathematical discoveries [1,15] and understanding [5]; they play, at times, a justificatory role in mathematical proofs [3,4]; they have a classificatory function [6]; and they support computations in distinctive ways [7].

In this paper, we consider a construction procedure found in a recently developed mathematical theory situated within algebra and combinatorics that involves constructing one mathematical object from another (Sect. 2). This procedure produces a graphical object called a *quiver* from a combinatorial object called a *triangulation*, and is commonly depicted with the use of diagrams. Knowing how to perform this construction is complemented by the propositional knowledge of which features of the triangulation are encoded in the resulting quiver. This case study illuminates the complementarity of knowledge-how and knowledge-that in the context of constructing and using diagrams in mathematics (Sect. 3). Brief remarks conclude the paper (Sect. 4).

2 Encoding Combinatorial Data Using Quivers

A *quiver* is like a directed graph: it is a well-defined mathematical object consisting of arrows and vertices. Formally, a quiver, denoted by Q, is a quadruple (Q_0, Q_1, s, t), in which Q_0 is a set of *vertices*; Q_1 is a set of *arrows*; $s : Q_1 \to Q_0$ is the *source* map; and $t : Q_1 \to Q_0$ is the *target* map. The source map, s, sends an arrow $\varphi \in Q_1$ to the vertex $v \in Q_0$ at which φ originates. The target map, t, sends an arrow $\varphi \in Q_1$ to the vertex $v \in Q_0$ at which φ terminates. In practice, a quiver may be shown by a diagram (Fig. 1).

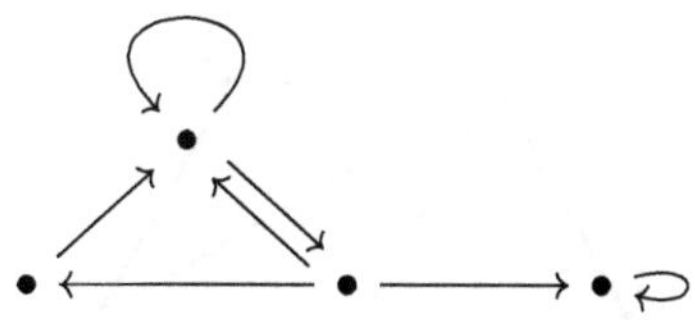

Fig. 1. A diagram of a quiver with loops and multiple edges.

Quivers are used for encoding data of various types in mathematics, among other purposes. We examine a specific use of quivers: encoding the combinatorial data given by a so-called *triangulation* $T(P)$ of a polygon P. The triangulation $T(P)$ is a collection of pairwise non-crossing diagonals between pairs of vertices in P. Conceptually, $T(P)$ inscribes a configuration of triangles within P (Fig. 2).

The diagonals of a triangulation give rise to salient combinatorial data that is used in a variety of mathematical contexts. Depending upon the given context and aims, this data may be more readily treated in some other form than is given by the triangulation. In certain cases, this data is instead captured by a quiver. A significant advantage of encoding the data by a quiver is that quivers afford distinct ways of being manipulated from those afforded by triangulations. This feature of quivers gives rise to certain conceptual opportunities that have proven to be fruitful in mathematics. In other words, quivers and triangulations possess different *affordances*, which refers to the space of possible epistemic moves that may be performed and, in particular, the mathematical operations which are available.[1] In brief, quivers are tractable and well-suited for encoding and manipulating diverse forms of mathematical data.

2.1 Constructing a Quiver from a Triangulation of an n-gon

Consider a regular n-gon (i.e., polygon), denoted by P_n, where n is, as usual, taken to be the number of vertices of the polygon. A *triangulation* of P_n, denoted by T, is a maximal collection of pairwise non-crossing diagonals of P_n. Figure 2 shows a diagram of a triangulation T of the polygon P_6. Observe that other triangulations of P_6 are possible; the one displayed in the figure simply represents a given choice concerning the arrangement of the diagonals.

To capture the relevant data of a triangulation T in a quiver $Q(T)$, one constructs the quiver $Q(T)$ from T according to a specified procedure.[2] This construction ensures that the adjacency relations found in T are preserved in $Q(T)$. In practice, the construction of $Q(T)$ is depicted using diagrams.

Two sequential steps determine the construction of $Q(T)$. In the first step, one defines the *vertices* of $Q(T)$ through their assignment to the diagonals of T and sides of P_6, one for each diagonal or side. This step involves two distinct

[1] The term *affordances*, coined by J. J. Gibson [9], has been discussed variously in the philosophy of mathematics literature concerning the epistemic roles of mathematical signs [7,8,10].

[2] The construction is described in general terms in [17].

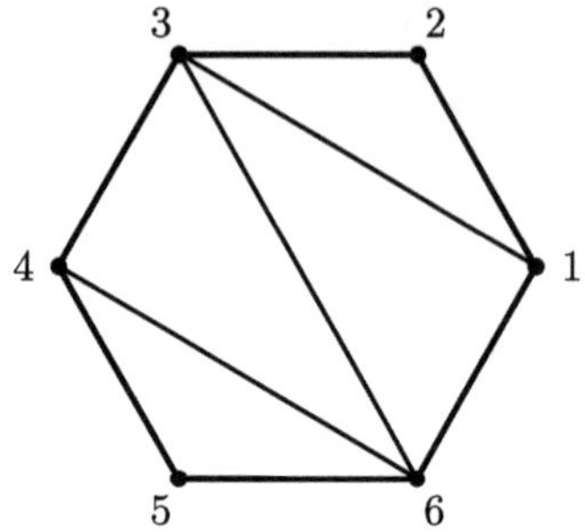

Fig. 2. A triangulation $T(P_6)$ of the hexagon P_6. The vertices of P_6 are labeled counterclockwise by $i = 1, 2, ..., 6$. By convention, the diagonals $d_{i,j}$ are labeled such that i and j are the endpoints of the diagonal, with $i < j$. Then $T(P_6)$ has three diagonals: $d_{1,3}$, $d_{3,6}$, and $d_{4,6}$.

kinds of vertices, since it is important for preserving the relevant data to denote whether a vertex sits along a diagonal or a side.[3] By convention:

- a vertex that sits along a *diagonal* is denoted by a *filled* circle, and
- a vertex that sits along a *side* is denoted by an *unfilled* circle.

In the second step, one defines the *arrows* of $Q(T)$, along with their *source* and *target* maps. Within each triangle of T, one inscribes a configuration of arrows which serve to connect the vertices that have just been defined. The arrows of $Q(T)$ are given a clockwise orientation in the diagram per convention. Carrying out these steps produces the quiver $Q(T)$, which is drawn in orange in Fig. 3.[4]

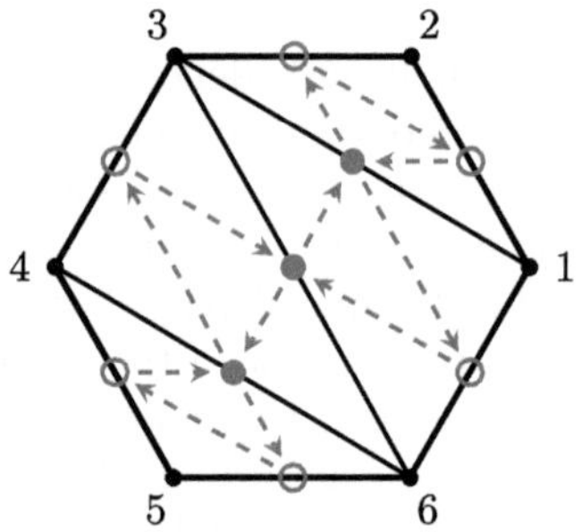

Fig. 3. The triangulation $T(P_6)$ with the quiver $Q(T)$ inscribed in it.

[3] To see why this is significant requires understanding the specific mathematical tasks where this combinatorial data plays a role, which is beyond our scope.

[4] Defining the construction in this way ensures that specific operations that are defined on these respective objects correspond to one another in a meaningful way.

3 Knowledge-How and Knowledge-That as Complementary Kinds of Knowledge

The kinds of knowledge that we are concerned with are (i) knowing how to perform an activity or set of actions and (ii) knowing that something is the case. Before assessing how these two kinds of knowledge relate to the construction procedure described previously, I shall highlight a difficulty in disentangling them with the aid of a non-mathematical example. Consider the following sentences:

(1) Janet knows that Paris is the capital of France.
(2) Janet knows how to travel to Paris from another city in France by train.
(3) Janet knows that train #1059 from Zürich arrives in Paris at 5:35pm.[5]

Evidently, the first sentence concerns propositional knowledge. The second sentence concerns practical knowledge, in that Janet has knowledge of how to reach Paris by a specified means, e.g., the national railway system. The third sentence illustrates how the distinction between knowledge-how and knowledge-that is not always clearcut in concrete examples. This sentence indicates that Janet has knowledge that a specific train reaches Paris at a given time. Can we say that Janet knows how to reach Paris on the basis of this propositional knowledge? Intuitively, it seems that she does, since she knows at least one way that this can be done. From this point of view, it seems plausible that knowledge-how is implicit in knowledge-that.

This subtlety may be even more difficult to discern in the context of mathematics, where symbolic manipulations are closely linked with handling mathematical objects. In some sense, knowing that a triangulation of a polygon consists of a maximal collection of non-crossing diagonals should be enough to draw this construction, assuming one has the physical and cognitive disposition to enable such an act. Furthermore, there is a notable difference between propositional knowledge in mathematics, which deals with necessary truths, and propositional knowledge dealing with contingent matters. Knowing that something is the case in mathematics entails that this 'something' always holds, since it (trivially) does not rely on contingent factors. In contrast, contingent states of affairs are just that; for example, political geography changes with time and trains can be delayed or canceled.

Knowledge-how and knowledge-that are complementary in the context of the construction procedure described in the preceding section. Taken on its own, the procedure *merely* concerns determining the vertices and arrows of some quiver. In the context of the mathematical theory where this construction occurs, the outcome of the procedure would be mathematically uninteresting if considered in isolation from further interpretation of which relations the quiver captures. Making progress in the relevant theory is done through exploiting knowledge of what the quiver encodes. Knowing how to perform the construction is thus complemented by propositional knowledge of what the construction yields: for

[5] The author wishes to thank one of the anonymous reviewers for suggesting such an addition to the example.

instance, knowing that the adjacency relations of the triangulation T are preserved in the associated quiver $Q(T)$. The way of constructing $Q(T)$ captures these relations *by design*. Notably, the level of detail of the propositional knowledge admitted could be subject to variability. For example, knowing that the procedure produces a quiver is distinct from knowing that the procedure produces a quiver which encodes the combinatorial data of the triangulation from which the quiver is constructed.

In carrying out the construction, a mathematician performs a sequence of steps, the outcome of which is the quiver $Q(T)$. Performing the construction presupposes that the mathematician *knows how* to perform the construction, which is commonly depicted with the use of diagrams. In this case, the diagrams do not show a general procedure, but rather they show specific instances of the general procedure being applied. The diagrams thus possess a high degree of specificity. This discussion relates to the work of Kozak [12], who draws attention to the role of knowing how in the context of geometrical constructions:

> [K]nowledge of constructions is general. Knowing how to construct a specific triangle implies that you know how to arrive at the same type of figure with different elements, e.g., with different lengths of line segments. By the same token, knowing how to apply an operation to a specific mathematical object implies that one knows how to apply it to any object that is given beforehand. ([12], p. 131)

We have focused only on knowledge-how as it relates to constructions, on the basis of the example given in Sect. 2.1, and not as it relates to mathematical operations, which would yield another interesting line of inquiry. As Kozak indicates, knowing how to perform a construction carries with it some degree of generality.[6] In the case of the quiver construction, one follows a general procedure and makes further choices in producing a specific object. One would be hard-pressed to produce a diagram that displays the general procedure in an arbitrary setting. Yet, this seems not to be a serious obstacle for the practice and neither should it be. The diagram shows a particular instance of the construction. In doing so, it shows the relationship between two objects, i.e., a triangulation T and the associated quiver $Q(T)$. While the steps of the procedure *describe* how these objects are related to one another, the diagram actually *shows* how they are related.

Constructing an object implies that one knows how to perform the construction. On the converse, having knowledge of how to perform the construction does not imply that one necessarily has the physical or cognitive disposition to produce a material representation of it:

> Knowing how to construct an object is dissociated from the actual ability to create it. One can understand that the diagram represents a triangle

[6] There may also be important differences between constructing objects where metric properties are essential, such as in geometry, and constructing objects which are *not* subject to such constraints, such as in combinatorics.

> construction even if one has no drawing skills or knowledge of how to use physical tools. ([12], p. 131)

This may be true in the context of mathematics, but this point seems somewhat dubious in light of conceptions of knowledge-how that relate to other skills such as riding a bicycle or playing a saxophone. In particular, *knowing how* has been characterized as knowledge that "cannot be communicated only through language [...] For example, learning how to ride a bike requires both *demonstration* and *practice*" ([11], p. 20; emphasis added). One could object that this refers to the *acquisition* of skills, which could be viewed separately from being in possession of the knowledge required for the skill. Still, it is unclear how knowledge-how should be cashed out in a mathematical context, if it is not closely tied to carrying out procedures.

Kozak appears to suggest that propositional knowledge is a form of knowledge-how when he writes that "knowing the properties of a construction *is* a kind of *procedural knowledge* of employing certain admissible procedures over the set of initial objects, leading to arriving at some new mathematical objects" ([12], p. 131; emphasis added). In performing a construction, one exploits knowledge of how to proceed, and the procedure yields a new object. It seems plausible that "knowing the properties of a construction" concerns factive knowledge, which is a form of knowledge-that. If this is the case, it seems evident that this knowledge is brought about, by Kozak's account, through actually performing the construction by applying one's procedural knowledge, or what we have been referring to as knowledge-how.

4 Concluding Remarks

In the context of mathematics, knowledge-how and knowledge-that are complementary in contributing to theoretical developments. This can be seen through investigating certain diagrammatic practices in mathematics. In the case examined here, the diagrams associated to the specific combinatorial procedure described in Sect. 2 show the relationship between two mathematical objects: the object being constructed (a quiver) and the initial object from which the construction is produced (a triangulation of a polygon). I have argued that this construction exemplifies a case in which knowledge-how enables one to obtain the construction and knowledge-that enables one to interpret the constructed object in a mathematically meaningful sense. This account provides a substantial basis for further inquiry into the nature and relationship of these two kinds of knowledge in the context of mathematics.

Acknowledgments. I wish to thank the three anonymous reviewers for their insightful questions and remarks. I presented parts of this work at the *History and Philosophy of Mathematics* seminar at Laboratoire SPHere, Paris, May 2026. I am grateful for the constructive feedback received on this occasion. This research was funded in part by grant no. FIS-2023-04053 – HUMATH – Humanizing Mathematical Knowledge: Fallibility, Technology, Know How (PI: De Toffoli) – CUP I53C24003170001.

Disclosure of Interests. The author has no competing interests to declare that are relevant to the content of this article.

References

1. Carter, J.: Diagrams and proofs in analysis. Int. Stud. Philos. Sci. **24**(1), 1–14 (2010)
2. Cath, Y.: Knowing how without knowing that. In: Bengson, J., Moffett, M.A. (eds.): Knowing How: Essays on Knowledge, Mind, and Action, pp. 113–135. Oxford University Press, Oxford (2011)
3. De Toffoli, S.: 'Chasing' the diagram–the use of visualizations in algebraic reasoning. Rev. Symbolic Logic **10**(1), 158–186 (2017). https://doi.org/10.1017/S1755020316000277
4. De Toffoli, S.: Who's afraid of mathematical diagrams? Philosophers' Imprint **23**(1), (2023). https://doi.org/10.3998/phimp.1348
5. Dutihl Novaes, C.: Diagrams as joint epistemic actions: a dialogical account of diagrams in mathematical proofs. J. Math. Behav. **80**(101271), 1–14 (2025). https://doi.org/10.1016/j.jmathb.2025.101271
6. Eckes, C., Giardino, V.: The classificatory function of diagrams: two examples from mathematics. In Chapman, P., et al. (eds.): Diagrams 2018, LNAI 10871, pp. 120–136. Springer, Cham (2018). https://doi.org/10.1007/978-3-319-91376-6_14
7. Elworth, M.: Cognitive artifacts and their affordances: cluster algebras as a case study. Synthese **207**(216), 1–27 (2026). https://doi.org/10.1007/s11229-026-05558-1
8. Giardino, V.: Manipulative imagination: how to move things around in mathematics. THEORIA Int. J. Theor. History Found. Sci. **33**(2), 345–360 (2018). https://doi.org/10.1387/theoria.17871
9. Gibson, J.J.: The Ecological Approach to Visual Perception. Psychology Press (2015). https://doi.org/10.4324/9781315740218. Classic ed
10. Johansen, M.W.: Cognitive artifacts in the history of mathematics. In: Knudsen, T., Carter, J. (eds.) Mastering the History of Pure and Applied Mathematics: Essays in Honor of Jesper Lützen, pp. 153–168. De Gruyter, Berlin (2024). https://doi.org/10.1515/9783110769968-008
11. Johansson, L.-G.: Philosophy of Science for Scientists. Springer, Cham (2016)
12. Kozak, P.: What does it mean that diagrams represent constructions? In: Lemanski, J., (eds.): Diagrams 2024, LNAI 14981, pp. 129–136. Springer, Cham (2024). https://doi.org/10.1007/978-3-031-71291-3_10
13. Ryle, G.: Knowing how and knowing that: the presidential address. Proc. Aristot. Soc. **46**, 1–16 (1946)
14. Stanley, J., Williamson, T.: Knowing how. J. Philos. **98**(8), 411–444 (2001)
15. Starikova, I.: From practice to new concepts: geometric properties of groups. Philos. Sci. **16**(1), 129–151 (2012)
16. Tanswell, F.: Mathematical Rigour and Informal Proof. Cambridge University Press (2024). https://doi.org/10.1017/9781009325110
17. Williams, L.K.: Cluster algebras: an introduction. Bulletin of the AMS **51**(1), 1–26 (2014). https://doi.org/10.1090/S0273-0979-2013-01417-4

Hobbes and the Physicality of Geometry

Viktor Blåsjö(✉)

Mathematical Institute, Utrecht University, Utrecht, The Netherlands
v.n.e.blasjo@uu.nl

Abstract. Hobbes's philosophy of geometry has often been regarded as bizarre and eccentric. His insistence that geometry is about figures constructed by motion in the physical world has been seen as materialist philosophy run amok. But Hobbes's claims to be following geometrical tradition are more credible when situated in the context of technical mathematics rather than philosophy. Generations of leading ancient geometers devised geometrical constructions with instruments that are explicitly physical and material. If one puts philosophical commentators such as Plato and Proclus aside and try to read a philosophy of geometry between the lines of these technical works, then it is not far fetched to arrive at conclusions like those espoused by Hobbes. The ancient obsession with constructions by physical instruments, taken seriously, arguably suggests embracing the physically constructed diagram as the bona fide ontology of geometry, and the empirically anchored generation of figures by motion as its epistemological bedrock.

1 The Standard View of Hobbes

Traditional scholarship on Hobbes's philosophy of geometry is beset with paradoxes. Hobbes famously declared that "Geometry ... is the only science that it hath pleased God hitherto to bestow on mankind" [12, III, pp. 23–24]. Consequently he professed to model his philosophical system on its example, by attempting to capture the methodological essence of classical geometry and extending it faithfully to philosophy as a whole. Yet most scholars maintain that Hobbes did nothing of the sort. Instead, in their view, he radically overthrew the foundations of geometry and replaced them with something completely different.

The generally accepted standard view has it that Hobbes was "a geometrical maverick" [29, p. 271] who espoused "a revisionist philosophy of geometry" [21, p. 99]. "Hobbes' philosophy of geometry was eccentric," "doubtless odd and quaint" [32, pp. 573, 575], "a rather shocking departure" from tradition, "eccentric, not to say bizarre" [15, pp. 170, 189], "thoroughly *sui generis*" [18, p. 207], and "in sharp opposition to the mainstream view" [9, p. 112].

There is also widespread agreement on the supposed reason for Hobbes's crazy philosophy of geometry.

> Hobbes's philosophy of mathematics is grounded in his strict materialism. He is well known for ... insisting that all the phenomena of the world must

P. Sobociński et al. (Eds.): Diagrams 2026, LNAI 16833, pp. 175–190, 2027.
https://doi.org/10.1007/978-3-032-34178-5_19

> be accounted for in terms of bodies and their motions. [Hobbes] extended to the philosophy of mathematics this metaphysical program. [15, p. 167]

In other words, Hobbes's philosophy of geometry is a mere side effect. It is forced upon him by "the fact that Hobbes held to a strict materialism" [16, p. 73]—the latter being apparently just that: a mere brute "fact," to which Hobbes was absolutely committed for reasons having nothing to do with the foundations of geometry.

Hence, if we accept the standard view of the "geometrical maverick" Hobbes, we face a number of puzzles. What possessed Hobbes to completely overthrow the foundations of what he himself considered to be "the only science God has bestowed on mankind"? Why would he do this if he was keen to follow "a method that hath been used only in geometry; whose conclusions have thereby been made indisputable"? [12, III, p. 33] How could he expect his attempts to use the authority of geometry to lend credibility to his philosophical system to convince anyone, if his picture of geometry was blatantly outlandish? And if he did overthrow the foundations of geometry, how come he always emphasises how traditional his views on the subject are, "little expecting that any professor of geometry should find fault therewith"? [12, VII, pp. 184–185] And if "geometry ... is the mother of all natural science" [12, III, p. 668], why did Hobbes let the philosophy of geometry be dictated by physicalism, which makes the offspring rule over its own mother science? Again, if, as he said, "senseless and insignificant language ... cannot be avoided by those that will teach philosophy without having first attained great knowledge in geometry" [12, III, pp. 668–669], why did Hobbes overturn geometry on preconceived philosophical grounds, which is precisely what he warned is bound to be senseless?

A simple solution to these puzzles is to take Hobbes at face value. Hobbes's philosophy of geometry is, as he says, not radical and revisionist but rather closely modelled on mathematical tradition.

2 Hobbes as a Conservative Philosopher of Geometry

Hobbes often spoke of ancient geometers with veneration. "There is nothing produced by Archimedes that I do not praise" [13, IV, p. 465], he professed. When listing the "most skilled masters" in the sciences, Hobbes mentions "in geometry, Euclid, Archimedes, Apollonius, Pappus, and other ancients from Greece" [13, V, p. 147]. Elsewhere, Hobbes "thought it fit to admonish the reader that ... he take into his hands the works of Euclid, Archimedes, Apollonius, and others" [12, I, p. 204]. The ancients compare favourably to the moderns, according to Hobbes: for example, "as regards analysis, it appears no less in the writings of Euclid, Archimedes, Apollonius, and other ancients, than in those of Vieta, Oughtred, and other algebraists" [13, IV, p. 196].

No doubt it was par for the course in the 17th century to praise ancient geometry. Nevertheless, these passages perhaps tell us more than this platitude. Note indeed that Hobbes is repeatedly citing the technical mathematical authors of antiquity and not, in this connection, philosophical commentators such as Plato,

Aristotle, and Proclus. It is the technical treatises that we should "take into [our] hands" if we want to understand ancient geometry, not the philosophical glosses. Generic allusions to the status of ancient geometry were indeed commonplace in philosophical contexts Hobbes's time, but much less common is a focus on specialised technical authors such as Apollonius and Pappus.

This suggests that we should contextualise Hobbes's philosophy of geometry in the technical history of mathematics rather than purely in philosophical tradition. I shall argue that this is indeed the key to seeing Hobbes's philosophy of geometry as in fact eminently traditionalist and conservative. If Hobbes's views are compared only with surviving philosophical passages on mathematics from Greek times he comes across as a *sui generis* maverick indeed. But when we study the technical geometrical tradition, and consider the methodological and foundational assumptions implicit in them, we find abundant precedent for Hobbes's views, to the point where little novelty of his own remains.

As Hobbes says, his philosophy of geometry is "to an attentive reader versed in the demonstrations of mathematicians ... without any offensive novelty" [12, I, p. vii]. Indeed, to appreciate the parallels between Hobbes and the ancients, one needs to be "versed in the demonstrations of mathematicians," meaning the technical Greek authors as opposed to merely relying on the accounts of mathematics given by philosophers. Furthermore, one must be "attentive," as Hobbes says, in drawing out the philosophical implications left implicit in these sources, since the technical mathematical works of antiquity are almost entirely void of any explicit philosophising. Indeed, Hobbes himself did not claim to have overthrown older conceptions of the foundations of geometry, only that he had explicated them better and with more care. I shall argue that on this point he was in many respects truthful and correct.

3 Maker's Knowledge

The classical problems of cube duplication, circle squaring, and angle trisection (or more generally multisection) had a singular status in Greek geometry. This is extensively attested in technical as well as cultural and philosophical sources in antiquity [20]. Hobbes claimed to have solved these classical problems. By his own reckoning, these were among his foremost achievements in mathematics [13, IV, p. 522].

That much is well known. But historians have not drawn the full consequences of this simple fact. If we take Hobbes's commitment to this problem tradition seriously, it is reasonable to give authority to ancient works in this tradition when interpreting the assumptions and methodology of geometry. This fits with Hobbes's emphasis on technical sources mentioned above, including Pappus, who is one of the main sources on this tradition.

Greek geometers devised at least 13 different cube duplications and at least 7 different angle trisections [3, p. 637]. The obsession with these problems is unique. No other mathematical problem or theorem in Greek mathematics was tackled so persistently and repeatedly. For example, as far as is known, Greek mathematicians gave one proof of the isoperimetric property of the circle. Why not 13 proofs? Indeed, subsequent history shows that this theorem can fruitfully be tackled in a multitude of interesting ways that were readily within the reach of Greek mathematicians [1]. But instead they preferred to double a cube for the 13th time. Why were the three classical construction problems virtually the only problems the Greeks were obsessed with proving over and over and over again? Why was a 13th way of doubling a cube a higher priority than a second way of proving the isoperimetric property of the circle, let alone a first way of doing something new, such as, say, drawing a tangent to a cycloid? I shall argue that trying to answer these questions leads naturally to several of Hobbes's notorious views on the philosophy of geometry.

First of all we must emphasise that the classical problems are *construction* problems. That is to say, they ask us to *make* something, to produce figures with certain properties. Plato explicitly denies that geometers are "diagram-makers"; rather, he wants to say, they "discover the realities of things" (*Euthydemus*, 290c). But the single-minded obsession with constructions in the Greek tradition suggests the opposite. In assigning preeminent status to the classical construction problems, ancient geometers effectively made "diagram-making" the heart of mathematics. The great targets of mathematical research in antiquity were not theorems, as one might expect from a modern point of view, but constructions. The ancient sources do not spell out why the classical constructions were so eagerly sought, but if one takes their singular status seriously it is hard to escape the conclusion that this otherwise odd obsession can only be explained by postulating an underlying constructivist philosophy. Historians of mathematics have felt the gravity of this evidence and concluded that constructions are fundamentally "what the ancients *mean* by mathematical knowledge" [20, p. 139]. It is hard to imagine how the classical construction problems could have acquired such disproportionate prestige without such a status boost from their embedding in a philosophical framework that connected constructions to the very meaning and essence of mathematics.

Thus Hobbes has ancient authority on his side when he singles out its constructive character as the distinguishing characteristic of mathematical knowledge, as he repeatedly does:

> Geometry ... is demonstrable, for the lines and figures from which we reason are drawn and described by ourselves. ... If the first principles ... contain not the generation of the subject, there can be nothing demonstrated as it ought to be. [12, VII, p. 184]

> From construction, that is, from generation alone, the affections of the constructed are known. [13, IV, p. 66]

If this was the opinion of ancient geometers, then the striking prominence of the classical construction problems in ancient mathematics makes perfect sense. If ancient geometers on the contrary agreed with Plato that they were not "diagram-makers," then it would be a strange paradox that the greatest problems of geometry were explicitly about diagram-making.

4 Physicalism

So far we have drawn some philosophical conclusions from the nature of the classical construction problems themselves. We must now consider what conclusions we can draw from the solutions to these problems proposed in antiquity. Indeed, we shall see that many aspects of this ancient tradition square very well with Hobbes's allegedly "maverick" ideas that geometry is about physical reality (not some idealised or Platonic realm) and that constructions of geometrical figures by motion constitute the de facto ontology of geometry.

Since the classical problems are not solvable by ruler and compass, the solutions proposed in antiquity all rely on some sort of new instrument or other auxiliary construction principle. About a dozen different types of solution methods for the classical problems are recorded in surviving sources [3, p. 637]. Of these, about half are directly and unequivocally physical as formulated in the source texts themselves. Eratosthenes speaks about the realisation of his construction "by a machine," namely triangles sliding along "grooves" inside "a box ... made of wood, or ivory, or bronze" [25, p. 296]. Nicomedes's solution likewise uses an instrument that is explicitly physical, involving several rulers interlocked with grooves and protruding parts that control their motion [25, p. 299], [34, p. 127]. The pseudo-Platonic solution also uses a contraption consisting of several "rulers" whose "motion" is constrained by various "grooves" and "knobs" [25, pp. 273–275]. Philon's solution manipulates a ruler in an explicitly hands-on manner: "Taking a ruler, ... I juggle it about, always keeping one part of it touching the corner" [22, p. 111]. The same goes for the solutions by Heron and Pappus [22, p. 41], [25, p. 282].

It is plausible that many or all of the remaining solutions were originally physical as well. This could have been evident to any reader without the need for formulations that make this completely explicit, just as physical realisability by ruler and compass is never explicit in the *Elements* but is nevertheless obvious. Indeed, Plutarch claims that Archytas, Eudoxus, and Menaechmus doubled the cube "by instruments and mechanical constructions" [38, p. 389], yet none of these three solutions have come down to us in a form that is explicitly physical.

People like Eratosthenes, Menaechmus, Eudoxus, Archytas, and Nicomedes were highly accomplished mathematicians at the heart of Greek mathematics. As such, they arguably have greater authority to decide what good mathematics looks like than philosophers such as Plato or Proclus. Their apparent commitment to generation by motion and outright physicality should be taken seriously. The physical aspects of their geometry could very well have been philosophically deliberate rather than, as many stubborn historians prefer to see them, mere secondary illustrations in principle separable from mathematics itself.

When Jesseph characterises Hobbes's physicalist philosophy of geometry as "thoroughly *sui generis*" [18, p. 207], he does so by contrasting it with the allegedly conventional view that "dimensionless points [and] breadthless lines ... could not be identified with material objects or the space of everyday experience" [18, p. 205]. Yet it is undeniable that many of the ancient solutions to the classical construction problems are explicitly based on precisely such an identification of the objects of mathematics with everyday experience. So Hobbes has ample ancient precedent for his views.

Euclid defined a point as "that which has no part," but that did not stop many ancient mathematicians from identifying physically extended objects with mathematical points. Euclid himself, as well as Ptolemy, affirmed that the Earth can be considered a point in relation to the sphere of the fixed stars [6, p. 186]. Aristarchus, in his treatise *On the Sizes and Distances of the Sun and Moon*, states as one of the hypotheses on which the work is based: "That the Earth has a ratio of a point and center with respect to the sphere of the Moon." [6, p. 45] Similar idealisations occur in other parts of ancient mathematics, such as treating weights as point masses in the theory of the lever.

It is therefore perfectly possible to think of the mathematics of the Greeks as no less empirical than their astronomy, mechanics, and optics. Euclid's definitions of point and line are then not a denial of physicality but a specification of the idealisations made. In this way, Euclid's definitions are not at odds with an empirical conception of geometry. On the contrary, they are exactly the same kind of idealisations that are explicitly made in empirical contexts such as Aristarchus's explicit assumption postulated at the beginning of his astronomical treatise. In other words, nothing is stopping ancient mathematicians—including those who take Euclid's *Elements* literally—from being hardline empiricists agreeing with Hobbes that "there is no conception in a mans mind, which hath not at first ... been begotten upon the organs of Sense" [12, III, p. 3].

This was indeed Hobbes's interpretation. He makes explicit both the idealising character of these definitions and their equivalence with empirical science:

> Those who say that the earth is a point do not speak improperly when it is treated, as in astronomy, as describing a line of annual motion. Nor is the width of a line zero, but is considered zero in the demonstration. [13, IV, p. 33]

This view is shared by several ancient authors. Heron states it clearly:

> Already in ordinary language use we have the notion of a line as something which has only length, but not at the same time width and thickness. For we say: ... a road of 50 stades, as we concern ourselves with the length only, but not at the same time its width. [11, p. 17]

Proclus makes the same point—also using the example of a road—and attributes this view to "the followers of Apollonius" [28, p. 82]: again a link to a highly authoritative technical author and not merely commentators.

In agreement with this interpretation, Hobbes writes that Euclid's definition of a point "not only to a candid, but also to a rigid construer, is sound and useful" [12, VII, p. 200]. "Euclid's definition of a point is accurately true, and the same with mine, which is, that a point is that body whose quantity is not considered." [12, VII, p. 201] Again: "his [Euclid's] meaning was, that the quantity of a point, the breadth of a line, and the thickness of a superficies were not to be considered." [12, VII, p. 211] That is to say, these definitions express not some profound ontological commitment but simply common-sense idealisations of the same kind that is involved in any other physical science. As these passages show, Hobbes sees his physicalist conception of geometry not as a radical departure from tradition but rather a mere restoration or clarification of what Euclid really meant.

The viability of such a physicalist reading of the Greek tradition has often not been recognised by modern scholars. Grant, to his credit, specifically "tried to suggest that some of [Hobbes's] apparently oddest ideas were in fact faithful echoes of the mathematical mainstream of centuries past" [9, p. 126]. This is precisely my thesis in so many words. But unfortunately Grant did not carry through on this intention to anywhere near its full potential, in my view. Instead he takes for granted that Hobbes's physicalist view of geometry must "place him in sharp opposition to the mainstream view" and constitute an "insistent challenge to the ancient legacy ... at its very foundations." [9, p. 112] The possibility that the physicalist view simply was the ancient mainstream view is apparently inconceivable even to Grant.

It is precisely the inability to conceive this possibility that leads Grant to claim, erroneously in my view, that Hobbes "balked at Euclid's definition of a line as 'breadthless length'." [9, p. 126] Hobbes took a physicalist view of points and lines, that much is true. But the inference that he therefore "balked" at Euclid does not follow. Grant is led to put these words in Hobbes's mouth by his implicit assumption that surely Euclid could not have been a physicalist. But, as we saw, Hobbes expressly approved of Euclid's definition of a point, and for the definition of a line only felt the need for a clearer formulation to bring out what "his [Euclid's] meaning was." There is no basis to speak of any "opposition to the mainstream view." Hobbes considered himself part of the mainstream view embodied in the Greek tradition, and, arguably, he was right.

Already in antiquity attempts were made to argue that Euclid's definition of a line contradicts geometrical diagrammatic practice. Sextus Empiricus made such an argument:

> The mathematicians talk idly when they say that they will bisect a given straight line. For the straight line shown to us on the board has length and breadth, whereas the straight line conceived by them is 'length without breadth'. And the line shown on the board will not be a line, and those who attempt to cut it are cutting not the real line but the unreal. [35, p. 139]

But Sextus Empiricus is a philosophical commentator with no mathematical authority. Hobbes mentions his argument and squarely dismisses it on the grounds that Sextus Empiricus has "misunderstood" Euclid [12, VII, p. 184]. Once again we see Hobbes dismissing a philosophical commentator in favour of aligning himself with a technical author, Euclid, whose views he considers himself in continuity with.

Hobbes also, with good cause, observes that the significance of Euclid's definitions of point and line is questionable since they are quite extraneous to the actual body of the *Elements* and play no meaningful part in any proof. Hobbes is arguably right to point out that "seeing [Euclid] maketh not, nor could make any use of them in his demonstrations, they ought not to be numbered among the principles of geometry" [12, VII, p. 184]. Similar points have been made by modern scholars [37, p. 222], [30, pp. 196, 206]. Despite being technically inconsequential, these are the very passages so often heavily relied on by those who allege that Greek geometry was anti-physicalist. The same goes for Euclid's definition of a straight line as a line that "lies evenly with the points on itself." This exceedingly vague definition has been criticised by many as empty verbiage of no mathematical value. Hobbes is right to say that "Euclid's definition is completely meaningless" [13, IV, pp. 396–397]. Some modern historical scholarship has even gone so far as to argue that these basic definitions are later additions that were not in the original text of the *Elements* at all [30], [31, pp. 320–326]: another case where Hobbes's view squares well with later historical research.

There is also a telling linguistic aspect to the notion of a point, which was carefully heeded by Hobbes. Russo observes that "the notion of a point (στιγμή) was analyzed at length in pre-Hellenistic times" in philosophical sources, but "Euclid avoids the word στιγμή in the Elements, using instead σημεῖον" "This replacement suggests that Euclid may have wished to cut himself off from the tradition of Platonic speculations on the true nature of the point." [31, p. 181] This is yet another instance where Hobbes finds himself aligned with modern scholarship. Hobbes was well attuned to subtleties of the Greek language, and indeed when discussing Euclid's notion of a point he specifically quotes Euclid's Greek term and argues that its meaning is that of a "mark" in a physical sense [12, VII, p. 200].

Equality is another fundamental notion that is naturally defined in physicalist terms. According to Hobbes, geometrical entities are equal if they are capable of physical superposition, that is, "capable of being coincident with the place" of each other [12, VII, p. 197], or in other words: "bodies are equal to each other, which can fit into the same place" [13, IV, p. 59]. This agrees very well with Euclid's Common Notion 4: "Things which coincide with one another equal one another." Indeed, even modern scholars such as Heath have felt that some of Euclid's language in connection with this notion "leaves no room for doubt that he regarded one figure as actually moved and placed upon the other" [10, I, p. 225]. Heath's view is not definitive (it is criticised on linguistic and other grounds in [36, p. 446]), but it does show that an interpretation similar to that of Hobbes was considered quite unavoidable even by a modern scholar who was specifically devoted to a faithful translation from the Greek and who shared none of Hobbes's philosophical conceptions in this regard. Clearly, then, Hobbes can reasonably claim textual support for his physicalist definition of equality.

5 Later Evolution of Hobbes's Views

The notion that Hobbes was a faithful interpreter of classical Greek geometrical method has been done no favours by the notoriously poor quality of Hobbes's own mathematical work. In the context of his wrongheaded attempts at solving the classical construction problems, Hobbes increasingly found himself "struggling against the tide of the geometers of this age, and even sometimes against Euclid and his interpreters—that is, the very fathers of geometry" [13, V, p. 94]. He found himself backpedaling as others exposed how his work was for example inconsistent with Archimedes's work on the area of a circle [16, pp. 273, 290], [13, IV, pp. 450–451]. To defend his erroneous work, Hobbes had to take an increasingly radical stance in his philosophy of mathematics. But this was a reactive stance forced upon Hobbes by having argued himself into a corner: his foolish attempts at solving outstanding problems like that of squaring the circle left him no other recourse, short of admitting error, but to explain away its inconsistency with other parts of mathematics somehow. This is indeed precisely what Jesseph has argued [17, pp. 434–437, 449–450], [16, pp. 248–249, 256, 273, 290]. Hobbes's initial framing of his own mathematical results was indeed that they were fully consistent with the outlook of ancient mathematicians: "neither they, nor I, [are] in the wrong" [12, I, p. 316]. This suggests that we should not take Hobbes's later, sometimes increasingly radical claims as showing an inherent readiness on Hobbes's part to dismiss ancient geometry and its foundations. Rather, it is reasonable to take Hobbes's many statements to be following the ancient tradition to be a sincere expression of his core outlook, while the exceptions to this can be seen as reluctant afterthoughts forced upon him in order to try to save face when the errors of his attempts at creative mathematics were exposed.

In this context Hobbes grew a bit more cautious in his interpretation of Euclid. Regarding the definition of a point, Hobbes now says more noncommittally that "it is difficult to know what Euclid meant by this definition," "but whether Euclid thought so or otherwise, it is clear that a point is divisible" [13, IV, p. 391]. Even so, he remained squarely a traditionalist in his own view:

> Gratitude is owed to Euclid, who was the first of all to show the world the method of demonstrating, that is, of reasoning well. [13, V, p. 202]

> To define well ... is very difficult. ... But we are relieved of the greatest part of this difficulty by the industry of the ancient geometers: except that Euclid's definition of a line needs some correction, or at least a correct interpretation. [13, V, p. 156]

> I have indeed criticised some things in Euclid, but not so much that I do not think that he should be highly esteemed, who was the first to teach the method of mathematical sciences. [13, IV, p. 465]

Thus Hobbes remain consistent in his insistence that had no intention of supplanting the philosophy of mathematics of classical antiquity, but only to explicate Euclid's own meaning "or at least a correct interpretation" of it.

6 Motion

We discussed above how a significant portion of the classical corpus on the famous construction problems is explicitly stated in physical terms. In this classification, I counted as physical only those cases where the text made clear reference to material objects. A similar analysis applies for the use of motion in these solutions. I did not count references to motion as itself physical. About half of the documented ancient solution methods of the classical problems explicitly involve constructions by motion, including several of the ones that are not explicitly physical [3, p. 673].

Hobbes indeed considers curves to be generated by physical bodies in motion. Sacksteder highlights this as the grounds for his assessment that "Hobbes' philosophy of geometry was eccentric" and "doubtless odd and quaint" [32, pp. 573, 575], since, according to Hobbes,

> geometry can be attentive to nothing which is not a motion or which is not derived by compounding various motions. This requirement for geometry seems very odd to us today. [32, p. 576]

Today, yes. But in antiquity and among leading early modern mathematicians definitions of geometrical entities by compounded motions are ubiquitous. There is nothing "eccentric" or "quaint" about it. It is merely an accurate observation about classical geometrical methodology.

Hobbes indeed appeals to this ancient precedent, specifically in the case of Archimedes:

> Archimedes has many things demonstrated in his books about motion and time, which not even Wallis himself, I believe, would deny are both well demonstrated and purely mathematical. [13, IV, p. 17]

Hobbes is right, and once again we see how he based his views on the authoritative technical writers, such as Archimedes. It is of little consequence that Proclus opens his commentary on the *Elements* by declaring that geometry is superior to "the kinds of things that move about in matter" [28, p. 3]. These words of a card-carrying Platonist matter little compared to the mathematical practice of the greatest geometer of antiquity.

Euclid is another authoritative mathematician who embraced motion in geometry. Like Archimedes, Euclid defined several geometrical entities in terms of motion. Hobbes notes this, and even criticises Euclid for not using the same approach when defining a circle as well:

> A circle is a figure described by the circumduction of a line, being in a plane, one end of which is at rest. This method of definition is also used by Euclid in the definition of a sphere, a cone, and a cylinder. [13, IV, p. 64]

> I ask ... why [Euclid] did not define a circle from the circumduction of a radius, as he defined a sphere from the circumduction of a semi-circle; for it could have been: that definition had been a declaration of the generation of a circle, and by it this definition could have been demonstrated briefly. [13, IV, p. 408]

That is to say, Euclid's definition of a circle, in terms of equidistance from a center point, can be demonstrated from the motion definition of a circle in terms of a line segment rotated about one of its end point. Such definitions in terms of motion have an impeccable ancient pedigree.

7 Instantivism

When Pycior calls Hobbes a "geometrical maverick," her grounds for this is his "rejection of universal ideas": "He thought that the geometer reasoned on specific lines and figures, or on their universal names, but never on universal abstract ideas as such" [29, p. 271]. In other words, geometrical theorems are statements about particular concretely constructed figures, not infinite classes of objects that preexist fully formed. This position—which we may call instantivism—was indeed Hobbes's view. But after thus accurately describing Hobbes's view, Pycior concludes that "this view of geometry ... put him at odds with the traditional Euclidian approach" [29, p. 271]. This is the part that I dispute.

Instantivism is little more than the constructivist paradigm taken to its logical conclusion. If we hold that geometry is about nothing but what we ourselves have constructed, then it follows that geometry cannot speak about universal abstract ideas. Just as, on a constructivist view, mathematical entities must be defined in terms of a recipe for making them, so must the meaning of theorems likewise be defined in terms of constructive operations.

Greek geometry is very amenable to such a reading. Consider for example the theorem that the angle sum of a triangle is two right angles (*Elements* I.32). Arguably, Euclid does not assume the existence of a universe of triangles and proclaim a universal relationship holding for all of them. The theorem can be read as saying merely: if you construct a triangle, then this property will hold for that one triangle. And if you construct another triangle it will hold for that one too, and so on. In this way the theorem is in a sense universal, yet strictly speaking "the geometer reasons only on specific lines and figures," just as in the Hobbesian view described by Pycior [29, 271].

This is arguably nothing but the extension to theorems of the view that the construction of figures is ontologically fundamental. On the constructivist view, it is the very constructive act that gives meaning to geometrical terms and statements. On this reading, "triangle" simply means the drawing of three lines with a ruler. If we accept this view, then we must, to be consistent, also accept that propositions about triangles are propositions about the outcomes of certain constructions, not universal and eternal truths about some abstractly existing Platonic universe of all triangles.

This reading agrees with Hobbes's account. As he puts it:

> If any man, by considering a triangle set before him, should find that all its angles together taken are equal to two right angles ... and it should happen afterwards that another triangle ... should be offered to his consideration, he would not know readily whether the same property were in this last or no, but would be forced, as often as a different triangle were brought before him ... to begin his contemplation anew ... [unless] he had the use of names [such as "triangle," which] serve as marks for the help of our memory, whereby we register to ourselves our own inventions. [12, I, pp. 79–80]

This view is a natural corollary of the constructivist commitment that mathematics only has meaning in terms of concretely constructed figures. Indeed, the question, then, is not: how does the man know that his argument applies to all triangles? But rather: how does he know that his argument applies again to the next concretely constructed triangle he encounters, and the next one after that, and so on? Universal names like "triangle" have no ontological reality. They are merely psychological shortcuts that help us highlight which aspects of the concrete situation before us are essential to our argument about it.

This position may seem radical today, but one would be hard pressed to find any inconsistency between it and ancient mathematical practice. On the contrary, once again recent scholarship on ancient geometry can be adduced to vindicate Hobbes. Instantivist-style readings of Euclid have recently been advocated as a viable historical hypothesis [26, pp. 57–58], [27, p. 62]. Indeed, Netz has observed that Greek mathematical texts never explicitly claim generality beyond the concrete proof based on a particular diagram [24, p. 242]. Doing so would raise the dreaded "generality problem" of how to justify the inferential leap from a particular diagram to an infinite class of objects—a problem that haunted Proclus and early modern thinkers alike [28, p. 162], [23, p. 257]. Instantivism provides a way around this dilemma. In this way instantivism can be motivated on internal mathematical grounds. Hence there is no need to write it off as yet another absurd stance that Hobbes was driven to advocate solely due to prior philosophical commitments external to mathematics.

8 Existence and Consistency

Philosophy of mathematics should enable one to "avoid the cavils of the sceptics" [12, VII, p. 185]. A challenge particularly central to mathematics is: how do we know that the axioms of geometry are consistent? Basing geometry on physical constructions enables an answer to this sceptical challenge [3, pp. 597–605]. Namely, in this way, we reduce as far as possible any contradiction among the principles and assumptions of geometry to a contradiction in physical experience itself. Thus we do not need to place inordinate trust in mathematicians as to whether they formulated a consistent axiom system in the first place. Instead we only need to trust that actual physical experience is not self-contradictory. As the eminent historian of mathematics Zeuthen put it:

> The certainty that these assumptions [the presuppositions of geometry] do not contradict one another, that is, are possible at all, follows from the fact that it is known in advance from their origin that there exists 'a geometry' for which they hold, namely the 'empirical geometry'. [40, p. 277]

> In order for the geometry based on [Euclid's axiomatic assumptions] to be actually possible, it is necessary that these [assumptions] can be reconciled with each other. The certainty of this Euclid really only has in the fact that he has arrived at them through analysis of empirical geometry, which as empirical must be possible. [40, p. 357]

Hobbes did not spell out this line of reasoning in so many words. Nevertheless, it may be interesting to note how many ingredients of this perspective are found in various places in Hobbes's writings. First of all, Hobbes was alert to the issue of consistency in general. He spoke for example of systems of knowledge "from which can be deduced, by lawfull argumentation, no absurdity" [14, I, p. 33], [16, p. 223]. He also observed that physical reality itself has a special status as far as consistency is concerned. As Hobbes says, "Nature itself cannot err"—that is to say, physical experiences "are not subject to absurdity" [12, III, p. 25]. Now, according to Hobbes, Euclid's postulates that allow constructions of lines and circles "belong to practice" [12, I, p. 82]. Thus it seems only natural to conclude that Euclid's postulates, by virtue of being defined in terms of their physical execution, automatically inherit the warrant of consistency that belongs to "Nature itself."

Closely related to consistency is the issue of existence. Indeed, inconsistencies in mathematics have often manifested themselves in terms of objects that do not exist unwittingly being admitted into mathematical discourse [3, pp. 594, 597, 605]. As Hobbes observes, constructions in geometry are a way to ensure the existence of the objects one speaks of [12, VII, p. 205]. This fits with his general precept that "the first principles of all knowledge are the phantasms of sense and imagination, which we know by nature to exist" [13, I, p. 59]. By restricting geometry to entities that are physically constructed in nature, one avoids the danger of discoursing about supposed entities that cannot actually exist due to hidden contradictions among their defining properties.

9 The Role of Geometry in Hobbes's Thought

As noted above, the standard view is that Hobbes's philosophy of geometry is forced upon him by his other, prior philosophical commitments. Namely, his philosophy of geometry "follows quite naturally from his thoroughgoing materialism" [16, p. 74]:

> Because his ontology recognizes only body as real, and because he holds that it is only through motion of bodies that anything can be brought about, Hobbes's program in the philosophy of mathematics must found all geometry upon the principles of matter and motion. [16, p. 77]

My argument that Hobbes's philosophy of geometry was anchored in tradition rather than eccentric gives us reason to re-evaluate this supposed causal relationship. My reading suggests, if anything, that it makes more sense to reverse cause and effect and say that Hobbes's philosophy of mathematics explains his materialism, rather than the other way around. For it would be remarkable indeed if Hobbes's philosophy of geometry was forced upon him by external necessity, yet had so much to commend it as an interpretation of the technical corpus of Greek geometry.

One can readily imagine the following order of development. First Hobbes recognises the power and epistemic authority of mathematics. Being thus impressed, he resolves to try to lay bare the underlying principles of the geometrical method, so that he may emulate its success in other fields. He becomes convinced that the constructivist character of geometry is the key to its success, which is a very reasonable interpretation amply anchored in tradition. In physics this leads naturally to the materialist position that everything must be accounted for by body in motion, just as in mathematics everything must be built up by physical constructions, that is, by motions. Materialism in physics is thus analogous to constructivism in geometry. Indeed, it is striking that other ardent advocates of materialist contact mechanics in physics, such as Descartes, Huygens, and Leibniz, were equally committed to constructivist ideals in geometry [3, pp. 592–593], [2, pp. 57–58, 206].

There are no chronological problems with the hypothesis that Hobbes's materialism was inspired by geometry. In Hobbes's own words, he studied Euclid's *Elements* and was impressed especially by its method in 1629–30 [13, I, p. xiv], well before any of his materialist writings. It is also perfectly possible that Hobbes was inspired by Descartes in this regard, perhaps during his time in Paris the year before the publication of Descartes's *Discourse* of 1637. The hypothesis of such an influence is consistent with the chronology of Hobbes's writings, as [5,39] show at length.

Descartes's commitment to a construction-based philosophy of geometry was no less pronounced than that of Hobbes [4]. Indeed, the constructions that Descartes sets out as the foundations of his geometry are palpably physical, as many of the figures of his *Géométrie* show vividly: the motions of instruments consisting of interlocking rulers and pegs trace the desired curves, much as in the physical constructions for the classical problems proposed in antiquity. One can imagine that this made an impression on Hobbes and supported his conviction that the physicalist conception of geometry was mainstream.

Perhaps it is relevant in this connection that Hobbes observes that "the ellipse and the hyperbola can be drawn with a thread" [13, IV, p. 410]. Indeed, string constructions of conic sections were a recurring standard topic in 17th-century geometry. But why does Hobbes restrict himself to the ellipse and the hyperbola, when the third conic section—the parabola—can likewise be constructed by strings? The standard string construction for parabolas was discussed for example by Kepler [19, pp. 95–96], Cavalieri [7, §XLV], and van Schooten [33, §XIV] in major published works long before Hobbes wrote these words. Meanwhile, Descartes, in his *Dioptrique* had shown precisely the two constructions mentioned by Hobbes [8, pp. 90, 101], and not the one for the parabola. Hence it seems not unlikely that Descartes was Hobbes's source on this point as well.

References

1. Blåsjö, V.: The isoperimetric problem. Amer. Math. Monthly **112**(6), 526–566 (2005)
2. Blåsjö, V.: Transcendental Curves in the Leibnizian Calculus. Elsevier (2017)
3. Blåsjö, V.: Operationalism: an interpretation of the philosophy of ancient Greek geometry. Found. Sci. **27**(2), 587–708 (2022)
4. Bos, H.J.M.: Redefining Geometrical Exactness: Descartes' Transformation of the Early Modern Concept of Construction. Springer, New York (2001)
5. Brandt, F.: Thomas Hobbes' Mechanical Conception of Nature. Levin & Munksgaard, Copenhagen (1928)
6. Carman, C.C., Buzón, R.P.: Aristarchus of Samos: On the Sizes and Distances of the Sun and Moon. Routledge (2023)
7. Cavalieri, B.: Lo specchio ustorio overo trattato delle settioni coniche, Bologna (1632)
8. Descartes, R.: La Dioptrique. Leiden (1637)
9. Grant, H.: The Cambridge Companion to Hobbes. Presented at the Hobbes and Mathematics (1996)
10. Heath, T.L.: The Thirteen Books of the Elements. Cambridge University Press, Euclid (1925)
11. Alexandrinus, H.: Opera Quae Supersunt Omnia, vol. IV: Heronis Definitiones cum variis collectionibus Heronis quae feruntur Geometrica. Bibliotheca scriptorum Graecorum et Romanorum Teubneriana (1912)
12. Hobbes, T.: The English Works of Thomas Hobbes of Malmesbury, 11 volumes, London (1839–1845)
13. Hobbes, T.: Thomae Hobbes Malmesburiensis Opera Philosophica quae Latina Scripsit, 5 volumes, London (1839–1845)
14. Hobbes, T.: The Correspondence of Thomas Hobbes. Oxford University Press (1994)
15. Jesseph, D.: Of analytics and indivisibles: Hobbes on the methods of modern mathematics. Revue d'Histoire des Sciences **46**(2), 153–193 (1993)
16. Jesseph, D.: Squaring the Circle: The War Between Hobbes and Wallis. University of Chicago Press (1999)
17. Jesseph, D.: The Decline and Fall of Hobbesian Geometry. Stud. Hist. Philosophy Sci. **30**(3), 425–453 (1999)
18. Jesseph, D.: Hobbes's Theory of Space. In: De Risi, V. (ed.) Mathematizing Space. Springer (2015)
19. Kepler, J.: Ad Vitellionem Paralipomena, Quibus Astronomiae Pars Optica Traditur, Frankfurt (1604)
20. Knorr, W.R.: The Ancient Tradition of Geometric Problems, Birkhäuser (1975)
21. Mancosu, P.: Philosophy of Mathematics and Mathematical Practice in the Seventeenth Century. Oxford University Press (1999)
22. Marsden, E.W.: Greek and Roman Artillery: Technical Treatises. Oxford University Press (1971)
23. Mumma, J.: Proofs, pictures, and Euclid. Synthese **175**, 255–287 (2010)

24. Netz, R.: The Shaping of Deduction in Greek Mathematics: A Study in Cognitive History. Cambridge University Press (2003)
25. Netz, R.: The Works of Archimedes: Volume 1. Cambridge University Press (2004)
26. Panza, M.: Rethinking geometrical exactness. Hist. Math. **38**(1), 42–95 (2011)
27. Panza, M.: The twofold role of diagrams in Euclid's plane geometry. Synthese **186**(1), 55–102 (2012)
28. Proclus: A Commentary of the First Book of Euclid's Elements. Princeton University Press (1970)
29. Pycior, H.M.: Mathematics and Philosophy: Wallis, Hobbes, Barrow, and Berkeley. J. Hist. Ideas **48**(2), 265–286 (1987)
30. Russo, L.: The definitions of fundamental geometric entities contained in book I of Euclid's elements. Arch. History Exact Sci. **52**, 195–219 (1998)
31. Russo, L.: The Forgotten Revolution: How Science Was Born in 300 BC and Why it Had to Be Reborn. Springer (2004)
32. Sacksteder, W.: Hobbes: geometrical objects. Philosophy Sci. **48**(4), 573–590 (1981)
33. Van Schooten, F.: De Organica Conicarum Sectionum in Plano Descriptione, Leiden (1646)
34. Sefrin-Weis, H.: Pappus of Alexandria: Book 4 of the Collection. Springer (2010)
35. Sextus Empiricus: Against Physicists, Against Ethicists. Loeb Classical Library 311. Harvard University Press (1936)
36. Sidoli, N.: Uses of construction in problems and theorems in Euclid's Elements I-VI. Arch. Hist. Exact Sci. **72**(4), 403–452 (2018)
37. Szabo, A.: The beginnings of Greek mathematics. Springer (1978)
38. Thomas, I.: Greek Mathematical Works I: Thales to Euclid. Loeb Classical Library 335. Harvard University Press (1939)
39. Tuck, R.: Hobbes and Descartes. In: Rogers, G.A.J., Ryan, A. (eds.) Perspectives on Thomas Hobbes. Oxford University Press (1988)
40. Hieronymus Georg Zeuthen, H.G.: Hvorledes Mathematiken i tiden fra Platon till Euklid blev rationel videnskab. Det Kongelige Danske videnskabernes selskabs skrifter, Naturvidenskab og Mathematik, Afd. 8, Raekke I.5. Copenhagen (1917)

Are Graphs, Built on Logical Independence, Capable of Replacing Quantum Thinking?

Jerzy Król(✉)

University of Information Technology and Management, Chair of Cognitive Science and Mathematical Modelling, ul. Sucharskiego 2, 35-22 Rzeszów, Poland
jkrol@wsiz.edu.pl

Abstract. It was shown by Paterek et al. in 2010 that the logical independence of finitely many axioms of a complete theory leads to the randomness usually assigned to the measurement of spin in quantum mechanics. In the present work I extend this result to infinitely many axioms of the incomplete ZFC set theory. On the other hand the randomness of QM can be fully translated into genericity in the ZFC models on infinite dimensional Hilbert space. This complements and extends the finite result of Paterek et al. giving rise to the statement that QM randomness envisaged in quantum measurements can be fully and faithfully reproduced from logical independence, in general. This in turn opens up the intriguing possibility that QM might be derived to some extent from classical independence in logical systems. To understand this connection, I define a q-digraph based on the multiverse of random forcings over a ZFC model M where nodes are certain sets in Ns (other ZFC models) and wedges are random forcing extensions. Such a graph carries quantum randomness obtained by purely classical constructions without any reference to QM. I investigate properties of such a directed graph and find that this q-digraph is not a random Rado graph due to the nonamalgamation property of the random forcing. Also, the modal logic of forcing multiverse is S4.2, but the modal logic of the random multiverse is not known to be S4.2 and it could be essentially weaker. It follows that the modal logic of QM could be S4.2. or weaker $S4$. I conclude with certain philosophical remarks regarding graphs and QM.

Keywords: Random forcing · Quantum mechanics · q-digraphs

1 Introduction

It is well established phenomenon that quantum mechanics (QM) is not reducible to any classical (non-quantum) theory. The story has a rather long and dramatic history starting from the Einstein Podolski Rosen [1] thought experiment up to the Bell inequalities [2] and their experimental verification. In this paper, we focus on the logical side of this irreducibility since theories of classical physics

P. Sobociński et al. (Eds.): Diagrams 2026, LNAI 16833, pp. 191–198, 2027.
https://doi.org/10.1007/978-3-032-34178-5_20

are domains also for classical logic based on Boolean algebras. Quantum logic, in contrast, does not have an honest logic to be assigned to. In the very first paper on quantum logic, Birgkhoff and Von Neumann represented the logic of QM as a lattice of projections $\mathbb{L}(\mathcal{H})$ on the closed linear subsets of the Hilbert space $\mathcal{H}$ of a quantum system. This lattice is nondistributive which is in sharp opposition to classical logic of Boolean algebras, which are distributive. The connected problem is that it is difficult to assign a reliable canonical logical consequence functor to such systems of projections, which raises the question about the well-definiteness of quantum logic. That is why we propose (following [4]) to perform a ZFC twist of the QM formalism and investigate features of Zermelo-Fraenkel set theory with the axiom of choice (ZFC) in the context of QM. The twist is based roughly on taking maximal complete Boolean algebras $B_{\max}$ chosen from $\mathbb{L}(\mathcal{H})$ and building the sheaves of sets on them, $Sh(B_{\max})$. Here we do not dig deep into the technicalities of this process, but we only need basic information about what appears in the final stage and refer the reader to [3–5] for more details. So, the starting point is to determine a family $\{B_{\max,\alpha}\}_{\alpha\in I}$ of the complete Boolean algebras in $\mathbb{L}$ and switch to the corresponding family of $\{Sh(B_{\max,\alpha})\}_{\alpha\in I}$ by ZFC twist

$$B_{\max,\alpha} \to Sh(B_{\max,\alpha}),\ \alpha \in I.$$

The basic fact is that $Sh(B_{\max,\alpha})$ are Boolean-valued models of ZFC. We thus turn to the dynamics of ZFC models as the set theory counterparts of the QM formalism. This helps to consider the relations between the models as expressing the 'quantumness' of QM: ZFC models are constructs in classical logic (and set theory), thus if QM is nonclassical the relations between ZFC models have to carry quantum aspects of QM. This is the feature of the QM formalism where one can try to employ certain graphs which would express the quantum randomness, entanglement, reduction of the wave-function, etc., without envoking quantum measurement or ucertainty. Paterek et al. [6] observed that for finite collection of axioms, quantum randomness follows from logical independence. In our approach, we deal with infinite schemata of axioms and logical independence on these axioms as carriers of quantumness. Set theoretic forcings become the relation between ZFC models capable of deciding questions about quantum behavior. We define a special class of directed graphs that would be well suited for this task. In the next sections, we present how QM randomness refers to logical independence not only for finite sets of axioms but also for infinite sets of axioms. In the subsequent section, we construct q-digraphs that reflect this relation of QM and logical independence. We close the paper with a discussion of these intriguing findings.

2 Logical Independence and QM

2.1 The Finite Case

Independent logical statements relative to a logical theory T in the most simplistic case rely on taking say two statements p and q in the first order language in T such that

$$\begin{aligned} p \not\to q \text{ and } p \not\to \neg q \\ q \not\to p \text{ and } q \not\to \neg p. \end{aligned} \tag{1}$$

These p, q are *independent* relative to a complete theory T which means that T can decide any statement s of T. Taking three sentences p, q, r from T, we can have more refined dependence or independence patterns between these p, q, r. For example, we can consider p, q as axioms and r as an independent statement on p, q. In the first order language we can consider two unrelated predicates $P(x), Q(x)$ such that $\exists_x P(x), \exists_x Q(x)$ are independent in the sense of (1).

Although the above is the weakest form of logical independence, the authors of [6] found it to be strongly related to QM randomness. The key is to characterize the quantum state of a system as carrying the maximal possible information about the system. The idea in [6] is to start with Boolean functions

$$f_i(x) = \begin{cases} 1 \\ 0 \end{cases} \quad \text{for } x = 1, 0, i = 1, 2, 3, 4$$

and corresponding elementary statements, like

$$\begin{aligned} p &: \text{ The value of } f_1 \text{ is 0 for } x = 0,\ f_1(0) = 0. \\ q &: \text{ The value of } f_2 \text{ is 1 for } x = 0,\ f_2(0) = 1. \end{aligned}$$

etc. Certainly, there can be in principle some relations between p, q in a complete theory T that might spoil their independence; however, the requirement of impossibility to increase the information content of each sentence reduces this possibility. Thus, there is the relative improvability of one sentence from the other, and this first plays the role of a (relative) axiom for the second. This is well-illustrated by more complex sentences allowing for 2-bits information content, e.g.:

$$p'' : \ f_1(0) = 0 \text{ and } f_2(1) = 0.$$

or

$$q'' : \ f_1(0) = f_2(0) \text{ and } f_1(1) = f_2(1).$$

Now, considering q'' as the axiom, we infer that all individual values for f_1, f_2 are undetermined and thus p'' is the 2-bit sentence independent of q''. p'', q'' are complementary and logically independent 2-bit statements.

Following [6] this can be assigned to the quantum measurement process which leads to the appearance of definite values for some physical quantities represented by Hermitian operators. The canonical situation is to measure the direction of spin of a particle such as an electron in x, y, z coordinates of 3-dimensional space. The operators representing spins are three complex hermitian Pauli matrices, $\sigma_x, \sigma_y, \sigma_z$:

$$\sigma_x = \begin{pmatrix} 0 & 1 \\ 1 & 0 \end{pmatrix}, \sigma_y = \begin{pmatrix} 0 & -i \\ i & 0 \end{pmatrix}, \sigma_z = \begin{pmatrix} 1 & 0 \\ 0 & -1 \end{pmatrix}$$

which have $+1, -1$ eigenvalues. Let $m, n = 0, 1$ and $\sigma^0_{x,y,z} = id, \sigma^1_{x,y,z} = \sigma_{x,y,z}$ and recall that $\sigma_y = i\sigma_x\sigma_z$. Let our quantum particle has spin in the x or y or

z directions. Then measuring spin in any other direction is completely random, in the sense that whether it is $+1$ or -1 direction along the measured axis is completely unpredictable. Now, let us take a Boolean function $f(x)$. The value $f(0)$ is encoded by the operator $\sigma_x^{f(0)}$ and the value $f(1)$ by $\sigma_z^{f(1)}$ so thus

$$(m,n) \mapsto i^{mn}\sigma_x^m\sigma_z^n$$

which results in encoding the Pauli operators in Boolean pairs (m,n):

$$(0,1) \to \sigma_z; (1,0) \to \sigma_x; (1,1) \to \sigma_y.$$

Now QM teaches us that when the initial spin of an electron is in the x direction (σ_x) and it is measured along y the resulting $+,-$ in the y-direction is unpredictable and random. Thus, depending on what Pauli operator is placed after $i^{mn}\sigma_x\sigma_z^n$ and what are the initial values m,n the result of the measurement can be unpredictable or definite. Assigning to the Boolean function $f(m) = 1, 0$ the statements p,q as before we found the intriguing possibility that certain statements r representing some Boolean functions $f(x)$ would be logically independent of p,q similarly as we discussed at the beginning of this section. Quantum measurements can show the logical independence of certain classical (not quantum) statements, but logical independence is also strong enough to express quantum randomness. There is, however, the additional external 'information content' condition which has to be placed on sentences.

Theorem 1. *Logical independence (1) augmented by the requirement of maximum amount of classical information in the axioms, generate quantum randomness involved in the measurement of spin-$\frac{1}{2}$ particles. This happens even without reference to any existing quantum system.*

The above phenomenon is very intriguing and shows how classicality can cover quantum phenomena at least in the quantum Pauli algebra case. In the next section, we will show that this information condition can be relaxed.

2.2 The Infinite Case and ZFC

The independence in the previous section, with the maximality information condition, is weak from the point of view of logic and can hold even for a complete theory T. The maximality of information in sentences/axioms can be obtained just by artificially cutting off the access to the ambient information that exists in a complete theory T. Without this cutting, T can decide any sentence in T, so thus, even though (1) holds, p,q,r are dependent on the axioms of T.

The stronger version is the independence relative to the entire incomplete first order theory. The canonical example is ZFC with infinite schemata of axioms. The independence in this case is comparatively much stronger than for a few sentences in a complete theory fulfilling (1), now it is independence on all the axioms of ZFC. Is this strong independence somehow related to QM? To understand the connection with QM and to answer the question, we should turn to

ZFC models. If there exists a single set model of ZFC, there must also exist a countable transitive model M [7]. But there also exists a model $M[G]$ *nontrivially* extending M, $M \subsetneq M[G]$. Here G is a generic filter in $M[G]$, $G \notin M$ that determines $M[G]$ [7]. $M[G]$ is the forcing extension of M with respect to G. Equivalently forcing extensions can be defined by complete Boolean algebras B and the Boolean-valued models V^B [8], where V is the universe of sets like the cumulative Von Neumann universe [7].

Forcing can be considered as a logical tool for showing independence results in set theory [8] (relative proofs) and this was originally invented by Cohen to show independence of the continuum hypothesis (CH) on the axioms of ZFC (and the axiom of choice from ZF axioms). Cohen built a model M that meets CH and its forcing extension, where $\neg CH$ is true. The other side of forcing is 'ontological' and shows how to build new models of ZFC from old ones. One can think of each model as a universe where almost all mathematics (also mathematics of QM) can be expressed. There are several models and, in each of them, it is possible to find different independent ZFC statements, the veracity of which is proven by means not available in the system. Similarly to CH, in one model it is true, while there exist other models where CH is false. This ontological side of forcing is well-suited for grasping certain features of QM formalism, especially QM randomness.

We say that a forcing G is nontrivial whenever $M \subsetneq M[G]$ and this property can be stated in terms of Boolean algebras B and Boolean-valued models M^B:

Lemma 1 ([7]). *$M^B/G \simeq M[G]$ and $M \subsetneq M[G]$ if and only if B is a complete atomless Boolean algebra in M.*

As we noted in Introduction, the ZFC twist of QM relies on the switch between B and V^B. But any maximal complete Boolean algebra $B \subset \mathbb{L}$ on $\dim \mathcal{H} = \infty$ contains a universal atomless component:

Theorem 2 ([4]). *Any maximal complete Boolean subalgebra $B^{(\infty)}_{max}$ of $\mathbb{L}$ contains the atomless part which is isomorphic to the measure Boolean algebra B_m.*

It follows from this theorem and from lemma 1 that *QM on infinite dimensional Hilbert spaces determines unique nontrivial random forcing extension of V, $V[G]$.*

Now the point is that in V one cannot decide by any logical means of ZFC which forcing extension $V[G]$ will be taken. This is a perfect counterpart for random behavior relative to M. Is this ZFC model-theoretic randomness strong enough to capture QM randomness? To answer this, we need to turn to the mathematical theory of algorithmic randomness (Martin-Löf) [10]

Theorem 3. *i. QM is 1-random [9].*
ii. QM is n-random and ω-random [4].
iii. QM on infinite dimensional Hilbert spaces is ZFC (Solovay) random [4].

The relation between ZFC randomness and n-randomness is the following

Theorem 4. *Relativized to a ZFC model M, the following implication holds true:*

ZFC randomness $\longrightarrow$ n-randomness and ω-randomness.

Then, taking into account Therems 3 and 4 we obtain:

Theorem 5. *Logical independence due to random forcing while relativized to a ZFC model M expresses the full randomness of QM.*

This is a generalization of Theorem 1 to infinite dimensions.

3 Q-Digraphs for QM

Let us rewrite the above classical data that generate QM randomness in the language of graphs. Let M be a transitive model of ZFC and let S be a set of such models. We define the graph subordinated to S.

Definition 1. *Let S be considered as the set of nodes. For $M, N \in S$ if N is a random forcing extension of M, $N = M[G]$, then there exists a directed edge $M \to N \in F$. The graph built in this way $Z = (S, F)$ is called a 'ZFC random graph' if there exist at least two different edges from any node $M \in S$.*

The ZFC random graph is a directed graph (digraph). Let $M \in S$ be a node in a ZFC random digraph $Z = (S, F)$. There can be many different random extensions of M and many different edges from M in F. The *amalgamation property* for Z holds when for any two different nodes M_1, M_2 there exist another N and two edges starting from M_1, M_2, respectively, such that they meet in N. The *nonamalgamation property* for Z holds when for any two different nodes M_1, M_2 there are edges and their extensions in Z starting from M_1, M_2 correspondingly such that they do not meet in any N in Z.

Lemma 2. *There exists a ZFC random digraphs Z such that*

i. Z has the nonamalgamation property.
ii. Every node in Z codes ZFC randomness.

Proof. i. is the application of the result of Hamkins, stating that for Cohen forcing the corresponding multiverse has this nonamalgamation property [11]. Here, we choose certain ZFC models M as nodes in Z and random forcing extensions of them as edges, that *i.* holds.

ii. is a general property of forcing extensions plus the existence of at least two different edges $M[G_1], M[G_2]$ starting from every node M in Z. In M there is no possibility to predict which forcing extension has been taken. In $M[G_1]$ or in $M[G_2]$ no randomness related to M survives, but a new one appears connected with the subsequent choice of $M[G_1][G_{11}]$ or $M[G_1][G_{12}]$. The strength of randomness connected with the choices in Z is ZFC random, which is more powerfull than Martin-Löf algorithmic randomness as stated in Theorem 4. This finishes the proof of Lemma 2.

However, there exist Zs that presumably have the amalgamation property. The question whether QM separates Z having the amalgamation property from those which do not is the subject of ongoing studies. Now we will show the relation of QM and Z. First, QM is ZFC-random (necessarily on $\mathcal{H}^{(\infty)}$) as stated in Theorem 3 (*iii.*) but also QM is n-random and ω-random as in Theorem 3 (*ii.*) for finite-dimensional $\mathcal{H}$. Both these properties are reflected in our digraph Z since ZFC randomness implicates n-randomness for any $n \in \mathbb{N}$ (relative to any node M in Z).

Second, the QM measurement produces the values of observables that cannot be preassigned before the experiment to the measured quantity. This value is no longer random after the measurement. This reflects the property of the graph Z that the ZFC randomness is relative to M and after the forcing extension M-random sequences are not random in $M[G]$.

Third, as shown in [4] in a generic QM measurement, the random forcing extension of V, $V[G]$, or equivalently a ZFC model $M[G]$ is always assigned. Thus, the displacement along the graph Z models generic measurements in QM.

Fourth, the nonamalgamation property of Z reflects the QM property that two possible results of a QM measurement cannot coexist as real in a single universe V.

Fifth, the graph Z could support the modal logic S4.2 which is the same as the multiverse of all forcing extensions over M [12,13]. But it can happen that Z has a weaker modal logic S4. Currently, this is an open question.

Thus, the logic of QM randomness can be approached by modal $S4$ logic on infinite dimensional Hilbert spaces. Since ZFC independence and built on it graphs take over some crucial aspects of QM phenomena, we elevate the modal logic of ZFC random digraph along with random forcing into the core of QM logic.

4 Conclusions and Perspectives

Quantum randomness is supported by deep quantum phenomena like the Heisenberg uncertainty principle or entanglement, and the possibility to approach classically this quantum randomness is, in fact, entering the quantum world by classical means. Logical independence, on the other hand, is an important but rather well-recognized topic in classical logic. The possibility that QM randomness generated by Pauli algebra of spin observables is fully captured by a weak form of logical independence (augmented by the restriction on the information content of logical axioms) in a complete first order theory is quite a surprise. Imagine a classical formalized theory of physics that contains many independent pairs of logical sentences. This formal part would be in power to generate the quantumness of the physical phenomena such as those connected with spin-$\frac{1}{2}$ particles. The purpose of this work is to understand this miracle better via a certain graph structure.

We have analyzed the finite dimensional case of the quantum particle above and we have attempted to extend it over infinite dimensional Hilbert spaces and the corresponding quantum randomness. There emerges even a stronger correspondence between quantum randomness and logical independence. We built graphs of ZFC models and their forcing extensions such that the traveling along the graphs represents the sequence of quantum measurements. The graphs carry the S4 or S4.2 modal logics, which should be considered as the basis for quantum logic. Investigations of this phenomenon are pending.

There is yet another feature of the extension of finite-dimensional Hilbert spaces onto infinite ones via ZFC independence. The negation of the Tsirelson conjecture, proved recently, states that on $\mathcal{H}^{(\infty)}$ there are certain finite correlations that can distinguish the product Hilbert spaces from non-product. The proof has recently been reformulated in terms of random forcing and genericity in ZFC [14]. This shows again that the analysis of quantum experiments via forcing and q-digraphs seems to be a worthwhile step in understanding the structure of QM. This also indicates that the foundation of QM presumably should be based on the ZFC multiverses rather than on the fixed, unchanged universe of sets. This paper is the first step in exploring quantum phenomena via forcing graphs. The further effort should be focussed on wave-packet reduction in quantum measurement or entanglement expressed in the language of the graphs.

References

1. Einstein, A., Podolsky, B., Rosen, N.: Can quantum-mechanical description of physical reality be considered complete? Phys. Rev. **47**(10), 777–780 (1935)
2. Bell, J.S.: On the Einstein Podolsky Rosen paradox. Physics **1**(3), 195–200 (1964)
3. Takeuti, G.: Two Applications of Logic to Mathematics. Princeton University Press, USA, Princeton (1978)
4. Król, J., Bielas, K., Asselmeyer-Maluga, T.: Random world and quantum mechanics. Found. Sci. **28**(2), 575–625 (2023)
5. Król, J., Asselmeyer-Maluga, T.: Negation of the smooth Poincaré conjecture in dimension 4 and negation of the Tsirelson's conjecture shed light on quantum gravity. Universe **11**(4), 126 (2025)
6. Paterek, T., et al.: Logical independence and quantum randomness. New J. Phys. **12**, 013019 (2010)
7. Jech, T.: Set Theory. Germany, Third Millenium Edition. Springer Verlag, Berlin (2003)
8. Bell, J.L.: Set Theory. Boolean-Valued Models and Independence Proofs. Clarendon Press, Oxford, UK (2005)
9. Landsman, K.: Randomness? What randomness? Found. Phys. **50**, 61–104 (2020)
10. Downey, R.G., Hirschfeldt, D.R.: Algorithmic Randomness and Complexity. Theory and Applications of Computability. Springer, New York (2010)
11. Habič, M.E., Hamkins, J.D., Klausner, L.D., et al.: Set-theoretic blockchains. Arch. Math. Logic **58**, 965–997 (2019)
12. Hamkins, J.D., Löwe, B.: The modal logic of forcing. Trans. Am. Math. Soc. **360**(4), 1793–1817 (2008)
13. Hamkins, J.D.: The set-theoretic multiverse. Rev. Symbolic Logic **5**(3), 416–449 (2012)
14. Król, J., Asselmeyer-Maluga, T.: Negation of the Tsirelson's conjecture and genericity in quantum mechanics. Kielnarowa Rev. **1**, 46–70 (2024)

∞-Simplexes, Completion-Games and Poly-Lobes: Enriching, by Diffraction, the Oppositional Space B_MN?

Alessio Moretti(✉)

Università Telematica eCampus, Via Isimbardi 10, 22060 Novedrate, CO, Italy
alessio.moretti@uniecampus.it

Abstract. Oppositional geometry is the framework of diagrams like the "square" and "hexagon" of oppositions. It is captured, as poly-simplicial space B_MN, by the ("horizontal sections" of the) "Pascalian simplexes" P_M (cf. [3]). Now we investigate the Pascalian ∞-simplexes through "completion-games". As an outcome, one finds two results: "poly-numbers" (entities consisting in an infinite, n-dimensional and all-directional distribution of "mono-numbers", cf. [4]) and "poly-lobes" (i.e. particular poly-numbers made of n-tuples of centrally symmetric ∞-simplexes). By its generality, the theory of poly-numbers allows reaching, for any ∞-simplex X_m, the "closure" $\pi\lambda(\pm X_m)$ of its poly-lobes. The inner structure of this closure is given by transformation polytopes $\kappa\lambda(\pm X_m)$ (made of Klein groups, cf. [1]) relating two by two the involved lobes. Here we study $\pi\lambda(\pm P_2)$, whose transformation structure $\kappa\lambda(\pm P_2)$ is an octahedron. We prospect the hypothesis of a consequent "poly-lobic diffraction" of the oppositional space B_MN.

Keywords: Oppositional Geometry · Pascalian ∞-Simplexes · Poly-Lobes

1 From "Oppositional Diagrams" to "Pascalian ∞-Simplexes"

2-valued "n-oppositional geometry", a mathematical framework for the "square (and hexagon) of oppositions", is encrypted (through its "horizontal sections", i.e. its numerical rows) in a famous numerical ∞-diagram: "Pascal's triangle" (cf. [2, 3]) (see Fig. 1).

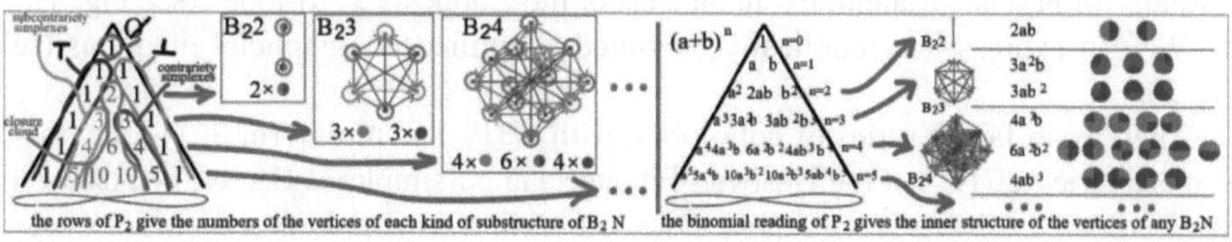

Fig. 1. Pascal's triangle encrypts, in its rows, 2-valued oppositional geometry (the space B_2N).

Pascal's ∞-triangle belongs to the series of the Pascalian ∞-simplexes P_m (see Fig. 2).

P. Sobociński et al. (Eds.): Diagrams 2026, LNAI 16833, pp. 199–203, 2027.
https://doi.org/10.1007/978-3-032-34178-5_21

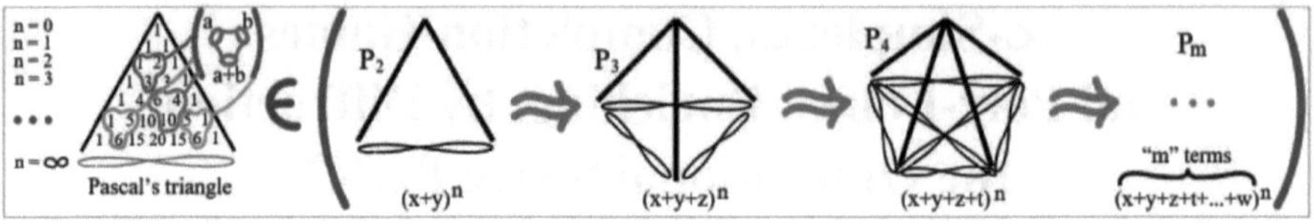

Fig. 2. Pascal's triangle P_2 is just one term of a series: that of the "Pascalian simplexes" P_m.

As for m-valued n-oppositional geometry (the space B_MN), it is encrypted in this series P_m (cf. [3]). But the P_m remain mysterious. In [4] we try to deepen their understanding by studying them through three new mathematical concepts: "completion-games", poly-lobes $\pi\lambda$ and, more fundamentally, (spatially infinite) n-dimensional "poly-numbers" $\pi\nu$. In this poster we will deal explicitly only with P_2's poly-lobes (for a soft introduction to poly-number theory, and for more ∞-simplexes and poly-lobes, cf. [4]).

2 "Completion-Games" over ∞-Simplexes Give "Poly-Lobes" $\pi\lambda$

By "completion" we will mean: "filling the void with structure-compatible numbers". Pascal's triangle P_2 is infinite (its structure is such that each inner number admitting above itself any integers "a" and "b" is equal to "a + b"), but it is surrounded by void (i.e. it does not fill the 2D plane, to which it belongs as "∞-fragment"). Let us try to abolish this void. This can be done in 2 moves: first laterally (see Fig. 3).

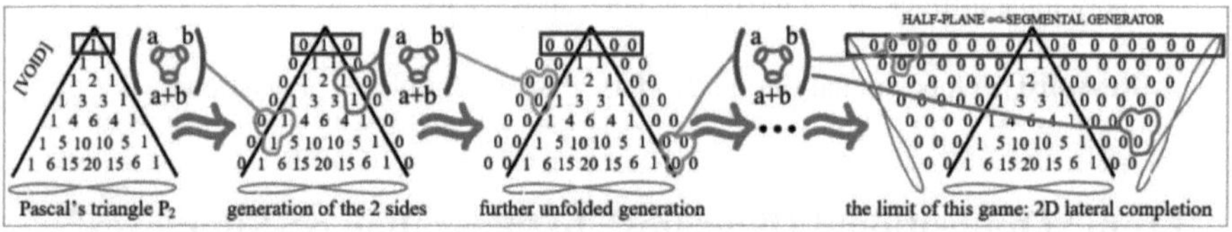

Fig. 3. First move of this completion-game: "lateral 2D completion" of Pascal's ∞-triangle P_2.

The outcome is a lower half-plane. Let us now try to perform 2D upwards-completion (so to recover a full-plane): among infinite possible solutions (we do not give here a full typology of them), 2 are arguably "optimal": they lead to the self-similar emergence of "avatars" of Pascal's triangle P_2. In the best of the 2 appears a "tri-lobe" (see Fig. 4).

We can express it symbolically by suited simplified ∞-simplicial diagrams (see Fig. 5).

There is, in fact, a series of poly-lobes, with $\pi\lambda(P_m)$ an m-dim (m + 1)-lobe (there also is a series $\pi\lambda(H_m)$ of the Hosoyan-Fibonaccian ∞-simplexes H_m, cf. [4]) (see **Fig. 6**).

Because P_2 undergoes "tri-lobic diffraction", a natural question is that of a possible tri-lobic diffraction also of the oppositional space B_2N based on P_2 (see Fig. 7).

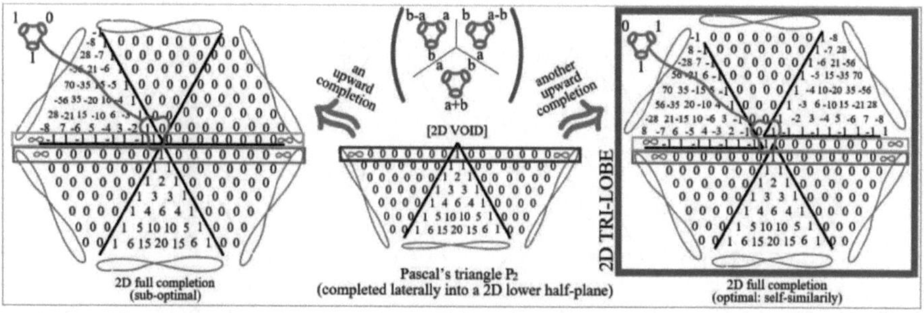

Fig. 4. One of the two best solutions of the 2D completion problem with P_2 gives a "tri-lobe".

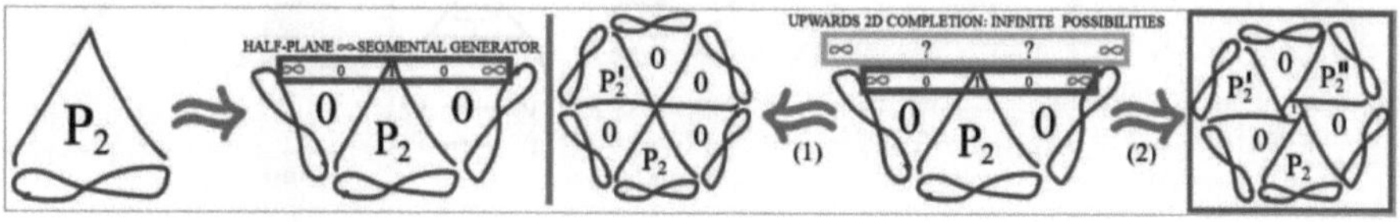

Fig. 5. Symbolic diagrammatic notation of the lateral and upward-optimal 2D completion of P_2.

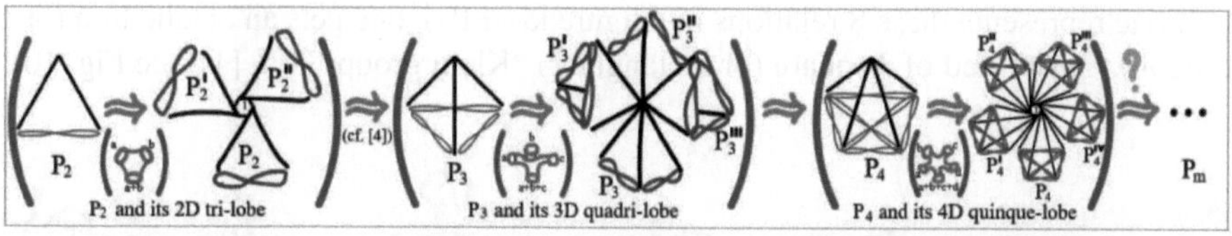

Fig. 6. A series $\pi\lambda(P_m)$ of m-dim Pascalian poly-lobes, correlated by bijection to the series P_m.

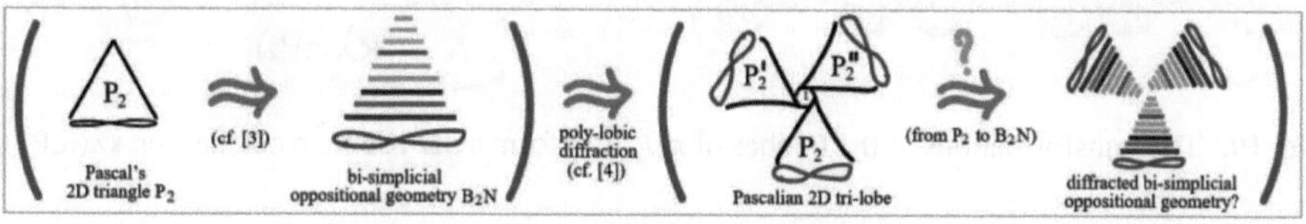

Fig. 7. Does P_2's 2D tri-lobe mean some kind of "diffraction" of the B_2N embedded in P_2?

As we study it in [4], poly-numbers show that any poly-lobe $\pi\lambda(X_m)$, being a non-0 poly-number, admits a negative counterpart $-\pi\lambda$: from this emerges a "closure" $\pm\pi\lambda$. This consists mainly in considering also the $\pi\lambda$ of the negative of X_m, i.e. $-X_m$ (cf. [4]).

3 The Inter-Lobic Group-Transformation Structures $\kappa\lambda$ for $\pi\lambda$

We know that P_2 gives 2 avatars, the 3 forming a 2D tri-lobe $\pi\lambda(P_2)$ and (because of $\pi\nu$-theory, cf. [4]) that $-P_2$ gives 2 more avatars, forming a tri-lobe $\pi\lambda(-P_2)$ (see Fig. 8).

These six 2D lobes of the poly-lobic closure $\pi\lambda(\pm P_2)$ are, 2 by 2, related by a particular transformation scheme: as it happens, there are 8 possible such relations (see Fig. 9).

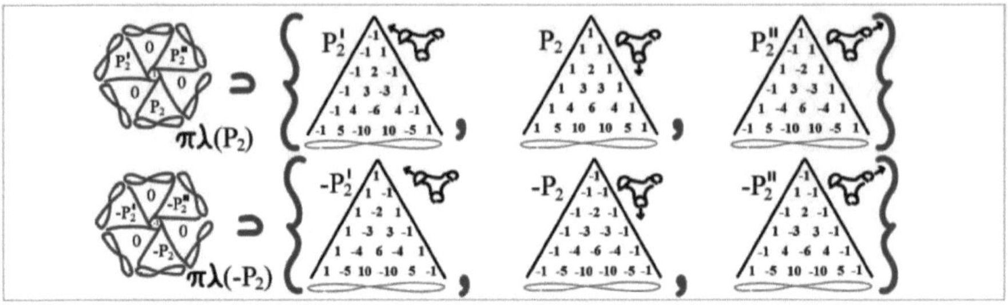

Fig. 8. The 2D tri-lobes $\pi\lambda(P_2)$ and $\pi\lambda(-P_2)$, of the ∞-triangles P_2 and $-P_2$, form 6 2D lobes.

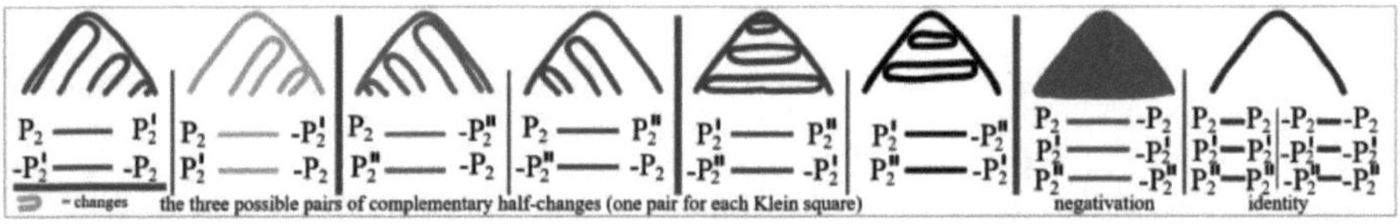

Fig. 9. The 8 possible relation-kinds holding between any 2 of the 6 2D lobes of $\pi\lambda(\pm P_2)$.

If one represents these 8 relations in a figure $\kappa\lambda(\pm P_2)$, one gets an octahedron (or a hexagon), constituted of 3 square (or rectangular) "Klein groups" (cf. [1], see Fig. 10).

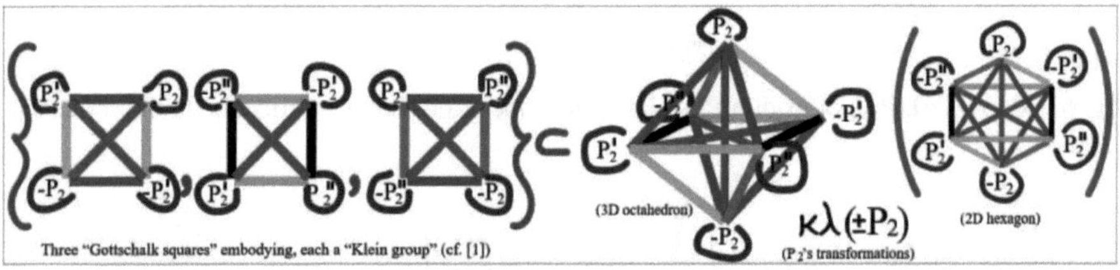

Fig. 10. The transformations of the 6 lobes of $\pi\lambda(\pm P_2)$ form a 3D Kleinian octahedron $\kappa\lambda(\pm P_2)$.

With this we have reached a minimal understanding of the poly-lobic closure of P_2.

4 A Poly-Lobic Diffraction of the Oppositional Space B_MN?

This allows coming back to the hypothesis of a poly-lobic diffraction of the oppositional space B_2N (and, later, B_MN). For this diffraction to be real, it must be inquired whether the presence of negative mono-numbers in the lobes can be meaningful for the oppositional universe: we claim that it can and that the diffraction is thus fully meaningful, but cannot study it here (we sketch it in [4], by asking whether there can be "negative" (1) dimensions, (2) simplexes, (3) truth value-sets, (4) metalogical *extrema*). For now, by a product-diagram we can at least give an image of the idea (see **Fig. 11**).

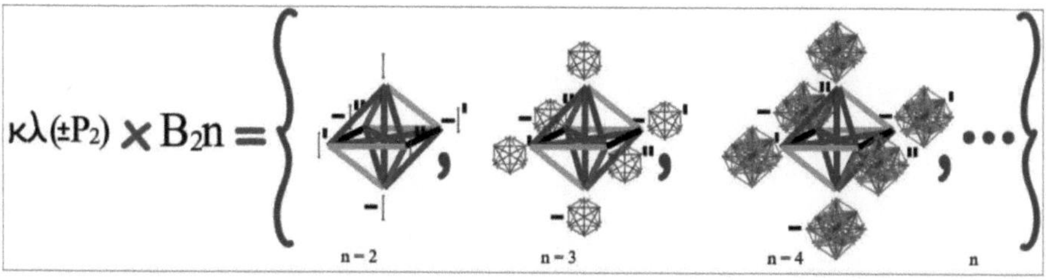

Fig. 11. The basic idea of "poly-lobic diffraction" of the (2-valued) oppositional space B_2N.

Disclosure of Interests. The author has no competing interests to declare that are relevant to the content of this article.

References

1. Gottschalk, W.H.: The theory of Quaternality. J. Symb. Log. **18**(3), 193–196 (1953). https://doi.org/10.2307/2267401
2. Green, T.M., Hamberg, C.L.: Pascal's Triangle, 2nd edn. Right Angle, Charleston (2014)
3. Moretti, A.: B_42: the geometry of 4-valued contradiction. In: Lemanski, J., Johansen, M.W. (eds.) Diagrammatic Representation and Inference 14th International Conference, Diagrams 2024, LNAI, vol. 14981, pp. 84–100. Springer, Cham (2024)
4. Moretti, A.: Pascal's Triangle as a "Mother-Diagram": ∞-Simplexes, Poly-Lobes and Poly-Numbers (soon posted in ArXiv) (2026)

Diagrams and Cognition

Pictographic Representations Enhance Understanding of Simple Dynamic Systems

Friederike Brockhaus(✉)

Chemnitz University of Technology, 09107 Chemnitz, Germany
friederike.brockhaus@psychologie.tu-chemnitz.de

Abstract. Understanding how stocks change due to inflows and outflows poses a persistent challenge. For example, many people struggle to grasp how atmospheric CO_2 levels (the stock) depend on natural and anthropogenic emissions (inflow) and CO_2 absorption, such as by plants and oceans (outflow). Stock-flow systems underlie many real-world phenomena, yet research using graphical representations – typically line graphs – has consistently documented poor performance in judging stock behavior from flow information. Drawing on Neurath's Isotype principles of iconic representation, I modified the standard format by using pictographic symbols instead of line graphs to depict flows. Pictographs were tested varying in icon type (specific icons like baby strollers and gravestones vs. abstract symbols like "+ / – ") and spatial arrangement (edge vs. center alignment). All four pictographic variants outperformed conventional line graphs. However, the variants did not differ significantly from one another in effectiveness. Regression analysis supported the results revealed by graphical data analysis. These findings suggest pictographic representation offers a promising alternative for communicating stock-flow dynamics in educational and media contexts.

Keywords: graphical representation · diagram comprehension · pictographs · stock-flow systems

1 Introduction

We all know stock and flow (SF) systems: settings in which an inflow and an outflow determine a stock. A familiar example is a bank account: deposits (inflow) and withdrawals (outflow) determine the balance (stock). They are omnipresent in our lives, from rather casual situations like our refrigerator to settings that are very important to life on this planet as CO_2 in the atmosphere. Despite their importance and omnipresence, these systems are difficult to understand, as numerous studies showed (e.g., [1–3]). In typical SF studies, participants view flow patterns as line graphs and either draw the stock's trajectory over time [1] or answer questions about the stock's maximum and minimum [2]. Figure 1 shows two typical examples of flow patterns. Gender and mathematical ability influence SF understanding [1, 4, 5], other factors like motivation or spatial abilities led to varying results (e.g [2, 6, 7].). Most intervention attempts have proven ineffective, even first attempts to animate SF tasks [6]. Studies on training programs also failed to yield a clear picture, although one approach produced promising results [7–9].

P. Sobociński et al. (Eds.): Diagrams 2026, LNAI 16833, pp. 207–214, 2027.
https://doi.org/10.1007/978-3-032-34178-5_22

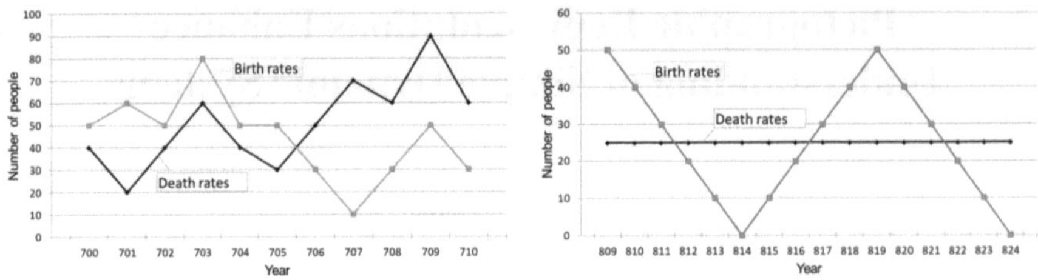

(a) (b)

Fig. 1. Two examples of different flow patterns: the discontinuous task (a) (modified from [2]), the shortened square wave pattern task (b) (modified from [1]).

Beyond explicit teaching, inspired by learning with multiple representations [10, 11], I explored whether modifying the representation format could improve intuitive understanding, particularly for lay audiences facing SF systems in media contexts. This approach has proven successful in other domains: for example, representing probabilities with countable items instead of percentages improves performance [12]. Similar format modifications have been tested for SF tasks. In one study graphs showed stick figures representing people getting on and off a bus, and participants drew the stock's pattern using countable symbols [13]. This seemed to facilitate correct solutions, and to prompt participants to calculate the stock at each time point. However, in a follow-up study where participants were only asked when stock reached its maximum and minimum (and therefore no calculations were necessary) the pictographic advantage disappeared [14]. Both studies followed some principles of Isotype, a method developed by Neurath [15] for communicating statistical information through pictograms. The graphs included repeated identical symbols instead of scaled icons to represent quantities and the symbols' were grouped in a way, that flows could be easily compared, but the time axis was arranged horizontally, not vertically as recommended [16]. In a subsequent study with a small sample, the spatial arrangement was modified again by orienting the time axis vertically in the pictographical condition, which led to a significant improvement in SF understanding compared to line graphs [17]. Given some evidence that pictographic representations following Isotype principles can enhance SF understanding, the present study aimed to replicate these findings with a larger sample, and to examine how robust the effect is. Therefore, two design factors were examined:

Icon Specificity: Do specific icons (e.g., baby strollers for birth rates; inflow) facilitate understanding more than abstract symbols (e.g., "+ "for inflow)? I refer to these as "specific" versus "general" pictographs. An earlier study [14] found no difference, but that study also failed to find any pictographic advantage over line graphs. Using the improved Isotype design from a preceding study [17], I tested whether icon specificity matters when the icons' arrangement is implemented more effectively.

Spatial Layout: Does icon arrangement influence comprehension? Understanding SF tasks requires grasping the principle of accumulation: recognizing when inflow exceeds, equals, or falls below outflow at each time point, and understanding that the stock results from cumulative netflow (the flows' difference) over time. To facilitate flow comparison, the middle section shows the area where inflow and outflow are in balance. When the netflow is positive, additional inflow icons appear right of middle section; when negative, additional outflow icons appear left of the middle (Fig. 2). MacDonald-Ross [18] suggests that visualizations showing identical data but differing in icon arrangement can lead to differences in understanding, sometimes even significant differences. He cites Vernon [19], whose analyses showed no advantage of pictorial charts over other graphs or tables. However, closer examination reveals that her charts violated several Isotype principles concerning the arrangement of icons, which may explain the lack of effectiveness. I therefore tested two arrangements:

Edge alignment: The middle section aligns with the dominant flow direction (icons right when inflow exceeds outflow, left when outflow exceeds). According to the Gestalt principle of proximity [20], this grouping may visually associate the balanced middle section with the dominant flow, more emphasizing the netflow's direction.

Center alignment: The middle section remains centered regardless of which flow dominates, less emphasizing the netflow's balance and maintaining a kind of visual stability.

The primary hypothesis was that pictographic representations would outperform line graphs. Additionally, I examined whether design variations (icon type, spatial arrangement) influence SF understanding.

2 Method

2.1 Participants

Students were invited via email. 134 persons participated (mean age: 23.6 years, SD = 5.2, range 18–47; 42 male, 90 female, 2 non-binary). A priori power analysis for the originally planned linear regression with three predictors ($\alpha = .05$, power = .95, medium effect size + = .15) had indicated a required minimum sample size of 119 participants. Participants studied psychology (n = 40), human medicine (n = 51), Sensorics and Cognitive Psychology (n = 14), economics-related subjects (n = 6), or other fields (n = 23).

2.2 Materials

The online questionnaire was implemented in LimeSurvey (version 2.05). Participants completed two tasks: a discontinuous task and a modified square wave pattern task (Fig. 1a, b). The baseline condition consisted of line graphs with a horizontal time axis, as typically used in SF studies. The four pictographic conditions used vertical time axes, following Neurath's recommendations [15, 16]. Two kinds of iconic signs were tested. Specific icons directly represented their meaning: baby strollers represented birth rates, gravestones death rates (Fig. 2). General icons used abstract symbols: "+ "for inflow and "+ "for outflow (Fig. 3). Both icon types were tested with two spatial arrangements (see Fig. 2a, b):

For both tasks, participants answered questions about the stock's maximum and minimum (correct answers for the discontinuous task: year 705 (maximum); 710 (minimum); for the square wave task: years 811 and 821 (maximum), year 816 (minimum)).

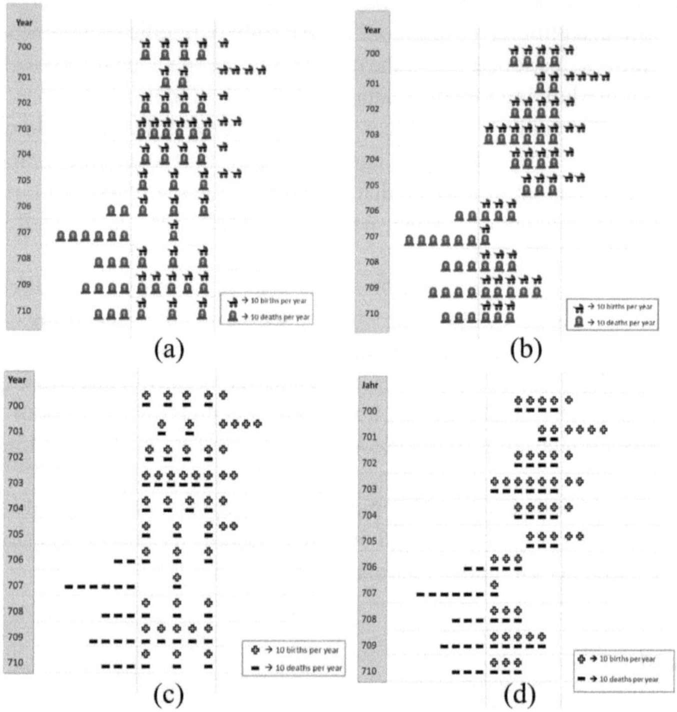

Fig. 2. Spatial arrangement: the balanced middle section stays centered – the "center" condition (a)/(c). The middle section aligns with the exceeding flow – the "edge alignment" condition (b)/(d). Either in the "specific" (a)/(b) or "general" condition (c)/(d).

The dependent variable was response accuracy. Each answer was scored as correct (1) or incorrect (0). The sum of correct answers provided each participant's SF score.

2.3 Procedure

Participants were randomly assigned to one of the five conditions. Due to randomization and incomplete responses, conditions had different sample sizes (Baseline: n = 25; specific-edge: n = 27; specific-center: n = 32; general-edge: n = 25; general-center: n = 25). Participants completed both tasks in the same representation format. After reading about birth and death rates in a medieval village, they answered two questions per task. Task order was randomized. Participants then provided demographic information (gender, age, field of study, self-reported mathematical ability) and answered additional questions (e.g., solution strategies).

3 Results

3.1 Influences on SF Performance

Sum of correct answers – the SF scores – could range from 0 (no correct answers) to 4 (all correct). Boxplots (Fig. 2) show the median and variation of SF scores across conditions. As can be seen, all four pictographic conditions led to higher solution rates than the Baseline condition, in which most participants scored zero, so the median and box are identical. Fig. 3 shows the proportion of correct solutions and exact 95% confidence interval for all five conditions, separated by task type (discontinuous vs. square wave) and question type (stock maximum vs. minimum).

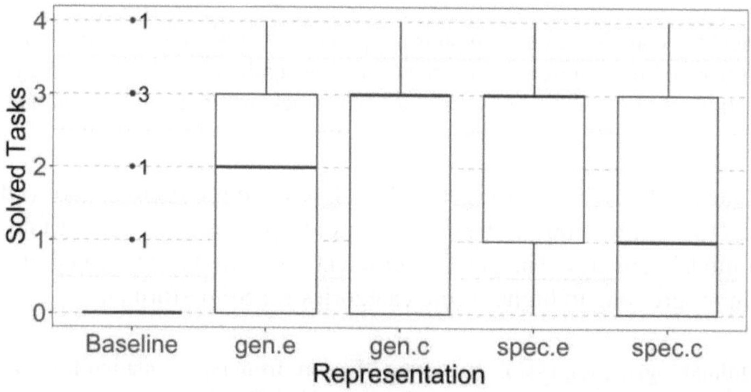

Fig. 2. Boxplots showing median SF scores across all five conditions, comparing baseline to pictograph conditions, including numbers of outliers in the Baseline condition. (gen.: general, spec.: specific, e: edge, c: center)

Graphical data analyses supported the hypothesis that pictographic representations enhance SF understanding but they did not support the assumptions that icon specificity or spatial layout influenced SF understanding significantly. Therefore, representation format was coded as a binary variable for regression analysis (Baseline vs. pictographic). Given that the dependent variable may not be interval-scaled and showed a skewed distribution (0 correct: n = 57; 1 correct: n = 7; 2 correct: n = 16; 3 correct: n = 32; 4 correct: n = 22), an ordinal logistic regression was conducted. The number of correct solutions served as the dependent variable, with representation format (Baseline vs. pictographic), gender, and mathematical skills as predictors. Two non-binary participants were excluded due to insufficient sample size for this category. The proportional odds assumption was tested using the Brant test (+ = 7.37, p = .600), implying that the assumption is correct. The ordinal regression analysis revealed that pictographic representation significantly increased the odds of achieving higher scores compared to Baseline (OR = 5.13, 95% CI 1.92 to 15.68, p = .002), indicating that participants in pictographic conditions had 5.13 times greater odds of scoring in a higher category. Male participants scored significantly higher than female participants did (OR = 4.20, 95% CI 2.08 to 8.65, $p < .001$). Additionally, each one-point increase in mathematical skills

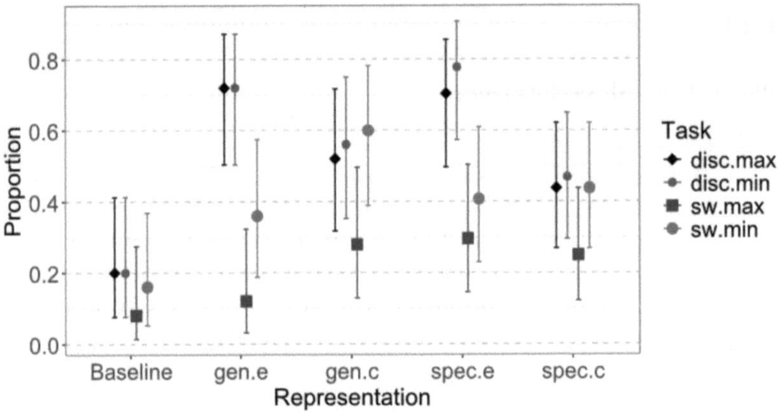

Fig. 3. Exact 95% confidence intervals showing proportion of SF scores for stock maximum and minimum, separated by representation format (gen.: general, spec.: specific, e: edge, c: center; disc.: discontinuous task, sw: square wave task, max: stock maximum, min: minimum).

was associated with 1.78 times higher odds of achieving a higher score (OR = 1.78, 95% CI 1.27 to 2.52, $p < .001$). The model showed a pseudo- + = 0.12. Table 1 presents additional model statistics. Threshold coefficients (see Table 2) revealed an increasing difficulty in progressing to higher score categories for SF performance.

Table 1. Ordinal logistic regression predicting SF score from representation format and control variables. Note: Representation format was dummy coded (0 = Baseline; 1 = pictographic).

Coefficients	Value	Std. Error	*p*-value	Odds Ratio	95% Confidence Interval
Representation	1.63	0.53	< 0.01	5.13	[1.92; 15.68]
Gender	1.43	0.36	< 0.01	4.20	[2.08; 8.65]
Math. skills	0.58	0.17	< 0.01	1.78	[1.27; 2.52]

Table 2. Intercepts resulting from the logistic regression.

Intercepts	Value	Std. Error	*p*-value
0|1	3.32	0.75	< 0.01
1|2	3.60	0.76	< 0.01
2|3	4.22	0.79	< 0.01
3|4	5.72	0.85	< 0.01

4 Discussion

The data support the assumption that pictographic representations enhance SF understanding. In some cases, substantial improvements were observed: for the discontinuous task, SF performance increased from 20% in the Baseline condition to approximately 70% in both the specific edge and general edge conditions. The largest odds ratio among all predictors was found for representation format. Mathematical skills and gender were also significant predictors, consistent with previous research [1, 4, 5]. No significant differences appeared between the two icon types – specific iconic signs (e.g., baby strollers) versus general abstract symbols (e.g., "+ / – "). These findings are consistent with prior research on iconic representations. Studies comparing specific pictograms to general countable elements have similarly failed to reveal clearly better performance for specific icons. For example, Brase [21] found no performance differences between realistic iconic signs and abstract representations in Bayesian reasoning tasks. Haroz et al. [22] similarly found that pictograph effectiveness depends rather on countability than iconic realism. These findings suggest that the relevant factor is the presence of countable items rather than the specificity of the symbols themselves. Likewise, spatial arrangement (edge vs. center) did not significantly affect performance. This might support the assumption that once basic Isotype principles are applied – such as uniform symbol repetition, grouping relevant elements, and a vertical time axis – the precise spatial configuration may be less critical.

Concerning solution rates depending on flow patterns, the square wave task appeared to be more difficult than the discontinuous task. Notably, the participants consistently achieved the lowest rates of correct answers when asked about the maximum stock. One possible explanation for this is the fact that this task is the only one in which two points in time are possible as correct answers. Future studies might include flow patterns as additional independent variables and use block randomization. It would also be beneficial to investigate whether the advantage of pictographic design persists when solving SF tasks by drawing the answer.

To summarize, the present results support the Isotype approach for diagram design, demonstrating its effectiveness in a new domain. Pictographic representations of flows improve SF understanding, and this effect seems to be robust across different design variations. For practical application, it might be a straightforward recommendation: when presenting SF systems to lay audiences – whether in media or educational contexts – avoid line graphs and rather use a pictographic representation format.

References

1. Booth Sweeney, L., Sterman, J.D.: Bathtub dynamics: initial results of a systems thinking inventory. Syst. Dyn. Rev. **16**(4), 249–286 (2000)
2. Cronin, M.A., Gonzalez, C., Sterman, J.D.: Why don't well-educated adults understand accumulation? A challenge to researchers, educators, and citizens. Organ. Behav. Hum. Decis. Process. **108**(1), 116–130 (2009)
3. Sterman, J.D.: All models are wrong: reflections on becoming a systems scientist. Syst. Dyn. Rev. **18**, 501–531 (2002)

4. Qi, L., Gonzalez, C.: Mathematical knowledge is related to understanding stocks and flows: results from two nations. Syst. Dyn. Rev. **31**(3), 97–114 (2015)
5. Lungwitz, V., Sedlmeier, P., Schwarz, M.: Can gender priming eliminate the effects of stereotype threat? The case of simple dynamic systems. Acta Psychol. **188**, 65–73 (2018)
6. Schwarz, M.: Vom stockenden Verständnis fließender Zusammenhänge (2016). https://nbn-resolving.org/urn:nbn:de:bsz:ch1-qucosa-203692. Accessed 22 May 2026
7. Lungwitz, V.: Entwicklung und Evaluierung einer Intervention zum besseren Verständnis einfacher dynamischer Systeme, (2024), https://nbn-resolving.org/urn:nbn:de:bsz:ch1-qucosa2-927083. Accessed 22 May 2026
8. Pala, Ö., Vennix, J.A.M.: Effect of system dynamics education on systems thinking inventory task performance. Syst. Dyn. Rev. J. Syst. Dyn. Soc. **21**(2), 147–172 (2005)
9. Sterman, J.D.: Does formal system dynamics training improve people's understanding of accumulation? Syst. Dyn. Rev. (Wiley) **26**(4), 316–334 (2010)
10. Ainsworth, S.: DeFT: a conceptual framework for considering learning with multiple representations. Learn. Instr. **16**(3), 183–198 (2006)
11. Schnotz, W., Bannert, M.: Construction and interference in learning from multiple representation. Learn. Instr. **13**(2), 141–156 (2003)
12. Gigerenzer, G., Hertwig, R., Hoffrage, U., Sedlmeier, P.: Cognitive illusions reconsidered. Handb. Exp. Econ. Results **1**, 1018–1034 (2008)
13. Brockhaus, F., Arnold, J., Schwarz, M.A., Sedlmeier, P.: Does the modification of the representation format affect stock-flow-thinking? In Eberlein, R., Martínez-Moyano, I.J. (eds.) 31st International Conference of the System Dynamics Society (2013). http://www.systemdynamics.org/conferences/2013/proceed/papers/P1253.pdf. Accessed 13 Mar 2026
14. Brockhaus, F., Sedlmeier, P.: Using pictograms improves the understanding of stock-flow systems. In: Ceccarelli, N., Jiménez-Martínez, C. (eds.) 2CO Communicating Complexity 2017, pp. 19–26. Universidad de La Laguna (2020). https://doi.org/10.25145/b.2COcommunicating.2020.004. Accessed 13 Mar 2026
15. Neurath, O.: Isotype: International Picture Language. Kegan Paul, London (1936)
16. Neurath, M., Kinross, R.: The Transformer: Principles of Making Isotype Charts. Hyphen Press, London (2009)
17. Brockhaus, F., Sedlmeier, P.: Diagrams including pictograms increase stock-flow performance. In: Chapman, P., Stapleton, G., Moktefi, A., Perez-Kriz, S., Bellucci, F. (eds.) International Conference on Theory and Application of Diagrams 2018, pp. 704–707. Springer International Publishing, Cham (2018)
18. MacDonald-Ross, M.: How numbers are shown: a review of research on the presentation of quantitative data in texts. Audiov. Commun. Rev. **25**(4), 359–409 (1977)
19. Vernon, M.D.: Learning from graphical material. Br. J. Psychol. **36**, 145–158 (1946)
20. Wertheimer, M.: Laws of organization in perceptual forms. (1938)
21. Brase, G.L.: The power of representation and interpretation: doubling statistical reasoning performance with icons and frequentist interpretations of ambiguous numbers. J. Cogn. Psychol. **26**(1), 81–97 (2014)
22. Haroz, S., Kosara, R., Franconeri, S.L.: Isotype visualization: working memory, performance, and engagement with pictographs. In: Begole, B. (ed.) The 33rd Annual ACM Conference on Human Factors in Computing Systems, pp. 1191–1200. ACM, New York (2015)

Can Planning with Diagrams Help Students Think more Critically about Moral Questions?

Emmanuel Manalo[1(✉)], Reena Cheruvalath[2], and Hiroaki Ayabe[3]

[1] Graduate School of Education, Kyoto University, Kyoto, Japan
manalo.emmanuel.3z@kyoto-u.ac.jp
[2] Department of Humanities and Social Sciences, BITS Pilani K.K. Birla Goa Campus, Goa, India
reena@goa.bits-pilani.ac.in
[3] Graduate School of Education, The University of Tokyo, Tokyo, Japan
ayabe.hiroaki@mail.u-tokyo.ac.jp

Abstract. Planning is a metacognitive strategy that can enhance performance in complex cognitive tasks such as moral reasoning, but students tend to neglect to use it effectively. This study examined whether advising students to plan their answers to moral reasoning questions would improve response quality, and whether diagrammatic planning offers specific advantages. One hundred thirty-six undergraduates were assigned to four conditions varying by planning format (diagrammatic vs. unspecified) and provision of content-related advice (advised vs. not advised). Answer quality was evaluated before and after planning advice. No consistent overall improvements were found, and the quality and usefulness of students' plans varied considerably, suggesting that simply instructing students to plan is insufficient. However, students who used diagrams demonstrated deeper engagement with the complexity of moral issues, including more frequent conditional reasoning (e.g., if-then structures). The findings indicate that diagrammatic planning may facilitate more critical and integrative moral thinking.

Keywords: Self-Constructed Diagrams · Planning · Metacognitive Strategy · Moral Reasoning · Critical Thinking

1 Introduction

Metacognitive strategies such as planning, monitoring, and evaluating are considered effective for enhancing performance on cognitive tasks [1, 2]. This becomes apparent when we consider the components of metacognition which are *knowledge of cognition* and *regulation of cognition*, both of which are necessary for understanding how to perform cognitive and other tasks more effectively [2]. Such understanding is particularly valuable when performing more complex cognitive tasks like moral reasoning, which requires – among other things – reflection and evaluation of the validity or invalidity of any moral judgment formulated, including the objectivity of the basis on which the judgment was made [3]. Moral reasoning relies on executive control processes, including

P. Sobociński et al. (Eds.): Diagrams 2026, LNAI 16833, pp. 215–227, 2027.
https://doi.org/10.1007/978-3-032-34178-5_23

attention regulation, inhibitory control, and working memory, to evaluate ethical options. When cognitive overload occurs, these executive resources are strained, leading individuals to rely more on intuitive or simplified moral judgments rather than engage in ethical reasoning [4, 5].

Thus, planning is particularly important in complex cognitive tasks because it supports executive control and reduces the risk of cognitive overload. Such tasks require the coordination of multiple interacting elements – including principles, contextual constraints, counterarguments, anticipated consequences, and conditional relationships. Without prior organization, these elements can compete for limited working memory resources. Planning helps by structuring the task before response construction: it enables goal specification, sequencing of reasoning steps, allocation of attention to relevant dimensions, and inhibition of premature conclusions [6, 7].

Moral reasoning exemplifies this kind of structural complexity. Moral dilemmas typically involve competing principles, stakeholder perspectives, and "if…then…" contingencies. Planning encourages the deliberate organization of these elements prior to judgment, thereby supporting reflective processing and reducing reliance on intuitive, rapid responses [4]. By making relationships, trade-offs, and conditional dependencies explicit, planning can facilitate more coherent and critically structured moral judgments [8].

Because moral reasoning exemplifies a structurally complex cognitive domain, it provides a particularly suitable context in which to examine the role of planning and possible variations in how it is implemented. Moral dilemmas typically require the coordination of competing principles, stakeholder perspectives, and conditional consequences [9, 10]. Higher-level moral judgment demands reflective integration rather than simple rule application and often requires explicit justification and counterargument [8, 11]. Responses to moral problems also naturally entail relational dependencies and conditional structures, making them well suited for examining whether structured planning – particularly when externalized through diagrams – might support the organization and integration of complex reasoning [12, 13]. Additionally, graphical representations of ethical decision-making processes can improve the decision-making process itself [14]. One important reason for this is that the constructed diagram can facilitate inference generation and make crucial details more explicit, thereby supporting model-based reasoning [15, 16]. Furthermore, as noted above, diagrams externalize relational structure and therefore can reduce working-memory demands [13]. However, integrating multiple sources of information may also increase cognitive load, as suggested by the split-attention effect [17].

Rational decision-making often involves selecting plans rather than individual actions [18]. From an educational perspective, it is therefore useful to examine not only how to encourage more effective use of planning in such complex tasks, but also which kinds of planning may be most beneficial. Prior research suggests that simply encouraging students to use a strategy may not be sufficient to improve performance [19, 20]. It is also important to consider whether the form of planning matters – for example, whether diagrammatic planning, which can promote integration of arguments and counterarguments [21, 22], offers advantages over unspecified planning. In addition, planning may be ineffective if students lack awareness of relevant aspects to consider [23], suggesting that provision of guidance could influence outcomes. Finally, it remains important to examine whether particular features of plans are associated with higher-quality responses.

With these considerations in mind, in the present study we sought answers to the following questions:

- RQ1. Would simply telling students to plan be enough to improve the quality of answers they write?
- RQ2. Would specifying use of diagrams in planning produce better results?
- RQ3. Would provision of advice on general aspects to think about when planning be helpful?
- RQ4. Are any features of plans related to better answers?

2 Method

Departmental human participants ethics committee approval was obtained for this study prior to its conduct.

Participants. The participants were 136 undergraduate students from a university in Japan (n = 88) and a university in India (n = 48). Forty of these students were female, and 96 were male. Their average age was 19.46 years. All the students participated voluntarily.

Collecting data from both Japan and India was to obtain a broad sample of students (i.e., rather than just one country). No plans were made to compare the responses from the participants in these two countries, and no efforts were made to ensure equivalence in the demographic profiles of students who were invited to participate. The participants in Japan came from a wide range of subject disciplines as the students who were invited to participate were taking education courses which were part of interdisciplinary course options they could take outside of their majoring subjects. In contrast, the participants in India were mostly from science and engineering disciplines, based on courses that the second author had access to.

Procedure. The procedure comprised two parts, both involving pen-and-paper tasks. In Part 1, the students were given a case requiring moral reasoning and a corresponding question to read and think about within a 5-min time frame. Following that, they were asked to write their answer, and for this they were also allowed 5 min.

In Part 2, the task was very similar: the students were given another case and a corresponding question (different from the one they received in Part 1), which they had to read and think about within a 5-min time frame. During this time, they were also asked to create a plan for their response to the question. Following that, they were given 5 min to write their answer.

We used two cases with corresponding questions (see Table 1). Half of the students received Case A in Part 1, and then Case B in Part 2. The other half of the students received Case B first, and then Case A second. To examine baseline comparability of the two cases, we compared their overall quality scores in Part 1 and found no significant difference between them (Welch's $t(130.44) = .51$, $p = .61$, $d = .09$). An equivalence test further supported their comparability within a medium effect-size bound (90% CI [−0.23, 0.44], equivalence bounds ±0.59) [24].

Table 1. The two moral reasoning cases used and corresponding questions.

Case A and Question	Case B and Question
An employer of an oil exploration company implements a policy of random drug testing in the workplace for employees. He says that the reason is because of critical safety issues. The employer is of the view that "any employee under the influence of illicit drugs or even prescribed medication can pose a serious risk of injury or death to themselves and/or to others in the workplace".	Imagine that a friend has lent you money, and you are about to pay him back. However, you found out that your friend will spend the money on drugs which will be very damaging to his health.
QUESTION: Do you consider it right for the employer to conduct drug testing? Explain your answer.	QUESTION: Will you return the money? Explain your answer.

For the planning instruction, we randomly assigned the student participants to one of four groups that varied in conditions given as shown in Table 2. These conditions manipulated whether the students were specifically asked to create a diagram for planning, and whether they received advice on how to plan their response. We managed the random assignment by creating four versions of the task sheet instructions for Part 2, producing equivalent numbers of each version, and randomly distributing them to the students. Thus, those in Group 1 were asked to plan their answer by constructing a diagram, and they also received advice on what to think about in planning their answer. Those in Group 2 were likewise asked to construct a diagram for their plan, but received no advice on what to consider during planning. Those in Group 3 were asked to construct a non-specified kind of plan, but they received advice on what to consider in planning. Finally, those in Group 4 were likewise free to create any kind of plan they wished, and they did not receive any advice about how to plan their answer. Note that the instructions provided to the students were limited to what is shown in Table 2: thus, no example or model diagram was shown to those in Groups 1 and 2.

In Japan, the task sheets were provided in Japanese and the students wrote their answers in Japanese. In India, the task sheets were in English and the students wrote their answers in English.

Data Analysis and Scoring. The students' written answers to the moral reasoning questions in Parts 1 and 2 of the study were scored by an independent scorer who was a paid research assistant (RA) with no vested interest in the outcomes of this study. She was provided rubrics to use in scoring and to ensure accuracy and reliability in her scoring, she was provided several practice sessions in scoring batches of 5 answers following which her scores were compared with what the researchers would have scored. Differences in scoring were discussed and appropriate scoring agreed to, and adjustments were accordingly made to the rubrics details. After four practice sessions, the RA's scoring became perfectly aligned with those of the researchers' scoring, and the RA was given the rest of the data to score.

Table 2. Instructions for the four groups in Part 2.

GROUP 1: Diagram + Advice	Plan your answer by constructing a DIAGRAM in the space provided below. Make sure that you think about possible answers to the question, reasons for those answers, arguments against those answers, and counter-arguments in response to those arguments.
GROUP 2: Diagram only	Plan your answer by constructing a DIAGRAM in the space provided below.
GROUP 3: Plan + Advice	Construct a PLAN for your answer in the space provided below. Make sure that you think about possible answers to the question, reasons for those answers, arguments against those answers, and counter-arguments in response to those arguments.
GROUP 4: Plan only	Construct a PLAN for your answer in the space provided below.

In the scoring rubrics, a score of 1 (present) or 0 (absent) was given for the presence or otherwise of certain features in the students' answers. Those features were: (i) provision of a clear answer, (ii) provision of reason(s) (1 point for every distinct reason given), and (iii) provision of alternative answer(s) to the first answer provided (1 point for every distinct alternative answer included). The total score for these three features combined became the "overall quality score" for each student answer.

Separately (i.e., not as a component of the "overall quality score"), the students' answers were also scored for inclusion of "conditions" (i.e., qualifications such as "if [certain conditions are met/present], then [answer is as stated]") and "elaborations" on the answers given (e.g., providing additional details such as the kinds of testing that might be acceptable or explaining what else they would do in connection with the decision they had made). We were particularly interested in any "conditions" and "elaborations" students included because these could represent deeper insights into the complexity of the moral reasoning issue. Furthermore, neither "conditions" nor "elaborations" were included in the planning advice provided to Groups 1 and 3, unlike "reasons" and "alternative answers." Therefore, inclusion of "conditions" and "elaborations" would have reflected spontaneous deeper processing and insight into the moral issue the students were dealing with. Thus, by scoring both "conditions" and "elaborations," we could examine whether planning – and more specifically, planning with the use of diagrams – might facilitate spontaneous deeper processing of pertinent issues beyond any specific planning advice some students had received.

The plans students produced in Part 2 were also scored for representation of the features noted above (i.e., whether they included representations of a clear answer, reasons, alternative answers, conditions, and elaborations). In addition, they were scored for use of visual (e.g., lines, arrows) and word (e.g., "but," "because") connectors. This scoring was intended to help us explore whether any quality indicators in students' answers might be associated with particular features of their plans. We focused particularly on connectors because they are essential components of planning. We hypothesized that encoding more connections could help students recognize potentially important relationships among different elements of the problems, which could in turn be reflected in some of the quality features we were scoring for. As with scoring of the answers to the moral reasoning questions, the RA undertook scoring of the plans following comparable training and practice procedures to ensure the necessary levels of accuracy and consistency.

3 Results

3.1 Did Planning Improve the Quality of Students' Answers?

The means and standard deviations (*SDs*) of the "overall quality scores" of the four groups in Parts 1 and 2 are shown in Table 3. We conducted a 2 (Diagram instruction provided: Yes, No) x 2 (Advice on planning: Yes, No) x 2 (Part 1, Part 2) ANOVA on these overall quality scores. No main effect due to Part (Part 1 scores compared to Part 2 scores) was found, $F(1,132) = 0.44$, $p = .509$, $\eta_G{}^2 = .002$. Likewise, the main effects due to Diagram instruction ($F(1,132) < 0.01$, $p = .950$, $\eta_G{}^2 < .001$) and Advice on planning ($F(1,132) = 0.07$, $p = .788$, $\eta_G{}^2 < .001$) were not significant. None of the interaction effects were significant, $F(1,132) = 0.06$–0.67, $p = .415$–$.814$, $\eta_G{}^2 =$ .000–.003.

Table 3. Means and SDs of the *overall quality scores* of the four groups in Parts 1 and 2.

Groups	Part 1 BEFORE instruction to plan		Part 2 AFTER instruction to plan	
	Mean	*SD*	*Mean*	*SD*
1 = Diagram + Advice	2.82	0.97	2.59	0.93
2 = Diagram only	2.71	0.84	2.59	1.02
3 = Plan + Advice	2.74	0.89	2.63	1.00
4 = Plan only	2.61	1.06	2.76	1.06

Note. The range of the total overall quality scores was 0–5.

These results indicate that simply telling students to plan was in general inadequate for improving the overall quality of their moral reasoning answers. The plans that the students created varied considerably in quality. A few examples of diagram and text-based plans are shown in Fig. 1. These examples suggest that some students probably could have benefited from some instruction or guidance on how to effectively plan answers according to question requirements.

3.2 Did Planning with Diagrams and the Provision of Planning Advice Matter?

As noted in the Method section, we also scored for inclusion of "conditions" for and "elaborations" on the answers the students provided as these can be indicative of deeper insights into the complexity of the moral reasoning issues they were dealing with – which planning and the use of visual representations/diagrams could conceivably have facilitated. We conducted separate 2 x 2 x 2 ANOVAs on these scores. The analysis results for "elaborations" revealed no main effect due to Part, $F(1,132) = 1.32$, $p = .252$, $\eta_G{}^2 = .004$. Likewise the main effects due to Diagram instruction ($F(1,132) = 1.01$, $p = .316$, $\eta_G{}^2 = .004$) and Advice on planning ($F(1,132) = 0.44$, $p = .508$, $\eta_G{}^2 = .002$) were not significant. Furthermore, none of the interaction effects were significant, $F(1,132) = 0.00–0.96$, $p = .329–.991$, $\eta_G{}^2 = .000–.004$.

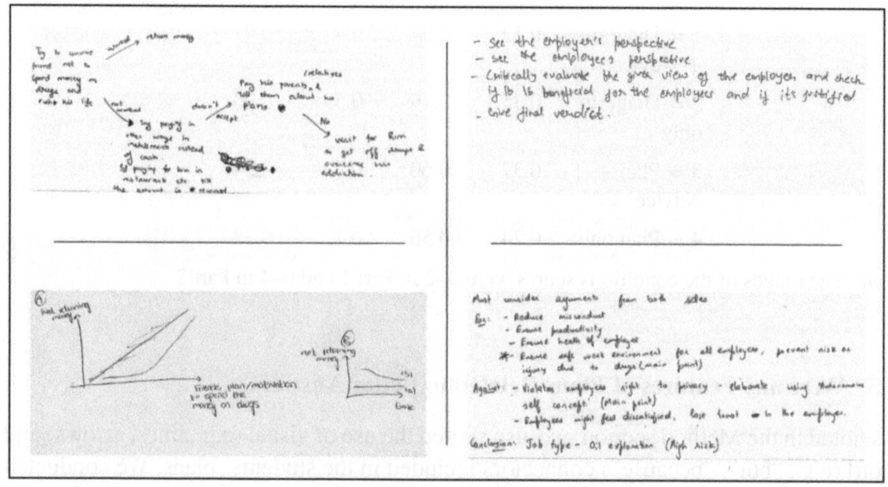

Fig. 1. Examples of diagram (left column) and text-based (right column) plans.

However, the analysis results for "conditions" revealed a significant main effect for Diagram instruction, $F(1,132) = 4.56$, $p = .035$, $\eta_G{}^2 = .019$; but no main effects for Advice instruction, $F(1,132) = 0.44$, $p = .509$, $\eta_G{}^2 < .01$, and for Part, $F(1,132) = 0.68$, $p = .410$, $\eta_G{}^2 < .01$. The interaction effect between Diagram instruction and Part was marginally significant, $F(1,132) = 3.57$, $p = .061$, $\eta_G{}^2 = .01$. No other interaction effect was significant, $F(1,132) = 0.00–2.62$, $p = .108–.988$, $\eta_G{}^2 = .000–.012$. Table 4 shows the means and corresponding *SDs* of the "conditions" scores of the four groups in Parts 1 and 2.

Simple main effects analysis of the interaction between Diagram instruction and Part revealed that the difference between the groups according to the provision of diagram instruction was *not* significant in Part 1, $F(1,132) = 0.11, p = .739, \eta_G{}^2 < .01$. However, it was significant in Part 2, $F(1,132) = 6.83$, $p = .010$, $\eta_G{}^2 = .05$. This means that in Part 1 *when no instruction had yet been provided to Groups 1 and 2 to draw a diagram* for planning their answers, their scores for the inclusion of "conditions" did not differ from the scores of Groups 3 and 4. However, in Part 2 which was *after they received instruction to construct a diagram*, their scores for "conditions" became significantly higher than the scores of those in Groups 3 and 4 (i.e., the Groups that did not get asked to draw a diagram for their planning). Note however that the interaction effect was only of marginal significance, so we need to interpret this finding with caution.

Table 4. Means and SDs of the *conditions scores* of the four groups in Parts 1 and 2.

Groups	Part 1 BEFORE instruction to plan		Part 2 AFTER instruction to plan	
	Mean	*SD*	*Mean*	*SD*
1 = Diagram + Advice	0.32	0.54	0.47	0.71
2 = Diagram only	0.35	0.49	0.59	0.93
3 = Plan + Advice	0.37	0.60	0.34	0.54
4 = Plan only	0.24	0.56	0.12	0.33

Note. The ranges of the conditions scores were 0–2 in Part 1 and 0–4 in Part 2.

3.3 Were any Features of Plans Related to Better Answers?

As noted in the Method section, we also scored the use of visual (e.g., lines, arrows) and word (e.g., "but", "because") connectors included in the students' plans. We conducted exploratory correlational analyses to examine whether the inclusion of these connectors might relate to the construction of better quality answers. Scores for both visual and word connector use correlated significantly with "conditions for answer" scores in Part 2 (both $r = .20$, $p = .02$). Figure 2 shows examples of how students used arrows as visual connectors in their diagram plans (solid black arrows) and how these subsequently appeared in their corresponding answers (grey arrows).

We also observed marginally significant correlations (i.e., $p < .10$) between the students' use of visual connectors in their diagram plans and their scores for "elaboration of answer" ($r = .16$, $p = .07$) and overall quality score of answer ($r = .15$, $p = .08$). These results suggest that students who used more connections such as lines and arrows in their diagram plans also tended to produce answers containing more of the quality features we scored for (i.e., clear answer, reasons for answer, alternative answers), as well as elaborations on their answers.

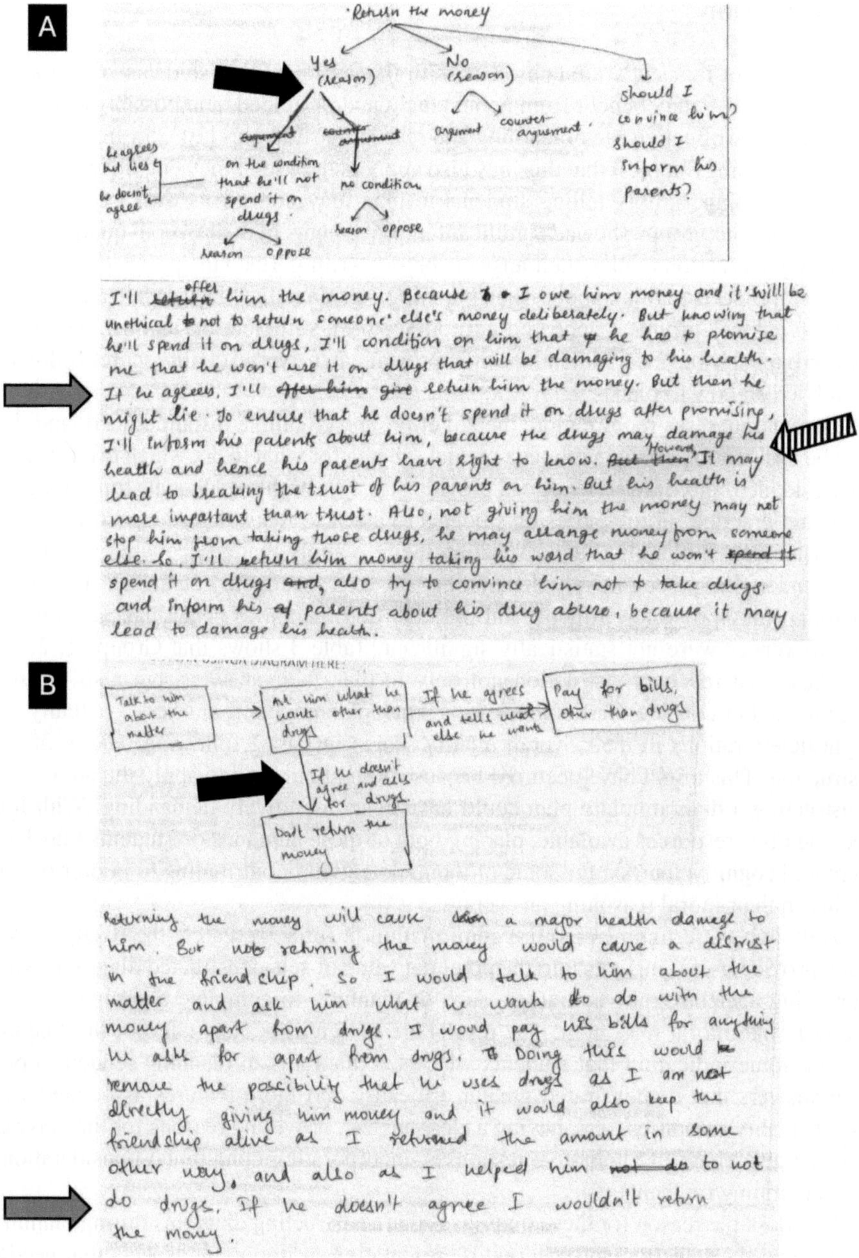

Fig. 2. Examples of visual connectors in diagram plans (black arrows), how these appeared in written answers (grey arrows), and an elaboration of an answer (striped arrow).

4 Discussion

The findings of this study are consistent with the argument that students – even at the university level – may benefit from being taught and/or guided, and possibly also given practice, in the effective use of learning and reasoning strategies [20, 25]. In the present study, the findings suggest that this may also apply to the use of metacognitive strategies such as planning: simply telling students to plan may not, on its own, be sufficient. None of the four groups showed significant improvements in their overall quality scores following instruction to plan their answers before writing. Even the provision of advice on general aspects to think about when planning – given to the "Diagram + advice" and "Plan + advice" groups – appeared not to have been sufficient on its own. Neither of these groups showed clear indications of improvement in overall quality scores following the advice on how to plan.

Demanding tasks require more mental effort and cognitive resources [26], and they may be difficult to perform without a mental schema for what to do, which prior instruction, guidance, and/or experience can provide [19, 27]. Without adequate training, guidance, and practice, simply advising students to use a strategy (e.g., suggesting aspects to consider when planning) and expecting them to apply that advice while simultaneously undertaking a cognitively demanding task (e.g., producing an answer to a moral dilemma) may prove too difficult and possibly detrimental to performance. Although the differences were not statistically significant, Table 3 shows that Groups 1, 2, and 3 – those that received instruction not only to plan their answers, but also to use a diagram and/or consider particular aspects when planning their answers – actually had slight deteriorations in their overall quality scores in Part 2 following receipt of that instruction. This might have occurred because both attempting to apply the advice and constructing a diagrammatic plan could have been cognitively demanding. With limited cognitive resources available, placing both of these demands on students may have increased cognitive burden for some of them, potentially contributing to poorer overall quality in their moral reasoning answers.

Although these findings require confirmation in future research, the results of this study provide useful insights into the potential value of self-constructed diagrams when employing a metacognitive strategy, such as planning to complete a complex cognitive task, like moral reasoning. The results are not entirely clear-cut, but the findings provide some indication that students who used diagrams in planning tended to produce answers that demonstrated greater criticality and more features associated with higher-quality responses (e.g., having a clear answer, providing reasons for that answer, showing awareness of alternative responses, incorporating conditional considerations, and elaborating on them).

One possible reason for these findings is that constructing diagrams during planning encouraged the selection and external representation of important aspects that needed to be considered [12]. The resulting diagrammatic representation may support inference generation and reasoning by presenting, in an integrated visual manner, all the components of the case that need to be considered together [28]. These aspects are available in one place and spatially organized, either positioned close to one another or connected by lines, arrows, or other visual connectors. For example, in moral reasoning, chains of actions and consequences may become more apparent, making it easier to infer alternative possibilities or additional consequences. When appropriate models are available, diagram construction can also support their systematic application. For instance, a diagrammatic plan might take the form of a flowchart that clearly shows the steps required, together with the considerations, requirements, and consequences associated with decisions at each step (e.g., see the top left panel of Fig. 1).

From the present study, we also gain insights into specific features of plans that may facilitate the production of better answers, namely the use of visual and word connectors. These connectors may support reasoning by helping establish a logical flow and clarify relationships between aspects or components that need to be considered together [12].

4.1 Conclusion

The present study contributes to understanding how metacognitive strategies such as planning can be used to support complex reasoning tasks. The results suggest that simply instructing students to plan may not be sufficient: they may require guidance, training, and opportunities for practice in order to use planning effectively. At the same time, the findings indicate that the use of diagrams when planning may offer particular advantages. Diagrammatic representations may make relationships, conditions, and consequences more explicit and visible, potentially helping students organize and integrate multiple aspects of a problem when reasoning about it. In this way, diagrammatic planning may function as a form of external cognitive support: once a diagrammatic plan becomes available, students may be able to inspect it, draw inferences from it, and use it to support more systematic and logical reasoning. Features such as visual and word connectors may be particularly helpful in this process, as they may clarify relationships between elements and help establish a coherent flow of reasoning. Although further research is required to confirm and extend these findings, they suggest the potential value of further exploring the incorporation of diagrammatic planning into educational practices aimed at developing students' critical thinking and reasoning about complex issues such as moral dilemmas.

Acknowledgments. The first author's work on this research was supported by grants-in-aid (20 K20516, 22KK0029, 23H00065) received from the Japan Society for the Promotion of Science.

The researchers published a preliminary study based on the same research demonstrating that incorporating personal and professional cases into the ethics curriculum can improve meta-moral cognitive skills [11]. This earlier study did *not* deal with planning as a metacognitive strategy or with diagram construction and use.

References

1. Panadero, E.: A review of self-regulated learning: six models and four directions for research. Front. Psychol. **8**, 422 (2017)
2. Schraw, G., Crippen, K.J., Hartley, K.: Promoting self-regulation in science education: metacognition as part of a broader perspective on learning. Res. Sci. Educ. **36**(1–2), 111–139 (2006)
3. Cheruvalath, R.: Meta-moral cognition: an introduction. Mind Soc. **18**, 33–42 (2019)
4. Evans, J., Stanovich, K.E.: Dual-process theories of higher cognition. Perspect. Psychol. Sci. **8**(3), 223–241 (2013)
5. Zucchelli, M.M., Matteucci Armandi Avogli Trotti, N., Pavan, A., Piccardi, L., Nori, R.: The dual process model: the effect of cognitive load on the ascription of intentionality. Front. Psychol. **16**, 1451590 (2025)
6. Winne, P.H., Hadwin, A.F.: Studying as self-regulated learning. In: Hacker, D.J., et al. (eds.) Metacognition in Educational Theory and Practice, pp. 277–304. Lawrence Erlbaum Associates Publishers (1998)
7. Zimmerman, B.J.: Attaining self-regulation: a social cognitive perspective. In: Boekaerts, M., et al. (eds.) Handbook of Self-Regulation, pp. 13–39. Academic (2000)
8. Kuhn, D.: The Skills of Argument. Cambridge University Press (1991)
9. Greene, J.D.: The cognitive neuroscience of moral judgment. In: Gazzaniga, M.S., et al. (eds.) The cognitive neurosciences, 4th edn, pp. 987–999. Massachusetts Institute of Technology (2009)
10. Kohlberg, L.: The Psychology of Moral Development: the Nature and Validity of Moral Stages. Harper & Row (1984)
11. Cheruvalath, R., Manalo, E., Ayabe, H.: The role of rationales for and criticisms of ethical decisions in the development of meta-moral cognitive skills. Ethics Behav. **35**(3), 240–258 (2024)
12. Manalo, E., Uesaka, Y., Chen, O., Ayabe, H.: Showing what it looks like: teaching students how to use diagrams in problem solving, communication, and thinking. In: Manalo, E. (ed.) Deeper Learning, Dialogic Learning, and Critical Thinking: Research-Based Strategies for the Classroom, pp. 231–246. Routledge (2019)
13. Tversky, B.: Visualizing thought. Top. Cogn. Sci. **3**(3), 499–535 (2011)
14. Carvalho, L.P., Santoro, F.M., Oliveira, J.: Representing ethical decision-making graphically. J. Interact. Syst. **13**(1), 166–178 (2022)
15. Quillin, K., Thomas, S.: Drawing-to-learn: a framework for using drawings to promote model-based reasoning in biology. CBE life. Sci. Educ. **14**(1), es2 (2015)
16. Van Meter, P., Garner, J.: The promise and practice of learner-generated drawing: literature review and synthesis. Educ. Psychol. Rev. **17**(4), 285–325 (2005)
17. Chandler, P., Sweller, J.: Cognitive load theory and the format of instruction. Cogn. Instr. **8**(4), 293–332 (1991)
18. Pollock, J.L.: Plans and decisions. Theor. Decis. **57**(2), 79–107 (2004)
19. Manalo, E., Uesaka, Y.: Hint, instruction, and practice: the necessary components in promoting spontaneous diagram use in students' written work? In: Jamnik, M., et al. (eds.) Diagrammatic Representation and Inference. Diagrams 2016 Lecture Notes in Artificial Intelligence, vol. 9781, pp. 157–171. Springer (2016)
20. Paris, S.G., Lipson, M.Y., Wixson, K.K.: Becoming a strategic reader. Contemp. Educ. Psychol. **8**, 293–316 (1983)
21. Nussbaum, E.M.: Using argumentation vee diagrams (AVDs) for promoting argument-counterargument integration in reflective writing. J. Educ. Psychol. **100**, 549–565 (2008)

22. Uesaka, Y., Igarashi, M., Suetsugu, R.: Promoting multi-perspective integration as a 21st century skill: the effects of instructional methods encouraging students' spontaneous use of tables for organizing information. In: Jamnik, M. et al. (eds.), Diagrammatic Representation and Inference. Diagrams 2016. Lecture Notes in Artificial Intelligence 9781, pp. 172–186 (2016)
23. Mumford, M.D., Schultz, R.A., Van Doorn, R.A.: Performance in planning: processes, requirements, and errors. Rev. Gen. Psychol. **5**, 213–240 (2001)
24. Lakens, D.: Equivalence tests: a practical primer for t tests, correlations, and meta-analyses. Soc. Psychol. Personal. Sci. **8**(4), 355–362 (2017)
25. Manalo, E., Uesaka, Y., Chinn, C. A.: Promoting spontaneous use of learning and reasoning strategies: Theory, research, and practice for effective transfer. Routledge (2017)
26. Paas, F., van Merriënboer, J.J.G.: Methods to manage working memory load in the learning of complex tasks. Curr. Dir. Psychol. Sci. **29**(4), 394–398 (2020)
27. Sweller, J., van Merriënboer, J.J.G., Paas, F.: Cognitive architecture and instructional design: 20 years later. Educ. Psychol. Rev. **31**, 261–292 (2019)
28. Larkin, J.H., Simon, H.A.: Why a diagram is (sometimes) worth ten thousand words. Cognitive Sci. **11**, 65–99 (1987)

An Empirical Examination of Diagrammatic Competency Using Cognitive Diagnostic Models: A Subcomponent Analysis of Diagram Interpretation, Mental Construction, and Spontaneous Use

Yuri Uesaka(✉) and Shun Saso

Graduate School of Education, The University of Tokyo, Tokyo, Japan
yuri-uesaka@g.ecc.u-tokyo.ac.jp

Abstract. Diagrammatic competency is recognized as an essential component of key competencies in school education. To cultivate this competency, it is necessary to assess the extent to which students have developed diagrammatic competency and to provide feedback accordingly. School tests as well as other general assessments can provide useful opportunities for such assessment. In this paper, students' diagrammatic competency was analyzed using cognitive diagnostic models, which statistically estimate students' mastery of the cognitive abilities and skills required for problem solving. Study 1 was conducted as a collaboration between educational psychologists and a high school mathematics teacher, in which a regular school test was modified to incorporate items requiring diagrammatic competency, enabling the assessment of students' achievement of this competency in an actual high school classroom. The results indicated that students' acquisition of diagrammatic competency was insufficient, suggesting the need to cultivate this competency in subject learning instruction in schools. Study 2 further examined subcomponents of diagram use using a test designed to assess the componential elements of mathematical problem-solving process. The results revealed that, within the broader construct of diagrammatic competency, students' ability to spontaneously use diagrams was particularly underdeveloped.

Keywords: Diagrammatic Competency · Cognitive Diagnostic Models (CDMs) · Higher-Order CDM with testlet effects · Subcomponent Analysis

1 Introduction

1.1 The Necessity of Evaluating the Diagrammatic Competency

Traditionally, school education has emphasized the acquisition of subject-specific knowledge across various disciplines. However, since the 2000s, global changes in educational goals have increasingly highlighted the development of students' learning competencies as a central objective of schooling. This perspective is reflected in the concept of "key

P. Sobociński et al. (Eds.): Diagrams 2026, LNAI 16833, pp. 228–245, 2027.
https://doi.org/10.1007/978-3-032-34178-5_24

competencies" proposed by the Organisation for Economic Co-operation and Development (OECD). Among these competencies, the ability to utilize external representations such as diagrams is considered one of the most important.

An important aspect that should be fostered in school education is the ability to effectively utilize diagrams, referred to here as diagrammatic competency. In this study, diagrammatic competency is defined as the ability to appropriately interpret, construct, and utilize diagrams as external representations in problem solving. A large body of research in cognitive science and educational psychology has demonstrated that diagrams can significantly support understanding and problem solving. For example, previous studies have shown that diagrams can make relational structures explicit and thereby support efficient inference processes (e.g., Larkin and Simon [1]; Cheng [2]). In addition, educational studies have shown that generating diagrams can promote deeper understanding by encouraging students to organize and integrate information (e.g., Van Meter and Garner [3]; Fiorella and Mayer [4]). However, previous research has also pointed out that many students experience difficulties in effectively using diagrams for problem solving (e.g., Uesaka, et al. [5]).

Based on these findings, Kragten et al. [6] emphasized that diagrammatic competency is critically important in secondary science education. Furthermore, based on findings regarding the effectiveness of self-generated diagrams, the ability to construct diagrams has also been incorporated into the concept of diagrammatic competency.

To cultivate diagrammatic competency, it is necessary to assess students' levels of achievement and provide feedback to both students and teachers. Regular school examinations and other general assessments can serve as valuable opportunities for such evaluation. However, many tests primarily focus on assessing students' understanding of subject content rather than the development of competencies such as diagrammatic competency. As a result, students' abilities to use diagrams are rarely assessed directly. At the same time, it is important to empirically isolate and analyze diagrammatic competency independently from subject content.

In addition, it is important not only to analyze diagrammatic competency as a whole but also to examine its subcomponents. The ability to use diagrams consists of several related skills. For example, these include the ability to interpret diagrams, the ability to mentally construct diagrams, and the ability to use diagrams spontaneously. By identifying which of these abilities present particular difficulties for students, it becomes possible to derive implications for instructional design.

Therefore, this study proposes a framework for statistically assessing students' diagrammatic competency using response data from regular school examinations and general achievement tests. In addition to examining overall diagrammatic competency, the study aims to empirically investigate its subcomponents, including diagram interpretation, mental construction, and spontaneous use.

1.2 Assessing Diagrammatic Competency Using Cognitive Diagnostic Models

How, then, can diagrammatic competency be empirically examined? Quantitatively evaluating students' ability to use diagrams is not straightforward. For example, in mathematics, the ability to use diagrams is often intertwined with mathematical competence itself. Therefore, capturing diagrammatic competency quantitatively requires the use of statistical methods, as it is necessary to separate this competency from the effects of specific items.

One approach that enables such analysis is the use of cognitive diagnostic models (CDMs) (Rupp et al. [7]). In CDMs, abilities are defined as a set of cognitive skills, and researchers specify which attributes are required to successfully solve each item. These relationships are summarized in a Q-matrix (Tatsuoka [8]). Based on students' responses to the items, the model estimates whether each attribute has been mastered by each student. CDMs are particularly suitable for this purpose because they allow researchers to estimate students' mastery of specific cognitive attributes and to obtain detailed diagnostic information about students' strengths and weaknesses.

Although the mathematical details of CDMs are described in the next section, Study 1 first aims to analyze diagrammatic competency using a regular high school examination. In this study, the DINA model (Junker and Sijtsma [9]), one of the most fundamental models in CDMs, is employed to demonstrate that diagrammatic competency can be empirically examined using this framework. In addition, the study seeks to clarify whether students encounter particular difficulties in acquiring diagrammatic competency.

Subsequently, Study 2 conducts a more fine-grained analysis by decomposing diagrammatic competency into multiple components. Specifically, a higher-order DINA model is employed, in which the attribute mastery probabilities are modeled as functions of a common higher-order latent trait. This model enables the analysis of both general diagrammatic competency and its subcomponents. Through this analysis, the study aims to empirically clarify students' strengths and weaknesses in diagram use and to derive implications for instructional practices.

2 Cognitive Diagnostic Models: Basic Concepts and the Model Used in this Study

2.1 Basic Concepts of Cognitive Diagnostic Models the Analytical Procedure

As described above, CDMs analyze students' mastery of the cognitive attributes required to solve specific items. In these models, researchers specify the attributes necessary for each item and estimate whether each student has mastered them.

The procedure of the analysis is described as follows. In CDMs, the relationship between test items and the attributes required to solve them is first specified using a matrix called the Q-matrix. The Q-matrix is a binary matrix that links items to the attributes required to answer them correctly and plays a central role in CDMs. Rows correspond to items and columns correspond to attributes, and each element of the matrix indicates whether a particular attribute is required for a given item: a value of 1 indicates that the attribute is required, whereas a value of 0 indicates that it is not required. The Q-matrix is specified based on theoretical and practical considerations regarding the cognitive processes required to solve each item. Table 1 presents an example of a Q-matrix specified by Saso, et al. [10]. In this example, five attributes are specified.

In the analysis, the Q-matrix is combined with students' item response data (correct or incorrect) in order to estimate the probability that each student has mastered each attribute. Several CDMs can be used for this purpose; however, in this study we adopt

Table 1. Example of a Q-matrix (adapted from Saso, Oka, & Uesaka, 2023)

Item	A1	A2	A3	A4	A5	Item	A1	A2	A3	A4	A5
1	0	0	0	0	1	15	1	1	0	0	0
2	0	0	0	0	1	16	1	1	0	0	0
3	0	0	0	0	1	17	1	1	0	0	0
4	0	0	0	0	1	18	1	1	0	0	0
5	0	0	0	0	1	19	1	0	0	0	1
6	0	0	1	1	0	20	1	0	1	0	0
7	0	0	1	1	0	21	1	1	1	0	0
8	0	0	1	0	0	22	1	1	1	0	0
9	1	0	1	1	0	23	0	0	1	0	0
10	1	0	0	0	0	24	0	0	1	1	0
11	1	1	0	0	0	25	0	0	1	0	0
12	1	0	1	0	0	26	1	0	1	0	0
13	1	0	1	0	0	27	1	0	1	0	0
14	0	0	1	1	0	28	0	0	1	1	0

Note. The attributes represent shallow understanding of mathematical terms (A1), deep understanding of mathematical terms (A2), shallow understanding of mathematical expressions (A3), deep understanding of mathematical expressions (A4), and calculation skills (A5).

the DINA model, which is parsimonious and one of the most widely used CDMs. The formulation of the DINA model is presented in Appendix I.

One of the main outputs of CDMs is the estimated probability that each student has mastered each attribute. Table 2 shows an example of students' attribute mastery probabilities (adapted from Saso, et al. [10]). In this example, five attributes are specified, and each student's test score and mastery probabilities are presented. The highlighted values indicate attributes that are considered unlikely to have been mastered. In Table 2, four students with the same test score are intentionally selected to illustrate that even when students obtain identical scores, their attribute mastery probabilities can differ substantially, demonstrating the advantage of CDMs in revealing differences in underlying competencies that are not captured by total scores alone.

Table 2. Example of estimated attribute mastery probabilities for each student (adapted from Saso, Oka, & Uesaka, 2023).

ID	Score	A1	A2	A3	A4	A5
25	20	0.98	0.68	0.99	0.32	0.94
34	20	0.79	0.40	0.97	0.82	0.92
36	20	0.85	0.78	0.86	0.25	0.92
72	20	0.85	0.40	1.00	0.99	0.90

In CDMs, the goal is typically to estimate whether each attribute has been mastered or not. Therefore, a threshold is used to convert the estimated probabilities into mastery or non-mastery. In general, an attribute is regarded as mastered when the estimated probability is 0.5 or higher, and as not mastered when the probability is below 0.5. As a result, each student is classified into one of the possible attribute mastery patterns. For example, when three attributes are considered, there are theoretically ($2^3 = 8$) possible mastery patterns (e.g., (A1, A2, A3) = (000, 100, 010, ..., 111), 0: non-mastered, 1: mastered).

Based on these classifications, it is also possible to calculate the proportion of students who have mastered each attribute. For example, in the example above, the mastery rate of each attribute can be obtained by calculating the proportion of students classified as having mastered that attribute.

In addition, prerequisite relationships among attributes can be specified. For example, in the study by Saso et al. [10], it is assumed that deep understanding is acquired only after shallow understanding has been mastered. Specifically, mastery of A2 requires mastery of A1, and mastery of A4 requires mastery of A3. Such prerequisite relationships can be incorporated by imposing constraints that prohibit certain mastery patterns (e.g., Patterns in which deep understanding is mastered while shallow understanding is not).

To evaluate model fit, the posterior predictive p-value was calculated. Values close to 0.5 generally indicate an adequate model fit, whereas values smaller than .05 or larger than.95 typically suggest an inadequate model fit (e.g., Zhan et al. [11]).

2.2 Higher-Order Cognitive Diagnostic Model Used in Study 2

In Study 1, regular school examinations were used to broadly analyze students' diagrammatic competency. In contrast, Study 2 examines diagrammatic competency by decomposing it into several subcomponents. To estimate both the overall level of diagrammatic competency and the mastery of its subcomponents, this study employs the higher-order cognitive diagnostic model proposed by de la Torre and Douglas [12].

In this model, similar to a second-order factor model framework, a higher-order latent attribute is specified above the individual attributes. While the subcomponent attributes are modeled as binary variables representing mastery or non-mastery, the higher-order attribute is treated as a continuous latent variable. This higher-order factor is typically assumed to follow a standard normal distribution with a mean of 0 and a variance of 1. This modeling framework enables the simultaneous estimation of students' overall diagrammatic competency and their mastery of each subcomponent.

In addition, the mathematics items used in this study consist of subitems nested within larger problem contexts. Such a structure may induce testlet effects, meaning that responses to items within the same problem context may exhibit local dependence. To account for this dependency, the present study incorporates the testlet-effect modeling approach, following Zhan et al. [11]. Because the original DINA formulation does not easily accommodate such effects, this study adopts the reparameterized DINA model (R-DINA). Taken together, this modeling framework enables the simultaneous estimation of students' overall diagrammatic competency and their mastery of each subcomponent while accounting for local item dependence. Empirical studies that combine these approaches remain limited, and this integration constitutes one of the methodological contributions of the present study. Detailed technical descriptions are provided in Appendix II. For simplicity, the model is referred to as the Higher-Order CDM with testlet effects throughout this paper.

3 Study1:Analysis Using Regular High School Examinations[1]

3.1 Purpose

Study 1 uses tasks from regular high school examinations. The ability to utilize diagrams is regarded as an important competency that teachers aim to foster in students. However, in regular high school examinations, not many items are necessarily related to the use of diagrams. In this school, the researchers collaborated with teachers to design sever items that incorporate diagrams. By applying a CDM to these items, this study empirically examines students' mastery of diagrammatic competency.

3.2 Participants, Items, and Analytical Approach

Forty Japanese 12th-grade high school students participated. Examples of the items are shown in Fig. 1. The test included different types of items. Some items, such as Item 1, required students to reason while actively using a diagram. Other items, such as Item 2, required students to mentally construct in order to solve the problem. In Study 1, five attributes were specified, as illustrated in Table 3. The Q-matrix was specified by a math teacher and two educational psychologists. Inter-rater agreement between the math teacher and one of the educational psychologists was substantial (Cohen's $\kappa = .66$, 95% confidence interval: .54–.78). Inconsistencies were resolved through discussion between the two educational psychologists. The first attribute represents overall diagrammatic competency. As shown in the Table 3, attributes were assigned to each item to specify the cognitive skills required to solve the item.

Table 3. Example of the Q-matrix used in Study 1

Item	A1: Diagrammatic Competency	A2: Comprehension of Math Terminology	A3: Application of a Mathematical Formula	A4: Understanding Relations between Numerical Expressions	A5: Computational Skills
1	1	0	0	1	1
2	1	0	1	1	1

3.3 Results of the Analysis

First, the probability that each student had mastered each attribute was estimated. An example of the output is shown in Table 4. As illustrated in this example, there were substantial individual differences in students' diagrammatic competency. Students such as ID 1 and ID 23 were estimated to have a low probability of mastery, whereas student ID 17 was estimated to have almost fully mastered the competency.

[1] This first study was presented as a poster at the Diagrams 2021 (Uesaka et al., [13]) as work in progress.

	Item 1	Item 2
Item	Let D be the domain represented by the three inequalities $y - x \leq 0, y + 2x \geq 0, 2x - y - 4 \leq 0$. Find the maximum and minimum values of $x + y$ when point (x, y) moves within this domain.	Let C be a parabola $y = f(x)$ and take a point $P(a, 2a^2)$ on C, where $a > 0$. When the tangent at the point P on C is l, choose one of the following (1)to (4) as the most appropriate representation of $T = \int_0^a \{2x^2 - (4ax - 2a^2)\}dx$ (1) Area of the square $OQPA$ (2) Area of the figure bounded by curve C and line l (3) Area of the figure enclosed by curve C, line l, and y-axis (4) Area of the figure enclosed by curve C, line l, and the x-axis
Necessary Diagram	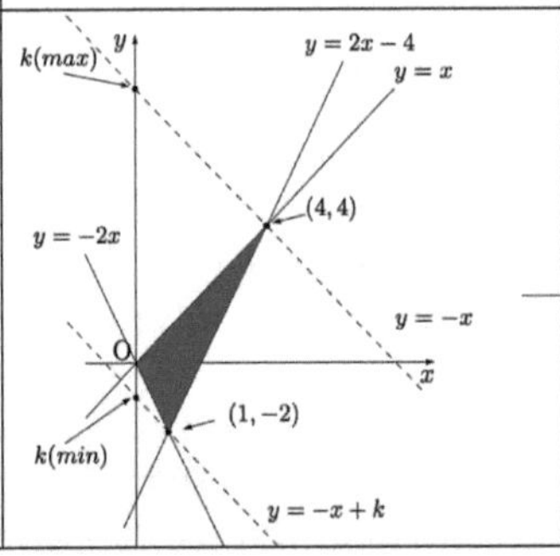	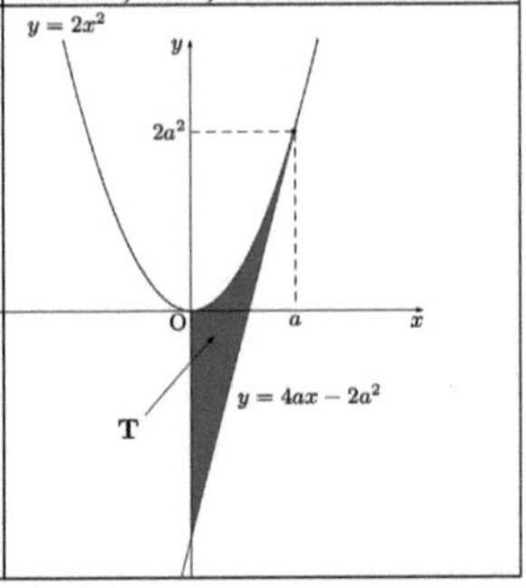

Fig. 1. Example items assessing diagrammatic competency

Table 4. Example output: estimated probability of attribute mastery for each student

ID	A1: Diagrammatic Competency	A2: Comprehension of Math Terminology	A3: Application of a Mathematical Formula	A4: Understanding Relations between Numerical Expressions	A5: Computational Skills
1	0.19	0.55	0.90	0.54	0.80
17	0.97	0.90	1.00	0.05	0.99
23	0.09	0.89	0.93	0.31	0.92
37	0.44	0.83	0.71	0.59	0.60

Next, using 0.5 as the cutoff point for mastery, the proportion of students judged to have mastered each attribute was calculated. As shown in Table 5, the proportion of students judged to have mastered diagrammatic competency was 0.525. This result indicates that the level of mastery cannot be considered sufficiently high. The posterior predictive p-value was 0.40, indicating an adequate model fit.

Table 5. Proportion of students judged to have mastered each attribute

A1: Diagrammatic Competency	A2: Comprehension of Math Terminology	A3: Application of a Mathematical Formula	A4: Understanding Relations between Numerical Expressions	A5: Computational Skills
0.525	0.525	0.675	0.450	0.600

3.4 Discussion of Study 1

The results indicate that even data from regular school examinations can be used to analyze diagrammatic competency by applying CDMs. The overall findings suggest that only about half of the students were judged to have mastered diagrammatic competency, implying that many students may not have sufficiently developed this competency.

However, because the number of items was limited, the analysis had to treat diagrammatic competency as a single overall attribute. To examine the structure of diagrammatic competency in more detail, it will be necessary to prepare a larger number of items that allow for the analysis of finer-grained subcomponents.

Furthermore, future work should explore how the information obtained from such analyses can be provided as feedback to both teachers and students in order to support improvements in learning. These limitations motivated the design of Study 2, which investigates diagrammatic competency by decomposing it into several theoretically motivated subcomponents.

4 Study 2: Decomposing Diagrammatic Competency into Subcomponents

4.1 Purpose

Study 1 analyzed students' diagrammatic competency using a regular school examination. The results suggested that students' diagrammatic competency was not sufficiently developed and indicated the need to further cultivate this competency in school education. While this finding is meaningful, the analysis did not sufficiently examine the internal structure of diagrammatic competency. Specifically, the number of items that required diagrammatic competency in the regular examination as an attribute was limited. As a result, it was necessary to analyze diagrammatic competency as a single integrated construct. This limitation reflects a methodological characteristic of CDMs, which generally require multiple items to estimate the mastery of a given attribute.

Diagrammatic competency is likely to consist of several components. For example, it may include the ability to interpret diagrams, to mentally construct images, and to generate diagrams spontaneously. To provide meaningful feedback for instruction, it is necessary to examine students' mastery of each of these subcomponents. Study 2 therefore aims to investigate this issue.

To achieve this goal, it is necessary to use items that require diagram use more extensively. For this purpose, Study 2 focuses on COMPASS (COMPonetial ASSessment) (Ichikawa, et al. [14]; Uesaka et al., [15]). COMPASS is an assessment framework designed to evaluate the component processes involved in mathematical problem solving based on psychological research on problem-solving processes. The abilities assessed at each stage were identified through practical experience in individual learning consultations, where educators observed elements that students often find difficult.

COMPASS includes items that assess abilities related to diagram use, such as interpreting diagrams and spontaneously generating diagrams. Although previous studies using COMPASS have discussed which types of items tend to be difficult at the group level, they have not statistically analyzed the extent to which individual students have mastered each underlying ability.

Therefore, in Study 2, items related to diagrams are selected from the COMPASS dataset and analyzed as subcategories of diagrammatic competency. Furthermore, diagrammatic competency is modeled as a higher-order construct above these subcategories, allowing the estimation of both students' mastery of each subcomponent and their overall level of diagrammatic competency.

4.2 Participants, Items, and Attributes Used in the Analysis

A total of 106 s-year junior high school students in Japan participated. As described above, this study uses COMPASS as the assessment framework. A total of 20 items were used in the analysis. All of these items involved diagrams in some form. To analyze diagrammatic competency, two psychologists discussed and defined three sub-attributes, one of whom also holds a teaching license in mathematics:

A1: ability to interpret given diagrams (diagram interpretation)

A2: ability to mentally represent diagrams (mental construction of diagrams)

A3: ability to use diagrams spontaneously (spontaneous use of diagrams)

An example of the items used in the analysis is presented in Fig. 2. For the three example items shown in the figure, Item 1.1 is assumed to require attribute A1, Item 1.2 is assumed to require attributes A1, A2, and A3, and Item 2 is assumed to require attribute A2. These relationships between items and attributes are specified in the Q-matrix, which is presented in Table 6.

	Example Items
Items	1. A water tank holds 100 litres of water. Water pipe A is used to fill the cistern with water. However, the water flows out because the bottom pipe is pulled out in the process. After closing the bottom pipe, water is filled using water pipe B as well, and the cistern becomes full. The graph below shows what happened. Item 1.1) How many minutes did it take the bottom pipe to come out after you started filling the tank with water? Item 1.2) If the bottom wire is not removed and only water pipe A continues to fill, how many minutes will it take from the time the water is added until the reservoir is full? 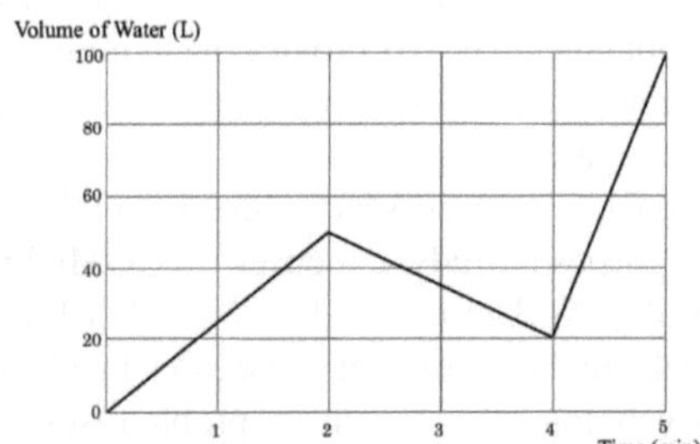 2. Answer whether the statement is 'correct' or 'incorrect'. The graph representing the relationship between two proportional quantities is a straight line, passing through the origin.

Fig. 2. Example items used and the attributes required to solve each item.

Table 6. Q-matrix corresponding to the example items.

Item	A1	A2	A3
1.1	1	0	0
1.2	1	1	1
2	0	1	0

The model specified in this study is illustrated in Fig. 3. A total of 20 items were selected, and each item was assumed to require one or more of the three subcomponents of diagrammatic competency. Specifically, the attributes were defined as α_1: diagram interpretation, α_2: mental construction of diagrams, and α_3: spontaneous use of diagrams.

Above these attributes, θ (diagrammatic competency) was specified as a higher-order construct. By estimating both the overall diagrammatic competency and the mastery of each subcomponent, the analysis aims to identify which aspects of diagram use require instructional support.

In addition, a prerequisite relationship among the attributes was assumed in the analysis. Specifically, the model assumed that the ability of spontaneous use of diagrams (α_3) requires prior acquisition of the ability of mental construction of diagrams (α_2).

To account for local dependence among items that share the same item context, a higher-order CDM model with testlet effects was employed.

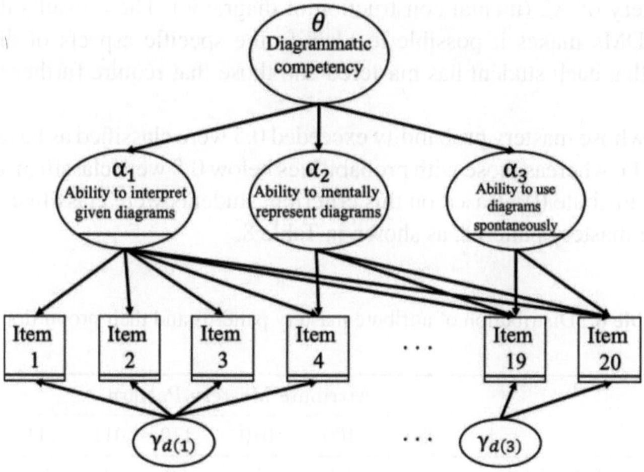

Fig. 3. Structure of the model adopted in this study (Higher-Order CDM with testlet effects)

4.3 Results of the Analysis Using Higher-Order Cognitive Diagnostic Model

Based on the Q-matrix, item response data, and the specified model, the attribute mastery patterns of each student were estimated. Table 7 presents an example of the analysis results for individual students. The results show that even when students obtain the same test score, their profiles of diagrammatic competency can differ substantially. For example, Students ID 2 and ID 3 both obtained a score of 16 points. However, Student ID 2 shows a high probability of having mastered all three attributes, whereas Student ID 3 shows a relatively low probability of mastering A3 (spontaneous use of diagrams). As a result, their levels of overall diagrammatic competency (θ) differ considerably.

Table 7. Example of estimated attribute mastery results.

Student ID	Score	θ	A1	A2	A3
2	16	0.59	0.94	0.89	0.68
3	16	0.38	0.87	0.95	0.43
5	6	−0.28	0.75	0.40	0.04
56	6	−0.45	0.18	0.77	0.16

A similar pattern can be observed for Students ID 5 and ID 56, both of whom obtained 6 points. Student ID 5 appears to have obtained this score mainly through mastery of A1 (diagram interpretation), whereas Student ID 56 appears to have obtained the score through mastery of A2 (mental construction of diagrams). These results illustrate that the use of CDMs makes it possible to identify the specific aspects of diagrammatic competency that each student has mastered and those that require further instructional support.

Students whose mastery probability exceeded 0.5 were classified as having mastered the attribute (1), whereas those with probabilities below 0.5 were classified as not having mastered the attribute (0). Based on this criterion, students were classified according to their attribute mastery patterns, as shown in Table 8.

Table 8. Distribution of attribute mastery patterns and their proportions.

	Attribute Mastery Pattern					
	000	100	010	110	011	111
N (= 106)	9	24	5	50	0	18
θ ($\sim \mathcal{N}(0,1)$)	−0.81	−0.23	−0.36	0.10	–	0.56
Score (Max: 20)	6.33	9.08	8.60	11.84	–	14.94

In this figure, for example, the pattern "000" represents students who have not mastered any of the attributes. This group consisted of 9 out of 106 students. The pattern "100" represents students who have mastered only A1 (diagram interpretation) but not the other attributes. This category included 24 out of 106 students. The pattern "010" represents students who have mastered only A2 (mental construction of diagrams) but not the other attributes. This group consisted of 5 out of 106 students, suggesting that only a small number of students acquired A2 independently.

Among all patterns, the most frequent was "110", indicating students who had mastered A1 (diagram interpretation) and A2 (mental construction of diagrams) but had not mastered A3 (spontaneous use of diagrams). This pattern was observed for 50 out of 106 students. In contrast, only 18 out of 106 students showed the pattern "111", indicating mastery of all three attributes.

It should be noted that, in the present analysis, a hierarchical structure among the attributes was assumed. Specifically, it was assumed that students cannot acquire A3 (spontaneous use of diagrams) without A2 (mental construction of diagrams). As a result, no students were classified into the pattern "001" and "101." The posterior predictive *p*-value was 0.63, indicating an adequate model fit.

Based on these results, the mastery rates for each attribute were calculated. The mastery rate for A1 (diagram interpretation) was 87%, and that for A2 (mental construction of diagrams) was 69%. In contrast, the mastery rate for A3 (spontaneous use of diagrams) was only 17%. These findings indicate that, among the subcomponents of diagrammatic competency, spontaneous use of diagrams is the least well developed.

These results provide empirical evidence that diagrammatic competency is not a unitary construct but consists of multiple subcomponents. Even when the hierarchical structure of the attributes is taken into account, the results suggest that many students who have already acquired the preceding components still have difficulty acquiring A3 (spontaneous use of diagrams). These findings suggest that instruction should particularly focus on supporting students in developing the spontaneous use of diagrams during problem solving.

4.4 Discussion of Study 2

By employing a higher-order CDM with testlet effects, this study not only analyzed overall diagrammatic competency but also empirically examined the mastery of its subcomponents. The results made it possible to identify differences in the mastery patterns of subcomponents among individual students. This approach also provided useful insights for instruction by clarifying which aspects of diagrammatic competency require further support for each student.

In addition, the analysis of overall mastery rates of the subcomponents revealed that A1 (diagram interpretation) and A2 (mental construction of diagrams) showed relatively high mastery rates, whereas A3 (spontaneous use of diagrams) showed a much lower mastery rate. This result suggests that students particularly experience difficulty in using diagrams spontaneously during problem-solving. These findings are consistent with previous research indicating that students often struggle to spontaneously utilize diagrams even when they are able to interpret them (e.g., Uesaka et al., [5]).

The framework proposed in this study makes it possible to identify more precisely which aspects of diagrammatic competency present challenges for individual students. By diagnosing the mastery of each subcomponent, the approach provides a useful basis for designing targeted instructional support aimed at improving students' diagram use in problem-solving contexts.

It should be noted that these subcomponents do not comprehensively cover all aspects of diagrammatic competency. Rather, they merely represent the diagram-related skills considered necessary to solve the specific items used in the present study. In CDMs, subcomponents can be defined flexibly depending on the characteristics of the item set. In addition, the component labeled the spontaneous use of diagrams does not refer to items that explicitly require participants to draw diagrams. Rather, it refers to problems in which drawing diagrams is considered likely to facilitate problem solving. This component was defined because the COMPASS included two tasks designed to measure the spontaneous use of diagrams.

From a theoretical perspective, these findings suggest that diagrammatic competency should be conceptualized as a multidimensional construct rather than a single unified ability. The results indicate that students may acquire the abilities to interpret diagrams and mentally construct diagrams without necessarily developing the ability to use diagrams spontaneously. This hierarchical pattern of acquisition highlights the importance of explicitly supporting the development of spontaneous diagram use in instructional settings.

5 General Discussion

5.1 Summary of the Findings

Study 1 opened a pathway for analyzing diagrammatic competency by adapting regular school examinations. The results revealed that students' diagrammatic competency was not necessarily sufficiently developed. Furthermore, the analysis showed that even when students obtained the same test scores, their levels of mastery of diagrammatic competency differed substantially. This finding suggests that the framework can provide useful insights for instruction.

However, regular school examinations have limitations in capturing the detailed structure of diagrammatic competency. In particular, they do not easily provide insights into how insufficient diagrammatic competency can be improved through instruction.

To overcome these limitations, Study 2 employed a higher-order CDM in which subcategories of diagrammatic competency were specified and an overall diagrammatic competency construct was defined at a higher level. In addition, the analysis incorporated testlet effects, reflecting the structure of mathematics tests in which items are grouped into task contexts. Furthermore, a hierarchical relationship among the subcomponents was assumed, such that some subcomponents (in this study, spontaneous use of diagrams) were assumed to depend on the acquisition of another subcomponent (mental construction of diagrams). These modeling choices enabled the analysis of diagrammatic competency and its subcomponents in a manner that more closely reflects real learning processes.

The results indicated that many students had acquired diagram interpretation and mental construction of diagrams, whereas spontaneous use of diagrams remained relatively underdeveloped. Moreover, the analysis revealed that students with the same test scores sometimes achieved those scores through mastery of different attributes. These findings indicate that the instructional needs of students may differ even when their test scores are identical. The proposed framework therefore provides a way to identify which aspects of diagrammatic competency require instructional support for each student.

5.2 Implications and Limitation for Research

This study analyzed diagrammatic competency using CDMs. The findings demonstrate that it is possible to analyze diagrammatic competency empirically using data from regular school examinations and mathematics assessments. By applying this approach, diagrammatic competency can be examined in a more systematic and evidence-based manner.

In particular, as demonstrated in Study 2, the use of a higher-order CDM makes it possible to identify specific subcomponents of diagrammatic competency and to examine their levels of mastery. Such analyses can contribute to improving diagrammatic competency by providing detailed diagnostic information that can guide instructional design.

Previous research using CDMs has often focused on very fine-grained attributes, such as fraction subtraction or common-denominator operations (e.g., Sun et al. [16]). On the other hand, some studies have analyzed large-scale assessments such as PISA using highly abstract attributes (e.g., Wu et al. [17]). However, these studies have not always clarified how their results can contribute directly to instructional improvement. In contrast, the present study demonstrates that by defining attributes at a level that is meaningful for instruction, CDMs can provide more actionable insights for educational practice.

Furthermore, the higher-order CDM with testlet effects used in this study has methodological novelty from the perspective of cognitive diagnostic modeling. While higher-order CDM and the testlet effect model have been proposed separately in previous studies, few empirical studies have combined these approaches in applied educational contexts. In addition, the present model incorporates a hierarchical relationship among subcomponents, resulting in a more complex model that better reflects realistic learning processes. For this reason, the proposed modeling framework may serve as a versatile approach for analyzing diagrammatic competency.

The first limitation concerns the fact that the attributes and their estimated mastery depend heavily on the items used in the analysis. Even if a student appears to have mastered diagrammatic competency in the present assessment, the results may differ when more complex items are used. This limitation is partly inherent to CDMs, and therefore the results should not be interpreted as definitive conclusions about students' diagrammatic competency.

Second, the present study focused on diagrammatic competency within the context of mathematics problem-solving. However, diagrammatic competency is not limited to mathematics and may also play an important role in other subject domains. Future research should therefore examine diagrammatic competency across a wider range of learning contexts and items.

5.3 Conclusion

In conclusion, this study demonstrated that diagrammatic competency can be empirically assessed using CDMs and that its internal structure can be examined by analyzing its subcomponents. By analyzing general academic achievement tests using higher-order CDMs, the study provided a framework for identifying students' mastery of diagram interpretation, mental construction of diagrams, and spontaneous use of diagrams.

The findings revealed that while many students were able to interpret diagrams and mentally construct diagrams, fewer students were able to use diagrams spontaneously during problem-solving. These results highlight the importance of supporting the development of spontaneous diagram use in instructional settings.

Overall, the framework proposed in this study provides a promising approach for analyzing diagrammatic competency in classroom contexts and for generating evidence-based insights that can support instructional improvement.

Acknowledgements. This work was supported by JSPS KAKENHI Grant Numbers 23H00065 and 24 K00485. The authors would like to express their sincere gratitude to Mr. Takeshi Akisawa and his students for their cooperation in the data collection for Study 1. The authors also gratefully acknowledge the students who participated in Study 2. The authors also acknowledge the use of ChatGPT for assistance with English language editing.

Appendix I: Basic Framework of the DINA Model

The mathematical notation of the DINA model is summarized as follows. Let x_{ij} denote the binary response of learner i to item j, where 0 represents an incorrect response and 1 represents a correct response.

Suppose that a test measure K attributes. Let α_{ik} denote a binary latent variable indicating whether student i has mastered attribute k (1, 2, ..., K), where 0 represents non-mastery and 1 represents mastery. In addition, let q_{jk} indicate whether attribute k is required to correctly answer item j; $q_{jk} = 1$ if the attribute is required and $q_{jk} = 0$ otherwise.

The DINA model assumes that a student who has mastered all attributes required for an item has a higher probability of answering the item correctly than a student who has not. The ideal response of student i to item j is defined as a variable that takes the value 1 (i.e., correct) when the student has mastered all required attributes and 0 (i.e., incorrect) otherwise. This ideal response is defined as

$$\eta_{ij} = \prod_{k=1}^{K} \alpha_{ik}^{q_{jk}}.$$

Here, $0^0 = 1$ is defined. In actual observed responses, even when $\eta_{ij} = 1$, a student may answer incorrectly (i.e., $x_{ij} = 0$), and even when $\eta_{ij} = 0$, a student may answer correctly (i.e., $x_{ij} = 1$). To account for these possibilities, two item parameters are introduced: the slip parameter $s_j = P(x_{ij} = 0 \mid \eta_{ij} = 1)$ and the guess parameter $g_j =$

$P(x_{ij} = 1 \mid \eta_{ij} = 0)$. Using these parameters, the probability that student i answers item j correctly, denoted by p_{ij}, is defined as

$$p_{ij} = \big(1 - s_j - g_j\big)\eta_{ij} + g_j. \tag{1}$$

That is, when $\eta_{ij} = 1$, the probability of a correct response is $1 - s_j$, whereas when $\eta_{ij} = 0$, the probability of a correct response is g_j. Note that the monotonicity constraint $0 \leq g_j \leq 1 - s_j \leq 1$ is typically imposed.

Appendix II: Higher-Order CDM with Testlet Effects

In the higher-order cognitive diagnostic model proposed by de la Torre and Douglas [12], a higher-order latent variable θ_i is introduced as a continuous factor underlying multiple attributes in the DINA model. Specifically, the probability that student i has mastered attribute k, denoted by p_{ik}, is defined as,

$$p_{ik} = \frac{\exp(\xi_k\theta_i - \beta_k)}{1 + \exp(\xi_k\theta_i - \beta_k)},$$

where ξ_k and β_k represent the discrimination and difficulty parameters associated with the mastery of attribute k, respectively. For model identification, the higher-order latent variable θ_i is typically assumed to follow a standard normal distribution.

Furthermore, the mathematics items used in this study consist of subitems nested within larger problems. Because of this structure, local dependence may arise among subitems belonging to the same problem. To account for such dependence, this study incorporates testlet effects into the model.

However, the original formulation of the DINA model in Eq. (1) does not easily allow the direct incorporation of such effects. Therefore, following Zhan et al. [11], this study adopts the R-DINA, in which the probability of a correct response is expressed using a logistic function so that the testlet effect can be incorporated. Specifically, the probability that student i answers item j correctly, denoted by p_{ij}, is expressed as

$$p_{ij} = \frac{\exp\big(\lambda_{j0} + \lambda_{jK}\eta_{ij} + \gamma_{i,d(j)}\big)}{1 + \exp\big(\lambda_{j0} + \lambda_{jK}\eta_{ij} + \gamma_{i,d(j)}\big)},$$

where λ_{j0} represents the baseline parameter for item j, and λ_{jK} represents the effect of the ideal response η_{ij}. The term $\gamma_{i,\,d(j)}$ denotes the random testlet effect for student i associated with the testlet $d(j)$ to which item j belongs, capturing the local dependence among subitems within the same problem. For simplicity, this modeling framework is referred to as the Higher-Order CDM with testlet effects in the main text.

References

1. Larkin, J.H., Simon, H.A.: Why a diagram is (sometimes) worth ten thousand words. Cogn. Sci. **11**(1), 65–100 (1987)
2. Cheng, P.C.-H.: Why diagrams are (sometimes) six times easier than words: benefits beyond locational indexing. In: Blackwell, A.F., Marriott, K., Shimojima, A. (eds.) Diagrammatic Representation and Inference. Diagrams 2004 Lecture Notes in Computer Science, vol. 2980, pp. 345–360. Springer, Berlin, Heidelberg (2004)
3. Van Meter, P., Garner, J.: The promise and practice of learner-generated drawing: literature review and synthesis. Educ. Psychol. Rev. **17**, 285–325 (2005)
4. Fiorella, L., Mayer, R.E.: Eight ways to promote generative learning. Educ. Psychol. Rev. **28**, 717–741 (2016)
5. Uesaka, Y., Manalo, E., Ichikawa, S.: What kinds of perceptions and daily learning behaviors promote students' use of diagrams in mathematics problem solving? Learn. Instr. **22**(5), 322–335 (2012)
6. Kragten, M., Admiraal, W., Rijlaarsdam, G.: Diagrammatic literacy in secondary science education. Res. Sci. Educ. **43**(5), 1785–1800 (2013)
7. Rupp, A.A., Templin, J., Henson, R.A.: Diagnostic Measurement: Theory, Methods, and Applications. Guilford Press, New York (2010)
8. Tatsuoka, K.K.: Rule space: an approach for dealing with misconceptions based on item response theory. J. Educ. Meas. **20**(4), 345–354 (1983)
9. Junker, B.W., Sijtsma, K.: Cognitive assessment models with few assumptions, and connections with nonparametric item response theory. Appl. Psychol. Meas. **25**(3), 258–272 (2001)
10. Saso, S., Oka, M., Uesaka, Y.: Development of assessment tools for depth of understanding quantitatively with cognitive diagnostic models. In: Arai, K. (ed.) Future Information and Communication Conference (FICC 2023) LNNS, vol. 651, pp. 766–774. Springer, Cham (2023)
11. Zhan, P., Jiao, H., Man, K., Wang, L.: Using JAGS for Bayesian cognitive diagnosis modeling: a tutorial. Appl. Psychol. Meas. **43**(7), 539–556 (2019)
12. de la Torre, J., Douglas, J.A.: Higher-order latent trait models for cognitive diagnosis. Psychometrika. **69**(3), 333–353 (2004)
13. Uesaka, Y., Saso, S., Akisawa, T.: How can we statistically analyze the achievement of diagrammatic competency from high school regular tests? In: Diagrammatic Representation and Inference (Diagrams 2021), pp. 562–566 (2021)
14. Ichikawa, S., et al.: Development of the COMPASS test for diagnosing mathematical achievement and learning competencies. Cogn. Stud. **16**, 333–347 (2009) (in Japanese)
15. Uesaka, Y., Suzuki, M., Kiyokawa, S., Seo, M., Ichikawa, S.: The state of students' fundamental mathematical competence as revealed by the COMPASS component-process test: is it true that "basic knowledge is solid but application is weak"? Jpn. J. Educ. Technol. **37**(4), 397–417 (2014) (in Japanese)

16. Sun, Y., Suzuki, M., Toyota, T.: Designing effective feedback for cognitive diagnostic assessment in web-based learning environment. In: Proceedings of the 21st International Conference on Computers in Education (ICCE 2013), pp. 115–120 (2013)
17. Wu, X., Zhang, Y., Wu, R., Chang, H.H.: A comparative study on cognitive diagnostic assessment of mathematical key competencies and learning trajectories. Curr. Psychol. **41**(11), 7854–7866 (2022)

Learner-Generated Diagrams in L2 Literary Discussion: Mediational Artifacts in Collaborative Meaning-Making

Junko Itokazu(✉)

University of the Ryukyus, Okinawa, Japan
itokazu@okilc.org

Abstract. Research in diagrammatic cognition suggests that diagrams support reasoning and conceptual representation by making relations visually explicit. The present study investigates how learner-generated diagrams (LGDs) function during L2 literary discussion among lower-proficiency learners. Twenty-two Japanese university students discussed chapters from *The Little Prince* in small groups using either diagram-based (DB) notes or SB (SB) summaries. Discussion recordings, learner-generated notes, and post-task responses were analyzed. Results suggest that DB preparation facilitated broader sharing of story information and supported collaborative meaning construction during discussion. Visible diagrams functioned as shared visual references that supported explanation and interaction.

Keywords: diagrammatic cognition · learner-generated diagrams · L2 discussion · visual representation · mediational artifacts · collaborative learning

1 Introduction

Research in diagrammatic cognition has highlighted diagrams as tools for reasoning and conceptual representation [1, 2]. LGDs may also function as mediational artifacts that support explanation, interaction, and higher-order cognitive processing during collaborative activity.[1]

From sociocultural and distributed cognition perspectives, interaction and external representations may support collaborative meaning construction [5, 6]. However, most studies of L2 interaction have focused primarily on verbal mediation rather than learner-generated visual representations.[2]

The present study examines how LGDs mediate discussion processes in L2 literary interaction by comparing two preparation formats: DB representations (drawings, symbols, and keywords) and SB summaries.

The study addresses the following questions:

[1] Prior studies suggest that peer explanation promotes spontaneous diagram use and collaborative explanation [3]. LGDs have also been associated with higher-order cognitive processing [4].

[2] From a sociocultural perspective, learning occurs through socially mediated activity in which learners externalize ideas and negotiate meaning collaboratively [7, 8].

P. Sobociński et al. (Eds.): Diagrams 2026, LNAI 16833, pp. 246–249, 2027.
https://doi.org/10.1007/978-3-032-34178-5_25

RQ1: How do LGDs function in L2 discussion?
RQ2: How do preparation formats influence interaction and comprehension?

2 Materials and Methods

The study involved 22 Japanese university students (approximately CEFR A2 level) participating in L2 literary discussions based on a simplified version of *The Little Prince* [10].[3] Participants were organized into seven small groups and prepared either DB notes (drawings, symbols, and keywords) or SB summaries (Fig. 1). Discussion activities consisted of pre-discussion explanation and main interpretive discussion phases. Discussions were recorded, and post-task comprehension activities assessed both basic comprehension and inferential understanding.

The analysis focused on the first three sessions covering Chapters 1–3. Groups experienced both DB and SB conditions through role switching in Chap. 3.

Fig. 1. Examples of LGDs and sentences describing chap. 1 and 2 of *The Little Prince*.

3 Results and Discussion

Quantitative analysis showed small differences between the DB and SB conditions. DB groups showed slightly higher scores in comprehension, inferential responses, and total performance, with similar discussion duration (Table 1).[4]

Table 1. Discussion results under DB and SB conditions.

Cond.	Q&A	Short Answer	Total	Time
Diagram	89.8	89.3	89.5	7.66
Sentence	85.0	88.7	87.0	7.60

However, discussion recordings suggested meaningful differences in interactional patterns.

[3] Part of the dataset was previously examined from a pedagogical perspective [9], while the present study focuses on LGDs during L2 discussion.

[4] DB groups averaged slightly higher overall scores (89.5% vs. 87%), while discussion duration was similar across conditions.

Qualitative analysis identified two major diagram types: narrative diagrams representing sequential story events and focus diagrams emphasizing symbolic or thematic elements (Fig. 2). Similar tendencies also appeared in SB notes (Fig. 3).[5]

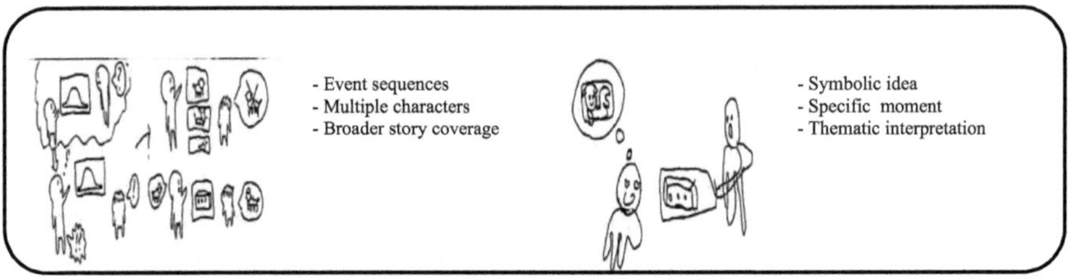

Fig. 2. Narrative (left) and focus (right) learner-generated diagrams.

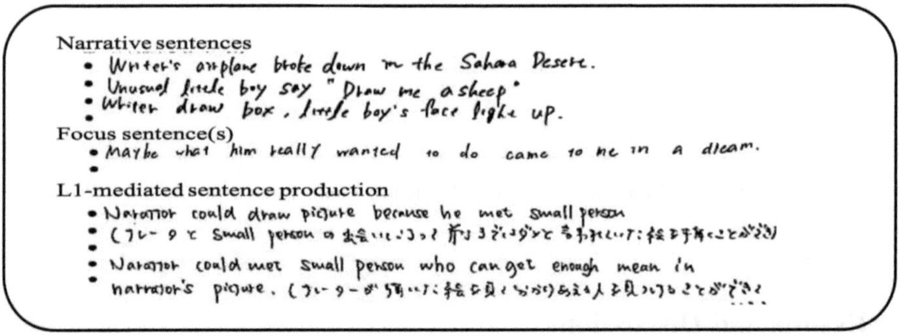

Fig. 3. Representative SB notes showing narrative, interpretive, and linguistically unclear L2 expressions supported by L1 annotations.

During pre-discussion, learners in the DB condition often explained chapter content by sequentially describing visual elements or depicting thematic scenes from their diagrams. DB learners frequently produced short symbolic L2 expressions linked to visible diagram components that could be readily understood by other group members. These expressions sometimes became shared linguistic resources reused during later discussion. In contrast, SB groups often read aloud from SB notes containing longer and more complex sentences with multiple embedded ideas. As a result, speakers were frequently asked to clarify their meanings in L1. During main discussions, SB groups often relied more heavily on L1 support, although such interaction sometimes facilitated conceptually elaborated interpretation.

The findings also suggest that learners adopted different representational tendencies across both DB and SB conditions. Some learners organized information narratively, while others selectively emphasized symbolic elements. One group in particular (Group

5 Some SB notes contained unclear L2 expressions despite coherent meaning supported by L1 comments.

4) conducted most discussion in L2 while actively referring to diagrams. Different representational styles appeared to contribute complementary perspectives: narrative-style diagrams supported detailed explanation, whereas focus diagrams introduced original symbolic keywords later reused by other members during main discussion.

The findings also suggest that the effectiveness of diagram-mediated interaction may depend partly on learners' communicative strategies. Learners strongly accustomed to translation-based processing sometimes appeared to struggle with more immediate symbolic interaction even when visual scaffolding was available.

Future studies may further investigate how group composition and representational diversity influence collaborative meaning-making in L2 discussion environments.

4 Conclusion

The present study examined how LGDs function in L2 literary discussion among lower-proficiency learners. The findings suggest that diagrams may support collaborative meaning construction by providing shared visual references and accessible symbolic resources during interaction. Although quantitative differences between conditions were modest, DB preparation appeared to facilitate interaction and interpretive discussion. Future research may further examine how representational diversity influences collaborative meaning-making in L2 discussion.

Acknowledgments. The author thanks the participating students.

Disclosure of Interests.. The author declares no competing interests.

References

1. Larkin, J.H., Simon, H.A.: Why a diagram is (sometimes) worth ten thousand words. Cogn. Sci. **11**, 65–100 (1987)
2. Tversky, B.: Visualizing thought. Top. Cogn. Sci. **3**, 499–535 (2011)
3. Uesaka, Y., Manalo, E.: How communicative learning situations influence students' use of diagrams: focusing on spontaneous diagram construction and protocols during explanation. In: International Conference on Theory and Application of Diagrams (pp. 93–107). Berlin, Heidelberg: Springer Berlin Heidelberg (2014)
4. Van Meter, P., Garner, J.: The promise and practice of learner-generated drawing: literature review and synthesis. Educ. Psychol. Rev. **17**, 285–325 (2005)
5. Zhang, J., Norman, D.A.: Representations in distributed cognitive tasks. Cogn. Sci. **18**, 87–122 (1994)
6. Vygotsky, L.S.: Thought and Language. MIT Press, Cambridge, MA (1986)
7. Hutchins, E.: Cognition in the Wild. MIT Press, Cambridge, MA (1995)
8. Swain, M.: Languaging, agency and collaboration in advanced second language proficiency. In: Byrnes, H. (ed.) Advanced Language Learning, pp. 95–108. Continuum, London (2006)
9. Itokazu, J.: Facilitating conceptual expression in L2 beginners through verbal symbolization training. La enseñanza bilingüe en el siglo. **XXI**, 80 (2025)
10. de, S.-E.,.A.: The Little Prince. Reynal & Hitchcock, New York (1943)

Under which Conditions Are Highlighted Multi-attribute Tables more Effective for Decision Making? An Eye-Tracking Study

Masahiro Morii[1(✉)], Takashi Ideno[2], Yuki Tamari[3], Kazuhisa Takemura[4], and Mitsuhiro Okada[5]

[1] Tokai University, 2-3-23 Takanawa, Minato-Ku, Tokyo, Japan
m.morii@tokai.ac.jp
[2] Keiai University, 1-5-21 Anagawa, Inage-ku, Chiba-shi, Chiba, Japan
t-ideno@u-keiai.ac.jp
[3] University of Shizuoka, 52–1 Yada Suruga-Ku, Shizuoka, Japan
[4] Waseda University, 1-24-1 Toyama, Shinjuku-Ku, Tokyo, Japan
[5] Keio University, 2-15-45 Mita, Minato-Ku, Tokyo, Japan

Abstract. Highlighting is widely used in tables and visualizations to guide users' attention, yet its role in multi-attribute decision making remains unclear. We conducted an eye-tracking experiment using five-alternative × five-attribute tables representing digital audio players. The experiment compared three table conditions: (a) tables highlighting the better value for each attribute, (b) tables highlighting the largest value for each attribute, and (c) tables without highlighting. In half of the tables, trade-offs existed only between two alternatives (Dominance tables). Eye-movement analyses revealed that participants showed different information-search patterns between the first and second halves of the trials across all conditions, suggesting the use of a two-stage decision-making strategy. In Dominance tables, decisions were made fastest in condition (a), and the number of participants who made irrational choices was also smallest in this condition. These findings indicate that highlighting can facilitate the identification of dominance relations among alternatives and thereby support faster and more accurate decision-making in multi-attribute tables.

Keywords: Highlighted multi-attribute tables · Decision making · Eye movements

1 Introduction

Many real-world decision-making situations can be formulated as multi-attribute decision-making tasks, such as consumer product selection, medical treatments selection, and voting decisions. Multi-attribute tables are widely used, particularly in consumer decision-making. Research on decision-making using multi-attribute tables has accumulated since the 1970s (*cf.* Bettman [1]). For studies on other types of diagrammatic representations in decision-making, see Jarvenpaa [2].

P. Sobociński et al. (Eds.): Diagrams 2026, LNAI 16833, pp. 250–258, 2027.
https://doi.org/10.1007/978-3-032-34178-5_26

In a series of studies, we have analyzed decision-making processes using multi-attribute tables with binary values and represented either in black-and-white or numerical formats [3–5]. (The black-white based tables were introduced in the cognitive study by Shimojima and Katagiri [6] on the binary-valued graphical representations using eye movement data analysis.) In the next step, a highlighted table is introduced by superposing a numerical table and a corresponding black-and-white table (*e.g.*, the table in Fig. 1(a) was made of superposing the tables in Fig. 1(c) and (d)).

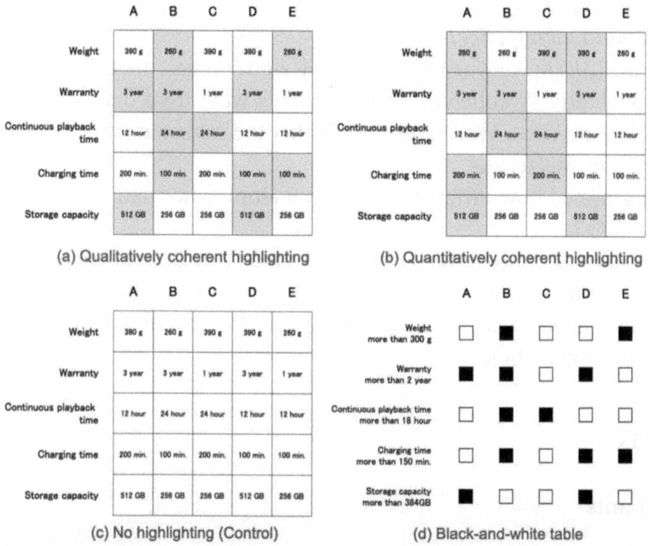

Fig. 1. Examples of multi-attribute tables of audio players used in the present study (a–c) and in a previous study (d). Tables (a–c) contain identical attribute values but differ in highlighting.

The present study compared three types of table representations (see Fig. 1). (a) A qualitatively coherent highlighted table of digital audio players, in which cells representing better attribute values for each attribute were highlighted; for example, smaller values for weight and charging time were regarded as better and therefore highlighted. (b) A quantitatively coherent highlighted table, in which cells with numerically larger attribute values were highlighted; in this condition, larger values for weight and charging time were also highlighted. (c) A control table without highlighting. In addition, two types of table structures were used (see Fig. 2 and Sect. 2.2 for details). Dominance table was defined as a table in which only two alternatives were in a trade-off relationship. In contrast, Non-dominance table was defined as a table in which trade-offs existed among all five alternatives. The present study addresses the following research questions.

RQ1: Is decision-making faster with highlighting than without highlighting in multi-attribute tables?

Ideno et al. [4] showed that decision time was shorter when black-and-white representations were used than when numerical representations were used. We examined whether decision-making is faster when highlighting is used than when it is not.

RQ2: Does highlighting lead to a two-stage decision-making strategy?

Ideno et al. [4] analyzed whether eye-movement patterns differed between the first and second halves of trials. Their results showed that participants employed a single decision-making strategy when using black-and-white tables. In contrast, numerical tables showed different fixation-shift patterns between the first and second halves, suggesting the use of a two-stage decision-making strategy. Based on these findings, we examined whether highlighted tables, which combine numerical representations with diagrammatic highlighting cues, would show characteristics similar to those of black-and-white or numerical Tables.

RQ3: Do qualitatively coherent and quantitatively coherent highlighting produce different decision-making effects?

Morii et al. [3] showed, using black-and-white tables, that decision-making was faster when qualitatively coherent attribute labels were used than when quantitatively coherent labels were used. We examined whether the same tendency would be observed when highlighting was used.

We also examined how differences between Dominance and Non-dominance tables relate to RQ1–RQ3.

RQ4: Does highlighting reduce irrational choices in Dominance tables?

In Dominance tables, only two alternatives were non-dominated, and selecting any of the other alternatives was an irrational choice. We examined whether highlighting could reduce irrational choices.

2 Methods

2.1 Participants

Twenty-seven Asian participants (15 males, 12 females; aged 20–25 years, $M = 21.07$) took part in the experiment. Data from eight participants whose eye fixations could not be successfully recorded were excluded from the analysis. Thus, data from 19 participants were included in the final analysis. Participants were tested individually and received JPY 1,100 (approximately USD 6.97) for their participation.

2.2 Apparatus and Stimuli

Participants' eye movements were recorded using an EyeLink 1000 (SR Research, Ontario, Canada). Stimuli were presented at the center of a 23-in. display (RDT234WX, Mitsubishi, Tokyo, Japan) viewed from 75 cm with head stabilized. The display resolution was 1,920 × 1,080 pixels. A fixation was defined by the velocity, acceleration, and duration of eye movements ($30\,^\circ / s$, $8000\,^\circ / s^2$, and 100 ms).

Participants viewed a five-alternative × five-attribute table of digital audio players (weight, charging time, continuous playback time, storage, and warranty). Attribute values were restricted to two levels. Each table contained 9, 11, or 13 better attribute values, with 16 tables per level, totaling 48 tables.

Twenty-four of the 48 tables were Dominance tables. A Dominance table was defined as a table in which only two alternatives had a trade-off relationship, while the remaining three alternatives were dominated by one of these two alternatives. In the Dominance tables, one of the two trade-off alternatives had better values on four of the five attributes. For example, in Fig. 2 (left), B dominated C and E, while D dominated A. There was no dominance relationship between B and D; instead, a trade-off existed. Thus, the decision was effectively reduced to choosing between two dominant alternatives. Therefore, selecting B or D was considered rational, whereas selecting A, C, or E was considered irrational. The remaining 24 tables were Non-dominance tables. A Non-dominance table was defined as a table in which trade-offs existed among all five alternatives and no alternative dominated the others (Fig. 2, right).

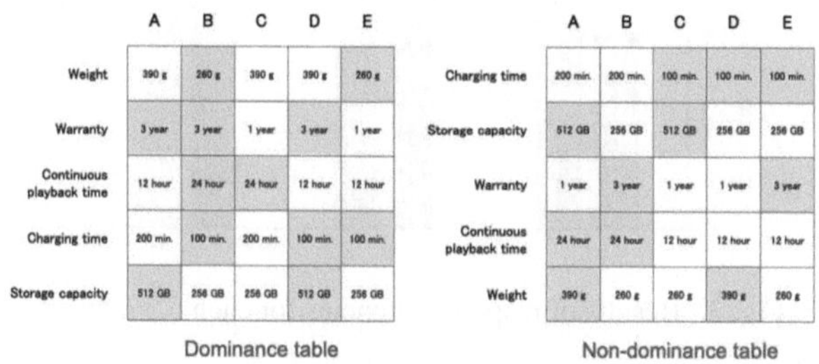

Fig. 2. Example of Dominance Table and Non-dominance Table in condition (a).

2.3 Procedure

After receiving instructions, participants sat in front of the display and completed a calibration procedure before the experiment. Each participant completed three blocks of 48 trials. Three types of multi-attribute tables were used in each block: (a) qualitatively coherent highlighted tables, (b) quantitatively coherent highlighted tables, and (c) control tables without highlighting. The order of the blocks was counterbalanced across participants. At the beginning of each block, an example table and instructions were presented. In each trial, a fixation cross appeared for one second, followed by a multi-attribute table. Participants selected the most desirable alternative using the corresponding key, without any time pressure. After each response, the next trial began immediately. Eye movements were recorded throughout. For the eye-movement data analysis, each trial was divided into the first half and the second half at the median time point between stimulus onset and the key press. We then compared decision-making processes between two halves of the trial.

3 Results

3.1 Response Latency

Response latency was defined as the time from when the multi-attribute table was presented on the screen to the participant's decision indicated by a key press. Fig. 3 shows the response latencies. We conducted a two-way (Table Type × dominance: Dominance vs. Non-dominance) repeated-measures ANOVA. The results showed that the main effect of dominance was significant ($F[1, 18] = 17.82, p < .01, {\eta_p}^2 = .50$); response latencies for Dominance tables were shorter than those for Non-dominance tables. In addition, the interaction between the two factors was significant ($F[2, 36] = 4.14$, $p < .05$, $\eta_p{}^2 = .19$). For the Dominance tables, response latencies were shorter in condition (a) than that in condition (b) ($p < .05$) and in condition (c) ($p < .05$).

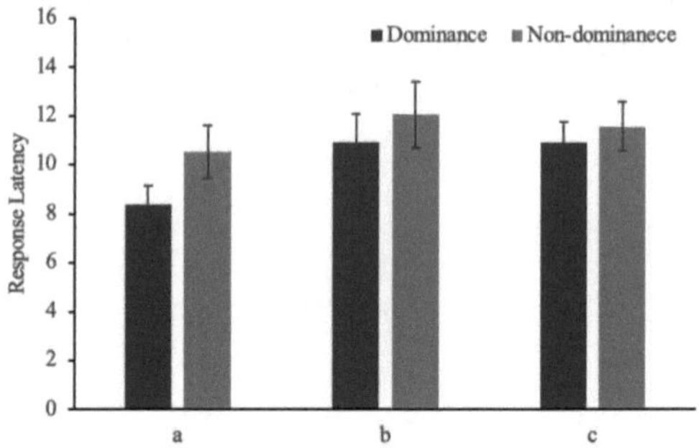

Fig. 3. Results of response latencies for each condition.

3.2 Irrational Choice in Dominance Tables

In Dominance tables, selecting a non-dominant alternative was defined as irrational. Mean irrational choices (± *SD*) were 0.42 ± 1.39 in (a), 1.32 ± 2.38 in (b), and 1.68 ± 2.47 in (c). A one-way repeated-measures ANOVA with condition revealed a marginally significant effect of condition ($F[2, 36] = 3.23$, $p < .10$, $\eta_p{}^2 = .15$). Post hoc multiple comparisons showed that condition (a) yielded marginally fewer irrational choices than condition (c) ($t[28] = 1.94$, $p < .10$). The number of participants who made at least one irrational choice was 3 in condition (a), 10 in condition (b), and 12 in condition (c). A Poisson regression analysis tested condition differences using the number of participants making at least one irrational choice as the dependent variable, with condition (a) as the reference. The results showed that the number of such participants was significantly larger in conditions (b) and (c) than in condition (a). The regression coefficients are reported in Table 1.

Table 1. Results of Poisson regression analysis for irrational choices

	b	*SE*	*z*	*p*	
Intercept	2.773	0.250	11.090	<0.001	***
condition (b)	−0.575	0.417	−1.381	0.167	
condition (c)	−0.827	0.453	−1.824	0.068	
irrational choice	−1.674	0.629	−2.661	0.008	**
cond. (b) × irrational choice	1.779	0.779	2.284	0.022	*
cond. (c) × irrational choice	2.213	0.789	2.806	0.005	**

*** $p < 0.001$, ** $p < .01$, * $p < .05$

3.3 Fixation Shift Patterns

The number of fixation shifts was calculated for each participant. The areas of interest (AOIs) were defined to correspond to each cell of the multi-attribute table. A vertical shift was defined as a fixation shift within the same column, whereas a horizontal shift was defined as a fixation shift within the same row. All other shifts were classified as diagonal. Because no significant differences were observed between Dominance and Non-dominance tables, they were analyzed together. A two-way repeated-measures ANOVA was conducted with table representation (a–c) and fixation shift direction (vertical, horizontal, diagonal) as within-participants factors. The results are shown in Fig. 4. Significant main effects were found for fixation-shift direction ($F[2, 36] = 24.45$, $p < .01$, ${\eta_p}^2 = .58$) and table representation ($F[2, 36] = 3.59$, $p < .05$, ${\eta_p}^2 = .17$). The interaction was also significant ($F[4, 72] = 24.08$, $p < .01$).

To further examine fixation shift patterns between first and second halves, a transition score was computed following the method proposed in [7]:

$$Transition\ Score = \frac{Vertical\ Shifts - Horizontal\ Shifts}{Vertical\ Shifts + Horizontal\ Shifts}$$

Transition scores indicate fixation-shift tendencies: lower values indicate more horizontal (attribute-based) shifts and higher values indicate more vertical (alternative-based) shifts. A two-way repeated-measures ANOVA was conducted with table representation (a–c) and trial phase (first half vs. second half). The results showed that the interaction was not significant ($F[2, 36] = 0.49$, *n.s.*, ${\eta_p}^2 = .03$). The main effect of table representation was significant ($F[2, 36] = 37.67$, $p < .01$, ${\eta_p}^2 = .68$). Transition scores for condition (c) were higher than those for condition (a) ($p <.05$) and condition (b) ($p < .05$). The main effect of trial phase was also significant ($F[1, 18] = 114.65$, $p < .01$, ${\eta_p}^2 = .86$). Transition scores in the first half were lower than those in the second half across all table conditions. These results suggest different decision-making strategies across trial phases.

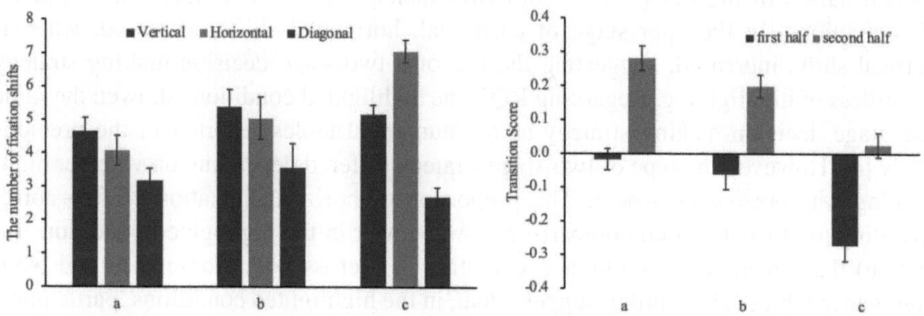

Fig. 4. The number of fixations shifts (left) and the transition scores (right).

4 Discussions

Based on the findings of our previous studies [3–5], we examined the effects of the presence and type of highlighting. The main findings are summarized as follows.

The results for response latency showed that, in the Dominance tables—tables in which trade-offs existed only between two alternatives—response times differed among the three conditions, with decisions being made fastest in condition (a) compared with conditions (b) and (c). In contrast, in the Non-dominance tables—tables in which trade-offs existed among all five alternatives—response times did not differ among conditions. Regarding RQ1, decisions were faster in the highlighted condition (a) than in the non-highlighted condition (c) for Dominance tables, whereas no difference was observed between these conditions in Non-dominance tables. Hence, the effect of highlighting on decision time depended on the type of table structure. Regarding RQ3, decisions were faster in the qualitatively coherent highlighting condition (a) than in the quantitatively coherent highlighting condition (b) for Dominance tables, whereas no difference was observed between these conditions in Non-dominance tables. Hence, the effect of highlighting type on decision time depended on the type of table structure, with qualitatively coherent highlighting being more effective in Dominance tables.

In addition, the number of participants who made irrational choices in Dominance tables was smallest in condition (a), with only three participants making such choices. Regarding RQ4, irrational choices were less frequent under the qualitatively coherent highlighting condition than under the other conditions, suggesting that qualitatively coherent highlighting may help prevent irrational choices.

These results suggest that highlighting may facilitate the rapid detection of dominance relations among alternatives, thereby supporting more efficient and accurate decision-making. In particular, the qualitatively coherent highlighting may have helped participants identify superior attribute values more easily, which may have contributed both to shorter decision times and fewer irrational choices.

To further examine the influence of highlighting on the decision-making process, we analyzed the eye-movement data. Eye-movement patterns differed between the first and second halves of the trials across both Dominance and Non-dominance tables under all conditions. In the later stage of each trial, horizontal shifts decreased, whereas vertical shifts increased, suggesting the use of a two-stage decision-making strategy regardless of highlighting. Regarding RQ2, the highlighted conditions showed the same two-stage decision-making strategy as the numerical tables reported in the previous study [4]. However, the type of two-stage strategy differed depending on whether highlighting was present or absent. The proportion of horizontal fixation shifts—corresponding to attribute-based comparisons—was lower in the highlighted conditions (a) and (b) than in the non-highlighted condition (c) across both Dominance and Non-dominance tables. This finding suggests that, in the highlighted conditions, participants relied less on attribute-based comparisons and may have adopted strategies other than alternative-based comparisons, such as counting the number of highlighted cells for each alternative.

The results of the present study indicate that, particularly in tables with a dominance structure, the use of qualitatively coherent highlighting may allow decision-makers to avoid irrational choices while reaching decisions more quickly. These findings suggest that highlighting can be an effective visual aid for multi-attribute decision-making. However, several limitations should be noted. First, the Dominance tables used in the present experiment represented a restricted situation in which the effective choice set was reduced to two alternatives. In real consumer environments, however, dominance relations may be more complex. Further research is needed to examine whether the highlighting effects observed in this study also occur in such situations. In addition, the effect of highlighting was not clearly observed in the Non-dominance tables. Future research should examine the effects of highlighting by considering differences in dominance relations among alternatives as an experimental variable. Second, attribute values were limited to two levels. In real-world product catalogs, however, attribute values often have multiple levels. Further research is therefore required to examine what types of highlighting strategies are most effective when attribute values have multiple levels. By addressing these issues in future studies, we aim to clarify effective diagrammatic representations of multi-attribute tables for supporting decision-making.

Acknowledgments. This work was supported by JSPS KAKENHI Grant Numbers JP19KK0006, JP21H00467, JP21K18339, JP22K13506, JP22K20170, JP23K20416, 23 K22164, JP24K16466, and JP25K00681.

Disclosure of Interests. The authors declared no potential conflicts of interest with respect to the research, authorship, and/or publication of this article.

References

1. Bettman, J. R.: An Information Processing Theory of Consumer Choice (1979)
2. Jarvenpaa, S.L.: Graphic displays in decision making—the visual salience effect. J. Behav. Decis. Making **3**(4), 247–262 (1990). https://doi.org/10.1002/bdm.3960030403
3. Morii, M., Ideno, T., Takemura, K., Okada, M.: Qualitatively coherent representation makes decision-making easier with binary-colored multi-attribute tables: an eye-tracking study. Front. Psychol. **8**, 1388 (2017). https://doi.org/10.3389/fpsyg.2017.01388
4. Ideno, T., Morii, M., Takemura, K., Okada, M.: On effects of changing multi-attribute table design on decision making: an eye-tracking study. In: Pietarinen, A.V., Chapman, P., Bosveld-de Smet, L., Giardino, V., Corter, J., Linker, S. (eds.) Diagrammatic Representation and Inference. Diagrams 2020 LNCS, vol. 12169. Springer, Cham. https://doi.org/10.1007/978-3-030-54249-8_29
5. Morii, M., Ideno, T., Tamari, Y., Takemura, K., Okada, M.: An eye-tracking study on the effects of using highlighted multi-attribute tables: a preliminary report. In: Lemanski, J., Johansen, M.W., Manalo, E., Viana, P., Bhattacharjee, R., Burns, R. (eds.) Diagrammatic Representation and Inference. Diagrams 2024 LNCS, vol. 14981. Springer, Cham. https://doi.org/10.1007/978-3-031-71291-3_40
6. Shimojima, A., Katagiri, Y.: An eye-tracking study of integrative spatial cognition over diagrammatic representations. In: Hölscher, C., Shipley, T.F., Olivetti Belardinelli, M., Bateman, J., Newcombe, N.S. (eds.) Spatial Cognition, pp. 262–278. Springer, Berlin (2010). https://doi.org/10.1007/978-3-642-14749-4_23
7. Payne, J.W.: Task complexity and contingent processing in decision making: an information search and protocol analysis. Org. Behav. Hum. Perf. **16**, 366–387 (1976). https://doi.org/10.1016/0030-5073(76)90022-2

Drawing Solutions: A Cross-Linguistic Diagram-Based Study of Ordinality in Problem-Solving

Ann Mary John[1,2(✉)], Maelle Dagnogo[3,4], Yu-Jr Lan[5], Mônica Macedo-Rouet[1], Emmanuel Manalo[5], and Hippolyte Gros[2]

[1] Learning Transitions Research Unit, CY Cergy Paris Université, Paris, France
ajohn@cyu.fr
[2] CRPN, Aix-Marseille University, CNRS, Marseille, France
[3] Université Paris Cité, Paris, France
[4] UNICOG - Neurospin, CEA, Saclay, France
[5] Graduate School of Education, Kyoto University, Kyoto, Japan

Abstract. Languages differ in how they describe time. While some rely on spatial metaphors, representing time as extending along a line, others express temporal relations through quantity-based metaphors. This raises the question of whether such differences shape how people reason about time. Building on research on ordinality in numerical cognition and theories of linguistic relativity, this cross-linguistic, diagram-based study examines whether temporal metaphors influence how participants represent and solve arithmetic word problems. We tested 306 children and adults across two languages: Japanese, which uses distance-metaphors, and Malayalam, which relies on quantity-metaphors to describe time. Participants solved word problems that allowed two possible strategies and created explanatory diagrams of their reasoning. We investigated how strategy choice and diagram production reflected the perception of ordinality in the problems across languages and age groups. Strategy choices reflected perceptions of ordinality in both languages; however, diagram production showed language-related preferences, with Japanese participants producing more ordinal representations. The results are interpreted in light of problem-solving literature and discussed in relation to linguistic relativity.

Keywords: Arithmetic Word Problem Solving · Linguistic Relativism · Ordinality

1 Introduction

Humans experience time continuously as they move through the world. Yet languages differ in the ways they talk about it. Some rely on spatial terms: it may stretch along a line or stack like blocks [1]. If the experience of time is indeed universal, does this universality extend to its visual representation despite the variation in description, or is it shaped by the language one speaks? Do linguistic differences in how time is described shape the diagrams people produce to represent it?

P. Sobociński et al. (Eds.): Diagrams 2026, LNAI 16833, pp. 259–266, 2027.
https://doi.org/10.1007/978-3-032-34178-5_27

1.1 Language, Cognition and Time Perception

The debate over whether language shapes thought has evolved from Whorf's [2] strong claim of linguistic determinism to the weaker version of the hypothesis, linguistic relativism [3]: language may influence, but it does not determine, how people think about concepts such as space, number and time [4].

According to the conceptual metaphor theory [5], abstract concepts like time are often understood through more concrete domains such as space, and linguistic metaphors could reinforce these understandings. However, on the other side of the debate, it has been argued that the evidence for the Whorfian hypothesis relied on verbal tasks [6], which may reflect language use during speech rather than thought and mental representations, and emphasised the need for non-linguistic evidence to support these claims.

Later studies using non-linguistic psychophysical time estimation tasks [7] have shown that speakers of different languages can be influenced by the temporal metaphors used in their language. They observed that speakers of languages that rely on distance metaphors (e.g., "long time") to describe time were influenced by growing lines during the time estimation task, while speakers of quantity metaphor languages (e.g., "much time") were instead affected by quantity cues, such as volume. Despite this empirical support for linguistic relativism, failures to replicate some of these findings [8] indicate that the relationship between language and cognition, especially time perception, requires further exploration using a wider range of methodological approaches.

1.2 Semantics, Numerical Cognition and the Perception of Ordinality

One such approach to studying mental representations examines how semantic content in arithmetic word problems influences how people represent quantities, especially time. Recent research shows that references to durations, as opposed to prices or other quantities, can influence how people represent word problems and select solving strategies [9]. These effects suggest that the context in which numbers are presented shapes how people mentally represent them, as quantities associated with time, heights or elevators tend to evoke ordered representations, whereas other quantities (such as prices, weights, and collections) elicit set-based representations.

Gros et al. [9] developed a strategy-based paradigm in which they used isomorphic problems admitting two distinct solving strategies. Figure 1 illustrates the abstract mathematical structure of the problems, along with examples of duration and price problems and their corresponding encodings and solving-strategies. By focusing on the distinction between ordinal and cardinal contexts [10], they probed the differences in the mental representations reflected in the two solving strategies. The 1-step strategy reflects an ordinal representation, in which solvers visualise quantities along an ordered structure and solve the problem in a single step. On the other hand, the 3-step strategy indicates a cardinal representation where quantities are visualised as discrete sets in a set-based representation and the solution is obtained by calculating the sum of individual parts using three steps. Across a range of tasks, they found that problems on durations, heights and elevators elicited the use of the 1-step strategy (ordinal), while weights, prices and collections elicited the 3-step strategy (cardinal). The Semantic Congruence model [11] suggests that participants consistently perceive

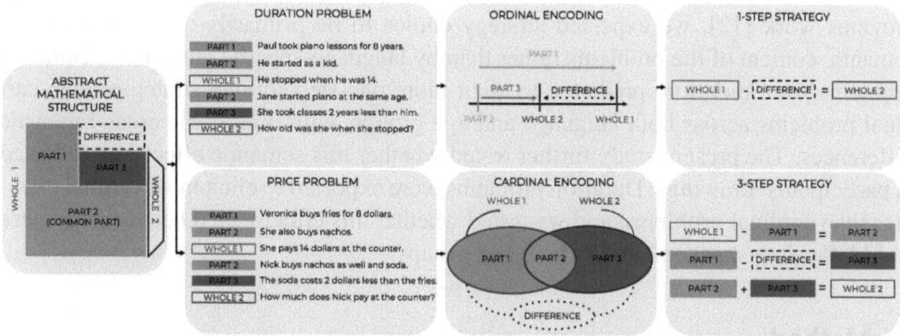

Fig. 1. Abstract Mathematical Structure. Duration and price problems lead to ordinal and cardinal encodings, respectively. (reproduced from John et al. 2025)

durations as ordinal because semantic meaning shapes their mathematical reasoning. More recent work [12] found that this effect is consistent regardless of the language spoken by the participant, thus providing evidence challenging the theories of linguistic relativism.

1.3 Visualising Thought: Diagrams as a Window into Mental Representation

A complementary approach to assessing how people mentally represent abstract concepts, such as time and number, is through drawings. Diagrams have been proposed as a means of externalising thought by transforming otherwise invisible mental representations into visible forms [13]. Since diagram production involves interactions between perception, memory, and knowledge [14], drawings may provide insight into how individuals internally represent and organise information. Schematic diagrams can also illustrate spatial or relational patterns, potentially making abstract concepts more accessible [15].

Diagrams have also played a crucial role in the study of numerical cognition, where they can be used to examine how people represent and reason about quantitative relationships. Within the context of arithmetic word problems, diagrams can help individuals construct mental models by making the elements of the problem and their relationships explicit [16]. While diagrams capture rich mental representations, they have historically been underused in psychology due to difficulties in quantifying them [17]. Recent work has leveraged diagram data as measurable output to investigate differences in the representation of arithmetic word problems during problem-solving tasks [18].

1.4 Present Study and Hypotheses

Building on a problem-drawing paradigm [18], we conducted a cross-linguistic study with children and adults to investigate how the use of temporal metaphors influences mental representations of ordinality in word problem-solving. We tested Malayalam speakers, who predominantly use quantity-metaphors, and Japanese speakers, who favour distance-metaphors. Participants solved arithmetic word problems and created explanatory diagrams, allowing us to investigate their perceptions of ordinality. In line with previous work [12], we expected strategy choice to be primarily determined by the semantic content of the problems rather than by language-specific metaphors. Duration problems were therefore predicted to elicit more one-step solving strategies than cardinal problems across both language and age groups, with no reliable cross-linguistic differences. The present study further tested whether this semantic effect was reflected in participants' drawings. Duration problems were expected to elicit more ordinal drawings than cardinal problems, and we tested whether this effect varied between Japanese and Malayalam speakers (across both age groups).

2 Methods

2.1 Corpus Analysis

Before the experiment, we conducted a corpus analysis via SketchEngine, a specialised corpus software [19], to categorise our target languages, Malayalam (മലയാളം), and Japanese (日本語), as either quantity- or distance-metaphor languages based on their use of temporal metaphors [7]. Analyses were conducted using the Malayalam and Japanese Web Corpora (mlWaC and jaTenTen, respectively). predominantly uses quantity-metaphors to describe time, whereas Japanese uses distance-metaphors more frequently.

2.2 Participants and Procedure

We recruited both child and adult participants from Japanese (children $N = 89$, $M = 12.3$; adults $N = 50$, $M = 20.7$) and Malayalam (children $N = 93$, $M = 12.7$; adults $N = 74$, $M = 20.2$). Japanese participants were recruited from schools and universities in Kyoto, and Malayalam-speaking participants from schools and universities in Kerala. Informed verbal consent was obtained from all adult participants, and permission was secured from the school authorities for child participants. Participants solved 12 isomorphic arithmetic word problems [12] translated into their native language, varying in terms of semantic content (durations, heights, prices and collections). They were asked to solve the problems in the booklets using as few operations as possible and to create a drawing that would "help someone understand the problem and solve it", guiding them to visually represent the relevant information. The order of problems was pseudorandomised to control for learning effects. The complete list of problems can be found at osf.io/vc4qj/files/vd3kc.

2.3 Strategies and Drawings

Strategy Coding. Each participant's response was identified as a 1-step strategy, a 3-step strategy, or an error. A response was coded as 1-step or 3-step only if the operations were explicitly stated. For 3-step strategies, partial solutions were coded only if both intermediate and final operations were present.

Drawing Scales. To analyse the drawings, we developed a structured coding scale adapted from [18]. Each drawing was evaluated on eight items, four on a cardinal scale and four on an ordinal scale. The scales were designed to capture prototypically cardinal and ordinal features (see Fig. 2). The cardinal scale included (a) an identifiable cluster of elements, (b) sets containing multiple elements, (c) the presence of embedded sets, and (d) a one-to-one correspondence between an element and a value. The ordinal scale, on the other hand, assessed for the presence of (a) axes, (b) graduations, (c) parallel axes/intervals/graduations, and (d) intervals. Each item on both the cardinal and ordinal scales was scored 0 (**absent**) or 1 (**present**), and the four items in each scale were summed to yield a final cardinal/ordinal score ranging from 0 to 4. Drawings were considered non-codable when responses were left blank or contained text only, representing approximately 11.5% of the dataset. Drawings containing both cardinal and ordinal features were scored independently on both scales. The complete dataset can be found at osf.io/bgvd7/files/osfstorage.

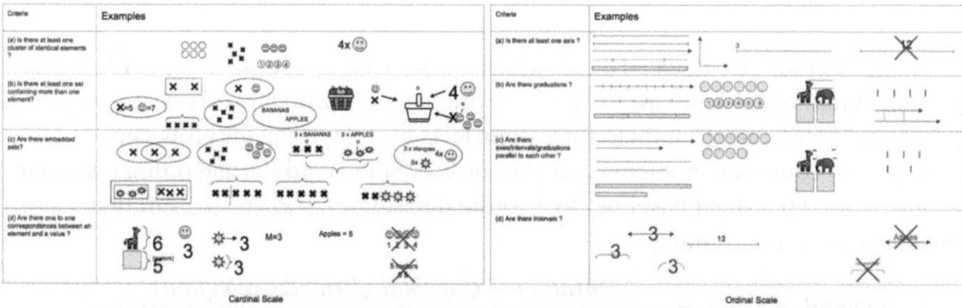

Fig. 2. Drawing Scales. Cardinal and Ordinal scales were used to rate the drawings.

Inter-Rater Reliability. To assess inter-rater reliability, three coders (including the first author and two co-authors) independently rated 20% of all drawings (N = 744) using the eight-item coding scale. The overall agreement rate was 89.26%, with an overall Fleiss' kappa of 0.765, indicating substantial agreement [20]. After resolving discrepancies, an additional subset (5%) was coded independently by all three coders, resulting in improved reliability (agreement = 93.01%, = 0.836). The remaining drawings were divided for independent coding between the three coders.

3 Results

Strategy Analysis. We analysed participants' use of the shortest strategy (1-step) across arithmetic word problems. Across both languages, participants showed a higher use of the 1-step strategy for height problems compared to cardinal problems. A similar pattern was observed across both age groups in each language (see Fig. 3).

We used a generalised linear mixed-effects model with a binomial distribution and random intercepts for participants and problem items. to examine the effect of problem type, age, and language on strategy use. Pairwise comparisons revealed that height problems elicited higher rates of 1-step strategies than cardinal problems across language and age groups. The full distribution of strategy responses across conditions can be found at osf.io/bgvd7/files/osfstorage.

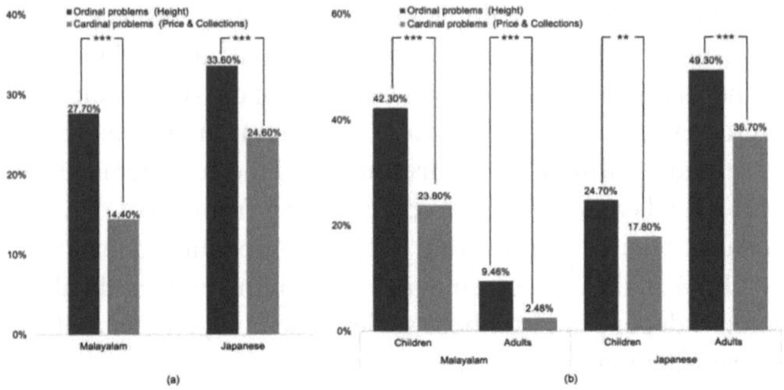

Fig. 3. Strategy Analysis. Proportion of 1-step strategy use across language and age groups.

Next, we computed a scaled duration score following John et al. (2025) [12] to assess whether duration problems are solved more ordinally or cardinally across languages and age groups. Scores were computed at a group level by comparing the proportion of 1-step strategy use in duration problems with the corresponding cardinal and ordinal baselines, ranging from 0 (cardinal baseline) to 1 (ordinal baseline), see Fig. 4. Duration score is calculated using the formula:

$$\text{Duration score} = \frac{Duration - Cardinal\ (Price\&Collection)}{Ordinal\ (Height) - Cardinal\ (Price\&Collection)}.$$

At the language level, Malayalam-speaking participants showed higher duration scores (M = 2.18) than Japanese-speaking participants (M = 1.56). Scores exceeded the ordinal baseline for both Malayalam-speaking children (M = 1.85) and adults (M = 3.26), as well as Japanese-speaking children (M = 2.41), indicating a greater use of the 1-step strategy for duration than height problems. In contrast, Japanese-speaking adults showed a duration score below the ordinal baseline (M = 0.74).

Drawing Analysis. Mean drawing scores (0–4) for cardinal and ordinal features varied by language, age and problem type (see Fig. 5). Malayalam-speaking participants showed generally low cardinal and ordinal scores, with adults showing slightly higher ordinal scores for height problems. Japanese-speaking participants showed higher ordinal scores for duration and height problems, while cardinal scores were higher for cardinal problems, particularly in adults.

Linear mixed-effects models revealed that ordinal scores were influenced by problem type, language and age with significant interactions, whereas cardinal scores were affected by problem type and language but not age. Post hoc comparisons showed that cardinal scores were higher for cardinal problems than for duration or height problems across groups. For ordinal scores, Japanese participants scored higher on duration and height problems, Malayalam-speaking adults scored higher on height problems, and children showed no reliable problem type differences.

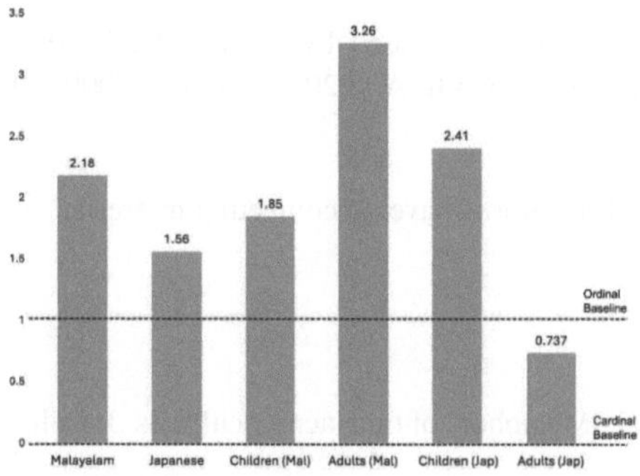

Fig. 4. Group-level mean duration scores compared to cardinal (0) and ordinal (1) baselines.

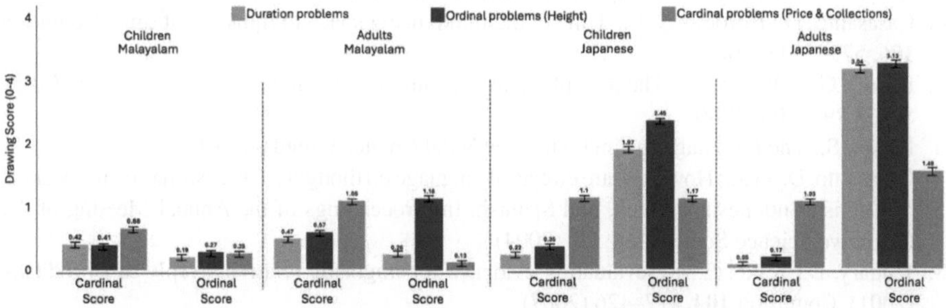

Fig. 5. Mean Drawing Scores across problem types, language and age groups.

4 Discussion

This study examined whether cross-linguistic differences in temporal metaphors shape how children and adults mentally represent durations in arithmetic problem-solving, reflected in strategy choice and diagrams. As predicted, problem semantics influenced strategy use: participants used the 1-step strategy more for height than for cardinal problems, and treated duration problems more like height problems. These patterns were observed across both Malayalam and Japanese, although the strength of the effect varied across groups particularly in the duration score analysis. Diagram analyses showed that cardinal features were consistently higher for cardinal problems across languages and age groups, reflecting a strong semantic effect. Ordinal features, however varied: Japanese participants drew more ordinal structures for duration and height problems, whereas Malayalam-speaking children showed low ordinal scores, and adults showed higher ordinal scores primarily for height problems.

These results suggest that strategy choice and diagrams provide complementary evidence about mental representations: strategies reflect ordinal thinking while diagrams capture meaningful differences in how these representations are externalised. Semantic content shaped both, with diagrams showing subtle differences across groups, but strategy choices provide a clear window into the universality of temporal reasoning and temporal representations.

Acknowledgements. This study was funded by Agence Nationale de la Recherche (ANR-25-CE28-7661–01), CY Initiative (CYIn-AAP2021-AmbEm-0000000026), and JSPS Kaitaku (20 K20516).

Disclosure of Interests.. The authors have no competing interests.

References

1. Khatin-Zadeh, O., et al.: Metaphors of time across cultures. J. Cult. Cogn. Sci. **7**(3), 219–231 (2023)
2. Whorf, B.L.: The relation of habitual thought and behavior to language. ETC: Rev. Gen. Semant. **1**, 197–215 (1939)
3. Lucy, J.A.: Linguistic relativity. Annu. Rev. Anthropol. **26**, 291–312 (1997)
4. Casasanto, D., Boroditsky, L.: Time in the mind: using space to think about time. Cognition **106**, 579–593 (2008)
5. Lakoff, G., Johnson, M.: The metaphorical structure of the human conceptual system. Cogn. Sci. **4**, 195–208 (1980)
6. Pinker, S.: The Language Instinct: How the Mind Creates Language (1994)
7. Casasanto, D., et al.: How deep are effects of language on thought? Time estimation in speakers of English, Indonesian, Greek, and Spanish. In: Proceedings of the Annual Meeting of the Cognitive Science Society, vol. 26, (2004)
8. January, D., Kako, E.: Re-evaluating evidence for linguistic relativity: reply to Boroditsky (2001). Cognition **104**, 417–426 (2007)
9. Gros, H., Thibaut, J.-P., Sander, E.: What we count dictates how we count: a tale of two encodings. Cognition **212**, 104665 (2021)
10. Fuson, K.C.: Relationships between counting and cardinality from age 2 to age 8. In: Pathways to Number: Children's Developing Numerical Abilities, pp. 127–149. Lawrence Erlbaum Associates, Hillsdale, NJ, US (1992)
11. Gros, H., Thibaut, J.-P., Sander, E.: Semantic congruence in arithmetic: a new conceptual model for word problem solving. Educ. Psychol. **55**, 69–87 (2020)
12. John, A.M., Macedo-Rouet, M., Gros, H., et al.: Challenging Linguistic Relativism in Numerical Cognition: a Preregistered Cross-Linguistic Study on the Perception of Ordinality. Preprint (Version 1). Research Square (2025)
13. Tversky, B.: Visualizing thought. Top. Cogn. Sci. **3**, 499–535 (2011)
14. Fan, J.E., Bainbridge, W.A., Chamberlain, R., Wammes, J.D.: Drawing as a versatile cognitive tool. Nat. Rev. Psychol. **2**(9), 556–568 (2023)
15. Wang, M., Zhao, H.: Are schematic diagrams valid visual representations of concepts? Evidence from mental imagery in online processing of English prepositions. Lang. Cogn. **16**(4), 1564–1587 (2024)
16. Ayabe, H., Manalo, E., Vries, E.: Problem-appropriate diagram instruction for improving mathematical word problem solving. Front. Psychol. **13**, 992625 (2022)
17. Bainbridge, W.A.: A tutorial on capturing mental representations through drawing and crowd-sourced scoring. Behav. Res. Methods **54**, 663–675 (2022)
18. Gros, H., Thibaut, J.-P., Sander, E.: Uncovering the interplay between drawings, mental representations, and arithmetic problem-solving strategies in children and adults. Mem. Cogn. **53**, 76–95 (2025)
19. Kilgarriff, A., et al.: The Sketch Engine. Lexicography **1**, 7–36 (2014)
20. Landis, J.R., Koch, G.G.: The measurement of observer agreement for categorical data. Biometrics **33**(1), 159–174 (1977)

Diagramming the Mind: A Framework for Visualizing Cognitive Change within and across Cognitive Networks

Liane Gabora(✉)

University of British Columbia, Kelowna, BC V0N 2J1, Canada
liane.gabora@ubc.ca

Abstract. This paper introduces a diagrammatic framework for modeling cognitive change using autocatalytic network representations—formal network structures in which elements mutually enable one another's transformation. It positions the diagrams as inferential cognitive artifacts that encode structure, constrain interpretation, and externalize reasoning. The framework specifies requirements for diagrams capable of representing mental processes, including the ability to distinguish internally generated from socially acquired elements, capture associative interactions that produce novel ideas, and depict how global cognitive organization emerges. Autocatalytic network diagrams satisfy these constraints because they model endogenous transformation within structured relational systems. The paper shows how such diagrams are used to represent cumulative cultural evolution, and argues that they provide a unified visual formalism for tracking the emergence of integrated worldviews and individual cognitive differences. The work contributes a principled representational tool for analyzing higher-order cognitive dynamics across individual and collective levels.

Keywords: Autocatalytic network diagram · cognition · cognitive network · creativity · mind · cumulative cultural change

1 Introduction

This paper introduces a diagrammatic method for modeling cognitive change that comes out of autocatalytic networks: a formal framework from network science for modeling the emergence and transformation of higher-level structure, and shows how such diagrams can be used to model cumulative cultural change. The paper positions the contribution within the field of diagrammatic reasoning and representation; diagrams are treated not merely as illustrations but as artifacts that structure inference, support constraint satisfaction, and enable externalized reasoning.

To model cumulative cultural change, a model must show not just how cultural lineages evolve over time, but what each creator contributes to that change Ganesh & Gabora (2022a). It must distinguish elements generated within a creator's mind from those acquired from others, represent the interactions through which novel ideas emerge, and depict how creative activity restructures the creator's conceptual network Gabora

P. Sobociński et al. (Eds.): Diagrams 2026, LNAI 16833, pp. 267–275, 2027.
https://doi.org/10.1007/978-3-032-34178-5_28

et al. (2022). The resulting diagrams are not merely visualizations of an underlying mathematical structure. They are diagrammatic representations in the technical sense: structured external artifacts whose topology, node–edge structure, and catalytic dependencies encode inferential constraints, making certain cognitive transitions explicit while excluding others.

2 Autocatalytic Network Diagrams

To meet these three requirements, we use a kind of network referred to as an autocatalytic network (Kauffman, 1993). The term autocatalytic network combines the notions of (a) a network, a set of parts that collectively comprise a whole, (b) catalysis, wherein one part facilitates the transformation of another, and (c) autonomy, wherein this transformation happens endogenously, within the network itself. Thus, roughly speaking, an *autocatalytic network* is a network wherein, through catalyzed interactions amongst the parts, the whole can autonomously sustain and regenerate itself.

Autocatalytic approaches to cognition build on earlier work on autopoiesis and self-organizing systems (Maturana & Varela, 1980; Varela et al., 1991). Mental contents exhibit tendencies toward self-organization, inconsistency reduction, schema preservation and revision, and the generation of remote associations (Festinger, 1957; Gabora & Merrifield, 2013; Mednick, 1962). The term cognitive autocatalytic network expresses that the elements of the network are mental representations and the relationships amongst them. Humans possess two levels of adaptive, self-organizing, self-mending structure: an organismic level—our bodies—and a psychological level—our minds (Barton, 1994; Freeman, 1991; O'Connor & Gabora (2009); Pribram, 1994). In a ***cognitive autocatalytic network*** the contents are mental representations and their relationships.

We now review why autocatalytic networks satisfy the requirements outlined above. Further mathematical developments of autocatalytic networks resulted in the formal framework of Reflexively Autocatalytic Foodset-derived (RAF) Networks (Steel, 2010; Hordijk, Hein, & Steel, 2010). In RAF networks, elements from *outside* the system are referred to collectively as the ***foodset*** since they serve as raw materials for the generation of new elements *within* the system. In our application of autocatalytic network theory, the system is a mind, so the foodset is whatever 'feeds the mind.' It includes not just innate knowledge, but also socially transmitted knowledge, as well as information acquired directly from the environment through individual learning—e.g., from a book, or observations of nature—so long as it's not modified or reinterpreted in the process. An inborn fear of snakes constitutes an *innate foodset item.* Learning from a teacher the scientific name for a snake produces a *socially learned foodset item* because pre-existing information is obtained from the environment through social means. Observing for oneself that lightning is followed by thunder is an *individually learned foodset item.* Thus, a foodset item comes into existence *outside* the individual's mind.

Elements generated *within* the system in question are referred to as ***foodset-derived*** elements. They're constructed anew from foodset elements or previously generated foodset-derived elements (Hordijk, Hein & Steel, 2010). An example of a *foodset-derived item* is the generation of a poem about snakes; here, new information results from the individual's own thought process. The defining feature of foodset-derived items is that they came into existence *within* the individual's mind. The different roles played by foodset and foodset-derived items is consistent with cognitive differences arising when learning is through (a) instruction or imitation, versus (b) opportunities to experiment or explore, or direct challenges that prompt students to learn for themselves. Note that the same item may be foodset-derived in one person, and part of the foodset of another. For example, if you come up with a joke, it's a foodset-derived item in your mind, but if you tell the joke to your friends, it's a foodset item in their minds, because they didn't think it up for themselves. What matters here is whether it materialized in its current form in the cognitive network of the individual in question. Thus, **autocatalytic network theory distinguishes mental contents acquired through innate predispositions, social learning, or individual learning from those generated through the individual's own thought processes**. The former constitute foodset items, while the latter are foodset-derived. They show how creative ideas cannot be attributed solely to nature or nurture; they arise through endogenous cognitive transformation within the network itself.

The second requirement for our network model is that it must incorporate **the creative process** by which new elements are formed. What differentiates autocatalytic networks from other network approaches is that the nodes are not just passive transmitters of activation; they actively galvanize, or ***catalyze*** the synthesis of new nodes from existing ones. The process by which a foodset-derived item is generated from one or more foodset items is referred to (in accordance with terminology developed in earlier applications to the origin of life) as a ***cognitive reaction***: a mental operation such as conceptual restructuring, induction, concept combination, or metaphor. Just as reactions between molecules generate new molecules, which in turn make new reactions possible, interactions between mental representations generate new mental contents, which in turn make new cognitive reactions possible. Just as a catalyst makes a certain reaction more likely to occur, a stimulus or memory can 'catalyze' a new insight or perspective. A mental representation or external stimulus serves as a ***cognitive catalyst*** if it facilitates a cognitive reaction but is not, itself, altered by the reaction. Thus, for example, if a trip to the library sparks the idea of turning a ladder into a bookshelf, the library serves as a catalyst because it's not altered by the reaction. You *might* just happen to invent a ladder-bookshelf out of the blue, but seeing bookshelves in a library makes it more likely. The concepts ladder and bookshelf are foodset items because they were socially acquired. Assuming you have never previously encountered a ladder used as a bookshelf, ladder-bookshelf is foodset-derived because it emerges through the individual's own cognitive activity. Unlike the catalyst (the library), the reactants are transformed through the reaction: ladder acquires the affordance of functioning as a bookshelf, while bookshelf acquires the affordance of being constructed from a ladder.

A catalyst need not come from the external world. Chemist Friedrich Kekulé's dream about a snake biting its tail catalyzed the realization that the benzene molecule is ring-shaped. The dream was internally generated, so it is a foodset-derived item, yet it functioned as a catalyst. Conceptual reactivity refers to the propensity of a mental representation to participate in the generation of new ideas. Concepts may become highly reactive by aligning with needs, drives, or emotions, thereby leveraging biological motivations in service of cultural goals.

The third requirement is that our network must be able to model the **emergence of integrated conceptual structure** that enables it to make connections, combine concepts, and adapt them to new situations. We need a framework that can model how cognitive structure grows through the incorporation of new knowledge and experiences, with efficient algorithms for decomposing a complex, hierarchical network into the simpler units of which it is made up. Autocatalytic networks also meet this requirement.

Consider the example portrayed in Fig. 1. Panel (a) depicts the mind of a newborn, Otto, with only innate knowledge. Panels (b) depicts knowledge acquired through individual learning; for example, Otto, now an infant, learns how to move an object by throwing it. Panel (c) depicts knowledge acquired through social learning, such as for example, Otto, now a young child watching a caregiver feed a dog a treat by hand. Let's say the top left piece of innate knowledge is an instinctive fear of large dogs, which stops Otto from simply imitating the caregiver. However, the caregiver's action catalyzes a cognitive reaction in Otto's mind, as shown in panel (d). It sparks the idea of throwing the treat to the dog instead, shown in panel (e), which provides the satisfaction of feeding the dog, but from a safe distance. Panel (e), and all subsequent panels, depict the special situation in which the criteria are met for a *Reflexively Autocatalytic Foodset Generated network, or RAF* (where the term *reflexively* is used in its mathematical sense, meaning that each part is related to the whole). To be a RAF it must contain: (1) *at least one cognitive reaction resulting in a product,* and (2) *all reactants and catalysts needed for each cognitive reaction (whether they be foodset items, or foodset-derived items from earlier reactions).* The significance of this is that **each RAF—each little network indicated by an orange circle—is *self-sustaining*;** it has what it needs to preserve and make more of itself. This means, for example, that Otto can voluntarily recall, and perhaps modify or embellish his idea of throwing a treat to the dog.

While panels (e) and (f), meet the criteria for a single RAF, panel (g) meets the criteria for a second RAF. In this second RAF, an individual learning experience catalyzes a new variant of socially acquired knowledge, e.g., seeing a bird hop on one foot and then the other might spark Otto to challenge himself by writing with his non-dominant hand (a creative twist on his socially acquired knowledge of handwriting). In panels (e) through (g), the reactants and catalysts are all foodset items. However, foodset-derived items can also serve as both reactants and catalysts. In this way, RAF networks grow and merge to form larger RAF networks. In panel (h), the product of the second RAF catalyzes a reaction in which the product of the first RAF serves as a reactant, e.g., writing with the non-dominant hand sparks in Otto the idea of throwing a treat to the dog with his non-dominant hand. Panel (i) depicts the formation of what is called a co-RAF because it is reliant on the continued existence of other RAFs. Panel (i) also depicts the *maxRAF:* the largest RAF that encompasses each of its other RAFs as components referred to as *subRAFs*. Note that, although this simple example does not portray cognitive networks as 'collapsing' into new configurations in response to changing contexts, the RAF approach isn't inconsistent with the view of concepts as dynamic constructions. However, this complicates things substantially, so for now, keep in mind that such figures depict snapshots in time.

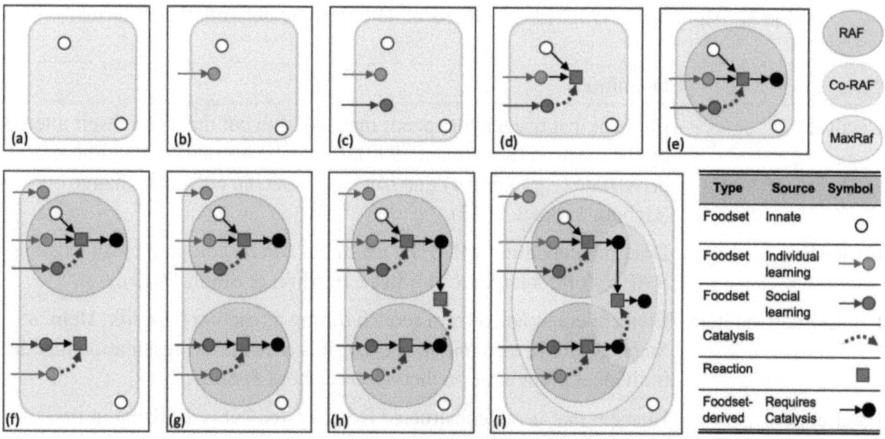

Fig. 1. Panel (a) depicts how, at birth, the mind (yellow rounded rectangle) consists only of innate knowledge (white dots). Panels (b) and (c) depict how, from infancy onward, foodset items are acquired through both individual learning (green dot), and social learning (purple dot), respectively. Panel (d) depicts an item acquired through social learning catalyzing (dotted arrow) a creative insight, described here as a *cognitive reaction* (blue square). In panel (e), this results in a new foodset-derived idea (black dot). Panels (e), (f), and (g) meet the criteria for a single RAF (large orange oval). Panels (f) and (g) depict a similar process resulting in the formation of a second RAF. In panel (h), the product of the first RAF serves as the reactant in a reaction catalyzed by the product of the second RAF. Panel (i) shows the formation of a co-RAF (pale blue oval) that is reliant on the continued existence of the earlier two RAFs. Panel (i) also depicts the maxRAF (grey oval) that encompasses each of the other RAFs as subRAFs. The innate item on the lower right of all panels, and the item acquired through individual learning on the upper left of panels (f) through (i) are not assimilated into a RAF, and may remain inaccessible to the stream of thought unless something in the environment triggers them.

This example shows how the RAF framework enables us to diagram how self-sustaining cognitive structure emerges and grows. Just as the individually self-organizing cells of a body cooperatively behave for the good of the whole (i.e., the body), 'cells of meaning' the mind—i.e., individual RAFs—cooperatively serve the needs of your world-view, coming into awareness when they're potentially useful, and 'staying quiet' when they're not. In the autocatalytic network representation, **closure** is visually instantiated as strongly connected substructures, making global coherence properties perceptually accessible. This diagrammatic encoding reduces the cognitive load required to detect systemic integration compared to propositional description. Table 1 provides definitions of terms from autocatalytic network theory. The terminology reflects its initial application to biochemistry, but it is not specific to that setting; it is a general framework that is equally applicable to cognition.

Table 1. Alphabetically listed definitions of autocatalytic network theory terms.

Term	Definition
Catalyst	Element that triggers or speeds up a reaction but that is not itself altered by the reaction (Kauffman, 1993). It may be a stimulus, thought, or drive state (e.g., hunger) that triggers a specific cognitive change (Gabora & Steel, 2017).
Co-RAF	Does not constitute a RAF by itself, but can be co-opted by an existing RAF to form a larger RAF (Steel, Hordjik, & Smith, 2013).
Foodset-derived item	Element constructed from scratch during a reaction (Hordijk, Hein, & Steel, 2010). In a cognitive context, it is a mental representation that the individual thought of on their own (Gabora & Steel, 2017).
Foodset item	Element that is not constructed from scratch but is available in the environment (Hordijk, Hein, & Steel, 2010). In a cognitive context, it is a mental representation that was either innate, or obtained from the environment, e.g., through social learning (Gabora & Steel, 2017).
IrrRAF	RAF that is irreducible, i.e., it cannot be reduced further without losing its RAF status (Hordijk, Steel, & Kauffman, 2012).
MaxRAF	Single unique union of all RAFs in a system (Hordijk, et al., 2012).
Persistent RAF	A RAF that does not depend on any particular element from the external environment to persist (Gabora & Steel, 2020a).
Reactants	Raw materials (either foodset items or foodset-derived items) that undergo change in a particular reaction; in a cognitive context, they may be concepts, beliefs, and so forth (Gabora & Steel, 2017).
Percolation threshold	Point at which there is a phase transition such that network elements form a single giant connected cluster, i.e., an integrated whole.
Products	New elements resulting from a reaction; in a cognitive context, they may be ideas (Gabora & Steel, 2022) or attitudes (Ganesh & Gabora, 2022b).
Reaction	Process wherein catalyst triggers transformation of reactants into products; in a cognitive context, a 'reaction' occurs through a mental operation such as deduction, analogical transfer, or concept combination (Gabora & Steel, 2017).
Reactivity	Capacity to catalyze reactions. In a cognitive context, the reactivity of an idea refers to its capacity to stimulate conceptual change (Gabora & Steel, 2020b).
SubRAF	Subset of a maxRAF that is itself a (smaller) RAF (Hordijk, et al., 2012).

3 Diagramming a Cultural Lineage

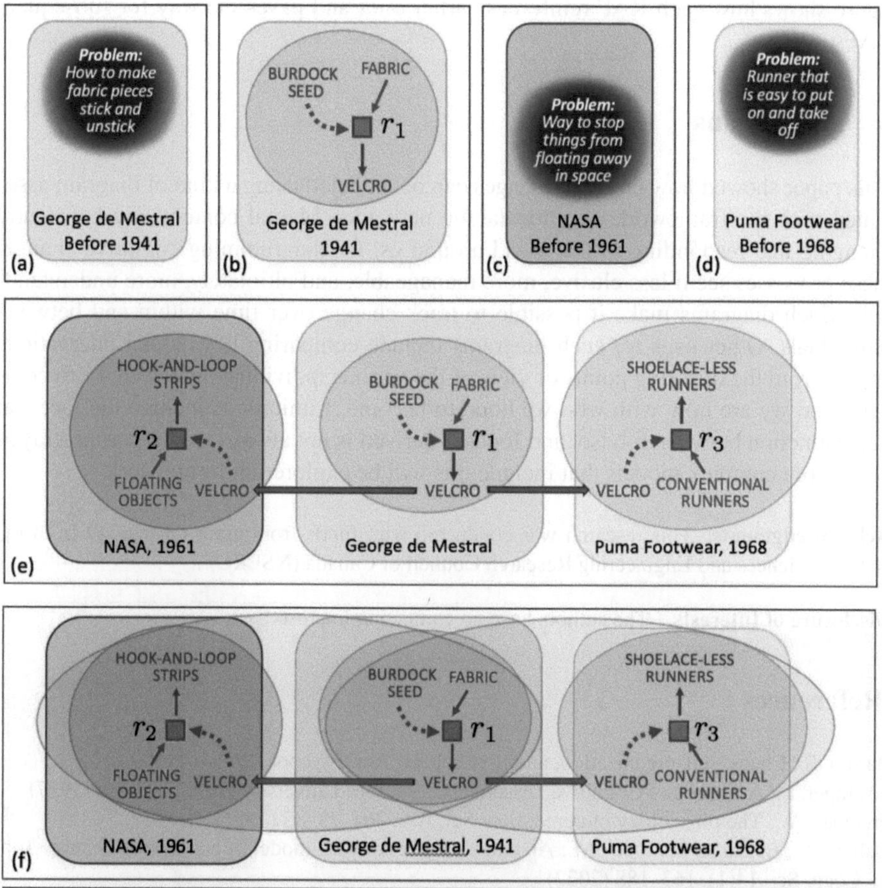

Fig. 2. (a) A problem, depicted as a gap in a worldview. (b) Texture of burdock seed, which sticks to clothing, catalyzes the invention of Velcro. For Puma and NASA, with problems of their own (c) and (d), velcro catalyzes the invention of hook-and-loop strips, and shoelace-less runners, each described by an irr-RAF, as shown in (e). The RAFs connecting these inventions to the invention of Velcro are shown in (f). The maxRAF that encompasses them all is shown in (g). Catalysts are indicated in red, reactants in green, and products in blue.

We now see how a cultural lineage is modeled in the RAF setting, using an example, George de Mestral's invention of Velcro. It was catalyzed by burdock seeds, which stick to clothing. Velcro subsequently catalyzed other inventions, as shown in Fig. 2. The figure shows how each RAF reinforces earlier ones and paves the way for subsequent RAFs.

4 Conclusions

This paper showed how cultural lineages can be modeled using a kind of diagram associated with the framework of autocatalytic networks. Mental contents are constantly changing and responding to the world around us. By diagramming cognitive change, these processes seem less elusive, more manageable, and ultimately, more understandable. Such diagrams make it possible to track change over time within and between individuals. Other uses for such diagrams include comparing how social interactions appear from the differing points of view of the various individuals involved, or to compare who we are now with who we hope to become. Limitations include the fact that the distinction between foodset and foodset-derived is not always as sharp as portrayed here; more complex models that include this will be explored in future work.

Acknowledgments. This research was conducted with funds from grant GR026749 from the Natural Sciences and Engineering Research Council of Canada (NSERC).

Disclosure of Interests. The authors have no competing interests.

References

Barton, S.: Chaos, self-organization, and psychology. Am. Psychol. **49**, 5–14 (1994)
Festinger, L.: A Theory of Cognitive Dissonance. Stanford University Press, Stanford (1957)
Freeman, W.: The physiology of perception. Sci. Am. **264**, 78–85 (1991)
Gabora, L., Beckage, N., Steel, M.: An autocatalytic network model of conceptual change. Top. Cogn. Sci. **14**(1), 163–188 (2022)
Gabora, L., Merrifield, M.: Dynamical disequilibrium, transformation, and the evolution and development of sustainable worldviews. In: Orsucci, F., Sala, N. (eds.) Complexity Science, Living Systems, and Reflexing Interfaces, pp. 69–77. IGI Global (2013)
Gabora, L., Steel, M.: Autocatalytic networks in cognition and the origin of culture. J. Theor. Biol. **431**, 87–95 (2017). https://doi.org/10.1016/j.jtbi.2017.07.022
Gabora, L., Steel, M.: Modelling a cognitive transition at the origin of cultural evolution using autocatalytic networks. Cogn. Sci. **44**(9), e12878 (2020a). https://doi.org/10.48550/arXiv.2007.06442
Gabora, L., Steel, M.: a model of the transition to behavioural and cognitive modernity using reflexively autocatalytic networks. J. R. Soc. Interface. **17**(171) (2020b). https://doi.org/10.1101/2020.07.10.185512
Gabora, L., Steel, M.: From uncertainty to insight: An autocatalytic framework. In: Beghetto, R., Jaeger, G. (eds.) *Uncertainty: A Catalyst for Creativity, Learning and Development*, pp. 125–158. Springer (2022)
Ganesh, K., Gabora, L.: A dynamic autocatalytic network model of therapeutic change. Entropy. **24**(4), 547 (2022a)

Ganesh, K., Gabora, L.: Modelling discontinuous cultural evolution: the impact of cross-domain transfer. Front. Psychol. **13**, 786072 (2022b)

Hordijk, W., Hein, J., Steel, M.: Autocatalytic sets and the origin of life. Entropy. **12**(7), 1733–1742 (2010)

Hordijk, W., Steel, M., Kauffman, S.: The structure of autocatalytic sets: Evolvability, enablement, and emergence. Acta Biotheor. **60**(4), 379–392 (2012). https://doi.org/10.1007/s10441-012-9165-1

Kauffman, S.: The Origins of Order: Self-Organization and Selection in Evolution. Oxford University Press, Oxford (1993)

Mednick, S.: The associative basis of the creative process. Psychol. Rev. **69**, 220–232 (1962)

O'Connor, B., Gabora, L.: Applying complexity theory to a dynamical model of the development of pathological belief systems. Chaos and Complexity Letters. **4**(3), 75–96 (2009)

Pribram, K.: Origins: Brain and Self-Organization. Lawrence Erlbaum, Hillsdale (1994)

Steel, M., Hordijk, W., Smith, J.: Minimal autocatalytic networks. J. Theor. Biol. **332**, 96–107 (2013). https://doi.org/10.1016/j.jtbi.2013.04.032

Varela, F., Thompson, E., Rosch, E.: The Embodied Mind. MIT Press, Cambridge (1991)

Diagrams and Computation

3D Euler Diagram Generation Using a Game Engine: Work in Progress

Matthew Hibbin(✉) and Peter Rodgers

University of Kent, Canterbury CT2 7NZ, UK
M.Hibbin@kent.ac.uk

Abstract. We describe work embedding general 3D Euler diagrams using a game engine. We create closed surfaces using 3D meshes to represent sets and so indicate set intersections by mesh overlap. Our goal is to represent the underlying data accurately with all required set intersections present and without any additional intersections. This work in progress report details dual graph production, mesh creation, accuracy measurements, and subsequent improvements to the meshes that are intended to fix incorrect intersections. We also discuss future work to further improve the generation process.

1 Introduction

We explore the research question: Can game engines aid in the automatic generation of accurate 3D Euler Diagrams? We describe our work in progress to generate 3D Euler diagrams using the Godot game engine.

Research into 3D Euler diagrams is an area not fully explored. Our research intends to further showcase the utility of 3D Euler diagrams by developing a general generation tool. We intend to demonstrate how diagrams with poor readability in 2D space can be better visualised in 3D. We will produce techniques to allow easy interaction with 3D diagrams so that all their elements can be clearly observed. Furthermore, the utilisation of a game engine will demonstrate its applicability to diagrammatic visualization and interaction. Compared to traditional graphing software, a game engine gives us more interaction methods, a physics engine and in-depth manipulation control. Godot was chosen as it is a lightweight, open-source game engine with suitable functionality for our needs.

Regarding related work, 3D Euler diagrams were first explored in [7], where they were formally defined and compared to a 2D approach. The drawability of these diagrams was further explored in [5] where a graph representation was used as the basis for wellformed 3D Euler diagrams. This followed a 2D approach [4] where, from an abstract description describing the required set intersections, a dual graph is generated. This dual is then used to generate a 2D Euler diagram, with a general 2D generation algorithm given in [8]. The work of implementing similar methods and algorithms for 3D Euler diagrams is the purpose of our

P. Sobociński et al. (Eds.): Diagrams 2026, LNAI 16833, pp. 279–283, 2027.
https://doi.org/10.1007/978-3-032-34178-5_29

research project. We aim to introduce new generation methods for 3D representation.

In the remainder of this paper, we first outline related Euler diagram research. We then detail the current method implemented to generate 3D shapes from an abstract description, how we evaluate the diagram and make adjustments to improve accuracy. We include example images and a discussion of future work.

2 Diagram Generation Method

To implement the generation of 3D Euler diagrams, we chose the Godot game engine [6] due to its 3D capabilities. It provides easy surface mesh generation, including convex hull generation with the help of an external library [3] and camera control.

Dual Graph Production: Following the 2D approach of [8], we first generate a dual graph from an abstract description (such as "$\emptyset, A, B, AB$"). Each letter is a set and each element is a zone or required set intersection. This uses a 3D representation of a dual graph using Godot's 3D nodes [6]. The edges were created by drawing 3D lines [2]. We utilise the spring embedder algorithm to lay out the dual graph [9].

Array Mesh for Shape Generation: Godot allows the creation of custom 3D shapes via its array mesh type which draws polygons between a set of defined points. A 3D mesh is used for each set where positions of the nodes in the dual graph that contain the set letter are used for the points of the array mesh. However, there were some immediate problems as some meshes contained a very small or very large number of nodes. The small sets have minimal nodes and therefore have an insufficient number of points for array mesh generation. This was solved simply by adding some artificial points for the array mesh closely surrounding the nodes to give the shapes a better definition in the 3D scene.

For the sets contained in a larger number of nodes, the dual graph has many nodes used for each array mesh where polygons would often overlap, not forming complete 3D shapes. This was solved by utilising a convex hull algorithm [1] which exposes the outermost points within a group of coordinates for a shape to be drawn around them [3]. However, the current implementation does not yet have support for non-convex meshes. This is something we plan to add in future (see Sect. 3).

See Fig. 1 for an example of output. It shows the dual graph in Fig. 1(a), the dual graph and the diagram in Fig. 1(b) and the diagram rotated compared to Fig. 1(b) in Fig. 1(c).

Correctness Detection and Improvement: After initial generation, the accuracy of the generated diagram is assessed. Inaccurate diagrams refer to those with missing zones in the abstract description or representing some zones that are not present in the abstract description. We build an abstract description of the generated diagram for comparison with the input abstract description. Our correctness test uses the points that were isolated by the convex hull algorithm for each array mesh. We find the meshes that contain a point, so indicating the zone which the point is contained within. As these are the points where the intersection of the array meshes are most likely to occur, the generated zones will be detected. However some refinement is required, as the are rare cases where the intersection of meshes may not be on these points.

As well as being able to evaluate the success of the embedding method, the correctness assessment can also be applied to adjust the generated graph so that it better fits the original abstract description. This work is in its infancy but is showing some promising initial results. The design observes the results from the correctness assessment that specifies the missing and gained zones. For each gained zone, it locates each point used in the correctness assessment where this zone was observed and "shrinks" the involved array meshes by finding the centroid of the array mesh's convex hull points and then moving the violating point towards that centroid with the aim that it will remove the zone which is not required. Meanwhile, for each missing zone, the associated array meshes representing the sets that are a part of that zone are queried for each of the closest convex hull points. These points are then "expanded", with their positions moved towards each other. Whilst this system improves accuracy, it does not correct inaccuracies entirely. We are working on further additions and fine tuning.

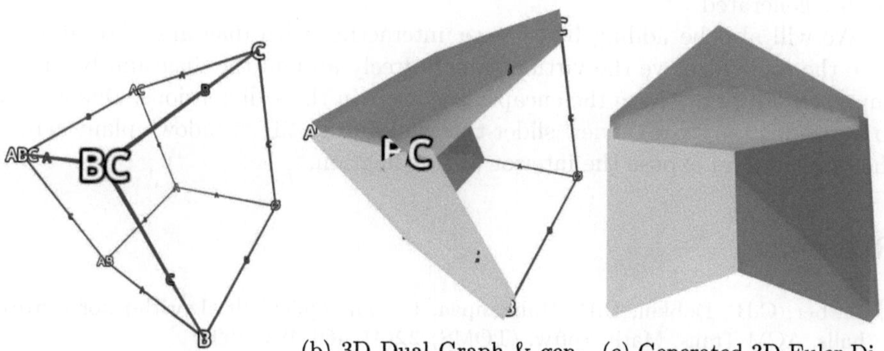

(a) 3D Dual Graph (b) 3D Dual Graph & generated 3D Euler Diagram (c) Generated 3D Euler Diagram at 90°

Fig. 1. Output with the abstract description: $\emptyset, A, B, C, AB, AC, BC, ABC$

3 Conclusions

We believe the initial results have proven promising, as we have successfully generated 3D Euler diagrams. The dual graph production, the spring embedder algorithm, and tools to observe the diagram all work well. Running our correctness evaluation on a sample of one hundred generated Euler diagrams with a max of 3 sets and 6 zones, we found that 82% were observed to be accurate by the system. We also believe we have so far proven the feasibility of game engines being suitable for 3D diagrams.

Future work includes improving the correctness evaluation. The current design does not allow the detection of zones when the intersections of meshes do not happen on the evaluated points. The testing of points beyond those used to generate the mesh should allow us to detect currently missed zones.

We intend to introduce concave shapes to support dual graph layouts that require non-convex set meshes. We will add more points to the array mesh that cause a "dip" in its geometry, causing a concave shape to form, so removing incorrect intersections.

Wellformedness of 3D Euler diagrams [5] will be addressed. This will examine the aspects of triple points, concurrency and duplicate curve labels that allow all abstract descriptions to be drawn. There are particular aspects of these in 3D that will be examined [7].

Looking further into the future, shape smoothing will be introduced thereby improving the readability of the diagrams. The array meshes from the generated diagram could be evaluated for any simple 3D shapes they may closely resemble and seeing if we can retain accuracy while changing their shape to more closely represent the chosen simple 3D shape. Whether this will be by adjusting the array mesh itself or replacing the mesh with Godot's in-built simple 3D shapes will have to be tested. Outside of shape smoothing, the readability of the generated 3D Euler diagrams can also be improved by removing the sharp edges of the meshes generated.

We will also be adding better user interaction with diagrams. We already have the tools to move the virtual camera freely around the diagram, but need improved solutions to see the encapsulated sets in three dimensions. One idea is to implement an "x-ray" view slider that will move a 2D "window" plane across the diagram and expose the interior of the diagram.

References

1. Barber, C.B., Dobkin, D.P., Huhdanpaa, H.: The Quickhull algorithm for convex hulls. ACM Trans. Math. Softw. (TOMS) **22**(4), 469–483 (1996)
2. betalars: Godot asset library - simple line renderer (2024). https://godotengine.org/asset-library/asset/2563. Accessed 14 Feb 2026
3. Campbell, M., Sehnal, D.: MIConvexHull: a.net fast convex hull library for 2D, 3D, and higher dimensions (2019). https://designengrlab.github.io/MIConvexHull/. Accessed 15 Feb 2026
4. Flower, J., Howse, J.: Generating Euler diagrams. In: Proceedings Diagrams, pp. 61–75. Springer (2002)
5. Flower, J., Stapleton, G., Rodgers, P.: On the drawability of 3D Venn and Euler diagrams. J. Vis. Lang. Comput. **25**(3), 186–209 (2014)
6. Linietsky, J., Manzur, A.: The Godot community: Godot docs - 4.5 branch (2026). https://docs.godotengine.org/en/4.5/index.html. Accessed 12 Feb 2026
7. Rodgers, P., Flower, J., Stapleton, G.: Introducing 3D Venn and Euler diagrams. In: Proceedings 3rd International Workshop on Euler Diagrams 2012, vol. 854, pp. 92–106. CEUR-WS. org (2012)

8. Rodgers, P., Zhang, L., Fish, A.: General Euler diagram generation. In: Proceedings Diagrams, pp. 13–27. Springer (2008)
9. Simon, F., Steinbrückner, F., Lewerentz, C.: 3D-spring embedder for complete graphs. BTU, Institute of Computer Science (2000)

Do Diagrams Help Large Language Models Reason? Evidence from Syllogistic Reasoning

Risako Ando(✉) and Koji Mineshima

Keio University, 2-15-45 Mita, Minato-ku, Tokyo 108-8345, Japan
risakochaan@keio.jp

Abstract. Diagrams are widely used to support logical reasoning, and prior studies suggest that representations such as Euler diagrams can improve human reasoning performance. Recent work has also explored their effects on large language models (LLMs). In this paper, we compare four representational conditions for syllogistic reasoning: natural language, logical notation, linear diagrams, and Euler diagrams. Using 285 problems from Ando et al. (2024), we evaluate two contemporary LLMs, Claude 3.5 Sonnet and GPT-4o-mini. Our results show that diagrammatic representations do not consistently improve performance. Although the models perform well on entailment and contradiction problems, they struggle with neutral problems and often make systematic conversion errors. Overall, the results suggest that the tested models gain limited benefit from diagrams in logical reasoning tasks.

Keywords: Diagrammatic reasoning · Syllogistic reasoning · Euler diagrams · Linear diagrams · Large language models

1 Introduction

Diagrams have long been used as external representations to support logical reasoning [8,9]. In diagrammatic reasoning research, visual representations such as Euler diagrams can make set-theoretic relations spatially explicit and thereby facilitate deductive reasoning. A number of empirical studies have demonstrated that diagrammatic representations can improve human performance on syllogistic reasoning tasks. In particular, Euler diagrams have been shown to support deductive reasoning effectively and may outperform traditional Venn diagrams [6,7]. Similarly, linear diagrams have been shown to provide reasoning support comparable to Euler diagrams in syllogistic tasks [5,6].

Recently, large language models (LLMs) have achieved strong performance on a wide range of reasoning tasks. However, it remains unclear whether diagrammatic representations can support reasoning in LLMs in the same way as they do for human reasoners. Ando et al. [1] recently investigated this question by examining whether Euler diagrams improve syllogistic reasoning in LLMs.

P. Sobociński et al. (Eds.): Diagrams 2026, LNAI 16833, pp. 284–292, 2027.
https://doi.org/10.1007/978-3-032-34178-5_30

Table 1. Four representational conditions used in syllogistic reasoning.

Natural language	Logical form	Euler diagram	Linear diagram
All S are P	$S \subseteq P$		`---- S` `------- P`
No S are P	$S \cap P = \emptyset$	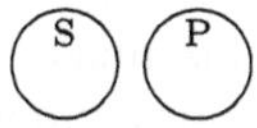	`--- S` `--- P`
Some S are P	$S \cap P \neq \emptyset$		`---x-- S` `--x---- P`
Some S are not P	$S \setminus P \neq \emptyset$	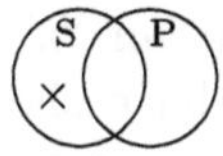	`--x----- S` `--- P`

Their experiments suggested that providing Euler diagrams alongside textual premises can improve LLM performance.

In this paper, we revisit this question by systematically comparing different representational conditions for syllogistic reasoning. While Ando et al. [1] compared natural language and Euler diagram representations, the present study extends this setup by including two additional representational conditions: linear diagrams and symbolic logical forms. This enables a more comprehensive comparison across textual, symbolic, and diagrammatic representations within a unified experimental framework.

Using a dataset of 285 syllogistic problems from the validity checking task introduced in [1], we evaluate two contemporary multimodal LLMs, Claude 3.5 Sonnet and GPT-4o-mini. The dataset includes annotations that enable us to analyze several well-known reasoning phenomena, including conversion errors, figural effects, and differences across inference labels and content types.

Our results show that differences across representational conditions are relatively small, and that diagrammatic representations do not consistently improve reasoning accuracy. In addition, the models exhibit substantial conversion errors and biases across inference labels, performing poorly on neutral cases. Overall, the findings suggest that the multimodal LLMs examined in this study gain limited benefit from diagrammatic representations for logical inference.

2 Background

Syllogistic reasoning is a classical form of deductive reasoning involving two premises and a conclusion that relate three terms. A typical example is: *All B are C*; *Some A are B*; *Therefore, some A* are *C*. The quantified sentence forms used in syllogisms are summarized in Table 1. Because syllogisms provide a well-controlled setting for studying logical inference, they have been widely used in cognitive psychology [2].

Diagrammatic representations provide an alternative way to express logical relations between sets. As shown in Table 1, Euler diagrams represent sets as regions in the plane, where spatial inclusion and exclusion represent subset and disjoint relations. Such diagrams make set-theoretic relations visually explicit and have been studied as tools for supporting logical reasoning [8,9]. Empirical studies have shown that Euler diagrams can facilitate human syllogistic reasoning and may outperform Venn diagrams in syllogistic reasoning tasks [6,7].

Another form of diagrammatic representation is the *linear diagram*, in which sets are represented by horizontal line segments (see Table 1). Inclusion and exclusion relations are encoded by the relative positions of the segments. In both Euler and linear diagrams, an "x" denotes the existence of at least one element. Experimental studies have shown that linear diagrams can support human reasoning performance at a level comparable to Euler diagrams [5,6].

Recent multimodal LLMs can process both text and images, making it possible to investigate whether diagrammatic representations affect reasoning performance [3,4]. Ando et al. [1] reported that Euler diagrams can improve performance on certain reasoning patterns, such as the neutral and conversion cases discussed in Sect. 3. In this work, we systematically compare textual, symbolic, and diagrammatic representations within a unified experimental framework.

3 Experimental Setup

3.1 Dataset

We evaluate the models on a dataset of 285 syllogistic reasoning problems derived from the validity checking (VC) task introduced by Ando et al. [1]. Each problem consists of two premises and a conclusion relating three terms, and the task is to determine the logical relation between the premises and the conclusion. Table 2 shows representative examples together with their annotations.

Following standard treatments of syllogistic reasoning, each problem is assigned one of three inference labels: *entailment*, *contradiction*, or *neutral*. An *entailment* label indicates that the conclusion logically follows from the premises, a *contradiction* label indicates that the premises and the conclusion cannot both be true, and a *neutral* label indicates that the conclusion is neither entailed nor contradicted by the premises.

The dataset also includes problems annotated as *conversion* cases. Conversion errors arise from incorrectly reversing quantified statements, such as interpreting *All A are B* as *All B are A*, or *Some A are not B* as *Some B are not A* (see [6]). In our dataset, these problems are labeled as *neutral*, although such incorrect conversions would make the conclusions appear entailed. For example, in the first problem shown in Table 2, incorrectly converting *All B are A* into

Table 2. Representative examples from the dataset with their annotations.

Example	Inference	Conversion	Figure	Content
P1: All B are A. **P2:** No B are C. **C:** No C are A.	Neutral	Yes	3	Symbolic
P1: All beer are liquor. **P2:** Some drink are not liquor. **C:** Some drink are not beer.	Entailment	No	2	Congruent
P1: All animals are dogs. **P2:** All robots are animals. **C:** Some robots are not dogs.	Contradiction	No	1	Incongruent

All A are B would make the conclusion appear entailed, although the correct inference label is *neutral.*

Syllogisms are also classified according to their *figure*, namely the arrangement of the middle term across the premises. Different figures are known to vary in difficulty for human reasoners, a phenomenon known as the *figural effect*, with Fig. 4 typically being more difficult than Fig. 1 (see [2,6]). Each problem is therefore annotated with one of the four syllogistic figures.

In addition, the natural language formulations are categorized into three content types: *symbolic*, *congruent*, and *incongruent* (see Table 2). Symbolic problems use abstract symbols (e.g., A, B, C), whereas congruent and incongruent problems differ in whether the described relations are semantically plausible. This distinction allows us to examine whether model performance is influenced by semantic plausibility in addition to logical structure.

The dataset is publicly available online[1]. All annotations used in this study, including inference labels, conversion cases, syllogistic figures, and content types, follow Ando et al. [1]; see their work for further details on the annotation scheme.

3.2 Representational Conditions

Each reasoning problem is presented under one of four representational conditions shown in Table 1. In all conditions, the premises and conclusion are presented in natural language, while additional symbolic or diagrammatic representations are provided depending on the condition.

Natural Language (NL). Only the natural language statements are shown.
Logic. Each premise is accompanied by a set-theoretic logical representation.
Linear. Each premise is accompanied by a text-based (ASCII) linear diagram.
Euler. Each premise is accompanied by an Euler diagram presented as an image.

The Linear and Euler diagram representations follow Sato and Mineshima [5,6].

[1] https://github.com/kmineshima/euler-diagrams-llm.

3.3 Models and Evaluation

We evaluate two multimodal LLMs: **Claude 3.5 Sonnet** and **GPT-4o-mini**, accessed through the OpenRouter API, representing widely used contemporary multimodal LLMs of different scales.

For each problem, the model is asked to determine the logical relation between the premises and the conclusion by selecting one of three labels: *entailment*, *contradiction*, or *neutral*. The models are instructed to respond using only the corresponding label.

Performance is measured by accuracy over the 285 problems. In addition to overall accuracy, we analyze results across several dimensions: representational conditions (NL, Logic, Linear, Euler), conversion vs. non-conversion cases, syllogistic figure (Figures 1–4), inference label (entailment, contradiction, neutral), and content type (symbolic, congruent, incongruent).

The prompt format follows Ando et al. [1], with additional instructions explaining the linear and Euler diagram representations. Figure 1 shows an example input for the Linear condition.

Example input (Linear condition)

```
Premise 1: No A are B.
Linear diagram for Premise 1:
A:  ----
B:          ----
Premise 2: Some B are C.
Linear diagram for Premise 2:
B:  ---x--
C:    -x-----
Conclusion: All C are A.
```

Fig. 1. Example input in the Linear condition (correct inference label: *contradiction*).

4 Results

Table 3 reports overall accuracy as well as accuracy on conversion and non-conversion cases across the four representational conditions.

Claude 3.5 Sonnet achieves relatively high performance across all conditions, with slightly lower accuracy in the Linear condition, whereas GPT-4o-mini performs substantially worse overall (65–71%). For both models, the Logic condition yields the highest accuracy, whereas the diagrammatic conditions fail to produce consistent improvements over NL and sometimes yield lower accuracy.

Overall, these results suggest that LLM performance varies only modestly across representational conditions, and that diagrammatic representations do

Table 3. Overall accuracy and accuracy on conversion vs. non-conversion cases (%).

	Claude 3.5 Sonnet			GPT-4o-mini		
Condition	Overall	Non-conv	Conv	Overall	Non-conv	Conv
NL	84.6	84.6	84.2	68.8	69.9	52.6
Logic	84.6	84.6	84.2	71.2	72.9	47.4
Linear	81.1	82.0	68.4	64.9	66.5	42.1
Euler	84.2	85.0	73.7	67.0	69.2	36.8

not consistently improve reasoning accuracy, in contrast to findings from human reasoning studies.

Regarding conversion problems, Claude 3.5 Sonnet shows only small differences between conversion and non-conversion cases in the NL and Logic conditions, whereas performance decreases under the diagrammatic conditions. GPT-4o-mini exhibits substantially larger gaps across all conditions, indicating stronger susceptibility to conversion-related reasoning errors.

Table 4 presents accuracy by syllogistic figure. Both models show systematic variation across figures, with Fig. 1 generally yielding the highest accuracy and Fig. 4 the lowest, consistent with the findings in human reasoning [6].

Table 5 reports accuracy across inference labels. For both models, entailment and contradiction cases are solved with high accuracy, whereas neutral cases are more difficult. This pattern is particularly pronounced for GPT-4o-mini, with accuracy on neutral cases below 30% across all conditions.

Table 4. Accuracy by syllogistic figure (%).

	Claude 3.5 Sonnet				GPT-4o-mini			
Condition	Fig. 1	Fig. 2	Fig. 3	Fig. 4	Fig. 1	Fig. 2	Fig. 3	Fig. 4
NL	91.3	80.0	89.8	82.7	89.1	66.7	69.5	58.7
Logic	93.5	82.9	88.1	78.7	82.6	70.5	78.0	60.0
Linear	91.3	79.0	89.8	70.7	73.9	66.7	74.6	49.3
Euler	91.3	81.0	94.9	76.0	87.0	64.8	66.1	58.7

We further analyze model performance across the three content types: *symbolic*, *congruent*, and *incongruent*. Table 6 summarizes accuracy across content types and representational conditions for both models.

Across models and conditions, performance generally decreases from symbolic to congruent and further to incongruent cases. For example, in the NL condition, Claude 3.5 Sonnet achieves 95.6% accuracy on symbolic problems, 85.8% on congruent problems, and 79.2% on incongruent problems. GPT-4o-mini shows a stronger drop, from 82.2% on symbolic problems to 56.7% on incongruent ones.

Table 5. Accuracy by inference label (%).

	Claude 3.5 Sonnet			GPT-4o-mini		
Condition	Entailment	Contradiction	Neutral	Entailment	Contradiction	Neutral
NL	97.9	92.6	63.2	81.1	100.0	25.3
Logic	98.9	92.6	62.1	86.3	100.0	27.4
Linear	97.9	96.8	48.4	78.9	96.8	18.9
Euler	95.8	100.0	56.8	82.1	98.9	20.0

Table 6. Accuracy by content type (%).

	Claude 3.5 Sonnet			GPT-4o-mini		
Condition	Symbolic	Congruent	Incongruent	Symbolic	Congruent	Incongruent
NL	95.6	85.8	79.2	82.2	75.8	56.7
Logic	86.7	87.5	80.8	73.3	74.2	67.5
Linear	86.7	83.3	76.7	68.9	68.3	60.0
Euler	91.1	85.0	80.8	75.6	72.5	58.3

Overall, these results suggest that model performance is sensitive to semantic plausibility. Problems with semantically implausible content (incongruent cases) are substantially more difficult for both models, and diagrammatic representations do not mitigate this decrease in performance.

5 Discussion

Our results provide several insights into the reasoning behavior of LLMs across different representational conditions.

Do Diagrams Help LLM Reasoning? A central question of this study was whether diagrammatic representations facilitate reasoning in LLMs in a manner similar to human cognition. In human reasoning, diagrams such as Euler diagrams or linear diagrams can externalize set relations and thereby support logical inference [5–7].

However, our results indicate that diagrammatic representations provide limited benefit for LLMs. Across both models, reasoning accuracy remains broadly similar across natural language, logical form, and diagrammatic conditions. In particular, neither linear diagrams nor Euler diagrams substantially improve performance compared to textual representations.

Our results also differ somewhat from those reported by Ando et al. [1], who found that Euler diagrams can improve LLM performance on the same validity-checking (VC) task. Since the experimental setup of the VC task is largely identical, one plausible explanation lies in differences between the models used in the two studies. This suggests that the effectiveness of diagrammatic representations for LLM reasoning may be highly model-dependent.

Reasoning Biases in LLMs. Although performance differences across formats are small, the models exhibit several systematic reasoning patterns.

First, both models show lower accuracy on conversion problems than on non-conversion problems (Table 3). The effect is particularly pronounced for GPT-4o-mini, but is also visible for Claude 3.5 Sonnet in the diagrammatic conditions. In human reasoning, diagrams are known to help prevent such errors by making the difference between statements such as *All A are B* and *All B are A* visually explicit. In contrast, we do not observe a comparable benefit for LLMs; for example, accuracy on conversion problems decreases under the Linear and Euler conditions for Claude 3.5 Sonnet, while GPT-4o-mini shows even larger conversion-related performance gaps in the diagrammatic conditions.

Second, both models show substantially lower accuracy on neutral problems than on entailment or contradiction (Table 5). Identifying neutral cases requires recognizing that a conclusion is neither logically implied nor incompatible with the premises, which appears to be considerably more difficult for current LLMs.

Third, performance decreases from symbolic to congruent and further to incongruent problems across both models and all conditions. Diagrammatic representations do not improve accuracy on incongruent cases, suggesting that model predictions depend more on semantic plausibility than on the structural relations expressed in the diagrams.

Implications for Diagrammatic Reasoning in LLMs. Taken together, our findings suggest that diagrammatic representations do not support LLM reasoning in the same way that they support human reasoning. While diagrams help humans by making set relations spatially explicit, LLMs appear able to extract sufficient relational information from textual or symbolic inputs alone.

More broadly, the results highlight a difference between human and machine reasoning. While diagrams support logical inference based on structural relations for humans, the LLMs we examined appear to rely more strongly on statistical patterns learned from textual data than on the spatial structure of diagrams.

6 Conclusion

This paper investigated whether diagrammatic representations improve syllogistic reasoning in LLMs. Using the validity-checking dataset introduced by Ando et al. [1], we compared four representational conditions: natural language, logical form, linear diagrams, and Euler diagrams.

Our results show that diagrammatic representations provide little advantage for current LLMs. Across two models, performance varies only modestly across representational conditions, with the diagrammatic conditions, particularly the Linear condition, yielding lower accuracy than NL or Logic. This contrasts with previous studies in human reasoning, where diagrams such as Euler diagrams and linear diagrams have been shown to facilitate syllogistic inference.

Our analysis also reveals systematic reasoning patterns in LLMs, including conversion errors and substantial difficulty with neutral inferences.

Future work may explore whether multimodal training or diagram-aware architectures could enable models to make better use of diagrammatic information.

Acknowledgment. We thank the anonymous reviewers for their helpful comments and suggestions, which have improved this paper. We also thank Kentaro Ozeki for providing valuable comments. This work was partially supported by JST CREST Grant Number JPMJCR2114, JST BOOST Grant Number JPMJBS2409 and JSPS KAKENHI Grant Number JP24K00004.

References

1. Ando, R., Ozeki, K., Morishita, T., Abe, H., Mineshima, K., Okada, M.: Can Euler diagrams improve syllogistic reasoning in large language models? In: International Conference on Theory and Application of Diagrams, pp. 232–248. Springer (2024)
2. Geurts, B.: Reasoning with quantifiers. Cognition **86**(3), 223–251 (2003)
3. Liu, H.: Visual instruction tuning. In: NeurIPS (2023)
4. OpenAI: GPT-4V system card (2023)
5. Sato, Y., Mineshima, K.: The efficacy of diagrams in syllogistic reasoning: a case of linear diagrams. In: Cox, P., Plimmer, B., Rodgers, P. (eds.) Diagrams 2012. LNCS (LNAI), vol. 7352, pp. 352–355. Springer, Heidelberg (2012). https://doi.org/10.1007/978-3-642-31223-6_49
6. Sato, Y., Mineshima, K.: How diagrams can support syllogistic reasoning: an experimental study. J. Logic Lang. Inform. **24**(4), 409–455 (2015)
7. Sato, Y., Mineshima, K., Takemura, R.: The efficacy of Euler and Venn diagrams in deductive reasoning: empirical findings. In: Goel, A.K., Jamnik, M., Narayanan, N.H. (eds.) Diagrams 2010. LNCS (LNAI), vol. 6170, pp. 6–22. Springer, Heidelberg (2010). https://doi.org/10.1007/978-3-642-14600-8_6
8. Shimojima, A.: Semantic Properties of Diagrams and Their Cognitive Potentials. CSLI Publications, Stanford, California (2015)
9. Stenning, K., Oberlander, J.: Diagrammatic reasoning. Cogn. Sci. **19**(2), 203–226 (1995)

Diagrams as a Service

Niklas Rentz[1], Maximilian Kasperowski[1(✉)], Reinhard von Hanxleden[1], Klara Modin[2], Samuel Miksits[2], Muhammad Afif Ramadhan[2], and Ingo Sander[2]

[1] Department of Computer Science, Kiel University, Kiel, Germany
{nre,mka,rvh}@informatik.uni-kiel.de
[2] KTH Royal Institute of Technology, Stockholm, Sweden
{smod,smiksits,ramad,ingo}@kth.se

Abstract. Diagrams are helpful tools serving as visual representations of structured program data and models in model-driven engineering (MDE). However, existing solutions to create diagrams programmatically are often constrained to specific programming languages or limited in the support for pragmatic and interactive features known from diagramming frameworks.

We here propose to provide *diagrams as a service*. The service is available through a web protocol. It provides a client that handles all diagram-related calculations for graph-based diagrams known from diagramming frameworks, including features such as automatic layout. JSON schemas for the diagram model and communication protocol facilitate automatic code generation and a direct connection to the service for custom diagram servers written in arbitrary programming languages. This enables interactive diagrams in any domain with established tooling.

We evaluate the service, which is provided through the open-source KIELER framework, with two custom server implementations. The first example is a prototype written in Python that showcases different features of the service. The second example presents ForSyDe, a textual modeling environment developed in Haskell for formal system design. ForSyDe utilizes the diagram service to automatically generate dataflow visualizations of their code in VS Code.

Keywords: Diagram Synthesis · Programming Language Agnostic · Communication Protocol · Diagramming Framework

1 Introduction

Traditionally, designers of programming languages and IDEs had to overcome a shared problem for scalability: For good language support in multiple IDEs, language designers had to integrate their language into multiple IDEs; for a versatile IDE with a good support of different programming languages, IDE designers had to integrate many languages into their IDE. As code editing in different languages often involves the same editing and navigation operations, a

P. Sobociński et al. (Eds.): Diagrams 2026, LNAI 16833, pp. 293–308, 2027.
https://doi.org/10.1007/978-3-032-34178-5_31

common interface between language designers and IDEs can solve this problem. The problem was solved with the introduction of the *Language Server Protocol* (LSP), as discussed by Bork and Lange [2]. With this standardized protocol, language designers only have to provide a single language server for their language; IDE designers only have to integrate the protocol features and implement a single language client. The LSP was a large success and disrupted the IDE and language design communities, so today both have widespread LSP support [2].

A similar problem and solution approach is also noticeable today in diagramming frameworks available for programmers in different programming languages. Many programmers want to work with diagrams, for example for model-driven engineering (MDE) or during reverse-engineering of existing code. However, there is no diagramming framework that can be programmatically used from arbitrary programming languages, so diagram designers are limited to simple exchange formats and frameworks available for their use case. Diagramming frameworks typically only provide a practical development interface for a few selected programming environments. Furthermore, simple exchange formats do not help here, as diagramming frameworks are required for pragmatic use of large diagrams. This includes features such as automatic layout, customizable styling and on-click interactions of graph elements, customizability for different level of detail renderings, and many more built-in optimizations for the diagrams' readability, scalability, and usability.

Contributions and Outline: This paper is a continuation to the paper about the KIELER diagramming framework [8] for graph-based diagrams. While the previous paper focused on the capabilities of the diagramming framework and the integration into specific modeling environments, in this paper we discuss how to generalize any diagramming framework to make it usable with arbitrary programming languages. We propose to answer the research question "**How can advancements of diagramming frameworks be applied to arbitrary domain-specific development environments?**" This paper first discusses the previous advancements and restrictions of related graph-based diagramming frameworks towards this question in Sect. 2. We then propose requirements for diagrams as a service (DaaS) and our concept for an implementation in Sect. 3. We evaluate the concept with our implementation in Sect. 4 and present a case study with one technical example showcasing the framework's features and one applied example for the textual programming environment ForSyDe, showcasing the evolution of a new diagram server. Finally, Sect. 5 discusses the results and concludes the paper.

2 Diagramming Framework Development Environments

Sprotty[1] is a low-level diagramming framework that adds specificity to graph-based diagrams (diagrams based on mathematical graphs, see Shahin *et al.* [19]). It enables the creation of domain-specific diagramming tools for any source model

[1] https://sprotty.org/.

with simple model-to-model (M2M) transformations with customizable interaction. Diagrams are created in a client-server architecture with a communication protocol that extends the LSP with diagram interactions. This communication protocol enables the creation of interactive diagrams rather than static diagrams that can be realized through various existing output formats. A benefit of this client-server architecture is the freedom to implement the server that synthesizes the diagram's graph structure in any programming language. However, the model rendering, styling, and custom interaction in Sprotty is required to be implemented in an extension of Sprotty's client in the JavaScript ecosystem, and a server development toolkit is only available for the Java and JavaScript ecosystems.

Rodriguez-Echeverria *et al.* propose the *Graphical Language Server Platform* (GLSP) as another approach to support graphical languages in a higher-level diagramming framework [15]. This framework ports the text-centric concepts of the LSP to diagrams using nodes and edges in a client-server architecture. The GLSP implements an extensible generic client and an application programming interface (API) for the communication of graphical modifications of domain-specific diagrams. The GLSP extends Sprotty and forwards its configurability and its full graph element styling customization on the client, but also contributes some pre-defined rendering primitives and server-configurable simple arrangements of those primitives within graph elements, which are subsequently automatically laid out and rendered on the client. However, they recommend defining more complex graph element styling and rendering in a custom client extension in the JavaScript ecosystem. Further domain-specific handling and interaction and the model-to-view transformation can be configured in the server. The default use case of the GLSP is a custom diagram application that extends this default behavior with custom diagram styling implemented in JavaScript and an M2M transformation implemented using the Java or the JavaScript development kit. Bork *et al.* also discuss their vision about flexible GLSP-based web modeling tools with requirements based on existing use cases [3].

The *KIELER* diagramming framework presented by Kasperowski *et al.* [8] also extends Sprotty and can be used for domain-specific diagrams, but has a few different core paradigms. For one, the GLSP uses the graph model as its fundamental model that allows for editing operations, often with hidden underlying source models in a diagram-first approach. In programmatic cases, KIELER views the (programmatic) source model as its ground truth and the generated transient diagrams as an artifact that stems from this source model [8]. The other different core paradigm is that KIELER does not expect its users to modify the client side for full customization of the diagrams, but that the client and its communication API already allow for arbitrarily complex renderings fully defined by the M2M transformation on the server. Therefore, the default use case of KIELER only requires a server that performs an M2M transformation, also called a *diagram synthesis*, and subsequently communicates its `KGraph` and `KRendering` structures to the client [17,18].

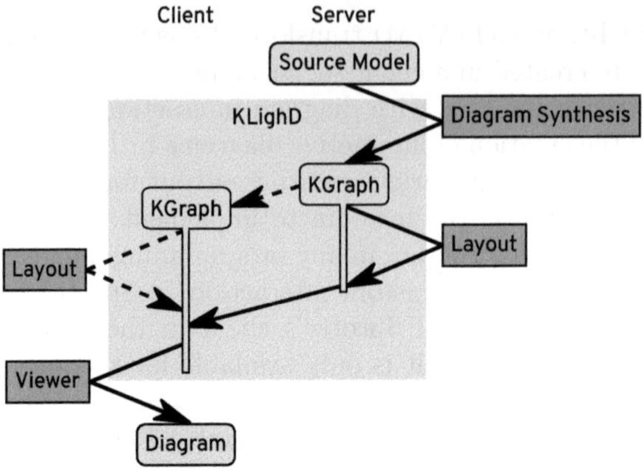

Fig. 1. The previous and new diagram generation paths.

The *KGraph* defines a directed graph to be automatically laid out by the Eclipse Layout Kernel (ELK) [4] in a step called *macro layout*. *KRenderings* and *KStyles* define the rendering primitives, their styling, and position constraints within graph elements. The layout of the rendering primitives within graph elements is called the *micro layout* of the graph. These layout steps are part of fully-automatic layout and were previously handled by the Java-based diagram server, even in its new web-based variant in KIELER [8]. This diagram generation path is illustrated in Fig. 1 by following the solid lines on the right side.

All of these three mentioned diagramming frameworks are established and have users in the scientific community. For example, BigER [6] and PASTA [13] implement tooling and use Sprotty directly. Indirect users of Sprotty via the GLSP are BigUML [12] and CINCO Cloud [1], and via the KIELER framework with SCCharts [7] and Lingua Franca [11]. However, these were only able to use the frameworks, because they are implemented in the Java and JavaScript ecosystems. Current users of diagramming frameworks from other programming languages are harder to come by, precisely because they have no such framework available.

3 Diagrams as a Service

To answer the research question, we first define the requirements for a diagramming framework in arbitrary development environments.

R1. The service should offer *pragmatic features of diagramming frameworks* for good usability and a rich feature set. This includes support for configurable automatic graph layout and the support for rich browsing and interaction techniques common to modern diagramming frameworks. Mechanisms to control and handle larger and more complex diagrams should also be considered for the scalability of the service. To simplify the API, such features should generally work without much configuration for the user in the source environment and have good defaults already implemented on the diagram framework application. Furthermore, this requirement includes a *powerful view model* that allows for arbitrarily complex renderings for each graph element. As the automatic graph layout may modify the absolute size of graph elements, this view model has to support flexible relative position constraints for the user.

R2. The diagram service needs to be *invokable from any programming language.* As it is infeasible to directly provide a framework with programmatic extensions in every programming language, the API of the diagram service can instead be defined as a communication protocol. This puts a first minor constraint on the source environment, it at least needs to be able to communicate with a framework application, for example via a socket connection.

R3. DaaS require *diagram modeling directly in the source environment.* There should be the functionality to create graphs and graph elements, rendering primitives and their configuration, and the communication structure. As this is specific to the source environment, it is also infeasible to provide this directly. However, there exist many code generators for such model code and communication structures from a JSON schema[2]. Using a JSON schema to define the communication API therefore automates the code generation to the source language for many programming languages, while at least providing a common and well-documented exchange format for those environments for which no code generators have been developed yet. Furthermore, using a common communication protocol such as the LSP further simplifies the integration of the communication protocol into the source environment.

R4. The diagram service needs to offer a *standalone application* to be generally applicable for any modeling environment. This application could also be embedded in other IDEs, but a standalone application that offers its own view is required so that no programmatic customization or configuration is necessary. The independent program using the service needs to be able to define view models from R1 with all configuration in its environment to avoid introducing another programming language into the custom diagram development.

If these requirements are fulfilled, the advancements of any particular diagramming framework can be applied to arbitrary domain-specific development environments, thus answering our research question. In practice, no current diagramming framework fulfills all requirements yet. For example, Sprotty is a low-level diagramming framework and does not fulfil R1. Both GLSP and KIELER extend Sprotty and have a larger set of pragmatic features, so they both partially fulfil R1 and would be a good basis to also support DaaS. However, the configurability of GLSP's communicated view model is limited to selected pre-defined renderings and is not as versatile as KIELER's view model, while the previous implementation of KIELER did not yet fully support client-based layout. R2 is generally supported by all presented options, as they are all based on the LSP

[2] A list of tools for JSON schemas is available at https://json-schema.org/tools.

communication supported by Sprotty. Sprotty and GLSP have a view model that does not fully define all renderings and therefore require client customization, which violates R3. The main use case of KIELER only requires customization in the diagram synthesis on the custom server, in accordance with R3. GLSP also supports some default renderings and style customization from the server, so it also technically meets R3, albeit it is not its intended main use case. A standalone client application for R4 is only offered by KIELER, but GLSP also offers a standalone package that could be bundled into a standalone application with low effort. In conclusion, KIELER and GLSP can technically be the basis for DaaS. For this paper, we chose to solve the remaining technical issues in KIELER and to provide an open-source communication API and a JSON schema for the possibility of language-independent model code generation.

3.1 Communication API for Diagrams as a Service

Fig. 2 illustrates the current architecture of KIELER as presented before [8], here with a focus on the CLI product that is required with R4. The framework offers web-based diagrams that communicate with a language server based on the KIELER Lightweight Diagrams (KLighD) subproject via Sprotty actions. KLighD integrates macro layout via ELK and features micro layout, while offering an abstract synthesis API to create diagrams programmatically in Java. We now propose to move the macro and micro layout from the Java server to the diagram client, modify the communication protocol accordingly, and use this protocol as the new API for diagram generation with the KIELER framework as illustrated in Fig. 3 to fulfil R1 and R2.

The proposed communication API extends the LSP and Sprotty's action messages. Its current version is available on GitHub[3] and may change in future releases of the software. For brevity, this paper only highlights a few selected modifications to the default LSP and Sprotty protocol.

For the basic diagram generation loop, KIELER reuses Sprotty's messages. We directly map the `KGraph` model onto Sprotty's `SGraph` model used in these messages. For the configuration of diagram synthesis options [8] cached on the client and other preferences, the protocol adds new parameters containing that information during the default LSP `initialize` message and adds the new LSP message `setPreferences`.

Other additional messages are for KIELER's pragmatic and scalability features and other technical aspects. Most pragmatic features can be utilized via properties in the `KGraph` and `KRendering` models and therefore do not directly require new messages. The other features with additional communication include but are not limited to

- basic diagram generation loop extensions for the possibility for different diagram syntheses for the same model with the `setSyntheses` message,

[3] https://github.com/kieler/klighd-vscode/wiki/Diagram-Server-Communication-%E2%80%90-Architectural-Overview.

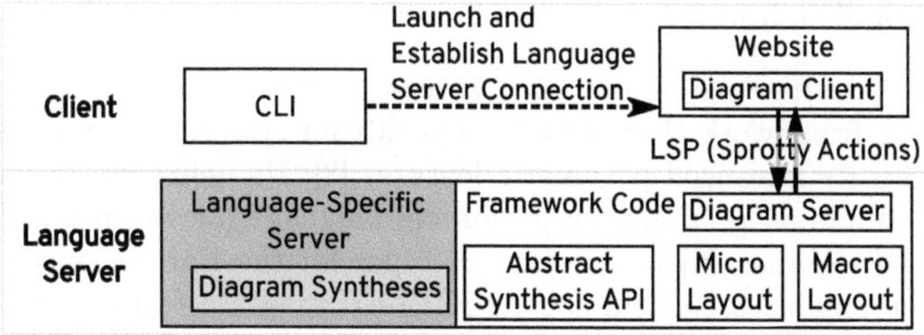

Fig. 2. The general KIELER diagram architecture with Java-based servers [8].

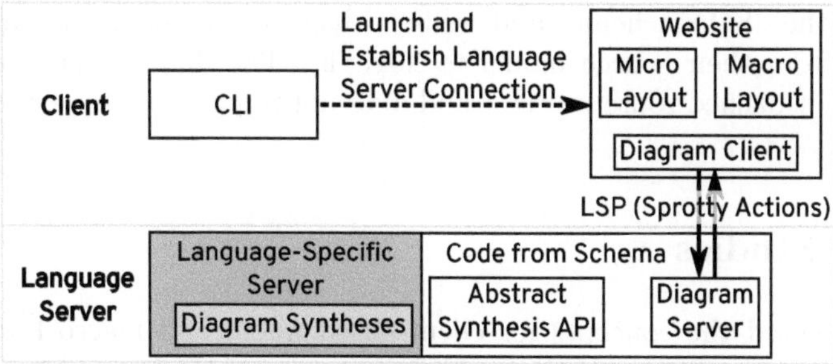

Fig. 3. The new diagram framework architecture for arbitrary diagram servers.

- custom options for the options sidebar with the `updateOptions` message, and
- client caching of pre-rendered images nested in the diagram with the `check-Images`, `checkedImages`, and `storeImages` messages.

KIELER-specific features also include messages for

- an incremental diagram generator with the `requestDiagramPiece` and `set-DiagramPiece` messages (following Sprotty's naming for the `requestModel` and `setModel` messages),
- custom action code execution on the server to modify or highlight something in the diagram or other side effects with the `performAction` message, and
- actions from the diagram sidebar, such as `setSynthesis` and `setSynthesis-Options`.

Next to the CLI hosting a website, there is a VS Code integration of KIELER diagrams [8]. This way, users of text-based models or programming languages with an automatically synthesized KIELER diagram can also edit and visualize their programs side-by-side with synchronization and navigation between the models from Sprotty. This integration does not change the diagram API, so any server working with the standalone CLI can also communicate with the VS Code extension. However, the integration requires a simple VS Code extension written in JavaScript that registers the language server and the textual sources to provide KIELER diagrams directly in VS Code.

3.2 Protocol Schema for Code Generation

Next to the communication API, we propose a JSON schema for the KIELER diagramming framework that contains the `KGraph` and `KRendering` structures and types for its advanced pragmatic features [8]. Its definition is available on GitHub[4] and lets users of any programming language for which a code generator for JSON schemas exists generate all types for the LSP messages, common Sprotty functionalities, and all special KIELER diagram features, models, and the messages, see Fig. 3. With this change, KIELER also fulfills R3. An application that uses KIELER diagrams now only needs to extend a plain language server for their programming language, generate the model and communication code from the JSON schema, and write a diagram synthesis (an M2M transformation from their source model to `KGraph`). The diagram generation then takes the new dashed route in Fig. 1 and does not require any further server-side calculations.

4 Case Studies

We implemented the concepts for client-based micro and macro layout in the KIELER diagram client. The last remaining parts of the micro layout are currently being ported from their Java implementation to the JavaScript client and the complete model layout from R1 is therefore not fully fulfilled yet, but we already validated the proposed new tool chain with two diagram projects. First, we implemented a proof-of-concept Python diagram server that shows how most pragmatic features of the KIELER diagramming framework work with the new schema and communication API. Next, we integrated a diagram server for a new visualization of specific ForSyDe models next to its compiler written in Haskell. These case studies show that a diagramming framework that fulfills all requirements listed above is powerful enough so that it is practical to use its pragmatic diagramming features in other programming languages.

4.1 Proof of Concept Example: Python

The Plyghd diagram server[5] is a language server extension that serves as a demonstrator that implements the proposed basic communication protocol in Python. It shows a working example for a KIELER diagram server that does not use a single line of Java or JavaScript code. The example implements a dummy diagram synthesis and examples for KIELER diagramming framework features such as diagram options and custom executable actions that are synchronized between client and server via the API. The entire communication API and the graph and rendering structure were generated from the JSON schema using the `datamodel-code-generator`[6] Python package .

[4] https://github.com/kieler/klighd-vscode/tree/main/schema.

[5] https://github.com/kieler/plyghd-ls-demonstrator.

[6] https://github.com/koxudaxi/datamodel-code-generator.

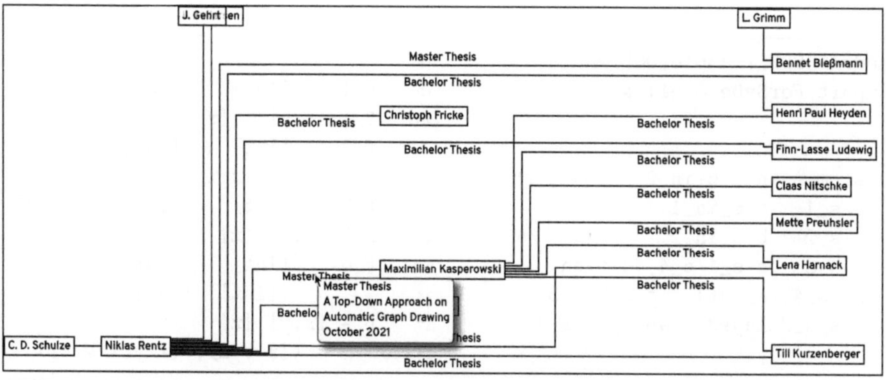

Fig. 4. A cutout of the thesis supervision relationships at Kiel University around the first authors of this paper.

We also utilized this demonstrator for a practical use case to generate a new visualization. The Real-Time and Embedded Systems working group from Kiel University advised at least 191 theses of different graduates since 2003. As each thesis was supervised by one or multiple people, often prior graduates of the same working group, the thesis supervision relationships induce a directed acyclic graph, which can be represented in a layered graph drawing [20]. Figure 4 shows a cutout of a diagram for that graph generated by a diagram server based on Plyghd. The diagram highlights a few pragmatic and navigational features of the KIELER diagramming framework. This includes proxies of otherwise off-screen nodes shown on the edges leaving the viewport at the top and left border and a text box that appears on hover. Other special features not shown in this image but featured by the demonstrator include custom key renderings for continuous level of detail renderings adapting the zoom level of the view and custom semantic tags for filtering and searching in the diagram.

4.2 Applied Example: ForSyDe

Formal System Design (ForSyDe) [16] is a design methodology for heterogeneous embedded systems. The starting point of the design process is a system model specifying the functionality of the system to be designed. Systems are modeled at a high level of abstraction as executable concurrent process networks with a well-defined semantics based on the tagged-signal model [10]. ForSyDe provides methods and tools for converting the initial system model into an efficient implementation consisting of hardware and software. ForSyDe-Shallow is a modeling library written in the functional programming language Haskell, utilizing Haskell's lazy evaluation for simulation to schedule the models dynamically. Synchronous dataflow (SDF) [9] is one of the models of computation supported by ForSyDe-Shallow, where each process takes a fixed number of tokens from input signals and produces a fixed number of tokens to output signals during each

```
1  module SDF_example_002 where
2  import ForSyDe.Shallow
3
4  -- Netlist
5  system s_in_1 s_in_2 = s_out where
6      s_1 = a s_in_1
7      s_2 = b s_in_2
8      s_3 = c s_1 s_4_delayed
9      (s_4, s_out) = d s_2 s_3
10     s_4_delayed = delay_1 s_4
11
12 -- Process/actor specifications
13 a = actor11SDF 2 1 f_1
14 b = actor11SDF 1 2 f_2
15 c = actor21SDF (2, 1) 1 f_3
16 d = actor22SDF (2, 1) (1, 2) f_4
17 delay_1 = delaySDF [0]
18 -- Function definitions
19 f_1 :: [Int] -> [Int]
20 f_1 [x,y] = [x+y]
21 f_2 :: [Int] -> [Int]
22 f_2 [x] = [x,x+1]
23 f_3 :: [Int] -> [Int] -> [Int]
24 f_3 [x,y] [z] = [x+y+z]
25 f_4 :: [Int] -> [Int]
26     -> ([Int], [Int])
27 f_4 [x,y] [z]
28     = ([x+y+z], [x+y,x+y+z])
```

Listing 1. ForSyDe sdf model as textual representation.

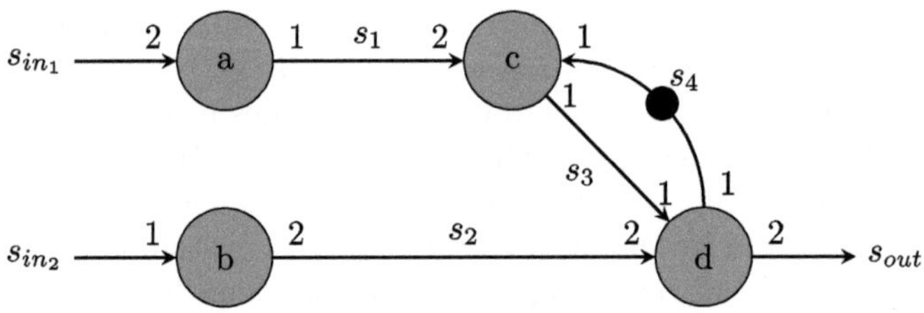

Fig. 5. Graphical representation of ForSyDe SDF system model (List. 1), manually drawn with Ti*k*Z.

firing. Given a valid and schedulable SDF model, a static and periodic schedule with fixed buffer sizes can be derived [9].

List. 1 shows a textual and executable ForSyDe system model. The model uses the SDF subset of the ForSyDe-Shallow modeling library. The model can be visualized as an SDF graph as illustrated in Fig. 5. The model contains four actors (`a`, `b`, `c`, `d`), one delay element (`delay_1`), two input signals (`s_in_1`, `s_in_2`), and one output signal (`s_out`). The delay element, modeled using the `delaySDF` constructor (Line 17), contains an initial token and is depicted as black dot on the edge s_4 in Fig. 5. An actor constitutes a ForSyDe process. Processes are created using process constructors, like `actor11SDF` on Line 13, which together with production and consumption rates and a function argument form a process. Processes communicate via signals. The process network is formed by a netlist defining the topology of the system model. The netlist specifies how processes communicate with other processes via signals (Lines 5–10). The actor's consumption rates are shown on the input edges, and the production rates are shown on the output edges in Fig. 5.

Since the system model forms the entry point for the system design process, it is key that the system model is correct and fully understood by industrial designers. Although the ForSyDe SDF model in List. 1 is well-structured, industrial embedded designers are, in general, not familiar with the underlying functional paradigm, and would benefit a lot from a visualization of the source code in the form of an informative diagram such as Fig. 5. Furthermore, a visualization can show additional information not directly available in the source code, such as required buffer sizes for the signals, using the available analysis methods for SDF [9].

Currently, there is no automatic tool which can visualize ForSyDe SDF models, so they have to be generated manually from the source code. The ForSyDe DevTools project[7] was formed to develop additional tool support for system design in ForSyDe with two goals: (1) to develop a compiler for generating C code from ForSyDe-Shallow SDF models, and (2) to develop a visualizer in the form of interactive diagrams created from the intermediate results of the compiler. The focus in this applied example is on the visualization tool using the proposed DaaS approach, where the tool integrates directly with the compiler. The integration with the compiler has the advantage that the visualization tool can show additional information not present in the input model, but derived by the compiler.

The pragmatic features and the powerful view model of R1 can be further specified for ForSyDe:

R1.1 *Real-time diagram updates*: The tool is intended to be used while writing the textual model as an aid in showing the current structure. The diagram should therefore reflect any changes in the source model as it is modified.

R1.2 *Diagram interaction*: The tool should not only display the diagram, but also link diagram elements back to the source model through diagram interaction.

R1.3 *Information from compilation steps*: The compiler computes information that is not present in the source model, such as required signal buffer sizes and a schedule. This information should be utilized and displayed in the diagram.

To check the feasibility of the approach, the ForSyDe SDF system model of List. 1 was manually transformed into the diagram sketch shown in Fig. 6 using the `KGraph` and `KRendering` structures. This experiment shows that KIELER can generate diagrams that have all the elements needed to represent SDF models visually. However, this initial sketch does not yet match the envisioned one in Fig. 5, and needs further configuration. In particular, there are additional requirements that can be formulated from the differences between the envisioned one and the sketch:

[7] See the results of the project at https://github.com/sthaeron/forsyde-devtools.

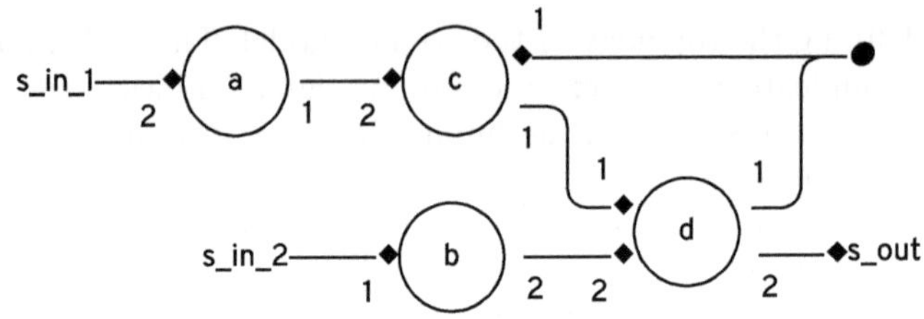

Fig. 6. SDF diagram manually modeled with KIELER.

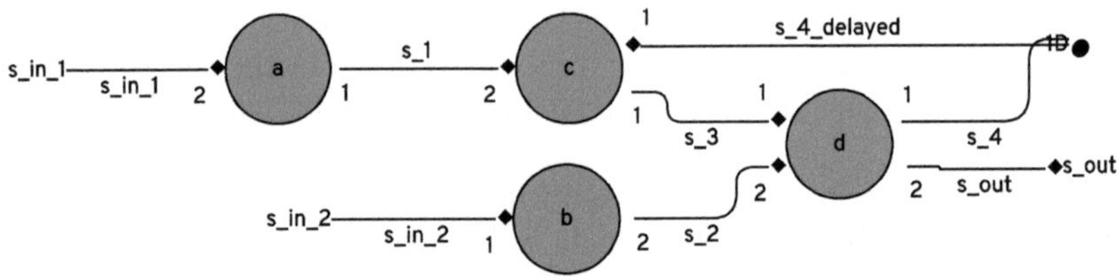

Fig. 7. SDF diagram automatically synthesized with KIELER (prototype tool).

R1.4 *Rendering and layout of delay elements*: In the ForSyDe source model (as seen in List. 1), delay elements are connected via signals similar to processes. However, initial tokens should appear as symbols on the edges and not be rendered as nodes, and connected by separate signals.

R1.5 *Layout of input and output signals*: To distinguish input and output signals from internal signals, they should originate from the left and right borders of the diagram.

A huge benefit of the DaaS approach is that the server does not need to perform the detailed layout. However, as a consequence, the server lacks full control over the layout process, although some constraints or ordering of elements [5] in the `KGraph` can be used to guide it. This means the output diagrams may not be the exact same as the envisioned one from Fig. 5, depending on the configuration of the automatic layout.

The first prototype tool (Fig. 7) focused on automating the synthesis, but not primarily on resolving graphical issues. To enable automatic synthesis, the compiler generates an internal representation (ForSyDe IR) from the ForSyDe SDF model. The ForSyDe IR is already similar to a graph with processes mapping to nodes and signals mapping to edges. Some graphical issues were also resolved at this point, such as adding labels to intermediary signals and node coloring.

The final design iteration (Fig. 8) focused on developing a tool compliant with the DaaS vision in Fig. 3 as well as resolving the graphical issues and new requirements in R1.4 and R1.5. It follows the architecture shown in Fig. 9. Haskell has good support for both JSON and the language server protocol, meaning that it was relatively easy to implement the communication protocol. This shows that R2 is fulfilled for the Haskell programming language. At the time of development, a satisfactory JSON schema to Haskell type generator was not identified, and the

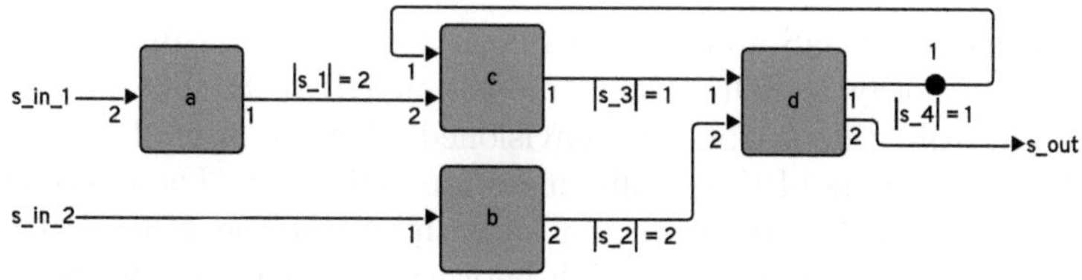

Fig. 8. SDF diagram automatically synthesized with KIELER (final tool).

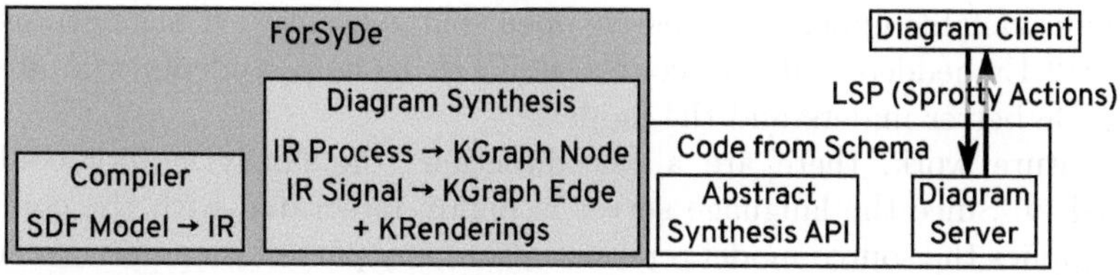

Fig. 9. Simplified ForSyDe language server architecture communicating with the diagram client from Fig. 3.

API types were instead implemented manually. Even though this code synthesis was not automatic, it still fulfills R3 because the types could be implemented from the JSON schema.

The different graphical issues and requirements R1.4 and R1.5 from Fig. 6 and still present in Fig. 7 were resolved in the final diagram in Fig. 8 using various preferences of KIELER and ELK, such as port side constraints, node placement constraints, and rectangular node rendering instead of a circular one.

With the new architecture of Fig. 9 where the language server is integrated into the compiler project, it is easier to invoke different parts of the compiler, such as the schedule and buffer size calculation. This addresses requirement R1.3 and enables the visualization of required buffer sizes in the diagram. This information, shown as e.g. `|s_1| = 2` in Fig. 8, notifies the designer that a correct implementation of the SDF system model requires at least a buffer of size 2 on the signal s_1.

Since ForSyDe models are text-based, it is beneficial to provide additional integration with IDEs. This ties back to requirements R1.1, real time diagram updates, and R1.2, diagram interaction. The ForSyDe diagram server was integrated into a new simple VS Code extension to operate in conjunction with the KIELER diagram extension. The real-time diagram generation is accomplished using standard LSP messages as implemented in the VS Code LSP client, which can be configured to send notifications once the source file is updated. The diagram interaction is achieved through messages sent by the KIELER diagram VS Code extension when elements in the diagram are selected. This enables tracing the element identifier back to the source model, and a reply with a message detailing which part of the source text model should be highlighted in VS Code can be sent.

In summary, the DaaS approach has been used to successfully implement a visualization of ForSyDe SDF system models in KIELER. The final ForSyDe SDF diagram still differs from the envisioned diagram from Fig. 5 in a few aspects, however, many of these differences are deliberate. The envisioned diagram (Fig. 5) uses TeX typesetting for subscripts, but the generated diagram (Fig. 8) does not, to keep the direct link between the source model and the diagram. The implementation serves as an example of how the new DaaS approach can be used and shows that the API and resulting diagrams are usable. The tool is publicly available under a permissive open source license[8]. It has been used in the IL2212 Embedded Software course at KTH, to help students who are new to ForSyDe better understand the models.

For future work, there are a few directions the ForSyDe tool could be expanded in. Since the language server is highly integrated with the compiler, which supplies the source model representation, any part of it can be invoked by the language server. It would be useful to display further general information, such as whether a schedule can be created from the model, and the respective schedule itself. There are also directions which would need more support from the compiler, such as supporting different models of computation and their combination in the same model, and visualizing simulation results in the diagram.

5 Conclusion

The usability of any software relates not only to the questions about the user experience, but also to whether users can use the software in their context at all. Interactive diagrams in the previous Eclipse-based KIELER framework were only usable in a single IDE, while the web-based implementation [8] opened it up for the VS Code IDE and provided the stepping stone for further usability. This paper advances that web-based implementation to be usable from arbitrary sources through a communication protocol and a JSON schema for automatic code generation in many programming languages. Furthermore, projects explained in the paper that did use early versions of the API show the relevance of an open diagram service for arbitrary programming languages. The KIELER diagram client and its communication protocol fulfil the requirements for diagram servers in arbitrary programming languages and face the challenge of modeling in arbitrary languages with a JSON schema. Furthermore, the applied ForSyDe example shows a novel visualization using the KIELER diagram service. Its use-case-specific requirements for their new diagrams and visions for future enhancements are fulfilled as well. This suggests our general requirements are sufficient, and highlights how diagramming frameworks such as KIELER and its new service can offer more than just a plain diagram view, but an interactive development environment for text-based models as well.

In conclusion, we can answer our stated research question how advancements of diagramming frameworks can be applied to arbitrary domain-specific development environments: The initial requirements discussed above need to be ful-

[8] https://github.com/sthaeron/forsyde-devtools.

filled by frameworks that want to offer DaaS, which we demonstrated with the KIELER framework. This links back to the core idea of the LSP: we offer a communication protocol and a web-based client that can be embedded in any environment, so that users can implement their own server in any language, now applied to graph-based diagrams.

Acknowledgments. The ForSyDe visualizer would not have been possible without the contributions of Michel Delli Abo, Sebastian Thaeron, and Zicong Zhang who worked on the compiler within the ForSyDe DevTools project.

Data Availability Statement. Next to the public GitHub repositories, the schema, communication API and the example code are available in an open data repository [14].

References

1. Bainczyk, A., et al.: CINCO cloud: a holistic approach for web-based language-driven engineering. In: Margaria, T., Steffen, B. (eds.) Leveraging Applications of Formal Methods, Verification and Validation. Software Engineering, pp. 407–425. Springer Nature Switzerland, Cham (2022)
2. Bork, D., Langer, P.: Language Server Protocol: An introduction to the protocol, its use, and adoption for web modeling tools. Enterp. Model. Inf. Syst. Architect. (EMISAJ) **18**(9), 1–16 (2023). https://doi.org/10.18417/emisa.18.9
3. Bork, D., Langer, P., Ortmayr, T.: A vision for flexible GLSP-based web modeling tools. In: Almeida, J.P.A., Kaczmarek-Heß, M., Koschmider, A., Proper, H.A. (eds.) The Practice of Enterprise Modeling (PoEM) - Proceedings of the 16th IFIP Working Conference. Lecture Notes in Business Information Processing, vol. 497, pp. 109–124. Springer (2023). https://doi.org/10.1007/978-3-031-48583-1_7
4. Domrös, S., von Hanxleden, R., Spönemann, M., Rüegg, U., Schulze, C.D.: The eclipse layout kernel (2023). https://doi.org/10.48550/arXiv.2311.00533
5. Domrös, S., Riepe, M., von Hanxleden, R.: Model order in Sugiyama layouts. In: Proceedings of the 18th International Joint Conference on Computer Vision, Imaging and Computer Graphics Theory and Applications (VISIGRAPP 2023) - Volume 3: IVAPP, pp. 77–88. INSTICC, SciTePress (2023). https://doi.org/10.5220/0011656700003417
6. Glaser, P.L., Bork, D.: The bigER tool - hybrid textual and graphical modeling of entity relationships in VS Code. In: 2021 IEEE 25th International Enterprise Distributed Object Computing Workshop (EDOCW), pp. 337–340. IEEE (2021)
7. von Hanxleden, R., et al.: SCCharts: sequentially constructive statecharts for safety-critical applications. In: Proc. ACM SIGPLAN Conference on Programming Language Design and Implementation (PLDI '14), pp. 372–383. ACM, Edinburgh, UK (2014). https://doi.org/10.1145/2594291.2594310
8. Kasperowski, M., Rentz, N., Domrös, S., von Hanxleden, R.: KIELER: a text-first framework for automatic diagramming of complex systems. In: Proceedings of the 14th International Conference on the Theory and Application of Diagrams, DIAGRAMS '24. LNCS, vol. 14981, pp. 402–418. Springer Nature Switzerland (2024). https://doi.org/10.1007/978-3-031-71291-3_33
9. Lee, E.A., Messerschmitt, D.G.: Synchronous data flow. In: Proceedings of the IEEE, vol. 75, pp. 1235–1245. IEEE Computer Society Press (1987). https://doi.org/10.1109/PROC.1987.13876

10. Lee, E.A., Sangiovanni-Vincentelli, A.: A framework for comparing models of computation. IEEE Trans. Comput. Aided Des. Integr. Circuits Syst. **17**(12), 1217–1229 (1998). https://doi.org/10.1109/43.736561
11. Lohstroh, M., Menard, C., Bateni, S., Lee, E.A.: Toward a Lingua Franca for deterministic concurrent systems. ACM Trans. Embed. Comput. Syst. (TECS) **20**(4), Article 36 (2021). https://doi.org/10.1145/3448128
12. Metin, H., Bork, D.: On developing and operating GLSP-based web modeling tools: lessons learned from bigUML. In: 2023 ACM/IEEE 26th International Conference on Model Driven Engineering Languages and Systems (MODELS), pp. 129–139. IEEE (2023). https://doi.org/10.1109/MODELS58315.2023.00031
13. Petzold, J., Kreiß, J., von Hanxleden, R.: PASTA: pragmatic automated system-theoretic process analysis. In: 53rd Annual IEEE/IFIP International Conference on Dependable Systems and Network, DSN 2023, pp. 559–567. IEEE, Porto, Portugal (2023). https://doi.org/10.1109/DSN58367.2023.00058
14. Rentz, N., et al.: Diagrams as a service paper material. Kiel University Research Data Repository opendata@uni-kiel (2026). https://doi.org/10.57892/100-340
15. Rodriguez-Echeverria, R., Izquierdo, J.L.C., Wimmer, M., Cabot, J.: Towards a language server protocol infrastructure for graphical modeling. In: Proceedings of the 21th ACM/IEEE International Conference on Model Driven Engineering Languages and Systems, pp. 370–380. MODELS '18, ACM, New York, NY, USA (2018). https://doi.org/10.1145/3239372.3239383
16. Sander, I., Jantsch, A., Attarzadeh-Niaki, S.H.: ForSyDe: system design using a functional language and models of computation, pp. 99–140. Springer Netherlands, Dordrecht (2017). https://doi.org/10.1007/978-94-017-7267-9_5
17. Schneider, C., Spönemann, M., von Hanxleden, R.: Transient view generation in eclipse. In: Proceedings of the First Workshop on Academics Modeling with Eclipse. Kgs. Lyngby, Denmark (2012)
18. Schneider, C., Spönemann, M., von Hanxleden, R.: Just model! – putting automatic synthesis of node-link-diagrams into practice. In: Proceedings of the IEEE Symposium on Visual Languages and Human-Centric Computing (VL/HCC '13), pp. 75–82. IEEE, San Jose, CA, USA (2013). https://doi.org/10.1109/VLHCC.2013.6645246
19. Shahin, M., Liang, P., Ali Babar, M.: A systematic review of software architecture visualization techniques. J. Syst. Softw. **94**, 161–185 (2014). https://doi.org/10.1016/j.jss.2014.03.071
20. Sugiyama, K., Tagawa, S., Toda, M.: Methods for visual understanding of hierarchical system structures. IEEE Trans. Syst. Man Cybern. **11**(2), 109–125 (1981). https://doi.org/10.1109/TSMC.1981.4308636

Pragmatic and Semantic Search in Diagrams

Maximilian Kasperowski(✉), Niklas Rentz, and Reinhard von Hanxleden

Department of Computer Science, Kiel University, Kiel, Germany
{mka,nre,rvh}@informatik.uni-kiel.de

Abstract. Textual search is a widely accepted and implemented user interaction in software development and maintenance. However, model driven engineering typically involves creating and viewing *graphical* models. As these models become larger, a search functionality becomes beneficial. However, many existing diagramming tools do not integrate a search function.

We here propose supporting pragmatic text-based search in diagramming tools. We propose a *semantic search* utilizing the diagram's underlying graph and its embedded semantic information. Our approach builds upon and enhances the pragmatic modeling approach and is realized in the open-source KIELER project.

We performed a user study comparing the performance of participants in information extraction tasks on domain-specific diagrams where participants were given either only pan-and-zoom or additionally a search function. Participants reported that they felt the search made the tasks easier and that they enjoyed using it. We also found that using the search function made tasks significantly faster.

Keywords: Diagrams · Pragmatics · Search · Model-driven engineering

1 Introduction

In model-driven engineering (MDE), diagrams are typically an important tool in the modeling process. There are different approaches such as the *text-first* [7] and *diagram-first* [9] paradigms. The text-first paradigm realizes the *modeling pragmatics* concept [4]. In particular, using modeling tools should feel seamless to developers and improve their productivity.

A central feature available in tools across many domains is a *search* function. In any context where the size of the document becomes larger than can be sensibly displayed in a readable manner and grasped at once by users, a search feature becomes useful. If the user has a notion of *what* they are looking for, the search can very quickly help them find the *where*. For many people nowadays textual search has become second nature and is integral to many workflows, be it searching the internet, scanning text documents, or searching large codebases.

P. Sobociński et al. (Eds.): Diagrams 2026, LNAI 16833, pp. 309–325, 2027.
https://doi.org/10.1007/978-3-032-34178-5_32

The Ctrl+F—or, in macOS, Cmd+F—shortcut for the search command is one of the few shortcuts that is available across a wide range of tools, and it appears to be one of the first shortcuts that users memorize and use frequently. However, despite this clear helpfulness of search and the ubiquity of search functionality, tools for modeling diagrams currently do not have strong search support yet.

The work presented here aims to close this gap with a search concept that is applicable to both text-first and diagram-first applications. We demonstrate the search concept with an extension to the existing text-first KIELER framework [7]. KIELER uses graph-based node-link diagrams [11], but the concepts we propose are applicable to other types of diagrams as well.

One of the goals of pragmatic modeling is that different views of a model should feel as though they represent the same model. This aims to strengthen the mental map of the user. Search provides an interaction mechanism that further enhances the connectedness between textual source, diagram, and mental map.

We aim to answer the following research questions:

- **RQ1** Does an automatic textual search facilitate fast solving of typical diagram tasks?
- **RQ2** How do users' perceptions relate to their actual task performance?

Contributions and Outline

In Sec. 2, we discuss existing modeling tools and search implementations. We then discuss how to implement a textual search for diagrams in Sec. 3, and how this can be extended using a logic-based graph query language in Sec. 4. In Sec. 5, we present the integration of the concepts in the KIELER diagramming framework. We distinguish between *pragmatic search*, which is a diagram-agnostic textual search applicable to any type of diagram containing text, and *semantic search*, which is diagram-specific and allows construction of more advanced queries. We verify its pragmatics with a small user study in Sec. 6 and conclude the paper in Sec. 7.

2 Related Work

The pragmatic modeling approach aims to enhance developer productivity by combining the best of textual and graphical worlds [4]. A core principle of this is to have automatically generated diagrams of the model. The textual source and the diagram have to feel connected so that developers have a single mental map of the model in their mind while working on it. Here, we will focus on the diagrams but with the goal of augmenting pragmatic modeling.

2.1 Searching in Diagrams

In diagrams symbols are indexed in two-dimensional space [8]. Winn suggests this makes it easier to search for information in diagrams than in text. "..., once the first piece of information has been found, the next useful piece of information will be in an adjacent location." [13] This suggests that a search tool must help in finding this first piece of information to provide the greatest benefit.

An everyday example of diagrams that people search are maps, and in particular digital maps. Nivala *et al.* have previously evaluated different digital maps and their search functionalities and used this to develop design guidelines for mapping software [10]. There were typically two types of search, a free search box, where users could type in anything, and search forms with multiple search boxes for different types of things. On maps users typically search for places or routes between places. Our vision for search in diagrams is similar to searching for places in maps with additional filtering options to narrow the search.

An important part of the search is the presentation of the results. While working with diagrams users build a mental map of the diagram. It is important that the presentation and ordering of the search results aligns with this mental map. In particular the reading direction, *e.g.,* left-to-right or right-to-left, can have an impact on spatial mapping and needs to be considered [12]. The diagrams we use are designed for left-to-right readers and in our study we restricted ourselves to such participants.

2.2 Diagramming Tools

There are several other MDE tools and diagramming frameworks that focus on similar use cases as the KIELER framework.

The Graphical Language Server Platform (GLSP) is a diagramming framework that uses the same technological foundations as KIELER but follows a diagram-first paradigm instead of the text-first paradigm of KIELER [9]. To our knowledge, the GLSP does not offer a method to search in their diagrams, however, there is a searchbar for the diagram editing palette.

Sirius Desktop and the newer Sirius Web are language workbenches, which allow easy development of domain-specific languages (DSLs) using graphical modeling [3]. Another web-based modeling tool that uses diagrams is JJodel [1]. For both Sirius and JJodel we also found no mention of the ability to search directly in the diagrams.

Diagrams have to reach a certain size for a search function to become helpful, so a reason for not including such a feature could simply be that it is not beneficial for the specific domain. From our experience, although most used diagrams are small, there are always some very large diagrams, which are too large to grasp without help by the diagramming framework. Precisely for these large diagrams we argue that a search feature is beneficial.

3 Textual Search in Diagrams

Although there are many graphs and diagrams that contain no text, the applications of diagrams in MDE generally make use of textual information in the diagrams, *e.g.,* to name nodes or to attach labels to edges. In general, text can be an important component of a diagram, describing the model and providing meaning and context to the graph. The drawn nodes and links concisely show relationships between model elements. Such diagrams provide developers with a powerful tool to understand models. To find a piece of information in a diagram not easily found by visual cues alone, a natural mechanism is to use natural language to express what is being searched for. Textual search ties into this. The most direct method is to search for keywords known to be in the diagram, *i.e.*, names of elements, descriptions, or other labels attached to graph elements.

Textual search is commonly applied to large bodies of text, *e.g.*, a plain text document, a PDF document, or a rendered HTML website. In these cases, the underlying format and document structure is different and needs to be taken into account, but they are all essentially linear passages of texts.

For diagrams, search cannot rely on existing search tooling, *e.g.*, in web browsers, as the rendered diagram may not necessarily contain all searchable elements. Any search tool must have access to the diagram's internal representation and thus be integrated into the diagramming framework directly.

The diagrams we consider are two-dimensional embeddings of graphs. We support *nested graphs*, where nodes can contain further subgraphs representing individual layers of hierarchy. To implement an effective search we need to solve two problems.

1. How can the relevant texts from the graph be extracted for the search?
2. What graph traversal order yields a sensible ordering of search results?

3.1 Search Results

During the search we check texts and perform substring matching to identify a search match. The search result is the graph element that contains the matching text. Text editors with integrated search often include more advanced text matching methods. For example, Visual Studio Code (VS Code) supports entering regular expressions and toggleable case sensitivity in its search.

Once the search has been performed, the results have to be presented to the user. The first way to present the results is to highlight them directly in the document. This gives users an immediate visual cue where to look. A diagram search should also add highlights directly in the diagram. These highlights can be applied to texts or to entire graph elements.

Search interfaces designed for large documents, often also present a dedicated view showing a summary of the search results. This allows stepping through the search results and automatically jumping to the corresponding location in the document. This view can also be used to communicate additional information about the search results to the user, such as the type of the found graph element.

3.2 Result Ordering

When stepping through the search results, the order should be consistent with the positions of the search matches in the graph. I.e., the order of the result

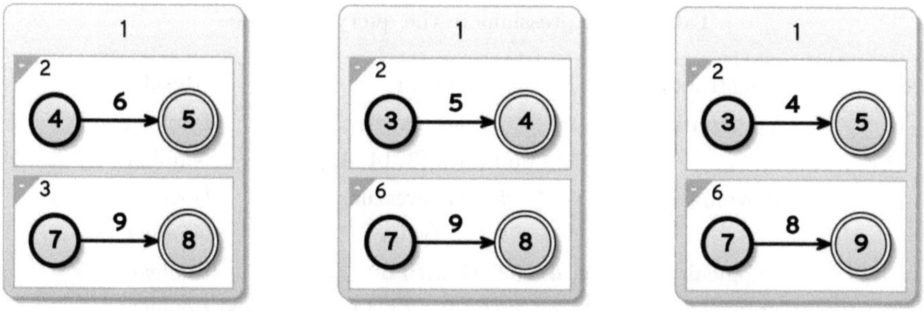

(a) Breadth-first. (b) Depth-first. (c) Coordinate sorted.

Fig. 1. Different possible traversal orders for graph elements.

should match the order of the corresponding graph elements in the diagram. This is to maintain a stable mental map and to prevent large jumps through the diagram while stepping through the results. We need to consider two dimensions.

Firstly, the traversal order within a single layer of hierarchy. The second traversing dimension is the tree structure of the nested hierarchy. To traverse the graph we consider three different traversal orders as shown in Fig. 1. The shown graphs are nested graphs where each graphical element is labelled with a number denoting the order in which the elements are visited.

A breadth-first traversal (cf. Fig. 1a) ensures that elements from the same subgraph are processed together so that neighboring nodes with their own nested subgraphs are listed next to each other in the search results. This is the option that we propose, since it ensures a top-down ordering through the hierarchy levels and elements within same hierarchy remain grouped. This ordering aligns with a mental map where overview comes before detail.

A depth-first traversal (cf. Fig. 1b) on the other hand groups the search results according to the hierarchy branch they belong to. This kind of ordering aligns with a mental map where users zoom into details first before moving to other areas of the diagram.

Finally, we could also sort the search results according to the coordinates of the elements in the diagram (cf. Fig. 1c) ordering from top-to-bottom and left-to-right. This way the order of the search results aligns with the reading direction, but the ordering of the hierarchies is lost.

A combination of a breadth-first traversal and a coordinate sorting per hierarchy level is probably the most desirable. To make breadth-first ordering feasible we rely on a property of the diagrams we use. *Model order* is the order in which graph elements are defined in the original model [2] and if a graph layout algorithm respects this model order, then the order of the elements in the final diagram actually matches the reading direction expected by the user who designed the model.

Table 1. Expressions in the query language.

Construct	Form	Result
Constants	`true`, `false`	Boolean
	numerics (`3.14`, 42)	Number
Tag evaluation	`#id` (is present)	Boolean
	`$id` (value)	Number
Logical	`!e`, `e1 OP e2` with `OP` $\in$ {`&&`, `||`}	Boolean
Comparisons	`e1 OP e2` with `OP` $\in$ {`=`, `!=`, `<`, `<=`, `>`, `>=`}	Boolean
Arithmetic	`e1 OP e2` with `OP` $\in$ {`+`, `-`, `*`, `/`}	Number
Quantifiers	`exists[x:L|p(x)]`	Boolean
	`forall[x:L|p(x)]`	Boolean
List evaluations	`#[x:L|p(x)]` (is non-empty)	Boolean
	`$[x:L|p(x)]` (count)	Number

In Fig. 1a and Fig. 1b the edges always follow the nodes in the ordering. This is due to the underlying graph, and as our evaluation of search strategies in Sec. 6 shows, this ordering actually aligns with the typical search strategy.

4 Graph Query Language

KIELER already supports attaching *semantic tags* to diagram elements allowing semantic information to be passed through the language-agnostic parts of the diagramming framework. The query language we present in this section is an extension of the filter rules that already exist in KIELER [7]. The search feature opens up new possibilities for users to directly interact with the semantic tags on the graph, *e.g.*, searching for all graph elements that have a particular tag. We propose a powerful query language that allows constructing logical expressions using the semantic tags and the underlying graph.

This allows advanced filtering of search results and finding interesting structural areas in a graph, *e.g.*, nodes with self-loops. Valid expressions in the language constitute a filter function that can be applied to graph elements. In the context of search, we take the set of search results and apply the filter function to each result. Only results that pass the filter are kept in the final result set.

The language operates on tags, boolean and numeric constants, and lists of elements. Table 1 contains a concise overview of the valid expressions. A simple filter could be `#myTag`. This would yield all graph elements that contain this tag. Tags can also contain numeric values allowing expressions such as `$myNumeric = 2`, which would yield all elements that contain this tag with the value 2. The common boolean and numeric operators can be used to construct arithmetic and logical expressions. To convert numeric results to booleans, comparison operators are available.

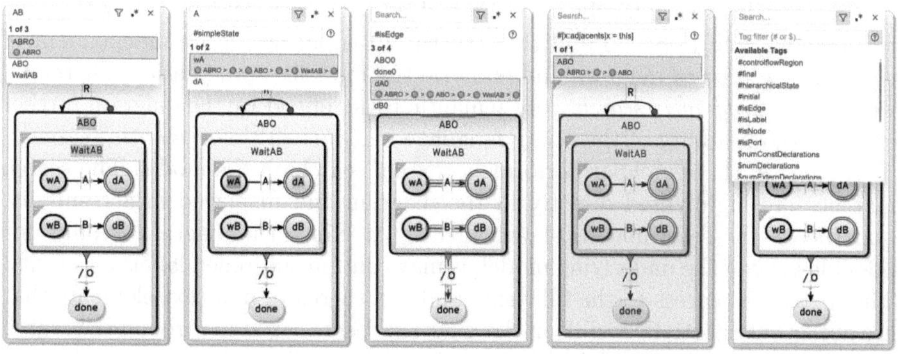

(a) Text search. (b) Filter search. (c) Filter only. (d) Filter query. (e) Help view.

Fig. 2. Searching for texts, with or without filters, or searching directly for particular graph elements. Note that these figures are best viewed in color.

To interact with lists of elements, we introduce the following additional operators. Similarly to the application of `#` and `$` on tags, these operators can be used to evaluate and reduce lists of elements. `#L` evaluates to true if the list `L` is not empty and `$L` evaluates to the number of elements in the list. Furthermore, list reductions can be performed by applying a predicate onto every element in a list. `[x:L|p(x)]` returns a list that is a subset of the input list. The predicate `p(x)` can be any valid filter expression and is applied to each element of the list.

Through pre-defined keywords we can expose the graph to the query language. The keywords `parent`, `children`, `siblings`, `adjacents`, `incoming`, and `outgoing` each return a list of graph elements that we can use to construct complex queries. The pre-defined structural tags `isNode`, `isEdge`, `isLabel` and `isPort` expose structural information about the graph elements.

The diagrams we use here, SCCharts, define their own semantic tags such as `initial` and `final` to distinguish different types of states. This allows constructing filters such as `#initial && $children = 2`—all initial states containing two children. Another example is an expression to find elements that have a self loop `#[x:adjacents|x = this]`. The keyword `this` returns the element the root expression is being evaluated on and allows element comparisons.

5 Pragmatic Semantic Search

The search feature is integrated into the KIELER framework as a searchbar UI overlay that can be opened using the common *Ctrl+F* key combination. This opens a simple searchbar with UI controls similar to the VS Code searchbar for text files. Fig. 2 shows the searchbar UI. The design follows the VS Code search UI and has a similar text box with buttons to toggle regular expression matching or closing the searchbar.

The feature was initially implemented as part of a student thesis [5]. The features outlined in Sec. 3 and the structural tags in Sec. 4 are independent of the concrete type of diagram and enhance the modeling pragmatics. Therefore, we call this *pragmatic search*. Any semantic tags defined by the diagram further enhance the usability of the query language and we call this *semantic search*.

Typing in the searchbar performs a textual search on the model. The search matches are highlighted directly in the diagram and displayed in a result list underneath the searchbar as shown in Fig. 2a. Since the diagram is only one possible view of the underlying model, it may contain shortened labels for clarity. The search has access to the full texts and can therefore find text elements that are not or only partially visible in the diagram. Users can step through the search results in the results panel and automatically jump directly to a selected result or pan through all elements sequentially.

Part of the existing pragmatics in KIELER is the *text-diagram sync* feature. Selecting elements in the diagram selects the corresponding section in the textual source and vice-versa. This also works when using the search, thus enhancing the modeling pragmatics. Panning to an element through the search automatically also pans to the corresponding line in the textual source model and vice-versa when using the VS Code search in the textual source.

Figure 2b shows how the semantic filters can be used to refine the search. Another text field can be opened with a button click to access the graph query language to further filter results. In this mode, the user can write a filter expression, here `#simpleState`, that reduces the search results to those elements that also pass the filter.

If the main search field is empty (cf. Fig. 2c), only the filter query is used, here `#isEdge`. In this case, the match highlighting works slightly differently. In both previous cases, the search results were text matches and those texts were highlighted in the diagram. Now, the matches can be any graph element, so matching graph elements are highlighted in their entirety. Fig. 2d shows how the single state with a self-loop can be found using the query `#[x:adjacents|x = this]`. Since different types of diagrams can define their own semantic tags, a help view (cf. Fig. 2e) displays all available tags to help on-board users.

6 Evaluation of Textual Search

We conducted a user study comparing the performance of solving information extraction tasks while browsing in the KIELER diagramming framework with and without the search feature. The software and models used for the study are available online [6]

Participants were given several diagrams and were asked a series of questions for each diagram. Before the experiment, the participants were given a short explanation of the structural elements of the diagram and their meanings. All participants were first shown a smaller training diagram (cf. Fig. 3a) with two questions. Afterwards, they had the opportunity to ask further questions about the tasks or the diagrams before starting with main diagrams. For the

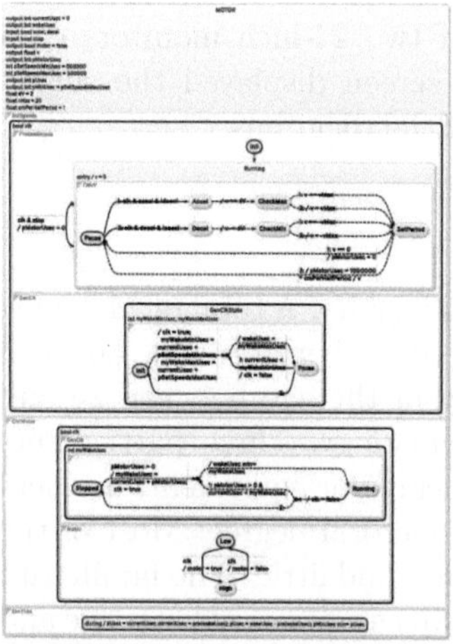

(a) The `Motor` diagram.

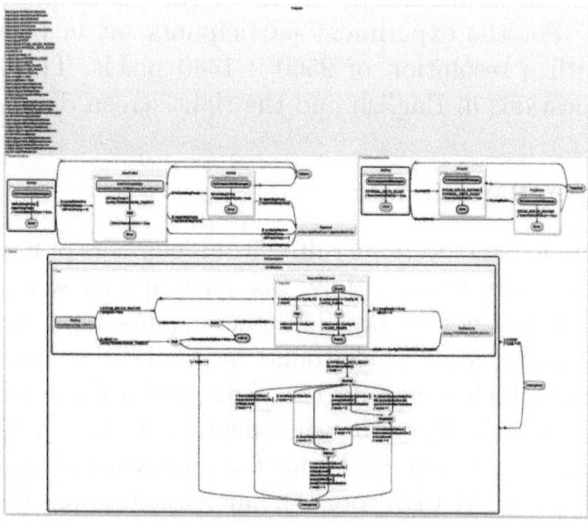

(b) The `Steamboiler` diagram.

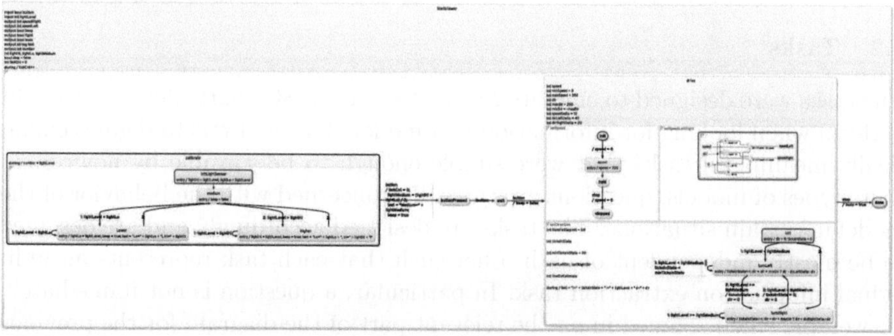

(c) The `Linefollower` diagram.

Fig. 3. The SCCharts diagrams used in the evaluation. `Motor` was used for training, whereas `Steamboiler` and `Linefollower` were used for the experiment.

main experiment, we used two diagrams: the `Steamboiler` (cf. Fig. 3b) and the `Linefollower` (cf. Fig. 3c). Half of the participants were first shown the Steamboiler and half were first shown the Linefollower. The participants were assigned to the groups at random. We measured the usefulness qualitatively via questions and quantitatively in terms of task completion time.

Furthermore, we also divided the participants into two further groups, giving the first group access to the *Ctrl+F* feature only for the first diagram and to the second group only for the second diagram. Both groups received an additional instruction on the search feature when they received access to it. This means that for the second group, the search feature was an addition to their toolbox, whereas the first group had it taken away after their first diagram. We decided to omit the filtering feature and support for regular expression search from the study to limit the amount of learning that was necessary to perform the experiment.

For the experiment participants sat in front of two 27-inch monitors each with a resolution of 2560×1440 pixels. The left screen displayed the survey questions in English and the right screen displayed the diagrams.

6.1 Participants

Participants were recruited from members of Kiel University. A total of 24 people took part in the study. Six participants were female, 17 were male, and one preferred not to say. The participants were mostly in the age between 25 and 34 and with a background in engineering and technology. Three participants held a high school degree, eight held a Bachelor's degree or equivalent, ten held a Master's degree or equivalent, and three held a doctoral degree. Most of the participants reported some familiarity with statecharts and little to no familiarity with the KIELER tool. All participants spoke German as a primary language and were fluent in English and thus accustomed to a left-to-right reading direction.

6.2 Tasks

The tasks were designed to emulate real tasks that an SCCharts developer might perform when looking for information in a model. The goal was to define semantically meaningful tasks that were simple enough to be solvable by novices. In these types of models, questions are typically concerned with the behavior of the model in certain situations. The tasks are designed accordingly and are designed to be mostly independent of each other such that each task represents an individual information extraction task. In particular, a question is not immediately answerable when zoomed in on the relevant part of the diagram for the previous question. The questions were always asked in the same order during the experiment. While answering the questions, users will naturally explore the diagram, consciously or subconsciously building a mental map, which can make later questions easier to answer. The following questions were asked. The expected answers are provided in brackets after each question.

Motor (Training Diagram)

- **G1Q1** Which state does the transition using the `accel` variable in its trigger lead to? (*`Accel`* or *`Decel`*)
- **G1Q2** Which variable is modified while the model oscillates between the states `Low` and `High`? (*`motor`*)

Steamboiler

- **G2Q1** In the initialization state, which effect is triggered if the `waterLevel` variable is less than the value provided by `Config.N1`? (*`OPEN_PUMPS`*)
- **G2Q2** Name one variable that can cause the `Steamboiler` to enter the `Degraded` state. (*`pumpDefective`*, *`steamSensorDefective`* or *`pumpControllerDefective`*)

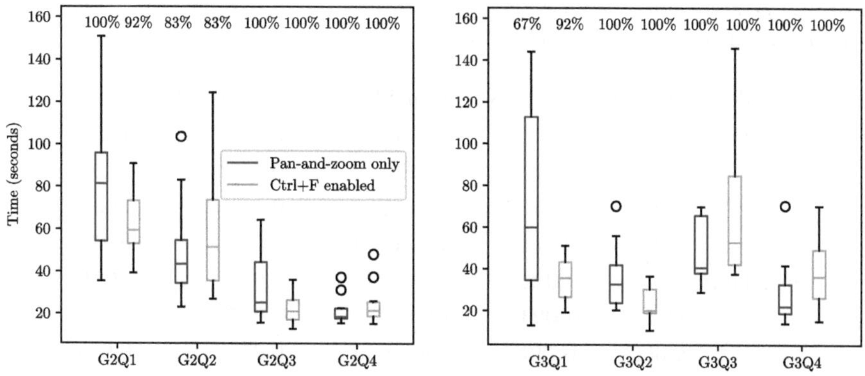

(a) **Steamboiler** diagram. (b) **Linefollower** diagram.

Fig. 4. Distributions of task completion times for both diagrams separated by the testing condition. The blue plots on the left represent the pan-and-zoom only group. The orange plots on the right represent the Ctrl+F group. Percentages above plots indicate the accuracy of the answers.

- **G2Q3** How many states named `Error` can be found in the model? (*6*)
- **G2Q4** Which variable is set to true every time an `Error` state is entered? (*transmissionFailure*)

Linefollower

- **G3Q1** In the `calibrate` state, which variable is repeatedly read?(*lightLevel*)
- **G3Q2** The variable `buzz` is only used in one transition. Which state does the transition lead to? (*done*)
- **G3Q3** Which state does the model transition to if the variable `lightLevel` is less than the value of `lightMedium` while the model is in the turnRight state? (*turnLeft*)
- **G3Q4** All states should be written in lowercase, but there is one state that begins with an uppercase letter. What is the name of that state? (*Lower*)

6.3 Quantitative Results

For each task, we measured the time it took the participants to complete the task. In addition, we measured the correctness of the answers. For each diagram users had access to either pan-and-zoom only or additionally to Ctrl+F. We separated the measured data by tool per task. We controlled and altered the ordering of tools and model to reduce learning effects.

Figure 4a and Fig. 4b show the distributions of task completion times for each task separated by the tools available (pan-and-zoom only vs. Ctrl+F). Above

Table 2. p-values for differences in time measurements for each task between each tool. Significant values are bold ($p < 0.05$).

Model	Task	Welch's t-test	Normality	Mann-Whitney U	Cohen's d
Steamboiler	G2Q1	0.141	normal	0.214	0.633
	G2Q2	0.512	normal	0.544	-0.272
	G2Q3	**0.043**	normal	0.112	0.903
	G2Q4	0.374	non-normal	0.260	-0.371
Linefollower	G3Q1	**0.020**	normal	0.069	1.091
	G3Q2	**0.021**	normal	**0.017**	1.038
	G3Q3	0.119	non-normal	0.237	-0.676
	G3Q4	0.123	non-normal	0.061	-0.656

each distribution plot there is a percentage that indicates the average accuracy for the task. To measure the accuracy, we compared the expected answer with the given answer ignoring spelling mistakes.

For the timing measurements we computed p-values using Welch's t-test for each task and tested the distributions for normality using the Shapiro-Wilk test. The results are shown in Table 2. We indicate normality violation in the table according to the Shapiro-Wilk test if one of the two data sets per task violated normality. In those cases, we additionally applied the non-parametric Mann-Whitney U test, but found no significances in these cases. While most results do not indicate a significant difference between the task completion times, for tasks where the tests indicate a significance, the participants who had Ctrl+F available were always faster. Furthermore, all these cases also showed no normality violations according to Shapiro-Wilk. This answers **RQ1**, indicating that an automatic search tool increases the efficiency of solving typical information extraction tasks in diagrams. We also applied the conservative Bonferroni correction, which indicates no significance for the experiment's results.

Table 2 indicates a significant difference in the task completion times for task G3Q1, and for this task the accuracy of the pan-and-zoom group is also quite low as can be seen in Fig. 4b.

For task G3Q3, the group that had Ctrl+F took longer than the pan-and-zoom group, although not enough to be significant. The task asked for a state, whose name started with an uppercase letter. This task was not solvable using search in the experiment as the regular expression matching was not available. Nevertheless, the participants seemed to struggle to simply fall back to pan-and-zoom only whereas their peers who only had access to pan-and-zoom for this task solved the task relatively quickly. This could be because they felt they were obliged to use Ctrl+F or because they very quickly became accustomed to the comfort of using it rather than searching manually.

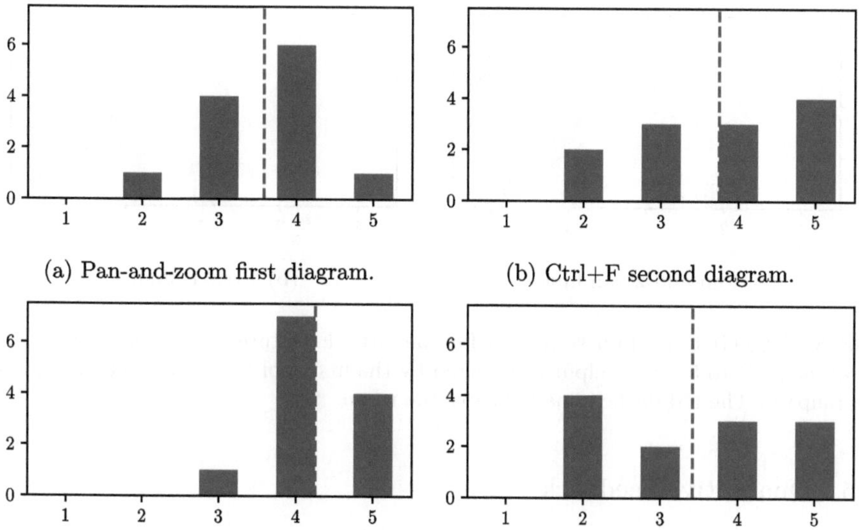

(a) Pan-and-zoom first diagram.

(b) Ctrl+F second diagram.

(c) Ctrl+F first diagram.

(d) Pan-and-zoom second diagram.

Fig. 5. Subjective experience ratings for each diagram on a scale from 1 (very frustrating) to 5 (very satisfying) separated by the first tool that was available for the participant. The red dashed line indicates the mean.

6.4 Search Strategies

After the experiment, participants were asked to describe the strategies they used to search through the diagram. For each technique, a common strategy was described.

While using only pan-and-zoom, the general approach was to *scan* across the diagram looking for important keywords and then to *narrow* the search to an interesting region by zooming in. The scanning direction and search order was commonly described as *left-to-right*, *top-to-bottom*, *outer-to-inner*. The graph elements were also scanned with different priorities. First states, then transitions, and finally variables.

Although the diagrams were technically small enough to be fully readable on the screen used during the experiment, all participants utilized the zoom and only one participant verbalized that they noticed that the screen was large enough to read all texts in the diagram.

The search strategy described for Ctrl+F was to type relevant keywords into the searchbar and jump through the results until the relevant area was found, and the answer could be read easily from the diagram. Little further panning and zooming was required.

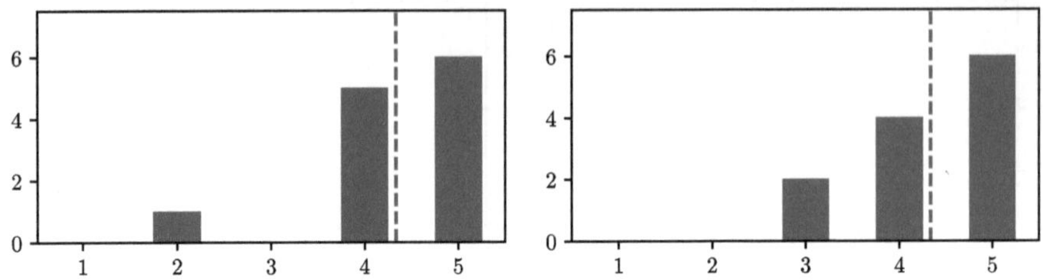

(a) Pan-and-zoom first.

(b) Ctrl+F first.

Fig. 6. Subjective helpfulness ratings for the Ctrl+F feature on a scale from 1 (not at all helpful) to 5 (very helpful) separated by the first tool that was available for the participant. The red dashed line indicates the mean.

6.5 Qualitative Feedback

During the experiment, several of the participants in the group that initially only had pan-and-zoom verbally expressed the desire for a search function or asked directly whether they could use Ctrl+F in the diagram.

The participants were asked to rate their experience with each of the diagrams with a score from 1 (very frustrating) to 5 (very satisfying). In Fig. 5 we can see how the two groups rated their experience with the first and second diagram they saw. The group that started with only pan-and-zoom gave a mean rating of 3.58 for the first model and the Ctrl+F group rated their first diagram with a mean of 4.25. The median rating for both groups was 4. Those that gained Ctrl+F then rated their second experience slightly higher with a mean rating of 3.75, while the group that lost Ctrl+F rated their experience noticeably lower for the second diagram with a mean rating of 3.42, decreasing the median to 3.5.

We also asked participants to rate how much the search feature helped them in answering the questions. Fig. 6 shows that both groups felt that the search feature was a helpful addition to solve the tasks. Overall, the participants expressed that they enjoyed using Ctrl+F and felt it made them faster and more efficient at solving the tasks. The times we measured support this perception, thus answering **RQ3**.

Participants were asked to provide any further feedback they had. Multiple participants were confused by task G2Q1. The question asks what happens when `waterLevel` is less than `Config.N1`. In the diagram the relevant transition contains the trigger `waterLevel <= Config.N1`. Even though the condition described in the task is clearly met by the trigger condition, this task was apparently often treated more as a text matching exercise. Those confused were expecting something like `waterLevel < Config.N1`. This was the only task where such an effect was so clearly observable.

As part of the feedback some participants left feature requests for the diagrams. Several requests were for the ability to filter the search results by the types of graph element. For example, to search directly for states with a certain name. Although this was not available in the study, this indicates a use case for the semantic filtering feature introduced in Sec. 4, which allows exactly the requested type of filtering. Examining the usability of the filtering language remains open for future work. The feedback provided by the participants further strengthens our proposal for semantic and pragmatic search in diagrams.

6.6 Threats to Validity

Although the presented scenario aimed to emulate realistic domain-specific tasks to the study participants, it was still an artificial setting. Instead of working on high-level tasks, we gave small tasks that they had to answer in a separate form. Furthermore, some tasks are not very realistic but rather a tradeoff to make the experiment possible with participants who were unfamiliar with the domain-specific diagrams we presented to them.

The tasks do not all have the same difficulty. Some tasks, especially G3Q4, were intentionally difficult to solve using the search feature. Since there were multiple tasks per diagram, there is always the possibility that the answer to a later question was already noticed during an earlier scanning of the diagram, making the timings for the later tasks less reliable.

During the experiment, users were not forced to actually use Ctrl+F at any point. For any task, we would expect pan-and-zoom to define a baseline for the task completion time. Since we cannot control for the way Ctrl+F is used, it can be difficult to compare the tool usage between different participants. In our observations, all participants did use the search feature.

All these aspects introduce uncertainty, and to account for them would require a larger study with expert users rather than novices. Nonetheless, the results do indicate that Ctrl+F is a helpful tool for diagrams.

7 Conclusion

Searching is a ubiquitous tool for digital data. We showed how search support can be added to diagramming software and in particular how it can be integrated into pragmatic modeling software. We also extended the textual search paradigm with a filtering language that enhances the search in a graph.

Our user study showed that users generally perceive access to a search function as helpful. The times we measured show that in some cases the search speeds up information extraction tasks even for relatively small diagrams as those used in the experiment. We also observed that users quickly came to rely on the search feature. The removal of the search was rated more negatively than the other group rated the gain of the feature. Some timing results also indicate that when tasks were not easily solvable using the search function users took longer when they were used to the search function and were forced to fall back to basic pan-and-zoom.

Future Work

For the experiment performed for this paper, we omitted the semantic filtering features due to their complexity. It would, however, be interesting to evaluate the usefulness of the filtering language and how easy or hard it is to learn. A further study with domain experts rather than novices would allow us to pose more complex and realistic tasks and thus would provide more insight in the usefulness of the search feature for real developers. What we also could not study in our experiment is the comparison between experts and novices and how Ctrl+F benefits these groups in different ways.

References

1. Di Rocco, J., Di Ruscio, D., Di Salle, A., Di Vincenzo, D., Pierantonio, A., Tinella, G.: JJodel-a reflective cloud-based modeling framework. In: 2023 ACM/IEEE International Conference on Model Driven Engineering Languages and Systems Companion (MODELS-C), pp. 55–59. IEEE (2023). https://doi.org/10.1109/MODELS-C59198.2023.00019
2. Domrös, S., von Hanxleden, R.: Diagram control and model order for Sugiyama layouts. In: Proceedings of the 9th International Conference on the Theory and Application of Diagrams, DIAGRAMS 2024. LNCS, vol. 14981, pp. 76–83. Springer Nature Switzerland (2024). https://doi.org/10.1007/978-3-031-71291-3_6
3. Giraudet, T., Bats, M., Blouin, A., Combemale, B., David, P.C.: Sirius Web: insights in language workbenches - an experience report. J. Object Technol. **23**(1), 1–20 (2024). https://doi.org/10.5381/jot.2024.23.1.a6
4. von Hanxleden, R., et al.: Pragmatics twelve years later: a report on Lingua Franca. In: 11th International Symposium on Leveraging Applications of Formal Methods, Verification and Validation (ISoLA). LNCS, vol. 13702, pp. 60–89. Springer, Rhodes, Greece (Oct 2022). https://doi.org/10.1007/978-3-031-19756-7_5
5. Harnack, L.: Ctrl+F for Diagrams—Textual Search for Diagramming Frameworks. Bachelor's thesis, Kiel University, Department of Computer Science (Sep 2025). https://rtsys.informatik.uni-kiel.de/~biblio/downloads/theses/lha-bt.pdf
6. Kasperowski, M.: Search in diagrams experiment material. Kiel University Research Data Repository opendata@uni-kiel (Feb 2026). https://doi.org/10.57892/100-338
7. Kasperowski, M., Rentz, N., Domrös, S., von Hanxleden, R.: KIELER: A text-first framework for automatic diagramming of complex systems. In: Lemanski, J., Johansen, M.W., Manalo, E., Viana, P., Bhattacharjee, R., Burns, R. (eds.) Diagrams 2024. LNCS, vol. 14981. Springer, Cham (2024). https://doi.org/10.1007/978-3-031-71291-3_33
8. Larkin, J.H., Simon, H.A.: Why a diagram is (sometimes) worth ten thousand words. Cogn. Sci. **11**(1), 65–100 (1987)
9. Metin, H., Bork, D.: A reference architecture for the development of GLSP-based web modeling tools. Softw. Syst. Modeling, 1–27 (2025). https://doi.org/10.1007/s10270-024-01257-y
10. Nivala, A.M., Brewster, S., Sarjakoski, L.T.: Usability evaluation of web mapping sites. Cartogr. J. **45**(2), 129–138 (2008). https://doi.org/10.1179/174327708X305120

11. Shahin, M., Liang, P., Ali Babar, M.: A systematic review of software architecture visualization techniques. J. Syst. Softw. **94**, 161–185 (2014). https://doi.org/10.1016/j.jss.2014.03.071
12. Tversky, B., Kugelmass, S., Winter, A.: Cross-cultural and developmental trends in graphic productions. Cogn. Psychol. **23**(4), 515–557 (1991). https://doi.org/10.1016/0010-0285(91)90005-9
13. Winn, W.: An account of how readers search for information in diagrams. Contemp. Educ. Psychol. **18**(2), 162–185 (1993). https://doi.org/10.1006/ceps.1993.1016

EvoEuler: Evolving Euler and Venn Diagrams with Specific Properties

Chi Ho Chan(✉), Peter Chapman, Kevin Sim, and Ben Paechter

Edinburgh Napier University, Edinburgh, UK
{c.chan3,p.chapman,k.sim,b.paechter}@napier.ac.uk

Abstract. Euler and Venn diagrams are widely used to visualize set-based data, but generating diagrams with desired properties (e.g., well-matchedness, well-formedness, symmetric diagram, and congruent shape) remains challenging. Existing methods typically aim to generate a single diagram with a fixed set of properties, offering users limited flexibility to choose which properties to consider or to explore trade-offs among solutions. To address this limitation, we present EvoEuler, a Python package that uses a multi-objective evolutionary algorithm (NSGA-II or NSGA-III) to search for Euler and Venn diagrams with specific properties using a chosen simple closed shape (e.g., circle, ellipse, or rectangle). EvoEuler provides both a web interface and an application programming interface (API). To the best of our knowledge, EvoEuler is the first method that (1) returns a set of non-dominated solutions (diagrams) in the context of both Euler and Venn diagram generation, with solutions evaluated using objectives that quantify violations of well-matchedness and well-formedness properties, and (2) allows solutions to be generated with optional constraints, namely symmetric diagram and congruent shape, in the context of Euler diagram generation. We conduct experiments to evaluate four configurations of EvoEuler on generating Euler and Venn diagrams. Our results suggest that rectangles are preferred over ellipses for generating Euler diagrams, and show that EvoEuler can find simple Venn diagrams for up to five sets.

Keywords: Euler Diagrams · Venn Diagrams · Set Visualization · Multi-Objective Optimization

1 Introduction

An effective Euler or Venn diagram should ideally be well-matched and well-formed. However, generating diagrams that satisfy these properties is already challenging, particularly as the number of sets grows, not to mention when additional properties are considered. Prior methods [13,22] aim to generate a single diagram with a fixed set of properties. In practice, not all properties are of equal interest to users, and users may want to explore alternative solutions with different trade-offs.

P. Sobociński et al. (Eds.): Diagrams 2026, LNAI 16833, pp. 326–341, 2027.
https://doi.org/10.1007/978-3-032-34178-5_33

To address this limitation, we propose a multi-objective evolutionary method for generating Euler and Venn diagrams with specific properties using a chosen simple closed shape (circle, ellipse, rectangle, rounded rectangle, a type of regular polygon with up to 10 sides or its rounded variant, or a custom simple closed shape provided by users). Our contributions are as follows:

- To the best of our knowledge, we propose the first method that (1) returns a set of non-dominated solutions (diagrams) in the context of both Euler and Venn diagram generation, with solutions evaluated using objectives that quantify violations of well-matchedness and well-formedness properties, and (2) allows solutions to be generated with optional constraints, namely symmetric diagram and congruent shape, in the context of Euler diagram generation.
- We implement our method as a Python package called EvoEuler[1], providing both a web interface and an application programming interface (API).
- We conduct experiments to evaluate four configurations of EvoEuler on generating Euler and Venn diagrams.

Our method has advantages over prior methods that return a single diagram with a fixed set of properties. First, our method returns a set of non-dominated solutions (diagrams), allowing users to explore trade-offs among solutions. Second, users can optionally enforce diagrams to be symmetric and to use congruent shapes. Third, determining whether a diagram satisfies a given property is straightforward. Specifically, a well-matched diagram can be identified from its objective values, while enabling a constraint (e.g., symmetric diagram) guarantees satisfaction of the corresponding property.

The remainder of this paper is organized as follows. Section 2 introduces concepts related to Euler diagrams, Venn diagrams, and multi-objective optimization. Section 3 reviews prior work on generating Euler and Venn diagrams. Section 4 describes the proposed method. Section 5 presents the implementation of EvoEuler and the functionalities provided by the web interface and API. Section 6 details the experimental setup. Section 7 discusses the experimental results. Finally, Sect. 8 concludes the paper, outlines the current limitations, and suggests future directions.

2 Background

2.1 Euler Diagrams

Following [20], an Euler diagram consists of labeled closed curves that partition the plane into minimal regions, where each minimal region is a connected component. One or more minimal regions form a zone representing a set intersection. An abstract description specifies a set of zones that should be present in the diagram (e.g., Venn-2 could be represented as $\{\varnothing, \text{A}, \text{B}, \text{A B}\}$).

[1] Code is available at https://github.com/superchchan/evoeuler.

Two well-known properties for Euler diagrams are well-matchedness and well-formedness. An Euler diagram is well-matched if it shows exactly the zones specified in the abstract description, that is, no target zones are missing (see Fig. 1a for a violation) and no unwanted zones are shown (see Fig. 1b for a violation). Well-formedness properties were first introduced in [11] and later formalized in [24]. There are six common well-formedness properties:

- No duplicated curve labels: Each curve has a unique label.
- No non-simple curves: Curves do not self-intersect.
- No triple points: There are no more than two curves that meet at any point.
- No concurrency: There are no pairs of curves that share a line segment.
- No disconnected zones: Each zone consists of one minimal region.
- No brushing points: There are no two or more curves that touch at a point.

Figure 2 illustrates the violation of each well-formedness property. Violating some of these well-formedness properties has been shown to impede user comprehension of Euler diagrams [21]. We consider an Euler diagram to be *relaxed well-formed* if it satisfies all the well-formedness properties except the no brushing points property. Chapman et al. [4] suggest that well-matchedness matters more than well-formedness for task performance with set visualizations.

(a) missing zone: C (b) unwanted zone: B C

Fig. 1. Examples of violations of well-matchedness properties for an abstract description {∅, A, B, C, A B}

Euler diagrams can also be area-proportional, such that the area of each zone is proportional to a given non-negative numerical value [5]. An area specification describes the value associated with each zone (e.g., {A 0.2, B 0.2, A B 0.6}). There are additional Euler diagram properties [24] such as the smooth property, which requires all curves to be smooth, and the S-shapes property, which requires all curves to use the same shape. An empirical study [2] shows that using smooth curves rather than jagged ones improves comprehension of Euler diagrams.

2.2 Venn Diagrams

A family of n simple closed curves that shows all possible non-empty intersections ($2^n - 1$) for n sets is called an independent family [14]. Venn and Euler diagrams differ in that Venn diagrams not only have to be an independent family, but also require each intersection to appear as a single minimal region.

(a) duplicated curve label: C

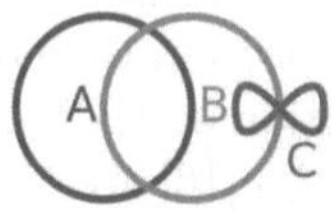

(b) non-simple curve: C

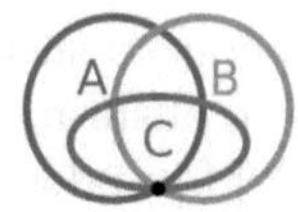

(c) triple point: a point in black shared by curves A, B, and C

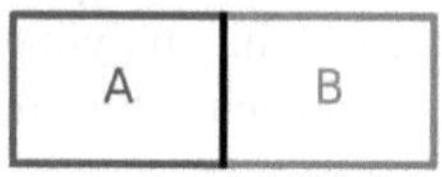

(d) concurrency: a line segment in black shared by curves A and B

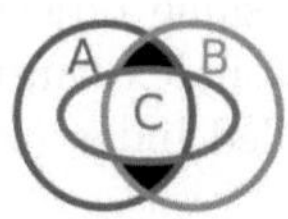

(e) disconnected zone: A B

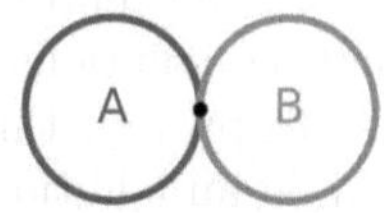

(f) brushing point: a point in black shared by curves A and B

Fig. 2. Examples of violations of well-formedness properties, adapted from [28]

An independent family or a Venn diagram is simple if no triple points exist [14]. An independent family or a Venn diagram with n curves is symmetric if the curves are congruent and rotating the diagram by an angle of $2\pi/n$ about a point produces the same diagram with curves relabeled [15]. Henderson [15] proved that if a Venn diagram with n curves is symmetric, then n must be a prime number. However, there exist symmetric independent families with n curves where n is not a prime number (e.g., $n = 4$) [14].

2.3 Multi-objective Optimization

Multi-objective optimization [9] is the task of minimizing or maximizing more than one conflicting objective simultaneously. In many applications, the goal is to find a set of non-dominated solutions where no objective can be improved without worsening at least one of the other objectives, allowing users to explore trade-offs and select solutions of interest.

Multi-objective evolutionary algorithms (MOEAs) [29] are a common heuristic approach to generate a set of non-dominated solutions for multi-objective optimization problems. Among MOEAs, NSGA-II [8] and NSGA-III [10] are frequently used and are often compared to each other [17]. Although NSGA-III is designed specifically for solving many-objective (with four or more objectives) optimization problems, Ishibuchi et al. [17] show that it does not always outperform NSGA-II on such problems, as their performance depends on the problem type, the number of objectives, and the algorithm implementation. MOEAs start by initializing a random population of solutions and evaluating each solution on all objectives. The population is updated each generation until reaching a termination condition such as a maximum number of generations or a time budget. In each generation, parent solutions are selected to generate offspring via genetic operators such as crossover and mutation. The offspring are evaluated, and selected offspring replace solutions in the population. Interested readers can refer to [29] for a detailed description of MOEAs.

Parallel coordinates plots (PCPs) [16] are one of the most popular techniques to visualize the objective values of all non-dominated solutions. In a PCP, each vertical axis corresponds to a dimension (e.g., an objective), and each solution is represented by a polyline. A polyline connects a point on each adjacent axis, where each point represents the solution's value for that dimension. It is possible that multiple solutions share the same objective values, causing polylines to coincide. To prevent this, a unique index can be assigned to each solution and displayed on an additional axis called Index (see Fig. 3).

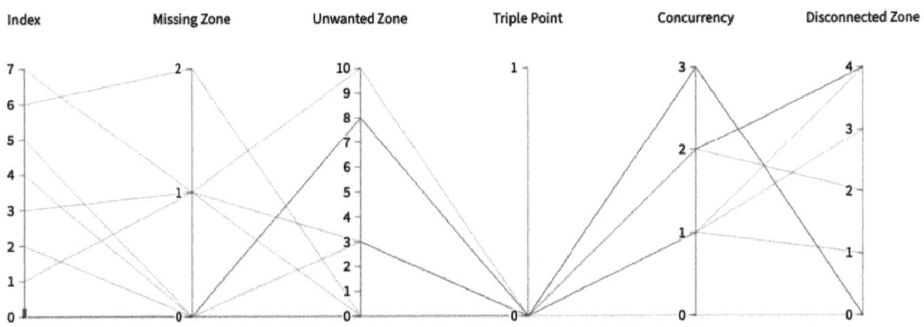

Fig. 3. Parallel coordinates plot

3 Related Work

3.1 Euler Diagrams

EulerSmooth [23] was developed to smooth the curves of existing Euler diagrams. SPEULER [18] generates well-matched Euler diagrams with smooth curves, ensuring well-formedness when possible. RectEuler [19] uses rounded rectangles to produce Euler diagrams without triple points, concurrency, and brushing points. However, the resulting diagrams may not be well-matched and may contain disconnected zones and duplicated curve labels.

Recently, Rottmann et al. [22] presented the first method that can determine whether a given abstract description can be drawn as a well-matched Euler diagram where each set is represented as a single connected region (allowing holes). However, even when the answer is yes, the resulting diagram may introduce concurrent line segments, triple points, and brushing points.

3.2 Venn Diagrams

There are constructions [1,26] that can generate Venn diagrams for an arbitrary number of sets, but the curves in the resulting diagrams differ in shape. Such diagrams are considered less attractive than diagrams with curves of the same shape. This has led to a long-standing interest in finding Venn diagrams for a given number of sets with a specific shape. Griggs et al. [13] provide a construction for generating symmetric Venn-n diagrams for any prime number n, although the resulting diagrams are not guaranteed to be simple. SPEULER [18] can generate Venn-5 and Venn-7 diagrams, with the optional symmetric diagram constraint.

4 Methodology

4.1 Problem Formulation

We formulate the problem of generating Euler and Venn diagrams with specific properties as a multi-objective optimization problem. Given a set of target zones Z (excluding the empty zone $\varnothing$), a shape, an algorithm (NSGA-II or NSGA-III) and its optional hyperparameters (number of generations, number of processes, time limit in seconds), and optional constraints (symmetric diagram and congruent shape), the goal is to find a set of non-dominated solutions (diagrams). A set of curve labels S is extracted from Z, and the set of all possible zones is defined as $Z_{\text{all}} = \mathcal{P}(S) \setminus \{\varnothing\}$. Recall that a symmetric diagram requires curves to be congruent, and therefore when the symmetric diagram constraint is enabled, the congruent shape constraint is also automatically enabled.

4.2 Representation

A solution is encoded as a real-valued vector $\mathbf{x} = (x_1, x_2, \ldots, x_{m \cdot n})$, where $m = |S|$ is the number of curves and n is the number of parameters per curve. Table 1 describes the parameters required for each simple closed shape. Each parameter in $\mathbf{x}$ is bounded: c_x and c_y are bounded by $[-2.0, 2.0]$; all size-related parameters are bounded by $[0.1, 2.0]$; θ is bounded by $[0.0, 360.0]$ to cover all possible rotation angles. The vector $\mathbf{x}$ is constructed by concatenating the parameters of each curve.

Decoding a solution takes the following steps:

1. Split $\mathbf{x}$ into m real-valued vectors $\mathbf{p}_1, \mathbf{p}_2, \ldots, \mathbf{p}_m$ of size n, where $(\mathbf{p}_i)_k = x_{((i-1)n)+k}$ for $k = 1, 2, \ldots, n$.
2. If the congruent shape constraint is enabled, size-related parameters are copied from $\mathbf{p}_1$ to all other vectors $\mathbf{p}_i$.
3. If the symmetric diagram constraint is enabled, for each $\mathbf{p}_i$ where $i = 2, 3, \ldots, m$, $(c_x^{(i)}, c_y^{(i)})$ are set by rotating $(c_x^{(1)}, c_y^{(1)})$ about point $(0, 0)$ by $\frac{360(i-1)}{m}$ degrees, and where applicable, $\theta^{(i)}$ is set to $\theta^{(1)} + \frac{360(i-1)}{m}$ degrees.
4. Create each shape C_i from its updated vector $\mathbf{p}_i$.

Table 1. Description of parameters required for each simple closed shape in EvoEuler. c_x and c_y are the x and y coordinates of the center, respectively. θ is the rotation angle (in degrees). Size-related parameters are in bold.

Shape(s)	Parameters	Description
circle	$c_x, c_y, \boldsymbol{r}$	$\boldsymbol{r}$ is the radius.
ellipse	$c_x, c_y, \boldsymbol{r_x}, \boldsymbol{r_y}, \theta$	$\boldsymbol{r_x}$ and $\boldsymbol{r_y}$ are the radii along the x and y axes, respectively.
rectangle, rounded rectangle	$c_x, c_y, \boldsymbol{w}, \boldsymbol{h}, \theta$	$\boldsymbol{w}$ is the width and $\boldsymbol{h}$ is the height.
a type of regular polygon with up to 10 sides or its rounded variant	$c_x, c_y, \boldsymbol{R}, \theta$	$\boldsymbol{R}$ is the circumradius.
a custom simple closed shape	$c_x, c_y, \boldsymbol{s_x}, \boldsymbol{s_y}, \theta$	$\boldsymbol{s_x}$ and $\boldsymbol{s_y}$ are scale factors along x and y axes, respectively.

4.3 Objectives

To quantify the violations of well-matchedness and well-formedness properties, we define and minimize the following objectives:

- Missing zone (O_1): number of target zones that do not appear in a diagram.
- Unwanted zone (O_2): number of non-target zones that appear in a diagram.
- Triple point (O_3): number of points shared by more than two curves.
- Concurrency (O_4): number of line strings (each composed of one or more line segments) shared by pairs of curves.
- Disconnected zone (O_5): number of zones that consist of more than one minimal region.

The no duplicated curve labels and no non-simple curves properties are not included as objectives, since our representation guarantees that each set is represented by a simple closed shape. Section 8 explains why the no brushing points property is not considered.

A zone is considered shown in a diagram if its geometry has positive area.

4.4 Zone Geometry Computation

In order to calculate O_1, O_2, and O_5, we need to first compute the geometry of each zone. Given an encoded solution $\mathbf{x}$, we decode it to create a shape C_s for each curve label $s \in S$. Let $I_z \subseteq S$ be the set of curve labels appearing in zone $z \in Z_{\text{all}}$ and $E_z = S \setminus I_z$ be the set of curve labels not appearing in zone $z \in Z_{\text{all}}$. Let $(i_1, i_2, \ldots, i_{|I_z|})$ and $(e_1, e_2, \ldots, e_{|E_z|})$ denote the curve labels of I_z and E_z

sorted in lexicographic order, respectively. For each zone $z \in Z_{\text{all}}$, its geometry is computed as:

$$G_z = \left(\bigcap_{j=1}^{|I_z|} C_{i_j} \right) \setminus C_{e_1} \setminus C_{e_2} \setminus \cdots \setminus C_{e_{|E_z|}} \quad (1)$$

The computation terminates early if the intermediate geometry becomes empty after any set intersection or difference operation.

5 Implementation

Our method is implemented as a Python package called EvoEuler, providing both a web interface and an API. EvoEuler uses pymoo [3] for implementing MOEAs, Shapely [12] for computing geometric objects, and Streamlit [25] for building the web interface.

5.1 Web Interface

Once EvoEuler is installed, the web interface (shown in Fig. 4) can be launched by executing the `evoeuler` command from the command line interface. The web interface provides the following functionalities:

- Draw, redraw, or smooth shape: draw, redraw, or smooth a custom simple closed shape.
- Round shape: round the corners of a custom simple closed shape.
- View shape: view all available built-in and custom simple closed shapes.
- Configure optimization settings: specify target zones, shape, algorithm, number of generations, number of processes, and constraints.
- Start optimization: start an optimization based on the optimization settings.
- View visualization of non-dominated solutions: view the PCP that visualizes the non-dominated solutions.
- View diagram: view the diagram of a solution.
- Customize diagram: choose whether to show zone labels and shade unwanted zones in the diagram of a solution.
- Export diagram: export the diagram of a solution as PNG or SVG files.
- View zone information: view whether each zone of a solution is a target zone, is shown in the diagram, and is connected.

It is worth noting that the PCP is interactive, allowing users to filter solutions by dragging lines along the axes and to reorder axes by dragging the axis labels.

By selecting a solution index from the drop-down list, users can view the zone information and diagram for that solution. Figure 4 shows the web interface with solution 2 selected. If solution 0 is selected instead, it results in a diagram with more unwanted zones and concurrent line strings but fewer disconnected zones, as shown by its highlighted polyline in Fig. 3 and its diagram in Fig. 5.

We also provide an API, an example of which can be seen in Listing 1.

```python
import matplotlib.pyplot as plt
from evoeuler import diagram, optimize, pcp
if __name__ == "__main__":
    # Start an optimization.
    result = optimize(zones={"A", "B", "A B"}, shape="ellipse",
    ↪   algorithm="NSGA-II", n_gen=100, n_process=1, time=180,
    ↪   symmetric=False, congruent=False)
    # Print the number of non-dominated solutions.
    print(f"Number of non-dominated solutions: {len(result)}")
    # Show the parallel coordinates plot.
    pcp(result).show()
    # Show the diagram of a solution.
    solution_idx = 0 # Solution index
    diagram(result[solution_idx], show_zone_labels=False,
    ↪   shade_unwanted_zones=True)
    plt.show()
```

Listing 1: Example of using the EvoEuler API to search for Venn-2 diagrams with ellipses

6 Experiment

We evaluate the effectiveness of EvoEuler on generating Euler and Venn diagrams under four configurations of algorithm and shape: NSGA-II with ellipses (II-E), NSGA-II with rectangles (II-R), NSGA-III with ellipses (III-E), and NSGA-III with rectangles (III-R). Ellipses are chosen over circles as a representative smooth shape because they provide more degrees of freedom for scaling and rotation, while rectangles are selected as a representative non-smooth shape, as they are also used in RectEuler. Comparing our method with existing methods is challenging; they generally do not provide the curve parameters, so we cannot reproduce their diagrams and evaluate them against our objectives and evaluation metrics using our code. All experiments are conducted using an AMD EPYC 7763 64-Core processor with 128 logical cores.

Based on initial experiments, for both NSGA-II and NSGA-III, the population size and the number of generations are set to 100, and parallelization is enabled using 128 processes. Reference directions for NSGA-III are generated using the Das-Dennis method [7] with 4 partitions, resulting in 70 reference points. All remaining hyperparameters are configured using the default values provided by pymoo [3]. The termination criterion for an algorithm is triggered when either 100 generations have been completed or a time limit of 180 s has been reached, whichever occurs first. If the time limit is reached during a generation, the algorithm stops after completing the current generation.

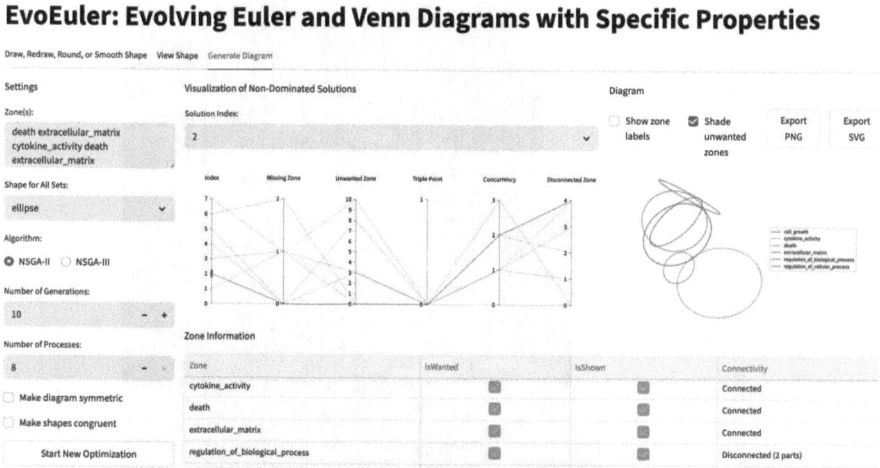

Fig. 4. Screenshot of the EvoEuler web interface

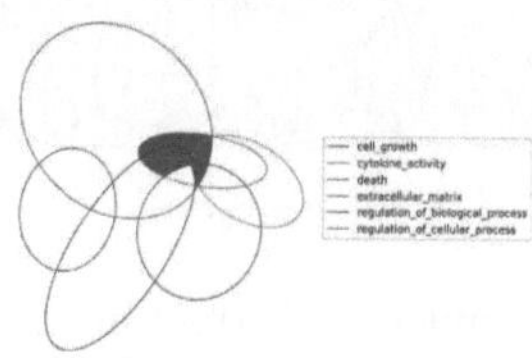

Fig. 5. Euler diagram of solution 0 whose polyline is highlighted in Fig. 3

6.1 Euler Diagrams

Derived from the GO database [6], the Gene Ontology dataset [27] contains 124 area specifications, which we convert into abstract descriptions by extracting zones that are associated with a non-zero value. For example, after conversion, an area specification {A 0.1, B 0.2, C 0.3, A B 0.4, A C 0, B C 0, A B C 0} becomes the abstract description {∅, A, B, C, A B}. This results in 124 abstract descriptions, but some of them are isomorphic up to curve relabeling (e.g., {∅, A, B, C, A B} and {∅, D, E, F, D E}). To obtain a set of unique abstract descriptions, we select one abstract description per unique combination of number of sets and number of set intersections, resulting in 76 unique abstract descriptions with the number of sets ranging from 1 to 20 and up to 150 non-empty set intersections, as shown in Fig. 6.

For each configuration, we report the success rate: the percentage of abstract descriptions for which a solution satisfying a specific condition is found in any of the 30 runs. Conditions include:

- No missing zones ($O_1 = 0$)
- No unwanted zones ($O_2 = 0$)
- Well-matched ($O_1 = O_2 = 0$)

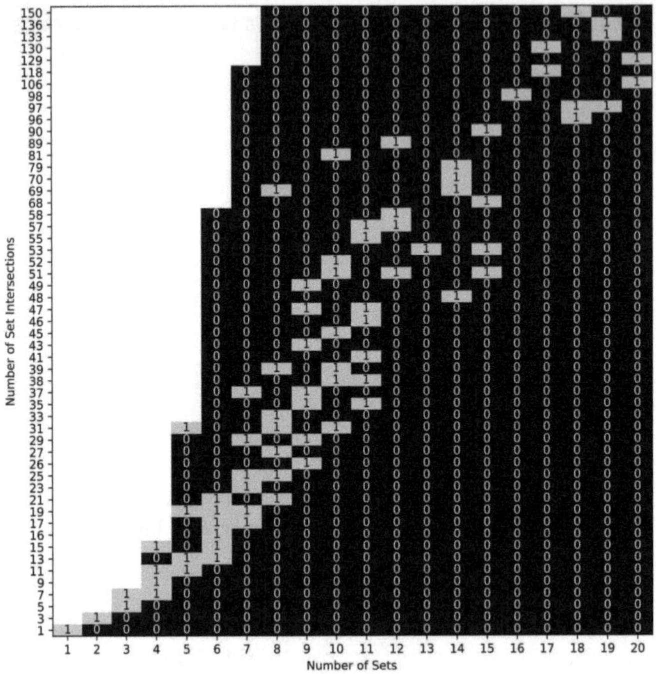

Fig. 6. Heatmap showing the number of abstract descriptions for each combination of set count and set intersection count on the Gene Ontology dataset

- Relaxed well-formed ($O_3 = O_4 = O_5 = 0$)
- Well-matched and relaxed well-formed ($O_1 = O_2 = O_3 = O_4 = O_5 = 0$)

Apart from success rates, we also measure the missing zone error rate (MZ-ER), unwanted zone error rate (UZ-ER), and runtime for every non-dominated solution. The missing zone error rate is calculated as $O_1/|Z|$. The unwanted zone error rate is computed as $O_2/(2^{|S|} - 1 - |Z|)$. If $2^{|S|} - 1 - |Z| = 0$, the unwanted zone error rate is set to 0. Runtime is the algorithm's execution time in seconds.

We evaluate the overall performance of non-dominated solution sets for each abstract description across runs using metrics including missing zone error rate, unwanted zone error rate, runtime, and each objective value. For each abstract description, we first compute the average value of a metric across all non-dominated solutions within a run, and then average these values across the 30 runs. This yields a distribution of 76 abstract-description-level values per configuration for that metric.

6.2 Venn Diagrams

We test EvoEuler on generating Venn-(4–6), Venn-(4–6) with congruent shapes, and symmetric Venn-(3, 5). For all configurations, we additionally apply the congruent shape constraint when searching for Venn-(4–6) with congruent shapes and both symmetric diagram and congruent shape constraints when searching for symmetric Venn-(3, 5).

We report whether a solution satisfying a specific condition is found in any of the 30 runs. Conditions include:

- Independent family ($O_1 = O_2 = 0$)
- Venn diagram ($O_1 = O_2 = O_5 = 0$)
- Simple independent family ($O_1 = O_2 = O_3 = 0$)
- Simple Venn diagram ($O_1 = O_2 = O_3 = O_5 = 0$)

7 Results

7.1 Euler Diagrams

Figure 7 shows that all configurations achieve high success rates for no unwanted zones (75–89%) and relaxed well-formed (78–96%), but lower success rates (< 62%) for no missing zones, well-matched, and well-matched and relaxed well-formed. II-R achieves the highest success rate in all conditions, with II-R and III-R tied for the highest success rate in the relaxed well-formed condition.

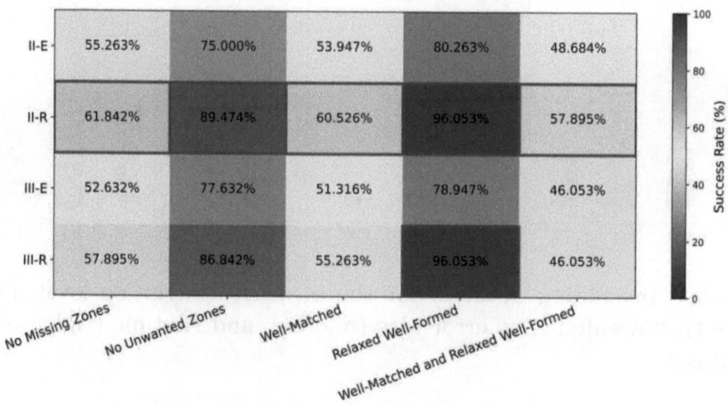

Fig. 7. Heatmap for success rate on the Gene Ontology dataset. Red boxes indicate the best values in each column. (Color figure online)

As well-matchedness and well-formedness are key properties for effective Euler diagrams, we examine how each configuration performs in finding well-matched and relaxed well-formed solutions for each abstract description. We can see from Fig. 8 that all configurations find a well-matched and relaxed well-formed solution for all abstract descriptions with 1–4 sets and 6 sets, but none find such a solution for any abstract description with at least 14 sets.

Figure 9 shows the boxplots for abstract-description-level missing zone error rate, unwanted zone error rate, and runtime. Configurations with rectangles

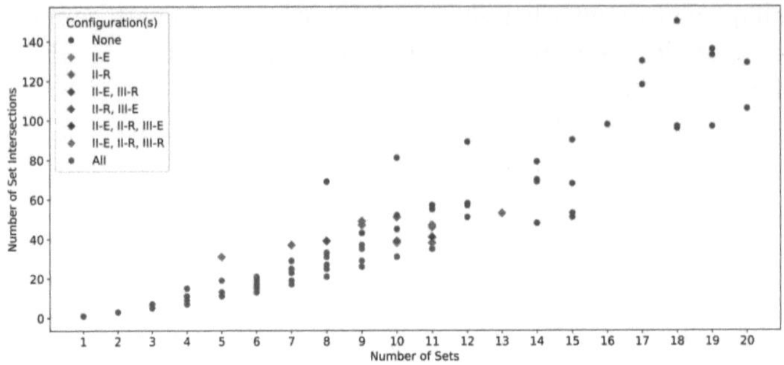

Fig. 8. Scatter plot showing whether each configuration finds a well-matched and relaxed well-formed solution for each abstract description on the Gene Ontology dataset

(i.e., II-R and III-R) outperform configurations with ellipses (i.e., II-E and III-E) across all metrics, while configurations that use the same shape perform similarly regardless of the algorithm used. Table 2 shows the same pattern for the average of abstract-description-level values for each objective.

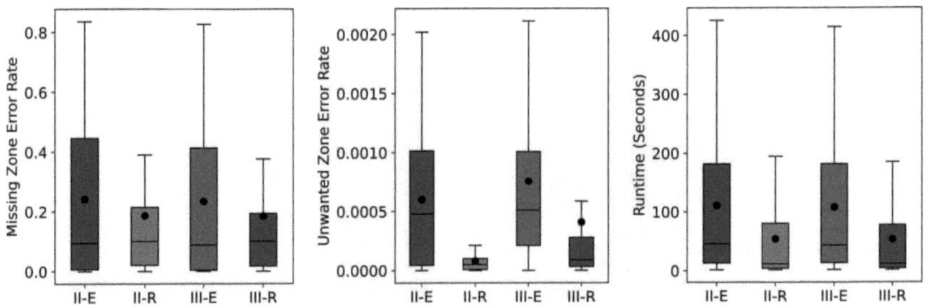

Fig. 9. Boxplots (excluding outliers) for the abstract-description-level missing zone error rate (left), unwanted zone error rate (middle), and runtime (right) on the Gene Ontology dataset

We conducted a Friedman test, which reveals significant differences across configurations for all abstract-description-level metrics ($p < 0.05$ for O_1 and missing zone error rate; $p < 0.001$ for all remaining metrics). We then performed pairwise post-hoc tests using Wilcoxon signed-rank tests with Bonferroni correction. Table 3 presents the pairwise comparison results for each metric, which confirms that configurations with rectangles significantly outperform configurations with ellipses on five out of eight metrics (O_1, O_2, O_4, unwanted zone error rate, and runtime).

Table 2. Average of the abstract-description-level values for each objective on the Gene Ontology dataset. The best value for each objective is in bold.

Configuration	O_1	O_2	O_3	O_4	O_5
II-E	21.322	19.255	0.037	3.430	2.704
II-R	16.978	3.350	**0.012**	**0.016**	**1.456**
III-E	20.808	17.774	0.042	3.385	2.577
III-R	**16.882**	**3.338**	0.024	0.025	1.716

Table 3. Pairwise comparisons for each abstract-description-level metric on the Gene Ontology dataset

Configuration	O_1	O_2	O_3	O_4	O_5	MZ-ER	UZ-ER	Runtime
II-E	A	A	A	A	A	A	A	A
II-R	B	B	B	B	B	BC	B	B
III-E	C	C	A	A	A C	B	A	C
III-R	B	B	A	C	C	C	C	B

7.2 Venn Diagrams

All configurations find simple Venn-4 and Venn-5 diagrams with or without congruent shapes. However, no configuration finds any solution that satisfies any condition when searching for Venn-6 with or without congruent shapes.

All configurations find simple symmetric Venn-3 diagrams. When searching for symmetric Venn-5 diagrams, only II-E and III-E find simple symmetric Venn-5 diagrams. II-R finds simple independent families, while III-R finds both simple independent families and non-simple symmetric Venn-5 diagrams.

Figure 10 shows some simple Venn-5 diagrams found by EvoEuler in this experiment, where Fig. 10a is generated without any constraints enabled, Fig. 10b is generated with the congruent shape constraint enabled, and Fig. 10c is generated with both symmetric diagram and congruent shape constraints enabled.

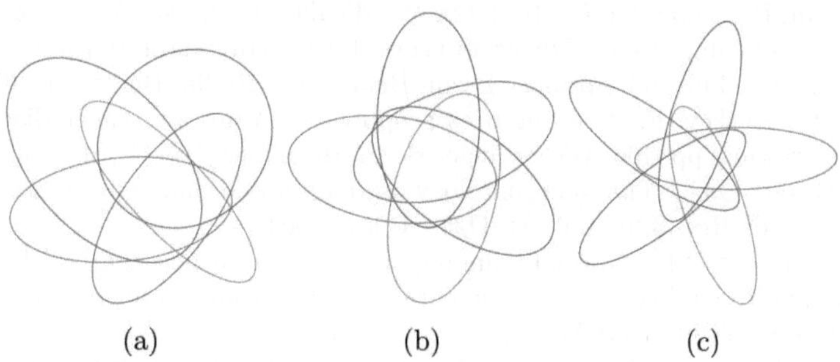

Fig. 10. Simple Venn-5 diagrams found by EvoEuler: (a) with ellipses, (b) with congruent ellipses, and (c) with rotational symmetry and congruent ellipses

8 Conclusions

We have introduced EvoEuler, a Python package for generating a set of non-dominated solutions (diagrams) with specific properties (well-matchedness, well-formedness, symmetric diagram, and congruent shape). For Euler diagrams, our results show that rectangles are preferred over ellipses. For Venn diagrams, EvoEuler successfully finds simple Venn diagrams for up to five sets.

Our method has two known limitations. First, it does not minimize violations of the no brushing points property. This is because we can only detect violations of this property when two curves touch at a single brushing point and do not cross. When two curves touch at a point and cross at other points, we cannot classify whether each point is a brushing point. Second, even though a zone may exist in a diagram generated by EvoEuler, its area can be too small.

We are extending EvoEuler to support the generation of area-proportional Euler and Venn diagrams by accepting area specifications as input and incorporating an objective that maximizes area accuracy. Our preliminary results are promising, suggesting that this is a viable direction.

In the future, we could conduct an empirical study comparing EvoEuler with existing methods. A user study could also be carried out to evaluate whether users benefit from exploring trade-offs among solutions and selecting solutions of interest. Moreover, to further improve flexibility, we could allow users to enable or disable some objectives before optimization starts.

Disclosure of Interests. The authors have no competing interests to declare that are relevant to the content of this article.

References

1. Anderson, D.E., Cleaver, F.L.: Venn-type diagrams for arguments of n terms. J. Symbolic Logic **30**(2), 113–118 (1965)
2. Benoy, F., Rodgers, P.: Evaluating the comprehension of Euler diagrams. In: 11th International Conference Information Visualization (IV '07), pp. 771–780 (2007)
3. Blank, J., Deb, K.: Pymoo: multi-objective optimization in python. IEEE Access **8**, 89497–89509 (2020)
4. Chapman, P., Stapleton, G., Rodgers, P., Micallef, L., Blake, A.: Visualizing sets: an empirical comparison of diagram types. In: Diagrammatic Representation and Inference, pp. 146–160. Springer Berlin Heidelberg, Berlin, Heidelberg (2014)
5. Chow, S., Ruskey, F.: Drawing area-proportional Venn and Euler diagrams. In: Graph Drawing, pp. 466–477. Springer Berlin Heidelberg, Berlin, Heidelberg (2004)
6. Consortium, G.O.: The gene ontology (go) database and informatics resource. Nucleic Acids Res. **32**(suppl_1), D258–D261 (2004)
7. Das, I., Dennis, J.E.: Normal-boundary intersection: a new method for generating the pareto surface in nonlinear multicriteria optimization problems. SIAM J. Optim. **8**(3), 631–657 (1998)
8. Deb, K., Pratap, A., Agarwal, S., Meyarivan, T.: A fast and elitist multiobjective genetic algorithm: NSGA-II. IEEE Trans. Evol. Comput. **6**(2), 182–197 (2002)

9. Deb, K.: Multi-objective Optimisation Using Evolutionary Algorithms: An Introduction, pp. 3–34. Springer (2011)
10. Deb, K., Jain, H.: An evolutionary many-objective optimization algorithm using reference-point-based nondominated sorting approach, part I: solving problems with box constraints. IEEE Trans. Evol. Comput. **18**(4), 577–601 (2014)
11. Flower, J., Howse, J.: Generating Euler diagrams. In: Diagrammatic Representation and Inference, pp. 61–75. Springer Berlin Heidelberg, Berlin, Heidelberg (2002)
12. Gillies, S., van der Wel, C., Van den Bossche, J., Taves, M.W., Arnott, J., Ward, B.C., et al.: Shapely (2025)
13. Griggs, J., Killian, C.E., Savage, C.D.: Venn diagrams and symmetric chain decompositions in the Boolean lattice. Electron. J. Comb. **11**(1), R2 (2004)
14. Grünbaum, B.: Venn diagrams and independent families of sets. Math. Mag. **48**(1), 12–23 (1975)
15. Henderson, D.W.: Venn diagrams for more than four classes. Am. Math. Mon. **70**(4), 424–426 (1963)
16. Inselberg, A., Dimsdale, B.: Parallel coordinates: a tool for visualizing multidimensional geometry. In: Proceedings of the First IEEE Conference on Visualization: Visualization '90, pp. 361–378 (1990)
17. Ishibuchi, H., Imada, R., Setoguchi, Y., Nojima, Y.: Performance comparison of NSGA-II and NSGA-III on various many-objective test problems. In: 2016 IEEE Congress on Evolutionary Computation (CEC). pp. 3045–3052 (2016)
18. Kehlbeck, R., Görtler, J., Wang, Y., Deussen, O.: Speuler: semantics-preserving Euler diagrams. IEEE Trans. Visual Comput. Graphics **28**(1), 433–442 (2022)
19. Paetzold, P., et al.: Recteuler: visualizing intersecting sets using rectangles. Comput. Graphics Forum **42**(3), 87–98 (2023)
20. Rodgers, P.: A survey of Euler diagrams. J. Vis. Lang. Comput. **25**(3), 134–155 (2014)
21. Rodgers, P., Zhang, L., Purchase, H.: Wellformedness properties in Euler diagrams: which should be used? IEEE Trans. Visual Comput. Graphics **18**(7), 1089–1100 (2012)
22. Rottmann, P., et al.: Generating Euler diagrams through combinatorial optimization. Comput. Graphics Forum **43**(3), e15089 (2024)
23. Simonetto, P., Archambault, D., Scheidegger, C.: A simple approach for boundary improvement of Euler diagrams. IEEE Trans. Visual Comput. Graphics **22**(1), 678–687 (2016)
24. Stapleton, G., Rodgers, P., Howse, J., Taylor, J.: Properties of Euler diagrams. Electron. Commun. EASST 7 (2007)
25. Streamlit. https://streamlit.io. Accessed 15 Feb 2026
26. Venn, J.: I. on the diagrammatic and mechanical representation of propositions and reasonings. London Edinburgh Dublin Philos. Mag. J. Sci. **10**(59), 1–18 (1880)
27. Wybrow, M., Rodgers, P., Dib, F.K.: Euler diagrams drawn with ellipses area-proportionally (EDEAP). BMC Bioinform. **22**(1), 214 (2021)
28. Yan, X., et al.: Eulermerge: simplifying Euler diagrams through set merges. In: Diagrammatic Representation and Inference, pp. 190–206. Springer Nature Switzerland, Cham (2024)
29. Zhou, A., et al.: Multiobjective evolutionary algorithms: a survey of the state of the art. Swarm Evol. Comput. **1**(1), 32–49 (2011)

Logic Sensitivity in Action: A Computational Tool for Aristotelian Diagrams

José David García Cruz(✉)

Universidad del Valle de Puebla, Dirección de Educación y Desarrollo Estudiantil, Puebla, Mexico
jose.garcia@uvp.edu.mx

Abstract. Aristotelian diagrams—such as the classical square of opposition and its generalisations—encode a rich network of logical relations between formulae. Recent work by Demey and Smessaert has shown that these diagrams are logically sensitive: the same set of formulae can yield geometrically distinct, and in general non-isomorphic, diagrams depending on the underlying logic. Despite its theoretical importance, this phenomenon has remained largely inaccessible to non-specialists because no interactive tool existed to visualise it directly. We present ARISTOBUILDER, a self-contained, browser-based application that computes and renders Aristotelian diagrams for propositional logic and five modal systems (K, KD, T, S4, S5). The engine implements the bitstring semantics of Demey and Smessaert over canonical finite samples of Kripke situations and maps logical relations to a standardised visual vocabulary. We describe the architecture, the key algorithms, and three worked examples that illustrate how logic sensitivity manifests across systems.

Keywords: Aristotelian diagrams · Square of opposition · Logical geometry · Logic sensitivity · Modal logic · Bitstrings · Kripke semantics · Interactive visualisation

1 Introduction and Background

The square of opposition is one of the oldest artefacts of formal reasoning, tracing its origins to Aristotle's *De Interpretatione* and *Prior Analytics*. In its classical form, it arranges four propositions at the corners of a square and connects them by four opposition relations: contradiction, contrariety, sub-contrariety, and subalternation. Over the past two decades, logicians have generalised this structure into an entire family of Aristotelian diagrams—hexagons, octagons, and beyond—governed by the same relational vocabulary [4,6].

A central insight of this research programme is that Aristotelian diagrams are not merely mnemonic devices but genuine geometric witnesses of logical structure. Demey and Smessaert have introduced the notion of *logical geometry* [5,7] to study these diagrams mathematically, and have shown that the geometry of

P. Sobociński et al. (Eds.): Diagrams 2026, LNAI 16833, pp. 342–349, 2027.
https://doi.org/10.1007/978-3-032-34178-5_34

a diagram depends critically on the logic in which the constituent formulae are interpreted. They call this dependence *logic sensitivity* [8]: a set of formulae that yields a square of opposition in one system may yield a hexagon, a degenerate diagram, or no connected diagram at all in another. More precisely, diagrams arising in different logics may be non-isomorphic with respect to the Boolean or Aristotelian isomorphism relations of logical geometry: two diagrams can be geometrically identical while still being logically distinct (e.g. a strong and a weak version of the same hexagonal shape).

Despite the elegance of this theory, the phenomenon of logic sensitivity has so far been difficult to demonstrate interactively. Checking whether two formulae stand in a given Aristotelian relation requires either a manual model-theoretic argument or a dedicated theorem prover, neither of which is accessible to students or researchers approaching the topic for the first time.

We address this gap with AristoBuilder, a self-contained HTML application (CDN dependency: Cytoscape.js [3]) that:

1. parses formulae of propositional and modal logic written in a simple ASCII notation;
2. computes Aristotelian relations using the bitstring semantics of Demey and Smessaert over canonical finite samples of Kripke models;
3. renders the resulting diagram interactively in the browser with a standardised visual encoding; and
4. allows the user to switch between logical systems in real time, directly observing how the diagram geometry changes.

Aristotelian and Related Relations. Let L be a logic with consequence relation $\vdash_L$. Two formulae φ, ψ stand in the following Aristotelian *opposition* relations: *Contradiction* if $\vdash \neg(\varphi \wedge \psi)$ and $\vdash \varphi \vee \psi$; *Contrariety* if $\vdash \neg(\varphi \wedge \psi)$ and $\nvdash \varphi \vee \psi$; *Sub-contrariety* if $\vdash \varphi \vee \psi$ and $\nvdash \neg(\varphi \wedge \psi)$; *Subalternation* ($\varphi \Rightarrow \psi$) if $\vdash \varphi \rightarrow \psi$ and $\nvdash \psi \rightarrow \varphi$. The tool also reports *Equivalence* ($\vdash \varphi \leftrightarrow \psi$), which belongs to the implication rather than the opposition vocabulary, and *Unconnectedness*, which signals the absence of any of the above; both are included for diagnostic completeness.

Bitstrings. Demey and Smessaert represent each formula φ by a bitstring [6] $\mathrm{bs}(\varphi) = \langle b_1, \ldots, b_n \rangle \in \{0,1\}^n$, where each position i corresponds to a *class* of situations (a partition cell of the full situation space) and $b_i = 1$ iff the formula is true in the representative situation of that class. Aristotelian relations then reduce to Boolean operations: φ, ψ are contradictory iff $\mathrm{bs}(\varphi) = \overline{\mathrm{bs}(\psi)}$; contrary iff their bitwise AND is $\mathbf{0}$ and OR is not $\mathbf{1}$; etc. This reduction makes the relations decidable and efficiently computable. The bitstrings produced by AristoBuilder are not guaranteed to be minimal: e.g. $\{p \wedge q, p \vee q, \neg p \wedge \neg q, \neg p \vee \neg q\}$ receives 4-bit strings from the engine, whereas the shortest faithful representation has length 3. Non-minimality does not affect the correctness of the classifier.

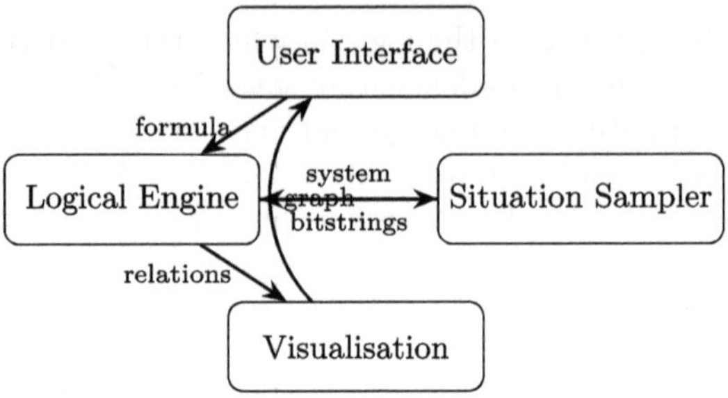

Fig. 1. High-level architecture of AristoBuilder.

2 System Architecture

AristoBuilder is a single ≈1200-line HTML file with no server-side component; Cytoscape.js is its only external dependency. Three functional layers interact as shown in Fig. 1: a *logical engine* (parser and relation classifier), a *situation sampler* (Kripke model enumerator), and a *visualisation renderer* (Cytoscape.js canvas).

2.1 User Interface

The interface is divided into three zones. A header bar hosts the formula input field, a system selector (Prop, K, KD, T, S4, S5), one-click symbol buttons ($\neg$, $\wedge$, $\vee$, $\rightarrow$, $\leftrightarrow$, $\Box$, $\Diamond$), and layout presets (square, hexagon, circle). Disjunction uses `|` in the ASCII input notation for parser compatibility, though we acknowledge that `|` is conventionally reserved for the Sheffer stroke; a future version will additionally accept `v`. A left panel shows, for each formula pair, the detected relation, proof-theoretic certificates (sequents), and bitgrids. The central canvas supports draggable nodes and a context menu for removing formulae.

2.2 Logical Engine

Parser. Formulae use ASCII notation: `~` ($\neg$), `&` ($\wedge$), `|` ($\vee$), `->` ($\rightarrow$), `<->` ($\leftrightarrow$), `[]` ($\Box$), `<>` ($\Diamond$). A recursive descent parser builds an AST with standard precedence ($\neg > \wedge > \vee > \rightarrow > \leftrightarrow$).

Relation Classifier. Given bitstrings bs(φ) and bs(ψ), the classifier tests four Boolean conditions (Listing 1.1).

```
function classify(bs_A, bs_B):
  bothTrue  := exists i. bs_A[i]=1 and bs_B[i]=1
  bothFalse := exists i. bs_A[i]=0 and bs_B[i]=0
  AtoB := forall i. bs_A[i]=1 => bs_B[i]=1
  BtoA := forall i. bs_B[i]=1 => bs_A[i]=1
```

```
  if not bothTrue and not bothFalse: return
     CONTRADICTION
  if not bothTrue and bothFalse:     return
     CONTRARY
  if bothTrue and not bothFalse:     return
     SUBCONTRARY
  if AtoB and BtoA:                  return
     EQUIVALENCE
  if AtoB:  return SUBALTERNATION(A, B)
  if BtoA:  return SUBALTERNATION(B, A)
  return UNCONNECTED
```

Listing 1.1. Relation classifier (pseudocode).

3 Semantics and Bitstring Computation

3.1 Propositional Logic

For n propositional variables the situation set is all 2^n truth-value assignments. Each formula is evaluated by truth-table recursion (Listing 1.2) and the resulting bits assembled into $\mathrm{bs}(\varphi)$.

```
function evalProp(node, valuation):
  if node.type = VAR: return valuation[node.name]
  if node.type = NOT: return not evalProp(node.
     child, valuation)
  if node.type = AND: return evalProp(node.left,v)
     and evalProp(node.right,v)
  if node.type = OR:  return evalProp(node.left,v)
     or  evalProp(node.right,v)
  if node.type = IMP: return not evalProp(node.left
     ,v) or evalProp(node.right,v)
  if node.type = IFF: return evalProp(node.left,v)
     = evalProp(node.right,v)

function propBitstring(formula, vars):
  bits := []
  for each valuation v over vars:    // 2^|vars|
     valuations
    bits.append(evalProp(formula, v))
  return bits
```

Listing 1.2. Propositional evaluation and bitstring construction (pseudocode).

3.2 Modal Logic: Kripke Semantics over Finite Model Samples

For systems K, KD, T, S4, S5, the situation set consists of pairs (M, w_0) with fixed $w_0 = 0$. Frame conditions are as follows:

System	Frame condition on R
K	(none)
KD	serial: $\forall w\, \exists v.\ wRv$
T	reflexive: $\forall w.\ wRw$
S4	Reflexive and transitive: $\forall w.\ wRw$; $\forall u, v, w.\ uRv \wedge vRw \Rightarrow uRw$
S5	reflexive, symmetric, and transitive

Tractability Constraint. For tractability the engine enumerates models with at most $N = 3$ worlds and at most **two propositional variables**. This restriction is fundamental: formulae with three or more distinct variables will be evaluated over an incomplete situation sample and yield incorrect results without warning. For example, in S5 the formula $\Box(p \wedge q \wedge r)$ is misclassified as *contrary* to $\Box(p \wedge q)$ rather than standing in the correct *subalternation* relation, because the three-variable situations required to witness subalternation are absent. Users must enforce this constraint manually in the current version; a future release will detect and flag violations automatically.

Within the two-variable limit, the sample comprises at most $512 \times 64 = 32{,}768$ situations per system (before frame filtering), well within browser performance limits and sufficient to distinguish all standard formulae of monomodal propositional logic with two variables [1]. Modal evaluation follows standard Kripke truth conditions (Listing 1.3).

```
function evalModal(node, model, world):
  if node.type = VAR: return model.val[node.name][
      world]
  if node.type = BOX:
    return forall v: model.R(world,v) => evalModal(
        node.child, model, v)
  if node.type = DIA:
    return exists v: model.R(world,v) and evalModal
        (node.child, model, v)
  // Boolean cases (NOT, AND, OR, IMP, IFF) as in
      evalProp
```

Listing 1.3. Modal evaluation at a world (pseudocode).

The bitstring of φ in system L over variable set V is then $\mathrm{bs}(\varphi)_{L,V} = \big[(M_i, w_i^0) \models_L \varphi\big]_{(M_i, w_i^0) \in \mathrm{Sit}(L,V)}$.

4 Visualisation

Aristotelian relations are rendered on the Cytoscape.js canvas using the visual vocabulary of Table 1. For each detected relation, the left panel additionally displays proof-theoretic certificates: the sequents that witness the relation, with provable sequents verified by exhaustion over the situation sample and refutable ones by explicit counterexample.

Table 1. Visual encoding of Aristotelian relations.

Relation	Edge style	Colour
Contradiction	solid line	Rose/`#d4748e`
Contrariety	dashed line	Steel blue/`#6fa8d8`
Sub-contrariety	dotted line	Teal/`#5bbfaa`
Subalternation	directed arrow	Lavender/`#c4a8e8`
Equivalence	double-headed arrow	Amber/`#e8c46d`
Unconnectedness	(no edge)	—

5 Logic Sensitivity in Action: Three Case Studies

5.1 Case 1: The Modal Square and Its Collapse

Consider the four formulae $\{\Box p, \Diamond p, \neg\Box p, \neg\Diamond p\}$. In system S5 they generate a proper square of opposition: the pairs $(\Box p, \neg\Box p)$ and $(\Diamond p, \neg\Diamond p)$ are contradictory; $(\Box p, \neg\Diamond p)$ are *contrary* (cannot both be true, but their disjunction is not a tautology); $(\neg\Box p, \Diamond p)$ are *subcontrary*; and $\Box p \Rightarrow \Diamond p$ is a subalternation.

Switching from S5 to K removes the reflexivity of R, which breaks the subalternation $\Box p \Rightarrow \Diamond p$: a model with no accessible worlds makes $\Box p$ vacuously true and $\Diamond p$ false. The square dissolves, retaining only the two contradiction pairs—a direct instance of what Demey has called the logic-sensitivity of subalternation [8].

5.2 Case 2: T Versus S4 for Iterated Modalities

Take $\varphi_1 = \Box p$, $\varphi_2 = \Box\Box p$, $\varphi_3 = \neg\Box p$, $\varphi_4 = \neg\Box\Box p$. In system T (reflexive frames), $\Box p \Rightarrow p$ holds but $\Box\Box p \not\Rightarrow \Box p$ in general, so φ_1 and φ_2 are unconnected. In system S4 (reflexive and transitive frames), transitivity gives $\Box p \leftrightarrow \Box\Box p$, collapsing φ_1 and φ_2 into a single equivalence class (amber edge). The diagram becomes a degenerate Aristotelian diagram in which the four formulae reduce to two equivalence classes, illustrating how the addition of transitivity alone produces a qualitative change in the diagram's logical structure.

5.3 Case 3: A Propositional Hexagon

For a purely propositional example, consider the six formulae $\{p \wedge q, p \wedge \neg q, \neg p \wedge q, \neg p \wedge \neg q, p, \neg p\}$ over two variables. Their 4-bit strings are:

Formula	Bitstring
$p \wedge q$	1000
$p \wedge \neg q$	0100
$\neg p \wedge q$	0010
$\neg p \wedge \neg q$	0001
p	1100
$\neg p$	0011

The classifier detects: p and $\neg p$ are contradictory; each minterm is contrary to every minterm with the opposite first conjunct; p subalternates both $p \wedge q$ and $p \wedge \neg q$ (likewise $\neg p$). Laid out in the hexagon preset, ARISTOBUILDER renders a hexagonal Aristotelian diagram with all relations correctly colour-coded.

This hexagon is *not* a Jacoby–Sesmat–Blanché (JSB) hexagon: a JSB hexagon requires that the formula set be closed under negation (every φ present implies $\neg\varphi$ also present), whereas here $p \wedge q$ appears without $\neg(p \wedge q)$. The structure is instead a *subalternation hexagon* built on the Boolean partition of two propositional variables: the four minterms occupy the lower corners, and p and $\neg p$ form the two upper vertices each subalternated to by two minterms.

6 Conclusions and Future Work

We have presented ARISTOBUILDER, a self-contained, browser-based tool for constructing and exploring Aristotelian diagrams across six logical systems. The tool implements the bitstring semantics of Demey and Smessaert over a canonical finite sample of Kripke situations (at most two propositional variables and three worlds), computes Aristotelian relations by Boolean operations on bitstrings, and renders the resulting diagram with a standardised visual vocabulary. Three case studies demonstrated how the same formulae produce non-isomorphic diagrams as the underlying logic changes—making logic sensitivity directly observable and interactive.

Several directions remain open. First, *variable-count extension*: lifting the two-variable cap via partial enumeration or symbolic methods is the most pressing engineering priority, as it would make the tool usable for richer formula sets without the current misclassification risk. Second, *non-classical logics*: adding intuitionistic, paraconsistent, and many-valued settings [2] would enrich the comparative dimension of the tool. Third, *axiom-based system definition*: allowing users to compose a modal logic from n independent axioms (e.g. $\Box p \rightarrow p$, $\Box p \rightarrow \Diamond p$, $\Box p \rightarrow \Box\Box p$) would enable exploration of up to 2^n distinct systems without hardcoded presets. Fourth, *export*: adding SVG or JSON output would make ARISTOBUILDER more useful for academic publication workflows. Finally, *empirical evaluation*: a user study with students of logic and philosophy would provide evidence about whether interactive logic-sensitive diagrams improve understanding of modal distinctions.

ARISTOBUILDER is available as a single distributable HTML file at https://github.com/0010x0101x0000x0110/aristobuilder/tree/main/aristobuilder.

References

1. Blackburn, P., de Rijke, M., Venema, Y.: Modal Logic. Cambridge University Press, Cambridge (2001)
2. Béziau, J.Y., Jacquette, D. (eds.): Around and Beyond the Square of Opposition. Birkhäuser, Basel (2012)
3. Franz, M., Lopes, C.T., Huck, G., Dong, Y., Sumer, O., Bader, G.D.: Cytoscape.js: a graph theory library for visualisation and analysis. Bioinformatics **32**(2), 309–311 (2016)
4. Demey, L.: Structures of oppositions for public announcement logic. In: Béziau, J.Y., Jacquette, D. (eds.) Around and Beyond the Square of Opposition, pp. 313–339. Birkhäuser, Basel (2012)
5. Demey, L., Smessaert, H.: The relationship between Aristotelian and Hasse diagrams. In: Dwyer, T., Purchase, H., Delaney, A. (eds.) Diagrams 2014. LNCS (LNAI), vol. 8578, pp. 213–227. Springer, Heidelberg (2014). https://doi.org/10.1007/978-3-662-44043-8_23
6. Demey, L., Smessaert, H.: Combinatorial bitstring semantics for arbitrary logical fragments. J. Philos. Log. **47**(2), 325–363 (2018)
7. Demey, L., Smessaert, H.: Metalogical decorations of logical diagrams. Log. Univers. **10**(2–3), 233–292 (2016)
8. Demey, L.: Aristotelian diagrams for semantic and syntactic consequence. Synthese **198**(1), 187–207 (2021)

Combined Network and Set Visualization with Hoop and Linear Diagrams

Markus Wallinger[1], Peter Chapman[2], Martin Nöllenburg[3], Peter Rodgers[4(✉)], and Andrew Blake[5]

[1] Technical University of Munich, Munich, Germany
[2] Edinburgh Napier University, Edinburgh, UK
[3] TU Wien, Vienna, Austria
[4] University of Kent, Kent, UK
p.j.rodgers@kent.ac.uk
[5] University of Brighton, Brighton, UK

Abstract. Set and network data co-occur frequently, with the sets representing node groupings and the network representing connections between node pairs. This paper investigates two different designs for jointly visualizing set and network data: HoopNet and LinearNet. HoopNet juxtaposes a hoop diagram with a circular network layout, whereas LinearNet juxtaposes a linear diagram with a linear network layout. We investigate two variations of each: a set-first and a network-first layout. Our human-subject studies show there is no difference between set-first and network-first optimization. However, participants achieved significantly higher accuracy with HoopNet, indicating it is a more effective visualization for set and network data than LinearNet.

Keywords: Linear Diagram · Hoop Diagram · Node-link Diagram

1 Introduction

Networks express relationships between pairs of objects, while set systems capture groupings of objects. Many real-world datasets combine these structures, including biochemical reaction networks [34] and social networks [16]. Such datasets require visualizations that support joint reasoning about both pairwise connections and overlapping sets. Although network and set visualization have each been studied extensively, their integration remains challenging [33].

In this paper, we investigate two designs for integrated set and network visualization. *HoopNet* combines hoop diagrams [27] with circular node-link layouts [3], while *LinearNet* combines linear diagrams [29] with arc-based network layouts (see Fig. 1). Both combine set and network aspects, revealing set membership and connectivity. These designs are grounded in prior empirical work showing that linear diagrams outperform some other set visualization designs [7,15]. They align naturally with circular and linear network layouts, respectively. Whilst related designs appear in prior work [26,32], we develop layout optimization

P. Sobociński et al. (Eds.): Diagrams 2026, LNAI 16833, pp. 350–365, 2027.
https://doi.org/10.1007/978-3-032-34178-5_35

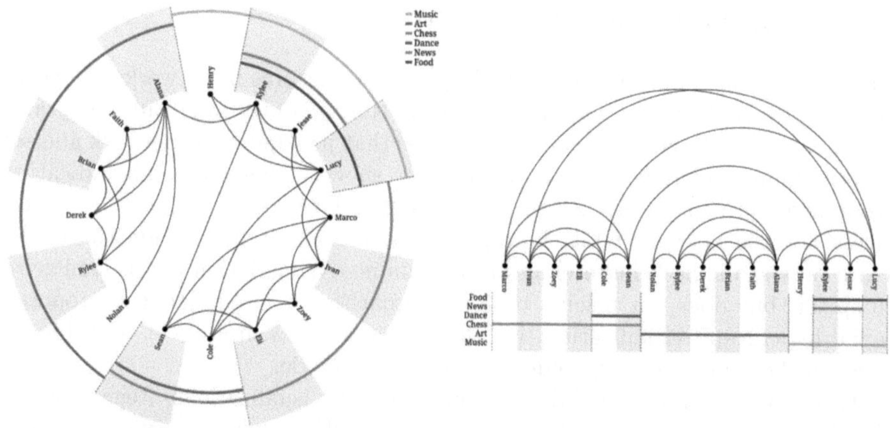

Fig. 1. Both HoopNet (left) and LinearNet (right) visualize networks and sets defined over nodes. HoopNet juxtaposes a hoop diagram with a circular network layout. LinearNet juxtaposes a linear diagram with a linear network layout. Both are set-first variants minimizing the number of gaps in the set lines.

methods and evaluate their comparative effectiveness through controlled studies.

We investigate the following research question: *How do radial and linear spatial organizations influence human accuracy and efficiency when reasoning about overlapping sets and network connectivity?*

To enable valid comparisons, we developed two exact optimization strategies based on integer linear programming: a *set-first* strategy that minimizes gaps in set lines, and a *network-first* strategy that minimizes edge crossings in the network layout. These strategies yield controlled layouts for studying how spatial organization affects task performance. Based on these layouts, we conducted three user studies focusing on accuracy and task completion time. The first two studies compared set-first and network-first optimization within each design. The third and main study directly compared HoopNet and LinearNet, using their set-first variants. Our results indicate that the radial design of HoopNet better supports comprehension in integrated set and network visualizations.

Our contributions include:

- **Diagram Design:** We detail the design of two closely related diagram forms: HoopNet and LinearNet and discuss how the radial spatial organization of HoopNet better supports integrated reasoning about sets and networks.
- **Optimization Framework:** We introduce two exact integer linear programming (ILP) strategies, *set-first* and *network-first* for the layout of HoopNet and LinearNet.
- **Empirical Evaluation:** Through three crowdsourced studies (N≈510), we systematically compare HoopNet and LinearNet in terms of accuracy and completion time. HoopNet achieved significantly higher accuracy than LinearNet (~10% overall, ~13% for larger networks).

2 Background and Related Work

The focus of this paper is on visualizing group structures in networks. A recent survey is by Vehlow et al. [33]. Early work in this area overlayed Euler diagrams with networks [22]. Here, we focus on designs that juxtapose the network and set aspects. Some techniques use arc diagrams to show the network while indicating group structure with trees [24] or treemaps [23]. TreeNetViz [16] uses a circular layout for the network while juxtaposing a tree hierarchy outside the circle. Work on visualizing gene interaction in immune dysregulation [32] is similar to HoopNet, but does not discuss design approaches. Also similar is a proposed radial hypergraph visualization [18] which places nodes in a circle, with binary edges in the centre and hyperedges around the outside.

Our work relies on combining set and network visualizations. Regarding set visualization, we use linear diagrams and hoop diagrams. A survey by Alsallakh et al. [2] categorizes linear diagrams as an aggregation-based set visualization technique, conceptually similar to matrix-based approaches. The core visual metaphor is a matrix in which each set is represented by a horizontal line in its corresponding row, and each element by a column. A horizontal line segment is drawn within a cell if the corresponding element belongs to the set. Unlike matrix-based techniques, linear diagrams merge consecutive elements of the same set into a single continuous line segment that spans all relevant cells. An empirical study [29] identified key design guidelines for linear diagrams, highlighting that minimizing the number of set line gaps significantly improves task performance. Furthermore, perceived visual clutter has been shown to correlate with the number of gaps [1]. However, minimizing the total number of gaps is an NP-hard problem [6,9]. One of the most widely used visualizations for general set systems are Euler diagrams. However, the scalability of Euler diagrams is restricted, and studies have demonstrated that linear diagrams outperform Euler diagrams as a more effective set visualization [7,15]. Recently, hoop diagrams [27] have been introduced as a variant of linear diagrams, where visual elements are arranged in a circular rather than linear layout. A comparative study found no significant difference in user performance between hoop and linear diagrams, suggesting both are effective for set visualization. Our work builds on these foundations. We follow validated design guidelines from the above prior studies when integrating linear and hoop diagrams with network visualization in HoopNet and LinearNet.

Regarding network visualization, node-link diagrams are a common design, where nodes are represented by small disks and edges are represented by curves connecting the respective nodes. A recent survey of surveys on network visualization [11] summarizes the current state of research for different network dataset types. For this paper, the most relevant types of node-link layouts are the circular layout [10,30] and the arc diagram [36]. Circular layouts arrange all nodes on a circle, while linear arc layouts arrange all nodes on a horizontal or vertical line. One of the key advantages of these layouts is that they are fully defined by a cyclic or linear order over the nodes. Combinatorially, circular layouts are considered equivalent to linear layouts [19] as all nodes are in a convex position

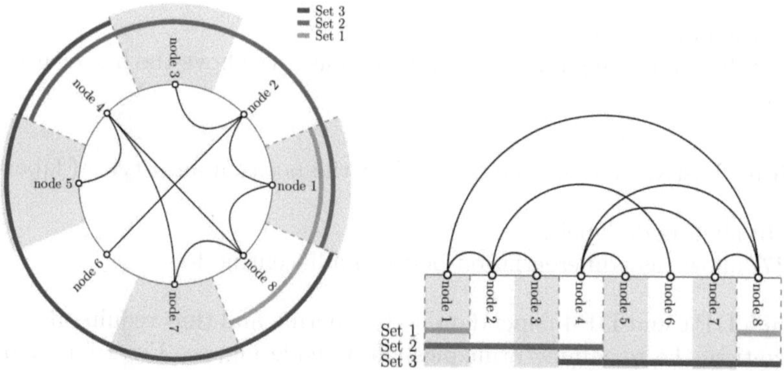

Fig. 2. HoopNet (left) and LinearNet (right) with the same instance and node ordering.

and induce the same number of edge crossings. Optimizing the layout to minimize crossings is considered to increase the readability of networks [3]. Most of the available algorithms for circular layouts are heuristics, but optimal ILP formulations have also been proposed [14].

3 Design Description

We combine hoop set diagrams with circular network layouts to create **HoopNet** diagrams. Similarly, we combine linear set diagrams with linear network layouts to obtain **LinearNet** diagrams. We juxtapose and attach the set visualization to the network visualization so that our designs consider both aspects in a coherent hybrid visualization that embodies two contrasting spatial metaphors, radial vs. linear, that we hypothesize support different cognitive strategies. The concepts of our design description are illustrated in Fig. 2.

Set Visualization. HoopNet and LinearNet diagrams are based on hoop diagrams [27] and on linear diagrams [29], respectively. Hoop diagrams are structurally similar to linear diagrams, as hoop diagrams can be considered linear diagrams wrapped around a circle by attaching the end of the linear diagram to its beginning. As there are no experimental results for hoop diagrams, we use design principles empirically validated for linear diagrams [29] and assume they also apply to hoop diagrams. These design principles are:

- **DP1:** minimize the number of gaps in set lines.
- **DP2:** use visual guide lines at the beginning and end of line segments.
- **DP3:** use thin set lines.

Network Visualization. We represent the network as a node-link diagram guided by the following principles. These have been validated by studies [25] in the case of **DP4** and by following standard linear and circle designs in the case of **DP5**, as curved edges considerably improve crossing angles:

- **DP4:** minimize edge crossings.
- **DP5:** draw nodes equidistantly and edges as arcs above the line or inside the circle.

Labeling. Lastly, we also need to consider the position and style of labels.

- **DP6:** align node labels.
- **DP7:** allow easy differentiation between adjacent nodes.

While **DP1** and **DP4** depend on node ordering and thus require algorithmic optimization, the remaining principles affect rendering; see Fig. 2 for examples.

To support **DP2**, we add dashed gray guide lines at the start and end of set line segments, indicating when two consecutive nodes differ in set membership.

For **DP5**, we render edges differently in the two designs. In HoopNet, edges are drawn as cubic splines with three control points: the two endpoints and a midpoint. The midpoint is obtained by first computing the straight-line midpoint, then projecting a perpendicular toward the circleâ€™center, and placing the control point halfway along this line. In LinearNet, edges are drawn as circular arcs centered at the midpoint between the endpoints.

Finally, to address **DP7**, we alternate background shading to distinguish between sectors of consecutive nodes. For even-sized networks, we alternate white and light gray; for odd-sized networks, we cycle among white, very light gray, and light gray to increase visual saliency.

Set-First and Network-First Layouts. To support a controlled comparison between HoopNet and LinearNet, we compute optimal node orderings that minimize either gaps (**DP1**) or edge crossings (**DP4**). These two objectives are often in direct conflict: a gap-minimal order can incur many edge crossings, and vice versa; see Fig. 3. Both problems are NP-hard [6,9], and we solve them exactly with integer linear programs; full formulations are in the supplemental material on OSF.

Crossing minimization follows the formulation of [14]. Binary variables $x_{u,v}$ encode whether node u precedes v in the order, with transitivity constraints enforcing a valid linear (equivalently [19], cyclic) order. For each pair of independent edges, an indicator variable is active whenever their endpoints interleave in the order, and the objective sums these indicators.

Gap minimization reduces to the Travelling Salesperson Problem [9] on the complete auxiliary graph $G^\star = (V, E^\star)$ whose edge weight $w_{u,v}$ is the Hamming distance between rows u and v of the set–node incidence matrix. Placing two nodes adjacently induces one gap for every set whose membership differs between them, so a minimum-weight Hamiltonian cycle corresponds to a gap-minimal cyclic order. For LinearNet, we add a zero-weight dummy node to mark the start and end of the linear order.

Two-Stage Combination. In the set-first variant, we solve the gap ILP first for a gap-optimal tour. Consecutive nodes with identical set memberships may be freely swapped without creating new gaps, so we then run the crossing ILP

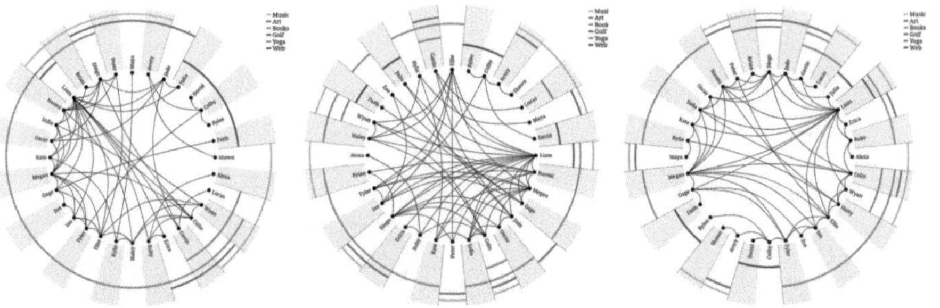

Fig. 3. Instance with 32 nodes and 6 sets. Ordering nodes randomly (middle) induces 439 crossings and 29 gaps. Optimizing gaps (left) results in 139 crossings and 8 gaps. Optimizing crossings (right) results in 82 crossings and 24 gaps.

with the relative order of all other node pairs fixed and select the layout with the fewest crossings. The network-first variant inverts this: We enumerate multiple crossing-optimal orders and pick the one with the fewest gaps. See Fig. 3 for the resulting layout differences.

Although computational performance was not our primary focus, we assessed HoopNet and LinearNet in terms of runtime. Detailed numerical results are provided in the supplemental material. Runtimes for both strategies quickly became impractical for larger instances (32 nodes and 5 sets), exceeding three hours for network-first. Thus, although optimal solutions provide reliable benchmarks, exact optimization may not be suitable for practical use in all cases.

4 Empirical Study Process

Our three empirical studies were designed to help address our research question.

We have two alternative layout approaches for both of these diagram types: set-first and network-first. We followed the tournament-based experimental methodology in [29]. Hence, in the first two studies, we examined which of set-first and network-first is the better design for HoopNet and LinearNet. For the final study, we selected the best design for both and compared HoopNet with LinearNet to determine whether a radial or linear spatial organization should be preferred. This led to the following six null hypotheses:

- **H0:A1** There is no difference in accuracy for HoopNet between optimizing network-first or optimizing set-first.
- **H0:B1** There is no difference in task completion time on HoopNet between optimizing network-first or optimizing set-first.
- **H0:A2** There is no difference in accuracy for LinearNet between optimizing network-first or optimizing set-first.
- **H0:B2** There is no difference in task completion time on LinearNet between optimizing network-first or optimizing set-first.
- **H0:A3** There is no difference in accuracy between HoopNet or LinearNet.

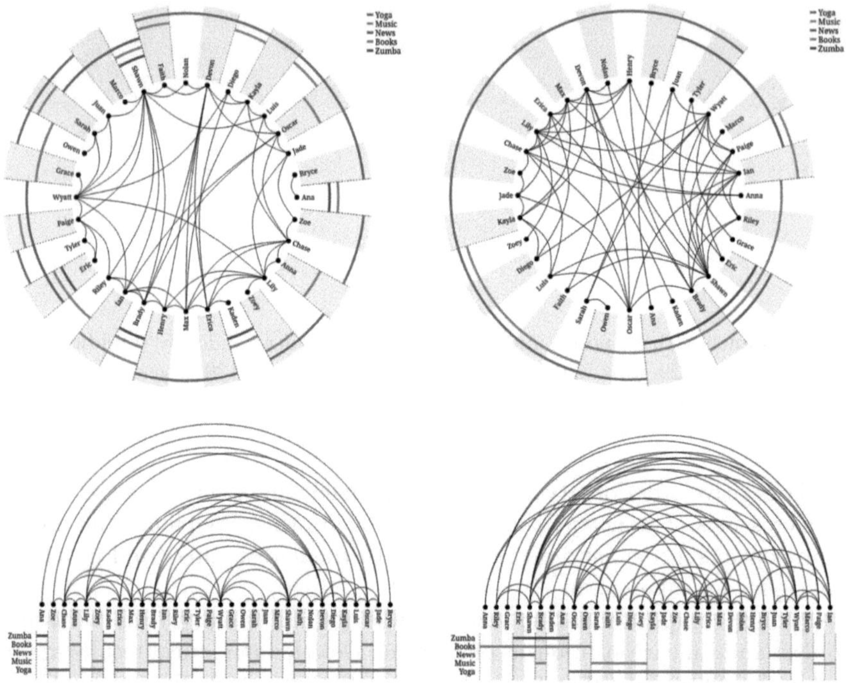

Fig. 4. One large ($|V| = 32$, $\mathcal{S} = 5$) instance used in our study visualized as HoopNet (top) and LinearNet (bottom). The left column shows network-first optimization while the right column shows set-first optimization.

- **H0:B3** There is no difference in task completion time between HoopNet or LinearNet.

We expected each of these accuracy and time hypothesis pairs to be answered with three separate studies. We developed an online study platform and chose the crowdsourcing platform Prolific (www.prolific.com) to recruit participants. Crowdsourcing is a widely used and reliable way of finding participants for information visualization studies [4]. Prolific is specifically designed for academic research, providing suitable filters and features.

4.1 Methodology

Data Preparation. Our data are drawn from the SNAP dataset [21], in particular, Twitter follows and circles. Twitter had connections between users, where one user followed the tweets of others. Twitter circles were smaller, and tweets could be restricted to selected user groups. To ease understanding for a wider audience, we reinterpreted this data as undirected friendship links rather than follows, and as subject interest groups rather than circles. Singleton nodes and non-overlapping sets were discarded, and further automatic filtering was applied to the simplest components to meet the size requirements listed below. The nodes were then renamed using a list of common first names, avoiding names that started with the same letter when possible. We used common interests for the sets, again avoiding those sharing a starting letter.

Diagram Size. To provide variety, we used *small* and *large* diagrams for the data collection tasks, with sizes typical for network visualization user studies [5]. Small diagrams had 16 nodes and 3 or 4 sets. Large diagrams had 32 nodes and 5 or 6 sets. Small and large are used to differentiate between our two datasets in this context. Diagrams were chosen at random as long as they could provide unambiguous, correct answers of sufficient complexity and enough potential alternative incorrect answers for the multiple-choice selection. The incorrect alternatives were chosen at random from the potential alternatives.

Tasks. To ensure variety in tasks, we developed four task types (T1–T4), with examples listed below. They were divided into *set-oriented* (T1, T2) and *network-oriented* tasks (T3, T4). All tasks required studying both the set and network information in order to complete successfully, however, we considered the set-oriented tasks to require study of the set information first, followed by the network information. Conversely, we considered network-oriented tasks to require studying network information first, followed by the set information.

In terms of developing tasks, we accessed existing task classifications for sets [2] and networks [20]. In all cases, the set part of the tasks falls into the "Tasks related to elements" classification because the shared information between the set visualization and the network visualization is through the elements (or nodes). The network part of the tasks again involves nodes, and the tasks are classified as "Adjacency" (both counting adjacency and finding adjacent nodes) and "Common connection". We calibrated the level of difficulty of both the set and network parts of tasks in the knowledge that non-expert users would need to complete all parts of the multi-section tasks to be successful.

Study Design. We chose a between-subject design, so each subject saw the same conditions throughout. This was because we thought a within-subject design would lead to too much confusion when participants were presented with both HoopNet and LinearNet diagrams.

From our experience with previous studies, we estimated that 12 data collection tasks were a suitable number for participants to complete in a reasonable time. Whilst a smaller study with 8 tasks would have been possible with the combination of 4 task types and 2 data sizes, we performed more tests to allow for more data collection in the time we felt was reasonable. Of the four task types, half had two small and one large diagram (T1, T3), whilst the others had one small and two large diagrams (T2, T4). We chose the details of each task (such as number, person, or set intersections) required for the tasks at random. However, we added restrictions on answer uniqueness and to ensure that the questions would be at the right level of complexity for participants to engage with the diagrams. For instance, for T4, the friendship count was restricted to

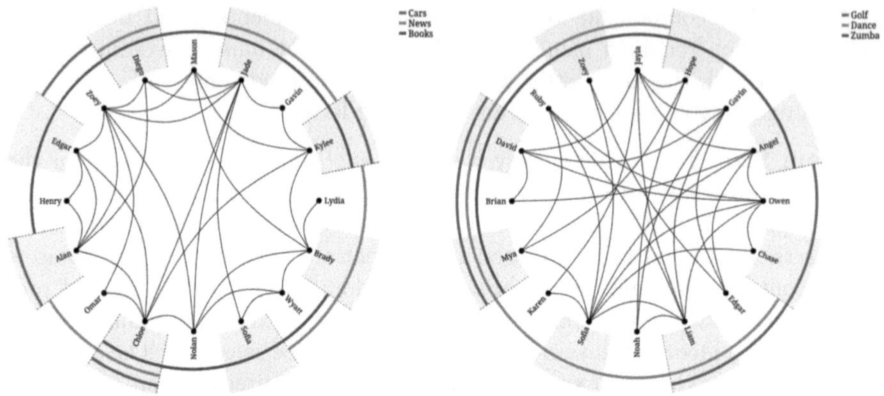

Fig. 5. One small ($|V| = 16$, $\mathcal{S} = 3$) instance used in our study visualized as HoopNet. In (left), we asked the participants: "What are the interests of the person who is friends with both Kylee and Edgar?" (T3). For (right), we asked the participants "Who is interested in Golf, Dance, and Zumba and is also friends with Jayla?" (T1).

a random number with exactly one correct answer in the diagram and between 3 and 8. Below, we list one example question for each task type.

- T1. *Who is interested in Golf, Dance, and Zumba and is also friends with Jayla?* Here, the set intersection and person vary. This is related to the set sub-task of finding set intersections, followed by the network sub-task of finding named nodes and discovering their links. An alternative, less efficient, network-first strategy is to find a named node, examine its connecting nodes, and then find all set intersections among them. We mitigate against this alternative strategy by putting the set intersection first in the question. This is for Fig. 5 (right), the first data collection task, a small diagram. Answer options: *David*, *Zoey*, *Edgar*, *Maya*, with *David* being correct.
- T2. *How many friendship links are there joining people who have interests in News only to people who have interests in Music only?* Here, the two set intersections vary. This relates to the set sub-task of finding named set intersections, followed by the network sub-tasks of identifying the nodes in the set intersections and discovering the node links. We could not identify a sensible alternative network-first strategy. This is for Fig. 4, the tenth data collection task, a large diagram. Answer options: *0*, *1*, *2*, *3*, with *1* being correct.
- T3. *What are the interests of the person who is friends with both Kylee and Edgar?* Here, the two people vary. This relates to the network sub-tasks of finding two named nodes and discovering network connectivity, followed by the set sub-task of identifying the node set intersections. We could not identify a sensible alternative set-first strategy. This is for Fig. 5 (left), the third data collection task, a small diagram. Answer options: (a) *Cars, News, and Books*,

(b) *Cars only*, (c) *News, Books, and nothing else*, (d) *Books only*, with (a) *Cars, News, and Books* being correct.

- T4. *What are the interests of the person who is friends with exactly 6 other people?* Here, the number varies. This is related to the network sub-task of discovering well-connected nodes, followed by the set sub-task of discovering the node intersections. We could not identify a sensible alternative set-first strategy. Figure 1 shows the fourth training task, a small diagram. Answer options: (a) *Art only*, (b) *Music, Food and nothing else*, (c) *Chess only*, (d) *Music, News, Food and nothing else*, with (a) *Art only* being correct.

Procedure and Conditions. We produced 18 tasks, each with separate diagrams for each of the four conditions: *HoopNet set-first*, *HoopNet network-first*, *LinearNet set-first*, *LinearNet network-first.* The same questions, response options, and underlying data were used for all conditions. Only the visualizations changed. The first four tasks presented were training tasks, with diagrams of increasing size, and the last training diagram was the same size as a small diagram in the study. In the case of training diagrams, after the user selected an answer, a response with the correct answer and an explanation was given. The training questions were one of each task type.

Regarding the remaining 14 tasks, twelve were for data collection, with task types and diagram sizes as described above. The final two tasks were attention checks that showed a standard question image, with three options appearing as standard options (without referencing any label in the diagram) and a fourth option labeled "Choose this option".

The training questions were always presented in the same order at the start of the study, straight after the initial information page and consent to start the study. The twelve data collection questions and two attention-check questions were presented in random order, with the answer options also randomized. The study was finished by presenting a demographics collection form and, finally, a completion link back to Prolific.

4.2 Study Execution

Overview. We conducted three studies to test our six hypotheses, each following a similar format.

- **Study 1:** HoopNet set-first vs. HoopNet network-first.
- **Study 2:** LinearNet set-first vs. LinearNet network-first.
- **Study 3:** HoopNet set-first vs. LinearNet set-first.

Each study would collect *accuracy* and *time* when answering questions. Accuracy is the frequency of the single correct answer out of four options presented. Time is the time from when the task first appears to the user until the user selects an option and presses a button to move on to the next task. We note that throughout this paper, we consider accuracy to be the more important indicator than time.

Participants. Our participant selection method used Prolific, which selected participants based on predefined filters we set and passed them to our study vehicle. We requested an even gender distribution from Prolific. The three studies comprised participation counts of: LinearNet 164 (network-first 83, set-first 81); HoopNet 164 (network-first 83, set-first 81); and HoopNet vs LinearNet 167 (HoopNet 87, LinearNet 80). Inclusion criteria were: fluent English, Prolific approval rate greater than 95% and no prior participation in an earlier study in the sequence. More details on participant filters, pilot studies, and data collection can be found online; see the link below.

Condition Selection for Study 3. The conditions of Study 3 were determined by the results of Studies 1 and 2. The analysis and discussion for Study 1 and Study 2 have been moved online to save space (see link to OSF below). There were no significant results between set-first and network-first in Study 1 and Study 2. The means for accuracy were better for set-first in both of these studies and so we used HoopNet set-first and LinearNet set-first in Study 3.

Study materials, including questions and diagrams, anonymized study results data and the discussion of Study 1 and Study 2, are available online on OSF[1]. Additionally, we also preregistered[2] our study design before collecting responses.

4.3 Layout Study Results

Two outcome variables were recorded: participants' accuracy (a binomial response variable) and the time taken to answer a question (in seconds). Since each participant answered twelve questions, they each supplied twelve accuracy responses and twelve timing responses. Each participant's responses are not independent, and thus traditional analyses, such as logistic regression (for the accuracy results) and ANOVA (for the time responses) might lead to incorrect conclusions. We use general estimating equations (GEE) [12], combined with generalized linear models, to account for these clustered data. Analysis was performed using the `geepack` package of R [17]. We can still calculate p-values and report them as for more standard techniques. The interpretation of a p-value is straightforward: it gives the probability of obtaining the data, assuming there is no difference between the populations' parameters. We consider results with a p-value less than 0.05 to be significant.

4.4 HoopNet vs. LinearNet Study Results

The descriptive statistics for Study 3, which compared HoopNet and LinearNet diagrams using set-first optimization, are shown in Table 1.

From Table 1, we see that the accuracy for HoopNet diagrams is significantly higher than for LinearNet diagrams. This result holds for the overall dataset and for the subsets based on diagram size. In percentage terms, there is around a 10%

[1] https://osf.io/6kr9g.
[2] https://osf.io/wha79.

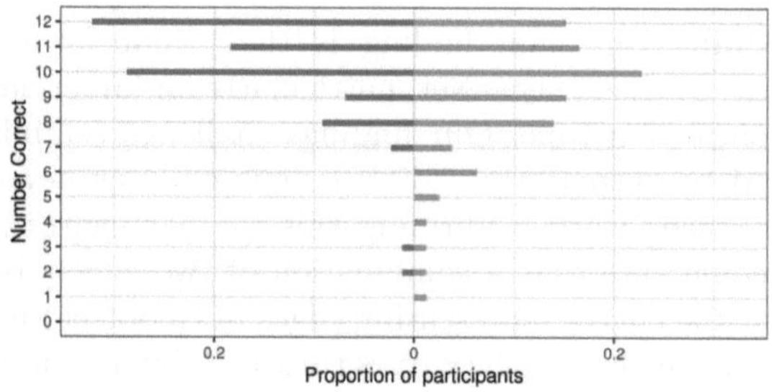

Fig. 6. Distribution of number of correct answers for HoopNet and LinearNet.

increase in accuracy of HoopNet over LinearNet. Thus, the accuracy rates when using HoopNet are significantly better than using LinearNet, and moreover, both use the same amount of time. We, therefore, have evidence to reject *H0:A3*.

For task completion time, there were no significant differences between participants using HoopNet and those using LinearNet. This result is the same regardless of diagram size. Whilst the *sample* mean time is quicker for HoopNet, the result is not significant. Hence, there is no evidence to reject *H0:B3*.

The distributions of correct answers are shown in Fig. 6. We can see that the modal category for HoopNet diagrams is all questions answered correctly. In contrast, for LinearNet diagrams, the modal category is one in which two questions were answered incorrectly.

Regarding diagram size, for large diagrams HoopNet had a mean accuracy of 83% compared to 71% for LinearNet. For small diagrams, the difference was lower as HoopNet had a mean accuracy of 89% compared to 83% for LinearNet.

The significant accuracy result provides evidence that *HoopNet is a more effective visualization than LinearNet.*

5 Discussion of Results

Set-First vs. Network-First. We conjecture that the lack of significant results in Study 1 and Study 2 on optimization strategy is due to the sub-tasks that involve solving both network and set sub-tasks. Hence, whether the optimization is for either network layout or set layout, there is always one part of the full task advantaged and one part disadvantaged.

Table 1. Descriptive statistics for HoopNet and LinearNet diagrams

Treatment	Mean Accuracy			Mean Time (s)		
	Overall	Small	Large	Overall	Small	Large
`HoopNet`	**0.8611**	**0.893**	**0.830**	**47.16**	**39.37**	**54.95**
`LinearNet`	0.7646	0.835	0.707	50.22	41.80	58.84
p-**value**	0.00041	0.026	0.00039	0.360	0.510	0.410

Linear vs. Radial. Our main finding is that HoopNet consistently supported higher accuracy than LinearNet, particularly for larger networks, without increasing task completion time. Our findings challenge established results, as linear designs tend to outperform radial designs on accuracy and completion time [8,13], with recent work confirming this for bar charts [35] and matrix layouts [31]. We conjecture that a combination of two effects is responsible for our results. Firstly, the curves representing edges in HoopNet are easier to follow than in LinearNet. In the latter, the curves turn 180° by design. In HoopNet, the shorter edges turn more while the longer edges are straighter. Secondly, radial layouts form a continuous loop, which makes it easier to follow sets around the circle and see how they overlap. In contrast, linear layouts rely on left-to-right scanning, which can make it harder to keep track of memberships, particularly when nodes in the same set are widely separated.

The large-diagram accuracy gap suggests LinearNet is nearing its understandability limit, whereas HoopNet could scale further.

6 Conclusion

We have presented two designs for visualizing set and network data: HoopNet and LinearNet. HoopNet juxtaposes hoop set diagrams with circular network diagrams, whereas LinearNet juxtaposes linear set diagrams with linear network diagrams. We have implemented two alternative ILP algorithms for exact optimization of our designs. For set-based tasks, we can minimize gaps in set lines using our set-first method. For network-based tasks, we can minimize edge crossings with our network-first method. Our empirical human-subject studies yielded statistically significant results: the radial design of HoopNet is a more effective visualization than the linear design of LinearNet.

Limitations. As with any empirical study, our results are valid within the constraints imposed by the study. In our case, the results are valid for the task types undertaken by our pool of participants drawn from the general population, although we mitigated this by introducing variety into the source data and tasks through randomization and introducing several different task types. Our studies avoided many use cases for these visualizations, including interactions and embedding them in a web page with additional subject context. This was done to minimize the number of variables present in the experimentation. The studies were limited in scale, meaning we chose data sets of a size that allowed the questions to be of a suitable difficulty and to be gathered in a reasonable amount of time from crowd-sourced participants. We expect our designs will scale beyond the tested size of 32 nodes, with an informal upper bound around 100 nodes and 12 sets, typical of small-to-medium sizes in graph visualization user studies [5]. This range exceeds the computability of our ILP and would require heuristic layout methods. For larger instances, we conjecture that interaction techniques can be a suitable way to handle visual complexity with detailed views on demand.

Our study did not look at designs without node ordering vs. the two orderings that were chosen to be examined. Given the lack of significance in the first two studies, the choice of optimization seems to have little effect, but the final significant result is only valid with regard to set-first optimization, and other optimization (or no optimization) combinations might differ in results.

Future Work. More empirical human-subject evaluation is necessary to examine the scalability of HoopNet diagrams, which may not yet have reached their maximum size in the current study (see Sect. 5). Other empirical work is also possible, comparing HoopNet against alternative set network visualization techniques, including embedded methods, such as Euler diagrams with networks and linesets on networks [28]. We found no statistical difference between set-first and network-first optimization for HoopNet or LinearNet, hence we can use either, depending on context. This might form the basis of an interesting interactive tool where a user can apply a set-first optimization to tasks that are wholly or mainly set-oriented, and similarly a network-first optimization to network-oriented tasks. ILP models can be slow to optimize, and it is algorithmically interesting to develop and implement fast optimization heuristics for HoopNet and LinearNet. Lastly, user interface interaction techniques could be used to handle the visual complexity and allow the designs to scale to larger instances. Whilst we consider that data presented in a book or on a static website should not greatly exceed the large data sets we tested in our study, for specialists and within interactive systems, larger datasets may be feasible.

References

1. Alqadah, M., Stapleton, G., Howse, J., Chapman, P.: The perception of clutter in linear diagrams. In: Jamnik, M., Uesaka, Y., Elzer Schwartz, S. (eds.) Diagrams 2016. LNCS (LNAI), vol. 9781, pp. 250–257. Springer, Cham (2016). https://doi.org/10.1007/978-3-319-42333-3_20
2. Alsallakh, B., Micallef, L., Aigner, W., Hauser, H., Miksch, S., Rodgers, P.J.: The state-of-the-art of set visualization. Comput. Graph. Forum **35**(1), 234–260 (2016). https://doi.org/10.1111/CGF.12722
3. Baur, M., Brandes, U.: Crossing reduction in circular layouts. In: Hromkovič, J., Nagl, M., Westfechtel, B. (eds.) WG 2004. LNCS, vol. 3353, pp. 332–343. Springer, Heidelberg (2004). https://doi.org/10.1007/978-3-540-30559-0_28
4. Borgo, R., Micallef, L., Bach, B., McGee, F., Lee, B.: Information visualization evaluation using crowdsourcing. In: Computer Graphics Forum, vol. 37, pp. 573–595. Wiley (2018). https://doi.org/10.1111/cgf.13444
5. Burch, M., Huang, W., Wakefield, M., Purchase, H.C., Weiskopf, D., Hua, J.: The state of the art in empirical user evaluation of graph visualizations. IEEE Access **9**, 4173–4198 (2021). https://doi.org/10.1109/ACCESS.2020.3047616
6. Chapman, P., Sim, K., Chen, H.H.: Minimising line segments in linear diagrams is NP-hard. J. Comput. Lang. **71**, 101136 (2022). https://doi.org/10.1016/J.COLA.2022.101136
7. Chapman, P., Stapleton, G., Rodgers, P., Micallef, L., Blake, A.: Visualizing sets: an empirical comparison of diagram types. In: Dwyer, T., Purchase, H., Delaney, A. (eds.) Diagrams 2014. LNCS (LNAI), vol. 8578, pp. 146–160. Springer, Heidelberg (2014). https://doi.org/10.1007/978-3-662-44043-8_18

8. Diehl, S., Beck, F., Burch, M.: Uncovering strengths and weaknesses of radial visualizations–an empirical approach. IEEE Trans. Vis. Comput. Graph. **16**(6), 935–942 (2010). https://doi.org/10.1109/TVCG.2010.209
9. Dobler, A., Nöllenburg, M.: On computing optimal linear diagrams. In: Proc. Diagrammatic Representation and Inference (Diagrams 2022). LNCS, vol. 13462, pp. 20–36. Springer (2022). https://doi.org/10.1007/978-3-031-15146-0_2
10. Doğrusöz, U., Madden, B., Madden, P.: Circular layout in the graph layout toolkit. In: North, S. (ed.) GD 1996. LNCS, vol. 1190, pp. 92–100. Springer, Heidelberg (1997). https://doi.org/10.1007/3-540-62495-3_40
11. Filipov, V.A., Arleo, A., Miksch, S.: Are we there yet? a roadmap of network visualization from surveys to task taxonomies. Comput. Graph. Forum **42**(6) (2023). https://doi.org/10.1111/CGF.14794
12. Galbraith, S., Daniel, J.A., Vissel, B.: A study of clustered data and approaches to its analysis. J. Neurosci. **30**(32), 10601–10608 (2010). https://doi.org/10.1523/JNEUROSCI.0362-10.2010
13. Goldberg, J.H., Helfman, J.I.: Eye tracking for visualization evaluation: reading values on linear versus radial graphs. Inf. Vis. **10**(3), 182–195 (2011). https://doi.org/10.1177/1473871611406623
14. Goodarzi, A.T.: Crossing Reduction in Circular Layouts under Grouping Constraints. Bachelor's thesis, Julius-Maximilians-Universität Würzburg, Würzburg, Germany (2022). https://www1.pub.informatik.uni-wuerzburg.de/pub/theses/2022-torabi-goodarzi-bachelorarbeit.pdf
15. Gottfried, B.: A comparative study of linear and region based diagrams. J. Spatial Inform. Sci. **10**, 3–20 (2015). https://doi.org/10.5311/JOSIS.2015.10.187
16. Gou, L., Zhang, X.L.: TreeNetViz: revealing patterns of networks over tree structures. IEEE Trans. Vis. Comput. Graph. **17**(12), 2449–2458 (2011). https://doi.org/10.1109/TVCG.2011.247
17. Halekoh, U., Højsgaard, S., Yan, J.: The R package geepack for generalized estimating equations. J. Stat. Softw. **15**(2), 1–11 (2006). https://doi.org/10.18637/jss.v015.i02
18. Kerren, A., Jusufi, I.: A novel radial visualization approach for undirected hypergraphs. In: Proc. EuroVis 2013 - Short Papers. Eurographics Association (2013). https://doi.org/10.2312/PE.EUROVISSHORT.EUROVISSHORT2013.025-029
19. Keys, C.D.: Graphs critical for maximal bookthickness. Pi Mu Epsilon J. **6**(2), 79–84 (1975). https://www.jstor.org/stable/24345165
20. Lee, B., Plaisant, C., Parr, C.S., Fekete, J., Henry, N.: Task taxonomy for graph visualization. In: Proc. BEyond time and errors: novel evaluation methods for information visualization, BELIV 2006, pp. 1–5. ACM Press (2006). https://doi.org/10.1145/1168149.1168168
21. Leskovec, J., Sosič, R.: Snap: A general-purpose network analysis and graph-mining library. ACM Trans. Intell. Syst. Technol. (TIST) **8**(1), 1–20 (2016). https://doi.org/10.1145/2898361
22. Mutton, P., Rodgers, P., Flower, J.: Drawing graphs in euler diagrams. In: Blackwell, A.F., Marriott, K., Shimojima, A. (eds.) Diagrams 2004. LNCS (LNAI), vol. 2980, pp. 66–81. Springer, Heidelberg (2004). https://doi.org/10.1007/978-3-540-25931-2_9
23. Neumann, P., Schlechtweg, S., Carpendale, S.: Arctrees: Visualizing relations in hierarchical data. In: 7th Joint Eurographics - IEEE VGTC Symposium on Visualization. pp. 53–60. Eurographics Association (2005). https://doi.org/10.2312/VISSYM/EUROVIS05/053-060

24. Pretorius, A.J., van Wijk, J.J.: Visual analysis of multivariate state transition graphs. IEEE Trans. Vis. Comput. Graph. **12**(5), 685–692 (2006). https://doi.org/10.1109/TVCG.2006.192
25. Purchase, H.C., Carrington, D.A., Allder, J.: Empirical evaluation of aesthetics-based graph layout. Empir. Softw. Eng. **7**(3), 233–255 (2002). https://doi.org/10.1023/A:1016344215610
26. Ren, D., Lee, B., Brehmer, M.: Charticulator: interactive construction of bespoke chart layouts. IEEE Trans. Vis. Comput. Graph. **25**(1), 789–799 (2019). https://doi.org/10.1109/TVCG.2018.2865158
27. Rodgers, P., Chapman, P., Blake, A., Nöllenburg, M., Wallinger, M., Dobler, A.: Hoop diagrams: a set visualization method. In: Proc. Diagrammatic Representation and Inference (Diagrams 2024). LNCS, vol. 14981, pp. 377–392. Springer (2024). https://doi.org/10.1007/978-3-031-71291-3_31
28. Rodgers, P.J., Stapleton, G., Alsallakh, B., Micallef, L., Baker, R., Thompson, S.J.: A task-based evaluation of combined set and network visualization. Inf. Sci. **367–368**, 58–79 (2016). https://doi.org/10.1016/J.INS.2016.05.045
29. Rodgers, P.J., Stapleton, G., Chapman, P.: Visualizing sets with linear diagrams. ACM Trans. Comput. Hum. Interact. **22**(6), 27:1–27:39 (2015). https://doi.org/10.1145/2810012
30. Six, J.M., Tollis, I.G.: Circular drawing algorithms. In: Handbook of Graph Drawing and Visualization, chap. 9, pp. 285–315. CRC Press (2013)
31. Ståhlbom, E., Molin, J., Ynnerman, A., Lundström, C.: Should I make it round? suitability of circular and linear layouts for comparative tasks with matrix and connective data. Comput. Graph. Forum **43**(3) (2024).https://doi.org/10.1111/CGF.15102
32. Tubbs, J.D., Ding, J., Baum, L., Sham, P.C.: Immune dysregulation in depression: evidence from genome-wide association. Brain, Behav. Immunity-Health **7**, 100108 (2020). https://doi.org/10.1016/j.bbih.2020.100108
33. Vehlow, C., Beck, F., Weiskopf, D.: Visualizing group structures in graphs: a survey. Comput. Graph. Forum **36**(6), 201–225 (2017). https://doi.org/10.1111/CGF.12872
34. Vehlow, C., et al.: ivun: interactive visualization of uncertain biochemical reaction networks. BMC Bioinform. **14**(S-19), S2 (2013). https://doi.org/10.1186/1471-2105-14-S19-S2
35. Waldner, M., Diehl, A., Gracanin, D., Splechtna, R., Delrieux, C., Matkovic, K.: A comparison of radial and linear charts for visualizing daily patterns. IEEE Trans. Vis. Comput. Graph. **26**(1), 1033–1042 (2020). https://doi.org/10.1109/TVCG.2019.2934784
36. Wattenberg, M.: Arc diagrams: visualizing structure in strings. In: Information Visualization (INFOVIS 2002), pp. 110–116. IEEE (2002). https://doi.org/10.1109/INFVIS.2002.1173155

24. Pretorius, A.J., van Wijk, J.J.: Visual analysis of multivariate state transition graphs. IEEE Trans. Vis. Comput. Graph. 12(5), 685–692 (2006). https://doi.org/10.1109/TVCG.2006.192
25. Purchase, H.C., Carrington, D., Allder, J.-A.: [illegible]

[illegible]

Applications

Legal Design and Diagrammatic Reasoning

Gloria Jacquet[1] and Lorenz Demey[2](✉)

[1] Leuven Institute of Criminology, KU Leuven
Herbert Hooverplein 9, 3000 Leuven, Belgium
gloria.jacquet@kuleuven.be

[2] Center for Logic and Philosophy of Science/Leuven.AI, KU Leuven
Kardinaal Mercierplein 2, 3000 Leuven, Belgium
lorenz.demey@kuleuven.be

Abstract. This paper presents the legal design movement, which aims to make the law more accessible to laypeople through the application of various design principles. We discuss two examples from different legal areas (comic contracts from employment law and an informative poster from criminal law). Finally, we highlight the potential benefits of collaboration between the legal design and Diagrams research communities.

Keywords: Legal design · diagrammatic reasoning · employment law · criminal law · depicting negation · first-person perspective · inclusiveness

Plain Legal Language and Legal Design. People in the legal profession have long been concerned with using a kind of language that is not just comprehensible to legal experts, but to laypeople as well [7]. Around the turn of the 21st century, the legal design movement came about. This movement is inspired by the same values of accessibility, inclusiveness and user-friendliness [3], but seeks to implement them in ways that go beyond the purely linguistic realm. Broadly speaking, the idea is to improve legal documents by applying tools from design thinking and user experience (UX) design, such as user interviews, visualization, creating personas, rapid and iterated prototyping, etc. [3,5].

The importance of visualization was particularly emphasized by Colette Brunschwig, one of the earliest pioneers of legal design [1], and 'visual-first' is listed as one of the key principles in the Legal Design Manifesto [8]. The visual elements to be used in legal design are often produced manually, but recently, there is also a trend to generate them automatically (based on semantically enriched legal data) [10]. Because of this heavy use of visualization, we have moved beyond the linguistic realm, but the same underlying values and principles are still at play. For example, to render a legal document fully understandable to a migrant worker, it might not suffice to translate it to the worker's native

The second author holds a Research Professorship (BOFZAP) from KU Leuven.

P. Sobociński et al. (Eds.): Diagrams 2026, LNAI 16833, pp. 369–373, 2027.
https://doi.org/10.1007/978-3-032-34178-5_36

language or to rewrite it from 'legalese' into plain language: comprehensibility can also be greatly enhanced by supporting the document with well-designed visuals.

Example 1: Comic Contracts. *Creative Contracts* is a social enterprise from South Africa which designs contracts and other legal documents in the form of comic strips [2]. Such visual contracts still need to present complex information, including logical operators such as universal quantification ('you need to come to work *every* weekday'), implication and negation ('*if* you are *not* at work, *then* you receive a warning'). To achieve this, legal designers can fruitfully draw upon theoretical work in cognitive science, diagrammatic reasoning, etc. For example, Sato et al. [11] have studied different methods to depict negative information in photographs and comics. One of the methods they discuss involves augmenting the picture with a conventional device, e.g., a dotted line, to highlight the absence of an object [10, p. 486–487]. This method has also been used in comic contracts, as illustrated in Fig. 1. This comic strip depicts the complex logical statement 'if you are not at work for the first time, then you receive a warning'. Some information is simply presented textually/numerically, such as the circled number '1' and the boxed word 'warning'. The use of an arrow to indicate a conditional is also quite standard (e.g., in flowcharts). More interestingly, a dotted line is used to indicate the negative fact that the worker is absent from their job.

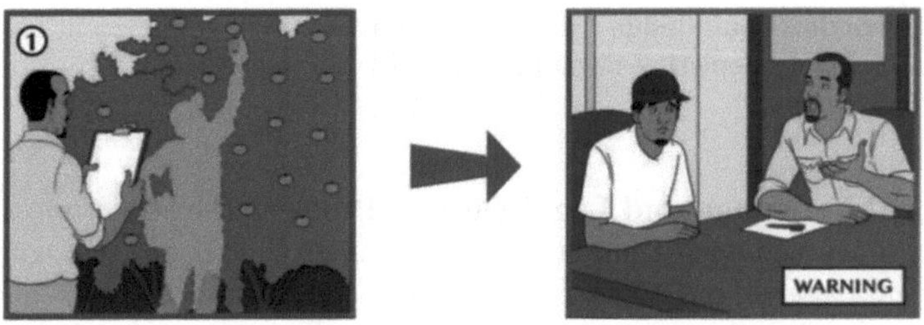

Fig. 1. Depicting negative information in a comic contract. Source: https://creative-contracts.com/clemengold/, last accessed 7 March 2026.

Example 2: Informative Poster. The second example concerns one of the first applications of legal design in Belgium. Already in 2013, Jacquet [6] developed an informative poster to help court visitors navigate a correctional courtroom (which treats rather serious crimes, such as rape, assault and violent drug crime); cf. Fig. 2. This idea was conceived while doing volunteer work with families of defendants in murder cases, and was also inspired by interviews with court officials and years of personally observing court proceedings. For example, judges, prosecutors and lawyers all wear nearly identical robes, and there seems to be a calming effect if one already knows who is who (i.e., what their role and main tasks are) prior to being called into the courtroom (e.g., to testify).

The poster's overall organization is focused around a visual depiction of the courtroom. This depiction balances abstract with more concrete aspects in

Fig. 2. Informative poster: 'Who's who in the correctional courtroom?'. Source: https://www.rechtbanken-tribunaux.be/sites/default/files/media/brochures/wie_is_wie_in_de_rechtszaal.pdf, last accessed 7 March 2026.

order to achieve maximal user-friendliness [4, Ch. 12]. For example, the poster is designed from the concrete perspective of the court visitor entering the courtroom, with the court usher and the barrier between court and audience serving as central points of reference. This egocentric (first-person) perspective was chosen in favor of an allocentric (e.g., bird's eye) perspective, because of its action-guiding qualities [11]. By contrast, the different people in the courtroom (judge, prosecutor, lawyers, defendant, victim, press) are differentiated not only by location, but also in a purely abstract way (color), to make their roles maximally clear.

Other visual elements include the use of recognizable icons and colors. At the top of the poster, there is a large icon to indicate that this is an information point (just like at a tourist office, in a hospital, etc.). The conventional colors of green and red are used to indicate what is resp. permitted and forbidden in the courtroom. Moreover, forbidden activities are depicted by a prohibition sign (recognizable from road traffic) overlaid on an icon (e.g., a text bubble) that indicates the activity (e.g., talking out loud during court proceedings).

Conclusion and Outlook. In this paper we have argued that legal design makes use of visualization techniques that are studied more systematically in cognitive science, diagrammatic reasoning, etc. [11]. We therefore conclude the paper by highlighting the great potential of increased interaction between the legal design and the Diagrams research communities. More intense collaboration between these two communities will prove to be mutually beneficial: on the one hand, diagrams research can provide legal design with more rigorous theoretical foundations [3, p. 412ff.], while on the other hand, legal design puts diagrams research to use in new application contexts of great societal relevance [9].

References

1. Brunschwig, C.R.: Visualisierung von Rechtsnormen. Legal Design, Schulthess (2001)
2. Brunschwig, C.R.: Contract comics and the visualization, audio-visualization, and multisensorization of law. U. of Western Australia Law Rev. **46**, 191–217 (2019)
3. Chung, S., Kim, J.: Systematic literature review of legal design: Concepts, processes, and methods. Des. J. **26**, 399–416 (2023)
4. Debecker, S., De Coensel, S., Jacquet, G. (eds.): Toegankelijk recht in woord en beeld. Legal Design in de praktijk. OWL Press (2025)
5. Hagan, M.: Design comes to the law school. In: Denvir, C. (ed.) Modernising Legal Education, pp. 109–125. Cambridge University Press (2020)
6. Jacquet, G.: De klant(on)vriendelijkheid van hoven en rechtbanken als organisatie in strafzaken. Een praktijkinitiatief voor een klantvriendelijkere justitie, University of Ghent Master's thesis, University of Ghent (2014)
7. Legal Design Alliance: Legal Design Manifesto (2018). https://www.legaldesignalliance.org/
8. Pasa, B., Perondi, L.: Legal design, criminal law and social empowerment. Legal Design J. **2**, 1–25 (2025)

9. Rossi, A., Palmirani, M.: From words to images through legal visualization. In: Pagallo, U., Palmirani, M., Casanovas, P., Sartor, G., Villata, S. (eds.) AICOL 2015-2017. LNCS (LNAI), vol. 10791, pp. 72–85. Springer, Cham (2018). https://doi.org/10.1007/978-3-030-00178-0_5
10. Sato, Y., Mineshima, K.: Depicting negative information in photographs, videos, and comics: a preliminary analysis. In: Pietarinen, A.-V., Chapman, P., Bosveld-de Smet, L., Giardino, V., Corter, J., Linker, S. (eds.) Diagrams 2020. LNCS (LNAI), vol. 12169, pp. 485–489. Springer, Cham (2020). https://doi.org/10.1007/978-3-030-54249-8_40
11. Yeap, W.K.: On egocentric and allocentric maps. In: Freksa, C., Nebel, B., Hegarty, M., Barkowsky, T. (eds.) Spatial Cognition 2014. LNCS (LNAI), vol. 8684, pp. 62–75. Springer, Cham (2014). https://doi.org/10.1007/978-3-319-11215-2_5

Discourse-Driven Decomposition of Diagrammatic Representations

Tuomo Hiippala(✉), Helmiina Hotti, Timo Kalliokoski, and Rosa Suviranta

Multimodality Research Group, University of Helsinki, Helsinki, Finland
tuomo.hiippala@helsinki.fi
https://www.helsinki.fi/multimodality

Abstract. This paper proposes a new approach to identifying discourse units in diagrammatic representations. A discourse unit refers to an instance of a mode of expression – such as written language, illustrations, shapes, arrows and lines – that functions as a part of the overall discourse structure of the diagrammatic representation. Identifying discourse units in diagrammatic representations is challenging, because diagrams are inherently multimodal: discourse units can be realised using various modes of expression and their communicative functions are determined on a case-by-case basis through contextual interpretation. To address the problem of identifying discourse units, we design and implement an annotation pipeline for collaborative annotation inspired by microtask crowdsourcing. We apply the pipeline to 1000 primary school science diagrams and show that the proposed approach can produce detailed descriptions of their multimodal discourse structure.

Keywords: Diagrams · Multimodality · Annotation · Crowdsourcing · Microtasking

1 Introduction

Diagrammatic representations are inherently multimodal, that is, they combine multiple 'modes' of expression – such as written language, diverse forms of pictorial expression, arrows and lines – into coherent organisations in two-dimensional layout space [18]. How such appropriate combinations of modes emerge and become interpretable is actively studied in the interdisciplinary field of multimodality research, which has developed a range of theoretical concepts for supporting the empirical analysis of communicative situations and artefacts [5]. These concepts have also been applied to analysing the multimodality of diagrammatic representations [10].

Just like for many other forms of multimodal communication, one major challenge in analysing diagrammatic representations is identifying the *units of analysis* that contribute towards the communicative goals set for the diagrammatic representation in question [2,6]. Our approach to identifying units of analysis

P. Sobociński et al. (Eds.): Diagrams 2026, LNAI 16833, pp. 374–390, 2027.
https://doi.org/10.1007/978-3-032-34178-5_37

differs from previous research in two ways. Firstly, we do not presume the existence of a pre-defined inventory of "meaningful graphic forms", such as circles, ellipses, lines, arrows, etc. [23, p. 222]. Instead, we assume that diagrams can flexibly draw on different modes of expression to instantiate forms as needed [10]. Secondly, we assume that these forms participate in a *discourse structure*, thus avoiding invoking the linguistic concept of grammar, which has been frequently used to describe the structure of diagrammatic representations [1,8]. As Bateman and Wildfeuer [4, pp. 375–376] have shown for the medium of comics, a discourse-oriented perspective enables accounting for the flexibility that many visual media naturally exhibit in combining multiple modes of expression. Hence, we refer to these units of analysis as *discourse units*.

Against this backdrop, we present a new approach to identifying discourse units in diagrammatic representations through collaborative annotation. The proposed approach relies on microtasks that are joined together into larger annotation pipelines. These microtasks are designed to be simple enough to be performed by non-expert annotators, and build on each other to gradually provide a comprehensive inventory of discourse units, their type and position in the diagram layout.

2 Identifying Discourse Units in Diagrammatic Representations

Empirical approaches to multimodality generally assume that capturing how multiple modes of expression co-operate in a given communicative setting requires a systematic approach to their description [5]. One way to pursue such analyses is to create corpora with multiple layers of annotation that describe the characteristics of the data at different levels of abstraction [3]. For diagrammatic representations, high-level annotations may include, for example, categories that describe entire diagrams (e.g. 'network' or 'cycle'). Low-level annotations, in turn, may include coordinates that define the position of a single element in the diagram layout and categories that define the element type [9,15]. Such corpora or datasets – the way such collections of annotated data are referred to varies from field to field – have also been developed for studying diagrammatic representations.

One prominent example of such a collection is the Allen Institute for Artificial Intelligence Diagrams Dataset (AI2D), which was originally developed for research on automatic processing of diagrams [15]. AI2D contains 4903 diagrams that represent topics in primary school natural sciences, such as food webs, carbon cycles and human physiology. The diagrams were collected by extracting chapter headings from primary school textbooks, which were used as seed terms for searching images online [15, p. 243]. The diagrams were annotated by non-expert workers recruited through Amazon Mechanical Turk, a crowdsourcing platform, who performed a series of tasks to annotate the diagrams [15, p. 243].

The annotation scheme applied to the diagrams in AI2D defines four categories for elements: TEXT, ARROWS, ARROWHEADS and BLOBS (see Fig. 1). In

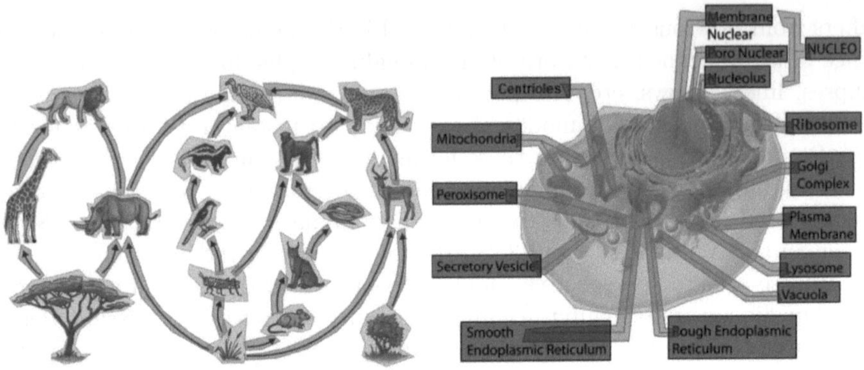

Fig. 1. Diagrams #862 and #3327 from the AI2D dataset, showing a food web and the structure of a cell. The original diagram images have been converted to grayscale to highlight the annotations for blobs (light blue), text (violet) and lines (orange). The annotations for arrowheads are not visualised. (Color figure online)

AI2D, the category of BLOBS covers illustrations, line art, photographs and other forms of visual representation, thus considerably extending the original definition in Tversky et al. [23]. The relationships between diagram elements are described using ten relations drawn from the framework developed by Engelhardt [8], which include relations such as INTRA-OBJECT LABEL and ARROW DESCRIPTOR. Together, the diagram elements and their relations are represented as nodes and edges of a *Diagram Parse Graph* (DPG) [15, p. 239].

The AI2D annotation scheme has been previously criticised for its inability to capture the key structural features of diagrammatic representations that depict phenomena or objects. Hiippala and Orekhova [12] argue that the AI2D DPGs cannot appropriately represent the discourse structure of such diagrams, because the annotation scheme does not capture how the elements of a diagram form hierarchical organisations. Without such a hierarchy, the annotation scheme cannot capture discourse relations that hold 'locally' between individual units and 'globally' between larger groups of units. This is exemplified on the left-hand side of Fig. 1, in which the labels and illustrations form local groups, which are then related to each other using the arrows as a part of the larger structure.

To address this issue, Hiippala et al. [9] build on the work of Hiippala and Orekhova [12] to present an alternative annotation scheme for the AI2D diagrams that provides multiple annotation layers. The resulting multimodal corpus, AI2D-RST, contains a subset of 1000 diagrams from AI2D. In contrast to the DPGs in AI2D, which use a single graph to represent the structure of the entire diagram, AI2D-RST uses separate graphs for representing hierarchical structures, discourse relations and connections indicated using lines and arrows. Each node has a unique identifier that remains the same across the graphs, which allows combining the annotations flexibly.

However, AI2D-RST uses the same units of analysis inherited from AI2D, namely text, lines and blobs, and the coordinates that designate the position of each unit of analysis in the diagram layout. Hiippala and Bateman [10, pp. 13–14] have argued that an accurate representation of the multimodal structure of diagrammatic represention requires decomposing them into more fine-grained discourse units. AI2D does not, for example, break graphic elements (blobs) down into their component parts, as exemplified by the diagram on the right-hand side of Fig. 1. This diagram represents a part-whole structure, in which the labels and lines pick out parts of the illustration. However, the parts referred to are not annotated separately, as the depiction in the middle is annotated as a single unit, although the communicative goal is obviously to describe the composition of this entity.

In light of this criticism, however, it should be noted that the AI2D diagrams were annotated by crowdsourced non-expert workers, whereas the ones in AI2D-RST were created by trained research assistants [9, p. 673]. Although crowdsourcing can help scale up corpus size, the use of non-expert workers requires making compromises about the level of detail captured by the annotations. In other words, the basic units of analysis must remain relatively simple in order to enable the non-expert workers to apply them to the data. Previous research has shown that despite training the annotators and designing effective instructions, crowdsourcing high quality annotations for diagrammatic representations remains challenging [21].

Being able to produce datasets that accurately reflect the multimodal structure of diagrammatic representations is crucial, because existing datasets such as AI2D and AI2D-RST are now being used as a foundation for developing further datasets for studying diagrams. For instance, Zala et al. [25] use a large language model to generate textual descriptions for entire diagrams and the individual elements in AI2D, whereas Sato et al. [20] use AI2D-RST as the basis for collecting captions for the diagrams in Japanese. Here the main problem is that AI2D-RST or any other derivative of the original AI2D dataset reproduces the fundamental issues concerning the units of analysis and their level of detail.

This leads to the main research question we seek to address in this paper:

> How to annotate diagrams for discourse units at a level of detail appropriate for the diagram in question?

In other words, we want to break down diagrams into units whose granularity corresponds to the communicative goals set for the diagram. Hiippala and Bateman propose that one possible answer to this question is to adopt a discourse-driven approach. This approach involves building an inventory of discourse units by having the annotators make interpretations about the diagrammatic representations [10, pp. 13–14]. More specifically, the annotators must reason about the meaning of particular instances of modes of expression in the diagrams – such as written language, illustrations and lines – in their context of occurrence. In what follows, we show how such a discourse-driven approach to decomposing diagrams may be implemented as a part of a microtasking pipeline, which breaks the process of interpretation into small, manageable tasks.

3 Implementing a Discourse-Driven Approach

We implemented a microtasking pipeline using the tool presented in Hotti et al. [13], which is written in Python and built on top of Prodigy, a proprietary annotation tool developed by Explosion AI.[1] The annotation pipeline contains 11 microtasks in two stages, which are illustrated in Fig. 2. Each rectangle identified by a number represents a single microtask, whereas the diamonds stand for aggregated decisions by the annotators, which are determined on the basis of a majority vote. The lines connecting the microtasks and the decisions show how the individual tasks performed by the annotators flow through the pipeline. The code for the pipeline is available online.[2]

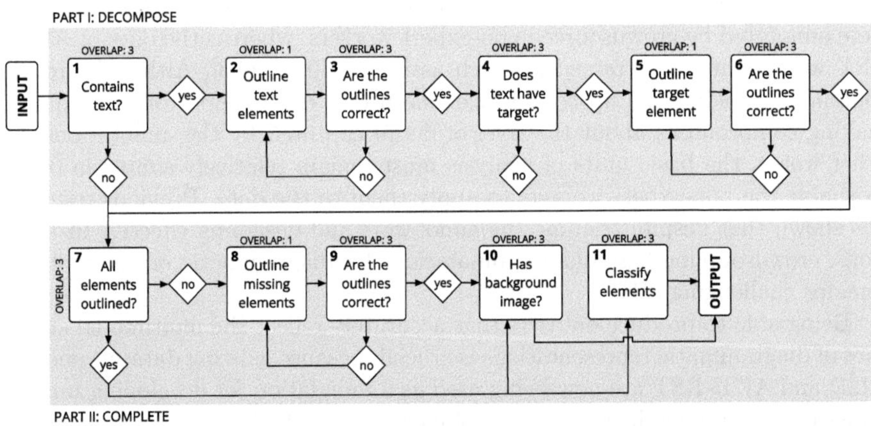

Fig. 2. An overview of the annotation pipeline. The arrows indicate how individual diagrams or their parts proceed through the pipeline. The label 'overlap' refers to how many annotators perform the same task in order to evaluate agreement between the annotators.

The first stage of the pipeline, shown in the upper grey box in Fig. 2, takes written language as the starting point for decomposing diagrams (1). Because diagrams use written language for various functions, such as titles, captions and labels, this provides an initial inventory of textual elements for each diagram. The annotators are then asked to outline any textual elements (2). These outlines are then reviewed by other annotators (3). Next, each textual element is shown separately to the annotators, who must determine whether the element has a 'target', that is, whether the text element stands in a relation to another specific, non-textual part of the diagram (4). In the following task, the annotators are asked to outline such target elements (5), which are then reviewed by others (6).

The second stage of the pipeline, shown in the lower grey box in Fig. 2, takes the output of the first stage as its input. At this stage, the annotations consists of

[1] https://prodi.gy.
[2] https://doi.org/10.5281/zenodo.20275603.

the outlines for text elements and any parts of the diagram they might refer to. These elements are labelled either TEXT or TARGET. Alternatively, if a diagram does not contain text, a diagram may have no annotations at all. In the first task of the second stage, all elements annotated in the first stage are shown simultaneously to the annotators, who must determine if all elements in the diagram have been annotated (7). If not, the annotators are asked to outline the missing elements and label them as OTHER (8), before these outlines are reviewed by other annotators (9). When all elements have been outlined, the diagrams are provided as input to two final tasks. In these tasks, the annotators must determine whether the diagram has a background image (10) and classify each element labelled as TARGET or OTHER into four categories defined below (11):

- TEXT: elements that consist of text, numbers or letters
- DEPICTION: pictorial representations, such as coloured illustrations or line drawings, which may include both entire objects and their parts
- ARROW/LINE: elements that indicate relations and connections between diagram elements, and non-connecting lines that separate elements
- SHAPE/SYMBOL: non-depictive abstract symbols and graphic shapes, such as rectangles and circles

Essentially, each microtask in the pipeline contains just two kinds of tasks: classification and segmentation. Whereas classification tasks mostly involve making choices that determine the flow of tasks in the pipeline (see e.g. microtasks 1, 3 or 4) or the properties of the diagram or its elements (10, 11), segmentation tasks require the annotators to draw outlines for parts of the diagram (2, 5, 8). Each microtask is designed to be self-contained: their scope is sufficiently narrow to be completed by relying on the instructions provided for the task. The annotators perform the tasks independently of each other, but they are exposed to annotations created by other annotators in review tasks, as explicated below.

To demonstrate the feasibility of the proposed approach, we recruited 26 non-expert annotators to work on a random sample of 1000 diagrams drawn from the AI2D dataset [15]. The annotators were chosen from a pool of annotators who had previously passed a brief examination, which measured their skill in performing similar annotation tasks and their ability to follow instructions [11, 21]. The annotation tasks were distributed to the annotators through a personal 'landing page', which listed all tasks allocated to the annotator in question. The annotators were paid 13€ per hour and were responsible for keeping track of their hours themselves. To reduce invisible work associated with microtasking [22], we paid the workers for 5 min of work if they checked the landing page and no tasks were available, and for 10 min if the tasks took less than 10 min to complete. The annotators could communicate with the researchers via the Slack messaging application.

4 Evaluating the Results

In this section, we evaluate the output from the microtask annotation pipeline qualitatively and quantitatively. The qualitative analysis in Sect. 4.1 focuses on what kinds of annotations the annotators can produce by making interpretations about the discourse structure of the diagrams, whereas the quantitative analysis in Sect. 4.2 assesses the scale and reliability of the annotations.

4.1 Can the Annotators Identify Discourse Units in Diagrams?

To demonstrate what kinds of annotations are produced at different stages of the annotation pipeline, Fig. 3 tracks the process for diagram #516 from the AI2D dataset, which is a network diagram that depicts a food web. First, the annotators must identify individual elements that consist of written language (see top right-hand corner in Fig. 3). This entails performing discourse interpretations about the function of text elements, which in this case act as labels for the accompanying illustrations. This prepares the annotators for the next task, which requires identifying just which elements in the diagram are being described by these labels. In this case, the discourse relation between the illustrations and their labels may be characterised as IDENTIFICATION [12, p. 1929]. This interpretation is cued by spatial proximity and cohesive ties across the illustration and the label, that is, they both convey similar meanings [19].

Resolving the discourse relations that involve textual elements provides an interim inventory of discourse units, as shown in the lower left-hand corner of Fig. 3. This also exemplifies what the annotators are presented with at the beginning of the second stage of the annotation pipeline in microtask 7. It is reasonable to assume that the contrast between what has already been annotated and those elements that remain without annotations can help the annotators determine the level of detail required from the annotation. For the diagram in Fig. 3, microtasks 7–9 populate the inventory of discourse units for arrows, which are not picked up for annotation in the first stage as they do not participate in any discourse relations involving textual elements. Nevertheless, the annotators must also perform interpretations about the functions of any elements that have not been annotated so far. In this case, the arrows act as connectors between the labelled depictions and correspond to particular processes that hold between the depicted entities [17].

In contrast to Fig. 3, diagrams that do not contain any textual elements enter the second stage without any annotations at all (see the outcome 'no' for microtask 1 in Fig. 2). However, as Fig. 4 illustrates, the annotators can identify discourse units at a level of detail that matches those in Fig. 3 even without support from pre-existing annotations for textual elements or their targets. Annotating the diagrams shown in Fig. 4 requires the annotators to recognise them as network diagrams, whose discourse structure is based on elements that function as *nodes* and *connectors* [8, pp. 40–41]. Identifying the elements that take on these functions is arguably facilitated by framing (empty space around elements) and the use of illustrations that are iconic in a Peircean sense, that is,

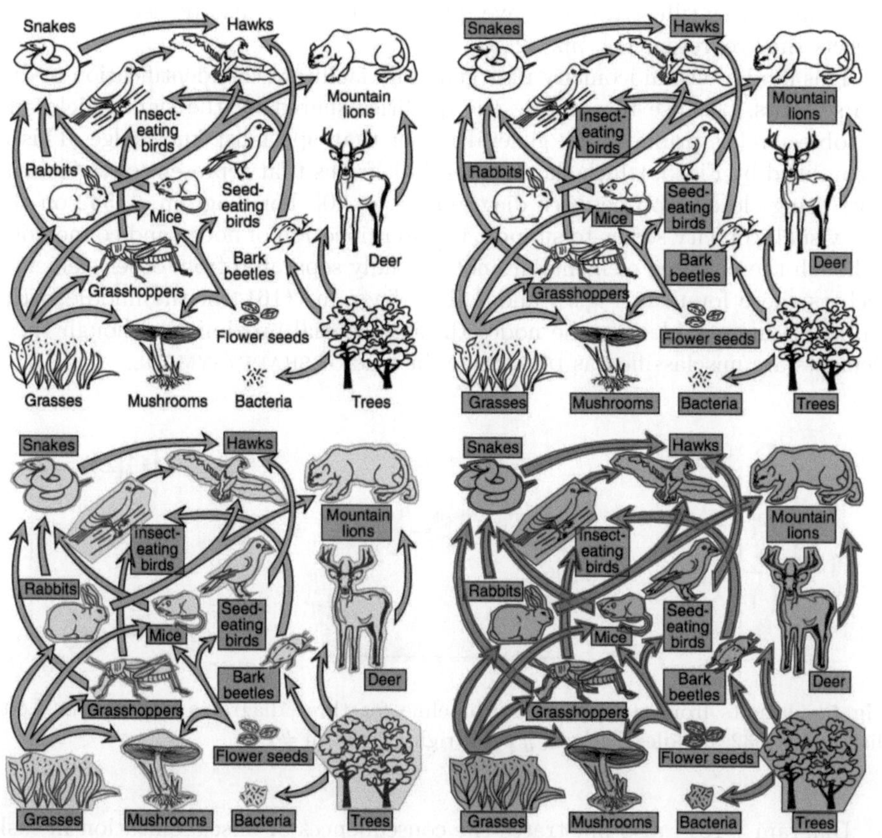

Fig. 3. Top left: AI2D diagram #516 provided as input to microtask 1. Top right: the output for microtask 3 consists of verified outlines for all text elements. Bottom left: the output for microtask 6 adds verified outlines for the target elements that the texts elements refer to. Bottom right: final output from the pipeline with annotations from microtasks 7–11.

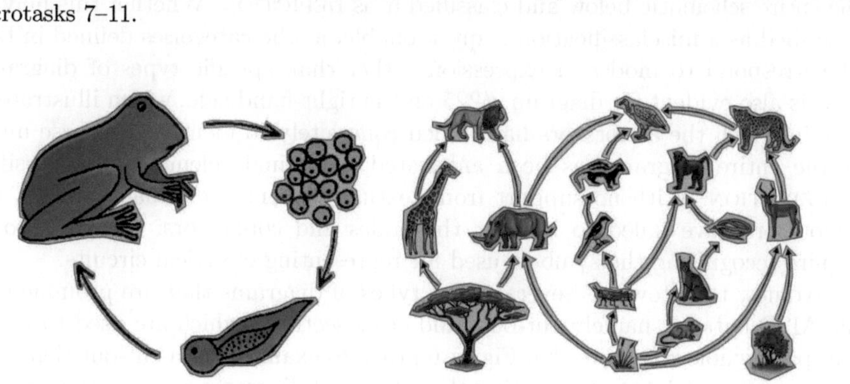

Fig. 4. Output from the second stage for AI2D diagrams #2277 (left) and #862 (right).

the sign-vehicles (illustrations) have qualities that may also be ascribed to the objects they represent [14, pp. 82–83].

This kind of visual iconicity may generally facilitate the identification of discourse units, because recognising the qualities shared by the sign-vehicle and the object relies primarily on general rather than specialist knowledge. This is exemplified by Fig. 5, which shows several diagrams that represent electrical circuits using closed-loop network diagrams [8, p. 40]. For diagram #1532 on the left, visual iconicity seems to support the identification of nodes and connectors, although the depicted elements are not spatially separated from other elements, such as those found in Figs. 3 and 4. For diagram #1614 in the middle, written labels help to identify the nodes through spatial proximity, although these elements are misclassified as DEPICTION instead of SHAPE/SYMBOL.

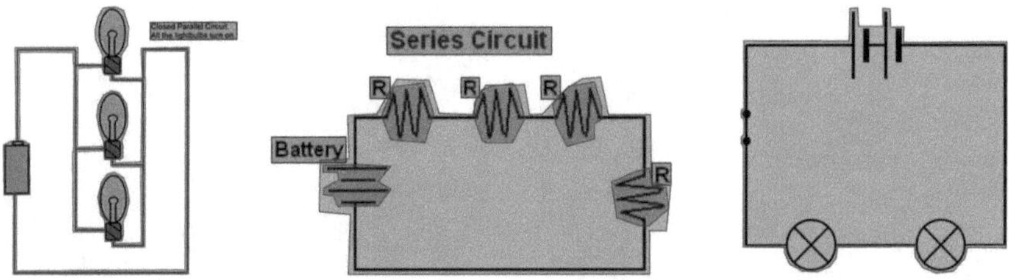

Fig. 5. Outputs from stage 2 of the pipeline for three diagrams from AI2D. Left: diagram #1532; middle: diagram #1614; right: diagram #225.

Diagram #1614 also illustrates the consequences of misclassification in task 4, in which the annotators must determine whether a text element has a target. In this case, the text "Series Circuit" does not refer to a *specific part* of the diagram, but functions as a title for the entire schematic representation below. Because the title has been classified as having a target, an annotator has outlined the entire schematic below and classified it as DEPICTION. Whether this may be described as a misclassification is questionable, as the categories defined in task 11 correspond to modes of expression rather than specific types of diagrams. This is also evident for diagram #225 on the right-hand side, which illustrates a case in which the annotators have failed completely to identify discourse units, as the entire diagram has been annotated as a single element and classified as DEPICTION. With no support from textual elements or visual iconicity, the annotators have failed to identify the nodes and connectors: doing so would require recognising the symbols used for representing electrical circuits.

We now turn towards several other types of diagrams that are prominent in the AI2D dataset, namely cut-outs and cross-sections, which are used to represent part–whole structures [9]. Figure 6 provides examples of a cut-out (left) and a cross-section (right). Annotating these kinds of diagrams requires the annotators to resolve the discourse relations, which are cued by connectivity: the labels and the objects they describe are connected by lines [8, p. 43].

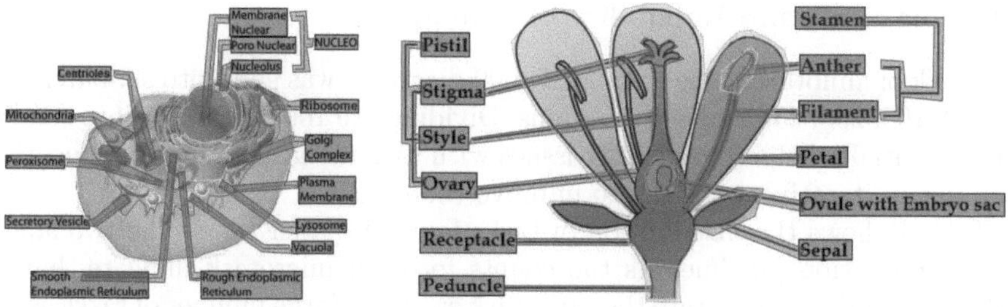

Fig. 6. AI2D diagrams #3327 (left) and #3425 (right). The elements classified as DEPICTION have been rendered using random colours to bring out the level of detail in the annotations. The original diagrams are drawn in greyscale to highlight the annotations. (Color figure online)

What is worth noting here is the level of detail achieved by a discourse-driven approach in contrast to the original annotations in AI2D (cf. diagram #3327 in Fig. 1, in which the illustration is annotated as a single element). This illustrates a key advantage of a piecemeal approach to identifying discourse units: instead of attempting to define an exhaustive set of categories for all possible functions that discourse units may have in diagrams, it is possible to initially operate with limited categories that focus on modes of expression that are known to contribute significantly to meaning-making. In the case of diagrams in AI2D, the key category is TEXT, which plays a crucial role in many kinds of discourse relations. Designing annotation tasks that focus on these relations allows identifying the discourse units dynamically. As Fig. 7 shows, the annotators can draw on their knowledge of the diagrammatic semiotic mode [10] to produce extremely detailed annotations without domain expertise.

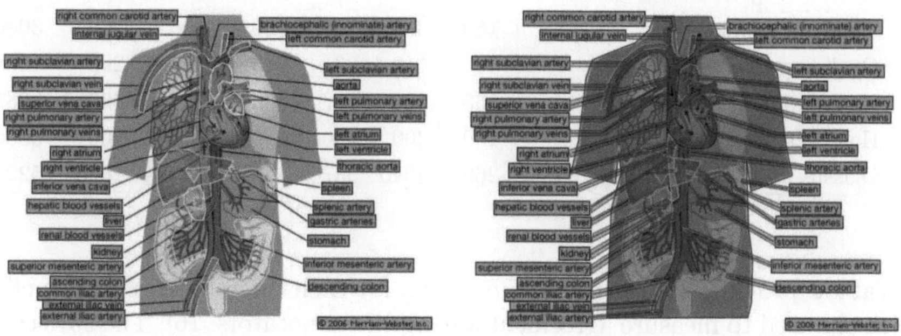

Fig. 7. AI2D diagram #3638 after the first stage (left) and the final output (right). The elements classified as DEPICTION have been rendered using random colours to bring out the level of detail in the annotations; original diagrams are in greyscale. (Color figure online)

4.2 The Scale and Reliability of Annotation

The work of annotating the sample of 1000 diagrams was split into six batches of 50, 100, 100, 200, 250 and 300 diagrams. Dividing the 1000 diagrams into smaller batches initially helped to identify issues with task design and instructions, thus enabling an iterative approach to improve the pipeline.

Table 1 shows the distribution of tasks for each batch across the two stages of the annotation pipeline. As the counts for each microtask indicate, having multiple annotators annotate the same task spawns a large number of tasks as the diagrams proceed through the pipeline (see the column 'overlap' for the number of annotators who performed the same task). The number of tasks also depends on what is being annotated: whereas in microtasks 1, 3, 7, 9 and 10 the annotators classify entire diagrams, microtasks 4, 6 and 11 involve classifying individual elements in the diagrams. In other words, it is the *scope* of the microtask that determines the number of tasks generated. In total, the 26 annotators performed 128591 tasks to annotate the 1000 diagrams.

Table 1. Number of tasks performed for each microtask and batch. The column 'overlap' reports how many annotators annotated the same data point. The rightmost column gives the total number of tasks performed.

#	Microtask	Overlap	Batch size						Σ
			50	100	100	200	250	300	
1	Contains text?	3	150	300	300	600	750	900	3000
2	Outline text	1	52	106	109	220	260	303	1050
3	Review text outlines	3	156	318	327	660	780	909	3150
4	Does text have target?	3	1431	2752	2697	5559	6504	8464	27407
5	Outline targets	1	444	806	813	1641	1773	2448	7925
6	Review target outlines	3	1323	2558	2415	4819	5259	7270	23644
7	All elements outlined?	3	150	300	300	600	750	900	3000
8	Outline missing	1	50	110	99	213	267	299	1038
9	Review added outlines	3	150	330	297	639	768	897	3081
10	Has background image?	3	150	300	300	600	750	900	3000
11	Classify each element	3	2691	5040	5376	11250	12588	15351	52296

Table 2 provides Krippendorff's α scores for each microtask in the pipeline, which are used to measure agreement among the annotators [16]. The 95% confidence intervals were estimated using 500 bootstrapped samples. What stands out is the nearly perfect agreement on simple microtasks such as 1, which requires the annotators to determine the presence of text in diagrams, and the considerably lower agreement scores for microtasks that involve reviewing (3, 6, 9). The review microtasks require the annotators to cross-check each other's work against the instructions, which appears to increase disagreement. Equally notable is the

Table 2. Krippendorff's α scores for all microtasks in the pipeline that involve classification. The microtasks are organised according to the α scores from highest to lowest. The column 'Items' lists the number of items to be annotated, whereas the column 'Tasks' reports the number of tasks performed to annotate these items.

#	Microtask	α	95% CI		Annotators	Items	Tasks
			Low	High			
1	Contains text?	0.98	0.95	1.00	24	1000	3000
11	Classify each element	0.93	0.94	0.98	20	17432	52296
4	Does text have target?	0.79	0.80	0.92	24	9135	27387
7	All elements outlined?	0.69	0.70	0.91	21	1000	3000
10	Has background image?	0.58	0.60	0.82	20	1000	3000
3	Review text outlines	0.40	0.47	0.75	23	1050	3150
6	Review target outlines	0.32	0.42	0.68	24	7822	23634
9	Review added outlines	0.25	0.35	0.67	21	1027	3081

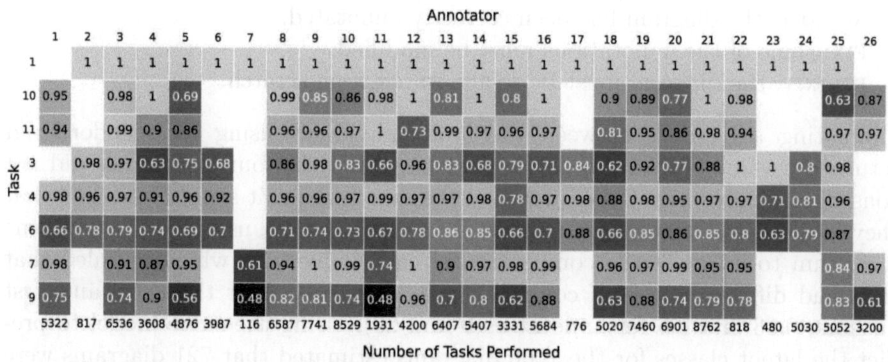

Fig. 8. Competence scores for different annotators as measured using the Dawid-Skene algorithm. Empty cells indicate that the annotator did not participate in the microtask. The task numbers correspond to those provided in Table 1.

lower score for microtask 10, which suggests that the definition of what constitutes a background image must be improved. In contrast, microtask 11 shows that the annotators can reliably apply the four-category scheme for classifying diagram elements to the data.

Figure 8 shows a heatmap with competence scores for each annotator in each microtask, which were measured using the Dawid-Skene algorithm [7] implemented in the Crowd-Kit library [24]. The Dawid-Skene algorithm was trained for 100 iterations to predict a latent label based on the consensus among annotators. The algorithm also estimates the reliability of each annotator by comparing their responses to the consensus. Here the competence score can be interpreted as the probability that the annotator selects the predicted latent label.

The competence scores in Fig. 8 show that the vast majority of annotators are highly competent in simple microtasks that require them to identify the presence of textual elements (1), but also in microtasks that require classifying individual diagram elements (11) or assessing the completeness of the annotations (7). Notably, the annotators were generally very competent in tasks that require performing discourse interpretations, that is, whether the text element has a target or not (4). At the same time, microtasks that involve reviewing annotations created by others were difficult for many annotators (3, 6, 9). Overall, examining the competence of individual annotators explains the disagreement revealed by Krippendorff's α scores in Table 2: some annotators tend to disagree with the consensus.

Because the pipeline is intended for annotating entire diagrams, we also wanted to assess the overall quality of the completed annotations. To do so, the first and the third author and two experienced annotators (9 and 25; see Fig. 8) independently classified each of the 1000 annotated diagrams into three categories:

1. ACCEPT: the diagram has been correctly annotated.
2. FIX: some of the annotations must be modified.
3. REJECT: the diagram must be re-annotated from scratch.

Evaluating agreement between the four individuals using Krippendorff's α returned a value of 0.38. While this indicates that the four individuals did not consistently agree about the quality of the annotations, it should be noted that they had different levels of expertise. For this reason, we used the Dawid-Skene algorithm to estimate the competence of each individual, which revealed that they had differing levels of competence (0.91 and 0.88 for the third and first authors, 0.83 and 0.5 for annotators 9 and 25). Using the same model to predict the latent classes for the 1000 diagrams estimated that 721 diagrams were correctly annotated and could be accepted, 273 should be fixed and 6 rejected. Given that the four annotators agreed that most diagrams assigned to the class FIX required minimal changes, such as drawing outlines for one or two elements or re-classifying them, the results may be considered very promising.

5 Discussion

Our results generally suggest that the proposed approach to identifying analytical units can produce detailed annotations for discourse units in diagrammatic representations. Nevertheless, the annotations must still be validated by domain experts. However, having a domain expert apply limited corrections to existing annotations is a minor task compared to annotating entire diagrams from scratch. Furthermore, as Hiippala et al. [11, p. 11] point out, the process of designing microtask pipelines is an iterative process of trial and error. From the perspective of creating multimodal datasets and corpora, collaborative annotation by non-experts also reallocates the experts' work from annotating data to designing pipelines for non-expert workers.

Although microtask pipelines allow distributing the annotation tasks effectively, breaking the annotation process down into self-contained tasks involves certain issues. Firstly, any annotation pipeline that employs multiple annotators will have bottlenecks: because tasks generate further tasks, a single inactive annotator may stall the process for everyone else. Because the annotation platform does not allow assigning tasks dynamically to active annotators, we ask the annotators to check the available tasks at regular intervals [13]. Secondly, erroneous annotations may be propagated down the pipeline, as exemplified by Fig. 5, which illustrates a failed decomposition. If erroneous annotations pass the subsequent review task, the annotators may be forced to make decisions that they know to be wrong. In future work, we seek to mitigate this by allowing the annotators to flag any decisions that they consider to be erroneous or against the instructions.

That being said, the role of instructions cannot be underestimated when designing microtasks [21]. Although the tasks include just two general types – classification and segmentation – the interfaces alone are not sufficient for communicating the task at hand to the annotators. In other words, the *instructions define the task* for the annotators. Without clearly defined instructions and task scope, the annotators begin to make assumptions about the nature of the tasks, which is reflected in the annotation quality. It is also important to keep in mind that the instructions themselves are multimodal artefacts, and thus a target of subjective interpretation.

Finally, it should also be noted that establishing an inventory of discourse units is just the first step toward a more comprehensive description of the multimodal structure of diagrammatic representations. As Hiippala and Orekhova [12] argue, capturing the hierarchical structure of diagrammatic representations is a prerequisite for describing the relations that hold between discourse units. For the AI2D-RST corpus, which describes these structures as a part of the grouping layer [9, pp. 667–668], the trained annotators exhibited a high degree of agreement as measured by Fleiss' κ (0.894) [9, pp. 674–675]. This raises the question whether the annotation of compositional structures may also be decomposed into a microtask pipeline. We plan to explore this in future work together with characterising the relations that hold between discourse units.

6 Conclusion

In this paper, we have presented a novel approach to identifying discourse units in diagrammatic representations, which involves designing annotation tasks with limited scope and distributing them to locally-recruited non-expert workers, who must then perform inferences about the diagrams under analysis. A qualitative and quantitative evaluation of the resulting annotations revealed most of them to be of high quality. As such, the annotations provide a robust foundation for developing further annotation schemes that capture the multimodal discourse structure of diagrammatic representations in greater detail.

Acknowledgments. This research is part of a project that has received funding from the European Research Council (ERC) under the European Union's Horizon 2020 research and innovation programme (Grant agreement No. 101122047). We also thank the CSC – IT Center for Science Ltd. for computational resources and everyone who participated in annotating the data.

References

1. Alikhani, M., Stone, M.: Arrows are the verbs of diagrams. In: Proceedings of the 27th International Conference on Computational Linguistics, pp. 3552–3563, Santa Fe, New Mexico, USA (2018)
2. André, E., Rist, T.: Generating coherent presentations employing textual and visual material. Artif. Intell. Rev. **9**, 147–165 (1995)
3. Bateman, J.A.: Using multimodal corpora for empirical research. In: Jewitt, C. (ed.) The Routledge Handbook of Multimodal Analysis, 2nd edn, pp. 238–252. Routledge, London and New York (2014)
4. Bateman, J.A., Wildfeuer, J.: Defining units of analysis for the systematic analysis of comics: a discourse-based approach. Stud. Comics **5**(2), 373–403 (2014)
5. Bateman, J.A., Wildfeuer, J., Hiippala, T.: Multimodality: Foundations. Research and Analysis - A Problem-Oriented Introduction. De Gruyter Mouton, Berlin (2017)
6. Carberry, S., Elzer, S., Green, N., McCoy, K., Chester, D.: Understanding information graphics: a discourse-level problem. In: Proceedings of the Fourth SIGdial Workshop of Discourse and Dialogue (2003). https://www.aclweb.org/anthology/W03-2101
7. Dawid, A.P., Skene, A.M.: Maximum likelihood estimation of observer error-rates using the EM algorithm. J. Roy. Stat. Soc. **28**(1), 20–28 (1979)
8. Engelhardt, Y.: The Language of Graphics: A Framework for the Analysis of Syntax and Meaning in Maps, Charts and Diagrams. Ph.D. thesis, Institute for Logic, Language and Computation, University of Amsterdam (2002)
9. Hiippala, T., et al.: AI2D-RST: a multimodal corpus of 1000 primary school science diagrams. Lang. Resour. Eval. **55**(3), 661–688 (2021). https://doi.org/10.1007/s10579-020-09517-1
10. Hiippala, T., Bateman, J.A.: Introducing the diagrammatic semiotic mode. In: Giardino, V., Linker, S., Burns, R., Bellucci, F., Boucheix, J.M., Viana, P. (eds.) Diagrams 2022. LNCS, vol. 13462, pp. 3–19. Springer, Cham (2022). https://doi.org/10.1007/978-3-031-15146-0_1
11. Hiippala, T., Hotti, H., Suviranta, R.: Developing a tool for fair and reproducible use of paid crowdsourcing in the digital humanities. In: Proceedings of the 6th Joint SIGHUM Workshop on Computational Linguistics for Cultural Heritage, Social Sciences, Humanities and Literature, pp. 7–12. International Conference on Computational Linguistics, Gyeongju, Republic of Korea (2022). https://aclanthology.org/2022.latechclfl-1.2
12. Hiippala, T., Orekhova, S.: Enhancing the AI2 diagrams dataset using rhetorical structure theory. In: Proceedings of the 11th International Conference on Language Resources and Evaluation (LREC 2018), pp. 1925–1931. European Language Resources Association (ELRA), Paris (2018)

13. Hotti, H., et al.: Building multimodal corpora using microtask pipelines and local annotators. In: Proceedings of the 15th International Conference on Language Resources and Evaluation (LREC 2026), pp. 6483–6495. European Language Resources Association (ELRA), Paris (2026). https://doi.org/10.63317/434uxg6yj2aj
14. Jappy, T.: Introduction to Peircean Visual Semiotics. Bloomsbury, London and New York (2013)
15. Kembhavi, A., Salvato, M., Kolve, E., Seo, M., Hajishirzi, H., Farhadi, A.: A diagram is worth a dozen images. In: Leibe, B., Matas, J., Sebe, N., Welling, M. (eds.) ECCV 2016. LNCS, vol. 9908, pp. 235–251. Springer, Cham (2016). https://doi.org/10.1007/978-3-319-46493-0_15
16. Krippendorff, K.: Content Analysis: An Introduction to Its Methodology, 3rd edn. Sage, Thousand Oaks, CA (2013)
17. Lechner, V.E.: modality and uncertainty in data visualizations: a corpus approach to the use of connecting lines. In: Pietarinen, A.-V., Chapman, P., Bosveld-de Smet, L., Giardino, V., Corter, J., Linker, S. (eds.) Diagrams 2020. LNCS (LNAI), vol. 12169, pp. 110–127. Springer, Cham (2020). https://doi.org/10.1007/978-3-030-54249-8_9
18. Martin, J.R., Unsworth, L.: Reading Images for Knowledge Building: Analyzing Infographics in School Science. Routledge, New York and London (2023)
19. Royce, T.D.: Synergy on the page: exploring intersemiotic complementarity in page-based multimodal text. JASFL Occasional Papers **1**(1), 25–49 (1998)
20. Sato, Y., Suzuki, A., Mineshima, K.: Building a large dataset of human-generated captions for science diagrams. In: Lemanski, J., Johansen, M.W., Manalo, E., Viana, P., Bhattacharjee, R., Burns, R. (eds.) Diagrams 2024. LNCS, vol. 14981, pp. 393–401. Springer, Cham (2024). https://doi.org/10.1007/978-3-031-71291-3_32
21. Suviranta, R., Hiippala, T.: Can digital humanities use microwork crowdsourcing in a fair manner? The effect of pedagogical training and multimodal instructions on annotation quality. Digit. Scholarsh. Human. **41**(1), 450–463 (2025). https://doi.org/10.1093/llc/fqaf110
22. Toxtli, C., Suri, S., Savage, S.: Quantifying the invisible labor in crowd work. Proc. ACM Hum.-Comput. Interact. **5**(319) (2021). https://doi.org/10.1145/3476060
23. Tversky, B., Zacks, J., Lee, P., Heiser, J.: Lines, blobs, crosses and arrows: diagrammatic communication with schematic figures. In: Anderson, M., Cheng, P., Haarslev, V. (eds.) Diagrams 2000. LNCS (LNAI), vol. 1889, pp. 221–230. Springer, Heidelberg (2000). https://doi.org/10.1007/3-540-44590-0_21
24. Ustalov, D., Pavlichenko, N., Tseitlin, B.: Learning from crowds with Crowd-Kit. J. Open Source Softw. **9**(96), 6227 (2024). https://doi.org/10.21105/joss.06227
25. Zala, A., Lin, H., Cho, J., Bansal, M.: DiagrammerGPT: generating open-domain, open-platform diagrams via LLM planning. In: First Conference on Language Modeling (2024). https://openreview.net/forum?id=NV8yRJRET1

Diagrams, Know-How & Beauty

Noah Greenstein(✉)

The Bronx, New York, USA
me@noahgreenstein.com
https://noahgreenstein.com

Abstract. This paper investigates how our state matters in the creation and analysis of diagrams: there is more than just our abstract knowledge that matters in a diagram, especially regarding our skills or know-how. It is argued that certain diagrams take advantage of this extra knowledge, while other diagrams expect the viewer to skillfully conform their imagination to them. The account is then generalized to sequences of diagrams and proofs, and how we are able to understand how these steps form a unified whole via a form of skilled intuition. This related the discussion to mathematical intuition and beauty, giving a new perspective on these wider questions.

Keywords: Diagrams · Knowledge How · Intuition · Beauty · Mathematics · Imagination

1 Introduction

The immediacy of some diagrams are critical to their function. Consider an emergency exit map: it needs to communicate the way out of the area as quickly as possible. An agent has to recognize the features of the diagram and be able to apply them to escape danger. This contrasts with diagrams that are meant to be studied and understood, like in a mathematical proof. In a proof we have to ensure every step is done according to established rules to guarantee the truth of the conclusion, and, for more significant conclusions, we have to be even more diligent. This diligence is not only to ensure truth but also so that we might understand the reasoning and underlying philosophical or mathematical significance of the proof.

This paper will look into this phenomenon where some diagrams facilitate ease of use and others facilitate deliberation. In this context: Why and what is ease of use, and why and what is deliberation? First I will introduce some plausible initial ideas and then propose my solution having to do with embodiment and know-how. Then this will be further developed to discuss multi-stage diagrams, like instruction manuals and proofs, eventually saying something about our intuition and how we connect different diagrams and the different steps of a proof together.

N. Greenstein — Independent Scholar.

P. Sobociński et al. (Eds.): Diagrams 2026, LNAI 16833, pp. 391–398, 2027.
https://doi.org/10.1007/978-3-032-34178-5_38

What, then, is the difference between diagrams designed for ease of application and diagrams to be deliberated over? From the perspective of them being, say, two dimensional pictures, there is nothing that would indicate one being immediately applicable while the other is not. This is to say, the trivial difference of them being differently shaped diagrams will not be sufficient to explain their difference in application.

Perhaps, then, it is the type of information contained in the diagram that makes one diagram immediately understandable and the other not. That is, it is easy to understand navigational directions but hard to understand complicated proofs, and so these different kinds of information are the source of the difference in how we understand the diagrams. However, this is not obviously true: certain navigational directions can be very difficult to follow and some proofs are trivial. Hence the triviality or complexity can be independent of the type of information communicated, and the difference cannot be just one of informational kind.

Alternatively we might think that diagrams that are hard to understand are the fault of a weak drafter. That is to say that the difficulty lies with the creator of the diagram and has little to do with the information communicated. This too cannot be correct: this implies that the creators of exit maps are all exceptional drafters of diagrams while proof-making geometers are all weak drafters. Though it must be the case that some people are better at making immediately accessible diagrams than others, the idea that all these people only work on emergency exit maps—as opposed to mathematical proofs—is absurd. Hence it does not seem correct to say that the difference between easily accessible diagrams and more difficult ones is entirely up to the drafter.

In a similar vein, a property of the user of the diagram can make the difference between what is easily accessible and what is more difficult. All diagrams do rely upon their user's background. On this point De Toffoli [2, p. 163] defines 'Transparency':

> Transparency quantifies how 'intuitive' a notation [or diagram] is. That is, to what extent it can be interpreted and used directly, by exploiting our cognitive abilities and our training. Therefore, the transparency criterion cannot be fixed once and for all, but it is indexed to the practitioner's background.

Plausibly, we've all had experience with navigating buildings and so we all already have the right sort of abilities and training to immediately use emergency exit maps when needed. This shared training could explain why these sorts of diagrams are immediately usable by nearly anyone.

However, our background cannot explain everything. As mentioned above, sometimes navigational maps are very complex and difficult to understand. Even though we may have experience with navigating buildings and using maps, this does not imply that all maps will be easy to understand. The purpose of training is to give us a better chance at understanding a novel map or diagram. Note though that this does not explain why certain diagrams are easier to understand. Conceivably, experts in geometric proofs also have been trained to understand geometric diagrams, but this does not mean that all geometric proofs are easy for them to understand. Hence, even though diagrams are constructed to take advantage of our cognitive abilities and our training, this holds for all diagrams and it does not explain why specific diagrams are easier to immediately understand and apply.

If no one factor can explain a diagram's ease of use as opposed to other diagrams, then let us consider a combination of factors: say both the type of information and the background. Exit maps both employ a simple kind of information and are something people are generally experienced in using; it is easy and accessible. This would oppose something like a proof in that the proof is complicated and requires much more background training. Hence the exit map seems more immediately understandable.

However, presupposing that an exit map communicates simple and easy information does not explain what about that information is simple or easy. Even if this is the case, that exit maps are simple and easy, merely describing it as such is insufficient as an account of what makes it so.

2 Know-How

Given these difficulties, a different approach is warranted. If we return to the type of information communicated by the diagram, we can also look at its epistemology. That is, it isn't the type of information that was described above, like navigational versus geometric, but the kind of knowledge being communicated. The exit map is telling us *how* to do something—how to leave the area quickly—while a proof is showing *that* the conclusion follows from the premises. This recalls the distinction between 'knowing-how' versus 'knowing-that' [8]. Knowing how to do something is to have the skill or be able to perform an action, like swimming, while knowing that something is the case is to know propositional facts about that thing. However, these two kinds of knowledge are often believed to be distinct: knowing facts about swimming will not mean that one knows how to swim, and vice versa.

Note also that this is not inherently a form of 'visualization' or visual thinking: knowing how to swim or knowing how to walk are not instances of visual knowledge. As mentioned above, all diagrams are different sorts visualizations and hence visualization cannot be the sole determining factor here (cf. [4, §3–4]).

Now, it is beyond my scope to get into the wider epistemic debate between proponents of knowing-how versus proponents of knowing-that (cf. [9,10]). For the current dialectic it is enough to point out that there is some physicality required in exiting a building. One has to be able to—have the skill to—get to and use elevator, stairs, doors, et cetera, and be able to physically move from one's current location to another.

The suggestion is that, in addition to Transparency where our cognitive abilities and training matter, something about the agent's *state* also matters: the diagram presupposes something of agent's current situation. For instance, exit maps often have a 'You Are Here' marker on them. As the map is affixed in a specific location, this You Are Here Marker indicates the location of the agent relative to their current surroundings. This helps correlate the position of the agent within the physical space and the orientation of the diagram because *the agent has to be in that position when reading the map*. Hence the drafter of the map can presuppose the location of the agent as they already know where the map is to be placed, and adjust their map accordingly.

The upshot is that the drafter has this super-diagrammatic information about the agent. Let us define this situation where information about the state or embodiment of the agent can be used in the diagram as a Post-Corpus Diagram (PC). Consider (1) below: when an agent is looking at the place indicated by the arrow and oval, the text is made true. It shows that information can be presupposed by the drafter, in this case me, about my reader and in doing so demonstrates the phenomenon: (1) is PC in that it makes use of the existing state of the agent as part of the diagram.

$$\text{You're looking} \longrightarrow \textit{(HERE)} \tag{1}$$

A second example of a PC diagram, one that assumes something of the state of the agent, are real-time economic market data diagrams. Imagine a diagram describing current market sentiment, either fear or greed, by a face showing either fear or greed. The point of the diagram is to communicate that the market is selling off very fast (fear) or buying very fast (greed). This sort of diagram is PC because it can assume the time and place of the agent: they are viewing the diagram on a financial information service site and this viewing is done at the same time as the market conditions. Therefore the agent can immediately gain understanding of current market sentiment by looking at the diagram.

The alternative to a Post-Corpus diagram is an Ante-Corpus diagram (AC). An Ante-Corpus diagram is one where the agent has to come to embody the diagram. Consider an instruction manual, like one to assemble an office chair: imagine a diagram depicting screwing the arms of the chair to the seat. The diagram expects the agent to conform to the diagram by embodying or realizing this step by actually placing the arm and seat in the way indicated and then screwing them together. Likewise we can imagine a diagram showing us the arm movements required in swimming stroke. We need to orient our arms and bend them in the way the diagram describes.

Similarly consider a geometric proof. When we see diagrams as part of a mathematical proof we are, in some sense, asked to imagine the mathematical figures and their properties. Our ability to understand how the proof progresses depends upon our ability to conceive of the steps of the proof, that is, to use our *manipulative imagination* [3, p. 836] to embody or envision how the mathematical figures change according to the diagrammatic steps. It is our ability to conform our imagination to the ways the diagrams' creator expects us to think about them that is the goal of the proof, to show how the conclusion follows from the premises.

Summarizing the PC/AC distinction: if the diagram is created already assuming something specific of the agent's state, it is Post-Corpus; if the diagram is created assuming the agent will have to change their state to conform to it, then it is Ante-Corpus. Cases of diagrams that are both PC and AC will be discussed below, exhausting the possibilities.

We can now answer the initial question of this paper: why are some diagrams immediately accessible whereas others seem to require effort? The diagrams that are immediately accessible are PC diagrams where something of the agent's state can be already assumed by the drafter of the diagram. Since the drafter has access to this extra information, they are able to make their diagram even more accessible over and above whatever Transparency features they are able to marshal in their diagram. The PC/AC distinction can therefore be seen as an extension, or further condition, of Transparency.

On the other hand, what then is the effort required by AC diagrams? It is not merely that less can be assumed of the agent viewing the diagram. Rather, it is that the agent is expected to conform themself to the diagrammatic representation in some way. This can be a physical change, as in holding one's arm in a certain orientation as with learning a swimming stroke, or mental, as with imagining the described structures. The effort is in our applying some skill to change our state or embodiment as the diagram requires.

3 Sequences and Proofs

This discussion raises a further question: What is going on in sequences of diagrams, such as in instruction manuals or multi-step proofs? Recall the example of an instruction manual for assembling an office chair. We had to screw the arms of the chair into the seat. Let us assume the next step is to screw the backrest into the seat and then the final step is to place the seat on the base with casters. These following steps are both PC and AC in that they assumes the top of the chair has already been assembled (PC), first with arms and then with the seat back, and then expects the agent to place that completed part onto the base (AC). It is a general pattern of diagram sequences that the diagrams are both PC and AC in that the previous step is assumed to obtain (PC) and the current step requires realization (AC).

Granted, that diagrammatic sequences presuppose or rely upon each previous step in the sequence is trivial. The point, though, is that we can now say something about the *continuity* between steps. For an instruction manual putting together a chair, the continuity is of the physicality of the chair: the chair is made of physical material that remains stable over the course of construction. For instructions on a swimming stroke, the continuity is biological: our bodies are only shaped in certain ways and can move in certain ways. Swimming diagrams have continuity with each other because we understand how our bodies biomechanically move from one state to the next.

Along the same line of reasoning, we can ask about the continuity of steps in a diagrammatic proof. However, while there is no physics or biomechanics here, De Toffoli and Giaquinto [3, p. 839–840] [4, p. 264] argue that we rely on our manipulative imagination to act as if we had actually constructed and handled the diagrams in physical space. The idea is that we are using our knowledge, i.e. our know-how, of physical and biomechanical manipulation to understand these abstract transformations.

But what is manipulative imagination? As imagination is a mental act, there is no 'body' to guide our actions. Still, in these embodied cases like swimming or walking, we are able to fill in the gaps between the explicit diagrammatic steps. That is, the know-how directs the abstract thought to fill in the gaps to tell us how our body should be placed: we each understand how to move our body to mimic the diagrams as needed. Returning to the exit map example, we understand our location on the map as indicated by the You Are Here Marker and then can abstractly understand how we can walk in the direction of the exit from that location.

Granted, there is no guarantee that the abstract thought being guided by the know-how exactly conforms to the physical or biomechanical reality—in fact it cannot. A diagram cannot tell us how each of our bodies will realize the act of walking to the exit; this is something each of us must understand. That is, the diagram cannot demonstrate our act of walking for us as how each of us moves is unique to ourselves. Hence, for us to understand a diagram, our manipulative imagination must inherently go beyond being just a proxy for these other, embodied modes of reasoning as it has to combine the abstract information of the diagram with our idiosyncratic embodied knowledge.

Let us call our ability to go beyong our embodied know-how in combination with abstract knowledge our *manipulative intuition*. Note that this merely defines the *skill* of using our individual manipulative imaginations, as given by De Toffoli and Giaquinto.

This reflection on *manipulative intuition* gains further significance with regard to more abstract proofs. Consider that all permissible steps in a proof must, by definition of that system, be trivially true. That the steps are trivial means that they are then all independent of each other: there is nothing in the math or logic that makes one trivial step follow from another trivial step. For instance, classical logic allows for Disjunction Introduction to be used at any point. One does not have to justify the use of DI as it is always allowed in classical logic, regardless of whatever rules were applied earlier in the proof, and it is truth-preserving. It is in this sense that the steps of a formal system are trivial: they are always truth preserving and can be applied independently of whatever the earlier steps were in the proof. As no proof has any obvious necessity relating their steps to each other, having something that goes beyond a mere proxy of physical or biomechanical manipulation—a *mathematical* intuition—would be both philosophically and mathematically significant.

But this is exactly what we have with *manipulative intuition*, at least to some degree. Our *manipulative intuition* gives us extra idiosyncratic insight, in cases where we have some know-how, to fill in the gaps between where we begin and our destination, be it navigational or in a proof. Hence, when we are deliberating over multiple steps using our manipulative imagination, we are able to create continuity between the steps via our *manipulative intuition*.

With this connection between manipulative and mathematical intuition, we can start to look at some wider questions in a new light. While the subsequent analysis will be a bit speculative, I believe it to be instructive to show how the above account may be applied. Consider the role that aesthetics, style or beauty have traditionally played in mathematics and mathematical proofs. The idea here is that our aesthetic sense has been used to guide our mathematical deliberations (see e.g., [5,6,11], [1, §19]).

Of particular interest to my account is the Platonic tradition where all particular occurrences of beauty in the world are united in being instances of the Form of beauty [7, p. 562, Symposium 210d]. The Form of beauty, as a singular thing, then relates and unifies all these instances together. Any particular instance can be situated and related to other objects with regard to how they all relate to the Form of beauty.

Now, while Plato expects us to use instances of beauty like rungs of a ladder to climb to the Form of beauty [7, p. 562-3, Symposium 211a-211e], I only expect our diagrams to act as stepping stones to get to further insights and to develop our deliberative skills. My point in raising the Platonic tradition is to suggest that our manipulative intuition, which we have as a result of our know-how, functions similar to how the Form of beauty acts for Plato. They both relate and unify apparently unrelated ideas or objects together. Hence the manipulative intuition can be seen as functioning like an account of beauty stemming from this tradition.

Extending this thought, that manipulative intuition and beauty are aligned, consider the second of the open questions [1, p. 992] Cain lists in his history of mathematical beauty [1, p. 996]:

> Does a judgement of beauty of a piece of mathematics remain unchanged across successive contemplations? Or, for instance, does a sufficiently large number of encounters with the same piece of mathematics breed *ennui* and hence a diminution of beauty? If there is a change, is it connected with increased or diminished knowledge?

As described by the PC/AC distinction above, our state plays an important role in how we interact with a diagram. When a diagram is AC, it cannot assume much of the viewer. However, if the viewer has seen the same diagram multiple times before, the diagram becomes PC to them: they have already learnt whatever the diagram has to offer, i.e., they no longer have to deliberate and conform their imagination to the diagram. Recall it is this deliberation, engaging the manipulative imagination and intuition, that leads to unification that is associated with beauty. Someone who is already familiar with the steps already knows how they all work together in a unified whole. Hence, whatever unifying aesthetic engagement one might have originally needed to perform will no longer be realized when one is already familiar with the material.

So, to answer Cain's question directly: our judgement of mathematical beauty will change over time. With practice our skill or *know-how* in manipulative imagination will increase, meaning that whatever aesthetic experience we had will no longer be realized in the exact same way as it initially was. While we can potentially return to our old mindsets, in an attempt to recover our original experience, once we become skilled the experience won't be the same. Granted, some mathematical insights may be so fruitful that we will continually find new relationships within its parts, with our insights and deliberative skills building upon each other, but these will be new aesthetic experiences.

To sum up: I argued that our state matters in the creation and analysis of diagrams. PC diagrams take advantage of the state of their viewers, while AC diagrams expect the viewer to skillfully conform to them. The analysis was then generalized to sequences of diagrams and proofs and how we are able to understand how these steps form a unified whole via our manipulative intuition. This related the current discussion to mathematical intuition and beauty, giving insight into these larger questions. Application of the primarily epistemic PC/AC distinction with respect to related concepts, such as easing cognitive load or grounding effective affordances, is left for future research.

solvitur ambulando ■

Acknowledgments. Thanks to the referees for helpful suggestions.

Disclosure of Interests. No competing interests nor funding apply.

References

1. Cain, A.J.: Form & Number: A History of Mathematical Beauty. AJC, Lisbon (2024). https://archive.org/details/cain_formandnumber_ebook_large
2. Toffoli, D.: Silvia: 'Chasing' the Diagram-the Use of Visualizations in Algebraic Reasoning. Rev. Symbol. Logic **10**(1), 158–186 (2017). https://doi.org/10.1017/s1755020316000277
3. Toffoli, D.: Silvia & Giardino, Valeria: Forms and Roles of Diagrams in Knot Theory. Erkenntnis **79**(4), 829–842 (2014). https://doi.org/10.1007/s10670-013-9568-7
4. Giaquinto, M.: Visual Thinking in Mathematics. Clarendon Press, Oxford (2007)
5. Giaquinto, M.: Mathematical proofs: The Beautiful and The Explanatory. J. Human. Math. **6**(1), 52–72 (2016). https://doi.org/10.5642/jhummath.201601.05, https://scholarship.claremont.edu/jhm/vol6/iss1/5
6. Lange, M.: Explanatory Proofs and Beautiful Proofs. J. Human. Math. **6**(1), 8–51 (2016). https://doi.org/10.5642/jhummath.201601.04, https://scholarship.claremont.edu/jhm/vol6/iss1/4
7. Plato: The Collected Dialogues of Plato. Edith Hamilton and Huntington Cairns (eds.) Princeton University Press, Princeton (1961)
8. Ryle, G.: The Concept of Mind. University of Chicago Press, Chicago (1949)
9. Stanley, J.: Knowing (How). Noûs **45**(2), 207–238 (2011). https://doi.org/10.1111/j.1468-0068.2010.00758.x
10. Stanley, J., Willlamson, T.: Knowing How. J. Philos. **98**(8), 411–444 (2001). https://doi.org/10.2307/2678403
11. Starikova, I.: Aesthetic Preferences in Mathematics: A Case Study. Philos. Math. **26**(2), 161–183 (2018). https://doi.org/10.1093/philmat/nkx014

Visual Metaphors for Abstract Conditions: Non-recoverable Replacement in Manga

Yuri Sato(✉) and Yuzuki Ono

Ochanomizu University, Tokyo, Japan
sato.yuri@ocha.ac.jp

Abstract. A persistent challenge in diagrammatic representation concerns how abstract conditions lacking spatially localized physical form, such as psychological states, social relations, or situational constraints, can be visually encoded through spatial visual features. Because many different design choices are possible for representing such abstract conditions, it is often unclear which graphical representations will be intuitively interpretable and widely adopted. This paper examines visual metaphor as a possible source of insight for such representations. Existing taxonomies commonly distinguish forms such as juxtaposition, fusion, and replacement, where replacement metaphors typically assume that the depicted substitute corresponds to a recoverable concrete referent. We identify a distinct subtype of visual metaphor that does not satisfy this assumption, which we call *non-recoverable replacement.* In this subtype, a concrete visual element substitutes for an abstract condition rather than for another spatial object, making the depicted imagery impossible to conceptually restore to a literal scene. To investigate this phenomenon, we constructed a human-annotated dataset of visual metaphors collected from Japanese manga, consisting of 556 annotated page samples. Qualitative analyses reveal recurrent uses of non-recoverable replacement to depict character attitudes, social relations, and situational constraints. These findings suggest that narrative visual media employ systematic strategies for representing abstract conditions through irreversible visual substitution, offering potential insights for diagrammatic representations of absence, uniqueness, and indeterminacy.

Keywords: visual metaphor · abstract conditions · diagrammatic representation · visual metaphor annotation · manga

1 Introduction

Representing the invisible—expressing entities or conditions that lack spatial location through spatial visual features—remains a persistent challenge in information visualization. Diagrammatic representations are particularly involved in this challenge, as they are often designed to visualize abstract concepts such as

P. Sobociński et al. (Eds.): Diagrams 2026, LNAI 16833, pp. 399–407, 2027.
https://doi.org/10.1007/978-3-032-34178-5_39

mathematical or logical relations. However, the design space of diagrammatic syntax is highly flexible. Designers can choose which graphical elements should constitute the representational vocabulary, but it is often unclear which choices will be widely understood and adopted. One possible source of design guidance is metaphor. As emphasized by Tversky [13,14], metaphorical mappings can play an important role in making abstract structures visually interpretable. Visual metaphor is a technique that represents one entity through another visible element, extending the well-known notion of metaphor in linguistic expression discussed by Searle [11]. In visual metaphor research, the entity being described is commonly called the target domain, while the entity used for comparison is called the source domain. Motivated by this perspective, the present study examines how metaphors are actually depicted in visual media, and whether such naturally occurring representations can provide useful ideas for the design of diagrammatic representations of abstract concepts.

Prior research on visual metaphor, much of it conducted in the context of advertising imagery, has commonly classified visual metaphors into three major types. Although naming conventions vary across studies, the terminology of Phillips and McQuarrie [7] and Forceville [2] is widely used. The descriptions below follow the more recent survey by [6], and the example cases are based on those discussed in [15].

(1) **Juxtaposition/Simile type**: both the source and target domains are depicted as separate, complete entities. For example, a car (target) may be visually compared to a dolphin (source) by depicting them side by side.
(2) **Fusion/Hybrid type**: the source and target are visually merged into a single hybrid object. For instance, a car (target) may be depicted as fused with an arm muscle (source).
(3) **Replacement/Contextual type**: one domain replaces the other in the visual depiction, while the absent domain is inferred from contextual cues. For example, a car (target) on a road may be replaced by a shark (source) (Fig. 1C).

However, it remains unclear whether these three types exhaust the possible forms of visual metaphor. In particular, we focus on cases in which a concrete visual element substitutes not for another spatial object but for an abstract condition, such as a psychological state, a social relation, or a situational constraint. Although such cases may superficially resemble replacement metaphors, they differ in an important respect: the substituted element does not correspond to a concrete object that could be conceptually recovered from the image. We therefore identify and analyze a distinct subtype of visual metaphor, which we call *non-recoverable replacement.* While this type may be relatively rare in the advertising imagery typically studied in previous work, we hypothesize that it may occur more frequently in narrative visual media that explore complex situations and internal states. To investigate this possibility, we constructed a human-annotated dataset of visual metaphors collected from Japanese manga. Preliminary annotation results further suggest that this subtype occurs far more

Table 1. Manga works included in the dataset. Numbers in parentheses indicate the total number of volumes of each work. Dem. denotes the demographic readership category: shōnen (boys), shōjo (girls), seinen (men), and josei (women).

Title	Author	Publisher	Dem.
Vagabond (37 vols.)	Inoue	Kodansha	seinen
Historie (12 vols.)	Iwaaki	Kodansha	seinen
Shissō Nikki (1 vol.)	Azuma	East Press	seinen
March Comes in Like a Lion (18 vols.)	Umino	Hakusensha	seinen
Chihayafuru (50 vols.)	Suetsugu	Kodansha	shōjo
Silver Spoon (15 vols.)	Arakawa	Shogakukan	shōnen
Kakukaku Shikajika (5 vols.)	Higashimura	Shueisha	josei
Blue Giant (10 vols.)	Ishizuka	Shogakukan	seinen
Hibiki (13 vols.)	Yanamoto	Shogakukan	seinen
Hanagami Sharaku (1 vol.)	Ichinoseki	Shogakukan	seinen
Blue Period (18 vols.)	Yamaguchi	Kodansha	seinen
Kore Kaite Shine (8 vols.)	Toyoda	Shogakukan	shōnen

frequently in our dataset than recoverable replacement metaphors. As emphasized by [1,5], Japanese comics employ distinctive visual techniques that are particularly effective in representing subjective experience and narrative perspective. This suggests that manga may provide a medium that systematically employs rich metaphorical visual narration. Focusing on Japanese manga also distinguishes the present study from recent visual metaphor datasets developed in AI research [4,16], which primarily analyze photographs, posters, or other static imagery rather than narrative visual media.

2 Manga Visual Metaphor Dataset

This dataset is intended as an initial exploratory resource for examining visual metaphors in narrative visual media rather than as a comprehensive corpus. To support further empirical research, the annotation metadata used in this study is publicly available at: https://github.com/yuri-ocha/manga-visual-metaphor-dataset.git.

2.1 Manga Works

To focus on manga works that are widely recognized in contemporary Japan, we selected titles that have received at least two major Japanese manga awards since 1997. The awards considered were: the Shogakukan Manga Award, the Japan Cartoonists Association Award (Grand Prize), the Kodansha Manga Award, the Tezuka Osamu Cultural Prize (Grand Prize), the Japan Media Arts Festival Manga Division (Grand Prize), and the Manga Taisho Award. Using this criterion, 19 works were initially selected. Among them, 12 works were judged by the authors to contain at least one instance of visual metaphor and were therefore included in the dataset (Table 1). The selected manga works were also categorized according to the demographic readership of the magazines in which they were originally serialized (e.g., shonen, seinen, shojo).

2.2 Annotation Scheme

First, the authors identified 556 manga pages that were judged to contain potential instances of visually expressed metaphor. These pages were used as annotation stimuli. Certain types of visual scenes were excluded from the dataset. Scenes in which characters literally perceive altered realities due to hallucination or supernatural abilities were not treated as metaphors. In addition, decorative visual signs often used in shojo manga—such as backgrounds filled with flowers around a character—were excluded, following the classification of visual signs discussed by [8].

Annotation was conducted by two Japanese native speakers (female university students, aged 21) who were familiar with manga reading. For each page, annotators were first asked whether the page contained a visual metaphor (i.e., whether an illustration visually expressed a relation similar to "A is like B"). If the answer was positive, annotators were asked to provide the following information:

1. Which panel contains the metaphorical expression
2. The target of the metaphor (the entity being described)
3. The source of the metaphor (the entity used for comparison)
4. The type of metaphor: A. Juxtaposition, B. Fusion, C. Replacement (recoverable), D. Replacement (non-recoverable)
5. Whether the annotator had previously read the manga work

For types A (Juxtaposition) and B (Fusion), the annotators were given descriptions and examples corresponding to those introduced in Sect. 1. For types C and D, the following instructions were provided to the annotators (a more detailed analysis of these categories is presented in the next section).

C. **Recoverable replacement.** The target entity is replaced by the source entity in the image, but the target could in principle be depicted directly as a visual object.
   Example (Fig. 1C): In a visual metaphor expressing "the car is like a shark," a shark is drawn on the road where the car would normally appear. Although the car itself is not depicted, it could be visually represented in the image instead of the shark.

D. **Non-recoverable replacement.** The target is replaced by a visual element, but the target itself cannot be directly depicted as a visual object.
   Example (Fig. 1D): A scene showing a man sitting alone in a bleak landscape with cloudy skies represents the man's feeling of loneliness. In this case, the target (the emotional state of loneliness) cannot be directly depicted in the image as a visual object replacing the landscape.

C

D

Fig. 1. Examples of replacement metaphors: (C) recoverable replacement and (D) non-recoverable replacement. The latter represents cases where the substituted element encodes an abstract condition rather than a spatial object.

2.3 Visual Metaphors with Annotator Agreement

Among the 556 pages initially identified by the authors as containing visual metaphors, 508 pages (91.4%) were judged to contain a metaphor by at least one annotator. Furthermore, 451 pages (81.1%) were judged to contain a metaphor by both annotators.

3 Non-recoverable Replacement

In this section we clarify the conceptual distinction between recoverable and non-recoverable replacement and illustrate it with examples from the dataset. We further examine the replacement type of visual metaphor in greater detail. In replacement metaphors, the depicted object in the image does not match the expected object in the depicted context. From this mismatch, viewers infer the presence of an absent target entity, which allows the image to be interpreted metaphorically.

When the target entity is a spatial object, the image can in principle be conceptually restored to a literal scene by replacing the depicted source with the expected object. We refer to this subtype as *recoverable replacement.* However, in some cases the substituted element does not correspond to a spatial object but to an abstract condition, such as a psychological state, a social relation, or a situational constraint. In such cases, the image cannot be conceptually restored to a literal depiction, because the target cannot itself be represented as a concrete visual object. We refer to this subtype as *non-recoverable replacement.*

In recoverable replacement, the validity of the viewer's inference can be verified by mentally reconstructing the literal scene. In contrast, in non-recoverable replacement such verification is not possible, because the target lacks a directly depictable visual form. As a result, this type of metaphor may require greater interpretive effort. While this may be less suitable for media such as advertising photographs that demand immediate recognition, it may be particularly compatible with narrative visual media such as manga, which often invite deeper interpretation.

Among the items labeled by the authors as non-recoverable replacement (Type D), 301 of 356 cases (87.1%) were also classified as Type D by at least one annotator, and 221 cases (62.1%) were classified as Type D by both annotators.

These results suggest that non-recoverable replacement can be identified with a reasonable degree of consistency. Figure 2(1) shows an example from *Blue Giant* (Vol. 3). In this scene, a man playing the saxophone is surrounded by a darkened background representing his feeling that he is alone in the world. Here, a concrete visual element (the darkened space) encodes an abstract psychological condition rather than a spatial object.

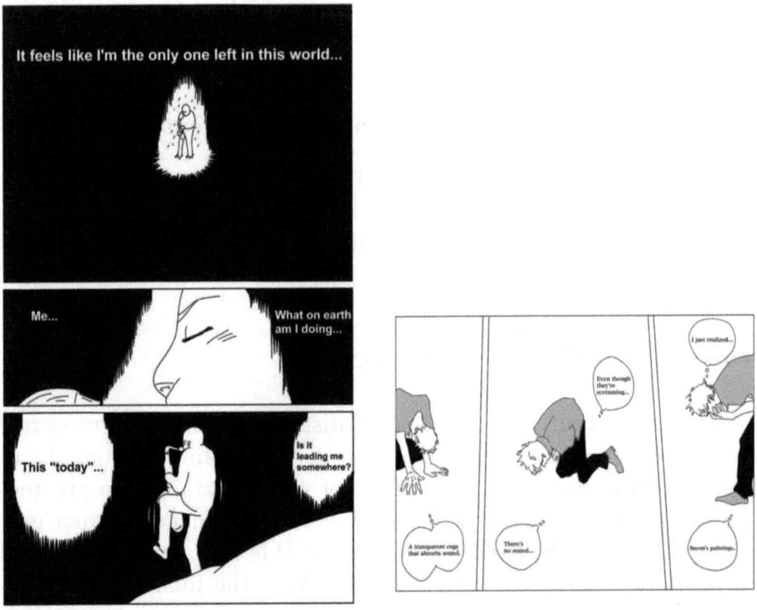

(1) (2)

Fig. 2. Example of non-recoverable replacement (1) from *Blue Giant* (Vol.3) and (2) from *Blue Period* (Vol. 16)

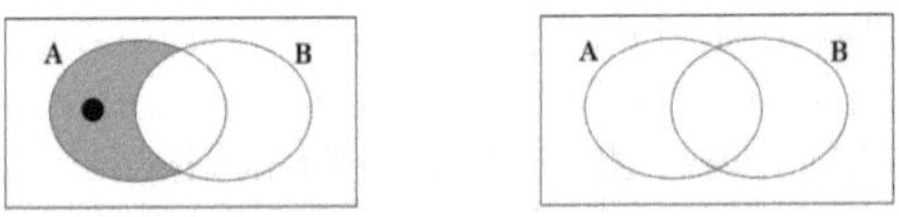

(1) (2)

Fig. 3. Examples of logical diagrams illustrating (1) exactly one element in the region $A \setminus B$ (corresponding to the black-background example in Fig. 2-1) and (2) minimal regions whose contents are unspecified (corresponding to the white-background example in Fig. 2-2).

Another example is shown in Fig. 2(2) from *Blue Period* (Vol. 16). In this scene, everything except the character is depicted as white space, representing the character's inability to hear sound. The perceptual condition of silence is metaphorically represented through the visual substitution of white space. However, the meaning of such visual substitutions is not fixed. For instance, in another case from *Chihayafuru* (Vol. 9), a darkened background expresses the character's shock rather than isolation. Similarly, in a scene from *Vagabond* (Vol. 12), a white background surrounding a character represents the absence of constraints on the character's actions. Despite these variations, the annotators were able to distinguish these cases consistently, suggesting that viewers rely on multiple cues when interpreting such metaphors. These cues may include visual structure within the panel, textual dialogue, or contextual information from surrounding panels.

Among the items labeled by the authors as recoverable replacement (Type C), 11 of 13 cases (84.6%) were also classified as Type C by at least one annotator, and 4 cases (30.8%) were classified as Type C by both annotators. The lower agreement for Type C may reflect the small number of such cases in the dataset and the relative rarity of recoverable replacement in manga. Figure 4 shows an example of recoverable replacement from *Kore Kaite Shine* (Vol. 8). In this scene, the person in the foreground shows her romance manga to her friends, who are depicted as animals such as rabbits and bears. The animal depiction metaphorically conveys that the friends fail to understand the intended romantic meaning. In this case, the depicted animals can be conceptually replaced by human characters, making the metaphor recoverable.

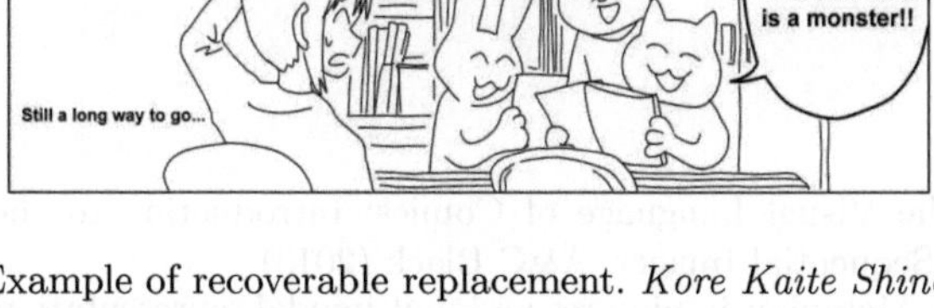

Fig. 4. Example of recoverable replacement. *Kore Kaite Shine* (Vol. 8)

4 Implications for Diagrammatic Representation

Modern variants of logical diagrams, such as spider diagrams [3] and concept diagrams [12], employ graphical devices such as shading and dots to express information about existence and cardinality. For example, in Fig. 3(1), shading applied to the region corresponding to $A \setminus B$, together with a single dot, indicates that exactly one element exists in that region. Interestingly, similar visual strategies appear in the manga examples discussed earlier. In Fig. 2(1), the area surrounding the character is filled with black, visually conveying that the character is the only entity present in the depicted space. This use of black background to indicate the absence of other entities resembles the use of shading in logical diagrams to mark regions where no additional elements may exist.

A related correspondence can be observed in the example shown in Fig. 2(2). In this scene, the surrounding space is rendered as blank white, representing the character's inability to perceive sound. This visual device can be interpreted as indicating that the content of the surrounding space is unspecified or indeterminate. In spider diagrams and concept diagrams, regions that contain no dots and remain unshaded similarly indicate that it is not specified whether any elements exist in those regions (Fig. 3(2)).

These parallels suggest that techniques used in visual narrative media, particularly the non-recoverable replacement metaphors observed in manga, may share representational intuitions with diagrammatic systems designed to express abstract logical relations. From this perspective, diagrammatic representations such as logical diagrams may not be purely artificial constructions invented by individual researchers, but may instead reflect visual conventions that are broadly intelligible to ordinary viewers. This may partly explain why, among the many proposed diagrammatic formalisms, only a limited number become widely adopted and persist over time (cf. [9,10]).

Exploring visual metaphor in real-world visual media therefore offers a potentially valuable empirical resource for the design of diagrammatic representations of abstract entities and relations. In particular, narrative visual media such as manga may provide useful insights into how viewers naturally interpret visual encodings of abstract conditions.

Acknowledgments. This study was supported by Grant-in-Aid for JSPS KAKENHI Grant Number JP24K15676 and JP24K00004 to the first author.

References

1. Cohn, N.: The Visual Language of Comics: Introduction to the Structure and Cognition of Sequential Images. A&C Black (2013)
2. Forceville, C.: Metaphor in pictures and multimodal representations. In: The Cambridge Handbook of Metaphor and Thought, pp. 462–482. Cambridge Univ. Press (2008). https://doi.org/10.1017/CBO9780511816802.028
3. Gil, J., Howse, J., Kent, S.: Formalizing spider diagrams. In: Proceedings of VL 1999, pp. 130–137. IEEE (1999). https://doi.org/10.1109/VL.1999.795884
4. Kundu, M., Shekhar, S., Bhattacharyya, P.: Looking beyond the pixels: evaluating visual metaphor understanding in VLMs. In: Proceedings of EMNLP 2025, pp. 23137–23158. ACL (2025). https://doi.org/10.18653/v1/2025.findings-emnlp.1257
5. McCloud, S.: Understanding Comics: The Invisible Art. Kitchen Sink Press (1993)
6. Peterson, M.O.: Aspects of visual metaphor: an operational typology of visual rhetoric for research in advertising. Int. J. Advert. **38**, 67–96 (2019). https://doi.org/10.1080/02650487.2018.1447760
7. Phillips, B.J., McQuarrie, E.F.: Beyond visual metaphor: a new typology of visual rhetoric in advertising. Mark. Theory **4**(1–2), 113–136 (2004). https://doi.org/10.1177/1470593104044089

8. Sakurai, S., Narumi, T., Tanikawa, T., Hirose, M.: Augmented emotion by superimposing depiction in comics. In: Proceedings of ACE 2011, pp. 1–2. ACM (2011). https://doi.org/10.1145/2071423.207150
9. Sato, Y., Mineshima, K.: Visually analyzing universal quantifiers in photograph captions. In: Giardino, V., Linker, S., Burns, R., Bellucci, F., Boucheix, J.M., Viana, P. (eds.) Diagrams 2022. LNCS, vol. 13462, pp. 373–377. Springer, Cham (2022). https://doi.org/10.1007/978-3-031-15146-0_34
10. Sato, Y., Mineshima, K., Ueda, K.: Can negation be depicted? Comparing human and machine understanding of visual representations. Cogn. Sci. **47**(3), e13258 (2023). https://doi.org/10.1111/cogs.13258
11. Searle, J.R.: Expression and Meaning: Studies in the Theory of Speech Acts. Cambridge Univ. Press (1979). https://doi.org/10.1017/CBO9780511609213
12. Stapleton, G., Compton, M., Howse, J.: Visualizing OWL 2 using diagrams. In: Proceedings of VL/HCC 2017, pp. 245–253. IEEE (2017). https://doi.org/10.1109/VLHCC.2017.8103474
13. Tversky, B.: Cognitive principles of graphic displays. In: AAAI Fall Symposium, pp. 116–124. AAAI (1997)
14. Tversky, B.: Spatial schemas in depictions. In: Spatial Schemas and Abstract Thought, pp. 79–112. MIT Press (2001). https://doi.org/10.7551/mitpress/6392.003.0006
15. van Mulken, M., Le Pair, R., Forceville, C.: The impact of perceived complexity, deviation and comprehension on the appreciation of visual metaphor in advertising across three European countries. J. Pragmat. **42**(12), 3418–3430 (2010). https://doi.org/10.1016/j.pragma.2010.04.030
16. Zhang, D., Zhang, M., Zhang, H., Yang, L., Lin, H.: MultiMET: a multimodal dataset for metaphor understanding. In: Proceedings of ACL 2021, pp. 3214–3225. ACL (2021). https://doi.org/10.18653/v1/2021.acl-long.249

A Diagrammatic Notation for Social Partner Dancing: Case Study in Representational Epistemic Design

Peter C. -H. Cheng[1(✉)] and Irvin R. Katz[2]

[1] Department of Informatics, University of Sussex, Brighton, UK
p.c.h.cheng@sussex.ac.uk

[2] Cognitive and Technology Sciences Consulting, Hopewell, NJ, USA

Abstract. How should representational systems for complex knowledge-rich topics be analyzed and designed? The Representational Epistemic (REEP) approach was previously proposed. It claims, first, that design should be grounded on a comprehensive analysis of the conceptual structure of the target topic. Second, design should aim to coherently encode that conceptual structure in representational schemes according to certain principles. A diagrammatic cognitive modelling tool supports analysis and design. The REEP approach has been used to design representational systems for various knowledge-rich topics successfully. This paper challenges the utility and validity of REEP by applying it to the design of a new graphical notation for a topic whose nature is distinct from those in the previous case studies. Additionally, the REEP design principles are used to guide the construction of a graphical editor for the new notation, further testing its scope. Implications for the design of representations for knowledge-rich topics, in general, are considered.

Keywords: Representational epistemology · conceptual structure · representational system design · cognitive modelling · social partner dancing

1 Introduction

Substantial research has been conducted on the nature and design of graphical representations, as exemplified by the Diagrams Conference series (beginning with [1]). A small sample of notable work, collections and reviews in the field includes: [2–7]. These theories and empirical findings have substantially advanced our understanding of how and why diagrams work, and our knowledge about what factors underpin effective representational systems. However, what is notable – understandably – is that much work in the field has focused on representations for topics that conceptually are relatively simple; such as hierarchies, sets, or quantitative datasets.

Thus, a challenge for the diagrams research community is to be able to systematically *analyze* the efficacy of representational systems for complex knowledge-rich topics. A grander challenge for the community is to be able to systematically *design* efficacious representational systems for complex knowledge-rich topics. Such analyses

P. Sobociński et al. (Eds.): Diagrams 2026, LNAI 16833, pp. 408–423, 2027.
https://doi.org/10.1007/978-3-032-34178-5_40

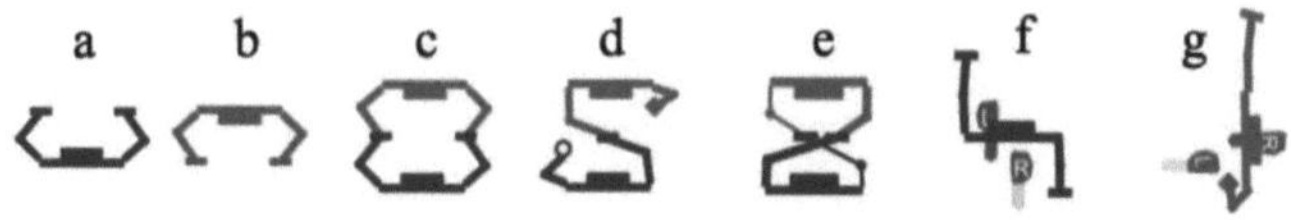

Fig. 1. Figurines representing dancers. Leads are blue (dark grey), followers red (light grey).

and designs could provide insights about how to represent intricate, multiscale, multilayer, heterogenous knowledge. In other words, we contend that factors exist that are relevant to the efficacy of representational systems, which are not reducible to models derived from representations for simple topics.

Representational Epistemological (REEP) analysis and design is an approach to the design of representational systems for knowledge-rich topics [8, 9]. REEP claims that such analysis and design of representational systems should primarily focus on understanding the inherent conceptual structure of the target topic [8, 9]. REEP contends that representational systems are effective when they encode the topic's concepts directly and coherently in the graphical structure of the representation. REEP has been used to analyze and design representational systems for diverse topics, including: physics (e.g., circuit electricity [8], quantum mechanics [10]); mathematics (e.g., probability theory [9], algebra and imaginary numbers [11]); logic (e.g., syllogisms [12], propositional calculus [13]); interfaces for information intensive problem solving (e.g., examination timetabling [14]). REEP is detailed in the next section of the paper.

To support the systematic analysis of conceptual structures and how they are encoded, a cognitive theory of the interpretation of representational systems has been developed, *RIST* [15–19]. It has an accompanying diagrammatic modelling notation, *RISN*, which has been implemented in a graphical editor, *RISE*. RIST/RISN/RISE are described in the 4th section of the paper.

The scope of REEP is challenged in this paper by applying it to the topic of *social partner dancing*, which has a rich, diverse and profuse conceptual structure. Importantly, it possesses features that are distinct from those in all the previous topics noted above. Using REEP to design an effective new diagrammatic notation for the topic, and developing a graphical editor program for the notation, provides further evidence of the utility and validity REEP approach. The new dance notation is introduced in Sect. 5, and the editor – *Choriolis* – is described in Sect. 6.

In social partner dancing, a dance is an unrehearsed *lead-follower* dance. The *lead* (typically a man) chooses, on the fly, what moves the pair will execute, which are communicated to the follower (typically a woman) by physical signals, mostly using the lead's hands. The particular form of social dancing considered here is Modern Jive [20], also known as Ceroc® or Leroc [21]. The development of this style of dancing began in the 1980s and has grown substantially in popularity; there are hundreds of venues with weekly classes and freestyle social dances in the UK. By de-emphasizing footwork patterns, Modern Jive can be danced to any music with a regular beat, but its repertoire does incorporate some Ballroom and Latin dance moves.

To introduce the dance and the new notation, consider Figs. 1 and 2. Dancers are represented by *figurines* (stick figures) in plan view, looking down. In Fig. 1a, the lead faces 12 o'clock and in Fig. 1b the follower faces in the opposite direction. In Fig. 1c

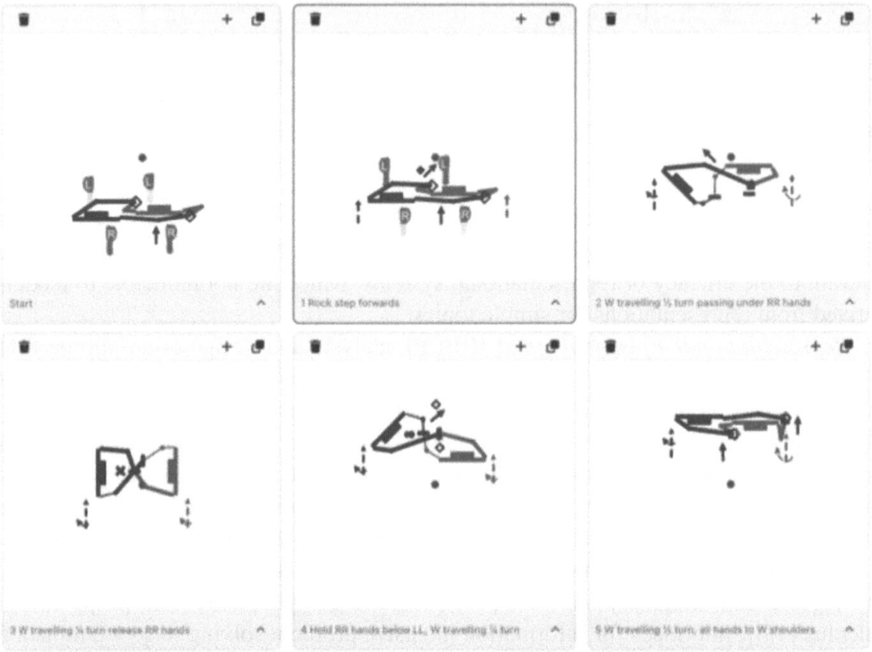

Fig. 2. The new notation drawn in Choriolis: *Low-level illusion* move (1st half)

they are holding both pairs of hands at waist level. Just right hands are held in Fig. 1d and the lead's free hand is at hip level and the follower's is above their head.

Figure 2 shows the *low-level illusion* move (invented by the first author). (Panel 1) To start, the dancers are side by side with both pairs of hands held and on the follower shoulders. (P2) They rock forward changing their weight distribution. The lead signals the follower to turn. (P3) The follower walks and turns clockwise under their raised left arms. (P4) Whilst travelling and turning their left hands are released. (P5) Continuing to move, the lefts hands are re-taken under the pair of rights hands. (P6) The dancers end up in the starting pose but facing the opposite direction. The sequence is physically impossible without the splitting of hands, which are hidden by the dancers' bodies, hence the illusion. The whole move is completed by reversing the whole sequence.

2 Representational Epistemic Analysis and Design

The core claim of the Representational Epistemic (REEP) approach is: *Cognitively effective representational systems for complex knowledge-rich topics should directly and coherently encode the fundamental conceptual structure of the target topic* [8, 9]. Cognitive effectiveness includes impacts on memory, interpretation, reasoning, problem solving, and learning. The claim applies to graphical displays of information, diagrammatic notations, computer user interfaces, and control panels. The fundamental conceptual structures of a topic are those ideas that permeate all considerations of a topic. These concepts underpin the topic such that if they were absent in our considerations we would essentially be thinking about a different topic. The analysis of the conceptual structure of a topic should uncover the *principles* underpinning the primary classes of concepts. These include invariants, regularities, symmetries, constraints, and laws that pervade all thinking about the topic. These ideas are exemplified in Sect. 3 of the paper, which analyses the conceptual structure of social partner dancing.

When these principles, of classes of concepts, are directly and coherently encoded in a representational system, REEP contends that the system will be *semantic transparent* and as a consequence also be *syntactically plastic* [8, 9]. When possessing this pair of properties, a representation will naturally support cognitive processes across timescales from perception (seconds) through to learning (days). Four REEP principles (design heuristics) have been proposed for semantic transparency [8, 9]. An effective representational system should provide:

1. **Distinct representational schemes** for each class of core concepts, in order to differentiate those classes from each other.
2. **Coherent representational schemes** for each set of core concepts, so the levels and aspects of the concepts are systematically integrated and differentiated.
3. **A global interpretive framework** to coherently integrate all the representational schemes.
4. **Subordination of secondary classes of concepts** within the global interpretive framework, or a particular representational scheme.

More detail and examples of the application of these design principles across diverse topics can be found in [8–14].

REEP builds on prior work on the nature of representational systems, to operationalize the design of component representational schemes for particular sets of concepts. For instance, all else being equal: location indexing should be used in preference to sentential representations [3]; to represent variables, graphic properties should be selected with quantity scales of (at least) matching expressivity, e.g., [2]; one should aim for isomorphic mappings between entities in the represented world and symbols in the representation [22]. However, what is novel about REEP is its prioritization of the *fundamental* knowledge of the topic, the principal classes of concepts, and the relations among higher order conceptual structures and representation schemes, which contrasts with previous work that asks questions about the mapping of more elementary information to graphic properties and representational formats.

3 Conceptual Analysis of Social Partner Dancing

The first step in the design of a representational system in the REEP approach is to analyze the conceptual structure of the target topic. We are after fundamental principles, in a broad sense, that permeate the topic, but that are describable in domain independent terms. The task of the analyst is to identify what principles, inherent notions, exist in the topic that: allow concepts to be distinguished from each other; determine what concepts are legitimate to consider; enable different classes of concepts to be meaningfully considered together. Here are some examples: *taxonomies* that specify what entities or processes exist, and their ordering and grouping; *relational systems* such as set theory, mereological hierarchies, algebras, geometry; *types of properties*, such as quantity scales, or causal versus statistical features; *scales of granularity*, over space, time and other properties; *frames of reference* that establish how perspectives are to be interpreted; *time* which can be expressed in continuous or discrete ways.

Mining the conceptual structure of a topic requires us to see through the overt contents of the topic to the underlying conceptual structures. This can be challenging because established terminology within the topic may give no hint of the presence of the principles. Further, some descriptions of a topic hide the principles in plain sight, because they are seemingly so obvious that they are not explicitly mentioned. However, they are all essential for the REEP design. For example, in dance, the fact that human bodies are physical and impermeable goes (largely) unmentioned in accounts of dance, but it is an inviolable constraint that can be exploited in the design of a representation system to aid the identification, or even prevent the generation of, impossible states.

We proposed six classes of core concepts for social partner dancing.

Space. *Everything in the topic is situated in three-dimensional space. Things have absolute positions and orientations with respect to the dance floor. From the dancers' perspective, their relative position, orientation and distance to each other is important. The stance of the body and positioning of parts of the body is also inherently spatial. However, in social dancing the body is typically upright, and the hands are carried at waist level by default. Normally, at least one foot is on the ground, so the overall elevation of dances' bodies typically varies little, but the altitude of the arms and upper parts of the body can vary substantially.*

Time. *Dancers follow the rhythm of the music with actions aligned to the beat, including quick actions on half beats, or slow actions drawn out over two beats. Notably, as a lead gives signals to the follower, both dancers attention will not just be on executing the actions in the moment, but must they have a sense of preparing for the future actions. There are subtle temporal relations to be encoded.*

Dancers *– statics. Human bodies have a mereological hierarchical structure, with a whole body being the trunk and the digits of the hands and feet being leaves of a tree-like structure. There are an immense possible range of poses, but our bodies establish many sets of natural constraints – a physical logic. The degrees of freedom of joints limits the range of poses that a body can adopt. Bodies are physical and so their parts are impassable, as noted above. The low-level illusion move,* Fig. 2, *plays on this idea with its brief cleaving of held hands.*

Many combinations of hand holds are possible by the physical logic of our arms: Figs. *1c-1e* *show three. One or two pairs of hands may be held, and one hand may hold two. If the arms are crossed, one pair must be above the other. A double crossing of the arms happens when there is a right-left and left-right hand hold, and one dancer does a full 360° turn without letting go.*

Movement *– kinematics. The movement of dancers is diverse, encompassing travelling and turning across the dance floor, and creating shapes with their bodies. A dance has a hierarchical structure that includes: a whole dance (≈3 min); learnt sequences of moves (lasting about 20 beats, ≈10 s); moves (3–7 beats), such as* Fig. 2; *"step" actions such as a footstep, a spin or an arm gesture (1 beat), e.g., panels in* Fig. 2; *quick actions, e.g.,* *releasing a hand hold (<1 beat). Moves can be complex: some require multiple actions by multiple body parts executed in parallel.*

***Support** – dynamics. As the dancers move, their weight shifts between their feet and parts of the feet. The correct distribution of weight is sometimes important to the execution of moves but also impacts a dancer's stylishness. With two feet, and support distributed to the toe, heel, both, or neither, or feet airborne, there are numerous possible support configurations.*

Interaction. *This is perhaps an unexpected category, but it is one that is critical for partner dancing, because clear ongoing communication between the dancers is essential. Signals are predominantly given by the lead pulling or pushing the follower's hands or other parts of their body. Verbal instructions are typically restricted to teaching. Signals may direct whole body moves and turns, and movements of body parts in three dimensions. They must also convey the extent and speed of the action: for instance, the splitting and re-holding of hands in the low-level illusion should be completed in a fraction of a beat. Most signals rely upon the context in which force or action is applied. Others are established by convention and taught, particularly non-touching visual signals. The timing of signals must be precise to allow for human reaction time, but not so early that they are out of context and misinterpreted.*

The dance also relies on various conventions. For instance, when travelling forwards or backwards the follower continues moving unless stopped (in a Newtonian fashion). The dance is "slotted" with the expectation that the follower will typically travel back and forth along a straight-line, unless otherwise led. Thus, the lead moves aside to clear a path, otherwise the follower must assume the move will be on the spot, unless a signal directs the follower to orbit the lead.

The classes of concepts establish a space with spatial, temporal, static physical, kinematic, dynamic, and interactional dimensions. A sense of the amount of information involved in the characterization of dance is suggested by the fact that a typical lesson lasting 30–45 min can only cover three moves each consisting of about 6 steps and taking 10 s to perform, at normal speed. The central issue for the design of a representational system is how to directly and coherently encode such a vast, complex and diverse informational space.

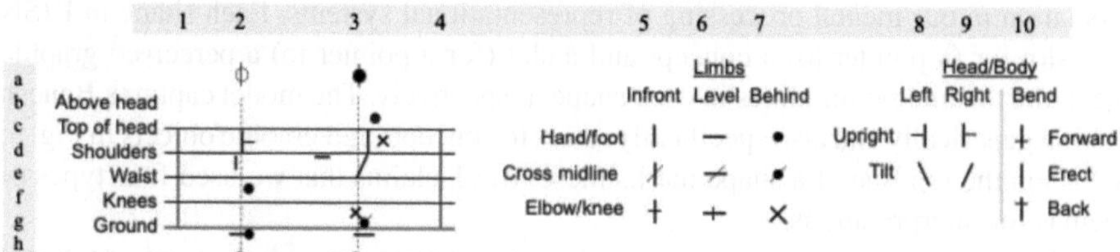

Fig. 3. A sample of Benesh notation and a selection of some of its symbols.

4 Modelling the Benesh Dance Notation

The REEP approach advocates examining existing representations as it contributes to the identification of a topic's classes of essential concepts, and because it may provide ideas for the design specific representational schemes and insights about what to avoid. For this purpose, the *Representational Interpretative Structure Theory*, RIST, has been developed for the cognitive modelling of representational systems. The models capture the contents and structure of the network of schemas that a reader builds in their memory as they interpret a representation. The degree of coherence of a network reflects the likely cognitive efficacy of its representation. RIST is instantiated in a diagrammatic Notation, RISN, and implemented as a specialized graphical Editor, RISE. This section uses RIST to analyze an established graphical dance notation and the following section applies RIST to the design of our new notation. Full details of how to model and evaluate representational systems with RIST/RISN/RISE can be found in [16, 17].

There is no scarcity of dance notations that we might analyze. Hutchison Guest identifies nearly 80 notations in the history of dance [23, 24]. Of these, Benesh is a well-known system that is among just a handful that are currently used, particularly in the realm of ballet [25]. Fig. 3 left shows a brief Benesh example. Benesh deploys a staff (Fig. 3, coordinates 1c-4 g) on which symbols for the location of one dancer's body parts and their movement are hung. Figs. 3.5a-10 g are examples of Benesh symbols.

Two poses are shown on the left of Fig. 3. In the first (2a-2i) represents an upright dancer with their upright head facing right (2c), their left arm stretched out in front at shoulder height to their left (2d), their right hand behind between their waist and knee to their right (2f), their left foot on the ground under their body and their right foot on ground behind (2 h), and the dancer is facing the forwards (2i). In second pose their head is simply upright (3c), they are leaning to the right from the waist (3e), their right hand (3b) is up above head height behind the body, its elbow is also behind on the right (3c), the left hand is outstretched to the left (3d), their weight is on their right foot (3 h), their left knee is behind (f3), with the left foot also on the right and behind just touching the ground but not supporting weight (3 g), and the dancer is facing to the right (3i).

The RISN model for these aspects of Benesh is shown in Fig. 4. Each shape is a schema and lines between them are connections between schemas. The unique theoretical proposition of RIST is that concepts about a topic are tightly coupled to the graphical objects representing them, so a primary function of the schemas is to maintain that association in our mental processing of representational systems. Each shape in RISN has a slot for (a pointer to) a concept and a slot (for a pointer to) a perceived graphic object, the top and bottom lines in each shape, respectively. The model captures Benesh notation generically and also specifically refers to concepts and graphic objects in Fig. 3; the "*" on the top line of a shape marks these. RIST claims that we used four types of schemas for interpretations.

A *Representation* schema – lozenge shapes – represents a whole representational system (Fig. 4.10a is Fig. 3) or a sub-representational system (e.g., 9c). Atomic concepts are represented by icons or graphic properties are *R-symbols* – rounded rectangles (e.g., 10f is for direction pins like Fig. 3.2i and 3i). A *R-dimension* is a variable or a class represented by an axis or a type of graphic object; e.g., icon Fig. 4.2i is a variable for

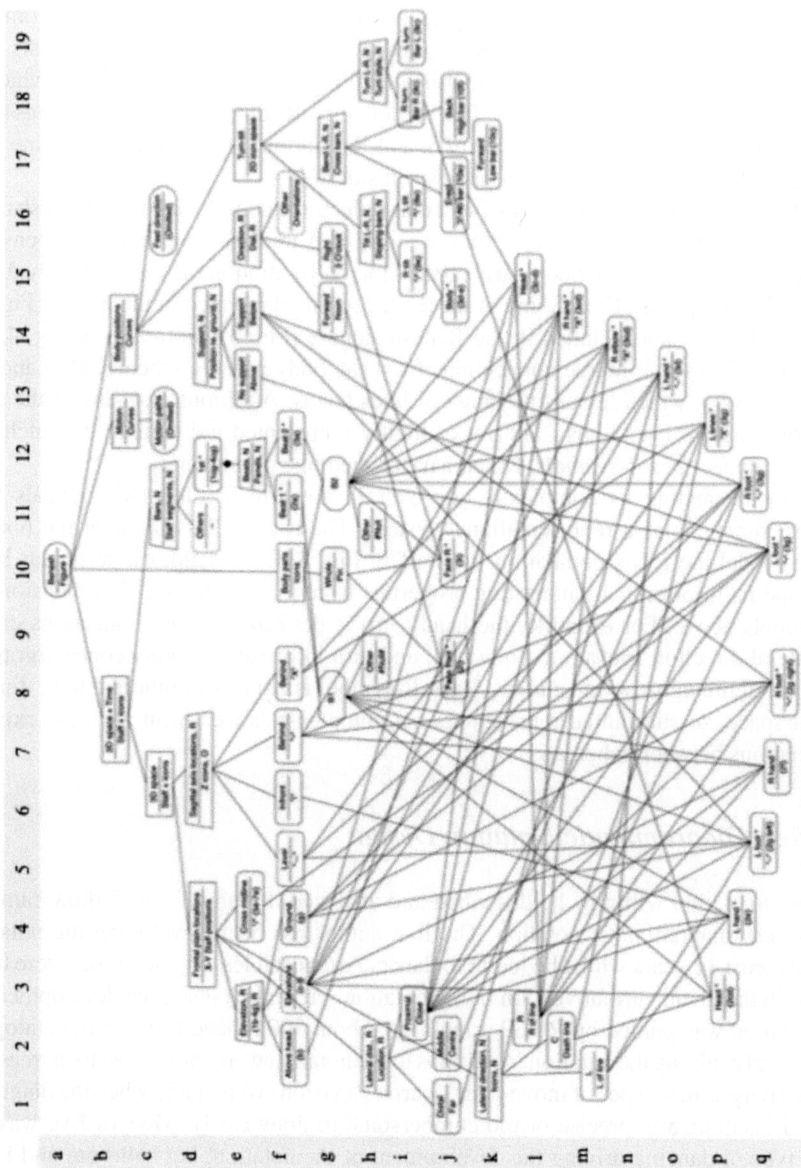

Fig. 4. A RISN model of the two Benesh poses in Fig. 3. Key: L – left; C – centre; R – right; M – lead; W – follower; * – graphical object in Fig. 3 left.

lateral directions represented by the position of icons relative to the midline. For this R-dimension there are R-symbols for *left*, *centre*, and *right* (1 l, 2 k, 3j).

R-schemes are schemas for complex concepts composed of some combination of the other schema types. From the modelling of diverse representations in RISN, an important discovery of RIST is that there are prototypical patterns of schemas, *idioms*, which are common across different representations [16]. They can be used to compare the underlying structures of representations even when they are in different formats. The staff in Benesh is a R-scheme (4c) that is a *triangulation coordinate system*, which is one type of four index systems [18]. It is modelled by R-dimensions for elevations (3d), lateral direction (2i), lateral distance (2f), and R-symbols for a reference midline (2d) and special symbol for when body parts swap sides (4d).

The complexity of the network of schemas reflects the complexity of the Benesh notation. In addition to the subnetwork for the staff, there are R-schemes and R-dimensions for sagittal locations (7c), body parts (10e), time (11b), motion (9b), whole body direction (14b), and poses (17b). Some of these are not full elaborated in the model (Fig. 4), because they are not included in the Benesh sample (Fig. 3). Note also in Fig. 4, the *B1* and *B2* icons that merge connections from the body parts R-scheme (10e) and the time (11d-12e), which lessens the mass of lines below. Additionally, many of the concepts/icons from Fig. 3 right are not explicitly represented individually but included collectively as *class R-symbols*, which have dashed line perimeters.

Notwithstanding its complexity, the overall structure of the model reveals how Benesh functions as a representational system. The row of R-symbols at the bottom of the model are icons populating the staff in Fig. 3. Each defines a particular body part, and its location is by inheriting properties from the R-schemes, R-dimensions or R-symbols above. For example, the head (3m) is defined by four connections carrying lateral direction, elevation, body part, and turn information. Other concept/graphic objects require up to seven sources. Each R-symbol is akin to a point in a high dimensional space, so substantial representational complexity arises from all these explicit associations between schemas.

5 New *Diagrammatic Notation Design*

The new notation will now be described and analyzed. Figures 1 and 2 show samples of the new diagrammatic notation. The first author has been developing the notation over the past 12 years whilst he learnt to dance. After each lesson, the moves were hand drawn in the, then, current version of the notation. From the outset, the development of the notation was guided by REEP principles. About 300 h have been spent cataloging moves and evolving the notation. Additions to the notation were introduced to increase its expressivity as new types of moves were learnt. Revisions were made when the diagrams proved insufficiently precise or too cumbersome to draw easily. Modern Jive was the main type of dancing driving the development of the notation, but ballroom and Latin classes also contributed.

Fig. 5 is a RISN model for the new notation. It captures the notation generically and focuses concretely on Fig. 2.P2 (blue border).

Again, a "*" to the right of a schema indicates a concept and graphical object in Fig. 2.P2.

The dance notation (9a) has R-schemes for all the major classes of concepts: 3D space (4c); time (16b); dancers (10e); movement (20f); interaction (9d). This largely satisfies the first REEP design principle concerning distinct representational schemes.

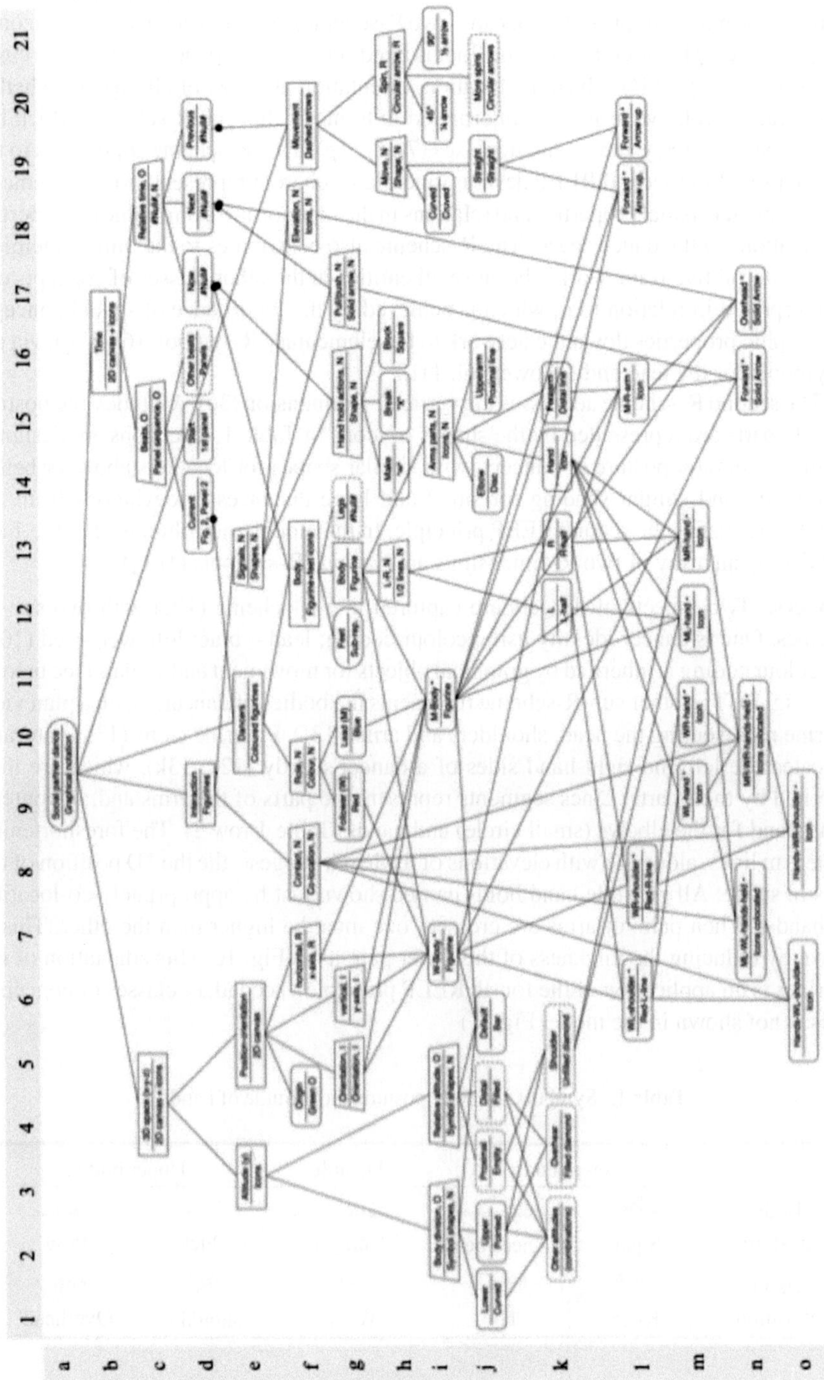

Fig. 5. RISN model of the new dance notation (left). Key: L – left; R – right; M – lead; W – follower; * – graphical object in Fig. 2 panel 2.

Space. The notation splits 3D space into two R-schemes. The first encodes the horizonal, x-y, plane (5e). The orientation of the floor is fixed across all the panels, and a green circle serves as an origin (4f). Thus, the location, orientation and size of all objects, whether in absolute or relative terms, are interpreted in terms of this sub-R-scheme, which has R-dimensions for x, y and orientation axes (7f, 6g, 5g). This R-scheme contributes to the satisfaction of the second REEP design principle – coherent representational schemes – because planar spatial properties and relations in the notation are isomorphic to properties and relations in the dance space. The R-scheme also contributes to the third principle – global interpretive framework – because all entities in the other classes of concepts can be interpreted in relation to it, which is achieved by the inheritance of spatial concepts and graphic properties down the network to the elementary R-symbols (6 l-17o), via the R-symbols for the lead and follower (6i, 11i).

The second R-scheme addresses the vertical, y, dimension (3e). Altitudes and posture of body parts are represented by the shapes of icons in Table 1. The icons are designed around the default posture of dancers, with similar shapes for locations above or below the default, and similar shading for small and large distances or deviations from the default, to satisfies the second REEP principle. In the model, the columns of Table 1 are encoded by an array of two R-dimensions and various R-symbols (1i-6j).

Dancers. Two aspects of dancers are captured in a R-scheme (10e) with two sub-R-schemes. One is dancer identity using colour coding; lead – blue; follower – red (10f). The colour coding is inherited by graphical objects for movement and signals (see below) (e.g., Fig. 2). The other sub-R-scheme represents the bodies of dancers, with a plan view figurine representing the head, shoulders and arms (13f). Figurine icons (13h) naturally indicated the left and right-hand sides of a dancer's body (12k, 13k), which are then inherited by their parts. Lines segments represent the parts of the arms and, in context, icons stand for the elbows (small circle) and hands (Table 1 row 2). The foreshortening of the arm lines, along the with elevations of the hand, suggests the the 3D position of the arms in space. All possible hand holds can be shown just by appropriately co-locating the hands. When pairs of arms are crossed, one must be higher than the other. This is shown by reducing the thickness of the lower pair, as in Fig. 1e. This adaptation of the figurines is an application of the fourth REEP principle - secondary classes of concepts. (This is not shown in the model Fig. 5.)

Table 1. Symbols for body posture and altitude of hands.

	Lower body		Default	Upper body	
Body posture	Squat	Knees bent	Upright	Duck	Bow
Hand elevation	Knee	Hip	Waist	Shoulder	Overhead

The plan view figurine representation of bodies exploits Modern Jive's deliberate de-emphasizing of foot work. The feet are represented by colour coded foot-shaped icons with shading to indicate the location of support (e.g., in Fig. 1f & 1g). The icons are included in a panel when an author deems it necessary (e.g., Fig. 2.P1 & P2). In the model (Fig. 5), for brevity, this sub-representation is noted as a sub-Representation schema (12g) but not elaborated.

Movement. A dancer's motion across the floor is encoded by colour coded dashed arrows drawn adjacent to the relevant dancer (20f). Straight and curved paths are shown by corresponding arrows (19h). Spins on the spot are part or multiple circles, with the arrowhead showing the direction of turn (20h). Combined moves and turns are represented by pairing translation and spin icons. Movements of arms and feet are not explicitly represented, because they are readily inferred from the comparisons of the figurines across panels, the interaction signals (see below), and are constrained by the reader's natural understanding of the capabilities of human movement.

Interaction. The idea of interaction (9d) has two parts, each an R-dimension. The first, is the location of contacts between the dancers (8f), which are simply encoded by colocation of body parts. In Fig. 2.P2, there are four points of contact: both pairs of hands are held (7n, 10n), and both the lead's hands are at the follower's shoulders (6o, 8o). The second aspect of interaction concerns the signals between the dancers (13e). These are represented by free-floating icons beside the point of contact, colour coded by the dancer initiating the action. Signals typically involve hands but also occur between many parts of the body. There are three signals in Fig. 2.P2. Solid arrows are for pushes or pulls in the horizontal plane; one is the push of the lead's right forearm on the follower's should (16n). (The pull of lead's left hand in Fig. 2.P2 is not in the model). Icons for signals about changes to hand elevation reused the elevations icons in Table 1, row 2; the blue diamond in our example means the lead's hand should rise above head height (17n), taking the follower's hand with it.

Other signals are instantaneous actions (15g), including: hold hands – "∞"; separate hands – "X"; *blocks* as actions to stop motions – solid square (14h–16h).

Time. The encoding of time takes two aspects. The first comes from the rhythm of music, with panels encoding absolute moments in time, typically at the end of each beat, or if actions occur rapidly at fractions of a beat. In the model, a R-dimension encodes the idea of panels aligned with beats (15c), with just the current panel (13d) elaborated in the model. Text at the bottom of panels records the beat count.

The second aspect of time is that of the dancers' immediate perception of the present (17d), immediate past (20d), and future (18d). Each panel indexes, relative to the present beat: (i) the current position and pose of the dances and any quick (within beat) actions to be performed (15g), (ii) the motions that were executed to achieve that state (20f), and (iii) the signals of actions for the next beat (18f, 17g), respectively. There are no explicit graphical objects associated with this scheme, hence the #Null# entries in its R-symbols (17d-20d). The lines with dots are *anchor* links that indicate the creation of a local context. This scheme is a key component of the overarching interpretative framework (REEP principle 3), that indexes the static, kinematic and dynamic classes of concepts temporally. It complements the other spatial integrations. The discovery of this *signal-move-pose-signal* scheme was a substantial breakthrough for the development of the notation, because it gives a continuous causal reading that compensates for the discrete time steps of panels. The reader's attention flows naturally across panels cycling through signals that produce movements, that produce poses, which frame the next set of signals. Other schemes for movement, pose and signal information across panels demand deliberate inferences to keep track of the time of actions.

That completes the outlining of the notation and its model. For comparison, the two Benesh positions (Figs. 3.2 & 3.3) are shown in the new notation, Figs. 1f & 1g. Like Benesh model, the model of the new notation is also complex. To warrant a direct comparison, the models must cover the same content from the topic for the sake of informational equivalence [3], but Figs. 4 and 5 are for different numbers of dancers and different poses. However, it is clear that the RISN network for the new notation has deeper paths from the trunk to the leaves with up to eleven links. Depths of four links are common in the Benesh model with none greater than seven. This is a sign that the new notation successfully exploits the hierarchical structure of the notation to encode the hierarchical structure of each of the main classes of concepts, which explains why the notation substantially satisfies the REEP design principles.

6 Graphical Editor

Choriolis is a graphical editor programmed specifically for the new notation. (The name blends *choreography* and *Coriolis effect*). The images of the new notation above are all screen shots from Choriolis. The original aim for Choriolis was to record dance moves efficiently with more detail and accuracy than hand drawn diagrams, so that dance moves could be physically reproduced more easily from the notation. For example, when hand drawing figurines it easy to confuse the identity of hands across panels and, for instance, accidentally swap a left-to-left hand hold to a left-to-right one, especially when the dancers change places and turn; which will appear like a magic trick to the reader. As the REEP approach appeared to be useful in the design of the system, this provides some further evidence of the utility of REEP, by extending the range of information intensive tasks to which it has been applied, e.g [14].

Initially, the application of REEP aimed to increase the accuracy of recording moves, by using the principles of the topic to define primitives and to constrain how they can be edited. Some of the physical logic of dancers' bodies was built into the interface objects. As parts of the body are attached to each other the components of figurines are implemented as complete units with articulated lines for the fore and upper arms permanently attached to the shoulders and hands. As the location of hands is critical and the whole arms typically moves as a coordinated whole, the hand icons are the main handles for manipulating the position of the arms relative to the fixed shoulders, with the relative length of the arm lines held constant. An elbow icon serves as a secondary handle to manipulate the bend of the arms with the other ends fixed by the shoulder and hand. The physical holding of hands is digitally encoded in Choriolis. The state of two (or more) co-located hand icons can be set as held or released. When held, the hands positions can be manipulated as one; when as figurines are rotated the arms remained joined. This eliminates the magical hand swap errors noted above. In tests, these designs of arm editing were obviously superior to alternative designs.

Choriolis includes much of the typical basic functionality of vector graphics editors, such as menus to add objects, drag handles to rotate objects, panel duplication, and zooming the canvas. REEP ideas were applied to tailor the functionality of basic editing commands to suit the topic of partner dancing and to facilitate the overall workflow of the recording whole dance moves. For example, the default of angle keyboard shortcuts for object rotations was set at 45°, because one eighth, quarter, and half turns of dancers are most common. Contextual (right click) menus were provided for dancers' actions that most frequently changed (e.g., hand altitudes). An object layer system was introduced so that icons for body, movement, signal, feet, and location could be individual locked, and brought to the front or sent to the back of the canvas. Not only does this deal with problem of occluding objects, this supports the typical workflow for recording a dance, which spans multiple passes through the panels, starting with dancers placement, then movements, signals and any footwork.

The implementation of Choriolis uses React for the UI, Zustand for centralized state management, and react-konva to render and manipulate shapes on an HTML5 canvas. The architecture cleanly separates visual rendering (Canvas, Dancer, Symbol components) from state logic (store slices), allowing interactive updates without tightly coupling drawing logic to application state.

7 Discussion

The REEP approach has been used to design a novel notation for social partner dancing. The notation has sufficient expressive capacity to capture a substantial range of Modern Jive moves and that of other styles. However, advanced *drop* and *dip* moves will likely require that the notation be adapted to represent body postures that are far from upright. From our extensive use of the notation, we contend that it is also a cognitively effective notation. We attribute this efficacy to the extent to which the REEP design principles have been satisfied. The classes of concepts have been distributed coherently across distinct representational schemes, and those schemes are in themselves reasonably coherent. Of note are: the adoption the plan view figurines for bodies; the signal-move-pose-signal scheme for the dancer-centric temporal distribution of other schemes; the universal colour coding of all information by dancer identity.

A direct comparison between the efficacy of the new notation and Benesh is problematic because their goals differ: paired dancers versus sets of individual performers. Nevertheless, the RISN models for the two notations, Figs. 4 and 5, do provide insights into the overall representational epistemic coherence of each system. In turn this lends additional support claims for the validity of RIST and the utility RISN and RISE.

The successful creation of the notation provides further evidence of the value of the REEP approach, building on previous studies (e.g., [8–14]), in two ways. First, the topic of social partner dancing spans diverse and complex classes of concepts not previously considered, including absolute and relative temporal perspectives, hierarchical physical structures, kinematics with dynamics, and interactions (contacts and signals). Second, the topic is not governed by a small number of formal or physical laws, which provide strongly constrain feasible designs of representational schemes. Rather the topic encompasses many specific principles distributed across the multiple classes of concepts.

Extant designs of dance notations, such as Benesh [23] (or Laban, Eshkol & Wachman, and others [24, 25]) coped with this distribution by adopting separate representations schemes for each class of concepts (e.g., Fig. 3). However, that leads to "sprawling" notational systems that do not satisfy the REEP design principles well, as shown by the tangled structure of the cognitive model of the interpretive structure of Benesh (Fig. 4). In contrast to the extant notations, the new notation is relatively unique in adopting a plan view and figurine-based design. It is these representational schemes that underpins the notation's facility to exploit our powerful natural cognitive ability to process hierarchical conceptual and graphics structures, with the inheritance of concepts and graphic objects and properties down layers of granularity in a representational system. Whether this idea can be generalized into a principle of representation design for topics of this kind is an interesting question for further study.

Another issue raised by the new notation is to what extent concepts that will be obvious to a reader should be depicted in a representation, even if its graphic objects are somewhat redundant. The absence of legs and the optionality of feet is an example.

Finally, the use of the REEP approach in the design of the Choriolis editor also provided some further evidence of the utility of the REEP approach. The editor can be accessed here: https://exidy80.github.io/Graphical-Editor-for-Dance-Notation/. An instruction manual is being prepared.

Acknowledgements. PCHC thanks the dance teachers – Colleen, Dave, Stacy, Alex, Ian, John, Sue, Andy, Mark, Carol, Leo, Becky, and James – from whom he had the pleasure of learning so much. We thank Tim Hewitt who built the initial version of the editor as a MSc project and the members of the RepSys lab for all their contributions to the REEP approach.

References

1. Anderson, M., Cheng, P.C.-H., Haarslev, V. (eds.): Theory and Application of Diagrams: First International Conference, Diagrams 2000. Springer, Berlin (2000)
2. Cleveland, W.S.: The Elements of Graphing Data. Wadsworth, Monterey, CA. (1985)
3. Larkin, J.H., Simon, H.A.: Why a diagram is (sometimes) worth ten thousand words. Cogn. Sci. **11**, 65–99 (1987)
4. Glasgow, J.I., Narayanan, H., Chandrasekaran, C. (eds.): Diagrammatic Reasoning. AAAI/MIT Press, Cambridge, M.A. (1995)
5. Engelhardt, J.: The Language of Graphics. ILLC, Unversity of Amsterdam, Amsterdam (2002)
6. Hegarty, M.: The cognitive science of visual-spatial displays: implications for design. Top. Cogn. Sci. **3**, 446–474 (2011)
7. Shimojima, A.: Semantic Properties of Diagrams and their Cognitive Potentials. CSLI Press, Stanford, CA (2015)
8. Cheng, P.C.-H.: Electrifying diagrams for learning: principles for effective representational systems. Cogn. Sci. **26**(6), 685–736 (2002)
9. Cheng, P.C.-H.: Probably good diagrams for learning: representational epistemic recodification of probability theory topics. Cogn. Sci. **3**(3), 475–498 (2011)
10. Cheng, P.C.H., Boehm, T.G.: Why Feynman diagrams are worth 10,000 formulae: a representational epistemological analysis. In: Lemanski, J., et al. (eds.) Diagrammatic Representation and Inference, pp. 11–27. Springer Nature Switzerland, Cham (2024)

11. Cheng, P.C.-H.: Algebra diagrams: a HANDi introduction. In: Cox, P., Plimmer, B., Rodgers, P. (eds.) Diagrammatic Representation and Inference: 7th International Conference on Diagrams, pp. 178–192. Springer, Berlin (2012)
12. Cheng, P.C.-H.: Graphical notations for syllogisms: how alterative representations impact the accessibility of concepts. J. Vis. Lang. Comput. **25**, 170–185 (2014)
13. Cheng, P.C.-H.: Truth diagrams versus extant notations for propositional logic. J. Lang., Logic Inf. **29**, 121–161 (2020)
14. Cheng, P.C.-H., Barone, R., Cowling, P.I., et al.: Opening the information bottleneck in complex scheduling problems with a novel representation: STARK diagrams. In: Hegarty, M., et al. (eds.) Diagrammatic Representations and Inference: Second International Conference, Diagrams 2002, pp. 264–278. Springer, Berlin (2002)
15. Cheng, P.C.-H., Stockdill, A., Garcia Garcia, G., Raggi, D., Jamnik, M.: Representational interpretive structure: theory and notation. In: Giardino, V., et al. (eds.) Diagrammatic Representation and Inference, pp. 54–69. Springer, Cham (2022)
16. Stockdill, A., Stapleton, G., Raggi, D., Jamnik, M., Garcia, G.G., Cheng, P.C.H.: Examining experts' recommendations of representational systems for problem solving. In: 2022 IEEE symposium on visual languages and human-centric computing, pp. 1–6 (2022)
17. Cheng, P.C.-H., Garcia, G.G., Raggi, D., Jamnik, M.: A human information processing theory of the interpretation of visualizations: demonstrating its utility. In: proceedings of the CHI conference on human factors in computing systems (CHI '24). ACM (2024)
18. Cheng, P.C.-H., Garcia, G.G., Raggi, D., Jamnik, M.: Index systems: Enumerating their forms and explaining their diversity with representational interpretive structure theory. In: Proceedings of the 46th Annual Conference of the Cognitive Science Society. Cognitive Science Society, Austin, TX (2024)
19. Cheng, P.C.-H., Garcia, G.G.: What and how schema networks are acquired during the learning of line graphs: Modelling using Representational Systems Theory. In: Proceedings of the 46th Annual Conference of the Cognitive Science Society. Cognitive Science Society, Austin, TX (2025)
20. https://en.wikipedia.org/w/index.php?title=Modern_Jive&oldid=1327675490
21. https://en.wikipedia.org/w/index.php?title=Ceroc&oldid=1304675366
22. Gurr, C.A.: On the isomorphism, or lack of it, of representations. In: Marriott, K., Meyer, B. (eds.) Visual Language Theory, pp. 293–306. Springer, New York, NY (1998)
23. Hutchinson Guest, A.: Dance Notation: the Process of Recording Movement on Paper. Dance Books, London (1984)
24. Hutchinson Guest, A.: Choreographics: a Comparison of Dance Notation Systems from the Fifteenth Century to the Present. Routledge (2014)
25. Ryman-Kane, R., Hughes Ryman, R.: Benesh for Ballet, Book I: (iBooks). iBooks (2014)

Diagram Design for Modelling Audiovisual Communication

Hans Smessaert[1(✉)] and Lorenz Demey[2]

[1] Department of Linguistics, KU Leuven, Blijde-Inkomststraat 21, 3000 Leuven, Belgium
hans.smessaert@kuleuven.be
[2] Center for Logic and Philosophy of Science, KU Leuven, Kardinaal Mercierplein 2, 3000 Leuven, Belgium
lorenz.demey@kuleuven.be

Abstract. In this poster we discuss the principles used in designing a cognitively effective diagram for modelling audiovisual communication in the context of teaching undergraduate introduction to linguistics courses.

Keywords: Models for audiovisual communication · diagram design · cognitive effectiveness

1 Components of an Audiovisual Communication Model

The diagram in Fig. 1 integrates the static, classical linguistic model of Jakobson [2, p. 22] with the more dynamic/procedural psycholinguistic analysis by Levelt [3, p. 9]. Jakobson's static components of ADDRESSER/SENDER, CONTEXT, MESSAGE and ADDRESSEE/RECEIVER constitute the top layer of "meaning" (Levelt's 'conceptualizer'), his CONTACT constitutes the bottom layer of "form" (Levelt's 'articulator') and his CODE the semiotically crucial intermediate layer where form and meaning are associated (Levelt's 'formulator'). On the sender/production side we go downwards from 'INTENTION' over 'CODING' to 'WRITING/SPEAKING', while on the receiver/perception side we go upwards from 'READING/LISTENING' over 'DECODING' to 'UNDERSTANDING'.

2 Diagram Design Principles for the Model

Building Blocks and Subdiagrams. The fundamental distinction between the static components from Jakobson [2] and the dynamic ones from Levelt [3], is visualised by the difference between grey and white rectangles, and reinforced by the contrast between sharp corners for the former and rounded corners for the latter.[1] The dynamic status of the white rectangles is furthermore emphasised by

[1] In terms of the conceptual dimensions in the Representational Epistemic Approach of Cheng & Barone, these contrasts reflect the distinction between the entity-taxonomic and the functional conceptual dimension [4, p. 105–107].

P. Sobociński et al. (Eds.): Diagrams 2026, LNAI 16833, pp. 424–427, 2027.
https://doi.org/10.1007/978-3-032-34178-5_41

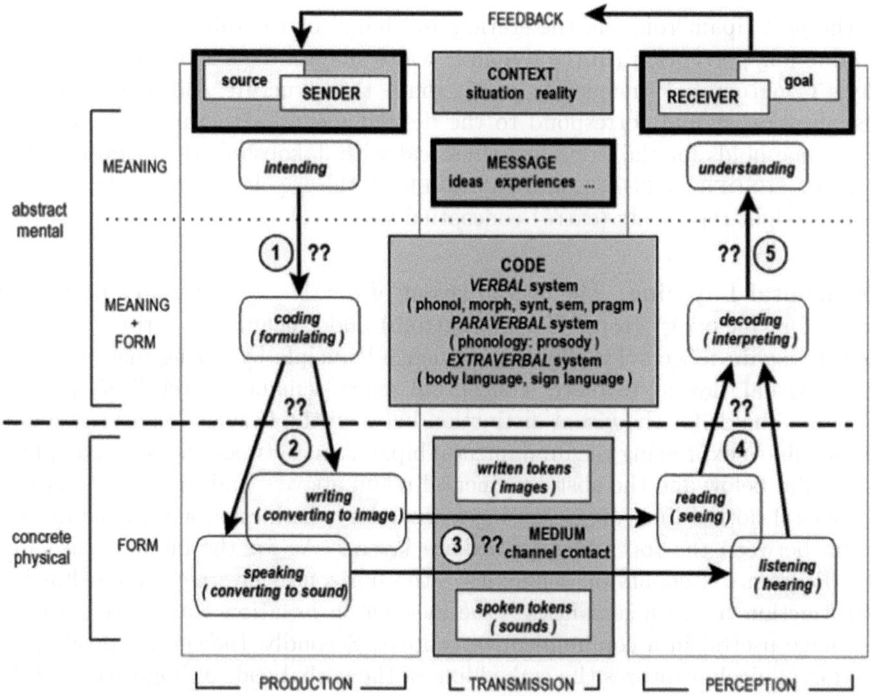

Fig. 1. A model for Audiovisual Communication [1, p. 16].

connecting them by means of arrows, a standard visual strategy for expressing motion or dynamics [6, p. 520], i.e. the transitions from one type of processing to the other. The question mark symbols co-occurring with them straightforwardly represent the concept of noise, i.e. the problems or impurities that may arise with these transitions.[2] Finally, the five circled numbers that accompany the various arrows express the natural flow of the communication cycle from sender intention at the top left to receiver understanding at the top right. The resulting visual integration of Jakobson's static grey T-shaped subdiagram in the middle with Levelt's dynamic white U-shaped subdiagram surrounding it, counts as an application of Tversky's Apprehension Principle [5, p. 37] that "the structure and content of the visualisation should be readily and accurately perceived and comprehended".[3] Both the T-shape and the U-shape contain overlapping rectangular components, namely SOURCE/SENDER (top left) and RECEIVER/GOAL (top right) with the former, and 'WRITING'/'SPEAKING'(bottom left) and 'READING'/'LISTENING' (bottom right) with the latter. This partial visual overlap of the rectangles represents the conceptual overlap, i.e. the possible simultaneity

[2] See also Moody's principle of *Semantic Transparency* [8, p. 765] that a symbol's appearance should suggest its meaning.

[3] See also Moody's principle of *Cognitive Integration* [8, p. 768] to help users integrate information across diagrams.

of the participant roles (in the static grey shape) or the different strategies for production/perception (in the dynamic white shape). This is in line with Tversky's Congruence Principle [5, p. 37] that "the structure and content of the visualisation should correspond to the desired mental structure and content". The same holds for the extra line thickness with Jakobson's three central components SENDER, MESSAGE and RECEIVER at the top layer of Fig. 1: "(extra) visual weight represents (extra) conceptual weight".

Horizontal Layering. The overall layout of Fig. 1 – with its three horizontal layers for "meaning" (top), "form" (bottom) and "meaning + form" (intermediate) – again reflects Tversky's Congruence Principle by "using diagrammatic space [visual 'layers'] to reflect conceptual space [semantic 'levels']" [5, p. 37].[4] The same holds for the visual distinction between the heavier/longer horizontal dashed line – expressing the fundamental bipartition between the concrete, physical realm below and the abstract, mental realm above – and the lighter/shorter horizontal dotted line – representing a secondary distinction within the mental realm between the top and intermediate layers.[5] As for the intended users of the diagram – students of linguistics – the horizontal layering allows drawing a distinction between semantics – the message in isolation – and pragmatics – language use(rs) in a communicative context. Secondly, the central position of the CODE nicely captures the embedding of the verbal code of linguistics within the broader semiotic context of (para- and extraverbal) sign systems. Finally, language-specific phonology on the intermediate level contrasts with language-universal phonetics on the concrete, physical bottom layer (cfr. below).

Vertical Layering. The overall layout of Fig. 1 also exhibits a vertical subdivision into a SENDER column – including the dynamic 'CODING', 'WRITING' and 'SPEAKING' components – on the left, a RECEIVER column – including the 'READING', 'LISTENING' and 'DECODING' components – on the right and a central MESSAGE column – including the CONTEXT, CODE and MEDIUM components from Jakobson T-shape. This fundamental left to right tripartition iconically reflects our canonical Western direction of writing and reading from a starting point at the left hand side towards an endpoint at the right hand side [6, p. 510–13]. This vertical layering into three columns again turns out to be crucial in teaching basic linguistic concepts. In particular, the tripartition at the bottom layer corresponds to the three stages in handling the speech sounds in the realm of phonetics, namely their PRODUCTION by the sender, their TRANSMISSION through the medium, and their PERCEPTION by the receiver. Production of speech sounds is studied in the subdiscipline of ARTICULATORY phonetics, transmission in ACOUSTIC phonetics and perception in AUDITORY phonetics. Notice

[4] See also Purchase's concept of *notational layout* [7, p. 66–8] as well as the central idea of the REEP approach to "preserve the conceptual structure of the domain in the design of the structure of the representational system [4, p. 104].

[5] Metaphorically, this horizontal layering also reflects the natural association of abstract versus concrete with up/above ('sky') versus down/below ('earth') [6].

that the communication cycle indicated with the numbered arrows in Fig. 1 crucially depends on the cross-cutting of two types of layering. From top left to bottom left, the horizontal layering is crossed by arrows ① and ②, from bottom left to bottom right the vertical layering is crossed by ③, and from bottom right to top right, the horizontal layering is again crossed by ④ and ⑤.

Center vs Periphery. Finally, the overall layout of Fig. 1 reflects the distinction between center and periphery [6, p. 509]. On the one hand, one can consider the grey T-shape with Jakobson's static components as the core of the overall diagram, and the white U-shape with Levelt's dynamic components as the periphery surrounding it. On a more radial interpretation, however, the crucial importance of the static CODE component – from a linguistic as well as semiotic perspective – is not only reflected in its location in the middle of the intermediate layer, but also by the bigger size of its grey rectangle in comparison with the others in the T-shape. This idea that bigger visual elements play a bigger semantic role can again be seen as an application of Tversky's Congruence Principle of "using diagrammatic space to reflect conceptual space" [5, p. 37].

Acknowledgments. L. Demey holds a KU Leuven Research Professorship (BOFZAP).

Disclosure of Interests. The authors have no competing interests to declare that are relevant to the content of this article.

References

1. Smessaert, H.: Basisbegrippen Taalkunde: Semantiek en Pragmatiek, 2nd edn. ACCO, Leuven (2025)
2. Jakobson, R.: Linguistics and Poetics. In: Rudy, S. (ed.) Roman Jakobson Selected Writings, vol. III: Poetry of Grammar and Grammar of Poetry, pp. 18–51. Mouton, The Hague (1981)
3. Levelt, W.J.M.: Speaking: From Intention to Articulation, The MIT Press (1989). https://doi.org/10.7551/mitpress/6393.001.0001
4. Cheng, P., Barone, R.: Representing complex problems: a representational epistemic approach. In: Jonassen, D.H. (ed.) Learning to Solve Complex Scientific Problems, pp. 97–130. Routledge, New York/London (2007)
5. Tversky, B.: Prolegomenon to scientific visualizations. In: Gilbert, J.K. (ed.) Visualization in Science Education, pp. 29–42. Springer, Dordrecht (2005)
6. Tversky, B.: Visualizing thought. Top. Cogn. Sci. **3**, 499–535 (2011)
7. Purchase, H.C.: Twelve years of diagrams research. J. Vis. Lang. Comput. **25**(2), 57–75 (2014)
8. Moody, D.L.: The "Physics" of notations: toward a scientific basis for constructing visual notations in software engineering. IEEE Trans. Softw. Eng. **35**(6), 756–779 (2009). https://doi.org/10.1109/TSE.2009.67

The epiDiagram and Some Other Conceptual Resources for Interdisciplinary Diagram Research

Dennis McNulty(✉)

CONNECT Research Centre, School of Engineering, Trinity College Dublin, Dublin, Ireland
demcnult@tcd.ie

Abstract. This paper introduces a Definition and associated General Model of the Diagram. Working in tandem, they decouple the roles of Diagram Creator and Interpreter, framing diagramhood as contingent on acts of interpretation and recognition. The transition from non-Diagram to Diagram is formalised through the concept of the epiDiagram, and Three Strands, based on three common emphases within the literature, are identified. These conceptual resources are introduced to support an interdisciplinary approach to Diagram research.

Keywords: Definition · Resources · Interdisciplinarity · epiDiagram · Three Strands · Common Model of the Diagram · General Model of the Diagram

1 Introduction

Diagram research is currently taking place in a media-saturated world where systems of meaning-making are being reconfigured on an almost daily basis. Traditional tacit assumptions as to what constitutes a Diagram[1] are being challenged by the animated and other more-than-two-dimensional diagrams that have proliferated in recent years. Against this backdrop, some conceptual resources are introduced to support an interdisciplinary (ID) approach to Diagram research that has arguably never been more urgent.

Acknowledgements that a comprehensive understanding of the Diagram requires an ID approach recur within the literature. Some publications have been framed in explicitly ID terms [1,2], but the question remains as to how an ID approach to Diagram research might be fostered more broadly. This paper presents some pragmatic resources developed within a larger project that addresses these

[1] For the purposes of clarity and disambiguation, Diagram (capitalised) refers to the concept and diagram (uncapitalised) refers to any specific diagram. Concepts proposed in this paper, such as the Three Strands, are also capitalised.

P. Sobociński et al. (Eds.): Diagrams 2026, LNAI 16833, pp. 428–436, 2027.
https://doi.org/10.1007/978-3-032-34178-5_42

calls for interdisciplinarity. The Three Strands are proposed as a heuristic macro-taxonomy to make the diversity of the literature visible and manageable. Following this, the assumptions, both stated and tacit, underpinning the majority of the existing work are captured in the Common Model. A Definition and a General Model are then introduced to challenge some of these assumptions. Both centre the act of interpretation, in terms of meaning-making and determining diagramhood. The concept of the epiDiagram is introduced to account for the consequent interpretative transition from non-Diagram to Diagram.

Inevitably, thinking about the Diagram more broadly incurs a loss of detail in zooming out to capture the bigger picture. Such an erasure of detail does a disservice to those who have worked so hard to discern those details. That said, this act may be outweighed by the possibility of developing some resources that eventually enable these details to be gathered and correlated more effectively with each other. The author does not claim expertise in all of the domains that are referenced here but the resources that emerge from this work are proposed as conduits and provocations for future dialogue across disciplinary boundaries.

2 Mapping the Literature

2.1 The Three Strands

The literature on the Diagram sprawls across myriad disciplines. As a researcher attempting to reach across disciplinary boundaries, it can be difficult to correlate, and even to become aware of the many different perspectives. The first obvious step in encouraging an ID approach to the research is to map the existing work. Blackwell and Engelhardt tackled this question over two decades ago in their papers proposing a taxonomy of diagram taxonomies [3,4].

The Three Strands below offer a less finely grained heuristic based on three common emphases I have identified within a broad survey of the literature across disciplines. In addition to gathering and organising the work done, they provide a useful shorthand for discussing the diversity of Diagram research and orienting oneself in relation to other perspectives.

This Tool Strand. Research in the Tool Strand frames the Diagram as a cognitive tool with untapped potential for learning and problem-solving. Work carried out in disciplines such as cognitive science, computer science, artificial intelligence, educational psychology, logic, and mathematics are gathered in this Strand. The Diagram is understood as an external representation that supports cognitive activity such as inference. Larkin and Simon's "Why a diagram is (sometimes) worth ten thousand words" is a foundational paper in the Tool Strand [5]. Historically, the vast majority of the work presented in the proceedings of the this conference has originated in this Strand.

The Language Strand. Research in the Language Strand frames the Diagram as a "visual language" with a "vocabulary" and a "syntax". In general, these "visual languages" are understood to emerge, either through the establishment of norms in the context of expert-to-expert communication, or through the design of diagrams to foster expert to non-expert communication such as infographics. The former case is addressed by work in disciplines such as anthropology, sociology, history of science and science and technology studies [6], while the latter is addressed primarily in design studies. Although this Strand is concerned with communication, there is an emphasis on the Diagram's rhetorical capacity and its role in producing social effects.

The Image Strand. Work in the Image Strand is concerned with formalising interpretation, as in Peirce's semiotic theory [7] and the art-historical methods that have been developed to systematically analyse visual art. In the Germanophone context, the latter were applied to non-art images, including diagrams, from the early 1970s onwards in bildwissenschaft. A similar shift was initiated in the Anglophone world in the early 2000s with the development of visual studies [8]. Art practice is also relevant here as a semiotic laboratory, as evidenced in the formal experiments of Hilma af Klint or the adoption of the Diagram as a tool for critique in the work of Mark Lombardi.

These Strands are not mutually exclusive. As is always the case with the Diagram, the boundaries are fuzzy and much of the literature lies in their overlaps. That said, they can help to consider what might be meant by an ID approach to the Diagram. Are we envisioning collaboration among disciplines within Strands? In the case of collaboration across Strands, other questions emerge. For example, how might the largely positivistic approach within the Tool Strand be correlated with those of the other two Strands?

2.2 The Common Model

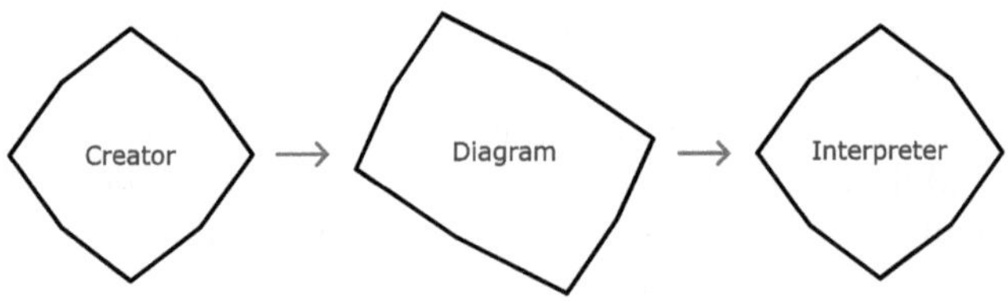

Fig. 1. The Common Model of the Diagram.

The Common Model (Fig. 1) is presented here as a complimentary resource to frame the literature. In most cases, it is assumed that the diagram has been intentionally created by a subject to capture some actual or conceptual relationships that will be "decoded" by some other subject. The Model therefore consists of three elements: the Diagram, the Creator and the Interpreter. Creator and Interpreter are best thought of as roles that can be occupied by one or more subjects.

Consider how this Model relates to the Strands. The Tool Strand is largely concerned with the Diagram/Interpreter relationship. In modelling the situation where a subject externalises thought by creating a diagram to solve a problem, the roles of Creator and Interpreter are occupied by the same subject. Within the Language Strand, emphasis is placed on the Diagram as a facilitator of the Creator/Interpreter relationship. Successful diagrams help the Creator to accrue social status and power through persuasion. Within the Image Strand, the researcher frequently takes on the role of the Interpreter to unpack a diagram's meaning in a particular cultural context.

2.3 Working Definitions and Other Strategies

The work in the Three Strands has taken place without a comprehensive widely-accepted definition of the Diagram. The lack of such a definition has been repeatedly acknowledged in the literature [9–12]. Such a definition, if it existed, would undoubtedly serve as a useful reference across disciplinary contexts.

Researchers have adopted a variety of strategies to work around this lack. Most commonly, texts tend to proceed assuming a consensus on what constitutes a diagram in a given context. Research centred on a specific Diagram type can proceed without a definition, as the status of the object being studied is clear. In situations where a definition might be useful, authors occasionally use a dictionary definition, some of which are recursively defined. In some cases, a prominent paper is cited in lieu of a definition, the implication being "my understanding of diagram is the same as theirs". Larkin and Simon's paper [5] is often cited in the Tool Strand in this capacity. Another common approach is to set out a working definition that is considered good enough for the task at hand [13,14]. Another, less frequently employed strategy, is to present a list of the Diagram's characteristics [15,16].

Generally speaking, the literature tends to frame the Diagram as a means for communicating or interacting with information that takes the form of a two-dimensional surface intentionally inscribed with markings. This forms the basis of the Common Model, where diagramhood is understood as a stable property of the marks on the surface. A Creator intentionally makes marks to capture some facets of a concept and the Interpreter decodes a meaning from these marks. The following section proposes a Definition and a General Model, developed from a different set of assumptions, that work in tandem to provide an alternative perspective on the Diagram.

3 Reframing the Diagram

3.1 A Definition and a General Model

This section revisits the Common Model's assumptions to introduce a Definition (fig. 2), a General Model (fig. 3) and the associated concept of the epiDiagram, to create an alternative set of affordances for ID research. The Definition and the General Model work together to frame the Diagram as generally as possible while retaining its essential characteristics.

The Definition posits that the Diagram exists to describe a set or subset of whole/part relations. The word describe is used here in its broadest sense. This

A Diagram is
a visual rendering that describes
some or all of the parts of a greater whole,
and any or all of the relations between them
that may include, or be wholly composed of
text,
whose unconventional spatial formatting
contributes to the Diagram's interpreted meaning.

Fig. 2. A Definition of the Diagram.

draws on Stjernfelt's reading of Peirce, who speaks of the shift in considering a painting in purely aesthetic terms to considering the relations between its parts, in terms of a shift to "regarding it as a diagram" [7].

The role of text is explicitly addressed, with the Definition stating that a Diagram may or may not include text, or may consist wholly of it. A good example of the latter is a word-cloud, where font-size reflects word-frequency in a source text. The phrase "unconventional spatial formatting" is included in the Definition to account for the effects of differences in textual formatting norms across writing cultures.

The Definition substitutes visibility for two-dimensionality as a criterion for diagramhood. Recent work on syllogistic diagrams presents evidence of diagramhood in the four-dimensional form of gesture [17] and time plays a role in animated and interactive diagrams, rendering them more than two-dimensional [18]. Non-two-dimensional phenomena such as brainstorming white-boards covered in Post-its that are interlinked with lines drawn in marker, and scenarios where a coach moves objects around on a table to convey strategies, describe whole/part relations and are indicators of the unsustainability of the constraint of two-dimensionality. Rather than trying to suppress the Diagram's dimensional porousness, the Definition and General Model embrace it.

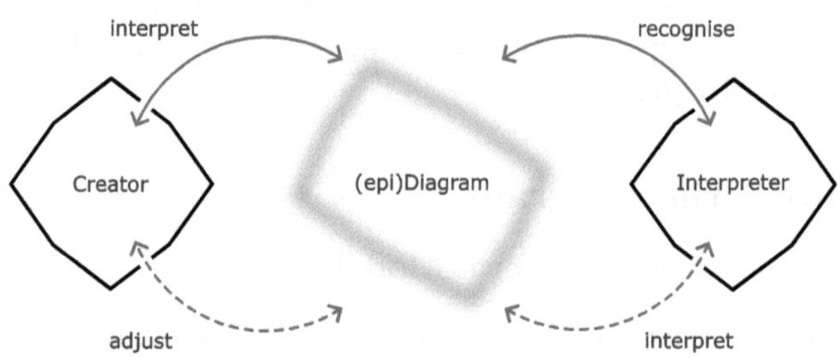

Fig. 3. The General Model of the Diagram.

The General Model can be thought of as having two parts, one centred on the Creator/Diagram relation and one centred on the Interpreter/Diagram relation.

Diagramhood is understood to emerge through a Creator's act of interpretation or an Interpreter's act of recognition, rather than being an inherent property of any particular visual phenomenon. This follows on from the Peirce quote above. Essentially, if a phenomenon is interpreted as a description of whole/part relations, then it is a Diagram. As diagramhood is a matter of interpretation, the same phenomenon can simultaneously be a Diagram for one subject and a non-Diagram for another. Although this emphasis on interpretation might more typically be associated with the Image and Language Strands, recent activity in the Tool Strand attests to its universal centrality [19].

The General Model frames the Creator/Diagram relation in terms of an iterative cycle of interpretation and adjustment. In the most extreme case, an existing visual phenomenon such as a set of objects might present itself as an already existing description of a set of whole/part relations. In such a scenario, Diagram creation is an act of interpretation. More usually however, the visual phenomenon in question needs to be adjusted to correspond with the set of relations the Creator wishes to convey, or to aid them in clarifying those relations.

For example, the relative positions of some coins on a tabletop can be interpreted as expressing the relations between the players on a team. If the coins are already in a configuration that describes the player relations the Creator has in mind, then Diagram creation is purely an act of interpretation. More likely however, they need to be adjusted until the relations between the coins match the relations the Creator wants to convey. This cycle of interpretation and adjustment generalises the scenario underlying the Common Model, in which the Creator makes and erases marks on a blank surface, adjusting the image until the marks adequately describe a desired set of whole/part relations.

Similarly, the General Model also splits the Interpreter/Diagram relation into two parts, to acknowledge the necessity of recognising a visual phenomenon as a Diagram in advance of any attempt at making meaning from it. This is premised on the assumption that diagramhood is not always self-evident. For example, an Interpreter might not recognise a specific visual phenomenon as a Diagram for cultural or contextual reasons, regardless of Creator intention.

In the lived experience of the Diagram, Interpreters often encounter a diagram that originated in an unfamiliar cultural context, as in the case of archaeologists interpreting the carvings on a prehistoric stone [20]. This kind of uncertainty is not well served by the Common Model's assumption of an intentional communicative trajectory that passes from Creator to Interpreter via the Diagram. The General Model's decoupling of Creator and Interpreter accommodates scenarios of this sort.

3.2 The epiDiagram

As discussed above, the transition from non-Diagram to Diagram takes place through an act of interpretation for a Creator, and through an act of recognition for an Interpreter. Both scenarios imply the existence of some visual phenomenon that possesses the potential to be interpreted as a Diagram. The term epiDiagram describes this state of potential diagramhood. The prefix epi- is an acronym that stands for entity with the potential to be interpreted (as a Diagram).

Generally speaking, all Diagrams can be understood retrospectively to have been epiDiagrams before achieving diagramhood in the eyes of a subject. That said, the criteria for epiDiagramhood are different for Creators and Interpreters. A visual phenomenon can only hold the status of epiDiagram for a specific Creator at a specific moment in time, contingent on the set of whole part relations the subject wishes to convey. Imagine a teacher explaining a concept to a student, scanning the room for a set of objects that they interpret as possessing the capacity to describe the set of relations they want to convey. Not every visual phenomenon in the room possesses the capacity to be interpreted as a Diagram describing the whole/part relations in question, but there may be a small number that do. In that moment, those phenomena hold the status of epiDiagrams for that teacher.

For an Interpreter, any intentionally created diagram holds the potential to be recognised and interpreted as a Diagram, and so holds the status of an epiDiagram. The likelihood of recognition is aided by contextual factors. Are they reading academic literature or a manual? Is a stranger gesturing to describe the relations between streets in an unfamiliar city? Conversely, not all epiDiagrams are Diagrams. Perhaps the marks on a surface are simply due to wear and tear? There is further scope for unpacking the epiDiagram's role in interrogating such processes of Diagrammatic meaning-making.

4 Conclusions

The Definition and the General Model introduced here decouple Creator and Interpreter to generalise subject/Diagram relations and the concept of the epiDiagram formalises the interpretative transition from non-Diagram to Diagram. These concepts are presented, in part, to extend the dialogue within the wider Diagram research community as to the kind of ID Diagram research that is necessary to tackle the complexity of the Diagram in a contemporary media-saturated society.

Acknowledgments. The work presented here was initially developed among the quantum networking research community at CONNECT as part of my PhD dissertation and developed further in my role as a research assistant in Prof. Dan Kilper's group at Trinity College Dublin. I would like to acknowledge the support of Dr. Linda Doyle, Prof. Kilper, the research community at CONNECT, my colleagues in the CoQREATE project and at the Trinity Quantum Alliance. Thanks also to Dr. Francis Halsall and the peer reviewers. Supported by Taighde Éireann – Research Ireland grants 20/US/3708, 21/US-C2C/3750, and 13/RC/2077 P2.

References

1. Krämer, S., Ljungberg, C.: Thinking with Diagrams: The Semiotic Basis of Human Cognition, De Gruyter Mouton (2016). https://doi.org/10.1515/9781501503757
2. Bender, J., Marrinan, M.: The Culture of Diagram, Stanford University Press (2010).https://doi.org/10.1515/97815015037572
3. Blackwell, A. F., Engelhardt, Y.:"A taxonomy of diagram taxonomies". In: Proceedings of Thinking with Diagrams 98: is There a Science of Diagrams?, pp. 60–70 (1998).).https://doi.org/10.1515/97808047732563
4. Blackwell, A. F., Engelhardt, Y." "A meta-taxonomy for diagram research". In: Anderson M., Meyer, B., Olivier, P. (eds.): Diagrammatic Representation and Reasoning. Springer, Berlin (2002)
5. Larkin, J. H., Simon. H, A.: Why a diagram is (sometimes) worth ten thousand words. Cognitive Sci. **11**, 65–99 (1987)
6. Latour, B., Woolgar, S.: Laboratory Life: The Construction of Scientific Facts. Princeton University Press, New Jersey (1986)
7. Stjernfelt, F.: Diagrams as centerpiece of a Peircean epistemology. Trans. Charles S. Peirce. Soc. **36**(3). 357–84. Indiana University Press. (2000)
8. Elkins, J.: The Domain of Images. Cornell University Press, New York (1999)
9. Bellucci, F., Burton, J.: "Observational advantages and occurrence referentiality". In: Pietarinen, A.-V. et al. (eds.): Diagrams 2020, LNAI 12169, pp. 202–215. Springer Nature, Cham (2020). https://doi.org/10.1007/978-3-030-54249-8_16
10. Kozak, Piotr. 2020. "The Diagram Problem". In: Pietarinen, A.-V. et al. (eds.): Diagrams 2020, LNAI 12169, pp. 216-224. Springer Nature, Cham. (2020).https://doi.org/10.1007/978-3-030-54249-81610
11. Johansen, M.W., Misfeldt, M., Pallavicini, J.L. "A Typology of Mathematical Diagrams". In: P. Chapman et al. (eds.): Diagrams 2018, LNAI 10871, pp. 105–119. Springer, Cham. (2018).https://doi.org/10.1007/978-3-030-54249-81711
12. De Toffoli, S.: What Are Mathematical Diagrams? Synthese **200**(2), 1–29 (2022). https://doi.org/10.1007/978-3-319-91376-61312
13. Tversky, B. "Diagrams: Cognitive foundations for design." In: Black, A., Luna, P., Lund, O., Walker, S. (eds.): Information Design: Research and Practice (1st ed.). Routledge, London. (2017) https://doi.org/10.1007/s11229-022-03553-w13
14. Sochański, M. "Experimenting with Diagrams in Mathematics". In: Pietarinen, A.-V. et al. (eds.): Diagrams 2020, LNAI 12169, pp. 507–510. Springer, Cham. (2020) https://doi.org/10.1007/978-3-030-54249-8_45
15. Tversky, B., Lee, P. U. "Pictorial and Verbal Tools for Conveying Routes". In: Freksa, C, Mark, D.M. (eds.): COSIT'99, LNCS 1661, pp. 51-64. Springer, Berlin, Heidelberg. (1999).https://doi.org/10.1007/3-540-48384-5_4
16. Tversky, B.: The Cognitive Design of Tools of Thought. Rev. Phil. Psych. **6**, 99–116 (2014). https://doi.org/10.1007/3-540-48384-5416
17. Reichenberger A, Lemanski J, Bhattacharjee R. "The role of gestures in logic". Multimodal Communication, vol. 14, no. 2, 2025, pp. 119-136. (2025). https://doi.org/10.1515/mc-2024-0027
18. Harriman, Hwei-Shin. "Ender website."https://www.hwei-shin.com/ender/, last accessed 2026/03/10
19. Cheng, P.C.-H., Stockdill, A., Garcia Garcia, G., Raggi, D., Jamnik, M. "Representational Interpretive Structure: Theory and Notation". In: Giardino, V., et. al. (eds) Diagrammatic Representation and Inference. Diagrams 2022. LNAI, vol 13462, 54–69. Springer, Cham. (2022). https://doi.org/10.1007/978-3-031-15146-0_4

20. Utrilla, P., Mazo, C., Sopena, M.C., Martínez-Bea, M., Domingo, R.: A palaeolithic map from 13,660 calBP: engraved stone blocks from the Late Magdalenian in Abauntz Cave (Navarra, Spain). J. Hum. Evol. **57**(2), 99–111 (2009). https://doi.org/10.1007/978-3-031-15146-0420

Author Index

P. Sobociński et al. (Eds.): Diagrams 2026, LNAI 16833, pp. 437–438, 2027.
https://doi.org/10.1007/978-3-032-34178-5

MIX
Papier aus verantwortungsvollen Quellen
Paper from responsible sources
FSC® C105338

If you have any concerns about our products,
you can contact us on
ProductSafety@springernature.com

In case Publisher is established outside the EU,
the EU authorized representative is:
Springer Nature Customer Service Center GmbH
Europaplatz 3, 69115 Heidelberg, Germany

Printed by Libri Plureos GmbH
in Hamburg, Germany